NEW CONNECTIONS

An Integrated Approach to Literacy

Kathy Pike
Roxbury Central Schools

Rita Compain
Kingston City Schools, New York

Jean Mumper
State University of New York, New Paltz

An imprint of Addison Wesley Longman, Inc.

New York • Reading, Massachusetts • Menlo Park, California • Don Mills, Ontario • Harlow, UK
Amsterdam • Bonn • Sydney • Singapore • Tokyo • Madrid • San Juan • Milan • Paris

Editor-in-chief: Priscilla McGeehon
Supplements Editor: Donna Campion
Text Designer: Electronic Publishing Services Inc.
Cover Designer: Scott Russo
Cover Photo: Photodisc, Inc.
Electronic Production Manager: Eric Jorgensen
Manufacturing Manager: Hilda Koparanian
Electronic Page Makeup: Electronic Publishing Services Inc.
Printer and Binder: R. R. Donnelley and Sons
Cover Printer: Phoenix Color Corp.

For permission to use copyrighted material, grateful acknowledgment is made to the copyright holders on pp. 511–513, which are hereby made part of this copyright page.

Library of Congress Cataloging-in-Publication Data

Pike, Kathy.
New connections : an integrated approach to literacy / Kathy Pike, Rita Compain, Jean Mumper.—2nd ed.
p. cm.
Includes bibliographical references and index.
ISBN 0-673-98421-4
1. Language arts (Elementary) 2. Language experience approach in education. 3. Literacy. 4. Children—Books and reading.
I. Compain, Rita. II. Mumper, Jean. III. Title.
LB1575.8.P55 1997
372.6—dc20 96-32591
CIP

ISBN 0-673-98421-4

3 4 5 6 7 8 9 10—DOW—99 98 97

To Sarah

and

all the men in our lives

CONTENTS

10

EXPRESSIVE/CREATIVE ARTS IN READING AND THE OTHER LANGUAGE ARTS 355

11

COMPUTERS IN THE WHOLE LANGUAGE CLASSROOM 392

12

MEETING THE NEEDS OF ALL CHILDREN 407

13

HOME TO SCHOOL: SCHOOL TO HOME 437

PREFACE

Welcome to the revised edition of *New Connections: An Integrated Approach to Literacy.* Helping children become literate has been the focus of our professional lives. The journey from our first steps as novices in our preservice educational training to our current positions as administrators and teachers of teachers has led to the birth of this book. Children and literature make an ideal combination to support the development of literacy; but in order for children to become independent, strategic learners, they must be provided with caring, supportive teachers who themselves are still learning and growing. This book is intended for these teachers—those who are just beginning their journeys as teachers and those currently in the classroom whose goals include furthering their own development as reflective educators.

TO OUR READERS

New Connections reflects our personal beliefs about learning and literacy; it also reflects the dramatic changes in the understanding of the learning process and the facilitation of this process that have occurred in recent years. Certain conditions make learning and literacy possible. This applies to learners of all ages, whether they are in elementary school or attending universities. All schools want their students to be able to read and write effectively, and the conditions that make this possible depend on the participation and support of knowledgeable educators and administrators who can help or guide the learners.

New Connections describes the conditions and supportive practices that enable literacy learning to occur. It is intended for preservice and in-service teachers who are interested in a child-centered approach to literacy instruction. It is our intent to provide information and support for educators who are preparing to teach as well as for educators who would like to move toward a balanced literacy program. As practitioners and as professors involved in teacher training, we have kept the needs of both audiences carefully in mind. Throughout the book we provide theoretical information with practical applications and balance holistic activities with skills addressed in meaningful contexts. A combination of indirect and direct teaching focuses on meaningful literacy experiences.

Since this is a text about literacy, it is imperative that our readers have an understanding of the term *literacy.* If we were to ask each of you what *literacy* means, we would probably get a response similar to this: "Literacy means the ability to read and write effectively for both learning and pleasure." Most schools would echo this response. In operation, however, the definitions may differ. In many traditional classrooms throughout the United States, literacy means the practice of reading and writing skills, which are frequently separated or isolated from the rest of the curriculum. Literacy is often associated with correct answers on worksheets and high test scores.

Our definition of literacy, which might sound the same as the preceding one, differs in concept. We define literacy as the ability to communicate effectively using all the language modes both for learning and for pleasure. Moreover, we believe that literacy is best attained through authentic reading, writing, listening, and speaking activities. Students should engage in meaningful language practices and should use literacy skills and strategies for many purposes throughout the curriculum. Even young children can use many behaviors that are characteristic of literate adults if they are afforded the right conditions and given adequate support.

Furthermore, we believe literacy is a lifelong challenge. No one should stop growing as a reader and writer. People develop language competence throughout their lives and use language skills to fulfill their needs, both in the workplace and at home. Through exposure to unfamiliar topics and ideas, people can broaden their literacy abilities in areas with which they previously were unfamiliar. In other words, they become more literate.

This book also addresses the latest trends in literacy instruction. Dramatic changes have occurred in classrooms and schools throughout the United States and world. The changes are of a holistic and process-oriented nature and tend to be discussed under such headings as literature-based reading, reading and writing across the curriculum, integrated language arts, emergent literacy, and whole language. Among the changes that are being initiated and that guide this text are:

- A constructivist perspective of reading whereby reading is considered an act of interpretation that relies both on the text and the prior knowledge of the reader
- Greater usage of tradebooks, as opposed to the reliance on basal reading programs and textbooks
- More attention to writing and its relationship to the reading process
- The provision of more student choice and responsibility in the learning process
- An increased integration of all the language arts across the curriculum
- The recognition that literacy is enhanced if students are involved in authentic learning experiences
- The belief that schools must prepare students for a technologically complex world and for lifelong learning

(Strickland, 1994; Putnam, 1994; Purcell-Gates, 1995)

New Connections seeks to help both preservice and in-service teachers move from traditional approaches to literacy to a more child-centered approach, generally called a whole language program or a balanced language program. This book evolved from many years of teaching and learning on our part, and we credit our students and colleagues with much of our learning.

This book also has an international flavor. Knowledge gained from several visits to New Zealand, recognized throughout the world for its noteworthy literacy practices, is also reflected throughout the text. New Zealand has had the highest literacy rate in the world for many years and serves as a model for effective literacy instruction.

ORGANIZATION AND SPECIAL FEATURES

New Connections: An Integrated Approach to Literacy begins with discussions on the nature of learning and the modes of language learning—reading, writing, listening, and speaking. This information provides a theoretical framework on which the text is based. The remainder of the book describes effective instructional practices for developing, supporting, and assessing learners at all stages of their development. Research has shown that children learn best when they are actively and purposefully involved in their learning. Children interact with their environment—exploring, investigating, hypothesizing—and as a result, actively construct knowledge. When they are provided with a language-rich environment filled with opportunities to explore language, children can construct their own knowledge about literacy with the support of adults who aid the learning. Throughout the book there is an emphasis on the interaction of the learners' background knowledge and experiences and the teacher's crucial role in orchestrating an exemplary literacy program.

Since we believe that teachers must constantly be growing and learning, we ourselves adhere to this philosophy. Therefore we have made some changes in this revised edition. Throughout the text, we have updated our resources and information, especially on such topics as assessment, meeting the needs of all learners, thematic instruction, and technology. We also celebrate the work of our colleagues in the classroom by expanding our *From the Class-*

room offerings. Of particular importance is the addition of Language Arts Outcomes and Descriptors for Grades K–6 in the Appendix. We feel teachers must be guided by relevant and meaningful objectives and therefore have chosen to include this information.

As with the former edition, each chapter has a predictable format and begins with a piece of children's writing—inspired by a piece of literature. We feel that a focus on children's writing is an excellent way to welcome our readers, and the beginning of each chapter also models for the readers some literature extensions. This is followed by an overview, "Questions to Ponder," the body of the text, a summary, and a bibliography. The "Questions to Ponder" are meant to serve as catalysts to help our readers relate the information in the book to their own lives, to analyze and generalize from the text, and to stimulate further thinking and reflection. We feel this is the type of questioning that all learners should be exposed to as they become more effective readers and writers. Throughout, each chapter has a special feature, "From the Classroom," which highlights the work of many practitioners. These features include effective practices we have viewed in elementary school classrooms and practices that teachers have shared with us.

An *Instructor's Resource Guide* to accompany this text has been prepared by the authors and is available to adopters. This *Guide* includes such features as Chapter Summaries, Significant Terms, Projects and Activities, Additional Reading Lists, Evaluation Guidelines, Instructional Masters, and a Glossary of Terms.

Finally, we have written a textbook to provide support and resources to those who desire to implement or move toward a balanced literacy program. We have also used this book as an opportunity to celebrate the work of teachers and students. Our own growth as learners is always "becoming," and we encourage you to share your success stories and effective practices with your colleagues and with us.

ACKNOWLEDGMENTS

The author Aliki wrote a book titled *How a Book Is Made.* A great many people helped us "make" both editions of *New Connections: An Integrated Approach to Literacy.* We now express our appreciation to them. First, we thank the many teachers and children who opened up their classrooms and shared their thoughts, practices, and writing. Without them this book would be far less rich and inviting. Special thanks go to our friends and colleagues Joan Cavagnaro, Adam Cody, Maria Constantinides, Julie Frankel, Joe Gasparini, Karen Pillsworth, Kathleen Scholl, Joyce Rubin, and Dean Witham. Their contributions truly enrich this book, and their exemplary teaching will continue to touch the hearts and minds of their students. Special thanks also goes to a special student, Laura Constantinides, who always was available to try out new techniques and to give a student's perspective to literacy learning.

To continue with the analogy of Aliki's *The Making of a Book,* the next step after the drafting and revising of the text is obtaining input from reviewers (similar to peer conferencing) who carefully read the text and provide suggestions that help shape the final writing. We thank the following reviewers for their time, efforts, and insights on our behalf: Dr. Sharon White Williams, Hampton University; Howard E. Blake, Temple University; Janet L. Nemec; and Sheila Fitzgerald, Michigan State University.

Our gratitude and appreciation also go to the editors of Addison Wesley Longman who made this book possible. Without them *New Connections* would have remained an idea.

Finally, we thank our families, who were there when we needed them, who were there when we needed encouragement, and who are now there to join in the celebration of a book no longer "in the making." With much love, we dedicate this book to them.

Kathy Pike
Rita Compain
Jean Mumper

BIBLIOGRAPHY

Purcell-Gates, V. (1995). Language arts research for the 21st century: A diversity of perspectives among researchers. *Language Arts, 72,* 56–60.

Putnam, L. (1994). Reading instruction: What do we know now that we didn't know thirty years ago? *Language Arts, 71,* 362–366.

Strickland, D. (1994). Educating African American learners at risk: Finding a better way. *Language Arts, 71,* 328–336.

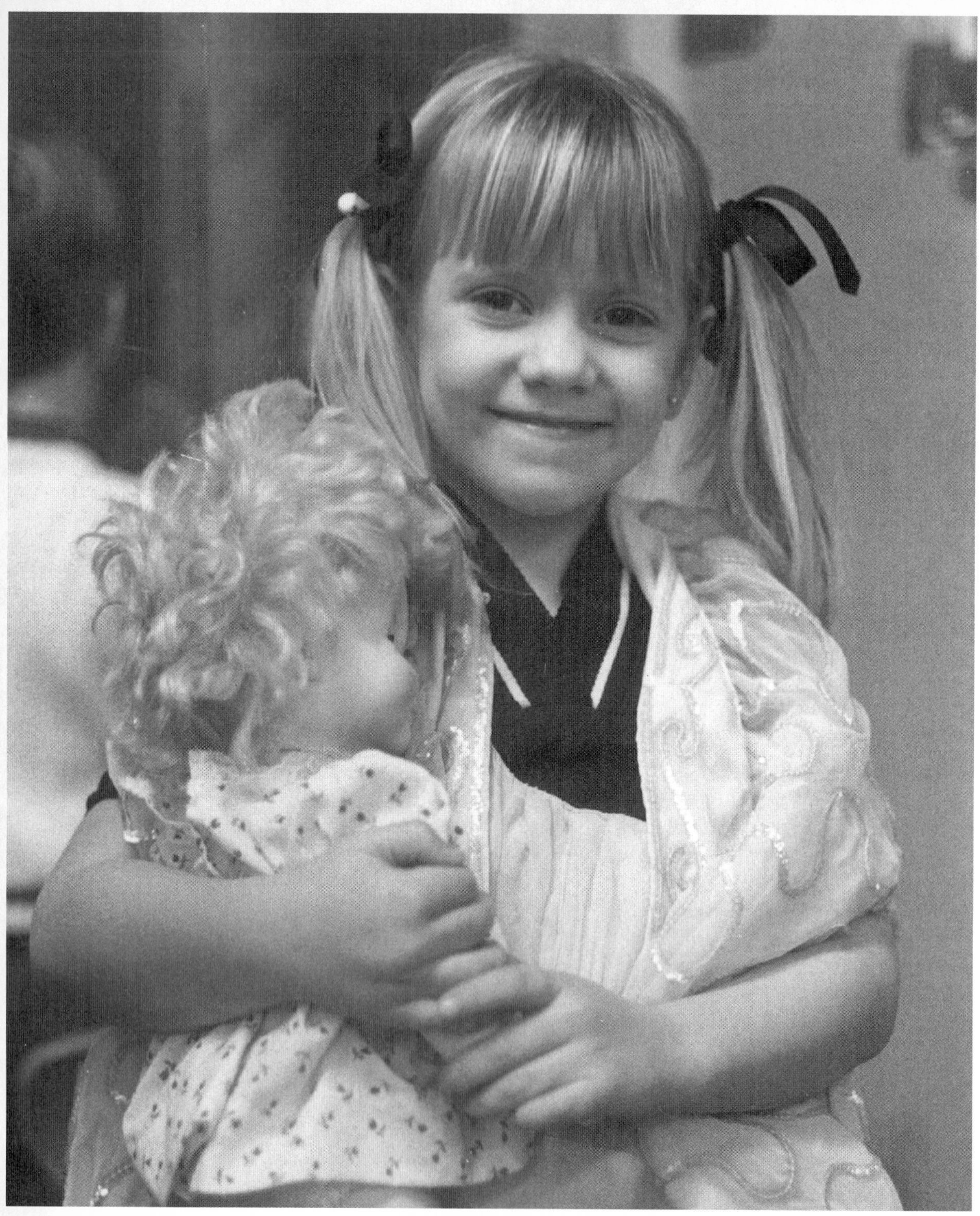

This is Sarah. She is in the process of becoming a proficient reader and writer. Throughout this book, you will see her grow into literacy—from looking at pictures in books to scribbling her first words to writing and reading for various purposes both at school and at home. You'll meet other learners like her as well on your journey through *New Connections: An Integrated Approach to Literacy.*

1 IN THE BEGINNING—WHAT WE KNOW ABOUT CHILDREN'S LEARNING DEVELOPMENT AGES AND STAGES

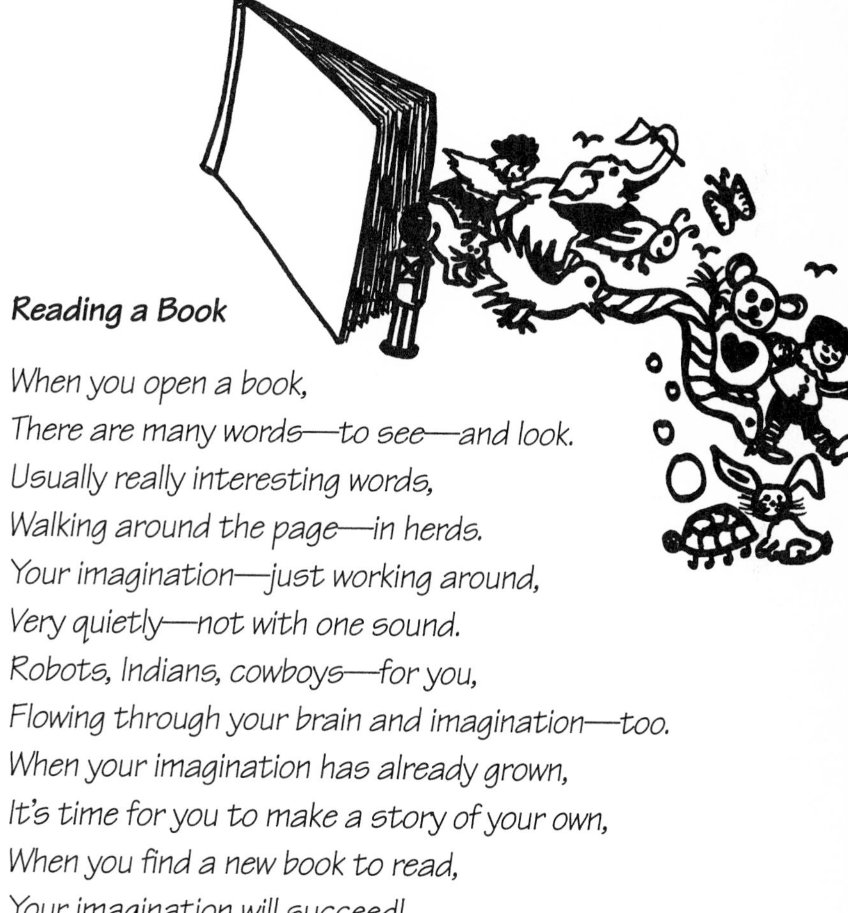

Reading a Book

When you open a book,
There are many words—to see—and look.
Usually really interesting words,
Walking around the page—in herds.
Your imagination—just working around,
Very quietly—not with one sound.
Robots, Indians, cowboys—for you,
Flowing through your brain and imagination—too.
When your imagination has already grown,
It's time for you to make a story of your own,
When you find a new book to read,
Your imagination will succeed!

Alison Schreck
Grade 4
New Lane Elementary
Middle Country School District
New York

Inspired by: *Invitation* in Shel Silverstein's *Where the Sidewalk Ends*

OVERVIEW

In the beginning—before children enter school—they have learned enough about their environment and mastered their native tongue sufficiently to communicate effectively. They have been successful as learners, basically using a hands-on approach; that is, they learned by observing, touching, smelling, tasting, experimenting, and practicing. Young children are actively involved in their learning. Then, when they reach a designated age (generally around 5 or 6), children enter school and are usually forced to sit quietly at their desks in front of worksheets and workbooks. This is contrary to children's active natures and what is known about child development. The child is expected to fit the curriculum rather than the curriculum, the child. In order to provide the right atmosphere for children to learn and the kinds of learning experiences that will make children effective learners, teachers must have an understanding of how children learn and be able to translate this understanding into classroom practice. This chapter explores the nature of learning, particularly language learning, and makes connections for classroom practice. Being aware of the nature of learning, the nature of language, and how language is learned is the key to providing instruction in literacy successfully.

Questions to Ponder

1. What do you do when learning something new?
2. How do children learn about their world?
3. What was necessary for this learning to occur?
4. Why are children successful in learning to speak?
5. How can schools capitalize on children's natural learning abilities; that is, what are the implications for the classroom?

THE NATURE OF LEARNING

In the beginning. . . . Congratulations! It's a girl! Think about a newborn entering the world—its helplessness is cherished and adults spend a great deal of time responding to its needs. Yet these same helpless creatures soon learn to move around, speak, and ultimately attain independence. How do babies who initially have to depend on a caretaker for their survival gain the ability to control their world?

Infants spend most of their waking time learning about the world around them. From the time they are born, babies explore and investigate. Through the use of their senses and their interactions with the environment around them, babies learn about their surroundings and develop their cognitive abilities. Through experimentation, exploration, and caring relationships, babies learn to form attachments with others and engage in activities that underlie all future learning and later development.

When you think about that totally dependent baby, you have to marvel at her ability to learn. She did not go to a formal "infant school" to learn to cry, roll over, babble, walk, or talk. She was not given lessons on the anatomy of the foot, on balance, on the correct placement of the feet when learning to walk. She was not given lessons in a prescribed sequence on babbling, on the proper use of nouns and verbs when learning to talk. Yet somehow, without formal schooling, without a prescribed sequence of skills, she learned to talk and become a master of her native tongue.

This experimentation and investigation play key roles throughout the preschool years. During this formative time, babies learn to walk, talk, dress themselves, and problem solve. The way they approach these tasks and keep on learning is through active manipulation of their environment. This continues as they approach school age. In order to illustrate how a school-age child actually goes about learning something new, let's look at an ordinary skill at which most children become experts—bike riding.

By the time children are ready for the challenge of riding a two-wheeler, they have already spent years watching others ride bikes. In most cases, they themselves have spent many hours performing stunts on tricycles or on some other three-wheeled vehicle. When it comes time to hop on that two-wheeler, many children have the support of training wheels or a guiding hand from an adult who is helping to balance the bike. Then they get on the bike and practice. There are unsuccessful attempts, a few falls and scrapes, many wobbly moments, and much support and encouragement from parents, siblings, and friends. Finally, after many attempts and lots of practice, children learn to ride a bike. Insights into bike riding are seen in Figure 1.1,

Figure 1.1 Sarah's Journal Entry

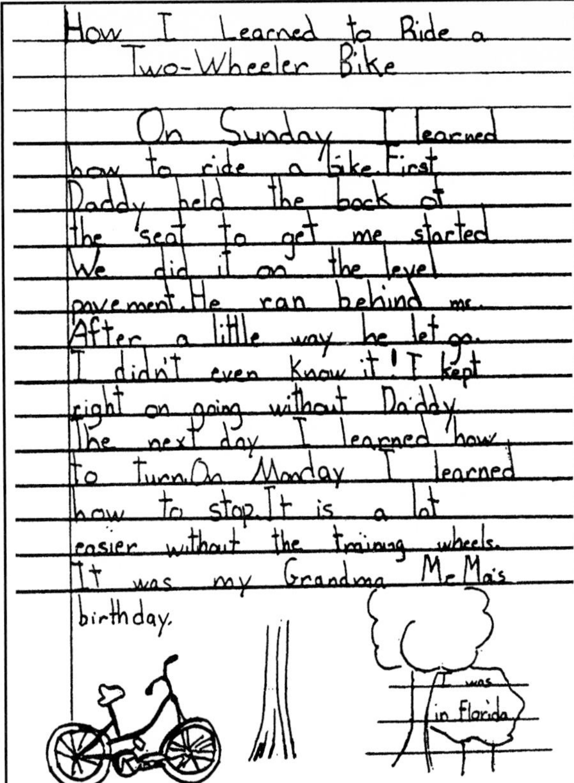
How I Learned to Ride a Two-Wheeler Bike

On Sunday I learned how to ride a bike. First Daddy held the bock of the seat to get me started. We did it on the level pavement. He ran behind me. After a little way he let go. I didn't even know it! I kept right on going without Daddy. The next day I learned how to turn. On Monday I learned how to stop. It is a lot easier without the training wheels. It was my Grandma McMa's birthday.

This figure depicts Sarah's journal entry at age 7, reflecting on how she learned to ride a bike.

which is a journal entry explaining how Sarah, a 7-year-old, accomplished this feat.

At the same time that children are learning to ride bikes, they are also ready to take on a new challenge—schooling. Do schools facilitate the same kind of learning opportunities young children have had in their homes? Let's return to the example of learning to ride a bike. Melvin (1985) describes such an experience. In her example, a young girl named Chris wants to learn to ride a bike. Because she realizes that schools are the places to go to learn something new, she enrolls in a bicycling class. There she goes through a series of exercises—naming the parts of the bike, learning about the nature of balance, learning how to mount a bike—but never has an opportunity to ride a bike herself. Frustrated, she wonders why. She ultimately gets an opportunity when a friend, Mike, rides by as she is walking home and invites her to come over to his house and ride bikes. He tells her she can use his old bike and that he'll show her how. "It's really easy. All you have to do is get on and try—I'll help you a couple of times, and you'll see how easy it is" (307).

Although the above example was intended to be humorous, many programs for young children do reduce learning to discrete skills. They do so with the mistaken belief that this makes learning easier. However, this is not how children learn best, nor does it take advantage of the types of learning experiences young children bring to school.

Since this book is about literacy acquisition, the rest of the chapter discusses the nature of learning and the conditions that facilitate this learning, particularly as it pertains to learning language. It is the intent of this book to describe practices that are being done—or that can be done—initially at home and then at school—that provide children with opportunities for learning language (i.e., listening, speaking, reading, and writing).

THE NATURE OF LEARNING LANGUAGE

Children learn through experience, observation, and language (Smith, 1975). Young children make daily discoveries about themselves and their environment. They learn that if they cry, Mommy will come and either feed them or change them. They learn that if they kick their mobile, the colorful objects will either move or make pleasant sounds. They learn that if they make an utterance, their needs most likely will be met. It is through such explorations and interactions that the groundwork for later learning is made. From simple cooing noises, babies begin babbling and later speaking, thus gaining more control over their lives.

Children are not taught how to talk directly. Rather, they learn to talk by interacting with others in a language-rich environment (Weaver, 1988). Children formulate the rules of language subconsciously and without direct instruction. Although children are not given formal instruction in oral language, there are conditions that facilitate this learning. These conditions are discussed in greater detail later in the chapter. Of particular importance is the fact that children are immersed in a language-rich environment in which language is used for real purposes in real-life situations. These purposes include the following (Halliday, 1975):

- **Instrumental.** Language is a tool allowing the speaker to get something done and to satisfy needs (e.g., notes, business letters, and conversations)
- **Regulatory.** Language that is used to control or regulate the behavior of others (e.g., demands, instructions, rules, and directions)
- **Heuristic.** Language that is used for the purpose of finding out things, asking questions, explaining facts, and for learning (e.g., webs, research, and learning logs)
- **Interactional.** Language that is used for establishing and maintaining social relationships (e.g., conversations, friendly letters, and discussions)
- **Personal.** Language that is used for the purpose of exploring and communicating the speaker's feelings and point of view (e.g., journals, literature responses, and show and tell)
- **Imaginative.** Language that is used imaginatively and creatively (e.g., storytelling, Reader's Theater, and poetry)
- **Informative.** Language that is used to inform others and convey information (e.g., oral and written reports, newspaper writing)

Children learn language because they experience a need to communicate and because language fulfills many functions. Language facilitates the communication of ideas, promotes an understanding of culture and society, enhances social relationships, aids in the classification of events, and assists in reasoning (Mussen, Conger, Kagan, and Huston, 1990). Through language, people discover, examine, reflect on, and refine their ideas. Language is a means of organizing and representing knowledge. Language is a vehicle for learning and facilitates the process for all learners. If you think about it, most of the learning you experience as adults involves language (listening, speaking, reading, and writing).

Children from all cultures on every continent learn to speak their native tongue while quite young. Many children begin to communicate using language before they are 1 year old. Most adults do not consider this a significant feat. Yet, if we consider the complex structure of language, this is indeed an accomplishment. How many of you have learned a foreign language? Was it easy? For most people, learning a second language is difficult because of the sounds, the grammar, the vocabulary, and the proper use of the new language. It is an exceedingly complex task, especially when the aim is to think like a native speaker. And young children master the complexities of their language by the time they are 5 or 6.

Children learn language because language meets certain needs—it is purposeful and meaningful. Let's look at the language development of a typical newborn. Most infants begin to learn language in their earliest months. Generally, they are only a few weeks old when they learn to look at the person who is speaking to them. Through positive parent-child interactions, they learn to distinguish their parents' voices from those of other people and begin to associate certain tones with particular actions. They then quickly learn to make their own sounds and to imitate laughter. They begin to babble or coo at about 5 or 6 months of age. At around 8 months, they say their first word. By the time they are 12 months old, they can repeat and understand about a dozen words. At approximately 18 months, they have a vocabulary of 40 to 50 words. At 24 months, they know 300 or more words. Approximately 60 percent of the speech of most 2-year-olds is intelligible.

At age 2, children may entertain their parents and siblings by mimicking animal noises, naming familiar objects, and combining words to form two-word sentences. Between ages 2 and 3, they can understand about 600 additional words. They notice colors and shapes and can repeat simple rhythms in songs. And they begin to ask questions! At age 3, although they make many sound substitutions, their speech is 70 percent intelligible. By the age of 4, they are able to use nearly 1,500 words (Bee, 1989). By the time they enter kindergarten, they are competent users of language. This astonishing achievement is accomplished without any formal instruction. It occurs almost effortlessly in their natural home environment within the context of their family.

This competence with oral language is typical of young children the world over. Although it was stated above that throughout the world children receive no formal instruction, certain conditions have to be present in order for them to learn language. There have been documented cases in which children living in certain environments and under certain conditions do not learn to speak and therefore do not communicate with language. Let's look at the conditions that make it possible for language development to occur.

CONDITIONS FOR NATURAL LANGUAGE LEARNING

Think about a time recently when you had to learn something new, whether learning to sail, ride a motorcycle, use a computer, or play a new game, such as golf, bridge, or tennis. Were you successful? Reflect for a moment, and jot down the steps you took to become proficient at the new learning. Did someone show you how? Did you do background reading? How much time did you practice? Were you successful right from the start?

Learning is a lifelong endeavor, and most learning occurs outside the classroom. This is natural learning. For young children, such major milestones as walking, talking, riding a bike, and hitting a home run do not happen in school. After people graduate from school, they continue to learn, whether this is job related or learning solely to enrich their lives.

Most of you chose to learn something new because you felt a need (to be like others, to belong, to acquire additional skills), for enjoyment, or a combination of both. You had a purpose for learning, and you chose to do it. You also took charge of acquiring the new knowledge. You decided to watch experts, take a class, ask questions. You practiced—you made mistakes—you practiced some more. Once the learning was completed to your satisfaction, you celebrated by sharing your successes ("Look what I did . . . or can do!") or by admiring your own accomplishment quietly. At this point you may have terminated the learning or wished to extend or refine it, and the cycle began anew at a more sophisticated or in-depth level. This type of learning occurs throughout life. What happens during this natural learning? Are certain necessary conditions present in order for people to learn successfully both as preschoolers and as adults?

Let's return to the bike-riding example. Children are successful in learning to ride bikes because certain conditions make it possible for them to do so. They are shown how by experts (other children or parents); they are given a bike and allowed to try. Although they are given support and feedback throughout the learning, no one expects them to become proficient immediately. They are given messages (either verbally or through body language) that they will someday be bike riders. And that day finally arrives.

These same conditions are present when children learn to talk—when children have their first experiences with learning language. Brian Cambourne (1987), a researcher at the Center for Studies in Literacy at the University of Wollongong, Australia, has studied the conditions under which children acquire oral language with the intent of applying those same conditions to aid them in acquiring written language. He has identified seven conditions under which children learn to talk.

1. **Immersion.** From birth, children are inundated with the sounds, the rhythm, and the words of their native tongue. For most of the time they are awake, children are surrounded with language as the people in their world are either talking with them or talking around them. This language is meaningful, purposeful, whole, and occurs in natural contexts.

2. **Demonstration.** While learning to talk, children are provided with many meaningful and functional examples or demonstrations of spoken language. The users of language provide many models of the spoken words as they go about their daily activities and as they interact with young children. In this way young children are provided with many demonstrations of the purposefulness and effectiveness of oral language. In the course of a day, young children see and hear many examples of the cause-and-effect relationship between spoken language and the world around them. For example, each time the

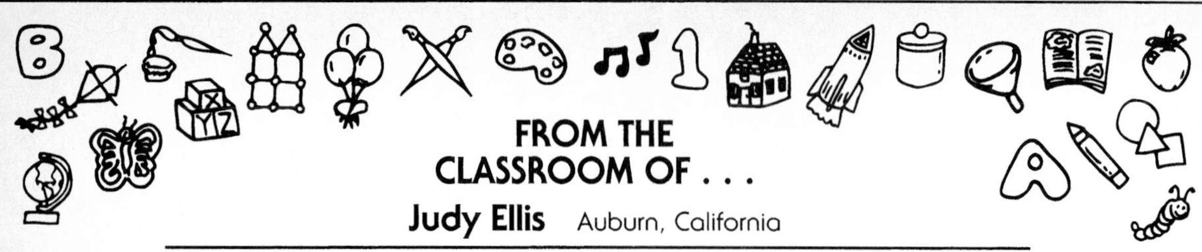

FROM THE CLASSROOM OF . . .

Judy Ellis Auburn, California

CONVERSATION COLLECTIONS

To help children develop their oral language, their ability to classify, and to interact with their peers, Judy uses an assortment of conversation collections. These collections consist of objects placed in plastic bags. Some of her favorite collections are boxes, bracelets, lids, vehicles, shells, gloves and mittens, and balls. They are used during a special collection time activity or occasionally are accessible to children at work/play time for their own exploration.

Children are generally paired up and given a collection to spread out before them. Some of the activities for these collections include:

- Children taking turns and describing the object
- Children giving clues and having their partner find the object
- Naming the collection, e.g., a collection containing binoculars, goofy glasses, and kaleidoscopes could be labeled "Things to See With" or "I Can See"
- Finding similar or different objects
- Seriating the objects
- Making up a story in which the objects could have been used, e.g., a dinosaur collection could have the children create dinosaur adventures

It is relatively easy for teachers to obtain items for collections. A note home explaining the activity or demonstrating the activity at an open house usually generates a wealth of objects. When children bring in new items, instead of the teacher placing them in the appropriate collection, the children should choose the appropriate bag and verbalize the reason for the choice. Many times an object could be placed in several collections.

This activity has many benefits for the children, particularly children who need to expand their ability to communicate orally. Children who are non-native speakers of English profit from the social interaction and the opportunity to use their growing facility with English to describe objects and think about relationships.

telephone rings, someone picks it up and says, "Hello," or if the children say, *"Baa-baa,"* someone gives them something to drink. Without demonstrations, learning will not occur.

3. **Expectation.** Expectations exert a powerful influence on learning and behavior. Research indicates that the expectations of others do influence the behavior of learners (Good and Brophy, 1986). Young children receive clear messages that they are capable of learning to talk and that they are expected to do so. Parents of newborns eagerly await the day of baby's first word. They have no doubt whatsoever that their baby will learn to speak. In fact, when parents were asked if they expected their baby to talk, the reply was always an unqualified positive response. Parents never questioned whether their young ones would be able to talk. However, the same unqualified expectation is not there when it comes to literacy acquisition. Parents hope their children will learn to read and write. Children tend to assume their parents' expectations and attitudes (or those of any significant others with whom they form a bond) as they grow up. This is carried over to both achievement and conduct (Good and Brophy, 1986) and from the home to the school.

4. **Responsibility.** Cambourne discovered that children learn to speak their native language by varied means along an uneven continuum. Yet by age 5 or 6, they are about equally proficient when allowed to learn naturally without any formal instruction. Whereas all children do master their native tongue, all children do not learn identical conventions at the same time. The order in which they learn language is left up to the children. They take responsibility for which set of conventions to master at a particular time.

5. **Approximation.** Young children are not expected to sound like experienced adults. Parents recall at least one memorable utterance by their child that resembled an actual word. Parents of young children expect and reward approximations in their speech. Parents trust that learning to speak will occur and really enjoy their children's early attempts at communicating. This willingness on the part of parents to accept—and cherish—approximations is necessary for learning language. It allows children to use the hypothesis-test-modification cycle that is characteristic of all natural learning. Without this acceptance of approximations, this cycle could not occur and neither could learning.

6. **Employment or use.** This condition actually means practice time—and a considerable amount of it. Young children chatter continuously once they begin to speak. They talk to themselves while lying in their cribs, they talk to their stuffed animals, and they talk to the significant others in their lives. Young children need the time and the opportunity to use their developing language ability.

7. **Feedback or response.** Positive, reaffirming language from older siblings, parents, and other adults in a child's environment constitutes the final ingredient to foster language learning. This condition is closely related to expectation. Body language and actual verbal responses must give the positive message to the learner that "I like what you're doing." The feedback provided to young learners is regular, constructive, and supportive of language growth.

These conditions that are present in the child's home environment enable him or her to learn to speak as well as lay the foundation for reading and writing. These same conditions can likewise be present in schools as children engage in additional experiences to further their language development—this time by learning to read and write.

READING AND WRITING DEVELOPMENT

Learning language does not mean learning only to speak. Language also includes the written mode—reading and writing. Although frequently considered otherwise, learning to read and write is not significantly different from learning to talk. Smith (1979) maintains: "The categories of the language arts are arbitrary and artificial; they do not refer to exclusive kinds of knowledge or activity in the human brain. Reading, writing, speaking, and understanding speech are not accomplished with four different parts of the brain. . . . They are not separate stages in a child's development; children do not first learn to talk, then to understand speech, then to read, and then to write (or any variation of that order)" (575).

While learning to speak, young children are also learning to read and write. Learning to read starts when children begin to notice print in their environment and recognize that this print stands for words. They recognize and can read some of the environmental print they encounter on a regular basis. How many parents have driven past a fast food sign and have had their offspring beg to stop for a hamburger? Children recognize brand names they see on television, signs that say *stop* or *exit,* and numerous other words (e.g., their names, Mom, Dad, logos, and names of favorite TV shows).

Children also engage in some prereading activities as they pretend to be reading books. Because children like to hear favorite stories and books repeatedly, they come to remember the words. They then practice reading, imitating the intonations and mannerisms they have heard from those reading the books. Pretend reading is essentially practice reading, which enables children later to become independent readers at some later time.

If we take a look at Sarah, our developing learner, we can see her beginning attempts at learning to read. Since Sarah was read to regularly from birth, she exhibited knowledge about handling books at a very young age. She knew how to turn the pages in her books, initially naming the objects on the pages and later telling the story from pictures and memory. Sarah was involved in readinglike behaviors, even though she could not match the print with the spoken words. Her focus was on getting meaning from the book, and she used both contextual information (the pictures) and prior knowledge of the story. By hearing stories over and over, Sarah began to internalize the way stories are structured so that when it was time for her to read the stories, she was able to provide reasonable facsimiles. If her father hurried and skipped parts of the story or paraphrased, Sarah would remind him that he had left out part of the story. Later Sarah began to pick out individual words and letters, still using the illustrations as an aid. Because Sarah experienced pleasure with books, certain books, such as *The Tales of Peter Rabbit* and *The Best Nest,* became old friends and remain on her bookshelves even as a teenager.

Just as children first babble when learning to speak, a child first scribbles when beginning

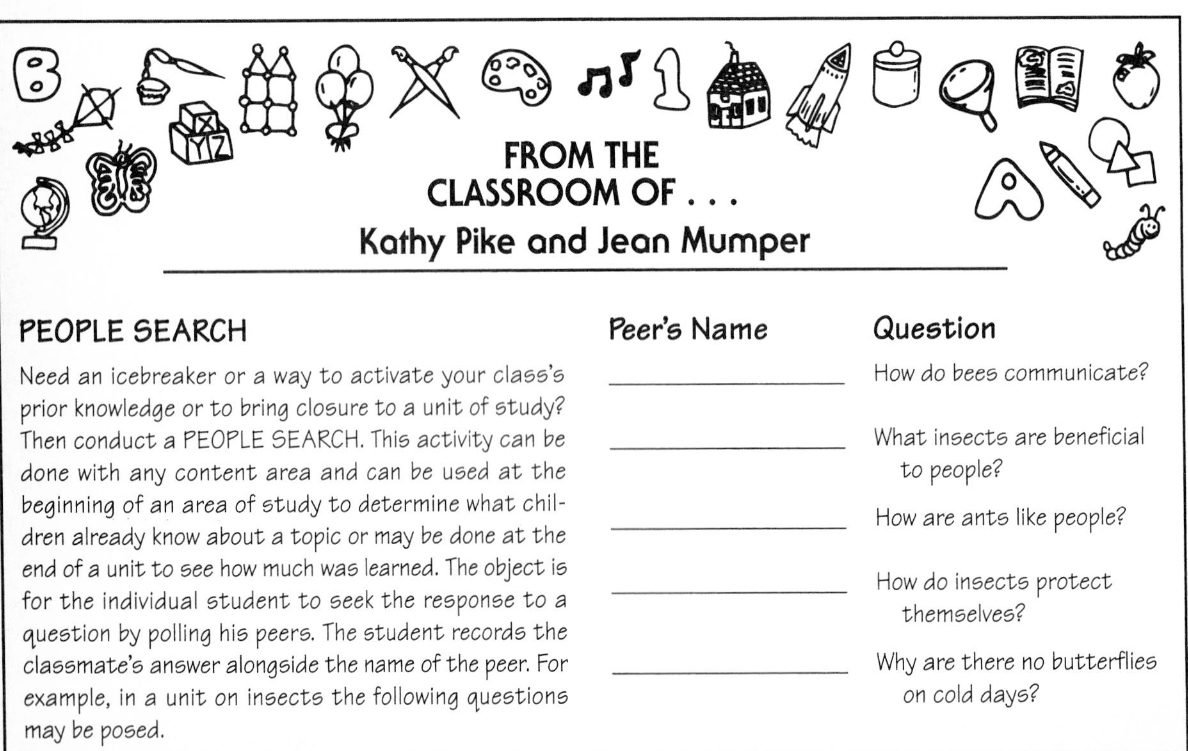

FROM THE CLASSROOM OF . . .

Kathy Pike and Jean Mumper

PEOPLE SEARCH

Need an icebreaker or a way to activate your class's prior knowledge or to bring closure to a unit of study? Then conduct a PEOPLE SEARCH. This activity can be done with any content area and can be used at the beginning of an area of study to determine what children already know about a topic or may be done at the end of a unit to see how much was learned. The object is for the individual student to seek the response to a question by polling his peers. The student records the classmate's answer alongside the name of the peer. For example, in a unit on insects the following questions may be posed.

Peer's Name	Question
________	How do bees communicate?
________	What insects are beneficial to people?
________	How are ants like people?
________	How do insects protect themselves?
________	Why are there no butterflies on cold days?

to write. These scribbles are children's first attempts at putting their thoughts down on paper. The squiggles and scribbles eventually emerge as identifiable pictures. Later these works of art will include printlike symbols, some random letters, beginning sounds, and the names of children. When children read their marks, they make the discovery that reading is essentially making sense of print.

Figures 1.2–1.6 show the beginnings of Sarah's writing development. Like many preschoolers, Sarah enjoyed picking up a crayon or marker and just scribbling. She experimented on sheets of paper, on her own books, and even on walls. But Sarah left her mark—at first they were scribbles, but slowly recognizable pictures, letters, and words began to appear.

The message is clear: Young children have a desire to communicate and are in the beginning stages of developing literacy. They are learning to speak, to read, and to write, and much of this learning overlaps or occurs concurrently. The beginnings of literacy are exceedingly important, not only for what is learned, but also for the positive attitudes toward reading and writing that are created.

These are among Sarah's earliest attempts (around age 2) to communicate through writing. A shoebox on Daddy's desk contained scraps of paper. Sarah would contentedly sit for long periods of time while Daddy attended to his correspondence and paid bills. As he wrote, Sarah wrote, using her paper in the shoebox. Her writing contains scribbles (first sample) as well as some numberlike figures.

Figure 1.2 Sarah's Writing Development

Figure 1.3 Sarah's Writing Development

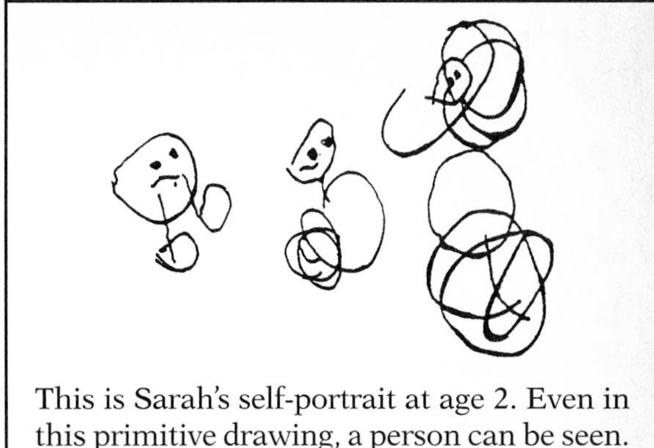

This is Sarah's self-portrait at age 2. Even in this primitive drawing, a person can be seen.

CONDITIONS FOR NATURAL LANGUAGE LEARNING APPLIED TO THE CLASSROOM

Whereas the real world provides many opportunities for children to learn oral language, it does not provide opportunities for other types of learning to occur, particularly learning to read and write. Therefore this becomes the function of schools. Schools become settings in which the opportunity to learn to read and write is created, insofar as they simulate the conditions that occurred naturally when children learned to talk (Cambourne, 1988).

Cambourne's conditions provide a foundation for learning literacy skills in the classroom. Classrooms that take into account these conditions immerse children in print, provide literacy models, regard approximations as evidence of growth, encourage children to assume responsibility for their own learning, offer supportive feedback, and give children ample opportunities to engage in real reading and writing tasks. Each condition is looked at separately, with examples of each applied to the school setting.

Figure 1.4 Sarah's Writing Development

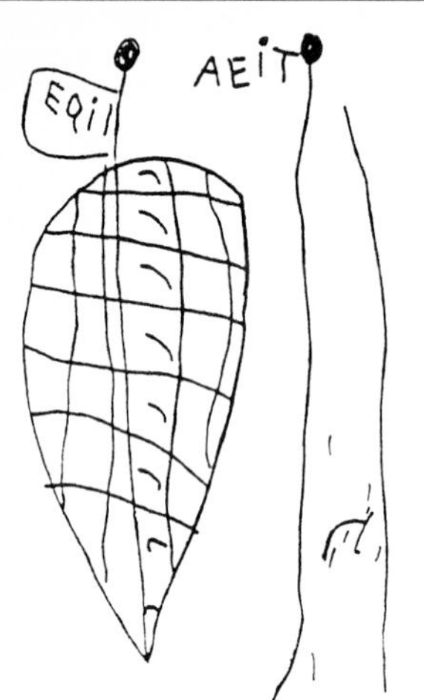

Just as young children experiment with oral language, when given the opportunity to use materials for writing and drawing, they naturally begin to experiment with picture images and even a primitive form of written language. This figure shows Sarah's story with a drawing, written at age 3. Sarah said it was a house and a tree. The letters have no resemblance to those words, but it is evident that an attempt was made to write words.

Immersion

When children are immersed in print that is referred to on a regular basis, they begin to make the association between the printed word and oral language. Identifying each child's name; allowing children to keep track of daily attendance, lunch, or milk counts; listing the names of those who have had a turn at the easel or learning center; providing empty packages of favorite foods for play areas; writing poems and songs on charts to be read while reciting or singing; and recording daily class news on charts are just a few ways to immerse the child in natural, meaningful, environmental print. This immersion must also include the regular reading aloud of printed words. Just as children progress along the continuum of language development, they will begin to read the printed words that surround them. At first, children recognize a single word—most often their own name or the name of a favorite cereal or drink, a specific toy, or a friend. As these important words appear in the context of written sentences, children begin to make associations on their own.

Young children should also be surrounded with environmental print from the adult world: road maps, tickets, warranties, bank forms—in short, all the throwaways that children find fascinating (Holt, 1989). The classroom should be alive with print displays since children will not learn to read and write unless they are exposed to print and given opportunities to associate that print with meaningful situations. "When the learning environment is one in which children are constructors of language in its spoken and print forms, they are immersed in the process . . . They are learning the processes of literacy and practicing what they have learned

A child may paint or draw an image and then say, "This is Mommy and Sarah and David with Tiger Kitty."

Clearly, Sarah may be relating an actual event or an imaginary story through her artwork. Often a child adds symbols resembling letters and asks an adult, "What does this say?" Another child may tell the adult exactly what he or she intends the "writing" to convey.

Figure 1.5 Sarah's Writing Development

Figure 1.6 Sarah's Writing Development

THEGrL FS HA LTL
SCOL EVE DAI
TEA AR FRDS.
TA PAT

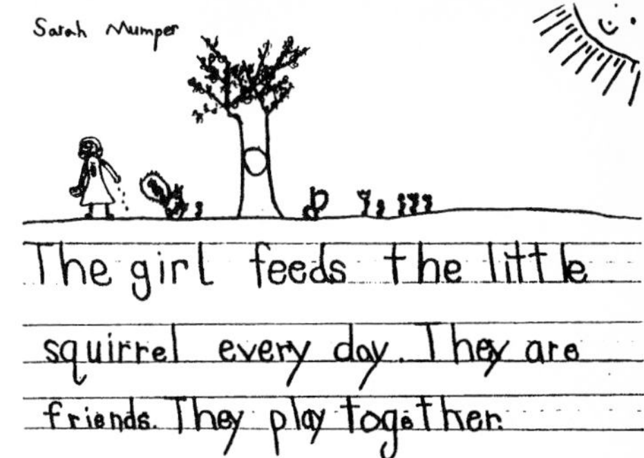

Sarah Mumper
The girl feeds the little
squirrel every day. They are
friends. They play together.

At age 5 and now a kindergartner, Sarah was asked to write a story on any topic she chose. Because she had a fascination with the squirrels in her backyard, she wrote a story about being able to be friends with these animals. In actuality, the squirrels disappeared whenever Sarah appeared, but her story fulfills a dream Sarah had of befriending the squirrels. Sarah's draft was written in invented spelling, but since she was asked to have her story published in a class book, she rewrote her story in conventional spelling with assistance from the teacher.

within the whole context of the curriculum" (Raines, 1995, 10 and 11).

Demonstration

During the course of a day the teacher needs to provide many demonstrations of how printed language makes life's routines richer and easier. Demonstrations occur when teachers share and discuss literature, write in front of the children, and think aloud. A kindergarten class lets the cafeteria know that 25 students are present, and exactly 25 cartons of milk are delivered. When the children deliver the message "We want 25 cartons of milk today" and this is done on a daily basis, they gradually make the association between the print and its meaning. Yes, everytime the message says "milk," they get milk. When the message says "juice," they get juice. Within two weeks every child is able to read and identify the words *milk* and *juice.* The names of absent children are written down and read aloud so that the school nurse knows who is ill. Get-well messages may also be sent home. When children are responsible for taking the attendance, they learn to read classmates' names quickly. Rather than merely having children deliver messages from school to their parents, teachers read the contents to the students. Written language need not be a mystery to children. Teachers provide demonstrations when they write a chart or poem, class news, or a brief memo. These are written in front of the students, and the message or poem is read aloud while it is being written. It is helpful to demonstrate the writing while thinking aloud. For example, a teacher might say, "I know that names begin with a capital letter, so I'll put a capital *K* at the beginning of Katie's name," or "I need to stop and take a breath now, so I know I need to put in a period." As children observe the writing and hear the oral language, associations occur naturally. If the teacher does voice pointing (touching each word as it is spoken) when reading aloud, the children develop such concepts of print as one-to-one correspondence (the spoken word matches the printed one) and are able to recall their favorite parts or repetitive lines and repeat them later all by themselves. Children consider themselves to be readers at this point, and indeed they are. Don't we say that children

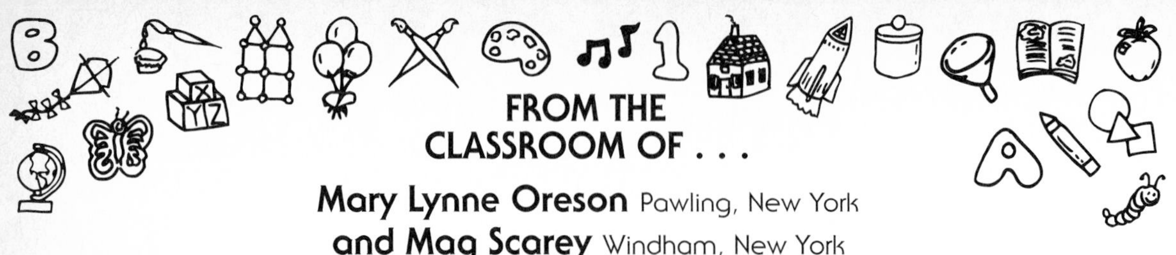

FROM THE CLASSROOM OF . . .

Mary Lynne Oreson Pawling, New York
and Mag Scarey Windham, New York

Travelmates

Need a perfect way to provide armchair travel adventures for your students and to learn geography in a highly motivating way? Then the *Travelmates* program might be just the program for you! Both these third grade teachers implemented different versions of this program after reading the article, *Travelmates,* in the professional magazines, *Teaching K–8*. The objective of this program is to make geography come alive through the sending of travel journals all around the world. A mascot or critter of a child's or class's own choosing is the "originator" of the journal, and his adventures are described as he travels around the world. A letter explaining the program is pasted inside the journal, along with a picture of the student or class. Key information about the school and its environs is also provided. As the critter travels, his adventures are described, either from his point of view, or that of someone he meets on his journey. Postcards, stamps, ticket admissions, etc. are pasted in the journal. Meanwhile, as he travels, the children back home receive postcards updating them as to the whereabouts of their critter. Adventures are marked on a map. The critter and journal are due back by the end of the school year—although they occasionally return throughout the year as well—so that the children can savor the contents and retrace the travel adventures.

Mary Lynne's students each have their own journal and critter so there are many journals for the children to receive and discuss, whereas Mag's student chose one animal, a dog named Snoopy, and the journal became a whole class activity. During the 1994–1995 school year, Snoopy visited Florida, Australia (twice), Germany, Spain, Switzerland, Italy, Greece, Israel, and Turkey among others. Each child in the classroom estimated the mileage Snoopy traveled, and then tallied the miles amassed. They wrote a challenge to the rest of the school to guess how far Snoopy had traveled, and had a map posted depicting his adventures. The children were amazed to find that their little friend traveled almost 60,000 miles!

This program can be adapted to meet the needs of the social studies curriculum of all classrooms. If United States history is the focus of study, the critter could travel solely throughout the United States, or if local state history is studied, then the critter travels only throughout the state. The children's faces and their enthusiasm are proof that this armchair travel adventure enriches their knowledge of their world, map reading, and even some math concepts.

Mrs. Scarey attached the following information to the travel journal.

> This project is part of a multidisciplinary unit that hopes to make the world more meaningful to a class of third graders at Windham-Ashland-Jewett Central School. It is a replication of a project carried out by two teachers who were trained by *National Geographic* as geography consultants for their states.
>
> The goal of the project is to travel and learn about the world around us without leaving home. Our Travelmate will make the journey. The diary is enclosed so the details of the trip can be recorded. Please tell us about yourself, what kind of community you live in, population, local industry, type of geography, time zones, and anything else you think we will find interesting.
>
> We will mark each location that has been visited on our map. Thank you for helping to make this project a success.

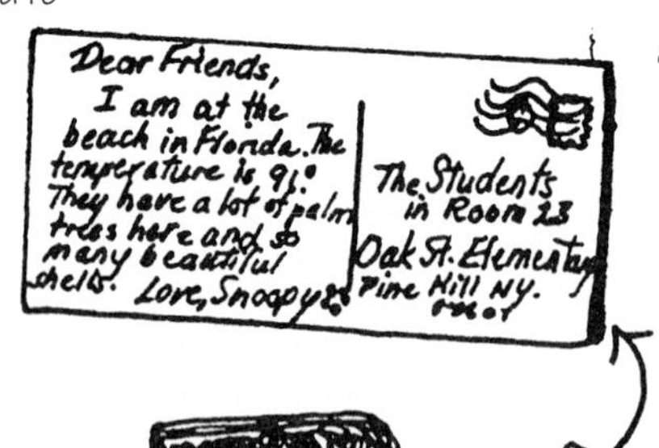

are beginning to talk when they utter their first words?

Expectation

An important element of whole language classrooms is the attitude of expectancy (Raines, 1995). The expectation by both the child and the teacher is that the child is capable of learning to read and write and is learning to read and write. Along with this positive message must come the realization that what is learned in the classroom is important, functional, relevant, and useful. Children will learn—and will want to learn—all they possibly can in this class because their lives will be enriched by the learning.

Teachers should convince young children that reading and writing are worthwhile activities and not merely subjects slotted into scheduled times. Teachers should take great care that they don't give the message that reading and writing are difficult and that the children will find them too hard or too complex. Teachers should also be wary of continually pointing out children's failures. However, teachers are responsible for providing experiences that are meaningful and relevant for their students. Therefore they do not have to be unquestioning approvers of anything their students produce. If students write *recieve* instead of *receive,* they ultimately will have to learn the correct spelling. Here expectations are related to helping learners achieve high self-esteem and develop a trusting relationship so that they can attain literacy.

An important concept to keep in mind with regard to expectations is that each child is an individual and expectations must vary accordingly. Children develop at varying rates. The adult must know the child extremely well in order to communicate appropriate messages to build the child's self-esteem and encourage intellectual growth (Hodgson, 1995).

Responsibility

Teachers may initially be uncomfortable with relegating responsibility for learning to the children. If teachers allow children to take responsibility to read what is important to them, children rarely make mistakes in their choices. Some 4- and 5-year-olds can read *Tyrannosaurus Rex, brontosaurus,* and *carnivorous* long before they can read *sun* or *happy.* Children can assume responsibility for choosing learning activities (some children may have to be provided with only a limited number of choices, but still the possibility of choice remains), books to read, topics to write about, and peers to work with. The degree of responsibility can vary depending on the capabilities and motivation of the students.

Responsibility is not synonymous with directionless learning on the part of the children. Cambourne (1988) maintains that responsibility involves two types of behaviors:

1. An eagerness on the part of young children to make appropriate decisions about their learning
2. A sense of trust by teachers that the children will engage in the available demonstrations and will select those that they think will be useful for them at that particular moment

What this means for teachers is that they need not involve all learners every day in the same demonstration at the same time. Children who are in need of certain demonstrations will be provided with the proper modeling when this is actually needed. At a later time, other learners might need that exact same demonstration. Therefore teachers should be prepared to provide similar demonstrations repeatedly over time—as needed.

Approximation

As a child begins to read or write, it becomes more difficult to accept approximations. Teachers have been conditioned or trained to eliminate all errors in learning. What is forgotten is that trial and error are necessary parts of the learning process. Acceptance of approximations also has an important impact on the child's self-esteem. If the attempt is not correct on the initial try, the learner is free to fail and try again, without any fear of humiliation or punishment. The child is free to be a risk taker.

A child will try reading words if the activity is pleasurable and meaningful and the atmosphere is one that allows for mistakes and approximations and is still supportive. Children's first attempts at spelling (from the scribbling stage to inventive spelling) are indications that they are developing as writers. Children's miscues (deviations from the printed text, sometimes referred to as oral reading errors) are used to look at the strategies they are using while reading. Approximations should not be perceived as failures but as indications of growth and opportunities to analyze the processes children are employing while becoming literate.

Employment or Use

Young children learn through all their senses. Piaget's studies (1969) underlined the importance of using objects and other aids to facilitate learning. When children touch, taste, and smell a strawberry, they will be likely to remember what a strawberry actually is. When they write about that experience, they will relate to it because they have lived it. When such an experience is recorded in this way, it can spur a child's memory to recall the experience long after it is past. It is unrealistic to think we can provide these kinds of concrete experiences for all learning situations. When the actual object is not available, a representation of the real thing, such as a photograph, book, or toy, might be used.

If this principle of learning is accepted and is to be followed, then educators of young children must provide ample opportunities for play and exploration in classrooms. Teachers must assist students in meaningful ways to record their experiences and to draw on them at a later time. Experience charts, personal journals, children's drawings accompanied by their own writing, and photographs are some ways to record daily explorations.

The importance of this condition as it applies to teaching lies in the activities provided for practice. If the activities are meaningless oral exercises, children will have little to say. The age-old show and tell (or sharing time) gives children a chance to talk about what is important to them. Writing and reading must be done for real purposes as well. Writing notes to each other and to parents about important events and writing about shared experiences are much more meaningful activities than are ditto sheets meant to drill a specific skill.

Significant time must be allotted for employment or practice on literacy-related activities. It is true that speaking, reading, and think-aloud writing should occur continuously during the day. However, children need practice time set aside for reading and writing just as they needed lots of practice when they started to talk. Significant times must be built into the daily schedule for exploring, enjoying, and reading books and for drafting, revising, proofreading, and publishing their writing. This should be done across the curriculum, thereby using reading and writing for authentic purposes.

Feedback or Response

The final condition to be discussed—feedback—is the food for growth. When people feel they are doing a good job and know they are pleasing an important person in their lives, they want to continue to improve. Positive feedback as children are beginning to read and write encourages them to take risks and explore reading in all arenas.

Feedback can take different forms. The most obvious is verbal statements expressing pleasure at a child's performance. Do not, however, overlook the importance of body language as feedback—a smile, pat on the back, or hug often says more than words. Teachers sometimes give children stickers, smiley faces, or food to indicate fine work, but the ultimate goal is to have children feel satisfaction in learning a new skill or perfecting one. The feedback or response to a child who is experiencing difficulty needs to be one of acceptance as well. "I can see you're having difficulty. Let's see how we can get help." The response must clearly send the message that it is okay to make mistakes, that children are accepted for themselves, and that the teacher is available for any needed help. The teacher assumes the role of a coach, not a critic. Teachers can facilitate learning by providing encouragement and reinforcement, and if needed, redirection (Hodgson, 1995). Feedback, in order to be effective, should be supportive, relevant, and constructive. Feedback should help children succeed as readers, as writers, and as learners.

Conditions for Natural Language Learning: A *Childs'* View

An excellent way to demonstrate the conditions for natural language learning is to look at how one teacher describes her use of these conditions. Paula Childs is a first grade teacher who states that whole language is not something she does from 9:00 A.M. until 10:00 A.M., but rather it is a way of life. It is a philosophy that she has embraced, and as such affects all the decisions she makes about her classroom. She makes every concerted effort to ensure that Cambourne's elements exist in her classroom:

1. Immersion—All day, every day the children are bombarded with print and language in my room. Songs, charts, morning messages, and stories are found all over my room. The children are encouraged to speak and discuss things in my class.
2. Demonstration—I model for the students how to write, read, and speak. An important part of our day is when I read aloud to them.
3. Expectation—From day one, I expect and communicate to the children that they are all readers and writers. Whole language teachers assume that children will learn to read and write (just as naturally as they learned to talk) if given the proper environment.
4. Responsibility—The students are encouraged to take responsibility for some of their own learning. For example, in my class each day a different child serves as the moderator who is responsible for leading the morning meeting. At this time, we do our calendar, the morning message, and math activities. I also use learning centers and computers in my classroom, which gives the children an opportunity to pace themselves.
5. Approximation—Just as when the children learned to talk, I praise all "attempts" to join the community of readers and writers.
6. Employment (use)—The children have many real and authentic opportunities to put into use the skills that they have learned.
7. Feedback (response)—It's important that children get feedback on their work. I believe most teachers do that. However, whole language teachers realize that children must learn how to praise their own work too. Students must learn to evaluate their own work and progress. This is why I encourage students to construct their own report cards. I find the more opportunities children have to reflect on their own progress, the better they get at self-evaluating.

Figure 1.7 summarizes the conditions for natural language learning applied to the classroom, and Figure 1.8 applies these conditions to a specific curricular objective. Now ask yourself the following questions, and see if you are providing these necessary conditions for natural language learning:

Do I *immerse* my students in:

- a language-rich environment?
- a variety of reading and writing experiences?
- a variety of literacy text types?

Do I *demonstrate* to or model for my students:

- in minilessons?
- by thinking aloud as I read or write?
- in groups or individually?
- process as well as product?
- the essential skills and strategies?
- different text types and genres?

Do I provide *feedback:*

- on a regular basis?
- that is constructive and personalized?
- that is positive?

Do I *expect* my students to:

- be successful as learners?
- achieve high standards of learning?
- assume responsibily for their learning and evaluation?
- be risk-takers?
- enjoy learning?

Do I allow my students to take *responsibility* for?

- choosing their own reading materials and writing topics?

Figure 1.7 Conditions for Natural Language Learning: Classroom Applications

Conditions for Natural Language Learning	**Classroom Applications**
Immersion	Displays of print all around the room: big books, wall stories, charts, books, labels, language experience stories, children's writing, letters, environmental print
Children are provided with a wide variety of rich, stimulating language experiences. They are surrounded by books and talk about books and writing. Reading and writing by children are valued and celebrated.	
Demonstration	Modeled Writing, Sustained Silent Reading, Shared Reading, Think Alouds, Brainstorming, Choral Reading, Reading Aloud
Children are provided with a multitude of examples, both oral and written. These examples are meaningful, done by a variety of experts, repeated as needed, and are both planned and spontaneous. In addition to humans, print resources are also considered demonstrations.	
Expectation	Positive expectations that teachers have and communicate (both through verbal comments and body language) that have an effect on children's learning. These focus on what children can do, not on what they are unable to do.
Children are provided with positive expectations that they can indeed learn to read and write and are expected to be able to do so. The teacher assumes the role of a coach or expert, while the child is the player or novice.	
Responsiblility	Children choose learning activities, topics for writing, books to read, classmates to work with, pieces to publish, conventions to master.
Children are provided with opportunities to be involved in their own decision making as it relates to their own learning. The intent is to help children become more self-directed and self-reliant.	
Approximation	Trial-and-error learning, miscues in reading, invented spelling
Children are provided with opportunities to "have a go" while they are learning, i.e., to become risk takers.	
Employment	Daily reading and writing throughout the entire day and throughout the entire curriculum
Children are provided with time for reading and writing and are encouraged to use real reading and writing for real purposes.	
Feedback	Supportive and constructive information given to children while they are learning. Forms of feedback include encouragement, confirmation, reinforcement, and redirection.
Feedback is provided to children to confirm or promote their language learning. It is meaningful, nonthreatening, and related to the children's needs.	

(Adapted from Cambourne and Turbill, 1987.)

Figure 1.8 Conditions for Natural Language Learning Applied to an Instructional Objective

Text Form: Biography

Conditions	Implementation
Immersion	Students and teacher gather biographies. Teacher reads one biography aloud; students read others independently and in literature groups. Students may also view life stories of people on video, television, or filmstrips.
Demonstration	Teacher reads biographies to expose children to the genre. Together, teacher and students discover elements (format) of the biographical genre. Teacher models researching and writing a biography.
Expectation	Teachers expect their students will suggest activities during the biographical study, participate in the activities, and develop an understanding of the genre, biography.
Responsibility	Children will locate biographies, share these in class, and compose a list of common elements in a biography. Children will choose someone to write a biography on, constructing either interview questions (and interviewing the person) or finding pertinent data in varied sources. They will choose a means to share their information—Big Book on the person, talk show guest, picture in the class gallery, or standard report.
Approximation	Children are not expected to be full-blown researchers with all research skills mastered. Drafting and revision of biography are accepted at the developmental level of the children.
Employment	Children will write a biography of the person of their choice. They will construct interview questions or research questions to obtain needed data. Children will interview community leaders or friends or conduct relevant research. Students will read biographies. Biographies of a single individual can be collected and compared. Children role-play events in the person's life. Videoshows can be created, entitled "This Is Your Life." A Famous Person Picture Gallery can be hung around the room, with the famous person coming to life and discussing significant issues in his or her life.
Feedback	The teacher provides feedback as needed—support, confirmation, redirection. Students can also receive feedback from peers.

- self-evaluation?
- making their own decisions?

Do I encourage my students to take risks and "have-a-go" *(approximate)* while they are learning:

- through invented spelling?
- new skills and strategies?
- as they are writing?
- as they are reading?

Do I give my students the time and the opportunity *(employment)* to:

- read a variety of genres?
- write for different purposes for different audiences?
- explore issues and topics?
- develop their own questions?
- learn and apply new skills, strategies, and information?
- experiment with and investigate new ideas?

(adapted from Hodgson, 1995)

SUMMARY

The beginning, as in most stories, sets the stage—it identifies the setting, the characters, and the focus of the story. This chapter introduced the main characters in this book—the children, their parents, and their teachers—and established the setting—the school and the home. It identified the purpose of the book—that learning to read and write is as natural as learning to speak. Specifically, it discussed the nature of learning, particularly as it relates to literacy, and the conditions that enable that learning to occur. The remainder of the book is devoted to showing how these conditions for natural language learning can be transferred to and implemented in the school setting.

BIBLIOGRAPHY AND SUGGESTED REFERENCES

Anderson, R.; Hiebert, E.; Scott, J.; & Wilkinson, I. (1985). *Becoming a nation of readers: The report of the Commission on Reading.* Champaign, Ill.: Center for the Study of Reading.

Bee, H. (1989). *The developing child,* 5th ed. New York: Harper & Row.

Cambourne, B. (1988). *The whole story.* New York: Scholastic.

Cambourne, B., & Turbill, J. (1987). *Coping with chaos.* Rozelle, Australia: Primary English Teaching Association.

Good, T., & Brophy, J. (1986). *Educational psychology,* 3rd ed. New York: Longman.

Halliday, M. A. K. (1975). *Learning how to mean: Explorations in the development of language.* London: Edward Arnold.

Hodgson, M. (1995). *Show them how to write.* Bothell, Wash.: The Wright Group.

Holt, J. (1989). *Learning all the time.* New York: Addison-Wesley.

Melvin, M. (1985). How do they learn? *Phi Delta Kappan, 67,* 306–307.

Mussen, P.; Conger, J.; Kagan, J.; & Huston, A. (1990). *Child development and personality,* 7th ed. New York: Harper & Row.

Naremore, R., & Hopper, R. (1990). *Children learning language,* 3rd ed. New York: Harper & Row.

Piaget, J. (1969). *The psychology of intelligence.* Paterson, N.J.: Littlefield, Adams.

Raines, S. (1995). Introduction: Reflecting on whole language. In S. Raines (Ed.), *Whole language across the curriculum—Grades 1, 2, 3,* 1–16. Newark, Del.: International Reading Association.

Smith, F. (1975). *Comprehension and learning.* New York: Holt, Rinehart, and Winston.

THE MODES OF LANGUAGE LEARNING: READING, WRITING, LISTENING, AND SPEAKING

I stared absentmindedly at the blank sheet of paper, as if in a trance. My mind was empty, unable to think of anything to write. The blue lines blurred and then doubled. Still nothing.

The center of the paper began to rip. A mere figment of the imagination, I reassured myself. But the tear became larger and a green-fleshed, moist claw protruded from the crevice.

Instantaneously, the paper crumpled away, revealing . . .

A giant block of wood. Seven talons stuck out from the wood. The longest, about eight inches long, had curved nails sharpened to points. It had a long pointed nose with a half inch diameter hole on the end.

Underneath was a jaw lined with two inch long teeth sparkling in the light.

Looking at the red, beady eyes sent a shiver up my spine. Before I was able to realize what had happened, the long talon reached out and snatched the blue ball-point pen I nervously gripped in my hand. The thing shoved it into the hole in its nose and snorted as the pen disappeared.

The blank paper stretched together and hissed as the rips began to fuse.

I soon realized what the horrible thing was—"Writer's block!"

I got another pen and hurriedly began scribbling.

Alan Lemley
North Country Rd. School
Miller Place School District
New York State

Inspired by: *Poem-making* by Myra Cohn Livingston

OVERVIEW

The main goal of teaching language in the elementary school is "to develop children's ability to understand, appreciate, and use language effectively" (Department of Education, Wellington, 1986, 10). Language refers to any system of oral and written communication. One means of looking at language is to consider the modes of language. These traditionally have been reading, writing, listening, and speaking, which constitute the language arts. In addition, there are nonverbal modes of language, which likewise contribute to a balanced literary program. These include moving, watching, shaping, and viewing. All these language modes are described and discussed in this chapter. In addition, the complex and varied relationships among the modes are presented.

Questions to Ponder

1. What is reading?
2. What makes an effective reader?
3. What is writing?
4. What makes an effective writer?
5. How do the nonverbal language modes contribute to the literacy program.

INTRODUCTION

Language is the major means of communication in all aspects of the elementary school curriculum. Consequently there is a component of language learning throughout the entire school day. Language development is facilitated when teachers integrate language objectives into all the subject areas. The foundation for learning language is provided in a child's first years of life, and by age 5 most children have attained some competency in their oral language. They have accomplished this, not through formal training, but because they were surrounded by language, had a need to communicate, and received positive feedback for their efforts. Language programs should build on these successful early learning experiences.

Although children have been quite successful in their ability to communicate in their home environment, schools may impose demands for language that are quite unlike children's prior experiences. It therefore becomes the role of the teacher to discover and accept all children's unique language backgrounds and accomplishments and to plan accordingly and appropriately. When this is done, children's abilities in oral, written, and nonverbal forms of communication will be developed and extended (Department of Education, Wellington, 1986).

One way to think about the teaching of language is to consider the major elements in language. These elements are reading, writing, listening, and speaking. A concerted effort has been made to integrate all of these modes. However, reading, writing, listening, and speaking are not the only modes of communication. In a balanced literacy program, nonverbal modes are included as well. These are moving, watching, shaping, and viewing. The balance of this chapter is devoted to describing all these modes of language, concluding with a discussion on the relationship among the modes.

READING

'Twas brillig, and the slithy toves
Did gyre and gimble in the wabe:
All mimsy were the borogoves,
And the mome raths outgrabe.

What did you do while you were reading this passage? Did you recognize it as a passage that was probably read to you as a child? Were you able to make sense of the text, or did you concentrate on pronouncing the words? Since this chapter is dealing with reading and the reading process, you were given an exercise that is somewhat similar to what young children experience when first learning to read. Most likely, you pronounced every word correctly and can answer the following questions as well without any real difficulty.

- What did the slithy toves do?
- Where did they do it?
- Describe the borogoves.

What if you were asked to tell in your own words what you read? Would you be successful? It's doubtful, since the passage wasn't intended to make sense. The passage, written by Lewis Carroll in *Through the Looking Glass,* is pure, delightful nonsense. Yet you were able to read that passage and answer some critical comprehension questions. Were you really reading? The purists would answer a resounding *No,* since no sense making occurred, but in reality you were using some sources of information that were available to you—sources that you internalized when you were learning to read.

The Three Cueing Systems

Remember learning to ride a bike? You learned how to get on, balance the bike, steer it, pedal, put on the brakes, and get off. You coordinated these efforts until you were a successful bike rider. Well, the act of reading is a coordinated effort as well—several sources of information are coordinated when you read. Written language contains three kinds of information or cues:

1. **Semantic information or cues.** These are cues that relate to meaning, that is, information from each sentence and from the context of the entire text that is being read, *along with* information readers bring to the printed page (their experiences and prior knowledge). Semantic cues answer the question, Does it make sense?

2. **Syntactic information or cues.** These are cues that relate to the underlying structure of language. Syntactic cues consist of the interrelationship among words and among sentences. This interrelationship is based on the grammar or language cues of the English language. Syntax involves placing words into sentences according to grammatical rules. These grammatical cues include word order, word endings, and function words (words having grammatical meaning but not lexical meaning, such as prepositions, conjunctions, and verb markers). Syntactic cues answer the question, Does it sound like language (English)?

3. **Graphophonic information or cues.** This is information obtained through letter-sound relationships. Graphophonic cues answer the question, What is the pronunciation of the word?

Readers have these three sources of information available as prior knowledge and use them interdependently. Good readers use all three cueing systems equally as needed. The semantic, syntactic, and graphophonic information in the text triggers information in the head of the reader. From this interaction between the visual information (the print) and the nonvisual information (the reader's background knowledge), meaning is constructed. The more information received from the semantic and syntactic cueing systems, the less reliance a reader has on the graphophonic cueing system. Therefore a reader is able to pay less attention to sounding out words and can focus on the meaning of the text.

When you were reading the sample passage by Lewis Carroll, you relied on graphophonic and syntactic information. You were able to pronounce the words because you have internalized the way words sound in our language; that is, you were successful at what is traditionally known as phonics. You also used your knowledge of the structure of English. You knew that *slithy* was an adjective describing toves, and you recognized that *gyre* and *gimble* were verbs and that *the wabe* was a place. However, no meaning took place—and therefore no real reading.

Try this next passage by reading it out loud, and think about your own reading behaviors as you attempt to read it.

The Clolf in Weep's Shothing

There was once a tolf who trew grired of funting for his hood. "It's such ward hork and it's no shun being fot at by fad marmers," he said.

Ho se thought of a plever clan. De hecided to hap wrimself in a leepskin and shive in a peep shen.

Therefore, hen whe hew grungry, ke could hill a fice nat lamb for dis hinner and not have to funt to hind it.

However, that name sight, the darmer also fecided that le would hike damb for linner and went down to the peep shen. It was dery vark and the grarmer fabbed and killed the shirst feep he found. Imagine sis hurprise when fe hound he had willed a kolf.

MORAL: Prever netend to se bomeone else.

FROM THE CLASSROOM OF . . .

Cathy Marino Ridgewood, New Jersey

SURPRISE BOX

What does an ordinary pencil box contain besides pencils? Well, just listen to or read the clues and find out. Cathy uses a pencil box for this activity, but any box, decorated or otherwise, will do. Children are encouraged to bring home the box and find an object to place inside. Three clues are written with the parents' or teacher's help and read to the class. For example, can you guess what's inside the box?

1. I am very long.
2. I go in and out.
3. You can find me on your feet.

Did you guess? The answer, in case you were tricked, is a shoelace. This activity is expanded into making a guessing book. The clues are typed on the computer by a class volunteer, and the child who brings in the object is the illustrator. To truly keep this a guessing game, the clues could be on one page and the readers would have to turn the page to see if they got the right answer.

CLUES
1. I am very long.
2. I go in and Out.
3. You can find me on your feet.

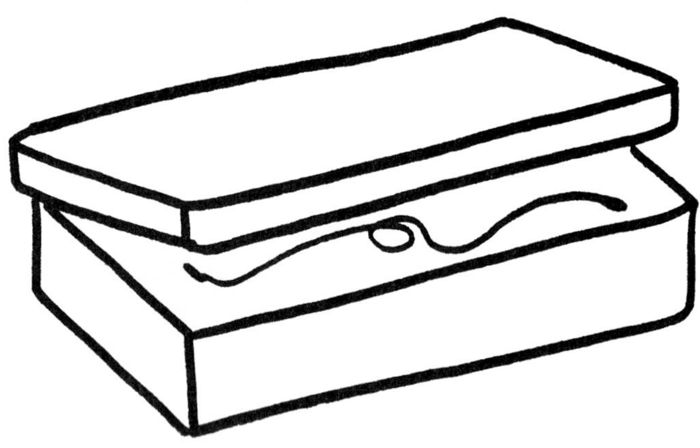

Now ask yourself these questions: Was your reading fluent or were you forced to read word-by-word? Did you find yourself making mistakes and going back to correct them? Did you feel like a successful reader?

Again you were forced to concentrate on pronouncing the words, and that made your reading somewhat robotlike. Have you ever listened to a first grader reading from a reading book? You probably sounded quite similar, since you were both forced to concentrate on word calling. Yet you probably made another discovery—that it was difficult to say each word, word-by-word. In addition, you said words you thought might appear. Since the text was mostly nonsense (and your initial guess was not confirmed), you went back and pronounced the word as it was written. You were actually *sampling* from parts of the text and *predicting* a probable word. You were attempting to make meaning based on your knowledge of language and your prior experience with the fable "The Wolf in Sheep's Clothing." Even though your task was to read the text out loud, you intuitively sought to make sense. That's what good readers do!

This exercise also raises a concern regarding the types of texts given to beginning readers. Beginning readers should be given reading materials that capitalize on their knowledge of language and their background experiences. Just as you coordinated your knowledge of the English sound system and the structure of language and used your background knowledge as you constructed meaning, young children need the same support as they are learning to read.

Reading as a Constructive Process

How do we read? Simply described, reading is the interaction of print with a brain. Through this interaction, meaning is made. To see for yourself, read the following passage. When finished, pretend you have been hired to illustrate the text. List what you would include in your illustration.

> Sitting across from one another, the siblings were playing Monopoly at the table. The older one was winning. Their mother came into the room. When she saw what was happening, she told him to try to let his sister win once in a while. Then she told them to clear the table because their father would be coming home shortly and it would be time to eat.

This activity has been undertaken by one of the authors many times in reading courses. Without fail, no two readers produce exact illustrations. However, although each rendition is personalized, there is enough commonality of vocabulary and concepts to recognize that the illustrations go with the same story. Some of the things depicted in the students' illustrations include:

- a smiling older child, a frowning younger one
- a dining room or a kitchen
- a mother with an apron on
- a clock showing five o'clock
- Monopoly board, hotels, houses, and money

Were these items similar to what you included in your illustration? Think about it: Nowhere was it mentioned that the story occurred in a dining room (or kitchen), nowhere were hotels or money mentioned, nowhere was a particular time mentioned. Yet these items are listed over and over. Where do readers get such information? Readers use two sources of information when constructing meaning (when using the semantic cueing system): the text and their own background knowledge. Here the author provided the general scenario and you, the reader, constructed the rest based on what you know about Monopoly, when fathers traditionally (in the United States) come home to eat, and what it feels like to lose a game (thus the sad face).

Reading therefore is a transaction between a reader and a text. But additional factors also affect a student's activation of his or her schema and the outcomes of the reading act (Weaver, 1988). These social and situational factors influence how a person reads and what he or she understands. Social factors include the readers' socioeconomic backgrounds, their culturally based expectations about reading, their ages, and their education. What the reader interprets from the text is also influenced by the reading situation or context. For example, people would read a novel differently from a chapter in a content area textbook. The reading context affects how the reader approaches the reading act and what he or she gains from the experience. Therefore no two readers will create identical interpretations of a text.

Reading, then, is an *interactive* process in which readers use information from the printed text along with what is in their heads to *construct* meaning in a given situational context. This is the definition of reading used in this textbook. Because reading is understanding, this also becomes the definition of comprehension used in this book. Reading and comprehension are synonymous. See Figure 2.1 for a model of the reading process.

Schema Theory

As stated above, reading is considered to be an active process in which readers make interpretations of the printed text in accordance with what they already know about the topic. To demonstrate the importance of the knowledge readers bring to the printed page, read the following passage.

> A newspaper is better than a magazine, and on a seashore is a better place than a street. At first, it is better to run than walk. Also you may have to try several times. It takes some skill but it's easy to learn. Even young children can enjoy it. Once successful, complications are minimal. Birds seldom get too close. One needs lots of room. Rain soaks in very fast. Too many people doing the same thing can also cause problems. If there are no complications, it can be very peaceful. A rock will serve as an anchor. If things break loose from it, however, you will not get a second chance.
>
> (Bransford and Johnson, 1972, p. 722)

Now close the book and retell in your own words what the passage was about. Again, you were able to pronounce all the words (you used graphophonic information). If certain words were deleted, you would provide words with the same part of speech (your syntactic cueing sys-

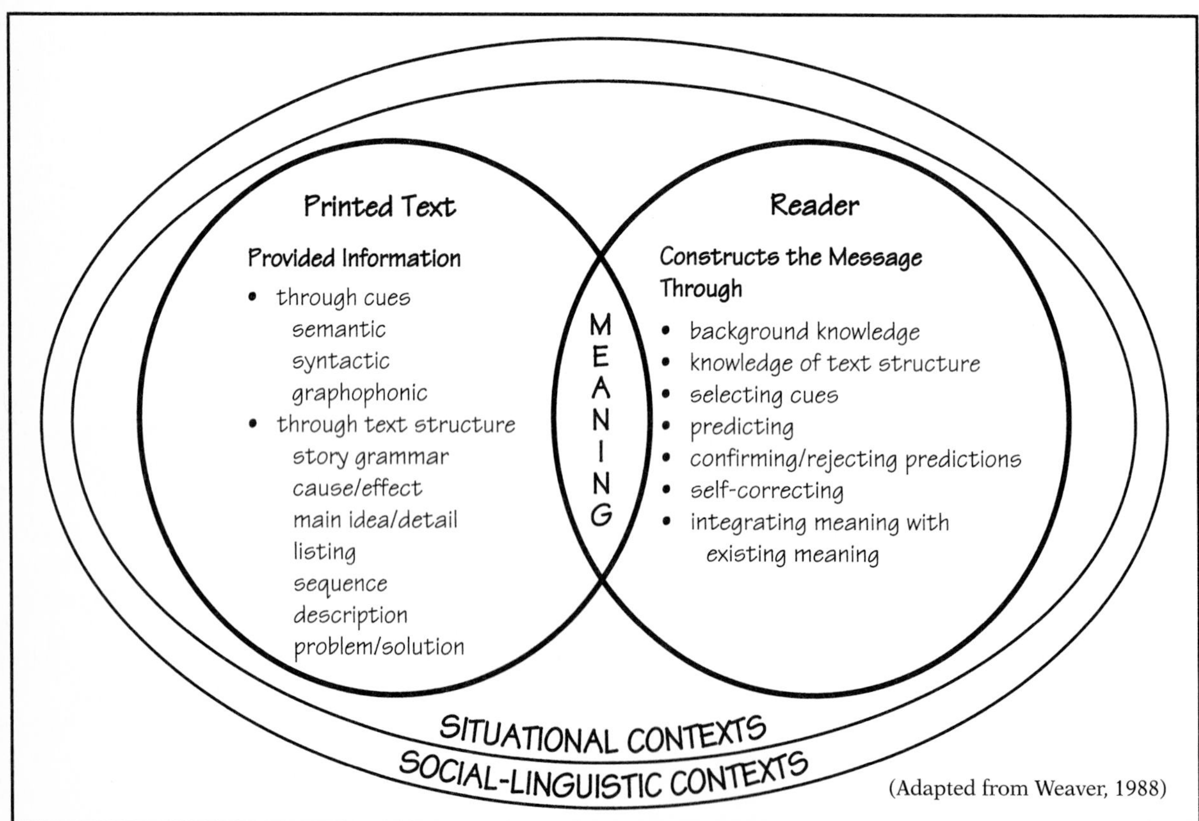

Figure 2.1 The Reading Process

tem). None of the vocabulary words taken alone was particularly difficult. Yet you still couldn't provide an effective reconstruction of the author's message. You were unable to make any connections. However, if you were told that this passage was about kite flying, everything would fall into place. Reread the passage and see if it now makes sense.

By activating what you, the reader, already know about the topic—kite flying—you were able to comprehend the text. You were able to tap into your Linguistic Data Pool (all the knowledge you hold in your head about language, about topics, about how texts are organized and constructed) (Harste, Woodward, and Burke, 1984) and retrieve the relevant information to make sense of that particular passage. This is known as **schema theory** (plural, *schemata*). *Schema theory* is a term used to describe how information is stored and organized in the brain. A schema is an organized body of a reader's information, conceptual knowledge, attitudes, and beliefs. It comprises the structure of a reader's knowledge. Schemata may be informational, linguistic, or affective (pertaining to a reader's emotions). Everyone possesses numerous schemata, some of which are quite comprehensive and some of which are relatively lacking in information.

Schemata are like individual file folders in which information is stored. Some file folders are thin, without much in them; some are thick. File folders are added to occasionally and items are removed when they are no longer needed or applicable. The same holds true for how learners store knowledge: They add to their schemata and the schemata are changed to accommodate the new information. Former beliefs and misinformation are removed as new data are added and new learning occurs. This chapter has added to your own file folder—your schema—for the reading process.

Schema theory proposes that a reader's existing knowledge and experiences have a direct influence over the content and form of any new knowledge that is to be learned. According to schema theory, what has been experienced and learned is stored in the brain in categories called schemata. These are incomplete and are constantly and continually being developed. Schema theory has significant implications for instruction. Teachers should be sensitized to the importance of a reader's prior knowledge. Before engaging students in any reading acts, teachers should activate, assess, and if necessary build background knowledge about the relevant concepts that will be presented and read. This will assure that the students' schemata are sophisticated enough to allow them to comprehend the printed text.

Models of Reading

In order to explain the processes and factors involved in what is called reading, models of reading have been formulated. Reading models—a way of providing insights into the reading process—have been developed for the purpose of describing how readers utilize language information while constructing meaning from the printed text. There are three main types of models describing how reading occurs. These are referred to as Bottom-Up, Top-Down, and Interactive—terms that refer to the flow of information during reading.

1. **Bottom-Up.** This model assumes that meaning is initiated by decoding graphic symbols into sounds. Children are expected to decode letters and words before they can obtain meaning from print. It is the belief that obtaining meaning begins with the print itself and that reading is the recognition of words. In this model, the teaching of subskills in a sequential and orderly manner is emphasized.

2. **Top-Down.** This model assumes that meaning begins with the prior knowledge of the reader because the reader's background knowledge is the starting point for understanding the text. Without prior knowledge, meaning cannot occur. The act of reading is begun with the reader making predictions about the author's intended meaning. Readers use graphophonic information to check their hypotheses about meaning.

3. **Interactive.** This model assumes that meaning involves using both the reader's prior knowledge and the print. The act of reading is begun by making predictions about the meaning in the text, by decoding the print, or both. The reader makes hypotheses based on the interaction of information from the three cueing systems (semantic, syntactic, and graphophonic).

In the latter two models—Top-Down and Interactive—meaning is given prime consideration. Reading is considered greater than the sum of its parts, with meaning as the core of the process. In these models, both speech and print are considered aspects of language, with print being merely an extension of language. Learning to read, like learning to speak, is a natural process. Reading is not considered a perfectible process, and deviations from the printed text are considered to be miscues, not errors. This is in contrast to the Bottom-Up model, in which words must be pronounced correctly and deviations from the text are considered to be errors.

There are instructional implications regarding these models. Teachers who subscribe to a Bottom-Up model would emphasize decoding and skills. Vocabulary would be controlled and stories would be adapted or abridged to accommodate the skills or the desire for a simplified text. Teachers who subscribe to a Top-Down or Interactive model of reading would choose materials with natural and familiar language. The materials would be chosen keeping in mind the children's prior knowledge and with the belief that the children will be able to discover the regularities in the printed text.

Instructional practices would vary as well, since these are largely determined by teachers' beliefs about the reading process. On the one hand, Bottom-Up teachers would emphasize decoding and sequential skill building as essential to obtaining meaning. Their students would spend a great deal of time on worksheets, drilling on phonics, vocabulary, and comprehension questions. On the other hand, Top-Down and Interactive teachers would have their students involved in meaningful, authentic literacy experiences. Their children will read real literature and engage in sampling, predicting, and confirming activities as they move toward meaning. Teachers would activate, assess, and build their students' prior knowledge as they engage their students in meaningful reading activities.

Children's approaches to reading are guided by what they believe reading is. Children's definitions of reading are obtained from what is emphasized during their reading instruction. If their teacher emphasizes decoding and word attack skills, then children will conclude that reading means pronouncing the words correctly. If their teacher emphasizes meaning and the use of strategies to construct meaning, then children will conclude that reading is making sense of printed text. Whatever approach teachers use instructionally will affect their students' implicit definition of reading and the strategies they use while reading. See Figure 2.2 for children's definitions of reading.

Reading: A Lifelong Process

Reading is a developmental process that is continually refined throughout life. Readers are always in the process of "becoming." Proficient readers continue to use the three cueing systems and to sample, predict, and confirm the author's intended message. The reader always expects print to make sense, and reading is therefore characterized by a concern for meaning.

The proficient reader not only expects texts to make sense and actively continues to seek meaning but also adds another dimension to the reading process—that of being a *dynamic* reader. Without being conscious of it, you most likely are dynamic readers. Do you read novels by Danielle Steele or Tom Clancy the same way you are reading this textbook? Hopefully not! You vary your rate, how you read, and what you do with the reading according to your purpose. Best-selling novels are intended to entertain, and no accountability is associated with the reading. Reading textbooks that are packed with facts and have a more formal style of writing is quite different. You read a textbook at a much slower pace, reread to clarify, and underline or take notes. Your purpose, reading rate, and use of reading strategies change depending on what you are reading. This is being a dynamic reader.

Throughout life, people are confronted with many reading tasks, some of which are comfortable and familiar to them. These reading acts will proceed fluently and efficiently, and meaning is created relatively easily. At other times—for example, when a reader is learning something new, taking college courses, or assembling something from complicated directions—reading will be more hesitant and less fluent and will result in less understanding. People continue as lifelong learners, and print will make different demands on their reading ability. By having been successful at reading, effective readers will

Figure 2.2 What Is Reading?

READING IS . . .

- if you don't need a grown-up or your Mommy to read it.
  (Ashley—Kindergarten)
- when you say the right words to your friends.
  (Heather—Kindergarten)
- if you can read you can be a leader.
  (Jonathan—Kindergarten)
- when you don't have to ask a grown-up what the words say.
  (Caitlin—Grade 1)
- when you can tell the story all by yourself.
  (Matt—Grade 1)
- exploring the world with no more than a move of the hand to turn a page.
  (Anna—Grade 3)
- sounding out words and reading them.
  (David—Grade 3)
- being able to pick up a book and being able to understand what it says.
  (Nicole—Grade 3)
- when someone sounds out a bunch of words to make a sentence.
  (Mike—Grade 3)
- the act of seeing and getting the meaning of something written or printed.
  (Michael—Grade 3)
- finding out things or just something to do when you want to or have time to for fun.
  (Sarah—Grade 3)
- unlocking a door to your imagination for just a little while or a long time each day.
  (Jessie—Grade 5)
- is helping to make us have better conversations and a bigger vocabulary.
  (Curtis—Grade 5)

Reading is my life!

Melanie

WHAT MAKES A GOOD READER?

- Somebody who enjoys reading and isn't afraid of picking up all different kinds of books.
  (Anna—Grade 3)
- Someone who enjoys books.
  (Shannon—Grade 3)
- Someone who understands what they're reading.
  (Samantha—Grade 3)
- A person who reads all the time. Someone who enjoys reading!! ME
  (Caitlin—Grade 3)
- Someone who was read to when they were little. Someone who likes to laugh or cry. Who really likes emotions. Someone who can sit down and read 14–20 pages and never put it down.
  (Alison—Grade 5)
- Someone who reads a book and tells friends about it.
  (Randy—Grade 5)
- Anybody can be a good reader by just reading real books.
  (Kalle—Grade 5)

I LIKE TO READ . . .

- I like to read because I have fun doing it and you can learn things from reading.
  (Nicole—Grade 3)
- I LOVE to read because I think it is interesting. Lots of books are appealing to me.
  (Megan—Grade 3)
- I did not like to read but now I read and get better grades. The reason I like to read is I like to have different emotions.
  (Alison—Grade 5)
- I like to read because there are so many books that are so well written that you feel like you're there with the characters. It is nice to sit in a cozy room here in America but be in some other place.
  (Jennifer—Grade 5)

approach unknown, complicated reading tasks in a positive, confident manner. If people have been unsuccessful at reading, then reading will be laborious and even avoided. Goals of a reading program should give primary attention to reading as a lifelong, meaningful act as well as cultivate a love of reading.

Proficient Readers

As a way of summarizing the reading process and what it means to be an effective reader, let's look at some good readers. Because of early literacy experiences at home and support at school, these children are typical of what educators consider to be good readers. They like to read and frequently choose reading over other activities. Although they have outside interests and participate in extracurricular activities, they prefer reading as a leisure-time activity. When reading, they are generally oblivious to everything around them. Good readers choose reading as an enjoyable activity and concentrate as they read.

If one were to observe them closely while reading, one would notice that their eyes move rapidly across and down the page. They do not read every letter, nor do they sound out every word on the page. If they were to do so, the process would be so laborious that they would not enjoy reading and would not choose to read.

As they read, not only do they sample from the printed text, but they also make predictions about possible events. They continue reading to confirm or make new predictions. Stories with predictable plots or familiar story lines are relatively easy to predict because good readers use both the text and their prior knowledge while reading. Unfamiliar stories with novel content are more challenging. Then these readers ask themselves what they already know about the topic and what they would like to learn. They adjust their reading rate to accommodate the more difficult text. At times they may have to ask the teacher or their peers for assistance, but for the most part they have learned enough strategies to be relatively self-sufficient.

When good readers come to unknown words, the strategy they usually use is to skip the word and see if they can get the meaning from the rest of the sentence or paragraph. Occasionally they might reread to see if they can determine the unknown word using both the context and their knowledge of phonics. If they stopped to unlock unknown words every time they encountered one, they would lose their train of thought, and the experience would be frustrating. When reading, if they misread a word, changing its meaning, they realize that something is wrong because the word doesn't make sense or doesn't sound right. They then reread to detect the error and correct it. They monitor their own reading and use self-correction when necessary.

These behaviors are typical of good readers. Good readers are knowledgeable about reading strategies that will help them comprehend text, and they are capable of monitoring their own reading progress. As they are exposed to more sophisticated texts and as their learning demands increase, they will add to their repertoire of strategies. They will grow in their role as lifelong learners and will continue to use reading for pleasure and to learn.

WRITING

Formerly, schools taught writing through the use of English or language textbooks. Teachers assumed the responsibility for choosing writing topics, and children were expected to produce a final copy on their first attempt, remembering all the mechanical skills that they were previously taught in isolation. After the piece was finished, it then became the teacher's responsibility for correcting, marking errors, and responding to the piece, usually with a letter grade. This traditional approach to writing was essentially writing on demand, and it focused on the written product.

Perhaps this was the type of writing program to which you were exposed, since it typified most writing programs in the past and still exists in some classrooms today. Fortunately, through the work of such notables as Donald Graves, Lucy Calkins, and Donald Murray, among others, writing is being viewed differently. The emphasis is no longer on the product (although written products are indeed valued) but on the process of writing. Writing is now perceived as a process and is described as falling into several stages or categories: prewriting, drafting, revising, editing, and publishing. These

FROM THE CLASSROOM OF . . .

Jane Kalfus Ridgewood, New Jersey

LET'S SHARE

Here's a variation of the traditional Show and Tell and Personal News Time. Each day, Jane puts up several pieces of paper on the chalkboard. If children have something to share, they write it on these sharing sheets when they enter school. At a convenient time, Jane writes up the sharing and sends the news home at the end of the week. A variation of this activity is to place a Sharing Box somewhere in the area where the class meets for community meetings. When children have objects to share, they place them in the box—to be retrieved when all the class is meeting and there is time available for the sharing of items in the box. Sharing children's experiences and personal belongings can develop both their written and oral language competencies.

stages represent a process that is nonlinear but is, rather, recursive; that is, authors go back and forth between the stages while composing. The author's movement from one stage to another is affected by what has previously occurred and what the author anticipates might happen. For example, the amount of information that has been gathered and the way the author has organized it may affect drafting and revising. While drafting, writers may see a need to include additional information, which can cause writers to retrace their steps and do some prewriting activities. Even when revising or editing, making corrections may take the writer back to the prewriting stage to gather more information or to reorder or resequence the information. Therefore the stages in the writing process influence and are influenced by one another.

"Writers are craftspersons; they are made, not born. Good writing doesn't just occur. It is fashioned out of the raw material of words with patience and the skill born of patience" (Temple and Gillet, 1989, 218). Writing is a craft that does evolve through the previously mentioned stages. However, it is of the utmost importance to remember that writing is cyclical and may not proceed through the stages in a neat, orderly fashion. Not all writing will reach the publishing stage. Writers may choose to abandon a topic or piece, temporarily or permanently.

Each stage in the writing process is described separately in the sections that follow. But before each stage is examined, a rationale for teaching writing is presented.

Why Teach Writing?

Why teach writing? Although the curriculum in the elementary schools is already quite crowded, there are valid reasons for including writing, and there are numerous benefits for children as well (Tompkins, 1990). First, writing is viewed as an activity that is natural for children to engage in. When Donald Graves asked children just starting school whether they knew how to read, only 15 percent said they could do so. This is in contrast to 90 percent of these same children who said they could write (Walshe, 1981b)! Not only do children perceive themselves as writers and therefore are motivated to continue writing in the school setting, but today's students also need to learn to communicate effectively using written language just as they did through oral language (Smith, 1982a). Life presents many opportunities for using writing to communicate, and these include future schooling, career-related writing, and writing informally at home.

Writing permits people to investigate and explore their understanding of the world and discover meaning in their experiences. It contributes to the growth of self-awareness and allows for the discovery, clarification, and sharing of personal thoughts and experiences (Learning Media, 1992).

Another reason for including writing in the curriculum is that children learn and apply their language skills through the act of writing (Calkins, 1980; Walshe, 1981a). The mechanics of writing, such as proper punctuation, capitalization, and spelling, are best learned in authentic situations rather than as isolated skill exercises. Not only is writing a more realistic situation in which to learn and apply these skills, but the skills also are best remembered when actively employed this way. Through writing, children also gain valuable knowledge about the reading process (Smith, 1983; Butler and Turbill, 1984; Hansen, 1987). Both reading and writing are constructive, meaning-making processes, with one process supporting the other. There is a strong relationship between reading (comprehending) and writing (composing), and, as Smith points out (1983), in order for children to become authors, they must read like real writers. This reading-writing connection is addressed in more detail later in this chapter.

Writing also enhances learning since writing becomes a tool for students to learn the content—that is, the body of knowledge—of a discipline (Walshe, 1981a; Fulwiler and Young, 1982; Gere, 1985). Through such writing activities as notetaking, learning logs, written conversations about a topic, research reports, and webbing, children have to think about what they are learning, relate it to what they already know about the topic, and raise pertinent questions. Writing also expands vocabulary. Every time writers choose one word over another, they are expanding their vocabulary knowledge. Writing helps in remembering and organizing information. Children use higher level thinking skills when they write because they must make decisions about choosing topics, organizing their writing, determining an appropriate audience, and revising their work (Langer and Applebee, 1987). A great deal of learning takes the form of problem solving and decision making (Walshe, 1981a). Problems can be approached by writing them out, recording guesses and insights, and finally drafting and rewriting solutions. The act of writing forces people to be clear and to go over the piece frequently, reworking, correcting, and polishing (Walshe, 1981a). These activities and thought processes make writing a valuable tool for learning.

Another exceedingly important reason for ensuring that writing receives attention in the elementary school curriculum is that writing is pleasurable (Tompkins, 1990). Many people write because it is an enjoyable activity. This writing may take the form of imaginative writing, letters, journals, newsletters, and poetry. Writing also provides a means of self-discovery, which empowers young authors. Through writing, authors can be put in touch with their feelings, their thoughts, and their concerns. Writing also builds self-esteem as writers get to see their thoughts and words in print. Children should not only be taught how to write during the elementary school years; they should also be given the gift of becoming lifelong writers. To do this, children should learn how to write and should be able to use writing both functionally and for enjoyment as part of the elementary instructional program.

Stages in the Writing Process

Traditionally, the teaching of writing assumed a one-draft-only mentality. The object was to get it done and move along. Children were forced into instant writing with one-shot drafts being published in a single sitting. The emphasis has shifted from analyzing children's finished products to looking at what children think and do as they write. Writing is now viewed as a multistage process. However, it is misleading to think of these stages as occurring in a sequential and linear fashion. The stages are interactive and frequently occur simultaneously. The writing process consists of prewriting, drafting, revising, editing, and publishing. Much of the following discussion is based on the work of such educators as Donald Graves, Lucy Calkins, and Donald Murray. See Figure 2.3 for a model of the Writing Process.

Prewriting

Prewriting is now considered the most crucial of the stages, although it previously was the most neglected. Just as athletes need to warm up before a game or an athletic event, writers also need to warm up and get ready. Prewriting is the stage when writers are getting ready to write. This is the time for rehearsal and incubation, for thinking and reflecting. First, writers must decide to write and then prepare for writing. In preparing for writing, writers have to decide on a topic, identify an audience and purpose for writing, determine the appropriate form for the piece, and gather ideas and data.

After writers have decided to write, they think about what to write and how to do it. Writers might have a great deal of indecision when determining topics—"Maybe I'll write about . . ." or "That's something I could write on." Doubts are quite common during the prewriting stage, and it is easy for teachers to

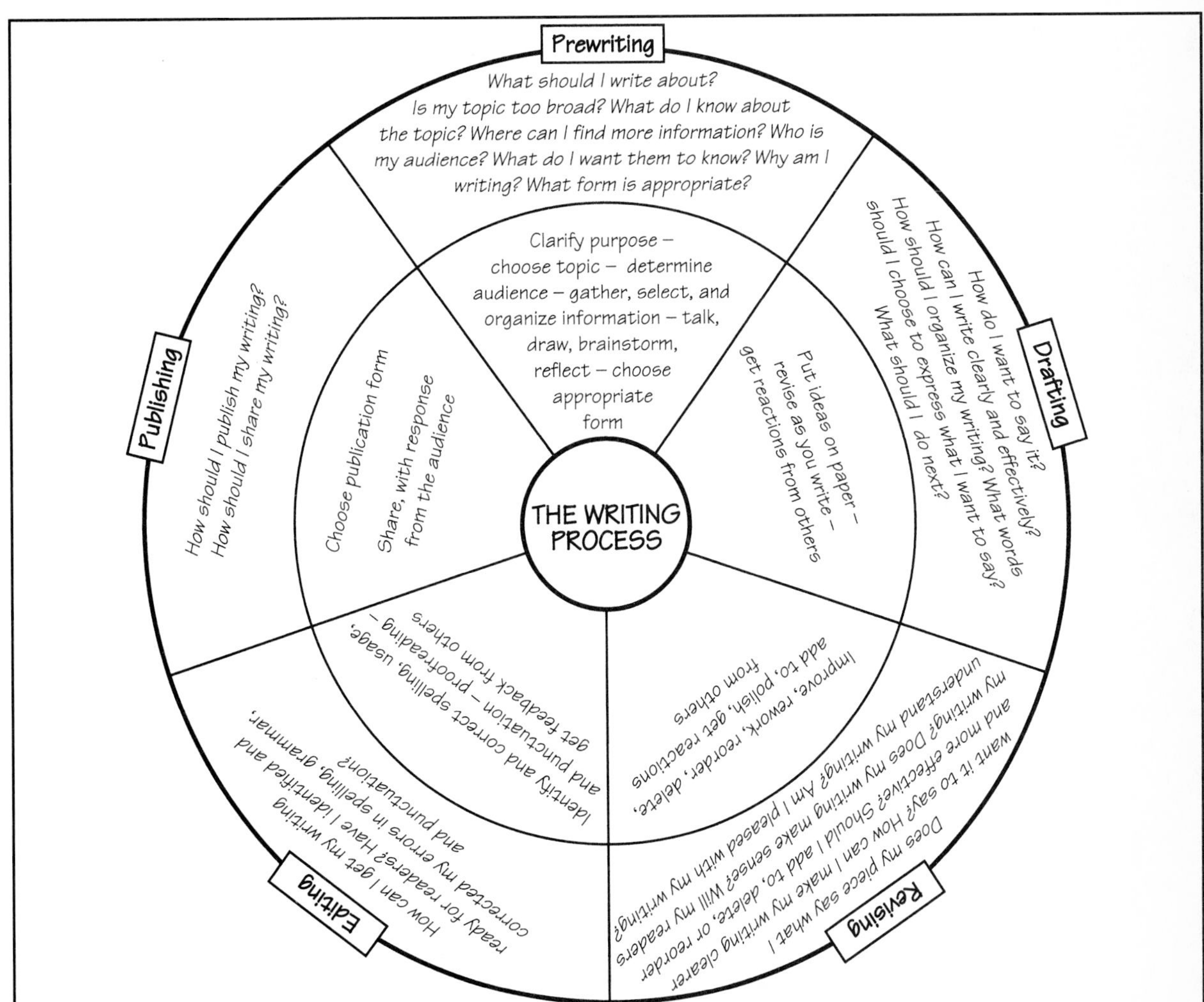

Figure 2.3 Model of the Writing Process—Questions Writers Should Ask and Possible Behaviors

revert to former practices and assign a topic to the young writer. Providing topics for children has been likened to "writing welfare" (Graves, 1976). Instead, it is preferred that teachers model how to get ideas for topics and help children develop their own "I Can Write About" lists. Figure 2.4 depicts where children can obtain ideas for their writing.

Although it is recommended that students generate their own topics, teachers can occasionally focus children and provide some direction during writing. Narrative writing is frequently the predominant kind of writing students choose (Learning Media, 1992). In order to have students experience and practice a range of writing forms and purposes, teachers sometimes need to provide students with opportunities to write for different audiences, for a variety of reasons, using various forms or registers. However, even during these occasions there still should be some element of choice for the writer within the boundaries established by the teacher. For instance, during writing instruction teachers can provide general guidelines. They can specify the form or function the piece should take while the writer determines the content (e.g., the teacher requests a piece of persuasive writing, and children can write to their parents, the principal, or a newspaper editor convincing them to support something, or they could write an editorial defending their position on an issue). Or teachers can determine the topic (perhaps one that is currently being studied in the classroom, e.g., landfills as part of a study on the environment) while the student determines the form (a research report, a persuasive letter to the editor stating why

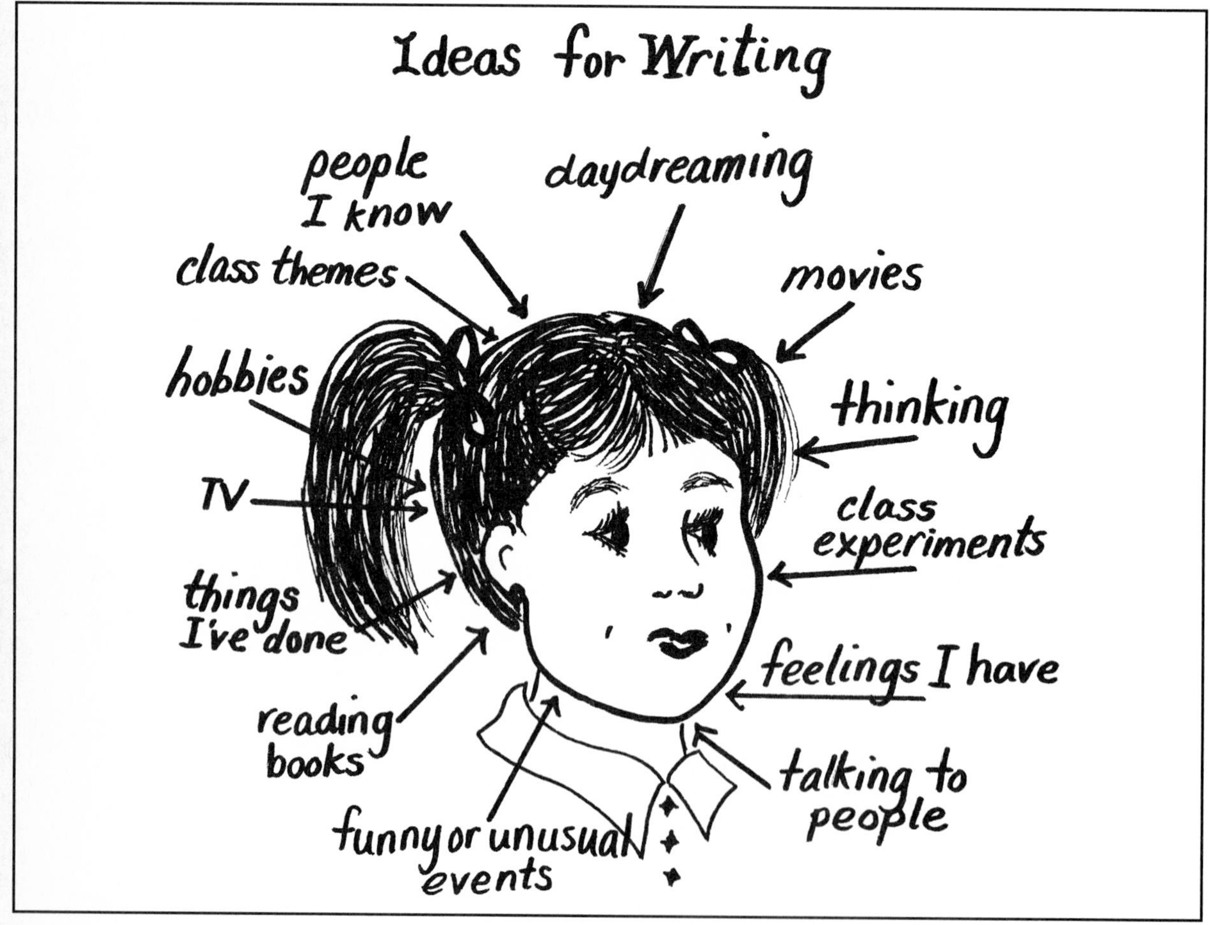

Figure 2.4

a landfill should not be located in the student's hometown, a public opinion survey on a landfill issue). Teachers need to stretch their students' writing repertoires, and they have certain mandated content to teach, so at times it may be necessary and desirable to focus students' writing.

In writing process classrooms, children now have wider audiences than previously, when their main audience consisted of the teacher. Today, in addition to the teacher, children write for themselves, their classmates, the community, school publications, and commercially produced magazines and newspapers. They also write for a variety of purposes that may take many forms. Following are listed, along with some typical forms, many of the reasons writing is used in people's daily lives.

PURPOSE	FORMS
to amuse or entertain	jokes, riddles, stories, comics, graffiti, plays, bumper stickers
to command, request, or direct	directions, warnings, rules, memos
to record events	diaries, research notes, semantic maps, lists, reports, histories
to predict or hypothesize	forecasts, predictions, theories, horoscopes
to inform or advise	announcements, invitations, pamphlets, surveys, catalogs, lists, graphs, broadcasts
to persuade	editorials, graffiti, signs, advertisements, arguments
to explain	textbooks, handbooks, recipes, captions, rules, excuses, brochures, newspaper articles
to narrate	stories of all genres
to create	plays, jokes, commercials, poems, stories, songs, puzzles
to find out or discover	interviews, questionnaires, surveys, observations, business letters
to invite reflection	quotations, questions, learning logs, journals

(Staab and Smith, 1986; Butler, A., 1988; Butler, S., 1991; Learning Media, 1992

Writing for these purposes using a variety of forms is a means for people to interact with the world. Writing that is encouraged and developed in school should not take place only during the time scheduled for writing, such as in a Writers' Workshop, but should occur throughout the school day in all curricular endeavors. An expanded range of written responses is provided in Figure 2.5.

During the prewriting stage, there are two general types of activities: background activities and informal writing activities. Background activities are those that give the writer the knowledge needed for writing. These include conducting research and reading about the intended topic. Informal writing activities include such rehearsal activities as drawing, talking, webbing or clustering, brainstorming, daydreaming, role-playing, and free writing.

Murray (1982) believes that 70 percent or more of the writing time should be spent in prewriting. Children need the time to think and talk about what they may write. They need to be engaged in research, brainstorming, reading, and viewing films for help in getting ideas and deciding on a topic. They need to consider the audience, their purpose, and the form the writing might take and then move on to the next stage—drafting or composing.

Drafting or Composing

Once writers begin to put their thoughts down on paper, they will frequently switch back and forth between rehearsal and composing since writing is both tentative and exploratory. During this stage, some children will have difficulty getting started, while others will plunge right in. Some will draw pictures and make doodles on their paper, while others will write continuously and seemingly without effort. While drafting, writers continually read back what they have written to see how their work is developing. This continues until writers are satisfied with their efforts or confer with their teacher or classmates to obtain assistance.

During this phase of the writing process, teachers generally move around the room providing help, encouragement, and support as needed. When conducting these brief sessions, referred to as roving conferences, teachers ask such questions as, How is your writing going?

Figure 2.5 A Range of Written Responses

advertisements
advice columns
alphabet books
agendas
anecdotes
announcements
apologies
applications
appointment books
autobiographies
autograph books
ballots
banners
bibliographies
book jackets
books
brochures
bumper stickers
captions
cartoons
catalogs
case studies
certificates
character sketches
charts
comics
commentaries
commercials
computer programs
contracts
conversations/dialogue
coupons
crossword puzzles
debates
definitions
deposit slips
diagrams
diaries
dictionaries
directories
editorials
envelopes
essays
experience stories
fables
fact sheets
flyers
folktales
food packages
fortune cookies
glossary
graphs
greeting cards
guidebook
handbook
horoscopes
index
innovating on text
interviews
invitations
itineraries
jingles
jokes
journals
jump–rope rhymes
junk mail
lab reports
labels
learning logs
letters
lists
lyrics
magazines
maps
math writing
- story problems
- solutions to problems
- learning logs

memoirs
memos
menus
messages
minutes of meetings
mysteries
myths
newsletters
newspapers
notes
obituaries
opinions
outlines
paragraphs
petitions
plays
poetry
postcards
posters
prescriptions
prophecy and predictions
puzzles
questionnaires
questions
quizzes
recipes
record albums
requests
research reports
responses to literature
résumés
reviews
riddles
rules
satire
science
- observations
- notebook
- lab reports

scripts
semantic mapping
sentences
signs
slogans
songs and ballads
speeches
stories
story frames
study guides
summaries
surveys
tables
tall tales
telegrams
telephone directories
thesauruses
tickets
time lines
tongue twisters
travelogues
valentines
wall stories
want ads
weather reports
word searches
wordless picture books
yearbook
"You Are There" scenes

What is going to happen next in your story? Do you need any help? The focus of these conferences is to help children get their ideas down on paper. Teachers may also conduct more formal conferences during the drafting stage. Children usually sign up for these conferences, and more time is devoted to helping them with their writing. The intent of these conferences during the drafting stage is on the child's message—the content of the piece—not the mechanics.

During the drafting stage, children must not be hampered with the mechanics of writing. The idea is to get their ideas down without letting concern about correct spelling, punctuation, and grammar get in the way of composing. Some children may be uncomfortable with imperfect drafts, and they will need support in their risk-taking behaviors. Writing resources should be available, and the children need instruction in how to use them. Invented spelling should be encouraged to enable younger children to use words from their oral vocabularies that will permit the free flow of ideas. To help children and their parents overcome their difficulties with imperfect pieces, teachers frequently use a stamp stating "Draft" or "Under Construction," which alerts readers that the piece will undergo corrections if it is to be published.

Children need to be made aware that first drafts are not finished products and that any piece of writing can be improved. They need to be shown the value of reworking their writing and how to improve on it. They are ready for the next stage of the writing process—revision.

Revising

This is the stage of the writing process when writers revisit or "see again" their writing pieces. "Writing, like the potter's clay, only becomes a thing of usefulness or beauty through repeated smoothing and shaping" (Walshe, 1981, 40). The purpose of revision is to clarify and shape the meaning and to organize the writing. It is the stage at which the author rethinks what has been written. Revision involves adding, substituting, deleting, and moving ideas and words around as writers rework and polish their pieces for clarity and interest.

During this phase of the writing process, young authors read their writing in pairs, in writing circles, and during conferences with their teacher. Listeners respond to the writer by noting what they liked about the piece, asking questions about the author's intent or confusing parts, and providing suggestions for improvement. Writers might also ask specific questions about aspects of the piece that they feel need reworking. In any case, the author always has the option of incorporating the suggestions or ignoring them. Once the piece has been reviewed, it is ready to be put into publishable form—it is ready for editing.

Editing

Editing is the process of getting the piece ready for the audience. Respect for the audience now guides the writer. The writer is expected to attend to the surface features of writing—mechanics, grammar, and spelling. Children must recognize that in order to communicate effectively with an audience, writing must be free of errors that can interfere with the understanding of the message or can distract from the writing itself. As Graves (1983) points out, "Poor spelling in the midst of a good piece of writing is like attending a lovely banquet but with the leavings of grime and grease from the previous meal still left on the table" (183). Depending on the age and development of the writer, the young authors now look over their pieces and make appropriate adjustments and corrections. Over time, children are taught to check capitalization, punctuation, spelling, paragraph structure, grammar, and vocabulary, as well as for complete sentences. Especially for young authors, the focus should be on some of these points, not all of them. Children should be taught some standard editing marks to use in proofreading their own or their classmates' pieces (see Figure 2.6).

The objective of this stage is getting the piece ready for readers. Young children will be unable to edit their pieces completely, but they should be expected to identify and correct some spelling errors, some missing capital letters, and the like. Their piece can then go to an editor (the teacher, a parent, an older child) for final correction. After taking into consideration all the editorial suggestions, the writer prepares this polished piece for sharing, publishing, or both.

Publishing

An important purpose underlying the writing process is to produce a finished product for an audience. Writers write to produce written mate-

Figure 2.6 Editing Marks

Mark	Function	Example
¶	Begin a new paragraph.	¶ Wolves are found in cold areas throughout the Northern Hemisphere. Because people have pushed the wolf farther into the wilderness, they are common only in Canada and Alaska.
≡	Capitalize a letter.	There are also wolf species that live in europe and Asia.
^,	Add a comma.	Wolves prey on deer, game birds rabbits, and other animals.
⊙	Add a period.	Wolves usually forage at night for their food ⊙
^	Add letter or word.	In winter, they frequently hunt in packs.
ᵛ	Add apostrophe.	The wolves mating season is in late winter or early spring, and the young are born about two months later.
∽	Trade position of letters or words.	Wolf families together remain until the young are mature.
sp.	Correct spelling.	Hunters and farmers object to wolves because they prey on wildlive and livestock. sp.
/	Make a capital letter lowercase.	In many Regions where wolves are found, bounties are offered for killing them.
ℓ	Delete a letter or word.	Wolves learn quickly by ~~through~~ experience, ~~rapidly~~ and stories have been told about how they have outwitted hunters and their dogs.

rial for an intended audience (Walshe, 1981). This final stage of the writing process—publishing—occurs when a completed text is reworked and edited to the satisfaction of the author. Although many young authors will want to publish everything they write, not all pieces will reach the publishing stage. Through conferencing, the children will indicate an intention to take a piece through to publication. Graves has suggested that on the average one piece in four is published; however, this can vary depending on the age of the writer and the style and format of some pieces. Some pieces, such as chapter books or research reports, naturally take longer to write, so the authors of these pieces will publish less often. The number of published pieces is really the children's decision, but negotiation may occur as to whether a piece should be published.

A high standard should be set for overall correctness and presentation for the pieces that are to be published. Once these standards have been achieved, the piece is ready for the public, and the author decides how the piece will be published, shared, or both. Many options are available, such as binding books, posting the writing on a specially created bulletin board, and submitting it to school newspapers, anthologies, commercial magazines, or newspapers. Children may choose to produce hand-scripted copies of their writing or have someone type their writing on a computer or typewriter. The writing may be placed in the class or school library and be available for others to check out to read at home. Authors may also share their writing by reading it in a special place in the classroom: the author's chair (Graves and Hansen, 1982). This chair is reserved for authors to read their pieces, and time is always set aside for this activity. Other audiences can include other classes, other teachers or support personnel in the school, the principal, parents and family, and community members.

Although the preceding discussion is about the process of writing, the ramifications are more important than the products that are produced. Writing can be a springboard to personal discovery, growth, and reflection when the writer's voice is encouraged, listened to, and respected. Writing is a means of empowering young learners as they assume control of and responsibility for their own learning. Thus, process writing is more than just an instructional method. It is a philosophy that helps determine both an approach and a practice—it is a philosophy that helps children develop into confident, capable writers. Figure 2.7 provides some comments from elementary students on what it means to be a writer.

The above information is intended to provide a general overview of the writing process. Instructional implications and techniques are presented in the chapters on emergent literacy (Chapter 6) and beyond emergent literacy (Chapter 8). In these chapters, specific techniques for both facilitating and teaching the writing process are offered, taking into consideration developmentally appropriate practices for the age and experiences of the children in the classrooms.

Framework for a Writing Program

There are some key points to consider when teaching writing:

1. **Time.** Time must be provided for children to write every day. They need time for thinking and talking about their writing and time for the actual drafting, revising, and publishing of their pieces. This time needs to be structured and predictable so that children can anticipate when they will be writing and can therefore be prepared for writing both mentally and physically. Time is also necessary for children to hear models of good writing through reading and discussing literature, teacher demonstrations of the writing process, and sharing other students' pieces.

2. **Process.** Students should be taught about the writing process and given the opportunity to use it in real-life activities with real audiences. Writing activities occur throughout the curriculum.

3. **Ownership.** Children should have control of the responsibility for their own writing. In general, they should be permitted to select their own writing topics, which will most likely stem from their own experiences and interests. Young authors need to decide on their own purpose for writing, their intended audience, the appropriate form or register, and the style of writing.

4. **Climate.** An appropriate writing climate needs to be established in which children are comfortable with taking risks and with working collaboratively with their peers and the teacher as part of a community of learners. Students work with their peers throughout the writing process, providing ideas, support, encouragement, and suggestions to one another. The teacher provides help to students through modeling, demonstration, corrective feedback, encouragement, and conferencing. Teachers focus their assessment and evaluation efforts on the process as well as on the product.

5. **Resources.** All classrooms should be equipped with a variety of resources to support the writing process. These include literature (fiction and nonfiction), reference materials (dictionaries, atlases, directories, thesauruses), and a range of writing materials (paper, pens, pencils).

6. **Writing instruction.** Writing strategies and knowledge about the writing process and the mechanics of writing are acquired as children read and write, as they talk to their classmates and share their writing. However, there

Figure 2.7

WRITING

WHAT IS A WRITER?

- Writing is sort-of expressing your feelings. Writing is sort-of like drawing, only when you write you put your thoughts in sentences, not in pictures, and in writing you create a picture in someone's mind.

  Karen—Grade 6

- To write means to:
  write a detailed story
  express my feelings on a sheet of paper
  to say if I am happy or sad or quiet
  or loud
  be able to paint a picture with my words
  to enjoy writing.

  Jenny—Grade 3

- To be a writer means a lot of hard work and a good imagination. You have to think about what you're writing and become what you're writing about. For example, I have never been to Disneyland. If I wrote a story about Disneyland, I would ride all the rides, meet the Disney characters, or maybe get lost by myself. By using your imagination you can go anywhere or do anything you want. By using my imagination and writing about it, I am able to go to Disneyland.

  Writing can make people laugh, smile, cry, upset them, but it also can help people when they write their feelings down like in a diary, journal, etc. Many good stories came from authors' true feelings and things that really happened in their life.

  Tarah—Grade 4

I AM A WRITER . . .

- I am a writer because I write in a journal. I write letters to people like my pen pal. I write stories. I write in a Literature Response Log, and I write everyday. I can play around with things that I write. I had to do a lot of writing this year but I didn't care. You can do anything you want with writing. You can change anything you want. I can write reports. I can write dialogue.

  Genevieve—Grade 3

- I am a writer because I have a good hand for writing. I am a good poet and author. My imagination helps to make my stories and poems come alive. I see myself as a writer because I enjoy writing and read other people's writing. I have a talent of writing about my friends, family, fantasy, and nature. I have lots of ideas. I believe in myself and I believe in others.

  Jennifer—Grade 3

- I am a writer because I write what I feel and I have many ideas. I also write what is going on in my head. I like writing. I can write dialogue. When I grow up I plan to be a writer.

  Zach—Grade 3

- I am a writer because I don't take a lot of time to think about what I want to write. I just write down my thoughts and I just write. My mom says I was born to be a writer. That's why I got a book published. I also have a mind of ideas.

  Dana—Grade 3

are times when children can benefit from more information about mechanics, new writing strategies, and different genres. Teachers need to provide such information and instruction. This instruction should occur at the time when children can use the instruction during real writing activities. Instruction is not based on an arbitrary list of skills, but on ongoing teacher observation.

(Butler and Turbill, 1984; Tompkins, 1990; Graves, 1994)

In addition, writing should not be used as punishment, and writing is not penmanship. Any negative associations to these two activities should be avoided. Requiring students to copy over such phrases as "I will not . . ." or "I will be good in school" does nothing to enhance the teaching of writing, nor does it contribute to positive discipline. Endless copying of exercises to improve handwriting likewise does not contribute to an effective writing program. Handwriting becomes important during the publication phase of the writing process when children need to produce legible copies for their audiences.

Therefore, the essential elements of a successful writing program include writing for authentic purposes for real audiences in a supportive environment that provides frequent writing opportunities (Calkins, 1983; Graves, 1983, 1994). Children are immersed in models of good writing, receive numerous demonstrations of all phases of the writing process, and are given the responsibility and opportunity to develop their writing ability.

Qualities of Good Writing

What is an effective piece of writing? What kinds of writing are memorable? Writing is good or effective because of its content, because of what it says. Good writing opens up a world of new facts and ideas for the readers and is written in a clear and memorable fashion. The following are considered qualities of good writing (Murray, 1979, cited in Walshe, 1981a; Reif, 1992; Learning Media, 1992):

1. **Meaning** (the content of the writing piece)
    - Does the piece of writing say something?
    - Does the form reflect the writer's purpose?
2. **Authority** (the provision of accurate and specific information)
    - Does the piece demonstrate that the writer is knowledgeable about the topic?
3. **Voice** (the use of individual voices)
    - Does the writing show a personal touch and reflect personal confidence?
4. **Design** (the form and structure of the piece)
    - Has the writer chosen the appropriate form?
    - Does the piece of writing have structure and is it well ordered and developed?
5. **Clarity** (the use of simplicity that is appropriate for the topic)
    - Is the writing clear?
    - Is the information correct?
6. **Conventions** (the use of correct conventions)
    - Is the spelling correct, or has the writer demonstrated the ability to identify misspelled words?
    - Is the punctuation correct?
7. **Attitude** (the way the writer approaches writing)
    - Does the writer enjoy writing?
    - Does the writer experiment with writing forms, purposes, words, and ideas?

Good writing is clear, honest, vibrant, authoritative, rhythmic, and memorable. The best of writing, whether prose or poetry, makes use of playful and imaginative language. Good writing is economical and does not waste words. It puts the readers right there in the writing. It makes believers out of them.

Development of Spelling and Writing

There are developmental characteristics of children's writing as they progress through various stages that ultimately culminate in standard spelling. Once children begin exploring with markers or crayons at very young ages (on walls, over books, on any unattended paper), they are beginning to develop their own writing abilities. First, children will merely *scribble*. The markings they create are done randomly with no real differentiation between drawing and writing. Two-year-olds scribble readily and, after a while, gradually differentiate between scribbling for drawing and scribbling for writing (Sulzby, Teale, and Kamberelis, 1989).

As children's drawings become recognizable, their scribbling also begins to look like writing. When young children make this distinction between drawing and writing, many begin to write on the left side of the page and proceed across to the right side. Many 3-year-old children use letterlike features when they scribble because that is the convention that was demonstrated to them, and they also begin to make more conventional letters. There is some knowledge of the alphabet, but there is no knowledge of letter-sound associations. Young children may write stories, letters, or messages using a string of letterlike formations and go back and forth among scribbling, drawing, and letter strings.

Over time, the writing of young children becomes shaped like writing—it tends to be linear, alike in size, repetitive, and symbolic (Fields, Spangler, and Lee, 1991). Children may start imitating conventional print and copying or memorizing familiar words, such as *Mommy, Daddy,* and their own names. Pseudoletters are invented. Their writing may include letters and letterlike forms and look more like real writing, but it is still unreadable. These letterlike forms include letters formed incorrectly or backward numerals. The stages described (scribbling, drawing, letter strings) are sometimes characterized as being precommunicative or nonspelling stages. However, even at these early stages of writing (or pseudowriting), given encouragement, children will write profusely and will even "read" their pieces to others, making up stories to accompany the writing.

The first stage of spelling begins when writing is made up entirely of letters and letterlike forms—the *prephonemic* stage. Although the writing consists of recognizable letters, the letters bear no resemblance to the sounds in the words. The children, who are prereaders, have not discovered that letters represent sounds in spoken words. Prephonemic spelling is typical of older preschool-age children, kindergartners, and some first graders. As children are provided with further experiences with print, they discover that letters represent sounds. At this point, they can now write words that are partially readable. When children first begin to spell phonetically, they use letters to represent sounds, but their spellings do not resemble conventional spelling. Generally, children at this stage attempt only to represent one or two sounds in a word, such as *m* for *my* or *mr* for *Mother.* Once children begin to associate some sounds with some symbols, they are entering a *semiphonetic* stage. Only one or two sounds in a word are represented, but some attempt is made to use the sounds heard in the words. This stage is typical of children beginning to read, some kindergartners, and most first graders.

Once children begin spelling words as they are heard, they are using *phonetic* spelling. All sounds are represented in the words. The word *apple* might now be spelled *apl,* representing all the sounds heard in the word. Children are using their auditory skills at this point, but once they start to visualize words they enter a *transitional* phase (which generally coincides with the children's advancement from beginning readers to independent readers). Some words are spelled using patterns found in conventional spelling, as in *unighted* for *united.* In this example, the young writer has discovered that *igh* stands for the long sound of /i and has overgeneralized this to other words. Examples of transitional spellings include adding silent *e* to words, doubling consonants before adding endings, and using alternate spelling forms for words. During the transitional phase, children will spell some words correctly and other words using their own invented (or temporary) spelling. With ample opportunities to write and with some spelling instruction on identified areas of need, children will start spelling conventionally (the *correct* stage). Although some children are termed good spellers—they tend to spell most words correctly most of the time—the goal is to help them become effective spellers—children who recognize misspelled words and have strategies to correct them. Figure 2.8 depicts Sarah's growth as a writer.

Figure 2.8A Sarah's Growth as a Writer (cont.)

At 2 years

2yr. 10 mo.

"Little People" Sarah L. Mumper

Sarah's message at 3 years

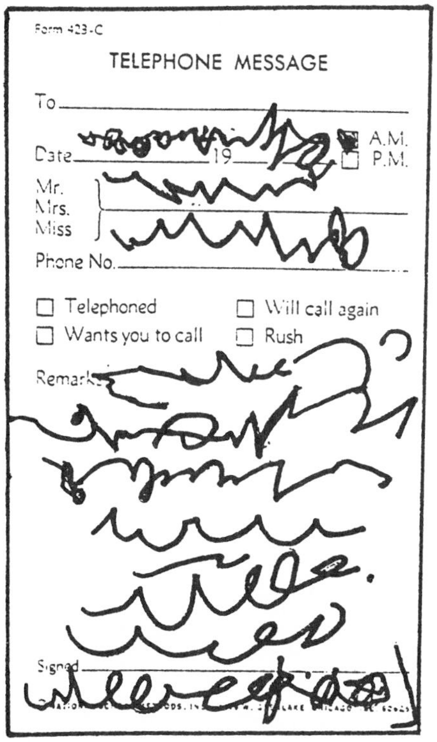

Form 423-C

TELEPHONE MESSAGE

To

Date 19 A.M. P.M.

Mr.
Mrs.
Miss

Phone No.

☐ Telephoned ☐ Will call again
☐ Wants you to call ☐ Rush

Remarks

Signed

Sarah's writing at 4 years

May 1980

Figure 2.8B Sarah's Growth as a Writer (cont.)

Age 5 years

"3 Little Kittys do ABC's"

Age 4½ yrs.

My name is Sarah.
I am five years old.
I want a dog.
I like to read.
I live in an A house.

A sentence by Sarah, age 6

This sentence was dictated by Sarah
"You can't see the girl pouring the coffee into the cup."

Figure 2.8C Sarah's Growth as a Writer (cont.)

By Sarah at age 8, first half of third grade

Sarah

Sponges

Sponges are really animals that live in the sea. They are millions of cells that live and grow together. Divers hunt for them to sell. When a sponge is taken out of the water it dies. Then people use the soft skeleton for cleaning. Real sea sponges have unusual shapes.

Jean, Robert, David.

I give my love to all of you. You're all sweet just like a cookie! Jean, I give you the name of tender loveing care. Robert, I give you the name of I love you. David, I give you the word of Hansom brother.

from,
Sarah

A love letter Sarah wrote
to her family for Valentine's Day
February 1984 (age 7 yrs. 10 mos.)

Original poem by Sarah, age 11

If I could have a wish
Come true on this night
I'd wish to hold a star
in my hands.

Then I'd let it go to fly
Up in the clear black
sparkling sky.

It would fly up
and hit the moon
Slivers of gold
would float down
Like a shower of
golden snow.

If I could have a wish
Come true on this day
I'd wish that I could
climb the tallest tree.

Then I'd be able
to jump on a
passing cloud.

It would take me
across the clear
blue sky.
I'd drift across
the land and
the shining sea.

Sarah [illegible]
1987

Sarah's writing at age 12

Sarah (Cinqain Poetry)

Ice
Cold, watery
Freeging, sucking, crunching
Cold in my mouth
Water

Sarah M. Sojourner Truth

Sojourner Truth was a black woman who spent the first half of her life in slavery. She lived around New Paltz. She had several children, but they were taken away and sold into slavery. She went to the judges and sued to get them back but only got one child back. During the rest of her life she went around making speaches about human rights.

SOJOURNER TRUTH

Sojourner Truth was a black woman who spent part of her life as a slave. She was born in New York State in about 1797. After the Civil War she spent most of her time helping freed slaves learn how to live in freedom. She traveled across America speaking about human rights. She died in 1883.

In February 1986, the United States Postal Service printed a stamp with a picture of her on it to honor her. This was the first stamp ever issued by the New Paltz Post Office. A Special ceremony was held for the first day of issue.

BY SARAH MUMPER

Figure 2.8E Sarah's Growth as a Writer (cont.)

Two of Sarah's poems, written at age 13

The Tiny Ship

One evening I sat by the river
and watched a small ship sail by.
The stones in the river bed made
huge waves that tossed the
ship about. I wondered as the
ship sailed by which tree it
had fallen from.

SADNESS

Sadness is the color of the night sky
It sounds like thunder roaring inside
It tastes like salty water
And smells like a rainy day.
Sadness looks like stormy skies
It makes you feel like emptiness.

Sarah Munper

The Reading-Writing Connection

Although the discussions of the reading and writing processes are presented separately in this chapter, both reading and writing are systematically related. Both processes can be learned in connection with each other rather than in isolation. The integration of reading and writing instruction has been receiving increased attention. Recent studies in the area of literacy have cast doubt on the traditional fragmentation of the language arts (e.g., the compartmentalization of reading and writing) and have demonstrated the positive aspects and benefits of connecting reading and writing (Stotsky, 1983; Eckhoff, 1984; Tierney and Leys, 1986). The studies show that better writers frequently are better readers and read more than do poor writers. In turn, better readers tend to produce more quality pieces of writing. Other findings support the contention that there are types of reading experiences that enhance writing and that there are types of writing activities that promote meaning (comprehension) in reading.

Although these studies reveal that there is a positive correlation between reading and writing, there are some exceptions. There are children who are good writers but not good readers, and vice versa. Since many reading and writing activities are isolated from one another, students may achieve more in one area than in the other. The good readers but poor writers and the good writers but poor readers could be products of a fragmented language arts program.

Today, both reading and writing are viewed as interactive, constructive processes. Both are acts of composing with enough similarities to lend support for integrating instruction of the two processes. Both readers and writers use similar cognitive and linguistic information and steps while constructing or reconstructing meaning. Readers use these steps to reconstruct meaning from print, while writers make use of these steps to construct meaning using print. For readers, meaning is created as they use their background knowledge along with information provided by the author. For writers, meaning is constructed as they use their own background knowledge to generate a message.

Readers and writers are involved in comparable thought processes during the acts of comprehension and composition (Squire, 1983). Both reading and writing make similar demands on thinking. Before reading, a reader prepares for understanding the text by establishing a purpose for reading and activating his or her prior knowledge (schema) of the topic. Before writing, a writer establishes a purpose for writing and thinks of what he or she knows about the topic. Quality time during both the prereading and prewriting stages is essential in preparing the student to construct meaning.

During reading, readers are actively involved in reconstructing the author's message and constantly monitor and self-regulate their reading. During writing, writers are actively involved in constructing meaning. They monitor their choice of words, how the writing piece is organized, and the sentence structure in order to fulfill the purpose they established during prewriting. During this stage, writers read and reread what has been written.

After reading, readers reflect on what has been read, consider whether they have achieved their purpose for reading, reconstruct the author's message for the entire text, and make value judgments (e.g., "I like . . . ," "I question . . . ," "I wish the author or article had . . ."). After writing, the writers check to see whether the piece makes sense and whether they have achieved their purpose for writing, and they also reflect and make judgments (e.g., "I like the way I . . .") (Heller, 1991).

In both processes, rereading is used to check understanding, whether the piece being read is one's own or another author's. When children are engaged in the reading process, they reread to verify and modify their predictions, to check on pertinent information that was provided, and to obtain data that will be used for other purposes (e.g., on reports, on tests, to add to their own background knowledge, or to apply in another context). As children write, they constantly read and reread their own work to be certain that what is being communicated actually makes sense to the intended audience. As writers reread, they also tend to rewrite.

Reading and writing are related, and certain types of reading activities promote growth in writing and vice versa. Let's look at how reading can enhance the writing process. Calkins

(1983) stated that the more readers interact with what they are reading, the better they do while writing. As children experience various forms of text structures (e.g., story grammars and the organization of expository texts), they gain an understanding of how specific texts work and are organized. This knowledge can be applied to students' own writing as they experiment with the various genres and registers. Literature provides examples of interesting and effective leads and endings and how authors set the mood, organize their pieces, and use certain literary techniques. Literature exposes readers to a variety of genres and serves as patterns and models for writing. Therefore, literature can be used to acquaint students with the various types and styles of writing.

Reading is also an indispensable part of the writing process because it is used throughout the writing process. During prewriting, children prepare to write through such activities as brainstorming, talking, thinking, and reading. After these rehearsal activities, they write a draft. Revision begins when the piece is reread, evaluated, and changed. Writers reread to review the writing and to ascertain whether their purpose for writing has been achieved. Writers also read their pieces to peers to receive input and feedback. During the editing stage, writers proofread their pieces in order to address the mechanics and to create copies ready for publishing and sharing. During the final phase of the process, the author reads the piece to an audience or publishes it in a form for others to read at a later time. Reading promotes writing by supplementing all the stages of the writing process, and writers must continually act as their own readers throughout the process (Goodman and Goodman, 1984).

Reading thus not only serves as a stimulus for writing, but it also plays a key role in helping students with the rules and the characteristics of good writing. Reading helps students obtain the strategies needed during the various stages of the writing process. Smith (1983) advises that students "read like a writer." By doing so, the reader becomes engaged in the author's writing and anticipates what the author's message will be. By reading like a writer, the student will learn to write like a writer. By reading like a writer, students will enhance their knowledge of writing skills and conventions.

In turn, writing teaches children about reading and can facilitate reading. Writing involves reading and reinforces and develops skills that have been perceived as reading skills (e.g., phonics, vocabulary, and comprehension). By using writing in the reading process, students are given a natural context in which to learn reading skills and strategies effectively. Students can learn and apply such aspects of reading as phonics, text structure, paraphrasing, summarizing, comparing and contrasting, and word knowledge and recognition.

Writing can be incorporated into all phases of the reading process: prereading, during reading, and after reading. Through the use of semantic maps and prereading writing assignments, writing can be used to activate prior knowledge of story topics and help in setting a purpose for reading. During reading, children can write predictions, record information, and respond to the piece being read. After reading, students can add to their semantic maps, respond to the entire text in a literature response log, or use writing during follow-up activities (e.g., writing a sequel, conducting further research, recasting the information into a different genre or form). When children learn to "read like writers," they become not only better writers but also better readers.

Writing provides students with a reason to connect with reading because writers need to know how texts are constructed and need to obtain information for their writing. In sum, reading and writing are closely related, and both can be enhanced by addressing the two processes in an integrated fashion rather than as isolated subjects. There is a need for an integrated approach to literacy, for experience with one process will foster development in the other. Figure 2.9 depicts the reading opportunities that exist in the various stages of the writing process.

LISTENING

Children have the ability to speak and listen long before they are able to read and write. Teachers in the elementary school classroom

Figure 2.9 Reading During the Writing Process

Stages of the Writing Process	Reading Opportunities
Prewriting	gathering information for topic • information books • pattern books • newspapers • primary sources (journals, memoirs, diaries) semantic mapping notetaking rereading notes
Drafting	reading piece silently while writing to see if piece makes sense rereading aloud to self, peers, teacher to check on message rereading to regain momentum researching for more information referring to word lists, reference books, for information and spelling
Revising	rereading silently to evaluate piece reading piece aloud in peer or teacher conferences reading piece in Authors' Circle
Editing	reading piece to check for spelling, mechanics, grammar reading word lists, dictionaries, to obtain spelling of words reading classmate's piece to proofread
Sharing/Publishing	reading piece in Authors' Circle reading piece to other audiences

(Adapted from Hornsby, Sukarna, and Parry, 1986.)

are beginning to recognize the importance of oral communication as a tool for learning and as the foundation for reading and writing. Children will have difficulty learning to read if the language used in the texts is different from their spoken language. Children likewise will have difficulty learning to write if these words are not part of their speaking vocabularies. In the early years of school especially, the oral modes of communication are exceedingly important.

Listening is the most basic and the most used of all the language modes. It is the first language mode that children acquire, and it provides the foundation for all the other language arts. Listening is an effective tool in seeking meaning. More time is spent listening than is spent reading, writing, and speaking together (Tompkins and Hoskisson, 1995). Approximately half of all the time spent communicating is spent listening. To illustrate the pervasiveness of listening in our daily lives, Lundsteen (1976, 75) has said, "We listen a book a day; speak a book a week; read a book a month; and write a book a year."

Being able to listen goes beyond the hearing of words. It is thinking about and interpreting what one hears. Listeners agree, disagree, enjoy, or dislike some of what they hear. As with reading and writing, listening is an active process that involves both the intake of material and the use of similar mental processing (Ministry of Education, Province of British Columbia, 1991). Listening is a learned receptive skill and can be defined as a process by which spoken language is convened to meaning in the mind (Lundsteen, 1989).

Although listening abilities affect children's performance in school, listening is often taken for granted and misunderstood. Many children do acquire listening skills without formal in-

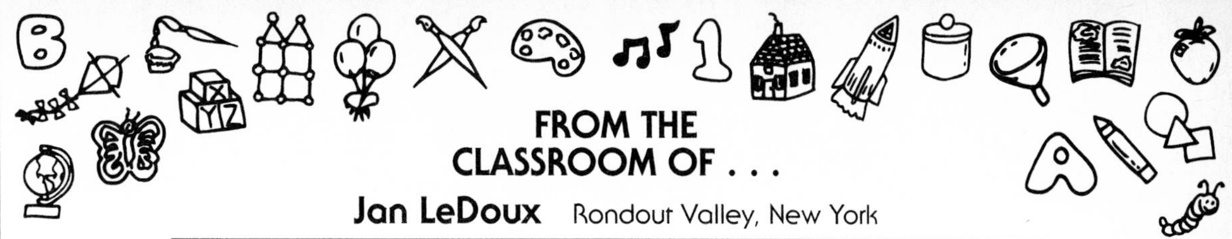

FROM THE CLASSROOM OF . . .

Jan LeDoux Rondout Valley, New York

LET'S LISTEN

To help young children develop an understanding of purposeful listening, Jan encourages her first graders not only to listen for information but also to record what was heard. This activity generally accompanies a thematic unit while she is reading a nonfiction book. The children are given a piece of paper, folded into quarters. In each section, the children record some interesting facts. They are encouraged to use invented spelling. Below is an example of what a student recorded during a thematic study on the sea.

aBaby whale is a calf breaching Lu mPing out	the Nose is Called blow
Whles are mammals they breathe air	Lobtailing slaPing the flueks

LUCY

struction, but many do not learn to use their listening ability effectively or efficiently. Children are capable of gaining proficiency in their listening skills when the importance of listening is recognized and when listening plays an integral part in the school's academic program. Listening can be enhanced by instruction, but most commonly it is developed incidentally by many activities in school, such as listening to read-alongs, serving as audience for peers, and participating in literature response groups. Listening should remain integrated with the other language modes and be used throughout the curriculum. It should not be taught outside real, meaningful language contexts.

By learning to listen, children are learning to understand and appreciate another person's point of view and that responses may be similar to theirs at times or amazingly different (Siemens, 1994). If children can become active listeners, they can internalize new thoughts and ideas, assimilate them with their prior knowledge, and formulate new ideas (Ministry of Education, Province of British Columbia, 1991). When conversation occurs in the classroom between the teacher and the students, children are provided with a model for language and listening. Children who are listened to soon recognize that what they have to say is important. These children then are more apt to listen to others, particularly if they feel they can gain worthwhile information from others.

An appropriate environment for listening needs to be established for effective listening to occur. This environment needs to be risk-free, nonthreatening, and supportive of the learners. Teachers need to prepare children for the listening experiences, encouraging them to feel as if they are personally involved. Children who are encouraged to talk about what they have heard gain valuable insights into the purposes for listening.

Although listening has been neglected in many literacy programs, teachers are recognizing its importance and are involving students in purposeful listening experiences. It is not enough merely to have something to listen *to*. Listeners must have something to listen *for*. They must have a reason or a purpose for listening. These purposes include:

- **Comprehensive or attentive listening** (listening to understand and comprehend, listening for information and to organize ideas, e.g., listening to a lecture)
- **Critical listening** (listening to evaluate or judge spoken material, e.g., detecting propaganda devices, persuasive language, conflicting ideas, and exaggerated statements)
- **Appreciative listening** (listening for enjoyment and creative response, e.g., listening to a story being read aloud)

(Donoghue, 1985; Tompkins and Hoskisson, 1995)

In classrooms where teachers are providing a balanced language program, there will be many opportunities for children to be involved in meaningful listening experiences. As a participation skill, listening can best be enhanced during activities in which all students have the opportunity to participate. Rather than correctness being emphasized, divergent thinking is encouraged and valued. Some of these activities (which are presented later in this book) include listening to stories and participating in shared reading, writers' share circles, and literature groups. Listening is being addressed today because it is a major means for children to gather information, appreciate language, and grow in their communicative competency.

TALKING AND SPEAKING

Speaking, like listening, tends to be taken for granted in the elementary school classroom. However, speaking is extremely important both in school and in the real world. Oral language forms the basis for a child's literacy growth and development. Speaking is important to thinking and learning (Vygotsky, 1962; Smith, 1982b; Wilkinson, 1984; Barnes, 1995). Putting thoughts and ideas into words helps people sort out and organize these ideas and assimilate new information with prior knowledge. By talking, people reconstruct their understanding, shaping it to make it available to others with whom the message will be shared (Barnes, 1995). Speaking makes significant contributions to children's abilities to communicate.

A child's speech development moves from becoming fluent to gaining control to attaining effectiveness. This growth is facilitated by encouragement and acceptance. Children gain control over their language competency gradually through demonstrations by and interactions with their teachers and peers. Through these interactions, children are able to use language for many reasons without any specific training.

As with reading and writing, speech develops by being used in meaningful contexts. Thus children learn to communicate by communicating. In general, children want to express themselves and learn about their world. This desire motivates them to communicate with others. Through such communication, along with their firsthand experiences, children's ideas and schemata are expanded. It is no longer believed that a silent classroom is an effective classroom. In fact, rooms where there are purposeful interactions, where discussions abound, and where there is plenty of oral language are now found to promote literacy and learning (Cazden, 1986; Heath, 1983). Speaking expands children's oral skills and develops their ability to use talk for many different language functions.

Teachers now believe in the value of speech and set up their classrooms to ensure that productive speaking can indeed happen. The atmosphere is one of acceptance and encouragement as opposed to an evaluative one. Children are released and encouraged to explore ideas. Children participate if they feel secure and valued versus being judged (Staab, 1991). There is a shift from teacher-dominated talk to shared responsibility for learning. Teachers permit their students to seek meaning, and they facilitate the process. To help children develop their oral language, teachers expose children to the types of talk activities that exist in elementary classrooms. These activities include:

- **Informal talk activities** (conversation and discussion, show and tell, buzz groups, community meetings)
- **Interpretative talk activities** (storytelling, reader's theater)
- **Formal talk activities** (oral reports, interviews, debates)
- **Dramatic talk activities** (dramatic play, role-playing, puppetry)

(Tompkins and Hoskisson, 1995)

Although oral communication requires both speaking and listening—that is, the sending and receiving of messages—these are not separate processes. Rather they are facets of being able to communicate. The goals of a balanced language program should include valuing and promoting children's own language, integrating the language arts, and giving children opportunities to communicate effectively in a variety of different language situations. It is important to remember when thinking about the modes of language that children learn language, about language, and through language simultaneously. Language develops through use and embraces all the areas of the curriculum.

Many of the listening and speaking activities that occur in the classroom are integrated with the other language modes and are used throughout the curriculum. Such is the case with the listening and speaking activities presented in this book. Although listening and speaking are discussed separately, their interdependence is recognized and instructional implications are addressed whenever listening and speaking are applicable (i.e., in shared reading, group discussions, peer conferences, drama, puppetry, and the like).

MOVING, WATCHING, SHAPING, AND VIEWING

Reading, writing, listening, and speaking are not the only modes of communication. When people speak, meaning is conveyed not only in the speaker's words but also through the use of such nonverbal cues as tone of voice, gestures, facial expressions, and body language. Nonverbal information is also used to help create meaning in both reading and writing (e.g., spacing between lines, spacing within the text, layout of the text, use of boldface, and so on). Therefore the nonverbal modes of moving, watching, shaping, and viewing need to be incorporated into a balanced literacy program. A brief description of each of these modes follows.

Figure 2.10 Language Modes and Classroom Activities

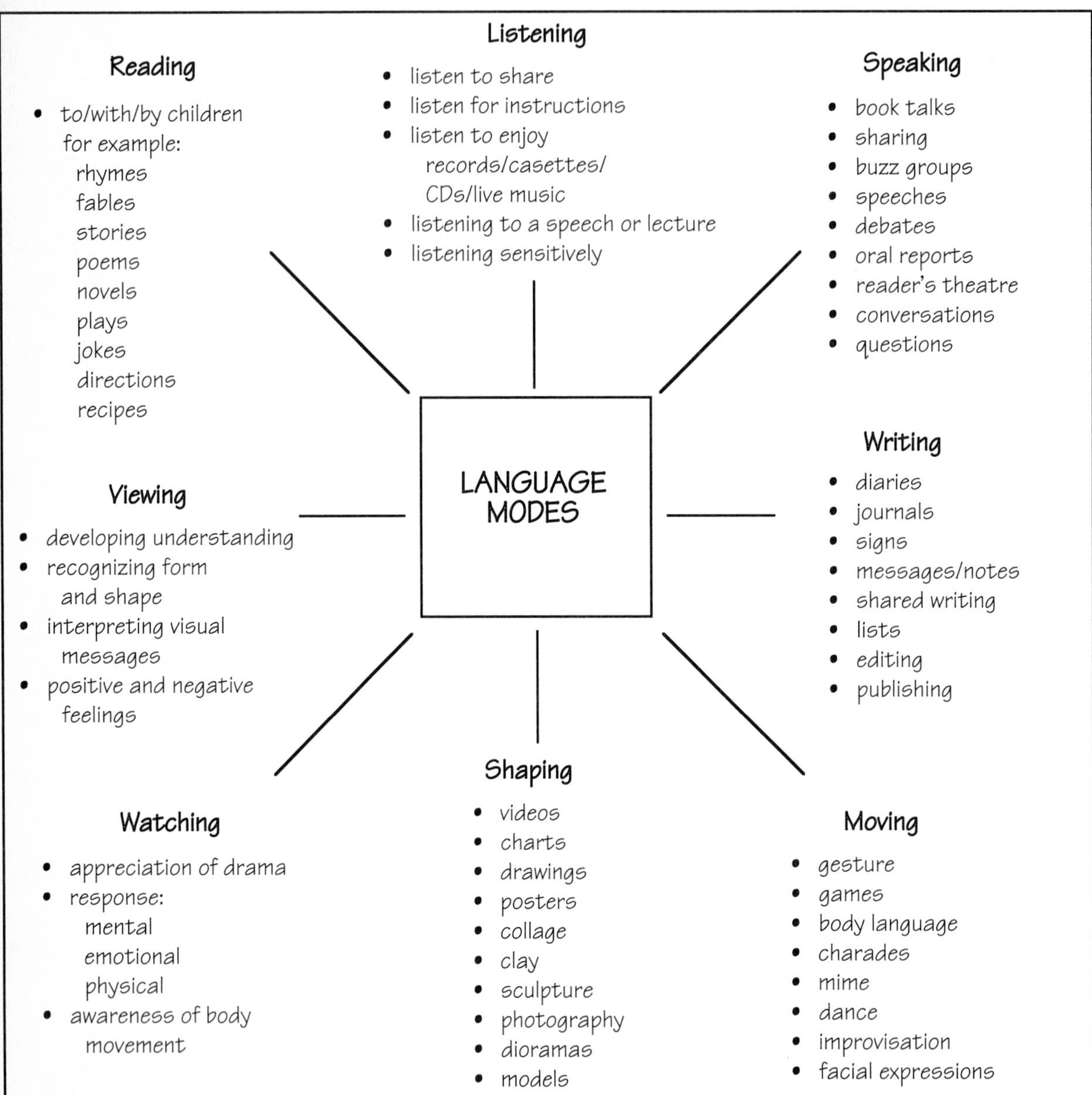

- **Moving.** Using gestures, facial expressions, and movement to convey meaning and express oneself (expressive)
- **Watching.** Becoming aware of nonverbal factors and their importance (receptive)
- **Shaping.** Using effects visually to convey meaning (expressive)
- **Viewing.** Becoming aware of and getting information from visual effects (receptive)

These nonverbal modes of communication are of particular importance because of the amount of time children spend watching television and films and working on the computer. Being aware of the influences on learning of nonverbal modes is important not only in the school environment but also outside the classroom (e.g., advertisements, propaganda, campaign speeches, and the like). See Figure 2.10.

RELATIONSHIP AMONG THE MODES

The relationship between reading and writing was discussed previously. As stated, reading and writing are complementary processes that involve the construction of meaning. The other modes of language are also complementary. For example, when people are listening, they are generally watching as well, noting the speaker's expressions and gestures in addition to listening to the spoken words. Similarly, speakers usually engage in some form of movement to emphasize a point or clarify a statement and also watch their audiences for reactions and feedback.

Shaping and writing are similar in that writers shape their writing. They may alter the size of the print they use or the fonts on a computer to emphasize a point. They may pay attention to the way they arrange their text to grab readers' interest or appeal to readers' emotions. Readers derive meaning from the way the words are arranged or highlighted. They obtain information from graphs, charts, and illustrations. Therefore reading and viewing accompany one another.

Shaping and viewing are language modes that represent the nonverbal, visual parts of language. They are important in written communication and in such media as television and film. Experience in all the modes of language, both verbal and nonverbal, helps children gain control over their language competence.

SUMMARY

The primary objective of language learning in today's schools is the development of children's ability to understand, appreciate, and use language effectively. A means of looking at language is to examine the modes of language learning, which was the focus of this chapter. In addition to discussing what are generally considered the language arts (reading, writing, listening, and speaking), the chapter also presented nonverbal forms of language (moving, watching, shaping, and viewing). Each is considered to be an active, meaning-making process. All make significant contributions to a language learner's ability to communicate. Although the modes were discussed separately, it is important to remember that they complement one another and are best addressed in an integrated fashion in the classroom throughout the entire curriculum.

An understanding of what occurs during both the reading and writing processes was developed. Through a series of activities, a definition of reading was obtained that serves as the framework for reading instruction throughout this book. Reading is an interactive process in which readers use information from their own background along with information from the text (the author) to construct meaning in a given situational context. The importance of a reader's background knowledge was stressed through the discussion of schema theory with resulting instructional implications. Learning to read is considered a lifelong process, with readers always seeking meaning throughout life with a variety of texts in various contexts. It was recommended that the goals of reading instruction in the elementary school give prime attention to reading as a lifelong, meaningful act, as well as the cultivation of a love of reading and books.

The various stages of the writing process (prewriting, drafting, revision, editing, and publishing) were presented, along with a rationale for incorporating writing instruction into the elementary curriculum. Some guidelines for an instructional program in writing and the developmental stages of writing were also presented. An argument for integrating reading and writing was offered with descriptions of how reading enhances the writing process and how writing enhances the reading process.

Oral communication is essential to success in the elementary school, and the importance of listening and speaking to develop communicative competence was emphasized. Although not treated as separate strands in elementary schools, listening and speaking enhance academic achievement because they are used in every aspect of the school curriculum. It was pointed out that throughout the rest of this book, listening and speaking play an integral part in the activities discussed.

Chapters 1 and 2 are both intended to provide the reader with the necessary theoretical background on which to base instructional practices and activities. The remainder of this book focuses on actual classroom instruction, but it is necessary first to have a solid understanding of how children learn and the modes of language learning in order to plan and implement an effective literacy program.

BIBLIOGRAPHY AND SUGGESTED REFERENCES

Applebee, A., & Langer, J. (1983). Instructional scaffolding: Reading and writing and natural language activities. *Language Arts, 60,* 168–175.

Barnes, D. (1995). Talking and learning in classrooms: An introduction. *Primary Voices, 3,* 2–7.

Booth, D., & Thornley-Hall, C. (Eds.). (1991). *The talk curriculum.* Victoria, Australia: Pembroke Publishers Limited.

Bransford, J., & Johnson, M. (1972). Contextual prerequisites for understanding some investigations of comprehension and recall. *Journal of Verbal Learning and Verbal Behavior,* 11, 717–726.

Britton, J. (1970). *Language and learning.* Harmondsworth, England: Penguin.

Butler, A. (1988). *The elements of whole language.* Crystal Lake, Ill.: Rigby.

Butler, A., & Turbill, J. (1984). *Towards a reading-writing classroom.* Portsmouth, N.H.: Heinemann.

Butler, S. (1991). The writing connection. In V. Froese (Ed.), *Whole-language: Practice and theory,* (pp. 97–147). Boston: Allyn & Bacon.

Calkins, L. (1980). When children want to punctuate: Basic skills belong in context. *Language Arts, 57,* 567–573.

Calkins, L. (1983). *Lessons from a child: On the teaching and learning of writing.* Portsmouth, N.H.: Heinemann.

Calkins, L. (1994). *The art of teaching writing.* Portsmouth, N.H.: Heinemann.

Cazden, C. (1986). Classroom discourse. In M. C. Wittrock (Ed.), *Handbook of research on teaching,* 3rd. ed., pp. 432–463. New York: Macmillan.

Department of Education, Wellington. (1986). *Language in the primary school: English statement of aims.* Wellington, New Zealand: Department of Education.

Donoghue, M. (1985). *The children and the English language arts.* Dubuque, Iowa: William C. Brown, Publishers.

Eckhoff, B. (1984). How reading affects children's writing. In J. M. Jensen (Ed.), *Composing and comprehending.* Urbana, Ill.: ERIC/RCS.

Fields, M.; Spangler, K.; & Lee, D. (1991). *Let's begin reading right: Developmentally appropriate beginning literacy.* New York: Macmillan.

Fulwiler, T., & Young, A. (Eds.). (1982). *Language connections: Writing and reading across the curriculum.* Urbana, Ill.: National Council of Teachers of English.

Gere, A. (Ed.). (1985). *Roots in the sawdust: Writing to learn across the disciplines.* Urbana, Ill.: National Council of Teachers of English.

Goodman, K., & Goodman, Y. (1984). Reading and writing relationships: Pragmatic functions. In J. M. Jensen (Ed.), *Composing and comprehending.* Urbana, Ill.: ERIC/RCS.

Graves, D. (1976). Let's get rid of the welfare mess in the teaching of writing. *Language Arts, 53,* 645–651.

Graves, D. (1983). *Writing: Teachers and children at work.* Portsmouth, N.H.: Heinemann.

Graves, D. (1994). *A fresh look at writing.* Portsmouth, N.H.: Heinemann.

Graves, D., & Hansen, J. (1982). The author's chair. *Language Arts, 60,* 176–183.

Hansen, J. (1987). *When writers read.* Portsmouth, N.H.: Heinemann.

Harste, J.; Woodward, V.; & Burke, C. (1984). *Language stories and literacy lessons.* Portsmouth, N.H.: Heinemann.

Heath, S. (1983). Research currents: A lot of talk about nothing. *Language Arts, 60,* 999–1007.

Heller, M. (1991). *Reading-writing connections: From theory to practice.* New York: Longman.

Hornsby, D.; Sukarna, D.; & Parry, J. (1986). *Read on: A conference approach to reading.* Portsmouth, N.H.: Heinemann.

Langer, J., & Applebee, A. (1987). *How writing shapes thinking: A study of teaching and learning.* (NCTE Research Report No. 22). Urbana, Ill.: National Council of Teachers of English.

Learning Media. (1992). *Dancing with the pen: The learner as a writer.* Wellington, New Zealand: Ministry of Education.

Lundsteen, S. (1976). *Language arts: A problem-solving approach.* New York: Harper & Row.

Lundsteen, S. (1989). *Language arts: A problem-solving approach.* New York: Harper & Row.

Ministry of Education. (1991). *Primary program foundation document.* British Columbia.

Murray, D. (1982). *Learning by teaching.* Montclair, N.J.: Boynton/Cook.

Noyce, R., & Christie, J. (1989). *Integrating reading and writing instruction in grades K–8.* Boston: Allyn & Bacon.

Reif, L. (1992). *Seeking diversity.* Portsmouth, N.H.: Heinemann.

Shanahan, T. (1988). The reading-writing relationship: Seven instructional principles. *The Reading Teacher, 41,* 636–647.

Siemens, L. (1994). "Does Jesus have aunties?" and "Who planned it all?": Learning to listen for "Big" questions. *Language Arts, 71,* 358–361.

Smith, F. (1982a). *Writing and the writer.* New York: Holt.

Smith, F. (1982b). The unspeakable habit. *Language Arts, 59,* 550–554.

Smith, F. (1983). Reading like a writer. *Language Arts, 60,* 553–564.

Squire, J. (1983). Composing and comprehending: Two sides of the same basic process. In J. M. Jensen (Ed.), *Composing and comprehending.* Urbana, Ill.: National Conference on Research in English.

Staab, C., & Smith, K. (1986). Functions in written language. *English Quarterly, 19,* 50–57.

Staab, C. (1991). Talk in Whole-Language Classrooms. In V. Froese (Ed.) *Whole-Language: Practice and theory,* pp. 17–49. Boston: Allyn & Bacon.

Stotsky, S. (1983). Research on reading/writing relationships: A synthesis and suggested directions. *Language Arts, 60,* 627–642.

Sulzby, E.; Teale, W.; & Kamberelis, G. (1989). Emergent writing in the classroom: Home and school connections. In D. Strickland and L. Morrow (Eds.), *Emerging literacy: Young children learn to read and write,* pp. 63–79. Newark, Del.: International Reading Association.

Temple, C., & Gillet, J. (1989). *Language arts: Learning processes and teaching practices.* Glenview, Ill.: Scott, Foresman & Company.

Tierney, R., & Leys, M. (1986). What is the value of connecting reading and writing? In P. L. Stock (Ed.), *Convergence: Transactions in reading and writing.* Urbana, Ill.: National Council of Teachers of English.

Tompkins, G. (1990). *Teaching writing: Balancing process and product.* Columbus, Ohio: Merrill.

Tompkins, G., & Hoskisson, K. (1995). *Language arts: Content and teaching strategies.* New York: Merrill.

Vygotsky, L. (1962). *Thought and language.* Cambridge, Mass.: MIT Press.

Walshe, R. (1981a). *Every child can write.* Rozelle, N.S.W., Australia: Primary English Teaching Association.

Walshe, R. (1981b). (Ed.) *Children want to write: Donald Graves in Australia.* Portsmouth, N.H.: Heinemann.

Weaver, C. (1988). *Reading process and practice.* Portsmouth, N.H.: Heinemann.

Wilkinson, L. (1984). Research currents: Peer group talk in elementary school. *Language Arts, 61,* 164–169.

CHILDREN'S LITERATURE CITED

Livingston, M. (1991). *Poem-making.* New York: HarperCollins.

CURRENT SCHOOL PRACTICES IN TEACHING READING AND THE OTHER LANGUAGE ARTS

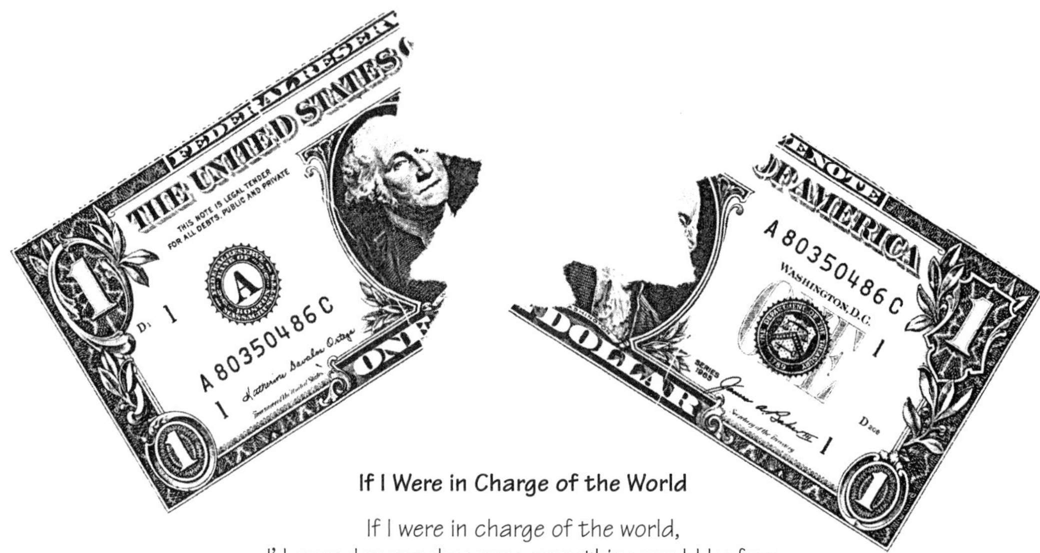

If I Were in Charge of the World

If I were in charge of the world,
I'd cancel money because everything would be free.
I'd cancel school because everybody would be born smart.
I'd cancel hurricanes, tornadoes, and volcanoes
so nobody would lose their homes.
I'd cancel drugs, cigarettes, tobacco, and alcohol.
I'd cancel weapons, wars, and bombs.

If I were in charge of the world,
There would be billions of vacations for everybody.
There would be an owner for every pet.
There would be every TV channel known to
man, available to everybody.

If I were in charge of the world,
I'd change the laws so everybody would have to recycle.
I'd change it so everybody wouldn't have to pay taxes.
I'd change it so nobody would be homeless.
I'd change it so everybody would be loved.

Corrinna Partridge
Grade 4
Windham, New York

Inspired by: *If I Were in Charge of the World and Other Worries* by Judith Viorst

OVERVIEW

If you walk into an elementary school classroom today, chances are that you will find reading taught through a basal reading program, through the use of children's literature in a whole language approach, or through some combination of these two approaches. Although we believe that a whole language approach comes closest to the ideal in helping children grow through reading, we are aware, and wish you to be aware, of other approaches. We believe in the need to value the professional decisions of the classroom teacher, even if we may not always agree with all of those decisions. In this chapter, therefore, we explain three current approaches to reading: the traditional, whole language, and transitional approaches.

In each instance, we explain where and how the other language arts fit into the curriculum. As you weigh these three approaches, we urge you to consider yourself a professional who continually observes and evaluates the children in your care. Whatever approach seems best or more expedient to you now deserves your ongoing scrutiny. Remember: when you meet the needs of the children in your care, they will tend to be more successful in the learning process. That makes your job inherently easier (although perhaps not less time consuming) and more fulfilling.

Questions to Ponder

1. What methods are used for teaching reading and the other language arts in today's schools?
2. How has literacy instruction changed over the years?
3. What are the reasons that various approaches coexist in schools today?
4. What are the roadblocks to implementing a whole language approach to literacy?
5. Is there an approach to teaching reading and language arts that is best for you as a teacher, keeping in mind your own strengths and weaknesses?

THE TRADITIONAL APPROACH

Reading and the Basal Reader Approach

Historically, basal readers have been the predominant means of delivering reading instruction in most elementary classrooms in the United States (Mason and Osborn, 1982; Shannon, 1983; Durkin, 1981, 1984; Anderson, Hiebert, Scott, and Wilkinson, 1985). In fact, basal readers have been so prevalent that they were used in more than 90 percent of elementary classrooms (Durkin, 1984; Flood and Lapp, 1986; Farr, Tulley, and Powell, 1987). In addition, 75–90 percent of the time students actually spend in reading instruction is dominated by basal reading programs (Mason and Osborn, 1982; Anderson et al., 1985). Note that the research cited is several years old, and with the advent of whole language programs, the estimates are probably considerably lower at the present time. The present-day basal reading program has evolved over a period of more than three hundred years, beginning with the Hornbook and the New England Primer. From these early days, when there were only a few instructional materials, has developed the modern, commercially produced basal program whose content and instructional quality have influenced reading instruction in the elementary schools. By their nature, basals—despite being produced by different publishers—tend to have a similar appearance. This is because they have similar characteristics and similar components. A basal reading program is designed to bring students to proficiency in reading through a series of books of increasing difficulty. Basal reading programs have three main features: scope; sequence; and organization (Searfoss & Readence, 1994). The term *scope* refers to the range of skills that are addressed in the series. *Sequence* pertains to the order in which the skills are introduced, taught, and tested. Basals are organized in such a way so as to integrate all the elements of the lessons, units, and books. The way the series is organized helps keep teachers on track by providing guidance as to when and how to teach certain skills. The predominant way this is accomplished is through the provision of a teacher's manual. Other characteristics of basal reading programs include:

- Series of readers of increasing difficulty (with each level viewed as a prerequisite for success at the succeeding level)
- Systematic skill development
- Abridged or adapted stories (primarily at the upper levels)

- An eclectic, comprehensive approach to literacy instruction, frequently including instruction in all the language arts as opposed to concentrating solely on reading instruction
- A variety of genres (fiction, poetry, and nonfiction)
- A variety of illustrations

The basal reading program moved from a reader for the student, a workbook, and a teacher's manual in the 1940s and 1950s to the elaborate set of materials typically available today. Most basal series consist of student readers, one or more student workbooks, a set of reproducible skill reinforcement pages, tests for each level and for each unit within the basal reader, and a teacher's manual for each level. The teacher's manual typically includes a lengthy explanation of the program and how it is to work, a scope and sequence chart (see Figure 3.1) that indicates which skills are taught or reinforced at each level, lesson plans with scripted dialogue for the teacher and students, and extra skill reinforcement lessons and extension activities for all students, but especially for those who are doing well and can spend extra time on interesting enrichment activities. Some programs have additional materials for vocabulary development and phonics instruction at the lower levels.

Due to intense criticism of basal readers over the past several years, newer programs have attempted to address the major criticisms. Therefore more recent editions of basal reading programs have incorporated other features:

- The use of literature as the basis for reading instruction, without editing and simplifying of vocabulary
- The provision of shared reading experiences
- The replacement of skill exercises with more meaning-oriented activities
- An emphasis on strategic learning, including student self-monitoring
- The use of reading across the curriculum
- The provision of opportunities for a variety of ways to respond to literature
- An emphasis on process writing
- Suggestions for alternative ways of assessing students
- The promotion of cooperative group activities

(Searfoss & Readence, 1994)

Basal reading programs are often perceived as being complete systems for teaching reading, since the range of available instructional materials is quite extensive. If the components of an entire basal program were stacked, they would measure 4 feet high (Anderson et al., 1985). The range of materials available to teachers who use basal programs is extensive (see Figure 3.2).

Generally, teachers meet with the children in reading groups on a daily basis. These groups, particularly in the early grades, tend to be formed by ability level. While the teacher is working with one group, the rest of the children are frequently engaged in seatwork. The quality of the seatwork can be another issue. Seatwork is intended to keep students occupied so that the teacher can devote time to one particular reading group.

The traditional format used in the basal reading program is the Directed Reading Activity (DRA). The teacher plans the instruction over a period of several days to include prereading, during-reading, and postreading activities. Prereading activities are intended to provide motivation, build the necessary background for the reading selection, and preteach vocabulary. Some newer basal programs now offer direct instruction in skills during this stage, with the skills being applied in the selection and on workbook pages. In the during-reading phase, teachers guide students through the selection, asking comprehension questions. After the selection has been read, students may be given additional skill and vocabulary instruction or reinforcement, enrichment activities, and workbook pages. Ideally, students are given the opportunity to extend the selection through literature projects and cross-curricular activities, but time frequently precludes this. More typically, students complete workbook pages and read the selection orally. The son of one of the authors was concerned when he learned his mother had to teach her college students about the basal program. He lamented, "Mom, you aren't really going to teach them that? I remember back in elementary school that we read the story quickly and then spent day after day an-

Figure 3.1A Sample of Scope and Sequence

SCOPE AND SEQUENCE

Level	K	R	1	2	3	4	5	6, 7	8, 9	10	11	12	13	14
Grade			PP1	PP2	PP3	P	Reader	2	3	4	5	6	7	8
Skills														
BEGINNING READING SKILLS														
Letter formation	○	○												
Sound matching	○	○	○	○	○	○	○							
Letter/sound correspondence	○	○												
Visual discrimination	○	○	○	○	○	○	○							
Phonograms		○	○											
Readiness words		●	○											
Initial consonants		●	○											
Final consonants			●	●	○	○	○	○						
DECODING/WORD STUDY														
Phonics														
Consonants		○	●	●	○	●	○	●						
Consonant clusters					●	●	●	●	○					
Consonant digraphs					●	●	●	●						
Short vowels		○	●	●										
Long vowels				●	●	●	●	●						
Vowel digraphs						●	●	●	○					
Variant vowels								●						
STRUCTURAL ANALYSIS														
Inflections			●	●	●	●	○							
Plural nouns			●	○										
Possessives					●	○	○	○						
-ed, -ing, -s, er, est				●	●	●	●							
Contractions			○	○	○	●	●	○						
Compound words														
Spelling generalizations						●	●	●	○					
Long word decoding strategies								○	●	○				
Suffixes/prefixes							○	●	●	●	●	●	●	●
Roots and combining forms										○	○	○	○	○
Context clues			○	○	○	○	○	○	●	●	●	●	●	●
VOCABULARY														
Word meaning	○	○	●	●	●	●	●	●	●	●	●	●	●	●
Synonyms/antonyms	○		○	○	○	●	●	●	●	●	●	●	○	○
Multiple meanings/homographs			○	○	○	○	○	○	●	●	●	●	●	●
Homophones								●	●	○	○	○	○	
Connotation								○	○	○	○	○	○	○
Classification		○	○	○	●	●	○	●	○	●	○	○	○	○
Analogies						○	○	○	○	●	○	○	○	○
Semantic mapping		○	○	○	○	○	○	○	○	○	○	○	○	○
Semantic features analysis						○	○	○	○	○	○	○	○	○
COMPREHENSION														
Getting Information from Text														
Picture details	○	○	○	○	○	○	○	○	○					
Main idea/details	○	○	○	●	●	○	●	●	●	●	●	●	●	●
Sequence	○	○	●	○	○	●	○	●	●	●	●	●	○	○
Word referents				○	○	○	○	●	●	●	○	●	○	●

○ Applied Skill ● Tested Skill

SILVER BURDETT & GINN

WORLD OF READING COMPONENTS

Components Level	K	R	1	2	3	4	5	6, 7	8, 9	10	11	12	13	14
Grade			PP[1]	PP[2]	PP[3]	P	Reader	2	3	4	5	6	7	8
Student Text			●	●	●	●	●	●	●	●	●	●	●	●
Pupil Book (consumable)	●	●												
Teacher Edition	●	●	●	—●	—●	●	●	●	●	●	●	●	●	●
Student Workbook (color)			●	●	●	●	●	●	●	●	●	●	●	●
Student Workbook/Teacher Edition			●	●	●	●	●	●	●	●	●	●	●	●
Kindergarten Kit (Hickory Dickory Village)	●													
Readiness Kit		●												
Big Book	●	●	●	●	●									
Big Shared Books (8)	●													
Teacher Resource Kit	●		●	—●	—●	—●	—●	●	●	●	●	●	●	●
Skills Practice*	●	●	●	—●	—●	●	●	●	●	●	●	●	●	●
Reteaching*			●	—●	—●	●	●	●	●	●	●	●	●	●
Challenge*			●	—●	—●	●	●	●	●	●	●	●	●	●
Achieving English Proficiency*			●	—●	—●	●	●	●	●	●	●	●	●	●
Writing Masters*						●	●	●	●	●	●	●	●	●
Language Arts Connections*			●	—●	—●	●	●	●	●	●	●	●	●	●
Curriculum Connections*			●	—●	—●	●	●	●	●	●	●	●	●	●
Teaching Charts*			●	—●	—●	—●	—●	●	●	●	●	●	●	●
Listening Cassette			●	—●	—●	—●	—●	●	●	●	●	●	●	●
Parent Letters	●	●	●	—●	—●	●	●	●	●	●	●	●	●	●
Teaching Posters			●	—●	—●	—●	—●	●	●	●	●	●	●	●
Poster Activities			●	—●	—●	—●	—●	●	●	●	●	●	●	●
Unit Project Cards			●	—●	—●	—●	—●	●	●	●	●	●	●	●
Storybooks			●	—●	—●	—●	—●	●						
Activity Cards	●													
Handwriting*	●													
Test Package* (Placement Test/Unit Skills Test–Form A)			●	●	●	●	●	●	●	●	●	●	●	●
Idea Factory for Teachers	●	●	●	—●	—●	—●	—●	●	●	●	●	●	●	●
Teaching Charts (24" x 32")	●	●	●	—●	—●	—●	—●	●	●	●	●	●	●	●
Word Cards		●	—●	—●	—●	—●	—●							
Assessment														
Placement Test		●	●	—●	—●	—●	—●	—●	—●	—●	—●	—●	—●	—●
Informal Reading Inventory			●	—●	—●	—●	—●	—●	—●	—●	—●	—●	—●	—●
Mid-Book Test										●	●	●	●	●
End-of-Book Test	●	●	●	—●	—●	●	●	●	●	●	●	●	●	●
Unit Skills Test (Forms A and B)			●	●	●	●	●	●	●	●	●	●	●	●
Unit Process Test						●	●	●	●	●	●	●	●	●
Reading Progress Card	●	—●	—●	—●	—●	—●	—●	—●	—●	—●	—●	—●	—●	—●
Instructional Management Systems (Apple®, IBM)			●	—●	—●	—●	—●	—●	—●	—●	—●	—●	—●	—●
Strategies for Thinking*			●	—●	—●	—●	—●	●	●	●	●	●	●	●
Spelling Connection*			●	—●	—●	—●	—●	●	●	●	●	●	●	●
Listening Program*			●	—●	—●	—●	—●	●	●	●	●	●	●	●
IT Kit (Interactive Teaching Kit)	●		●	—●	—●	—●	—●	●	●	●	●	●	●	●
Classroom Library	●	—●	●	—●	—●	—●	—●	●	●	●	●	●	●	●
Reading Skillsware: Vocabulary								●	●	●	●	●		
Reading Skillsware: Comprehension								●	●	●	●	●		

*Black-line Masters with Answers

●—● One Item

SILVER BURDETT & GINN

Figure 3.2 Components of Basal Reading Programs

- Graded series of readers for the students
- Teacher's Editions for each level that contain detailed lesson plans; informational articles on the teaching of reading; activities for reinforcement, review, and enrichment; annotated lists of trade books for children; scope and sequence charts for teaching the skills; and additional information as sample letters to parents
- Workbooks for each of the student readers
- Teacher's Editions for the workbooks
- Writing journals for the students
- Management systems including record-keeping devices, Informal Reading Inventories (for initial placement in the program), and criterion-referenced pre- and posttests to assess student performance as students move through the program
- Dittos or reproducibles to reinforce skill development and to provide enrichment
- Instructional aids, such as word cards, charts, puppets, or pictures of characters in stories (at early levels only), game boxes, and big books (enlarged reproductions of stories at the early levels)
- Supplementary library books
- Media, such as films, filmstrips, audiotapes, and computer software

swering dumb questions and doing tons of workbook pages!" Figure 3.3 illustrates a typical basal reading lesson.

Advantages of a Basal Reading Program

A basal reading program offers the beginning teacher a great deal of support. The beginning teacher, attempting to cope with all the exigencies of the classroom and having little experience with the grade level being taught, is often relieved to find that a large portion of the curriculum has already been planned. A more experienced teacher moving to a new grade level or one who may not have had the opportunity for recent professional development may also find that a basal offers much help. And the classroom teacher may find that the teacher's manual serves as a resource for lesson planning and as a good source of enrichment activities. Instead of having to search for poems, stories, and nonfiction material to interest students, the teacher has much material right at hand. There is often a good balance of genres in the reader: fantasy, historical fiction, realistic fiction, science fiction, adventure stories, poetry (both ballad and lyric), biography, and informational nonfiction with subject matter that appeals to students at each level. The artwork, too, is varied and balanced, ranging from photographs to realistic drawings in different media, from black and white to full color. Evaluation is provided for the teacher, from the ongoing evaluation of comprehension questions written into the lesson plans in the manual, to the unit and level tests provided with the series. In addition, most of the basal programs provide teachers with other ways of assessing their students, for example, performance tasks and portfolios. It is easy for parents to understand this approach to reading since it is most like what they themselves encountered in school. This means the beginning teacher is not left in the uncomfortable position of having to produce an on-the-spot explanation of the reading program for the principal or parents.

Disadvantages of a Basal Reading Program

The disadvantages of a basal reading program have partly to do with its inherent flaws and partly to do with its abuses. Let's look at the flaws first. The basal reading program is built on the idea that certain types of materials will work with children at different ages. It does not take into account the diversity of the U.S. school population. Certain areas of the country have a disproportionate influence on the material included in reading textbooks. In a number of states, such as California and Texas, not all reading series are made available for considera-

Figure 3.3A

Theme Connection

Hopes and Dreams

In this variation of "Sleeping Beauty," one character's dreams are realized when she gets what she wishes for. Another character gets what she deserves.

Selection Summary

Once upon a time there lived a beautiful princess named Miserella who was very mean and a poor orphan named Plain Jane who was very kind. One day Miserella gets lost in the woods and finds a fairy who takes her to Jane's house. Miserella angers the fairy so much that she accidentally puts them all to sleep for one hundred years. Only a kiss from a prince will wake them. One hundred years pass and Prince Jojo enters the scene. It is his kiss that breaks the spell. But who does he kiss? The beautiful princess? No. He kisses Plain Jane, and the two fall in love, marry, and live happily ever after.

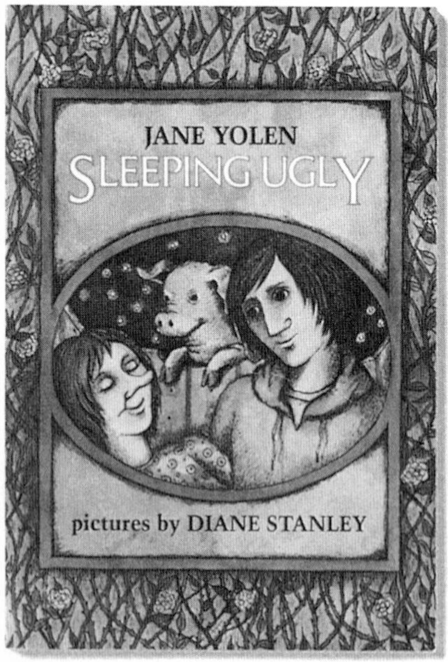

Diane Stanley, the illustrator of *Sleeping Ugly*, studied almost everything *but* art at college. During her senior year, she took an art course and discovered that drawing was what she wanted to do. She studied art for one year in a castlelike building in Scotland. She earned a degree as a medical illustrator.

Awards Ms. Yolen Has Won

Parents' Choice • Lewis Carroll Shelf Award • Golden Kite • Kerlan Award

Other Favorites by Jane Yolen

Wizard's Hall (Harcourt, 1991). Henry reluctantly goes to Wizard's Hall to learn to be a wizard. (average)

Encounter (Harcourt, 1992). The story of Columbus's arrival on San Salvador is told by a Taino Indian boy. (challenging)

What Rhymes With Moon? (Putnam, 1993). This poetry collection contains nineteen poems, all related to the moon. (average)

Figure 3.3B (cont.)

Lesson Planning Guide

Sleeping Ugly

	Teaching Strategies	Materials	Integrated Language Arts/ Integrated Curriculum
BEFORE Reading pages 28e–f	**Activate Prior Knowledge**		**Speaking/Listening** retell fairy tales
	Develop Vocabulary	Instructional Transparency 3 Practice Book, p. 7	**Vocabulary** determine word knowledge
	Link Spelling and Vocabulary	Spelling Practice Book, pp. 6–7	**Spelling** double consonants
DURING Reading pages 28–43	**Prereading Strategies**	Student Anthology, pp. 28–43	
	Strategic Reading	Practice Book, pp. 8–9 Purple Tape 4: Side 1	
	Teachable Moments to Develop Skills Humor Predict from Previewing Compare and Contrast Understanding Time Writers and Reading		**Writing** lists **Speaking** book talks
	Thinking About It		
AFTER Reading pages 43a–h	**Response Activities** Literature Circles Trade Book Link Story Starters Map and Retell Respond Using Vocabulary	Graphic Organizer Transparency 10 *Sarah, Plain and Tall* by Patricia MacLachlan	**Speaking/Listening** group discussion, retelling **Writing** fairy tale rewrites, tale morals, TV scripts
	Comprehension Strategies Skill Focus: Predict from Previewing Supporting Skill: Prior Knowledge	Practice Book, p. 10	
	Integrated Language Arts Compare and Contrast Characters Plurals T	Integrated Language Activity Book, p. 37 Integrated Language Teacher's Resource Book, pp. 11, 60	**Writing** comparison paragraphs **Viewing** student-performed dramas **Grammar** singular and plural nouns
	Integrated Curriculum Art: Culture/Heritage Social Studies: History Health: Mental Health/ Social Health Language Arts: Writing		

T = Holistic Test
T = Skills Test

INTEGRATED CURRICULUM
Art: Illustrate Fairy Tales
Social Studies: Construct a Time Line
Health: Explore Rules of Etiquette
Language Arts: Write Fairy Tales

28c • Anthology A *Sleeping Ugly*

Figure 3.3C (cont.)

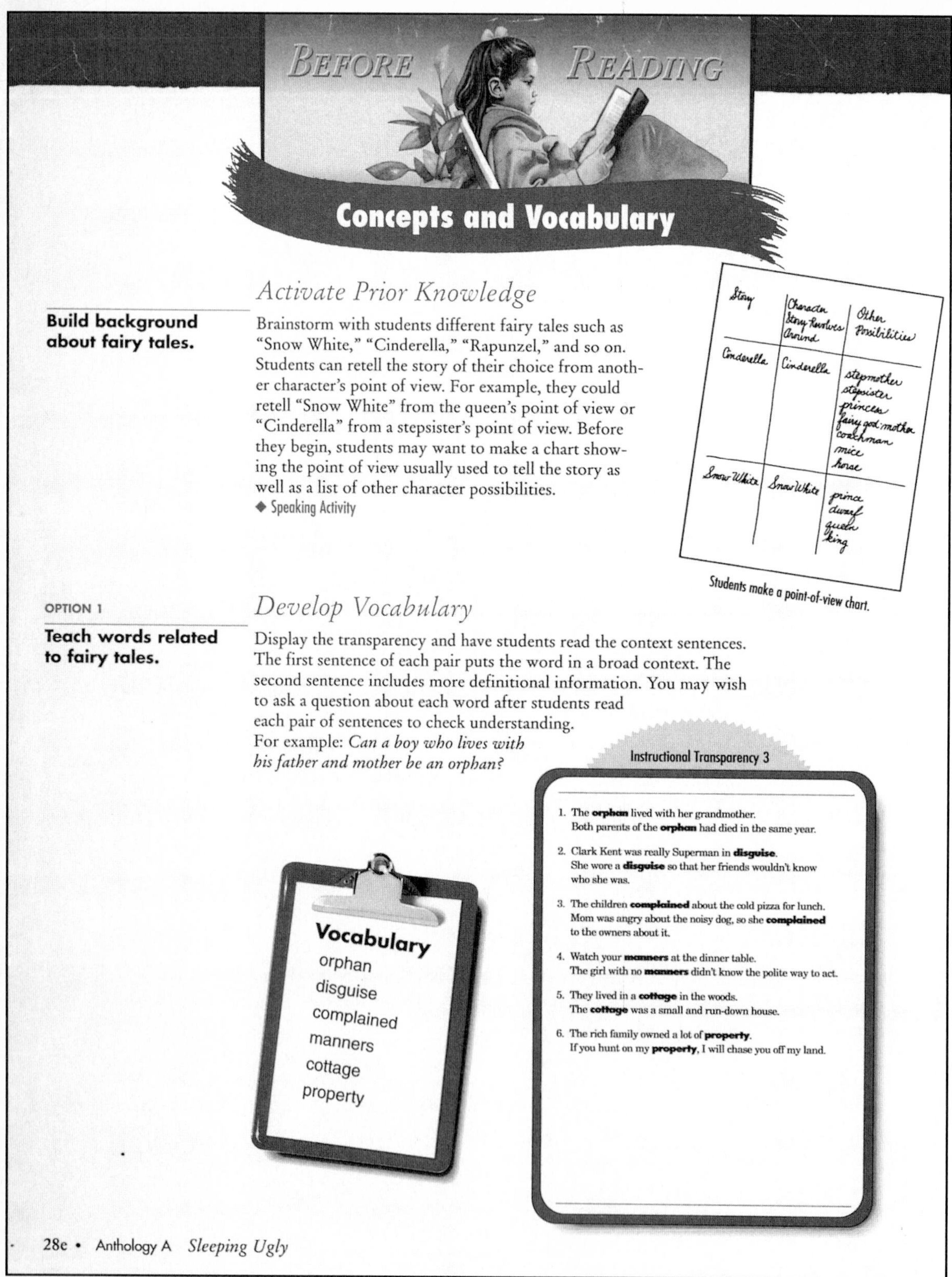

Concepts and Vocabulary

Activate Prior Knowledge

Build background about fairy tales.

Brainstorm with students different fairy tales such as "Snow White," "Cinderella," "Rapunzel," and so on. Students can retell the story of their choice from another character's point of view. For example, they could retell "Snow White" from the queen's point of view or "Cinderella" from a stepsister's point of view. Before they begin, students may want to make a chart showing the point of view usually used to tell the story as well as a list of other character possibilities.

◆ Speaking Activity

Story	Character Story Revolves Around	Other Possibilities
Cinderella	Cinderella	stepmother stepsister princess fairy godmother coachman mice horse
Snow White	Snow White	prince dwarf queen king

Students make a point-of-view chart.

OPTION 1

Develop Vocabulary

Teach words related to fairy tales.

Display the transparency and have students read the context sentences. The first sentence of each pair puts the word in a broad context. The second sentence includes more definitional information. You may wish to ask a question about each word after students read each pair of sentences to check understanding. For example: *Can a boy who lives with his father and mother be an orphan?*

Vocabulary

orphan
disguise
complained
manners
cottage
property

Instructional Transparency 3

1. The **orphan** lived with her grandmother.
   Both parents of the **orphan** had died in the same year.
2. Clark Kent was really Superman in **disguise**.
   She wore a **disguise** so that her friends wouldn't know who she was.
3. The children **complained** about the cold pizza for lunch.
   Mom was angry about the noisy dog, so she **complained** to the owners about it.
4. Watch your **manners** at the dinner table.
   The girl with no **manners** didn't know the polite way to act.
5. They lived in a **cottage** in the woods.
   The **cottage** was a small and run-down house.
6. The rich family owned a lot of **property**.
   If you hunt on my **property**, I will chase you off my land.

28e • Anthology A *Sleeping Ugly*

tion by local textbook committees. Instead, these states have lists of reading series and textbooks that are approved for adoption statewide. Publishers are understandably eager to have their textbooks on these lists. This means that certain selections might be deleted or certain words changed in order to overcome the objections of the buyer. In general, this practice has often led to textbooks that opt for cautiousness.

In older basal reader series, the selections were frequently adapted and vocabulary made simplified and also unnatural, particularly in books for the early grades. Sentence structure tended to be short and choppy because publishers believed that short, simple sentences are easier for children to read. In reality, this makes it harder for the reader to predict and comprehend the text. When written language is dissimilar to spoken language or the language used in trade books, this makes the child's task more difficult. A basal reading program included stories written specifically for that series or used portions of stories from children's trade books, often changing the wording and the spirit of the original books. Newer basal programs, responding to criticisms of adapted children's literature, now include original work of outstanding children's authors. Selections written by in-house authors are written in natural language.

Vocabulary still frequently is taught out of context by listing words on the board and encouraging definitions of the words that fit a given story. We believe that difficult words could be part of prereading discussions and dealt with in context during or after reading, along with the strategies readers can use to deal with the unfamiliar words. Also with an emphasis on skills, many stories are unnecessarily dissected, which could turn children off from reading for pleasure.

Other disadvantages of basal use center on the abuse of the system. Basals tend to encourage a traditional and unreflective approach to reading. Therefore such practices as round-robin reading (each child reading a paragraph or a page aloud, one after another), continue. The problem with this kind of reading is that it asks the child to perform material cold and creates tension and discomfort. Children who are not reading aloud are often not reading along but are daydreaming. The teacher may interrupt this by suddenly calling on a child who is not paying attention and asking that child to read, thereby embarrassing the child in front of his or her peers. What happens to building a love for reading in this procedure?

Teachers may also deliver reading instruction through whole-class instruction with just one level of the basal. This can be problematic in the early grades when some youngsters are emergent readers while some of their classmates are well into independent reading. Teachers cannot address the needs of individual students if reading instruction is not differentiated or individualized.

Another problem with the basal reading program is the belief many teachers develop that the basal is always right. It has been put together by experts, they are told, and if they just use it properly, they will get good results, as measured by standardized tests. The idea that these experts may not be able to make the best judgments for your class is not promoted by the publishers. The realization that publishers include material to try to meet the demands of every teacher is also not understood in its implications. And now a related problem arises: The time for reading in the classroom is limited, and this has implications for those using the basal. Many teachers follow the basal manual in sequence. In order to get through the book by the end of the year, they may discover that they have no time for the enrichment activities located at the end of a story or unit. These are the story extensions that whole language advocates believe are essential to a deeper understanding and enjoyment of the story.

Perhaps the most noticeable problems with the basal involve skill instruction, reinforcement, and testing. Fortunately, most of the publishing companies give teachers assessment options and even choice of the type of workbook, for example, a skills version or a journallike version. Basals still claim to be comprehensive, and they are indeed, but in their attempt to satisfy every consumer's appetite some sacrifices have had to be made. It is up to teachers to make decisions whether to use basal programs and, if so, how to use them successfully to meet the needs of their particular students.

FROM THE CLASSROOM OF . . .

Kathy Pike and Jean Mumper New Paltz, New York

VOCABULARY QUILT

One way to expose children to interesting words and develop their vocabularies is to make a VOCABULARY QUILT. A quilt can be outlined on chart paper or poster board with squares (4-inch squares work well) partitioned off. Each student is given a square of colored paper or wallpaper. During the course of a week (or whatever time frame is used), the students find one word to enter on their square and attach it to the class quilt. The word can be an unfamiliar one or one the student found particularly interesting or amusing. Words can be chosen from books read during Sustained Silent Reading, Literature Groups, content area subjects, or the newspaper. Words can also be chosen that pertain to a certain theme, e.g., a unit on the environment could contain such words as *acid rain, endangered species, destruction.* When the students attach their vocabulary choices to the quilt or during a sharing time, the words could be discussed and the original source for the word could be read. The quilt could also contain illustrations of the word if so desired. Once the quilt has been completed, the students could choose one word, not necessarily their own, and write about it.

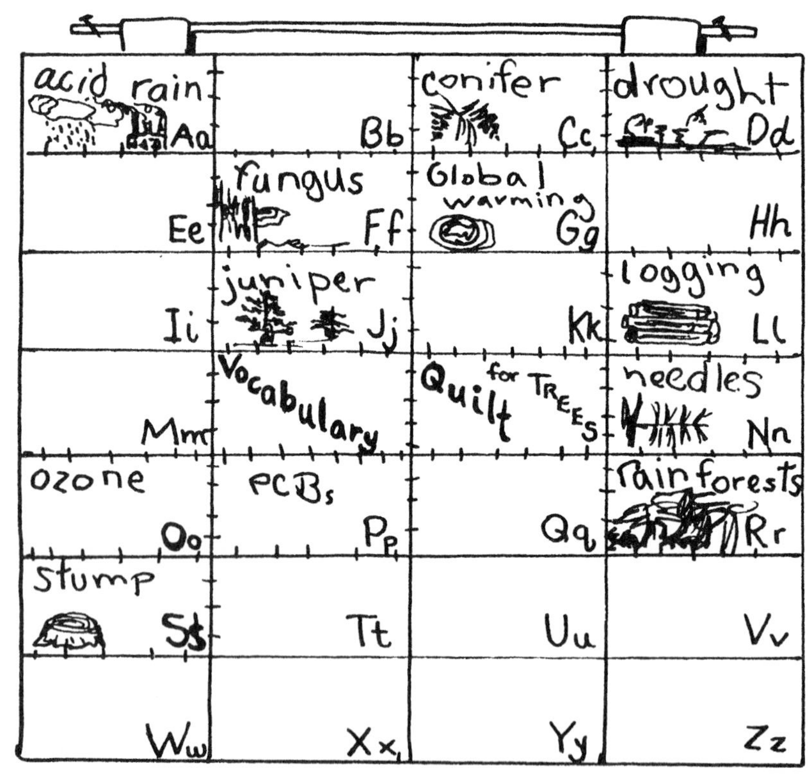

Language Arts in a Traditional Approach

The language arts are generally thought of as reading, writing, listening, and speaking. In practice, this means that in the portion of the day assigned to language arts, attention is given to areas not generally covered in reading instruction: spelling, handwriting, and language/English (which includes both composing and grammar). It is not uncommon for teachers to use separate textbooks for each of these areas. In a traditional classroom, these areas are rarely integrated. For example, spelling words are not integrated with writing and reading, and grammar instruction is frequently addressed as sequential, separate topics, not as needed when children are writing. Since these areas are addressed separately in traditional classrooms, they are presented separately in this section.

Spelling

"Okay, boys and girls, it's spelling time. Open your spelling books to page 76. Yesterday you took a pretest, and now you are going to practice your words. The directions say to write the spelling word that completes each phrase. After that you can do the crossword puzzle using your new words." This hypothetical scene represents what typically happens in the classroom when it is time to teach spelling. The most commonly used practice in contemporary schools is the spelling textbook approach. This practice involves a commercial spelling textbook with a daily period of work on word lists and related activities.

Not long ago, spelling instruction involved only the use of a hardcover text or perhaps a consumable softcover text. Today's publishers now provide many other components as well (see Figure 3.4).

Although some variation exists among spelling programs, they are similar in philosophy and format. The major goal is to have students learn a collection of words, usually 10–20 per week. The words to be learned are essentially the same for all the children, although some programs may suggest the use of diagnostic pretests in order to assign students to easier or more difficult books. Typically words are organized and grouped according to spelling patterns or common structural characteristics. This visual organization is used to help students identify similarities in word structure. For example, a unit might revolve around a particular phonic element, such as *oi* or *aw*, or around such structural elements as prefixes or the inflectional ending *ing*. The publishers state that studying words by patterns rather than just memorizing words helps create an understanding of spelling and promotes long-term retention. By studying words with similar features, it is hoped that students will become aware of the spelling patterns in the English language.

Textbook publishers also include spelling generalizations as an aid for remembering the spelling words and for application to other words. However, they rarely provide strategies for determining when to use a particular rule, nor do they discuss the limited accuracy of many of the rules. Generally the same rules are repeated at other grade levels, using different spelling words each year.

Many spelling textbooks use the test-study-test plan, whereby students are pretested on Monday, study the missed words during the week, and are retested on Friday. Some teacher's editions of commercial programs even cite relevant research supporting the use of pretests for building positive attitudes toward spelling and for ensuring high achievement in spelling (Gentry, 1984; Henderson, 1985; Templeton, 1986). Variations of this plan also exist. Some teachers use a study-test plan, omitting the pretest. The students study all the words—even those they can already spell. Other teachers add a midweek trial test (test-study-test-study-test plan).

Spelling textbooks are organized into weekly plans that include lessons for each day of the week. On Mondays, the children take a pretest and are guided through self-correction of the test. Step-by-step suggestions are provided to help the teacher guide students through this process. Along with the weekly word list in the students' spelling textbooks, there frequently are structured questions that review and reinforce the spelling generalization discovered during self-correction of the pretest. The textbooks also contain other activities that give students practice with the spelling rule or provide an opportunity for writing the week's words in order to help in the memorization of the words. Other activities include sentence com-

FROM THE CLASSROOM OF . . .

Jane Eakins Kingston, New York

I SPY

I SPY is an activity for children to use both context and initial sounds in guessing a secret item. Jane uses a bulletin board entitled *I SPY* for this activity. Two huge eyes are accompanied with a series of clues, one for each day. The children predict what the secret item might be by drawing their prediction. The children are encouraged to write their prediction as well in their own invented spelling. The children's daily predictions are collected and placed in their own individual *I SPY* booklets.

I spy with my little

something that

Starts with b.

is an animal

Steven bull

can fly

It is a bat!

Figure 3.4 Components of Spelling Programs

- Student texts or workbooks
- Teacher's Edition
- Teacher's Resource Binder (which may include such items as tests, aids for enrichment and management, writing activities, challenge activities, parent involvement packs, ideas for creative teaching, suggestions for preparation and practice activities for standardized tests, tools for spelling across the curriculum, and even colorful posters for the classroom)
- Spelling reproducibles (for additional practice and reinforcement)
- Computer software (for motivating practice of the spelling words or for integrating spelling with writing and word processing)
- Transparencies (stating spelling generalizations, steps to study a word, passages to demonstrate editing and proofreading, and patterns for bulletin boards)

pletion, puzzles, cloze activities, proofreading, dictionary activities, writing, and handwriting practice. These exercises comprise the spelling instruction that is undertaken between the pre- and posttests. All students are then tested at the end of the week. A sample spelling unit is shown in Figure 3.5.

Spelling texts also provide a systematic strategy for learning to spell words. This strategy focuses on the whole word as opposed to breaking it into syllables or sounds. It also makes use of the various modalities—visual, auditory, and kinesthetic. Research supports the whole-word approach to spelling instruction since it is more successful than a phonetic or syllable approach (Horn, 1969). A strategy for learning words is presented in Figure 3.6. This example is similar to strategies presented in most spelling textbooks.

Spelling textbook publishers suggest that students receive between 60 and 75 minutes of spelling instruction per week. They base this recommendation on research concluding that this amount of time will produce efficient spelling instruction (Horn, T., 1947; Horn, E., 1960).

Although the spelling textbook approach is by far the most common means of delivering spelling instruction, other approaches also exist. Some teachers do implement individualized spelling programs, while others construct their own spelling word lists from such curricular areas as science, social studies, and even basal readers.

Handwriting

Although we are in an age of technology when electric typewriters and computers are the norm, schools still feel the need to address the topic of handwriting. Illegible handwriting has contributed to reduced employability in our society, contributes to underachievement in schools, and costs the government and businesses millions of dollars annually (Barbe, Lucas, and Wasylyk, 1984). In addition, each year millions of pieces of illegibly addressed mail wind up in the dead-letter office at a considerable cost for handling. The goal of legible handwriting is certainly worthwhile if motivated by consideration for the reading audience rather than by a desire to help all children achieve model penmanship. Despite the need for legible and fluent handwriting, handwriting is the most overlooked component of the language arts. Handwriting is usually taught only occasionally, depending on the grade level and the time available for teaching it.

As in other areas of the language arts, handwriting is frequently taught using a commercial program that provides separate texts for each grade level. These texts contain skill pages that provide a systematic introduction to every letter of the alphabet and application pages to ensure that these skills are used.

Handwriting instruction generally begins in first grade, but unfortunately many kindergartners are also required to undergo formal instruction. Most handwriting programs begin with manuscript or printing, with a switch to cursive (which means flowing, or writing that is connected) in second or third grade. A new style of handwriting, called D'Nealian, appeared in

Figure 3.5A

■ **INTRODUCTION**

Short e and Long e

■ **FOCUS** Say each word and phrase. Notice how the **long e** and **short e** sounds are spelled in these words.

credit	buy new furniture on **credit**
speak	**speak** to a neighbor
alley	trash cans in the **alley**
fence	a white picket **fence**
least	the **least** expensive shirt
hockey	play ice **hockey**
went	**went** to see a play
contest	a juggling **contest**
beat	**beat** eggs until fluffy
honey	put **honey** on toast
reason	a good **reason** for that
valley	a river in the **valley**
money	**money** to buy food
engine	a car **engine**
them	gave it to **them**
steal	**steal** someone's property
monkey	a **monkey** in the jungle
treat	**treat** a friend to lunch
season	the fall **season**
donkey	a braying **donkey**

1. ____
2. ____
3. ____
4. ____
5. ____
6. ____
7. ____
8. ____
9. ____
10. ____
11. ____
12. ____
13. ____
14. ____
15. ____
16. ____
17. ____
18. ____
19. ____
20. ____

■ **DISCOVER** The **long e** sound is spelled **ea** in **speak.** How is it spelled in **honey?** What letter spells the **short e** sound?

■ **WRITE** Sort the words by writing
- seven words with **long e** spelled **ea**
- seven words with **long e** spelled **ey**
- six words with **short e** spelled **e**

CHALLENGE!

bleachers
squeaked
escaped
celery
jersey

48

Figure 3.5B (cont.)

WORD HISTORIES A **word history**, or **etymology**, tells us the origin and history of a word. Most dictionaries display word histories at the end of an entry.

The word histories for the names of our months can be traced back to the ancient Romans. Julius Caesar was a famous Roman emperor. A month was named *Julius* in his honor. *Julius* eventually became *July*.

Following are etymologies for other months in our calendar. Write the name of the month that completes each history.

1. In Roman times the Latin phrase *Martius mensis* meant month of Mars. In Old French this became *marche*, and in English it became ___.
2. In honor of the ruler Augustus, the Romans named a month *Augustus*. In English it became ___.
3. The Latin word *Januarius* is from *Janus*, a two-faced god said to look back at the old year and ahead to the new. This became the month of ___.

1. ________________
2. ________________
3. ________________

ENRICHMENT Pick one.

Back to the Present
Look up the word histories for *punish* and *kitchen*. Write a sentence describing your discoveries.

Where Is It From?
Work with a partner to look up these words in a dictionary: *denim*, *nicotine*, *jumbo*, *hamburger*, and *bloomers*. Which words came from the name of a city? Which came from the name of a person?

CHALLENGE!
Research the terms Old English and Middle English. When were they spoken? Find examples of English words spoken today that came from Old and Middle English.

43

Figure 3.5C (cont.)

■ **INTRODUCTION**

8 Words with Double Consonants

■ **FOCUS** Look at each word and read the meaning phrase. Notice the double consonant letters in each word.

different	many **different** animals
offer	**offer** to help
suffer	**suffer** from illness
slippers	wear **slippers** around the house
supper	have **supper** at 5:00
grasshopper	a **grasshopper** on a leaf
tomorrow	finish up **tomorrow**
worry	**worry** about someone's safety
current	study **current** events
borrow	**borrow** someone's pencil
written	a **written** party invitation
matter	does not **matter**
bottle	a **bottle** of juice
lettuce	a **lettuce** salad
ridden	has **ridden** a horse
paddle	**paddle** a canoe
shudder	**shudder** in the cold
odd	an **odd** cat with no hair
bubble	blow a big **bubble**
hobby	painting as a **hobby**

1. ______
2. ______
3. ______
4. ______
5. ______
6. ______
7. ______
8. ______
9. ______
10. ______
11. ______
12. ______
13. ______
14. ______
15. ______
16. ______
17. ______
18. ______
19. ______
20. ______

■ **DISCOVER** The double letters in **offer** and **supper** have only one sound, but to spell the words correctly you must use two letters. What letters are doubled in **bottle, worry, shudder,** and **grasshopper?**

■ **WRITE** First write the words in the list you think are easy to spell. Then write the words you think are difficult. Underline the double consonants in each word.

CHALLENGE!

allowance
antennas
impossible
Mississippi
recess

44

Figure 3.6 Instructional Strategy for Learning Words in Spelling

LOOK at the word, say it aloud as you do.
CLOSE your eyes and picture how the word looks.
SPELL the word to yourself.
LOOK at the word. Is it spelled correctly?
COVER the word and then write it.
CHECK your spelling. If you have made any mistakes, repeat the steps.

1968. In D'Nealian the letters are slanted as in cursive and all but five of the manuscript letters are formed in the same way as are cursive letters. Therefore, the transition from manuscript to cursive is simplified. Some handwriting series now offer a version similar to D'Nealian in addition to their more traditional versions. Figures 3.7 and 3.8 illustrate several handwriting forms.

Again, as in the other language arts areas, publishers of handwriting series also offer other components in addition to the student texts. Teacher's editions contain lesson plans, extended activities, background information, and teaching tips. Other components may include a Teacher's Resource Kit with support materials, an alphabet wall chart (sometimes grouping the letters by similarity of strokes), color transparencies with letter models and ruled lines, overlays for evaluating handwriting, an evaluation scale that allows students to compare their writing with that of their peers, and worksheets with guidelines to help parents and teachers improve their own handwriting.

Handwriting publishers also provide other materials, such as handwriting paper, jumbo alphabet cards, pens and pencils, pencil grips, writing frames (to help with proper pen or pencil slant), alphabet desk strips, alphabet flip charts, and a line scriber for making lines on the board. A word should be said about two of these handwriting tools—paper and pencils.

There is no conclusive evidence on the value of using lined versus unlined paper, but ultimately all handwriting instruction uses lined paper. In addition, paper for very young writers may have an extra dotted line in the middle in order to help in letter formation.

Kindergartners and first graders commonly use fat beginner pencils (13/32″ in diameter). However, some children prefer the regular-size pencils that older children use, and research indicates that beginner pencils are not necessarily better than regular pencils for younger children (Lamme and Ayris, 1983). There is also no evidence that specially shaped pencils and pencil grips are effective.

The time allocated for handwriting instruction varies depending on the grade level and the degree of expertise the students have in either manuscript or cursive. Students just beginning to learn to write manuscript (as in kindergarten and first grade) and students making the transition to cursive (usually in second or third grade) will be given more handwriting instruction time—generally 10–15 minutes daily. In the upper grades, students are given brief lessons and practice or no instruction at all.

Although commercial handwriting programs are popular for handwriting instruction, many school districts do not provide separate handwriting texts. Sometimes the district will require teachers to follow a certain style of handwriting and will provide alphabet cards to place around the room. Teachers refer to these as they model proper letter formation on the overhead projector or board. Students practice on worksheets constructed by the teacher or on regular handwriting paper. Some districts do not promote one handwriting style over another, and teachers are left to their own resources. Frequently, teachers will purchase specialized alphabet strip cards and place these over the board or use the form in the basal reader.

Language/English

Once upon a time what are known today as elementary schools were called grammar schools, an appropriate name since a large portion of the curriculum was devoted to memorizing rules, learning grammatical terms, and working on grammar exercises. It was thought that these activities would lead to acceptable speaking and

Figure 3.7 Samples of Manuscript and Cursive Handwriting Forms

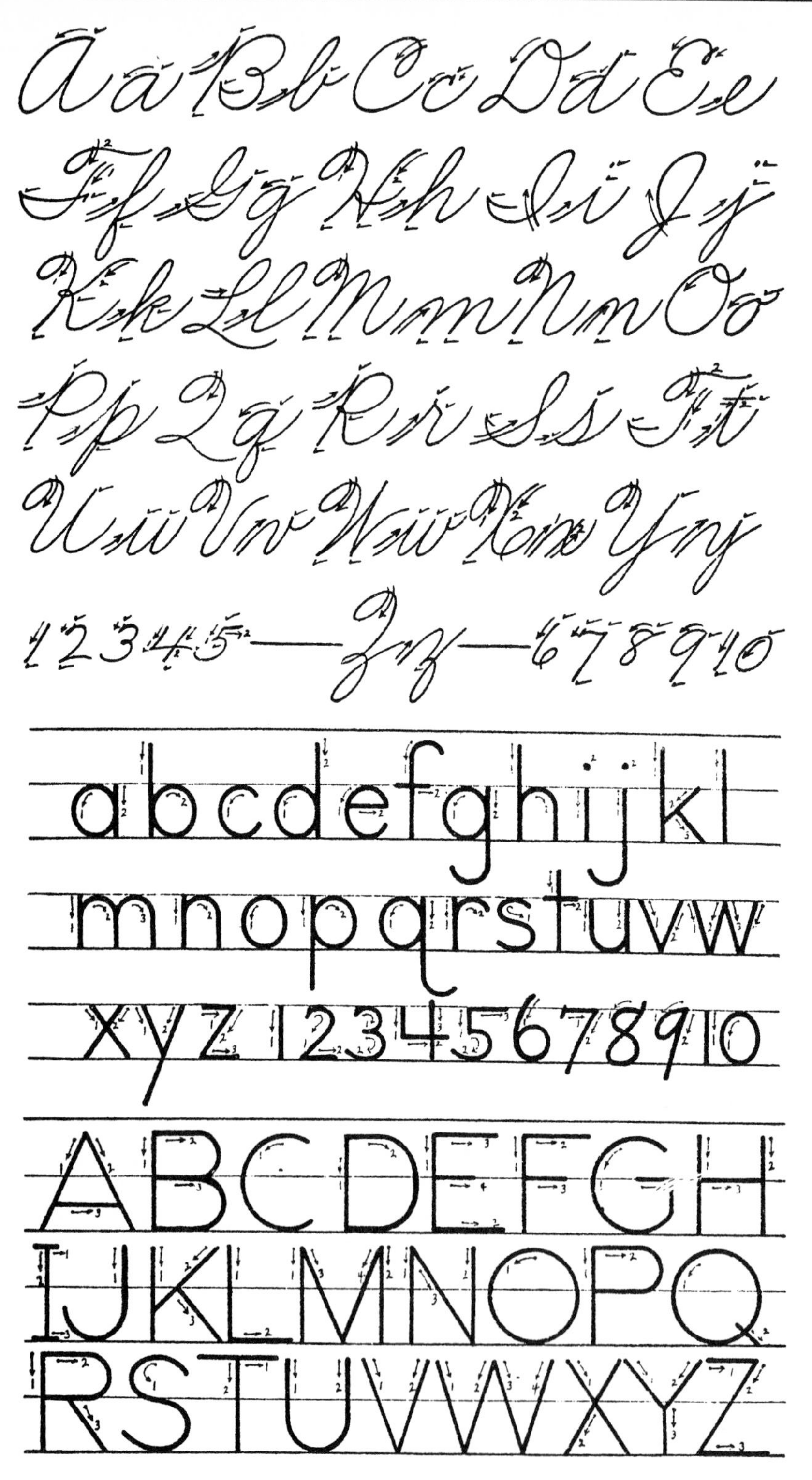

Figure 3.8 Sample of D'Nealian Handwriting Form

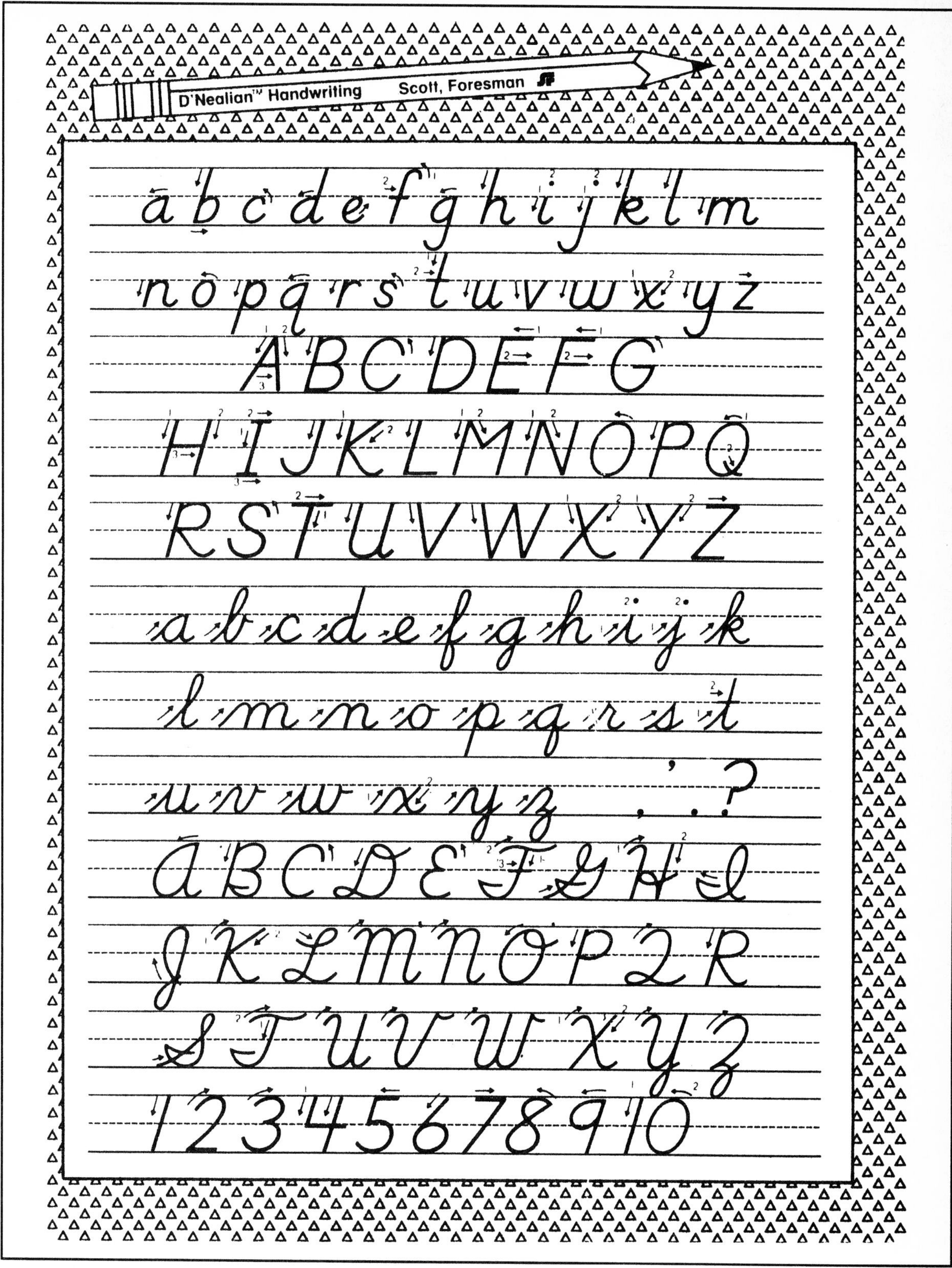

writing. This conclusion is questionable. Unfortunately, this tradition continues today in many classrooms. The development of language (English) is predominately conducted through the use of commercially prepared texts, referred to as English or as language. As with the basal reader program, the English program has graded student texts. Whereas years ago only student editions were available, now an abundance of materials accompany English programs. An example of some components that may accompany commercial programs appears in Figure 3.9.

In a typical English series, various strands are carried throughout the student texts. These strands are grammar (usage, mechanics, and grammar), composition, and related resources and skills (vocabulary, speaking and listening, research skills, study skills, literature skills, and thinking skills). Grammar instruction refers to such activities as studying sentences, the parts of speech, and usage rules; mechanics includes capitalization and punctuation.

- Student Editions, available in softcover, consumable format for grades 1 and 2 and hardcover for grades 2–8
- Teacher's Editions that provide teaching support with objectives, teaching suggestions, and strategies for individualizing each lesson
- Teacher's Resources Binder to reinforce, extend, and evaluate, including writing process transparencies, blackline masters, enrichment and reinforcement activities, ideas for creative teaching, suggestions for teaching and evaluating writing, lesson plans for integrating the language arts, and colorful posters
- Skills Practice Book with exercises to reteach and reinforce concepts in writing, grammar, usage, and mechanics
- Teacher's Edition for Skills Practice Book
- Tests (pretests and mastery tests for each chapter, midyear and end-of-year tests
- Instructional software with tutorial writing programs

Figure 3.9 Components of Language/English Programs

Although many contemporary schools approach the teaching of English in a similar fashion to the older grammar schools, there have been changes in the content and format of current English programs. Some programs include the writing process and use selections from literature (usually abridged) for extension activities.

English instruction is delivered in allotted time slots, approximately 30 minutes, with all the children working through the program at the same pace. Evaluation is determined through the use of tests that accompany the commercial program.

Advantages of the Traditional Approach to Language Arts Instruction

Language arts textbooks are designed to present systematically the basic content, concepts, and skills of each of the various language arts (language, spelling, and handwriting). These texts bring together a great deal of information for the teacher and the student, and this may be perceived as an advantage of the traditional approach to language arts instruction. The teacher's manuals provide a wealth of suggestions and activities, and this may prove to be beneficial for inexperienced teachers or for those making a grade-level change. The scope and sequence of each language arts component is readily available for the teachers, and thus teachers do not have to decide what to teach, in what order to teach it, or even how to teach. The manual guides the teacher through the day, the week, and even the year. Lesson plans can be noted on the small squares in the lesson plan book the teacher keeps. There is plenty of room to simply note "Spelling book, p. 34." The curriculum is predetermined, and all teachers have to do is follow the adopted language arts program(s).

Another advantage of the traditional approach is its built-in accountability. Each area has built-in testing, which makes assigning and defending grades easier. Teachers have actual, measurable products for grading: the spelling test, handwriting samples, and tests of grammatical usage. These types of testing materials are easily marked right or wrong. In these days of increased emphasis on accountability, having documentation in the various areas of the language arts is attractive to both teachers and administrators.

Disadvantages of the Traditional Approach to Language Arts Instruction

The disadvantages of this approach are found in the very areas that give rise to the advantages. Although the teacher now is sure of covering the different areas of the language arts, the areas are divided artificially, making it much less likely that children will see the connection of the parts or the importance of the pieces.

Let's take handwriting as an example. Why would a teacher believe handwriting is worthy of a student's attention? Because when you are producing something, you are generally concerned with communicating your ideas to another. At a minimum, you want to be able to read your own ideas later. Even if you are writing poetry for your own pleasure, you want to be able to reread your poems later. Therefore, legibility is a legitimate and natural concern for the writer. However, it will become an issue and will carry with it motivational power for change when it arises in the natural context of keeping material for one's own use and sharing material with others.

Setting small, individual goals for improvement is a much more fruitful tack for the teacher. A whole-class discussion on techniques students use to produce legible handwriting is also beneficial. Time is often a factor in good handwriting. If a student is rushing to finish an assignment, the handwriting may be illegible. An attitude of analysis of one's own writing, along with the ownership of the material and the desire to communicate the ideas well, goes far in helping the student develop legible handwriting that will remain throughout the student's life.

Another advantage of the traditional approach that becomes a disadvantage is in the area of testing. Although spelling lists, handwriting samples, and tests of grammatical usage are easy to grade and defend, they are not necessarily the best items to use for deciding on a grade in the area of the language arts. They are not even the best means to use in planning instruction in the language arts. Instead of devoting so much time to the topics covered on the tests, teachers might better focus on such areas as the writing process and how to incorporate the expressive arts into a language arts program. Grades in a traditional program may not even be indicative of a student's progress in the language arts since they may not reflect growth in a student's ability to draft, revise, proofread, and so on. They do not reflect a student's ability to apply correct spelling in functional writing tasks.

Because the testing aspects of the language arts necessitate using a great deal of class time, teachers may not have adequate time to devote to such topics as poetry and drama. These are important and legitimate areas of the language arts. They may be considered a fringe benefit since they are more difficult to grade and thus may not be included in the scope and sequence of a given language arts program. This is a difficult situation for teachers who believe in the importance of the arts in the education of all students.

Some practices associated with traditional language arts programs may not be beneficial for growth in these areas and may even be harmful for children. The practice of having children write a word repeatedly has not proven helpful in the learning of spelling words. Spending time on spelling exercises has not readily transferred to correct spelling in writing activities. Nor has isolated practice of correct grammatical usage in textbooks been readily transferred to students' writing. The practice of copying from the board, as in handwriting instruction, may be detrimental for young children because they might not be developmentally ready for this task.

Finally, the use of manuals can quickly become a disadvantage. The beginning teacher who found it helpful to know what words children at this level often misspell or what grammatical constructions they have problems with tends to follow the manual carefully and perhaps inflexibly and may not make the break within a year or two to designing his or her own lessons. Because the manual spells everything out for the teacher and often gives even more work than can be accomplished in the time,

FROM THE CLASSROOM OF . . .

A New Zealand Teacher Auckland, New Zealand

Birthday Card Display

Happy birthday! So today is your special day. Well, just go to the birthday card display and pick your own birthday card. Seen in a New Zealand classroom, this activity not only honors the birthday child or someone important in the child's life but also provides an opportunity for children to be engaged in some functional writing. The children are encouraged to create birthday cards whenever they like and add to the card collection. The cards may contain poems, jokes, and famous quotes, or may be in languages other than English. A note attached to the display area might say, "Make a birthday card for our display. When it's your birthday you get to choose a card."

teachers find themselves struggling simply to fulfill the expectations of the manual instead of taking charge themselves—observing and thinking through what the children are doing and how to help them to most effectively work through the process they are engaged in.

SCHOOLS IN TRANSITION

Beginning Integration of Reading and the Other Language Arts

"I just had my first head-on collision with a basal," wrote a student teacher in her journal during the first week of her student teaching experience. That comment and many more like that reflect the dissatisfaction many teachers have with current reading programs. Teachers are concerned with illiteracy rates, aliteracy (having the ability to read but choosing not to read), reading programs that divide reading into bits and pieces, and reading programs that do not take into account the natural learning behaviors of children. Teachers are moving away from the reading programs of the past and are presently *in transition.*

A transitional program is one that is moving away from a basal reading program toward whole language. Changes are taking place in educational philosophy and in the methods and materials used in the classrooms. Before describing transitional classrooms, it is necessary to explain why teachers are in transition.

Classrooms in Transition

The statistics for illiteracy and the drop-out rates in U.S. schools today are overwhelming. Kozol (1986), in *Illiterate America,* estimates that 60 million people in the United States are functionally illiterate and quotes statistics from the United Nations that rank the United States as forty-ninth in literacy levels among 158 United Nations countries. These statistics are of great concern to educators, to parents, and to the public. The reading program has been around long enough to affect these rates, but it has not done enough to alleviate the problem.

More recent statistics show higher literacy rates and an increased love and reading of books. These statistics, however, are not from the United States. They are from the small country of New Zealand, whose educational philosophy and educational programs have accomplished something about the issues of illiteracy and aliteracy. New Zealand is using a whole language approach to literacy, and this appeals to U.S. educators. Teachers are becoming more knowledgeable about this movement through workshops, an increasing number of whole language newsletters, and articles in educational journals. Teachers are meeting in support groups (e.g., Teachers Applying Whole Language [TAWL]) to learn about the why and how of whole language. And teachers are becoming excited about this approach to literacy development.

Although many teachers are now embracing a whole language philosophy and wish to implement whole language in the classroom, it may not be feasible to just "do whole language." There are many existing reasons and stumbling blocks that create transitional classrooms. Although teachers may be convinced that whole language is the way to approach literacy development, parents and administrators are more conservative and more resistant to change. Therefore teachers may be mandated to use the basal and have to fit the basal in with portions of a whole language approach. There is a fear that test scores will be affected by a change in reading programs, and until the issue of assessment and evaluation of whole language is resolved, basal reading programs will not entirely disappear.

Aside from the realization that students need more than a basal reading program, and aside from the resistance to change from administrators and parents, transitional programs exist for other reasons as well. Teachers are not comfortable enough as yet to abandon totally the familiar for the unknown. More training and staff development efforts are necessary to help teachers move further along into whole language. Teachers still need a support system as they move along the continuum from a basal program to whole language.

Another major stumbling block that helps account for the existence of transitional classrooms is the lack of resources available for teachers to make the change. A whole language approach means that many books must be available in the classroom. Whole language advocates are becoming creative in the ways they acquire books, but this takes time and money. Publishers are now addressing the production of whole language materials. Although many publishers feature high-quality literature, unfortunately many others are merely putting a whole language label on materials that do not reflect the whole language philosophy. Over time, resources may no longer be such a critical issue as teachers amass classroom libraries of good literature. So teachers are making the transition into whole language, and the reasons discussed are determining the rate of change and the possible extent of the transition.

Viewing Transitional Classrooms

There are as many versions of transitional classrooms as there are teachers. Teachers vary in their personal philosophies, their beliefs about language and literacy learning, and the constraints imposed on them because of their unique teaching situations. Transitional classrooms will reflect these differences. However varied in nature, transitional classrooms can be categorized. Following are some of the possibilities:

1. **Basal and literature.** Teachers may use the basal program as designed for a specific number of days, alternating its use with the reading of literature. For example, teachers may choose to use the basal for three days, with literature used the remaining two days. Or teachers

may undertake a two-week unit using the basal, followed by a literature unit.

2. **Alternative ways of using the basal.** Teachers may use the basal in alternative ways. They may group stories thematically or allow students to select stories they wish to read. This means that the stories are not used in the sequence provided by the publishers. Cooperative activities, such as peer reading, may be adopted. Teachers may also devote a considerable amount of time to the enrichment section of the basal, which would include many activities involving listening, speaking, reading, and writing, as well as cross-curricular activities.

3. **"Basalizing literature."** Teachers may choose not to use a basal program but to use literature instead. Rather than focusing on the reading, sharing, and discussion of stories, teachers still preteach vocabulary for the books, use a preponderance of questions (especially literal), and have students complete innumerable worksheets. Spelling words may be taken from the selections, and skills are emphasized. A basal philosophy is used, but the basal reader is replaced with a trade book.

4. **Literature and techniques to show accountability for basal scope and sequence.** Because of the issue of accountability, some transitional teachers ensure that their students can pass the tests provided by the basal publishers. Therefore they spend some time on test-taking strategies and on familiarizing their students with the basal test formats. The majority of their reading program is, however, devoted to literature.

Combinations of the above may exist, as do other possibilities for transitional classrooms. Teachers may still use the basal reading program as designed and add such activities as sustained silent reading and reading aloud. They may teach using thematic units, which incorporate all the language arts with the content areas, in addition to using the basal program.

Many teachers may make the transition into whole language through the writing program rather than through the reading program. There is less structure and fewer mandates are imposed on teachers in writing than in reading, and teachers may therefore feel more secure in implementing change through writing. Standardized test scores generally are reported for reading and mathematics but not for writing, so the accountability issue is lessened. Writing process classrooms and writers' workshops may coexist with a basal reading program. Some teachers claim to have writing process classrooms, but on close examination some of the basal philosophy can still be seen. Rather than give children responsibility for choosing topics and moving through the process at their own rates, some teachers feel the need to control writing by providing writing topics and imposing a daily structure to the writing period. For example:

- **Monday.** All children write a draft (on a topic generally supplied by the teacher).
- **Tuesday.** All children revise their draft.
- **Wednesday.** Drafts are shared and revised with a peer.
- **Thursday.** Drafts are edited.
- **Friday.** The writing pieces are published.

Many classrooms can be classified as transitional as they move from a basal program into a whole language one. For whatever reasons, teachers are moving into whole language. They are moving away from basal programs into transitional classrooms, and many are becoming whole language teachers.

THE WHOLE LANGUAGE APPROACH

Integrating Reading and the Other Language Arts

Now we have crossed over the bridge and are moving into whole language territory. This reminds us of the familiar tale "The Three Billy Goats Gruff." We will leave it to your imagination to identify the troll who is lurking under the bridge.

Greener pastures awaited the three billy goats gruff. What does the territory look like for the whole language teacher who has also made the crossing? Before describing whole language classrooms and providing a definition of whole language, we must note that there are as many types of whole language classrooms as there are teachers. Whole language is interpreted differently because it is a perspective on teaching and learning, not a prescribed set of practices (Raines, 1995). But despite this variety, whole language teachers share a common philosophy.

Whole language is a philosophy based on the findings from psycholinguistic, sociolinguistic, and literacy research, as well as from the research of practictioners. It is rooted in the belief that language must be natural, meaningful, and *whole.* It must be applied in situations that are authentic and relevant to the young learner. A major theoretical premise on which whole language is based is that learning to read and write is as natural as learning to speak. Throughout the world, language learning takes place through meaningful use, not through practicing separate parts and putting them together at a later date.

Think about it. Does a baby learn to say the word *Mommy* by first being taught the sound /m/ and hearing a lot of words beginning with *m?* The answer is a resounding no! Rather, it's the association of repeatedly hearing "Give Mommy a kiss," "Bring the bottle to Mommy," "Mommy has a cracker for you" that enables the baby eventually to associate the word *Mommy* with the person who nurtures him or her on a daily basis. In this way, the idea that language communicates meaning is being learned. This is the earliest development of the schema of language.

In a whole language classroom the process continues. There is no longer talking about reading and then the language arts, but rather reading and the language arts are treated as an integrated whole. A whole language approach is based on the premise that people communicate naturally and that they have been doing this for a long time. If we can discover what people use to communicate effectively, we will be able to translate that into effective language learning in the classroom.

Beliefs About Whole Language

Frequently, teachers who use Big Books claim, "I'm doing whole language." But whole language does not consist merely of using Big Books, keeping journals, reading aloud to children, or setting up classroom centers. Using whole language requires that teachers examine their beliefs and assumptions about teaching, learning, and the use of language both oral and written for the purpose of learning (Newman, 1985).

Since whole learning involves more than just altering appearances, it is necessary to examine the beliefs about language acquisition, about learning, and about the learner that are the foundation on which whole language is based.

The following are beliefs about what constitutes learning and the resulting roles of the teacher and the students in the learning process.

- Listening, speaking, reading, and writing, which have traditionally been taught as separate disciplines, are now integrated and complement and support each other.
- Students learn by constructing meaning from their experiences and the world around them.
- Reading and writing develop simultaneously.
- Language learning thrives in a setting where risk taking and exploration are encouraged and supported.
- Risk taking is a natural part of the learning process.
- Errors are indicative of a learner's attempts to make sense of his or her world.
- Students learn to read by reading and to write by writing.
- The process, product, and content to be learned are interrelated.
- Students use language for many purposes and audiences, encountering many opportunities to read natural, complete texts and produce many meaningful, whole communications.
- Allowing students to make choices about their reading and writing gives them ownership and permits them to assume responsibility for their own learning.
- The classroom is a community of learners, where there is respect for and trust of both teachers and students.

It is imperative that teachers examine their own beliefs and note the gaps that may occur in what they *say* they believe and what they actually *do* in their classrooms. There are no short cuts to implementing whole language. There are no manuals presenting "101 Easy Ways to Do Whole Language." There are no sets of materials that will ensure that whole language instruction does indeed occur. It isn't enough just to buy new books and prepare hands-on activities. In order to implement whole language, teachers must continually and systematically analyze their own teaching methods and philosophies. Teachers must constantly question how and why they are doing what they are doing: Is the way I work with children reflective of how children actually learn? Do I have a theory of learning that can be applied to my teaching? Are my students happy and confident about their own learning? A teacher's personal philosophy empowers that teacher, and an increasing professional knowledge base and philosophy elevate teachers in the greatest sense of the word (Routman, 1988).

Definitions of Whole Language

The whole language movement in the United States is a grass-roots movement that has developed significantly in the last few years. This is partly owing to the influence of such whole language proponents as Ken and Yetta Goodman, Don Holdaway, Frank Smith, Dorothy Watson, and Brian Cambourne, among others. It has also been motivated by a view of teaching and learning that is quite positive and additionally by the attempts of informed teachers to use what is known about learning and language development to provide more satisfying and effective experiences for both their students and themselves (Goodman, 1989). In order to get a clear perspective and gain an insight into the whole language movement, it is important to note the definitions of whole language that occur in the educational literature. These definitions may vary somewhat (owing to the diverse backgrounds of their authors), but the essential philosophy of language and learning remains intact.

> Whole language is clearly a lot of things to a lot of people. It is not a dogma to be narrowly practiced. It's a way of bringing together a view of language, a view of learning, and a view of people, in particular two special groups of people: kids and people.
>
> (Goodman, 1986, 5)

> Whole language weaves together a theoretical view of language, language learning, and learning into a particular stance on education.
>
> (Edelsky, Altwerger, and Flores, 1991, 7)

> First it is important to emphasize that whole language is a philosophy, a belief system about the nature of learning and how it can be fostered in classrooms and schools.
>
> (Weaver, 1990, 3)

> Whole language is a label for mutually supportive beliefs and teaching strategies and experiences that have to do with kids learning to read, write, speak, and listen in natural situations. And it is much more. Over the years it has become: Whole language is a perspective on education that is supported by beliefs about learners and learning, teachers and teaching, language, and curriculum.
>
> (Watson, 1989, 132–133)

> In a teaching-learning context, a whole language approach means that the literacy act or artifact being demonstrated needs to be sufficiently "whole" to provide enough information about the various systems and sub-systems of language, so that learners, if they decide to engage, will have the data available for working out how all the pieces fit together and interact with each other.
>
> (Cambourne, 1988, 204)

The different definitions in the literature allow people who are involved in whole language to arrive at their own personal definition and revise it over and over as needed. The definition of whole language that is used in this text is:

> Whole language is a philosophy in which listening, speaking, reading, and writing are integrated in natural language learning situations that are stimulating, supportive, and encourage risk taking and independence.

Looking into a Whole Language Classroom

While no two whole language classrooms are identical, the literacy instruction that provides the foundation for the curriculum is quite evident. Despite the fact that whole language classrooms do vary and do have their own personalities, certain elements and activities can be observed. These elements are consistent with the beliefs discussed earlier and reflect the teachers' respect for the students and for the learning process. Such elements include:

- daily speaking and listening
- reading aloud
- sustained silent reading
- the use of predictable books
- shared book experience
- modeled writing
- process writing
- language experience
- guided and individualized reading
- response journals and learning logs
- content area reading and writing

These elements, as well as others that are found in whole language classrooms (See Figure 3.10), are discussed in depth in later chapters.

In whole language classrooms children learn to read by reading and to write by writing. It is also true—and this is crucial information for whole language learning—that children learn to read by writing and to write by reading. When a child produces a piece of writing, not only has the child done a great deal of reading and rereading to finish the piece, but the child has also learned about the structure of text in the process.

Imagine having to construct a fairy tale for a course you are taking. You would probably base your tale on motifs that were common in the tales you knew as a child. Perhaps you would have a castle, a king, a princess, a witch, and a youngest son. You would almost certainly have the fairy-tale markers "Once upon a time" and "They lived happily ever after." Can you say that you would approach the fairy tales that others in the class read or that the teacher read to the class in the same way after this experience? You would now be more aware of things about fairy tales that you had paid little or no attention to before. You would be in a better position to notice the new and the fresh, the unusual twist, the humorous.

So, if the language learner can learn to read by writing, then it is also likely that the child learns to read by using language in its other manifestations: speaking and listening (in their many forms, such as discussion, drama, and storytelling) and exposure to electronic media. Other areas that should be integrated into the whole language approach are art, music, dance, mathematics, science, and social studies. This is the key to whole language thinking—that communication is more powerful if it is relevant to the learner, if it is interesting and motivating, and if it can be integrated within the classroom.

What about the other modes of language arts (listening and speaking) in the whole language classroom and such conventions and writing tools as spelling, grammar, and handwriting? Listening and speaking are very much a part of a balanced language program and are integral to all aspects of the curriculum. Both informal and formal talk are used socially, to learn from, and to learn by. Children learn through talking as they share and explore ideas. Children listen to and support one another by being audiences for writing and project sharing and by being part of literature groups and writing share circles. They listen to each other brainstorm and problem solve. They learn about language purposefully and meaningfully the entire day.

As for the tools of writing—spelling, grammar, and handwriting—these too are part of a balanced language program. Rather than being addressed through commercial programs and practiced on worksheets, they are addressed in authentic classroom situations as needed.

Writers should respect their audience. This means putting work in a readable, publishable form. This means writing that is free of errors in spelling and grammar. This means writing that is legible. Particularly with inexperienced writers, some modeling by the teacher and practice by the student may occur in whole language classrooms. Teachers might provide demonstrations through minilessons and modeled writing. Here writing conventions are addressed and discussed. Teachers also motivate students with relevant feedback in individual conferences on specific writing conventions the student may be having difficulty with.

Children might even keep notebooks for spelling and handwriting in which they note words they themselves misspell in their writing and letters of the alphabet they are learning to form or may be forming incorrectly.

Figure 3.10 What Does a Whole Language Classroom Look Like?

Students are reading and writing every day. The teacher reads to the students and writes with them regularly.

The curriculum is more and more integrated as the teacher builds learning centers around the basic themes that are common to two or more of the following in that grade: social studies, science, language arts, math curricula.

The classroom is full of literature that is easily accessible.

Children's work—individual in look—is prominently displayed.

Peers helping peers is evident through group work, through writing, at the computer, at centers, and with other classes (e.g., fourth graders reading to kindergartners).

On-task discussion is encouraged throughout the day, except for such times as sustained silent reading, read-aloud, class presentations.

Cooperative learning is valued, and a strong sense of respect for other learners is evident.

The teacher often acts as a facilitator rather than an authority figure.

The teacher attempts to reach the whole child, watching for ways to raise self-esteem through a student's work in art, music, drama, and sports and a student's interaction with peers.

The students and teacher are eager to involve parents in the learning process.

The students and teacher are eager to share what they have learned with others in the school: other classes, the principal, custodian, secretary.

The students and teacher love to read and know some great books they want to share with a visitor.

(Courtesy of Dr. Kathleen Scholl, Assistant Professor of Reading and Language Arts, Westminister College, PA.)

Whole language promotes a climate for learning. If a classroom is generally business as usual with children sitting in rows or in clusters of desks, as they did with basal reading programs, and the teacher has changed only a few things in the classroom, the classroom is probably in a transitional stage. A whole language teacher is sensitive to new needs that can never allow business as usual again.

In sum, whole language involves learners who, when provided with continual and authentic opportunities in an environment that is natural and safe, can initiate their learning, become curricular informants, and control, evaluate, and regulate their own behaviors, efforts, and learning (Harste, Woodward, and Burke, 1984; Watson, 1989). "Teachers who have a whole language perspective operate their classrooms with an abundance of children's literature, use a writing process approach, usually organize the curriculum in integrated, thematic units, teach strategies approaches to inquiry, and find authentic, meaningful ways for children to communicate about their lives and what they are learning" (Raines, 1995, 2). In whole language classrooms, students are at the very heart of curriculum planning, as teachers develop curriculum *with* their students. Whole language also involves teachers who are facilitators, coaches, researchers, participants, and learners.

Because whole language is a shared responsibility between the teacher and the learner, puts children at the center of the curriculum, and has a high regard for the learner, whole language generates excitement in its proponents. Teachers who are implementing whole language say that it produces an exciting and productive learning atmosphere and rekindles pleasure in the written word.

Advantages of the Whole Language Approach

Now that teachers and children are truly immersed in natural language learning, the advantages discussed for the transitional program that are prefaced with such words as *could, can,* or *may* be occurring are now definitely occurring. For example, whereas transitional classrooms may capitalize on the way children learn, whole language classrooms definitely consider the way children learn. Children are immersed in authentic literacy experiences through all the language arts. Learning in whole language classrooms is based on the kind of learning that occurs in the real world, and the curriculum is presented and structured so that optimal learning can take place.

In the whole language approach, children learn to read by reading and to write by writing. Real literature is used as the basis of the reading program, and reading is done for real purposes with all the accompanying benefits (e.g., the enhancement of background knowledge and story structure and the development of the human experience and a true love of reading). Writing is also done for real purposes: Children are given opportunities to write for many audiences, and writing is used throughout the curriculum. There is an emphasis on process, and children are provided with demonstrations of both the reading and writing processes that have been internalized by literate people. In this way, the student novices are given insights into reading and writing by the experts, in this case, the teachers. Therefore children learn language, both oral and written, by using real, meaningful, and relevant materials and experiences.

There is a sense of empowerment in whole language classrooms as teachers assume more responsibility for making professional decisions about their students' learning and their classroom literacy program. Students likewise are empowered as they become the focal points for planning instruction. Students are essentially curricular informants whose needs and interests are at the heart of literacy instruction. Students are encouraged to assume more responsibility for their own learning as they self-select strategies to implement, books to read, and topics to study and write about. Students can elect different working situations as well, such as individually, with a peer, or in a small group.

Another advantage is that the curriculum is integrated, not artificially separated. Whereas teachers frequently stated that they did not always have time for such subjects as social studies, science, or the expressive arts, by integrating curriculum, time is now available for these exceedingly important curricular areas. Reading and writing are no longer perceived as subjects that are taught at specific times but are woven into the true fabric of the entire instructional day.

In the whole language approach, literacy is celebrated—and this celebration awaits the teacher who has crossed over the bridge. At this celebration is a community of learners who assume responsibility for teaching and learning, who are empowered, and who demonstrate a true love of books and learning.

Disadvantages of the Whole Language Approach

With any good investment there are things to take into account in addition to the advantages that accompany the investment. This is true for the whole language approach as well. However, while these considerations are stated in this section as disadvantages, to whole language proponents many of these issues are merely roadblocks to overcome.

One major deterrent to implementing whole language is time. Teachers need time to become familiar with children's literature. They need time for retraining, planning, and conferencing. Time is also needed for teachers to procure books, set up centers, establish routines, and plan with support staff and other teachers on their grade level.

Adequate resources are also an issue. Many schools do not have sufficient resources to replace the commercially structured program now in place. Many teachers and administrators have a problem with the lack of a predetermined scope and sequence, even though research has shown that language is not learned according to a standard scope and sequence. The seeming lack of structure is perceived by teachers as a negative.

As mentioned previously, change is difficult for most people. Teachers have been using the skills-based, bottom-up approach since the 1920s. Many teachers tend to teach the way they were taught. Parental resistance is likewise a major problem. Some parents want their children to be taught the way they were taught. They are familiar and comfortable with the basal program. They are fearful as to what will happen to test scores with the whole language approach. And what about children moving from a basal classroom to a whole language classroom and vice versa? Many administrators join in parental concern for similar reasons, but particularly over the accountability issue. Whole language evaluation is in the process of being determined and refined. Traditional testing provides data that can rank children, schools, and districts. Since evaluation has been conceived in such a manner for so many years, there is discomfort on the part of many with the "kid-watching" and portfolio assessment that occur in whole language classrooms.

Although teachers applying whole language may find it more taxing, they also find it more rewarding. It allows them to become independent decision-makers, which raises their level of professionalism. And that brings us to another issue. Since parents, administrators, the community, and even some colleagues may be wary of this approach, teachers must be able to articulate why and how they are conducting their classrooms as they do.

These are the roadblocks that whole language advocates are meeting head-on through support groups, conference attendance, and the acquisition of additional knowledge and expertise. When the goal of producing learners who are confident, are independent, and love learning and literacy is considered, then the roadblocks must be treated as temporary inconveniences. Many districts and teachers have already eliminated these roadblocks—and others are making strides to do so. The community of learners regarding whole language issues is not just in the classroom. It extends into the community—to parents, to administrators, to anyone interested in literacy—so that the objectives are to develop empowered learners who read, enjoy reading, and become lifelong readers.

SUMMARY

This chapter described the various approaches to literacy and their advantages and disadvantages. The labels *traditional* and *whole language* were given to generally acceptable practices. In reality, few classrooms fall completely into the traditional or whole language descriptions. Many classroom teachers are moving along the continuum from traditional programs toward whole language—they are in the process of translating theory, research, and their literacy practices into more effective classroom instruction for their students.

BIBLIOGRAPHY AND SUGGESTED REFERENCES

Anderson, R.; Hiebert, E.; Scott, J.; & Wilkinson, I. (1985). *Becoming a nation of readers.* Urbana, Ill.: University of Illinois, Center for the Study of Reading.

Barbe, W.; Lucas, V.; & Wasylyk, T. (1984). *Handwriting: Basic skills for effective communication.* Columbus, Ohio: Zaner-Bloser.

Cambourne, B. (1988). *The whole story.* New York: Scholastic.

Crafton, L. (1991). *Whole language: Getting started . . . Moving forward.* Katonah, N.Y.: Richard C. Owen.

Durkin, D. (1981). Reading comprehension instruction in five basal reader series. *Reading Research Quarterly, 14,* 515–544.

Durkin, D. (1984). Is there a match between what elementary teachers do and what basal reader manuals recommend? *The Reading Teacher, 37,* 734–744.

Edelsky, C.; Altwerger, B.; & Flores, B. (1991). *Whole language: What's the difference?* Portsmouth, N.H.: Heinemann.

Farr, R.; Tulley, J.; & Powell, D. (1987). The evaluation and selection of basal readers. *The Elementary School Journal, 87,* 267–282.

Flood, J., & Lapp, D. (1986). Types of texts: The match between what students read in basals and what they encounter in tests. *Reading Research Quarterly, 21,* 284–297.

Gentry, R. (1984). Developmental aspects of learning to spell. *Academic Therapy, 20,* 11–19.

Goodman, K. (1986). *What's whole in whole language.* Portsmouth, N.H.: Heinemann.

Goodman, K. (1989). Preface. In K. Goodman, Y. Goodman, and W. Hood (Eds.), *The whole language evaluation book,* pp. xi–xv. Portsmouth, N.H.: Heinemann.

Goodman, K.; Freeman, Y.; Murphy, S.; & Shannon, P. (1988). *Report card on basal readers.* Evanston, Ill.: National Council of Teachers of English.

Harste, J.; Woodward, V.; & Burke, C. (1984). *Language stories and literacy lessons.* Portsmouth, N.H.: Heinemann.

Henderson, E. (1985). *Teaching spelling.* Boston: Houghton Mifflin.

Holdaway, D. (1979). *The foundations of literacy.* Portsmouth, N.H.: Heinemann.

Horn, E. (1960). Spelling. In C. W. Harris (Ed.), *Encyclopedia of educational research.* New York: Macmillan.

Horn, T. (1947). The effect of the corrected test on learning to spell. *The Elementary School Journal, 47,* 277–285.

Horn, T. (1969). Spelling. In *Encyclopedia of educational research.* New York: Macmillan.

Kozol, J. (1986). *Illiterate America.* New York: Dutton.

Lamme, L., & Ayris, B. (1983). Is the handwriting of beginning writers influenced by writing tools? *Journal of Research and Development in Education, 17,* 32–38.

Mason, J., & Osborn, J. (1982). *When do children begin "reading to learn"? A survey of classroom reading instruction practices in grades two through five.* Technical Report No. 261. Urbana, Ill.: University of Illinois, Center for the Study of Reading.

McCallum, R. (1988). Don't throw the basals out with the bath water. *The Reading Teacher, 42,* 204–209.

Newman, J. (1985). *Whole language: Theory in use.* Portsmouth, N.H.: Heinemann.

Raines, S. (1995). Introduction: Reflecting on whole language. In S. Raines (Ed.), *Whole language across the curriculum—Grades 1, 2, 3,* 1–16. Newark, Del.: International Reading Association.

Routman, R. (1988). *Transitions: From literature to literacy.* Portsmouth, N.H.: Heinemann.

Searfoss, L. & Readence, J. (1994). *Helping children learn to read.* Needham Heights, Mass.: Allyn & Bacon.

Shannon, P. (1983). The use of commercial reading materials in American elementary schools. *Reading Research Quarterly, 19,* 68–85.

Templeton, S. (1986). Synthesis of research on the learning and teaching of spelling. *Educational Leadership, 43,* 73–78.

Venezky, R. (1987). A history of the American reading textbook. *The Elementary School Journal, 87,* 247–265.

Watson, D. (1989). Defining and describing whole language. *The Elementary School Journal, 90,* 129–141.

Weaver, C. (1990). *Understanding whole language.* Portsmouth, N.H.: Heinemann.

CHILDREN'S LITERATURE CITED

Viorst, J. (1981). *If I were in charge of the world and other worries.* New York: Macmillan.

ASSESSMENT AND EVALUATION

LADYBUG

Flying through the air
ladybug flies with great grace
Black and orange wings

Nick Domenech

From the classroom of
Jean Mumper
Grade 3
Wallkill, N.Y.

Inspired by: *The Icky Bug Alphabet Book* by Jerry Pallotta

OVERVIEW

Integral to any literacy program are the issues of assessment and evaluation. Knowing what children have learned, how to help them learn, and how to plan for instruction are important aspects of education today. Not only are teachers concerned with assessment and evaluation, so are administrators, parents, students, and the public. Accountability is very much in the forefront in the educational scene. This chapter presents alternative assessment and evaluation practices that teachers and students may use to help inform instruction.

Questions to Ponder

1. Is it true that whoever controls assessment in effect controls education?
2. Is there a difference between assessment and evaluation?
3. Does information based solely on standardized test scores portray a limited view of the literacy accomplishments of U.S. schools?
4. What are some ways teachers can collect information about their students?
5. How can students become involved in the assessment and evaluation process?

WHAT ARE ASSESSMENT AND EVALUATION?

Assessment and evaluation are vital to the effectiveness of literacy programs. However, discussion of these terms often causes confusion and anxiety for teachers. Confusion exists because frequently the two words—*assessment* and *evaluation*—are paired or even used synonymously. Even the dictionary tends to define one term with the other. For instance, *The Random House Dictionary* (1987) defines the two words as follows:

- **assessment**—the act of assessing; appraisal; evaluation
- **assess**—to estimate or judge the value, character, etc., of; evaluate
- **evaluation**—an act or instance of evaluating or appraising
- **evaluate**—to judge or determine the significance, worth, or quality of; assess

Anxiety arises because the issue of accountability is of great concern, not only to teachers and administrators, but also to parents and the general public.

Although the two terms are often used interchangeably, there is a distinction between them. Assessment is the process of collecting information about the progress of learners toward learning goals, whereas evaluation is the analysis and interpretation of this information to identify learner strengths and needs and to determine whether teaching modifications are necessary (Department of Education, Wellington, 1989; Traill, 1993; Hancock, Turbill, & Cambourne, 1994). Assessment is part of evaluation, since it is necessary to gather evidence before making a judgment (Bouffler and Knight, 1991).

Both terms stand for a collection of data on which to base informed judgments about student learning. Both terms are different from the notion of testing. Testing is not synonymous with assessment and evaluation because it does not provide information on which teachers can make intelligent decisions about their students' learning and their own instructional practices. Later on in this chapter the principles of assessment are provided, and these will shed further light on the definition and meaningfulness of these terms.

LAND OF ASSESSMENT AND EVALUATION

You are about to embark on an adventure into the Land of Assessment and Evaluation. Before you take off, think about any trip or vacation you have taken or plan to take. Before you went, you did some planning. First, you decided on a destination, which probably was limited by the amount of vacation time you had, as well as your finances. You planned the means of transportation. Did you go by car, plane, boat, or train (or a combination)? You had to pack appropriate clothing for the places you planned to visit. If you planned to dine out or attend a formal event, then proper attire was necessary. Your recreational interests influenced what other things to pack (skis, skates, bathing suit, hiking boots, and so forth). Did you also prepare by reading guidebooks, sending for brochures, and checking maps? Being prepared helped you have an enjoyable vacation.

Traveling into the Land of Assessment and Evaluation demands similar preparation. The travelers on the journey are teachers and their students. Since most teachers have their students for one year, the duration of this journey is already predetermined—approximately 180 days. The destination may be the state's goals and objectives (generally stated in specially prepared publications), the district's mandated curricula, the teachers' or students' personal goals, or a combination of these. Ultimately the goal—and therefore the true destination—of all literacy programs is to produce independent, reflective learners who can and do read and write effectively and for pleasure. Therefore the classroom is a convenient stopover on the lifelong goal of literacy. The things that will be packed in the assessment and evaluation baggage—that is, the means of assessing and evaluation—are the focus of most of this chapter.

Before you pack your bags to go on this journey, you must read a guidebook to help you reach your destination. The first section of the guidebook provides relevant information on assessment and evaluation and offers a framework for thinking about these issues.

PRINCIPLES OF ASSESSMENT

Assessment and evaluation are integral parts of the educational process, for they help teachers look back at what has already happened, forward to what is going to happen, and at how students can be supported to ensure that it will happen (Cutting, 1989). Assessment and evaluation should not be added on at the end of a sequence of learning as has frequently occurred in traditional classrooms but should occur all day every day. Assessment and evaluation are not the responsibility of only the teachers; students themselves should play a key role in the process. The following principles should be kept in mind when assessing and evaluating:

- The student must be at the center of all educational assessment and evaluation.
- Assessment and evaluation must be ongoing and cumulative.
- A wide range of assessment instruments and strategies must be utilized.
- Assessment must draw from multiple information sources in a variety of contexts.
- Assessment and evaluation must be linked with instruction.
- Results must be such that the information can be clearly communicated to students, parents, administrators, and policymakers.
- Effective assessment is anchored in authenticity (i.e., grows out of real reading and writing instruction and real reading and writing tasks).
- Both teachers and students must be active, collaborative partners in the process. Reflective self-evaluation is necessary for both teachers and students.
- Assessment and evaluation are undertaken to determine student progress, to make educational decisions, and to communicate information about language growth.
- Assessment and evaluation must be doable in all classrooms and in all school contexts, meeting the needs of the school district, the teachers, the students, and the parents.

(Department of Education, Wellington, 1989; Goodman, K. 1989; Harp, 1990; Johnson, 1991; Cochrane and Cochrane, 1992; Valencia, Hiebert, & Afflerbach, 1994; Hancock, Turbill, & Cambourne, 1994; Learning Media, 1994).

The message stated in these principles is apparent. For assessment and evaluation to be sound educational practices, they must be ongoing, authentic, multidimensional, and interactive. Assessment and evaluation are not something teachers enter into their plan books for ten o'clock in the morning and then forget about for the rest of the day. Assessment and evaluation occur throughout the entire day across the entire curriculum. Literacy development is fostered and assessed across the curriculum, not only using measures that focus only on reading and writing. Assessment and evaluation are integral parts of the curriculum, not separate entities.

Teachers who use assessment and evaluation effectively constantly observe and interact with their students to discover not only what their students know but how their students are learning. The emphasis is on the process of learning. Teachers are constantly gathering data to use as the basis for future instruction. This information is also shared with students so that the students can then evaluate their own progress.

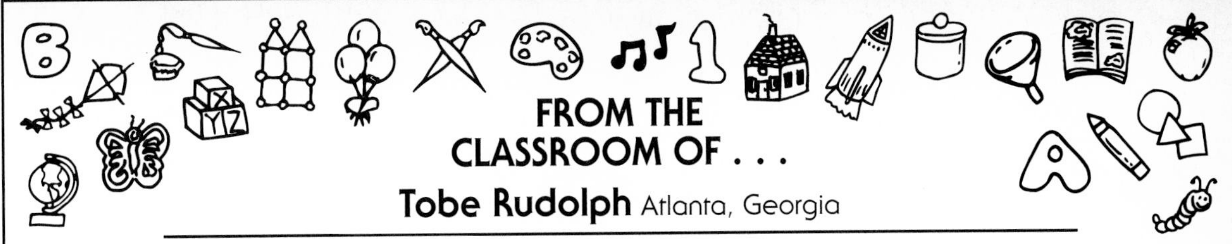

FROM THE CLASSROOM OF . . .

Tobe Rudolph Atlanta, Georgia

Getting the Message

Prior to the children arriving at school, Tobe writes a message on the board. The content of the messages can be seasonal, science or social studies related, mood pieces (funny, emotional, etc.), student issues or concerns, point of view, or the teacher's personal view on an issue or problem. As the children enter the classroom, some of them immediately begin reading it aloud, chatting about the content.

After the morning routines, the class sits in a circle and the children are asked to read the message silently, as best they can. It is then read aloud by a small group or the whole class. This choral reading helps the less able reader feel a part of the class activity. After reading the message, decoding difficult words with Tobe's prompts, the children are asked, "What is this message about?" A lively discussion ensues. After some conclusion is reached about its general meaning, Tobe reads the message aloud sentence by sentence, eliciting help from the children to figure out the unfamiliar and underlined words. Again the children are asked about the meaning of the message. Those who had a low level of involvement and comprehension now respond as though they were being pulled in by the tide of the more enlightened. They all come away with new knowledge.

The children get a copy of the message, which they copy into their message books. They are expected to reproduce it without any errors, unlike journals and other writing. Each student has an opportunity to read the message back to Tobe, self-correcting and making any written corrections if necessary. Saving messages in a special book gives children the opportunity to review prior messages and to see their own growth in reproducing and reading them.

In the early months, many children can't finish copying the messages in the required time. By the end of the year, they can complete all required tasks and are writing their own messages. They now take turns writing their own message on the board and leading the group while Tobe monitors the process. The students love this!

Vocabulary improves as many of the words that appear in the messages begin to show up naturally in the children's conversation and original writing. In addition to increase in vocabulary growth, the students learn to use the messages as resources for spelling words, for practicing their oral and silent reading, and for expressing their own thoughts and ideas when they begin composing them by themselves. Through this Getting the Message activity, learning becomes meaningful and enjoyable, with all students experiencing success. Below is a sample of a message that Tobe wrote in the fall.

Dear Students,

How many of you realize that the *autumnal equinox* is upon us? No, that is not a horrible disease, even though the words may sound *unfamiliar* and strange. Something happens the same time each year that gives these words meaning. It has to do with the *elliptical orbit* of the earth around the sun.

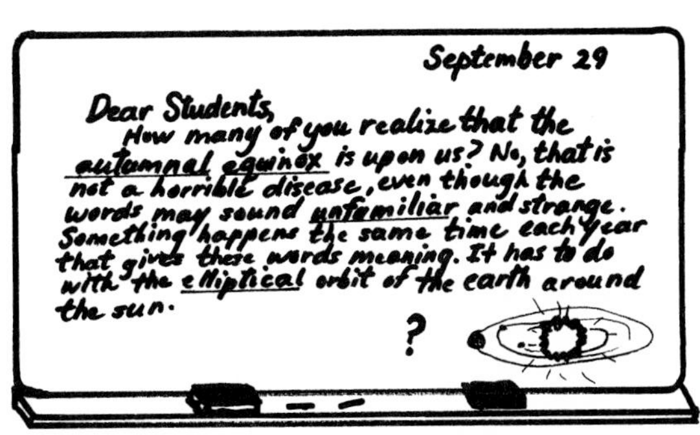

It is important to remember that assessment and evaluation are interrelated. Collecting assessment data serves many purposes, including obtaining information on students' achievements, needs, and progress. This information helps to draw a picture of what a student can do and what needs he or she may have. It can be used to monitor student growth and development and can provide insight into developing student-centered instructional programs. Collecting assessment data can also provide teachers with information so that teachers can examine how students interact with one another (Department of Education, Wellington, 1989).

Based on objective and accurate assessment practices, evaluation means making judgments and is essential for establishing the link between student learning and planning for future instruction. Through sound evaluation, the following questions can be answered:

- What has been—and what still needs to be—learned?
- Does the learning achieve the desired objectives?
- What are the new objectives that need to be set for learning to continue?
- What resources or strategies can or should be used?
- How can teachers be helped to identify their own strengths and needs?
- How can teachers be supported in their endeavors to organize their classrooms and assess and evaluate their students?

(Department of Education, Wellington, 1989)

Any improvement on teaching and learning depends on both effective assessment and evaluation. Such effective assessment and evaluation has to do with the teachers' knowing and accepting what their students do in reading and writing and how the students can be supported as they meet future challenges.

Now that you have done some background reading about your journey to the Land of Assessment and Evaluation, it is time to think about what to pack in your suitcase. Figure 4.1 depicts the range of assessment and evaluation possibilities. Each is discussed in a separate section. It must be noted, however, that these are presented as possibilities. They do not drive the curriculum—they grow out of and are part of it (Maeroff, 1991). Individual teachers have first-hand knowledge about themselves, their students, their classrooms, and their resources, and therefore it is up to each and every individual teacher to make informed decisions about what assessment practices and strategies to use.

Some sound advice is necessary before your journey. Remember traveling in the backseat of your parents' car or traveling with your own children? How many times were you told to look at the scenery, to look at what was going on around you? In order for you to get the most out of your journey, you must stop and look around. *Observation* is your passport to a successful and rewarding trip. Mixing with the local population is necessary in order to get a full taste of what you are experiencing. Talk to these persons (who may be 5 or 15 years old). They have much to share and communicate, much of which is indeed valuable for planning instruction.

FORMS OF DATA GATHERING

Many forms of data gathering are available to classroom teachers. Among those that can provide valuable information and assistance in instructional planning are the following:

- daily observations
- anecdotal records
- miscue analysis/running records
- student self-evaluation
- think-alouds
- portfolios
- conferences
- information from parents
- questionnaires, surveys, and inventories
- teacher judgment
- spelling analysis

Daily Observations

As stated previously, observation is integral to the assessment and evaluation process. To take the travel analogy even further, we must pay attention to signs along the way—such as "Stop, Look, and Listen"—as we journey along the road to literacy. The term *kidwatching* was coined by Ken and Yetta Goodman—and observing or watching kids in the classroom is of the utmost importance. Included in the process

Figure 4.1 Range of Assessment and Evaluation Measures

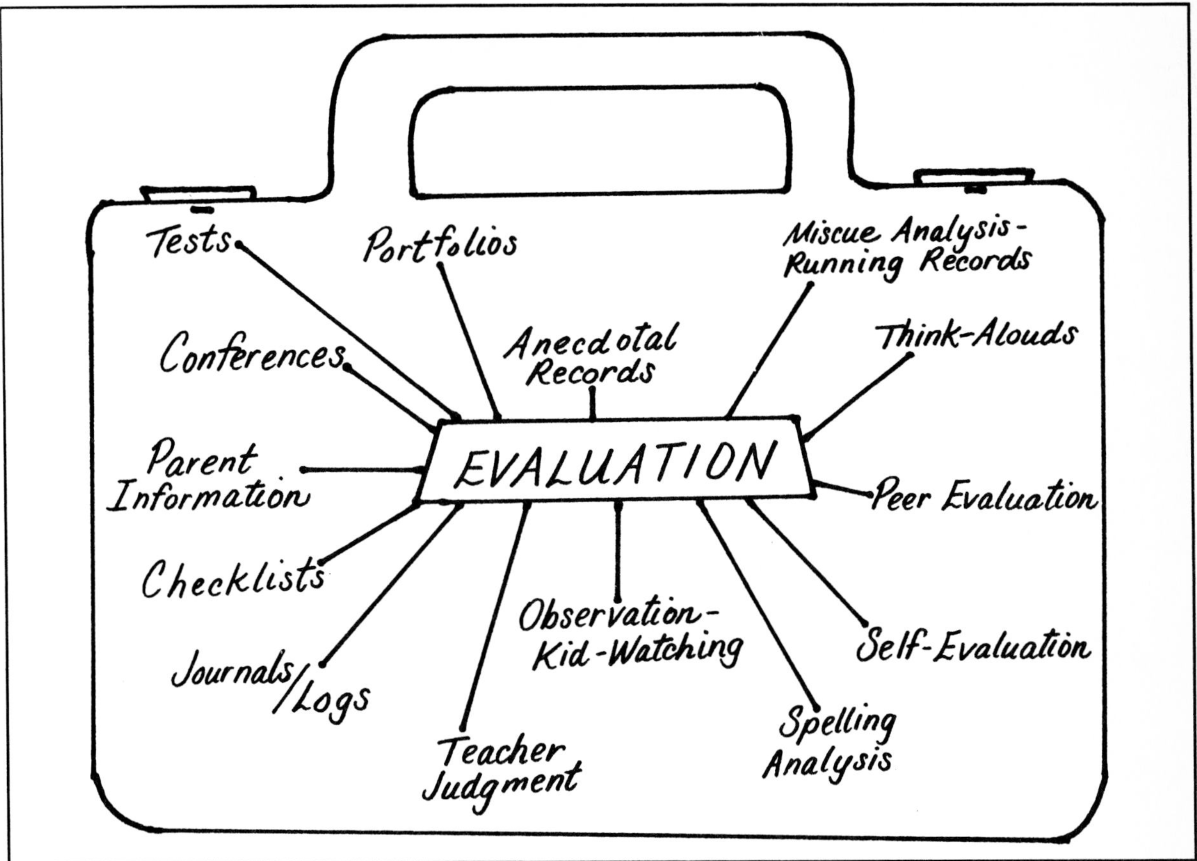

of kidwatching is structured observation whereby the teacher is an observer on the sidelines and watches and notes what the students are doing. In addition, the teacher may be a participant in the observation process. Here the teacher and students share information through conferences, discussions, question-and-answer sessions, and dialogue journals.

Since observation is crucial to the assessment and evaluation process, some guidelines may need to be established to help teachers in their observations. Teachers might ask themselves the following questions and use them to increase their understanding of their students' learning and to make modifications in their instructional practices:

- What is there to see?
- How best can we understand what we see?
- How can we put our understanding to use?

(Drummond, 1994)

Teachers must constantly observe their students, asking themselves, "What does it mean?" They should look for their students' strengths, confusions, and difficulties; for documentation of what the students can do and understand; and for the processes and strategies their students utilize (Clay, 1993). The desire is to have responsive and supportive teaching. Effective assessment and evaluation are processes in which an understanding of children's learning is acquired through observation and reflection, which can be used to evaluate and enrich the curricular offerings provided to students.

In order to watch each and every student systematically, teachers need to implement a system to ensure that this does indeed occur. Many teachers set aside a certain portion of the language learning time (when reading and writing instruction generally take place) to focus on individual students. Each day they have a designated number of students to observe. The data that are obtained may be recorded on checklists. Innumerable commercial checklists are available, but it is preferable that districts review the commercial products and then adapt elements of each to suit their individual needs. Figure 4.2 shows a checklist that was adapted by the Arlington School District in New York.

Data may also be recorded on teacher-designed data sheets or with recording methods that work well for individual teachers. For instance, one teacher uses sheets of cardboard (one for each student) held together by metal rings. One reason for using rings as opposed to a standard notebook is that when put down, the ring book is more noticeable and thus more easily located. The teacher records anecdotal observations, behaviors observed while the child is reading aloud or engaged in the writing process, spelling development and needs, suggestions for future handwriting practice, attitude, and so forth. Once a card is filled, it can be removed from the ring book and filed in the child's folder for future reference and entrance into more permanent records, and a blank card is then inserted into its place in the ring book.

Another system uses entries in standard notebooks. Teachers generally put tabs on sheets to indicate individual students. These notebooks may be written in directly, or data may be collected first and entered later. Teachers may choose to carry a clipboard with index cards on which to note observations, and these cards may be stapled or pasted into the notebook. Post-its may also be used to record initial observations, followed by a more permanent entry in the notebook.

Teachers who use index cards may prefer to file the cards in a box. The students' cards are arranged alphabetically and form the basis for writing up students' growth and progress.

Another kidwatching scheme is the use of gummed labels on which relevant data are recorded. These labels may be glued onto cards or file folders. Properly dated, these become a record of a child's progress over time.

It is important to remember that observations need not take place only during language learning time. Learning occurs all day, and reading and writing are integrated across the curriculum. Therefore it is imperative that teachers note what and how their students are doing during other instructional periods. By having a system in place for recording observations, teachers need only to take their recording instruments and note the observed behaviors. In addition to making structured observations, teachers must be alert to their students' behaviors throughout the day in and outside the classroom. Observations may therefore be recorded as they spontaneously occur. By being aware of the many observational possibilities and being prepared with a means of recording observations, teachers can amass valuable data on which to plan instruction and inform both the students and their parents.

Anecdotal Records

Anecdotal records are notes made about a student while observations are being made. As opposed to writing voluminous notes, which take both precious classroom time and time later for analysis (which may become unwieldy), it may be preferable to jot down significant behaviors. For example, let's look at Jimmy during Writers' Workshop time.

11/13	Having difficulty getting started.
11/15	Topic decided on. Worked well initially but later work trailed off.
11/17	Still drafting. Talked to friend about his writing piece.
11/20	Difficulty sticking to one topic. Paragraph structure weak. Asked Carlos to listen to his story.
11/23	Read piece in Writers' Circle. Ready to revise.

Jotting down significant information can reveal a pattern of development. Strengths and weaknesses can be determined so that the teacher can note and report on progress and help the student proceed in a beneficial direction.

In Jimmy's case, he may be a slow starter and may need additional rehearsal time in the prewriting stage. It may become apparent by examining the anecdotes over time that Jimmy has difficulty sticking to a chosen topic, and paragraph structure may be posing problems. The observations also reveal that Jimmy profits from interactions with his peers. Therefore these areas become future minilessons for Jimmy, as well as things to work on during con-

Figure 4.2A Reading Record

(Courtesy of Jane Barber Smith, Arlington School District, N.Y.)

Reading Record

Name ______________________________

	First Quarter	Second Quarter	Third Quarter	Fourth Quarter	Comments
ATTITUDE Demonstrates enjoyment of books by reading at other times, sharing with others, borrowing books freely Maintains silent reading for an increasing length of time Takes initiative in reading Reads silently for a sustained period					
SHARED BOOK EXPERIENCE Responds to text Comments about the story Asks questions about the story Comments or asks questions about the pictures Comments or asks questions about the print Joins in during subsequent readings Selects story to read independently Retains high use words in sight vocabulary					
BOOK SELECTION Selects a variety of books independently Generally selects appropriately Seeks advice when necessary Cares for borrowed books Uses library effectively					
CONCEPTS ABOUT PRINT Understands that print contains a message					
Understands directional conventions					
Understands concepts of *word, letter, sentence*					
Understands concepts: first, last, space, line, top, bottom					
Knows meaning of period and question mark					
Demonstrates concepts about print in own writing					
USE OF TEXTUAL CUES Uses context cues:					
☐ Semantic cues					
☐ Syntactic cues					
☐ Pictorial cues					
☐ Graphophonic cues					

(continued)

Figure 4.2B Reading Record (cont.)

(Courtesy of Jane Barber Smith, Arlington School District, N.Y.)

	First Quarter	Second Quarter	Third Quarter	Fourth Quarter	Comments
READING STRATEGIES **Reads for meaning:** Makes predictions and self-corrects unsatisfactory predictions					
Reads with phrasing					
Can locate specific parts of text					
When in difficulty: Reads on to end of sentence; starts sentence again and rereads; uses phonetic, pictorial, semantic, syntactic cues					
After reading: Retells story in own words; discusses character development, describes setting; understands sequence; recognizes main idea; recalls details; makes comparisons; recognizes cause and effect; makes judgments re: fact/opinion, values, reality/fantasy					
Knows whether she or he likes story					
ORAL READING Participates in choral reading					
Reads effectively with teacher					
Prepares beforehand					
Reads specific text to support a position taken					
Considers audience					
Gives attention to volume, pitch, intonation, expression, pace, breathing					
RUNNING RECORD **Title and Level:**					

ference time. Some examples of ways that anecdotal records can be kept are seen in Figure 4.3.

Figure 4.3

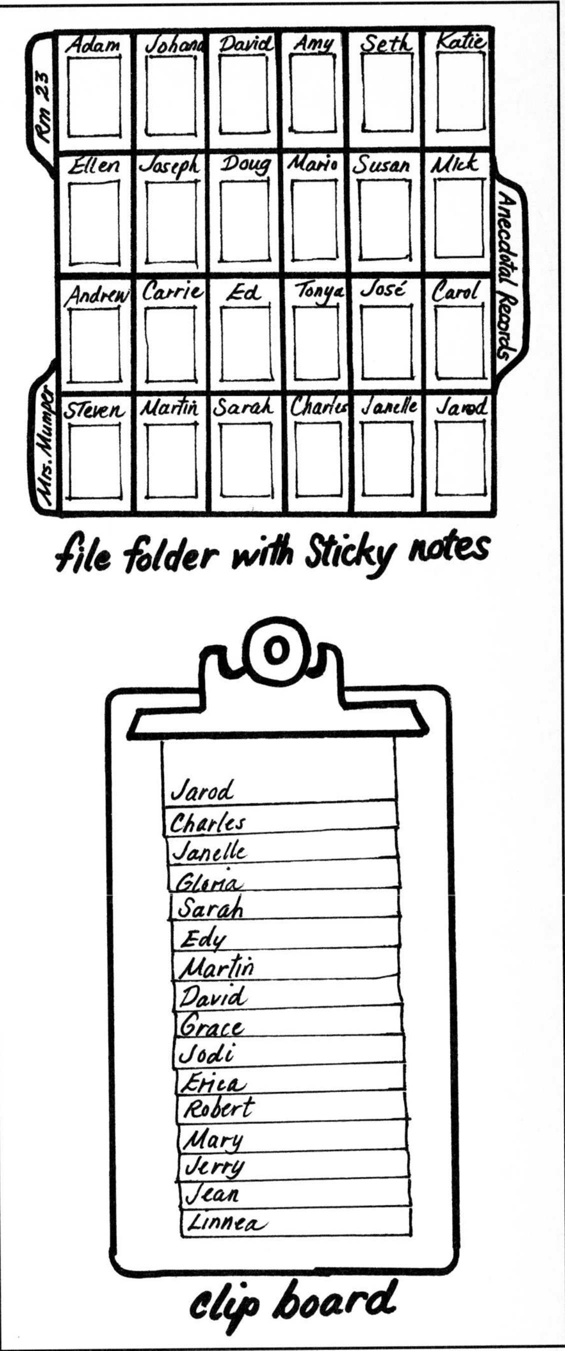

Miscue Analysis/Running Records

Miscue Analysis

As discussed in Chapter 2, readers use three major cueing systems in order to construct meaning:

1. **Semantic.** Constructing meaning from each sentence and from the entire text
2. **Syntactic.** Constructing meaning through use of grammatical information, such as word order and sentence structure
3. **Graphophonic.** Constructing meaning through letter-sound associations

In order to examine what readers do as they read, it is necessary to listen to students read aloud and to analyze the results of this oral reading and subsequent retelling of the text. As students read, they may not reproduce exactly what is stated in the text; that is, they do not read the author's exact words. This departure from what the author wrote is called a miscue (an oral reading error). Most miscues can be categorized into one of the following groups:

- **Substitution.** The reader substitutes a different word from the one in the text.
- **Omission.** The reader omits a word or a phrase.
- **Insertion.** The reader adds or inserts a word that did not appear in the original text.
- **Repetition (or multiple attempts).** The reader repeats a word or phrase that she or he has already read.
- **Correction.** The reader corrects the miscue.

The most significant use of miscue analysis is the help it gives teachers in gaining insight into the reading process. It allows teachers to examine the strategies that frequently cause readers to make miscues; that is, it provides a window into the mind of the reader (Goodman, 1973). By knowing what strategies students are using, teachers can help them develop more effective strategies or enlarge the repertoire of strategies they already possess.

People tend to read more effectively when they are reading silently, since reading aloud frequently interferes with obtaining meaning. However, if teachers are to determine their students' strategies for handling text by analyzing the students' miscues, then students must of necessity read aloud. Miscue analysis begins with a student reading a piece of text aloud while the teacher records what transpires. An example of a typical marking system appears in Figure 4.4.

Reading aloud, recording miscues, and analyzing miscues comprise only one part of the process. It is necessary that the reader retell what is remembered from the text. Retelling provides additional essential information. Some readers are adept at reproducing the text—that is, at pronouncing the words correctly—but are not good at obtaining meaning. Other readers may make a number of miscues but are still able to preserve meaning. Thus, by having both types of information—miscues and retelling—a teacher is able to obtain a balanced view of a student's reading. After listening to a student read and retell the text (both unaided and guided through follow-up questions), the teacher analyzes what has occurred. The number of miscues are counted and categorized according to whether they are graphophonic, syntactic, or semantic. Any self-corrections are noted, since these are indicative of student self-monitoring. A quantifiable score may be obtained by noting how many miscues occurred in a specified number of words. A self-correction score may also be obtained. Teachers may also make judgments about the quality of miscues. A student may have made many miscues that did not interfere with comprehension. Thus, although the miscue score might be high, the resulting impact on reading is nonexistent.

Teachers also look at the amount of information retold as well as at the significance of the information. Some students' retelling may be sketchy but may include all the major points, while others may regurgitate a large number of insignificant details. Using both types of information allows teachers to build up a picture of the students' reading ability and enables them to plan students' literacy programs.

Miscue analysis originated through the research of Ken Goodman. Later his wife, Yetta Goodman, along with Dorothy Watson and Carolyn Burke, published *The Reading Miscue Inventory: Alternative Procedures* (1987), which has been used by researchers and specialists. However, this taxonomy is too complicated to meet the everyday needs of classroom and reading teachers. Variations and modifications have been made to miscue analysis that now make the procedure useful in assessing students.

One such instrument is the *Classroom Reading Miscue Assessment* (CRMA), developed in Denver, Colorado, to serve several important purposes:

- give teachers a framework to understand the reading process
- help teachers with their instructional planning
- help students self-evaluate
- provide information about students' reading progress to both parents and policymakers

(Rhodes and Shanklin, 1990)

The instrument takes about 10–15 minutes to administer, and unlike many other miscue procedures, the sessions are not audiotaped. The developers suggest that passages chosen for the CRMA have a sense of completeness, such as whole stories or book chapters. The selections, of about 300–500 words in length, should not have been read previously. The passages should use natural language patterns and should have a strong, well-developed narrative or expository structure. They should be challenging enough so that the reader will make miscues. A suggested rule of thumb is that the reader should not make more than one miscue in ten words that disrupts the meaning of the passage.

Prior to reading the text, readers are instructed to read the passage aloud, and if they come to a word they do not understand, to do what they would normally do if they were alone. They are also told that they are expected to retell the reading material.

After the session is completed, the teacher decides whether each sentence is semantically acceptable or unacceptable. The number of semantically acceptable sentences is then divided by the total number of sentences read, and a comprehension score is obtained. Proficient readers obtain a score of 80 percent or above, adequate readers 60–80 percent, and poor readers 60 percent or below (Rhodes and Shanklin, 1990). The procedures and scoring guides are identical to those in *The Reading Miscue Inventory: Alternative Procedures* (Goodman, Watson, and Burke, 1987). It is also important for the

FROM THE CLASSROOM OF . . .
Best Town in the World

What makes an area so special to its inhabitants or to its former inhabitants? Read the book, *The Best Town in the World* by Byrd Baylor to your students. Prior to reading the book, have the children brainstorm why a town or city might be the best town/city in the world. A post-reading activity could be to list the reasons why the narrator in the story considered The Canyon, a Texan town, the best place in the world, and compare his reasons with the one they generated.

Another possibility is to have the students make an origami book, e.g., an eight page book. On the pages in the book, the students could do the following:

- first page: title and their own name as author
- pages two and three: free response to the story
- pages four and five: questions they might ask the narrator
- pages six and seven: connections to their own lives, other pieces of literature, etc.
- page eight: interesting language or their own illustration

Although the characters are not named in this story, there are people in the town that are depicted. Students in the classroom could be assigned to "become" one of the characters, while the rest of the class interviews the townsfolk. For example, the mayor could be asked, "What makes your town so special?" or a child could be queried as to what kinds of activities he or she did in his or her free time. The narrator could be questioned as to why he left the town if the town was so special.

A natural extension could be made with the social studies curriculum. If local history is the focus of the social studies program, the children's own town could be studied, and a brochure prepared as to why the town was so special. If United States or World History is targeted for study, students could choose a town or city, and research its history, unique features, contributions, and the like. These could be shared at a "Town Meeting," or at a mock "Convention of Mayors, Governors, or Heads of State." This becomes a wonderful culminating activity for a unit of study or for an end of the year activity.

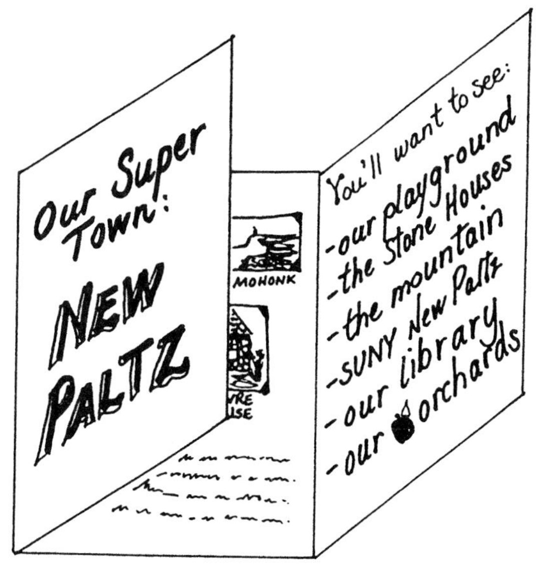

Figure 4.4 Marking System for Recording Reading Miscues

Substitution -- The word the subject says is written over the word in the text.

Jack and Jill went (climbed) up the hill.

Omission -- The omitted word is circled.

To fetch (a) pail of water.

Insertion -- A ^ is inserted with the added word written above.

Jack fell down ^ (the hill) and broke his crown.

Self-correction -- The incorrect response is recorded as if it were a substitution (the incorrect word written above) followed by SC .

And Jill came tumbling (running SC) after.

Repetitions -- When students repeat words or phrases, a wavy line is placed underneath the repeated word or words or an arrow is drawn around the repeated words to indicate the repetition. If a word is repeated several times, the number of times it is repeated is also indicated, e.g., broke his R2

Jack fell down and broke his crown.

Teacher assistance -- If a teacher pronounces a word for a student, the word that is pronounced is followed by T .

To fetch T a pail of water.

Teacher encouragement (Try that again) -- Teacher prompts are indicated by a TTA following the prompted word or words.

And Jill came tumbling after. (Jack can take) TTA

teacher to examine the student's use of strategies and cues.

The teacher then completes the form (see Figure 4.5), recording observations about the retelling. Since this is in a checklist format, the teacher may want to make additional anecdotal comments about the session at the bottom of the sheet.

This particular instrument does not call for audiotaping the session, but teachers may want to have a periodic sample of a student's oral reading and retelling as part of the student's permanent record. These audiotapes can be valuable in demonstrating progress to students and their parents.

You may be convinced that analyzing students' miscues is important but wonder how you can possibly fit the procedure into an already full day. In order to do this in an efficient yet effective manner, many teachers focus on one or two students daily, using time scheduled for Readers' Workshop, basal reading group time, or Writers' Workshop. There may be opportunities to use recess or special class time as well. Most teachers probably use some of the Readers' Workshop or basal group time for the purpose of hearing students read aloud. It is not necessary for teachers to meet with each group daily. Therefore during the time already allocated for basal groups or Readers' Workshop, teachers may choose to use one group's scheduled time for miscue analysis (or Running Records, which are discussed next). This procedure should be done whenever it is convenient to hear children read. What is important is that it be an integral part of the assessment and evaluation process. Therefore teachers must organize their classrooms and their instruction to allow time for miscue analysis.

Running Records

Running Records are an essential part of the assessment and evaluation process in all classrooms in New Zealand and in many U.S. classrooms today as well. The philosophy behind and the purpose of Running Records are similar to those of miscue analysis. Running Records are an insightful, informative procedure for monitoring students' progress in learning to read (Traill, 1993). Running Records help teachers in the following ways:

- observe precisely what students are saying and doing while they are reading
- observe what students can do, not just what they cannot do
- make observations during real reading tasks, not testing situations
- develop insights into the nature of the reading process, which affects classroom instruction
- help determine whether students are reading at their instructional levels, and helps match instructional materials to the student's needs
- identify students who may need special help

(Davidson, 1985; Traill, 1993)

As with miscue analysis, teachers can gain powerful information on children's understanding of the reading process, the strategies they use when encountering print, and the amount of self-monitoring they do.

A major difference between miscue analysis and Running Records is that the teacher does not use a prepared text on which to record the results of the oral reading. The teacher merely uses a blank sheet of paper, ticks off correct words (one tick for each word), and writes in other significant data, such as substitutions, insertions, omissions, self-corrections, and the like. An advantage to Running Records is that the reading session can be spontaneous, and any piece of text can be used at any time. However, by not having the text as a guide, the teacher needs practice to keep up with the more fluent readers of more challenging text. Also, if a teacher wants to analyze the miscues later, the text is not with the recorded data and the original source must then be located. Weaver (1990) warns that by recording miscues out of context, teachers may also analyze them out of context. The quantity of the miscues may be considered rather than their quality. Therefore a major advantage of Running Records could in actuality become a disadvantage.

Another difference is that Running Records do not include retelling as part of the process. This is not to say that aspects of miscue analysis and Running Records cannot be combined. Teachers may find both have value in the assessment and evaluation program and may incorporate elements of both.

Figure 4.5 Miscue Analysis Data Sheet (Rhodes and Shanklin, 1990)

Classroom Reading Miscue Assessment
Developed by Coordinators/Consultants Applying Whole Language

Reader's name ____________________ Date ____________________

Grade level assignment ______________ Teacher ____________________

Selection read: ____

I. What percent of the sentences read make sense?

	Sentence by sentence tally	Total
____ Number of semantically acceptable sentences		
____ Number of semantically unacceptable sentences		

____ % Comprehending score: $\frac{\text{Number of semantically acceptable sentences}}{\text{Total number of sentences read}}$ x 100 TOTAL ____

	Seldom	Sometimes	Often	Usually	Always
II. In what ways is reader constructing meaning?					
A. Recognizes when miscues have disrupted meaning	1	2	3	4	5
B. Logically substitutes	1	2	3	4	5
C. Self-corrects errors that disrupt meaning	1	2	3	4	5
D. Uses picture and/or other visual clues	1	2	3	4	5
In what ways is reader disrupting meaning?					
A. Substitutes words that don't make sense	1	2	3	4	5
B. Makes omissions that disrupt meaning	1	2	3	4	5
C. Relies too heavily on graphic clues	1	2	3	4	5

III. If narrative text is used:

	No		Partial		Yes
A. Character recall	1	2	3	4	5
B. Character development	1	2	3	4	5
C. Setting	1	2	3	4	5
D. Relationship of events	1	2	3	4	5
E. Plot	1	2	3	4	5
F. Theme	1	2	3	4	5
G. Overall retelling	1	2	3	4	5

If expository text is used:

	No		Partial		Yes
A. Major concepts	1	2	3	4	5
B. Generalizations	1	2	3	4	5
C. Specific information	1	2	3	4	5
D. Logical structuring	1	2	3	4	5
E. Overall retelling	1	2	3	4	5

Teachers take Running Records in a similar fashion to the procedure described for miscue analysis, again with the major exception being not having a prepared script on which to record the data. Children read aloud and the teacher records their reading behaviors. After the session the teacher also analyzes the performance to use as a basis for planning instruction and to determine the reader's strengths, needs, and progress. An example of both miscue analysis and Running Records appears in Figure 4.6. The procedure for taking Running Records appears in Figure 4.7.

Self-Corrections

It is important that teachers note any attempts readers make to self-correct. Self-correction, if it is efficient, is indicative of effective reading behavior. If it is inefficient (i.e., the readers correct all miscues, even those that don't interrupt meaning), it is an indication that the readers are monitoring their reading although they are focusing on word calling more than is necessary or desirable. If self-corrections are not present at all in a reading that contains errors, the teacher needs to provide the student with assistance in self-monitoring.

Both miscue analysis and Running Records provide valuable information about a reader. They give teachers insight into individual readers and help teachers plan or modify their instructional programs. Data obtained from observing students read aloud should be part of the assessment and evaluation process. Teachers should listen to their students' reading at the

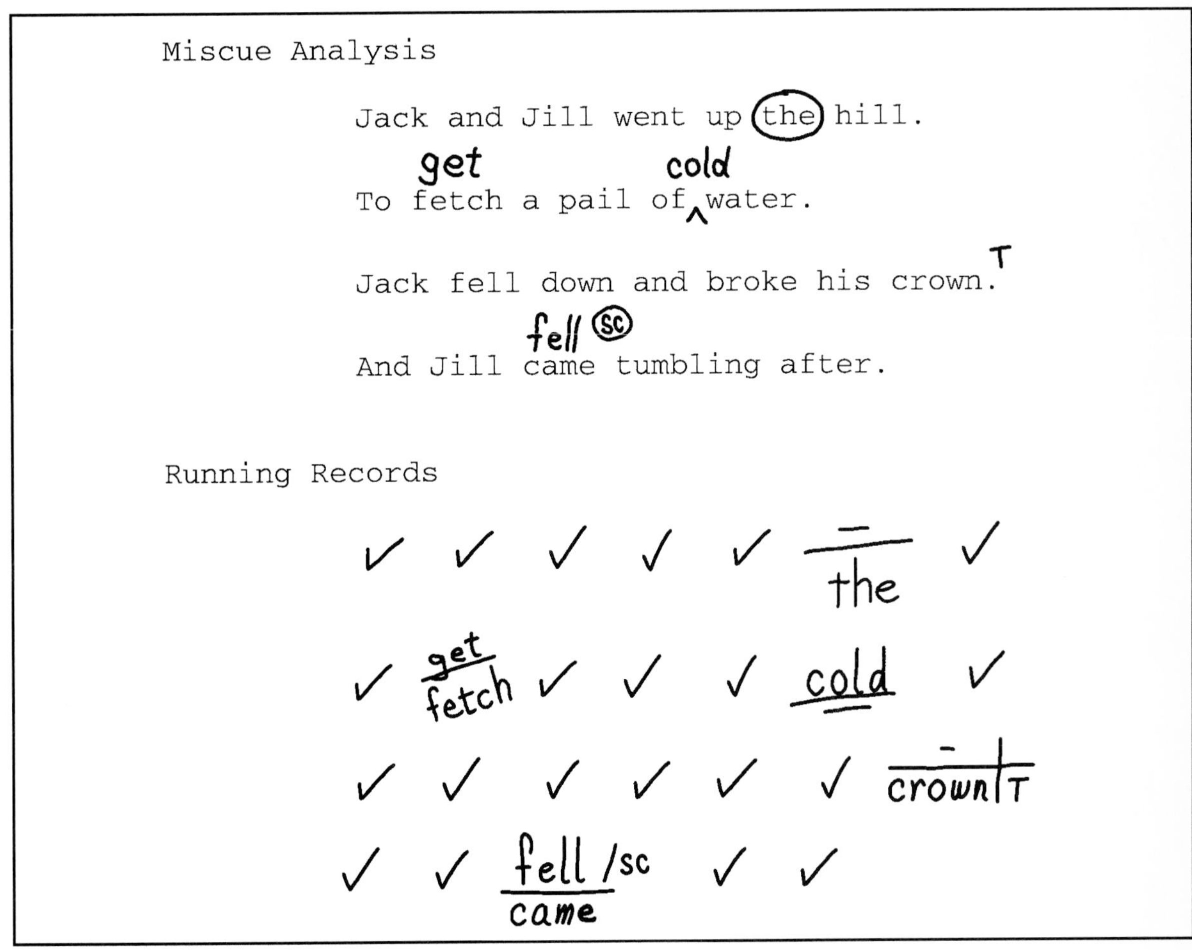

Figure 4.6 Miscue Analysis and Running Records

Figure 4.7 Sample Running Record

Running Record

Date 1/6/96 Text Cats and Kittens Recorder CJU. TL
Name Danny #of words 51 Grade 1

LEVEL: 9 Acc: 90% SC RATE 1:4

		TOTALS	5	2	INFORMATION	USED
Pg.	TITLE: Cats and Kittens	WORDS	E	SC	E MSV	SC MSV
2	cat/Cats SC ✓			1	MSV	MSV
3	✓ ✓✓					
4	✓ ✓✓					
5	✓ ✓ ✓✓					
6	✓ ✓ R2 ✓ ✓ ✓ —/their A/T ✓		1		MSV	
7	✓ Kittens/Cats SC ✓ R ✓ ✓ ✓✓			1	MSV	MSV
8	✓ ✓					
9	✓ ✓✓					
10	✓ ✓ ✓ ✓ ✓ sticks/stands up/On in/T ✓		2		MSV MSV	
	✓ tails/tail puffs/puff ✓		2		MSV MSV	

Scoring

✓ read correctly

sc self correction (child corrects a previous error, not counted as an error)

T Child knows he made an error but will not attempt the next word so he is told the word

A the child in some way makes an appeal for help

R the child's repetition is noted as an R. If he goes back over several words it is indicated with an arrow

Cues

M Meaning of the text remains the same (can also involve using the picture to help get the meaning of the story)

S Structure or syntax of the the text or the substitutions sounds like correct English

V Visual information from the tex (the words and letters)

Summary

Danny is reading at an L-9 instructional level. He is monitoring his reading by using meaning, structure and visual cues. He is cross checking meaning and structural cues with visual ones. He is making sense out of what he is reading. He reads with good expression and is fluent.

Teresa Leroy is a remedial reading teacher at John F. Kennedy Elementary School in Kingston, New York. She has been a reading recovery teacher for the past two years.

beginning of the year, and then the procedure should be continued on a regular, ongoing basis. The information obtained should be shared with both the students and their parents. Since both of these procedures provide worthwhile data, teachers should decide for themselves which procedure to use or whether to incorporate elements of both.

Student Self-Evaluation

An important element in the assessment and evaluation process is having students evaluate their own learning. If the ultimate goal for schooling is to produce independent and reflective learners, then teachers must provide opportunities for students to look at themselves as learners and to evaluate their own progress and development. Self-evaluation encourages students to observe themselves constantly.

Initially students are similar to Pinocchio, who needed Jiminy Cricket to be his conscience. While Jiminy Cricket's help and guidance were necessary for Pinocchio to learn to live in society, there came a time when Pinocchio had to learn to think for himself and to make his own decisions. The same goes for students in the classroom. Students ultimately will have to make their own decisions, and the classroom is the ideal place for students to undertake learning how to self-evaluate. There are many opportunities throughout the day and throughout the year for students to self-evaluate. Students can self-evaluate in conferences (both with teachers and with their peers), on checklists and on questionnaires, in their writing folders, and in their learning logs.

During conference time, they can be asked such questions as, What do you do well in reading? in writing? What do you need to work on? What skills or strategies do you already use as a reader? as a writer? Which ones do you need to learn? Teachers can probe into what the students actually did during the reading and writing processes. They can ask the students to retell and reconstruct their learning and help the students gain insights into their learning as a result.

Students can be given questionnaires similar to the one in Figure 4.8, which asks students to reflect on their reading and writing behaviors. Checklists can also be used for student self-evaluation and sources for some of these checklists can be found in the bibliography. An adaptation of one such self-evaluation sheet is shown in Figure 4.9.

Teachers can post charts around the room asking students to think about certain items as they read or write. These charts may also be reproduced for students to fill in and place in their portfolios. Sample reading and writing charts are depicted in Figure 4.10.

To help students recognize what strategies they may or may not be using, students may respond to statements similar to those that appear in Figure 4.11.

Students may also be taught to self-evaluate through the use of learning logs, and this may be done in any subject, for example, social studies, math, or science. At the end of the instructional period, students write comments in their learning logs pertaining to what they learned during the session, what they don't understand, and what they would still like to know.

Since the school day is so busy and since a desired goal is for students to evaluate them-

READING

1. What are some things you do well when you read?
2. What are some of the areas in reading that you find difficult?
3. Where are you improving in your reading?
4. What would you like to work on to improve your reading?

WRITING

1. What are some things you do well when you write?
2. What are you having difficulty with in your writing?
3. Where are you improving in your writing?
4. What is your best piece of writing so far?
5. Why is this your best piece?
6. What would you like to work on in your writing?

Figure 4.8 Self-Evaluation Questionnaire

Figure 4.9 Student Self-Evaluation Questionnaire (adapted from Eggleton, 1990)

LOOK WHAT I CAN DO!
(Checklist for beginning writers)

I Can:

- Print letters
- Leave spaces between words
- Put down the first letter in a word
- Put the last letter in a word
- Write some of the middle letters
- Put a period where it belongs
- Put capitals in the right places
- Write a sentence
- Write two sentences
- Write more than two sentences
- Write a story

LOOK WHAT I CAN DO!
(Checklist for developing writers)

I Can:

- Use capitals to begin sentences
- Use capitals for names
- Use periods
- Use speech (quotation) marks
- Write an interesting beginning
- Write a good ending
- Recognize errors
- Correct errors
- Use paragraphs

LOOK WHAT I CAN DO!
(Checklist for fluent writers)

I Can:

- Make notes or brainstorm some ideas
- Research a topic by reading other books or talking to others
- Think about how my piece might develop
- Write continuously for a while and then reflect on what I wrote
- Talk with a buddy about my writing
- Cut and paste pieces of my writing together
- Circle and correct spelling errors
- Work with a buddy to proofread my piece
- Publish my writing in many different ways
- Share my piece with an audience

selves, students should take over some of the responsibilities of record keeping. If writing folders are kept, students can keep a list of possible writing topics, writing skills they possess, drafts undertaken, pieces published, types of genre written, and so on. Students can also keep track of the books they have read and how they have shared the books (e.g., book talks, dioramas, art projects, or any of the numerous book extension projects discussed in Chapter 10). Students can keep a weekly grid of how they used their time during language learning time (either Writers' or Readers' Workshop). For example:

- **Monday.** Wrote prediction on book. Read 2 chapters. Wrote in log.
- **Tuesday.** Shared log in group.
- **Wednesday.** Read 3 chapters. Wrote in log.
- **Thursday.** Discussed chapters in group.
- **Friday.** Read picture book to child in grade 2.

Paper with blocks drawn on it can be provided for this purpose.

At the end of the school year, students can write letters to the teachers they will have next year giving personal data and information about themselves as students and learners. Fig-

Figure 4.10 Reading and Writing Charts

WRITING CHECKLIST

1. Did I pick an interesting topic?
2. Did I think about my topic before I began to write?
3. Did I stick to my topic?
4. Does it make sense?
5. Have I left out anything?
6. Did I read my writing aloud?
7. Did I make changes from the suggestions from my writing group?
8. Did I find and correct misspelled words?
9. Did I capitalize?
10. Did I check my punctuation marks?

If the above is to be used as a checklist, the following format may be used:

	YES	SOME	NO
Did I pick an interesting topic?	________	________	________
Did I think about my topic before I began?	________	________	________
Did I stick to my topic?	________	________	________

READING CHECKLIST
(for a narrative selection)

1. Did I begin my retelling with an introduction?
2. Did I tell where the story took place?
3. Did I tell when the story took place?
4. Did I name the main character(s)?
5. Did my retelling include the story problem?
6. Did I tell my story in order?
7. Did I include story episodes?
8. Did I tell how the problem was solved?
9. Did I tell how the story ended?
10. Did I talk about the theme of the story?

ure 4.12 presents actual letters written by second graders to their future third-grade teachers.

As you can see, many opportunities and management systems are available for students to become involved in their own learning. Teachers and students should look over what is available and make modifications to suit their own needs and goals. Once students become familiar with self-evaluation, they may design their own system, which should continually evolve and change.

Self-evaluation requires that teachers model the process, involve their students in discussions about self-evaluation and self-reflection, and provide their students with a great deal of practice. Students do not come to school armed with metacognitive knowledge and vocabularies to be able to articulate how they are learning and what they can do to improve their learning. But the benefits are many, as student self-evaluation encourages student responsibility for their own learning, promotes critical reflection, and enables students to become actively involved in their own learning (Hill and Ruptic, 1994). Self-evaluation gives students opportunities to recognize and determine patterns in their learning and as a result, set realistic goals.

Think-Alouds

Another means of gathering data about children's literacy development, which is also similar to self-evaluation, is to have students think aloud—verbalize their thoughts as they read or write. This can be done before, during, or after reading or writing. This practice can be likened to a sports announcer giving a play-by-play account of an athletic event. Students give play-by-play accounts of their own reading and writing behaviors. For example, after reading a piece of text, a child might say, "I looked at the pictures first and read the title, and I guessed at what the story might be about. When I read, I came to a few words I did not know, but I just

Figure 4.11A Reading Self-Evaluation Form

(adapted from Jeroski, Brownlie, and Kaser, 1990)

Name: ______________________________

Title of Text: ______________________________

Date: ____________________

WHAT I DID	HOW IT HELPED			
	Not at all	Sometimes	Frequently	Most of the time
Before I read				
I looked at the title and predicted what the selection might be about.	1	2	3	4
I thought about what I knew about the topic.	1	2	3	4
I thought about why the author wrote it.	1	2	3	4
I made pictures in my mind.	1	2	3	4
I asked myself some questions about what I want to learn about the topic.	1	2	3	4
As I was reading				
I restated what the text said.	1	2	3	4
I changed my predictions.	1	2	3	4
I made new predictions.	1	2	3	4
I noticed when I didn't understand				
—a word.	1	2	3	4
—a sentence.	1	2	3	4
—a longer idea.	1	2	3	4
When I didn't understand, I				
—did nothing.	1	2	3	4
—quit reading.	1	2	3	4
—remembered similar things I already knew.	1	2	3	4
—decided if the text made sense.	1	2	3	4
—thought about the writing in the text.	1	2	3	4
—formed an opinion about the text.	1	2	3	4
—talked to a buddy.	1	2	3	4
—asked the teacher.	1	2	3	4

(*continued*)

Figure 4.11B Reading Self-Evaluation Form (cont.)
(adapted from Jeroski, Brownlie, and Kaser, 1990)

WHAT I DID	HOW IT HELPED			
	Not at all	Sometimes	Frequently	Most of the time
After I read				
I reread the selection	1	2	3	4
I wrote down				
—what I learned.	1	2	3	4
—what confused me.	1	2	3	4
—what I'd like to do next.	1	2	3	4
I thought about other selections that were alike.	1	2	3	4
I thought about how this selection fit into what I already know.	1	2	3	4
I shared the information with a friend.	1	2	3	4
I thought about what I would do with the new ideas.	1	2	3	4

skipped them. Later I went back to see if I could figure them out. I had to reread a part of the story several times because it was confusing. At the end, I tried to retell the story in my mind."

Children will not naturally think aloud as they read and write. They must first be shown how to think aloud, and this is done through teacher modeling. If teachers use think-alouds as they demonstrate the reading and writing processes, this procedure will become familiar to students. In addition, teachers can ask such probing questions as these:

- What did you do before you read the story?
- Did the pictures and title help you?
- What did you do when you didn't know a word?
- How did you figure out what confused you?
- What could you do to help you understand that confusing part?

Helping students get in touch with their own thinking (metacognition) will provide both students and teachers with information that is useful for individual students' instruction.

Portfolios

Think about an artist who is packing his or her bag (to continue the travel analogy). It is the artist who makes the decision as to what to include and who then arranges the materials (the samples of the work) to exhibit both the depth and the breadth of his or her abilities. The artist's bag—a *portfolio*—presents a complete portrait of the artist and represents both development as an artist (the process) and the artistic endeavors (the products). Developing a portfolio makes it easier for artists, their teachers, and their critics to understand the artist's artistic growth and to plan experiences that will encourage further progress.

This approach to assessment and evaluation can likewise be developed in the literacy classroom. Portfolios reflect what is valued in reading and writing instruction and more accurately demonstrate the kinds of reading and writing that are desired and valued today. Portfolios are representative of a philosophy that necessitates viewing assessment and evaluation as integral components of instruction and they

Figure 4.12 Sample Letters

Hi!
My name is Dustin. I'm
very, very, smart.
I always get my work
done. I have brown hair
and torquise eyes. I love
doing activities. I'm always
working hard unless someone
desperatly needs help on their
work. I am very nice and
love animals. I'm eight
years old and I love writing
stories.

Larry

All About Me!
I have blond hair.
I have blue eyes. I have
lots of friends. It is hard
to make friends. I am not
messy. I am not so good at
school. It is hard.

provide a process for both teachers and students to use in guiding learning (Valencia, 1990a). Portfolios take into account both the learning process and the products of learning, as well as encourage the participation in assessment of both the teacher and the learner.

There are many reasons portfolio assessment appeals to educators. First, portfolio assessment grows out of authentic reading and writing tasks and activities. Real reading and writing are used as opportunities for assessment. Assessment is integrated into classroom instruction and incorporated into any curricular area. Assessment is not added on at the end of an instructional period, and time does not have to be taken away from regular instruction in order to assess student learning.

When using portfolios, assessment is an ongoing process and is multidimensional, since portfolios sample a wide range of evidence, both cognitive and affective in nature. In addition, portfolios provide for collaboration and reflection by the teacher and the student. Through collaborative assessment, a bond develops between the teacher and the learner. Teachers and students become partners in learning. Portfolios are compatible with a teacher's desires to capture and capitalize on the things that students do best and encourage teachers to use various means of evaluating student learning (Valencia, 1990a; Tierney et al., 1991; DeFina, 1992; Farr and Tone, 1994).

What Is a Portfolio?

Portfolios are defined as collections of evidence gathered across varied contexts before, during, and after instruction. They are used by both teachers and students to monitor the development of student knowledge, use of strategies, and attitude toward the accomplishment of goals. Portfolios capture the richness, the breadth, and the depth of a student's learning within the context of classroom instruction (Valencia, 1990a; Roettger, 1992; Clemmons,

Laase, Cooper, Areglado, and Dill, 1993; Porter and Cleland, 1995). "Portfolios help learners see how they think, feel, work, and change over a period of time" (Hill and Ruptic, 1994, 32). By focusing on both process and product, and by being collected over a period of time, there is a shift from getting snapshots of student learning, as in standardized testing, to an emphasis on growth and progress, which can be likened to a videotape of a student's progress and efforts over the year. Because of the philosophy on which portfolios are based, they frequently contain evidence of growth in areas that are not and cannot be measured by standardized tests.

What Do Portfolios Look Like?

For years teachers have kept samples of student work in work folders. Portfolios differ from work folders in that portfolios are archival in nature and are added to periodically in contrast to work folders, to which samples are added more frequently, even daily. Portfolios contain only carefully selected pieces of student work, and both the teacher and the student select the pieces to be included.

The range of things to put into a portfolio is limitless. However, it is important that what is included is representative of all the processes and products involved in a student's reading and writing so that a complete picture of the student can be drawn (Jongsma, 1989). Items to consider for placement in portfolios include:

PRODUCTS AND ARTIFACTS

- pieces of writing at different stages of completion
- written responses to reading
- selected daily work
- unit projects
- photographs
- audio- or videotapes
- classroom tests
- self-evaluation through self-analysis and reflection
- samples from learning or reading logs
- Authors' Circle comments
- written conversations
- evidence of metacognition, self-monitoring, and self-correction
- wild cards—any samples the students want to include

STUDENT LISTS

- list of reading and writing skills that the student can do
- list of writing topics
- personalized spelling lists
- records of books read and how they were shared
- records of published writing pieces
- checklists (self-evaluation, attitude, interests)
- goal-setting lists

TEACHER ASSESSMENT MEASURES

- checklists
- conference forms and notes
- observational data
- interviews, surveys, or questionnaires
- miscue analysis or Running Records data

PARENT CONTRIBUTIONS

- artifacts produced at home
- portfolio conference comments
- questionnaires
- anecdotal information

ORGANIZATIONAL ITEMS

- table of contents
- introductory note or letter to reader of portfolio
- summary sheet

(Tierney et al., 1991; DeFina, 1992; Clemmons et al., 1993; Rhodes and Shanklin, 1993; Farr and Tone, 1994; Hill and Ruptic, 1994; Porter and Cleland, 1995)

At the beginning of the school year, to get acquainted with the students, a teacher may have them represent themselves in a cluster or web. Students can include any pertinent or interesting information they wish to share with the teacher or class. For instance, they may give data on family members, interests, favorite music stars, pets, pet peeves, and the like. These may be placed in a portfolio as a way of introducing the student to anyone reviewing the portfolio. Figure 4.13 shows several examples of "getting to know me" maps. Maps can be done again at the end of the year to show changes or to introduce the students to subsequent teachers.

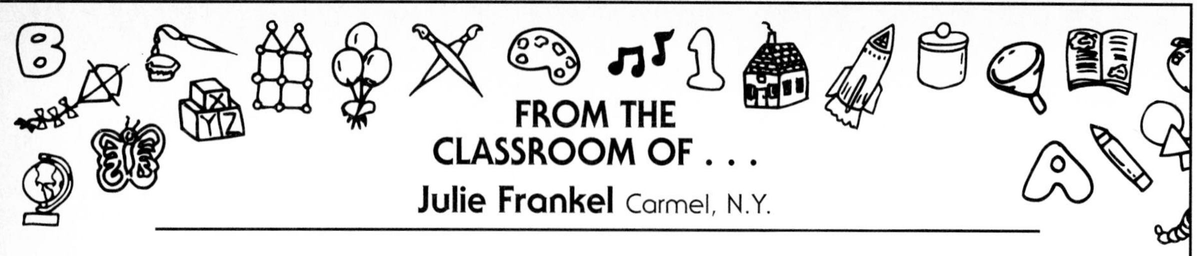

FROM THE CLASSROOM OF . . .

Julie Frankel Carmel, N.Y.

Election Day: Kindergarten-style

To help young children gain an understanding of the voting process, and to give them an opportunity to experience voting, Julie Frankel has her children participate in the naming of their class pet. Every child submits a favorite name for the pet, and these are compiled onto a ballot sheet. The ballot sheet not only has each child's suggested name for the pet, but a self-portrait of the child who has suggested the name. With the help of their parents, the children circle their three favorites. The results are tabulated and graphed, and the winner chosen.

Official Ballot: Guinea Pig Name
Circle 3 of your choice - Return by 11/7

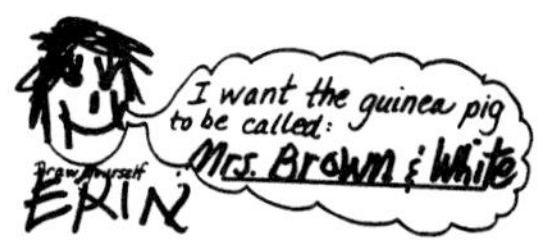

I want the guinea pig to be called: Mrs. Brown & White
ERIN

I want the guinea pig to be called: Fluffy
john

I want the guinea pig to be called: PEANUT
Ken

I want the guinea pig to be called: Ben

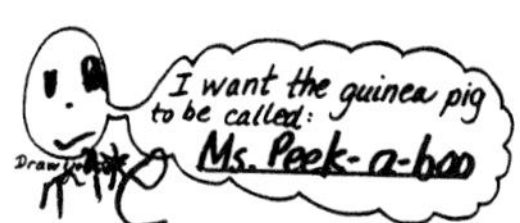

I want the guinea pig to be called: Ms. Peek-a-boo

I want the guinea pig to be called: Fluffy

I want the guinea pig to be called: Rosebud

I want the guinea pig to be called: CRYStal
Ben

I want the guinea pig to be called: Kathrine
Katie

I want the guinea pig to be called: Spot

Figure 4.13 Samples of Student Cluster Maps of Themselves

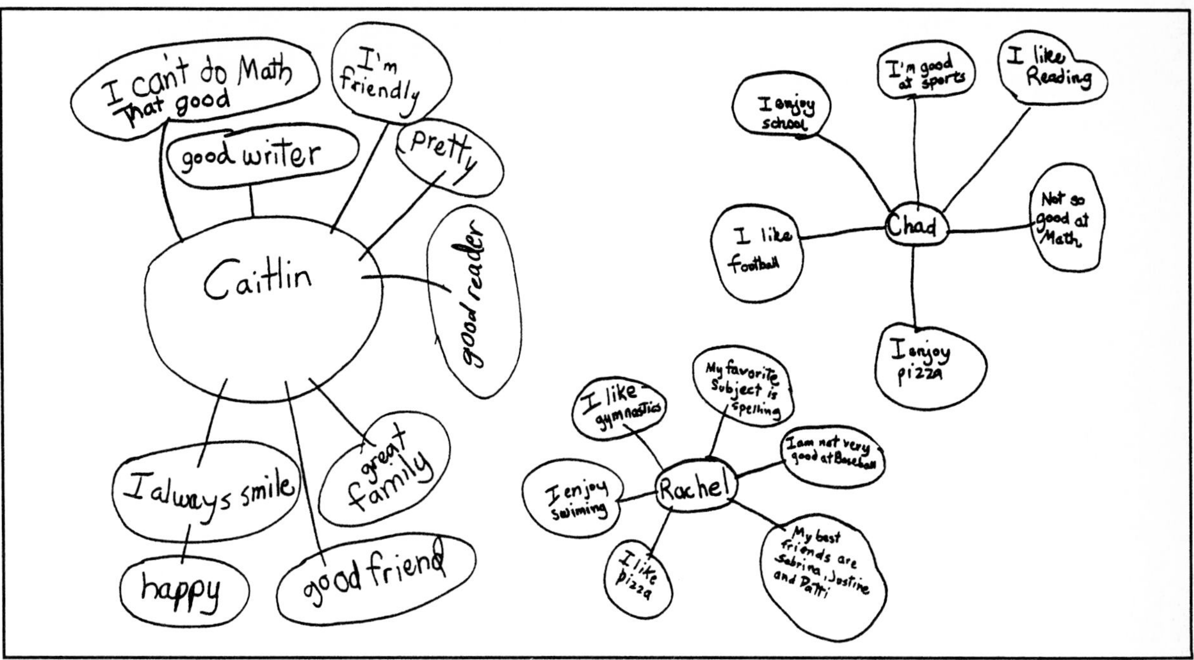

How Do You Organize and Manage Portfolios?

Decisions must be made as to what to include in a portfolio because it is important to be selective. The portfolio must be goal based; that is, the items included must evolve out of the key goals of instruction. There must be a focus on meaning making using a variety of texts in many different contexts (Valencia, Hiebert, and Afflerbach, 1994). Therefore a teacher must identify and specify the instructional goals. If goals are not specified, portfolios tend to become holding bins for papers. Examples of writing goals are presented in Figure 4.14.

Physical holders for the portfolios are important and there are many possibilities, depending on the storage space available and the size of the items to be included. Some possible holders include expandable file folders, folders with pockets which may be bound together, large envelopes, cardboard file boxes, three-ring binders, and tinted plastic boxes (See Figure 4.15). The holder should be large enough to accommodate the items without folding, if possible, and flexible to hold a variety of materials, including audio- and videotapes. They should also be sturdy enough to withstand frequent

The student will be able to:

- Write on a variety of topics using a variety of forms
- Demonstrate editing skills
- Write leads that arouse interest
- Attempt a variety of genre
- Gather/brainstorm for information
- Write descriptively with appropriate details
- Write satisfactory endings
- Reveal a growing writing vocabulary
- Show proper writing organization, e.g., for narratives using beginning, middle, and endings and for expository determining a topic, the main idea, and supporting details.
- Show a sense of audience
- Use a variety of sentence structures
- Make their characters come alive through description or dialogue

Figure 4.14 Goals in a Writing Program

Figure 4.15 Portfolio Holders

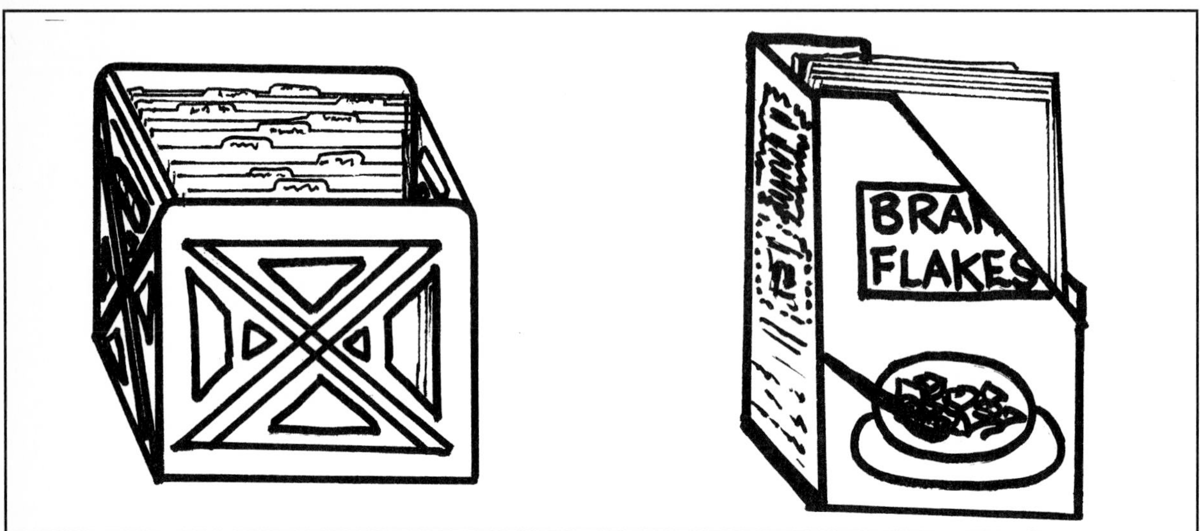

handling. Students should be encouraged to personalize their portfolios.

The holders should be stored where they are readily available. Space on shelves may be used for storing the portfolios, carts can be targeted for this use, or plastic crates may serve the purpose for housing portfolios.

Since it is important to be selective, students must also be guided in selecting items for inclusion, as there is a concern about the quality of the items selected if these are left solely to the students' discretion. Young children, after all, are not really familiar with the most desirable and pertinent criteria on which to document their growth and development. They need guidance in choosing selections for the portfolio. Salinger (1991) suggests that a Portfolio Selection Day be conducted periodically throughout the term and the school year. On this day, students are to look over pieces saved in work folders for possible inclusion in their portfolios. Teachers give students a framework around which the students can select the actual pieces. For example, students may be told to include samples that are illustrative of the following:

- a record of personal writing strategies
- a record of books read (updated reading log)
- a sample from the literature response journal
- something that was of particular interest in science or social studies
- best finished piece of writing
- some writing that shows the drafting (revision, proofreading) process
- a piece of writing from some area of the curriculum

Figure 4.16 summarizes and offers suggestions on evaluating the contents of portfolios.

After the focus of the portfolio has been determined, it is recommended that the contents include both actual evidence (the work samples) and analysis of that evidence (Valencia, 1990a). It is helpful to place *captions* on the pieces selected. Captions are brief written statements that accompany the evidence or documents (Roettger, 1992). Information to place on captions includes (1) identification of the document, (2) description of the context in which the document was obtained, (3) an explanation of the purpose, that is, why the document was chosen, and (4) the date it was written. Students may also write letters, perhaps addressed "Dear Reader of My Portfolio," explaining why the selections were chosen.

Captions give the portfolio reviewers sufficient information to interpret what the documents were intended to show. These questions can guide the selection of pieces for a portfolio:

Figure 4.16 Evaluating the Contents of a Portfolio (Salinger, 1991)

1. Decide what you *want* to see and make a tentative list.
2. Help students understand the criteria for selecting entries for the portfolio.
3. Schedule a selection schedule or selection day.
4. Let the students make selections, include whatever evidence of work you have decided must be included, and gather the portfolios together.
5. Read through a sample of the portfolios to see what students actually selected; make notes about:
   (1) the kinds of **work samples** students selected such as essays, graphic organizers, list of ideas, and so forth and
   (2) the **reading and writing behaviors** they have demonstrated, such as thinking and writing about what they have read, attempting to explore different "voices" in their writing, adopting a different point of view in examining an historical event, and so forth.
6. Compare this list with the list generated in Step 1 to determine the kinds of information actually available for evaluating students' progress.
7. Tally work samples and/or evidence of reading and writing behavior to evaluate the effectiveness of the first selection day as a measure of students' progress. If the information does not seem adequate to evaluate students' growth, restructure the selection process so that more specific **kinds** of work samples are included.

- What does the document show about the student's learning?
- How does using this document inform instruction?

Students can also be given prompts to help them in writing captions or "Dear Reader of My Portfolio" letters. Criteria for selection can be for the following reasons:

1. *Pride.*
   - I chose this piece because I am really proud of . . .
2. *Growth.*
   - This piece was chosen because it shows how much I have improved at . . .
3. *Continued effort.*
   - I chose this because I really worked hard to do well. It was difficult for me, but I want to show you that I am trying hard to . . .
4. *Process.*
   - I chose this piece because it shows that I made several tries to revise before publishing.
   - This piece was selected because it shows that I brainstormed using a cluster to jot down my ideas before I started writing.
5. *Wild card.*
   - This piece of work was selected because I enjoyed doing it so much.
   - I chose this piece because Justin and I made some wonderful drawings to go along with it.

(Adapted from Kaser, Jeroski, Gregory, Cameron, and Preece, 1991.)

An example of a caption is as follows:

- **Label.** Writing sample for Writers' Workshop
- **Description.** Document selected to show where Jamie is in the writing process
- **Comment.** Jamie's writing at this time is not as advanced as her language ability. However, she now is using a web to help plan her writing. She was willing to read her work during sharing time but had some difficulty.

In addition to captions, a summary sheet should accompany the portfolio that synthesizes the information contained in the portfolio. A summary sheet forces teachers to organize the documents in a way that helps them make instructional decisions and improves communications with parents and administrators.

Portfolios should be readily accessible to others, and guidelines should be established as to who should view portfolios (students, other teachers, parents, or administrators) and how portfolios can be made accessible to these different audiences. Farr (1990) suggests that regular sessions for portfolio discussions be scheduled throughout the school year. This would be a time for both evaluation and discussion. Portfolios could be shared with parents at conference time, and administrators might be invited to view portfolio assessment and to look in depth at several portfolios.

How Do You Use Portfolios?

Portfolios should be used throughout the year. Teachers may use them at planning time to review and reflect periodically on the contents of the portfolio. Teachers and students may visit the portfolio together every few weeks, and students may visit the portfolio at other times, either alone or with a friend. During such visits, students' progress and future plans and efforts might be discussed. At the end of the year, teachers and students together might decide what to retain in the portfolio to pass on to the next teacher and what the student will take home (Valencia, 1990a).

Portfolios are also important sources of information during conference time with parents and administrators. The dialogue that ensues from visits to the portfolio is an important element of assessment and evaluation.

Portfolio assessment can be messy, but if teachers establish guidelines to determine their instructional priorities and use these goals to guide assessment and evaluation, portfolios will become commonplace and exceedingly valuable in the classroom. Figure 4.17 summarizes what portfolios can do in the assessment process. A review of the steps in conducting portfolio assessments and an example of a Portfolio Assessment Analysis Form can be seen in Figures 4.18 and 4.19. Portfolios can be used effectively in all instructional areas and in all curricular contexts. Portfolio assessment can spark metacognitive learning and awareness and can create a classroom atmosphere that facilitates personal reflection and a sense of ownership.

Conferences

Conferences offer many opportunities for both teachers and students to assess learning and to plan future instructional activities. Conferences are an integral part of both Readers' and Writers' Workshops. Conferences held during either reading or writing time can focus on what the student has accomplished thus far, strategies the student is or is not using, the types of reading and writing the student is doing, and the like. At this time, discussions can be held, interviews conducted, checklists filled in, and anecdotes recorded. Reading and writing conferences are discussed in detail in later chapters on Readers' and Writers' Workshops. The important point to remember now is that conferences provide interactive opportunities for both teachers and students to gain insights into the student's learning programs.

Information from Parents

Research has demonstrated the powerful effect the home has on children's learning. Parents are the children's first teachers. They provide models of language use, provide an environment in which children first learn to communicate, and help establish attitudes and motivation for learning. Therefore, ongoing discussions between the school and the home are an integral part of the assessment and evaluation process. The emphasis should be on the word *discussion*—or conversation. The purposes for obtaining parental input are both to get information on the child and to help establish a two-way communication between the home and the school. Parents should be encouraged to share their knowledge of their children and their observations, as well as their concerns and expectations.

Parents may provide this information by filling out questionnaires requesting information on family background and the child's health history, development, interests, attitude toward learning, time spent reading or watching television, and so on. Or the teacher and parent may engage in a discussion that is later written up anecdotally. Some possible topics for the discussion include:

Figure 4.17 Functions of Portfolios

FUNCTIONS OF PORTFOLIOS

Should Function As:	**Should Not Function As:**
A collection of samples that reflect both process and product	A collection of graded papers
A video of a student's learning efforts over a period of time	A snapshot of a student's work on one task in one context
A reflection of ongoing authentic literacy activities	Only as a repository of short answer, predetermined responses on a teacher or commercially made exercise
A means to involve students in evaluating there own efforts and accomplishments	A vehicle for teacher evaluation only
A vehicle for involving parents in the assessment and evaluation process	A vehicle used only at conference time
A framework for student/teacher conferences	The only vehicle for teacher evaluation and grading
A shared teacher/student responsibility for its organization and management	The teacher's sole responsibility for maintenance
An instrument that changes when needed to reflect insightful understanding in the teaching and learning process	A rigid design with predetermined standards to achieve a product
A piece of the assessment puzzle used in conjunction with other assessment measures	The only assessment tool

Figure 4.18 Steps in Conducting Portfolio Assessments

Dr. Nancy Gropper
Early Childhood Coordinator

State University of New York
College at New Paltz

There is no single way to conduct portfolio assessments. It is a process that reflects the individual character of a school and classroom, just as it reflects the individual character of each child in the class. The steps that are listed below are therefore suggestive and can be altered where necessary.

1. Select goals.
   Identify the goals the portfolios will address. Goals should be long term and broadly stated. A hierarchy of goals can be delineated, but narrow skills need not be specified.

   Goal: Promotion of lifelong literacy
   - A. Progress in receptive language abilities
     1. Decoding the written word
     2. Comprehending what is read
   - B. Progress in expressive language abilities
     1. Encoding words
     2. Expressing ideas
2. Brainstorm about the types of children's work to collect to provide information about progress toward goals.
3. Set up system for collecting children's work.
   - Set up a folder for each child. Children can help to make or decorate their own folders. The size of the folder will depend on the anticipated sizes of work that might be included.
   - Set up convenient place for storing folders.
   - Create a system for dating each work sample that goes into the folder. For example, you might keep a date stamp and ink pad near the portfolio storage area so that each piece of work collected can be easily dated before storing.
   - Create a system for writing notes with additional information about the work samples, such as: context in which the work was done; comments the child made, etc. You might keep a note pad and stapler near the portfolio storage area for writing such notes and attaching them to the work samples before they go into the portfolio.
4. Collect portfolio items.
   - Retain all work samples that seem relevant to the goals. These should represent the breadth as well as the best of each child's work. (You can weed out items when you periodically review the portfolio as described in Step 5.)
   - Include other relevant items, such as observation notes, checklists, diagnostics, tapes, photos of work that cannot be preserved.
5. Conduct periodic reviews and analyses of portfolios.
   - Write a brief analysis of the individual work samples retained in the portfolio. This can be done as you put the samples into the folder or as soon as possible thereafter.
   - Review folders with children and retain work samples in folder that represent both the best and the breadth of the child's work in relation to the goals, and that lend themselves to comparision over time.
   - Look at individual children's work and make plans to promote further progress.
   - Plan additional activities that will facilitate your ability to assess progress from the beginning to the end of the school year.

(*continued*)

Figure 4.18 Steps in Conducting Portfolio Assessments (cont.)

6. Use portfolios in parent conferences.
   - Show parents samples of children's work and discuss the children's progress in relation to the goal.
   - In addition to report cards, analysis forms can be shared so that parents can get a qualitative sense of their children's progress.
7. Share portfolio assessments with future teachers.
   - You can forward final analysis forms to the child's future teacher at the end of the school year.
   - You can forward the portfolio with exemplary items to the child's future teacher, particularly if the teacher is also going to conduct portfolio assessments.

- the child's favorite stories
- the kinds of reading the child enjoys at home
- parents' observations about their child's use of language at home
- opportunities for reading and sharing stories in the home
- opportunities for writing in the home and whether the child chooses writing as an activity at home
- the child's interests outside school, including TV watching, participation in athletics, music or dance lessons
- changes observed in the child's literacy development and concerns parents may have

(Barrs, Ellis, Tester, and Thomas, 1988)

Conversations between parents and teachers provide an opportunity for parents to share their observations about their children and to state what their priorities are for their children. These interactions also give parents opportunities to ask about areas of the school program they feel the school does well or areas they would like to know more about, or to express their wishes for their child's development.

Questionnaires, Surveys, and Inventories

Students may also be given questionnaires, surveys, and inventories to complete. These may be done orally with the teacher (which allows the teacher to probe for additional information) or may be completed by the student alone. Questionnaires, surveys, and inventories may be constructed by the teacher, or the teacher may make use of those that have appeared in professional journals. Topics that may be addressed include interest inventories, attitude inventories, questionnaires on beliefs about reading, and questionnaires dealing with content area reading. Several of these instruments are illustrated in Figures 4.20 and 4.21.

Teacher Judgment

Contrary to traditional assessment and evaluation procedures, there is room for teacher judgment in today's concept of assessment and evaluation. Teachers have become informed participants in their students' learning, and through observation and the other instruments discussed are capable of making decisions about their students' instructional program and progress. Teachers make judgments about the difficulty level of the instructional materials and as to whether a child needs or is ready for certain reading or writing strategies.

In addition to making judgments about student performance in real reading and writing tasks, teachers have instruments that can help them make judgments about their students' dependency and about their students' level of experience as readers. Barrs, Ellis, Tester, and Thomas (1988) developed some rating scales that are of use to teachers in analyzing their students' literacy development. One scale—*Be-*

Figure 4.19A Portfolio Assessment Analysis Form

Dr. Nancy Gropper
Early Childhood Coordinator

State University of New York
College at New Paltz

Portfolio Assessment:
Individual Item Analysis

Child ______________________ Grade ________ School Year __________

Teacher ______________________ Date ________________

Goals:

Item (description/date of work):

Strengths:

Needs:

(*continued*)

coming a Reader—shows aspects of a child's movement along a dependence-independence continuum. It is intended to help describe what young children and beginning readers are capable of doing with increasing ease as they become fluent readers. After age 8, it is recommended that teachers use another scale—*Experience as a Reader Across the Curriculum,* which focuses on a child's increasing involvement with a range and variety of reading materials. The authors state that children may not fall into one specific category but may actually be between categories. This should be noted with perhaps a brief explanation of the reason why the child is bridging categories.

Spelling Analysis

Many parents become concerned when they see papers with unconventional spellings. Parents have to be trained to perceive invented or temporary spelling as being part of a process in which children are discovering how their language works. In whole language classrooms, spelling is no longer assessed by weekly tests with a single grade. There is another means of

Figure 4.19B Portfolio Assessment Analysis Form (cont.)

Dr. Nancy Gropper
Early Childhood Coordinator

State University of New York
College at New Paltz

Portfolio Assessment:
Summary Analysis

Child ______________________ Grade ________ School Year __________

Teacher ______________________ Date __________________

Goals:

Progress made to date:
(Make reference to specific portfolio items and describe child's strengths with objective examples.)

Ideas for promoting future progress:
(Make reference to specific portfolio items and describe the child's needs with objective examples.)

showing that students are progressing in their ability to spell correctly: analyzing students' spelling in authentic writing tasks.

A great deal of research has been conducted into the nature of spelling development. Spelling appears to develop in clearly defined stages in which children experiment with English orthography (Gentry, 1982). The stages are:

- **Stage 1.** Precommunicative spelling
- **Stage 2.** Semiphonetic spelling
- **Stage 3.** Phonetic spelling
- **Stage 4.** Transitional spelling
- **Stage 5.** Correct spelling

A description of each spelling stage appears in Figure 4.22. It is important to remember, however,

Figure 4.20 Reading and Writing Interviews

READING INTERVIEW

1. What do people do when they read (or why do people read)?
2. How well do you think you do in reading?
3. Are there any areas you would like to improve in your reading?
4. Do you have any favorite reading materials (books)?
5. How do you choose what to read?
6. What do you do when you have to read books that don't interest you?
7. What do you do when a book looks hard?
8. When you want to read, what do you do to get prepared?
9. What do you do when you come to a word you don't know?
10. What do you do when you come to something you don't understand?
11. Do you read at home?
12. Does anyone read to you at home? Who?
13. If you were going to teach someone to read, how would you do it?

WRITING INTERVIEW

1. What is writing (or why do people write)?
2. How well do you think you do in writing?
3. Are there any areas in writing that frustrate you?
4. When you are ready to write, what do you do to get prepared?
5. When you are writing and you stop for a reason, what do you do next?
6. What are some of your favorite pieces of writing? Why?
7. If you were to teach someone how to be a writer, what would you do?

that children can and will revert to previous stages when attempting to spell unknown words, and it is not uncommon for a single piece of writing to show several stages of spelling development.

Classroom teachers have several options in analyzing their students' spelling abilities. First, any piece of student writing may be used. The piece chosen should be in draft form before any proofreading has occurred. After all, teachers want to identify in which spelling stage the child is functioning. The teacher then makes a chart by dividing a piece of paper into the various spelling stages. Each word the child wrote is placed in the appropriate column. If the teacher has a question about which stage the word should be placed in, the higher stage should be used. Proper nouns and numerals should not be included in the tally.

After each word has been categorized, the teacher adds the total word count for the piece and then computes the score for each stage. Depending on which stage the child is functioning in, the teacher then plans appropriate instruction. This should be done on a regular basis in order to note the student's spelling progress. Sometimes a piece of writing may not include enough words for spelling analysis. This may occur in the beginning of the year when the child is not used to the teacher or to the classroom and cannot think of enough to write about. The problem is solved by reading a familiar tale to the students, such as "The Three Little Pigs" or "Little Red Riding Hood." The teacher then asks the students to retell the story in their own words. The result becomes the basis for spelling analysis.

By having results of spelling from actual writing endeavors, teachers have meaningful data on which to base future instruction. They also have a means of showing parents that students do move along toward correct spelling. The teacher could also look at the types of errors the student makes, and these could become the basis for minilessons and classroom practice.

Figure 4.21 Content Area Interview

(Courtesy of Elizabeth Maresco Kimiciek)

(Teacher should have a content area text, of appropriate difficulty, available for the student at the time of the interview.)

1. Tell me exactly what you do when you have something to read in social studies, science, or math.

2. What do you like about your social studies, science, and math books?

3. What do you *not* like about your social studies, science, and math books?

4. What do you usually do before you begin to read an assigned chapter?

5. When you are reading a textbook, such as science or social studies, what do you do when you come to material you do not know?

6. Have you ever tried looking through the chapter before you started to read? How has this helped you?

7. What types of things in the chapter can be good clues to what the chapter is going to be about?

(*continued*)

Figure 4.21 Content Area Interview (cont.)

(Courtesy of Elizabeth Maresco Kimiciek)

8. Are there any parts of a textbook that are helpful to you when you need to find out more information about a topic?

9. (If child does *not* use the names of parts of the textbook, ask the child if he or she knows how an index, glossary, appendix, summary, or preface can be helpful.)

10. (If child does use a term such as *appendix, index, glossary, summary,* or *preface,* ask him or her to locate each one mentioned in the book and explain how each one is helpful.)

11. What do you do after you read a chapter?

12. How do you use the chapter to prepare for a test?

13. Are there some things you would like to improve on in your use of this (content area) type of textbook?

14. Have you ever heard of SQ3R? If so, how do you use it?

Figure 4.22 Learning to Spell: Stages of Spelling

Precommunicative Stage of Spelling

(This is the stage of spelling development that represents children's first attempts to use alphabetic symbols to represent words or a message. Although these first attempts at writing are purposeful, precommunicative spellers lack knowledge of letter-sound relationships, resulting in messages that are not readable. This stage is typical of children around the ages of 3 and 5.

The speller:

- randomly strings together scribbles, letter-like forms, letters, and even numbers when spelling a word or creating a message.
- demonstrates some knowledge of the alphabet by producing letter forms to represent a message.
- demonstrates no understanding of sound-symbol correspondence.
- mixes uppercase and lowercase letters but generally prefers uppercase.
- may have a large repertoire of letter forms and letters or may repeat the same letters over and over.
- may write from left to right and top to bottom on the page, or may write randomly over the page.

Examples include:

P5CXOPC	(spider)
EIII3	(street)
7IEXP17	(toad)

Semiphonetic Stage of Spelling

(At this stage, children begin to have an understanding of sound-symbol relationships. Semiphonetic writing is similar to telegraphic writing in that it omits the major sounds. This stage generally includes children around the ages of 5 and 6.)

The speller:

- develops an awareness that letters are used to represent sounds in words.
- abbreviates spellings of words, typically using one, two or three letters to represent entire words; the letters give a partial phonetic mapping of these words.
- uses a letter-name strategy to spell words instead of representing vowels and consonants separately.
- starts to separate message into words.
- begins to grasp the left-to-right arrangement of letters and words.

Examples include:

R	(are)
U	(you)
hp	(happy)
td	(toad)

(continued)

Teacher Self-Evaluation

A nineteenth-century poet once said:

> He who learns from a teacher
> who has learned all he can,
> drinks from a green stagnant pool.
> But he who learns from a teacher
> who is himself still a learner,
> drinks from the clear water of a running brook.
>
> Author Unknown

The message is clear. It is not only necessary to evaluate student learning, but teachers, if they are to be effective, also need to assess and evaluate their own programs and their teaching strategies (Bouffler and Knight, 1991). Along with evaluating their students' progress and attitudes, teachers will also be gathering information about the effectiveness of their own practices and use of resources.

Because of the roles teachers play in planning, implementing, and assessing literacy pro-

Figure 4.22 Learning to Spell: Stages of Spelling (cont.)

Phonetic Stage of Spelling

(At this stage, children spell words the way they sound. Usually children are about 6 or 7 years of age.)

The speller:

- provides all the essential sound features of words.
- develops certain spellings for vowels, plurals, and markers for past tense, such as "hopt" for "hoped."
- uses letters strictly on the basis of sound, disregarding the acceptable letter sequences of English or other spelling conventions.
- frequently omits nasal sounds, e.g., writes "wet" for "went."
- uses correct word spacing.
- is able to read his/her writing even though conventional spelling is not used.

Examples include:

cum	(come)
stret	(street)
tod	(toad)

Transitional Stage of Spelling

(At this stage, children begin to internalize the basic conventions of standard English orthography. Children are usually 7 or 8 years of age when entering this stage.)

The speller:

- relies to a greater extent on visual and morphological information instead of phonological information.
- uses correct letters in words, but they may not be in the correct order, such as writing "braed" for "bread."
- adheres to the conventions of English orthography.
- uses vowels in every syllable.
- provides nasals before consonants, such as "bank" instead of the phonetic "bak."
- is able to use alternate spellings for the same vowel sounds but only partially understands the rules or conditions for using them.
- is beginning to identify words that "do not look right."
- uses many correct spellings.

Examples include:

shcool	(school)	reskyou	(rescue)
yuo	(you)	tode	(toad)

Correct Stage of Spelling

(At this stage, children are more aware of the English orthographic system and its basic rules, and they spell most words correctly. Children generally reach this stage by age 8 or 9.

The speller:

- uses many strategies to spell words.
- successfully understands the English spelling system and its rules and conventions.
- shows a knowledge of word structure, including the correct spellings of prefixes, suffixes, compound words, and contractions, and can distinguish homonyms.
- becomes more accurate in using silent consonants and in doubling consonants.
- continues to master words with irregular spellings.
- recognizes word origins.
- recognizes misspelled words.
- spells most words correctly with confidence.
- uses spelling resources effectively.

(Gentry, 1982, 1987; Wing Jan, 1991)

Figure 4.23 Teacher Self-Evaluation: Questions Teachers Can Ask

Think about the following questions. These questions can be answered using **yes** or **no,** or a check could be placed next to those questions you would like to work on developing.

Physical Environment

______ Is my classroom print-rich, displaying a variety of my students' work so that they can see and interact with the print?

______ Have I organized my classroom using learning centers?

______ Does my classroom contain an assortment of manipulatives and other objects for children to investigate and write about?

______ Do I have an array of materials and equipment such as writing tools, spelling resources, math and science equipment, overhead projector, tape recorders, etc., for the children to use in their language program and across the curriculum?

______ Is the library center attractive and readily accessible to the students?

______ Are the books displayed so that they entice children to read them?

Emotional and Intellectual Atmosphere

______ Do I provide a teaching and learning environment that fosters independence and risk-taking?

______ Do I encourage peer learning by providing my students with opportunities to collaborate with one another?

______ Do I provide learning activities that inspire curiosity and lead to exploration of ideas and materials?

______ Am I flexible in providing teaching and learning activities to accommodate all the children in the classroom?

______ Do I give children time to talk about, develop, and reflect upon their ideas and feelings?

______ Do I value individual differences?

______ Are the children involved in the planning of the literacy program, and do they help establish the rules and routines?

______ Are the children encouraged to make choices about their reading and writing?

______ Am I a good model of what it means to be literate, that is, do I set an example of good reading and writing behaviors?

(*continued*)

Figure 4.23 Teacher Self-Evaluation: Questions Teachers Can Ask (cont.)

The Teaching/Learning Process

_____ Is my instructional program based on how children learned oral language so that language is kept whole and meaningful for the children?

_____ Are the students' reading and writing activities relevant to their world rather than practice of isolated reading and writing skills?

_____ Does my role in the classroom include being a facilitator as well as one who models, demonstrates, and provides direct instruction?

_____ Do I inform parents about what is being accomplished in the classroom?

_____ Do I promote listening and speaking as a means of learning?

_____ Are skills addressed during reading and writing activities?

_____ Am I helping my students acquire learning strategies such as self-monitoring, predicting, visualizing?

_____ Am I flexible in my teaching so that I can take advantage of an unexpected teaching opportunity?

_____ Do I organize the curriculum around themes that become focal points for exploration and language development?

Assessment and Evaluation

_____ Do I observe my students, noting strengths and identifying needs upon which I can base my instructional planning?

_____ Are running records or miscue analyses used to note students' reading behaviors and use of strategies?

_____ Are the students given opportunities to self-evaluate and set their own goals?

_____ Do I periodically evaluate my instructional program and teaching practices?

Professional Growth and Development

_____ Do I participate in staff development or inservice activities and then try to implement the new ideas?

_____ Am I keeping up to date by reading professional journals and attending conferences?

_____ Have I established professional goals? If so, am I working towards fulfilling them?

Figure 4.24 Assessment Measures and Information They Provide

Assessment Measure	Information It Provides
Kid-Watching (Observation)	Motivation, interest, oral and written language development, learning style, interactions with peers, strengths, needs, problem-solving strategies, organizational skills, need for assistance
Anecdotal Records	Attitudes, interests, growth in language development, social development, understanding of curriculum, initiative, level of understanding
Running Records/Miscue Analysis	Use of reading strategies, self-monitoring, accuracy rates, retelling ability, level of difficulty of text being read
Portfolios	Interests, progress in reading and writing, ability to self-evaluate, creativity, application of skills
Think-Alouds	Comprehension of text, use of cues and monitoring
Checklists, Interviews, Questionnaires, Surveys	Attitudes, interests, strengths, needs, use of strategies
Conferences	Attitude, understandings, degree of progress, use of strategies, degree of independence/dependence, level of achievement, application of skills, organizational skills

grams, it is important that teacher performance be examined in much the same way as what is occurring in their classrooms. Elements that teachers might examine include their beliefs, the links between these beliefs and actual classroom practices, the connections between instructional practices and assessment and evaluation, and the selection and use of resources and teaching strategies (Anstey, 1991).

A teacher's personal philosophy plays a significant role in establishment of the classroom climate and the practices that are implemented. Therefore teachers need to examine their beliefs to ensure that their practices are in tune with their growing knowledge base. To do this, teachers can develop a set of belief statements about teaching and learning and review these regularly. In constructing these belief statements, they can reflect on such items as these:

- how students acquire language
- teaching strategies that will help children develop their language abilities, both oral and written
- the role of the teacher in the learning process
- the role of the student in the learning process
- the expectations they have for their students
- the kinds of resources that are appropriate for furthering literacy learning

(Anstey, 1991)

Periodic reflection helps teachers evaluate their beliefs, practices, and programs. Figure 4.23 provides some questions that can guide teachers in self-evaluation. One key role that teachers assume in a whole language classroom is that of learner. By examining what occurs in the classroom in light of their teaching and learning philosophy, teachers obtain valuable information for evaluating their own teaching strategies and literacy programs. This allows them to plan appropriate instructional practices to assist learners and to continue to grow as learners themselves.

SUMMARY

This chapter extended the traditional view of evaluation to incorporate more than just the issue of accountability. A range of assessment and evaluation tools were presented that included observation; anecdotal records; miscue analysis/Running Records; self-evaluation; think-alouds; portfolios; conferences; information from parents; questionnaires, surveys, and inventories; teacher judgment; and spelling analysis. Figure 4.24 outlines the range of assessment instruments and reviews the kind of information obtained from each. Using information obtained from these measures, teachers and students are able to make sound instructional decisions. A shift in the assessment and evaluation movement is occurring to include students in the evaluation of themselves as learners. Both teachers and students are now embarking on the journey to provide the most meaningful educational experiences for promoting learning.

BIBLIOGRAPHY AND SUGGESTED REFERENCES

Antsey, M. (1991). *Blueprint for assessment.* New York: Ashton Scholastic.

Au, K.; Scheu, J.; Kawakami, A.; & Herman, P. (1990). Assessment and accountability in a whole literacy curriculum. *The Reading Teacher, 43,* 574–578.

Barrs, M.; Ellis, S.; Tester, H.; & Thomas, A. (1989). *The primary language record: Handbook for teachers.* Portsmouth, N.H.: Heinemann.

Baskwill, J., & Whitman, P. (1990). *Evaluation: Whole language, whole child.* New York: Scholastic.

Bird, L.; Goodman, K.; & Goodman, Y. (1994). *The whole language catalog: Forms for authentic assessment.* New York: SRA.

Bouffler, C. (1992). (Ed.). *Literacy evaluation: Issues and practicalities.* New South Wales, Australia: Primary English Teaching Association.

Bouffler, C., & Knight, B. (1991). *Assessment and evaluation in reading.* New South Wales, Australia: Primary English Teaching Association.

Calfee, R., & Perfumo, R. (1993). Student portfolios: Opportunities for a revolution in assessment. *Journal of Reading, 36,* 532–537.

Cambourne, B., & Turbill, J. (1990). Assessment in whole language classrooms: Theory into practice. *The Elementary School Journal, 90,* 337–349.

Church, J. (1991). Record keeping in whole language classrooms. In B. Harp (Ed.), *Assessment and evaluation in whole language programs,* pp. 177–200. Norwood, Mass: Christopher-Gordon.

Clay, M. (1993). *An observation survey of early literacy.* Portsmouth, N.H.: Heinemann.

Clemmons, J.; Laase, L.; Cooper, D.; Areglado, N.; & Dill, M: (1993). *Portfolios in the classroom: A teacher's sourcebook.* New York: Scholastic.

Cornelius, K. (1985). Record keeping and evaluation. *Reading Around Series, No. 2.* West Perth, Australia: Australian Reading Association.

Crafton, L., & Burke, C. (1994). Inquiry-based evaluation. Teachers and students reflecting together. *Primary Voices K–6, 2,* 2–7.

Cutting, B. (1989). *Getting started in whole language.* Bothell, Wash.: The Wright Group.

Davidson, A. (1985). *Monitoring reading progress.* Auckland, New Zealand: Shortland Publications.

DeFina, A. (1992). *Portfolio assessment: Getting started.* New York: Scholastic.

Department of Education, Wellington. (1989). *Keeping school records.* Wellington, New Zealand: Author.

Depree, H., & Iversen, S. (1994). *Early literacy in the classroom: A new standard for young readers.* Ontario, Canada: Scholastic Canada.

Drummond, M. (1994). *Learning to see: Assessment through observation.* York, Maine: Stenhouse Publishers.

Eggleton, J. (1990). *Whole language evaluation: Reading, writing, and spelling.* Bothell, Wash.: The Wright Group.

Farr, R. (1990). Setting directions for language arts portfolios. *Educational Leadership, 48,* 103.

Farr, R., & Tone, B. (1994). *Portfolio and performance assessment—Helping students evaluate their progress as readers and writers.* Fort Worth: Harcourt Brace.

Feuer, M., & Fulton, K. (1993). The many faces of performance assessment. *Phi Delta Kappan, 74,* 478.

Flood, J., & Lapp, D. (1989). Reporting reading progress: A comparison portfolio for parents. *The Reading Teacher, 42,* 508–514.

Glazer, S., & Brown, C. (1993). *Portfolios and beyond: Collaborative assessment in reading and writing.* Norwood, Mass: Christopher-Gordon.

Gomez, M.; Graue, M.; & Bloch, M. (1991). Reassessing portfolio assessment: Rhetoric and reality. *Language Arts, 68,* 620–628.

Goodman, K.; Goodman, Y.; & Hood, W. (Eds.). (1989). *The whole language evaluation book.* Portsmouth, N.H.: Heinemann.

Goodman, Y. (1989a). Evaluation of students: Evaluation of teachers. In Goodman, Goodman, and Hood (Eds.), *The whole langauge evaluation book.* Portsmouth, N.H.: Heinemann.

Goodman, Y. (1989b). Evaluation in whole language classrooms. *Teachers Networking—The Whole Language Newsletter, 9,* 1, 8, 9.

Goodman, K.; Bird, L.; & Goodman, Y. (1992). *The whole language catalog: Supplement on authentic assessment.* New York: SRA.

Goodman, Y.; Watson, D.; & Burke, C. (1987). *Reading miscue inventory: Alternative procedures.* New York: Richard C. Owen Publishers.

Hancock, J.; Turbill, J.; & Cambourne, B. (1994). Assessment and evaluation of literacy learning. In S. Valencia, E. Hiebert, & P. Afflerbach (Eds.), *Authentic reading assessment: Practices and possibilities,* pp. 46–62. Newark, DE: International Reading Association.

Harmon, S. (1989–1990). The tests: Trivial or toxic? *Teachers Networking—The Whole Language Newsletter, 9,* 1, 5–7.

Heald-Taylor, G. (1987). *Whole language handbook for administrators.* New York: Richard Owen, Publishers.

Hill, B., & Ruptic, C. (1994). *Practical aspects of authentic assessment: Putting the pieces together.* Norwood, Mass: Christopher-Gordon.

Jeroski, S.; Brownlie, F.; & Kaser, L. (1990). *Reading and responding: Evaluation resources for your classroom.* Scarborough, Ontario, Canada: Nelson Canada.

Johnson, T. (1991). Evaluation in the classroom: Describing and judging the repertoire. Workshop presented in Albany, New York, March.

Jongsma, K. (1989). Portfolio assessment. *The Reading Teacher, 43,* 264–265.

Kaser, L.; Jeroski, S.; Gregory, K.; Cameron, C.; & Preece, A. (1991). *Learner focused evaluation: Issues, strategies, audiences.* Pre-Conference Institute, International Reading Association Annual Conference, Las Vegas.

Lamme, L., & Hysmith, C. (1991). One school's adventure into portfolio assessment. *Language Arts, 68,* 629–640.

Maeroff, G. (1991). Assessing alternative assessment. *Phi Delta Kappan, 73,* 272–281.

Mathews, J. (1990). From computer management to portfolio assessment. *The Reading Teacher, 43,* 420–421.

McKenna, M., & Kear, D. (1990). Measuring attitude toward reading: A new tool for teachers. *The Reading Teacher, 43,* 626–639.

Morrow, L., & Smith, J. (1990). *Assessment for instruction in early literacy.* Englewood Cliffs, N.J.: Prentice Hall.

Pikulski, J. (1990). The role of tests in a literacy assessment program. *The Reading Teacher, 43,* 686–688.

Porter, C., & Cleland, J. (1995). *The portfolio as a learning strategy.* Portsmouth, N.H.: Heinemann.

Rhodes, L., & Shanklin, N. (1990). Miscue analysis in the classroom. *The Reading Teacher, 44,* 252–254.

Rhodes, L., & Shanklin, N. (1993). *Windows into literacy: Assessing learners K–8.* Portsmouth, N.H.: Heinemann.

Rief, L. (1990). Finding the value in evaluation: Self-assessment in a middle school classroom. *Educational Leadership, 47,* 24–29.

Roettger, D. (1992). Involving students in evaluating their own performance. *A comprehensive look at portfolio assessment.* Pre-Conference Institute, International Reading Association Annual Conference, Orlando, Fla.

Salinger, T. (1991). Getting started with alternative assessment methods. Workshop presented at the New York State Reading Association Annual Conference, Lake Kiamesha, N.Y.

Sharp, Q. (1990). *Evaluation: Whole language checklists for evaluating your children.* New York: Scholastic.

Tierney, R.; Carter, M.; & Desai, L. (1991). *Portfolio assessment in the reading-writing classroom.* Norwood, Mass.: Christopher-Gordon Publishers.

Tompkins, G., & Hoskisson, K. (1991). *Language arts: Content and teaching strategies.* New York: Merrill.

Traill, L. (1993). *Highlight my strengths: Assessment and evaluation of literacy learning.* Crystal Lake, Ill.: Rigby.

Valencia, S. (1990a). Alternative assessment: Separating the wheat from the chaff. *The Reading Teacher, 44,* 60, 61.

Valencia, S. (1990b). A portfolio approach to classroom reading assignment: The whys, whats, and hows. *The Reading Teacher, 43,* 338–340.

Valencia, S.; McGinley, W.; & Pearson, P. D. (1990). Assessing reading and writing. In G. Duffy (Ed)., *Reading in the middle school,* 2nd ed., pp. 124–153. Newark, Del.: International Reading Association.

Valencia, S.; Hiebert, E.; & Afflerbach, P. (Eds.). (1994). *Authentic reading assessment: Practices and possibilities.* Newark, Del.: International Reading Association.

Weaver, C. (1990). *Understanding whole language: From principles to practice.* Portsmouth, N.H.: Heinemann.

Wiggins, G. (1989). Teaching to the (authentic) test. *Educational Leadership, 46,* 41–47.

Wolf, D. (1989). Portfolio assessment: Sampling student work. *Educational Leadership, 46,* 35–39.

CHILDREN'S LITERATURE CITED

Pallotta, J. (1986). *The icky bug alphabet book.* Chicago: Childrens Press.

SUPPORTING EMERGENT LITERACY: ORGANIZATION AND CLASSROOM MANAGEMENT (GRADES PRE-K–2)

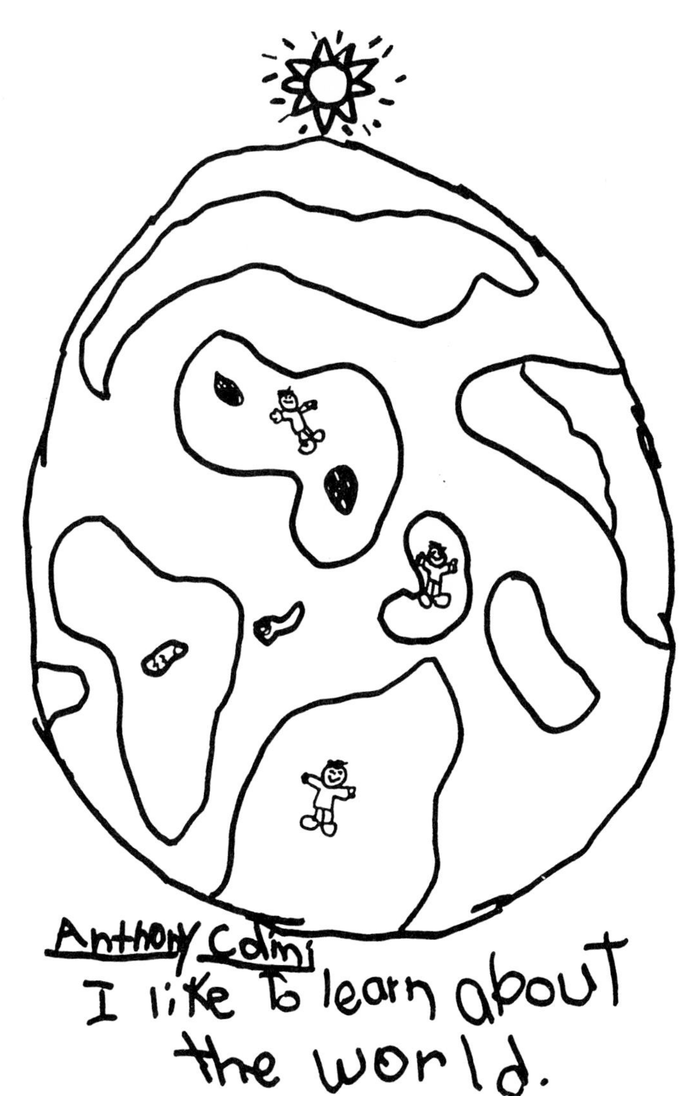

Anthony Colmi
I like to learn about the world.

Inspired by: *I Started School Today* by Karen Frandsen

OVERVIEW

In this chapter we explore the many ways to organize and manage a classroom that will best promote literacy development. Classrooms usually reflect the teaching philosophy of the classroom teacher. The learning environment, rather than the placement of desks and chairs, is a clue to the type of literacy program being implemented: traditional or whole language. Children sitting in rows may indicate a traditional classroom, but not always. Children grouped or seated in clusters may indicate a classroom in transition or a whole language classroom, but not always. Even in the seemingly traditional room, students may move furniture around to suit a particular activity. The room arrangement is not nearly as important as the ongoing classroom activities. As stated previously, there are as many different whole language classrooms as there are individual teachers. This chapter looks at the physical setup and materials present in various classrooms as well as at instructional planning and the teacher's role.

Questions to Ponder

1. Why is the physical design of the classroom so important for maximum learning?
2. What are some ways teachers can arrange the physical space in their classrooms?
3. How are the teachers' roles affected by the classroom design?
4. What are learning centers?
5. How can literacy be fostered in learning centers?

ORGANIZATION AND MANAGEMENT OF THE LITERATE CLASSROOM

Physical Setup

Traditional Classrooms

A traditional classroom gives a sense of formality. The desks may be lined up in rows, one behind the other, in pairs, or in groups of up to six or eight. The room is usually relatively quiet, and children are most often doing work at their seats. Teachers manage the class from their desks or the front of the room. The lesson is taught by the teacher, either lecture style, reading aloud from a textbook, or using the chalkboard or the overhead projector. The whole class receives instruction on the same topic regardless of variations in their knowledge of the subject. Some children receive hours of instruction in areas in which they are already proficient. Workbooks and skill sheets are the mainstay of the children's seatwork. Each page or worksheet is checked for errors. If the work is correct, children go on to the next page or assignment; if the work is incorrect, the teacher may question the students and assist them in making corrections. The focus tends to be on what children do not know, not on what they do know.

Environmental print in the traditional classroom is usually commercially produced and is used to decorate the room so that it looks attractive. Phonics charts and alphabet and number strips are posted above the chalkboard or around the room. Written on the chalkboard are assigned workbook pages, vocabulary words to be learned, a paragraph to copy or complete, or the daily schedule. Bulletin boards may present a theme for the month, may have a posting of weekly work jobs for the students, or may be decorated for a current holiday.

Children's work on display is usually similar in intent and format. The displays may include the best handwritten papers (often on the same topic), math or spelling papers with a grade of 100 percent, or worksheets or compositions stamped with smiley faces or stickers. There is little originality or variability, and frequently only the best papers are displayed. Each paper bears a stark resemblance to the others.

Students' artwork may also be prominently displayed. Here again there is much similarity among the children's products. There may be 25 versions of the same art project (e.g., turkeys for Thanksgiving), and the project usually has little tie-in with other curricular areas. The exception to this is in early childhood classrooms, where 25 windmills or watermelons might be created to teach the letter *W*.

If there is a library corner, it is not a focal point of the classroom. There may be shelves with books, although these may not be attractively displayed. There may be literature books for pleasure reading and for curriculum-related reading, but these usually have been selected by the teacher. The books are usually housed near the teacher's desk and may even be given out by the teacher. Books may also be kept with the spine out, on a high shelf or window ledge, inaccessible and unappealing to young readers. The focus of the reading program is the basal readers. Real books are sometimes read aloud by the teacher or assigned for book reports. Children usually visit the school library on a weekly basis (always scheduled, rarely spontaneous), and the books that are signed out may be kept in the classroom or taken home.

There may or may not be learning centers. If there is a science center, it may have objects related to the seasons or to a topic in the science text. Children may stand around looking at the objects and touching them. Each item may have a written label. Games and manipulatives may be kept on shelves and used only at specific times with the teacher's permission, frequently as a time filler when the child's work is completed.

Teachers' desks are placed so that teachers can observe everything that is going on, sometimes in the front or back of the room. On the desks will be an open plan book that can be referred to as teachers change lessons. Teachers' manuals for the various curricular areas may also be kept on the desk or on a nearby shelf. There may also be a place for children to deposit their completed work.

Materials are usually kept in a specific place and distributed as needed. The paper monitor hands out paper, and the extras are returned to the teacher. Paper is kept in a closet or on a shelf that children cannot reach.

Perhaps this type of classroom brings up memories of your own school experience. Although such classrooms still do exist, many classrooms are undergoing remodeling and are now in transition as teachers are embracing a more child-centered environment.

Classrooms in Transition

Classrooms in transition have some features of traditional classrooms and some features of whole language classrooms, although they are likely to be more inviting and child centered than traditional classrooms. Books are attractively displayed and readily accessible. There may even be a reading corner with comfortable cushions or chairs. More print is in evidence: labels, schedules, charts, thematic bulletin boards with children's work proudly exhibited. Instead of the focus on neatness typical of many traditional classrooms, the children's work and writing on display may now feature the most interesting or creative. However, the displayed work may all be on the same topic.

Centers are more in evidence but may not be fully implemented. Paper and crayons are on open shelves and somewhat accessible. The placement of the teacher's desk is less important since the teacher spends more time conferring with children individually and in groups. Classrooms today may be placed on a continuum from largely traditional to almost completely whole language. What keeps some classrooms in transition from being classified as whole language classrooms is again the philosophy that guides whole language.

Whole Language Classrooms

The whole language classroom provides a language-rich environment, and the physical setup facilitates language learning. Print is everywhere in the room. Children's writing—as well as word banks, content area webs, and experience charts—covers the walls. Objects may be labeled. Ideally these labels are made either by the children themselves or in front of the children. In this way, children do not think print appears magically but soon associate the label and the object or the message. Often the labels are complete sentences (e.g., "This is where we keep the paste"), but not always. Class rules, jointly established by the children and the teacher, are displayed.

The library area is the most inviting and attractive part of the room. Books (with covers facing out as much as possible) are attractively displayed, in great quantity and representing a wide range of reading levels and interests. Posters—commercial or made by the children—mobiles, and book reviews may be displayed to motivate readers and encourage use of the library area.

Other centers are quite visible and are integral to the instructional program. All classroom supplies are accessible: paper, pencils, pens, markers, math manipulatives, games, scissors, stapler, tape, paper clips.

Whole language teachers recognize that the arrangement of the physical aspects of their classrooms—the space, the furniture, the equipment, and the materials—facilitates implementation of a variety of activities and allows them to group students effectively for participation in these activities (Jewell and Zintz, 1990). Careful attention is paid to the allocation and design of the space and to the placement of the equipment and the materials because this contributes to the success of the instructional program. The physical design and arrangement are not merely background or scenery. They are purposefully arranged and influence the activities and attitudes of both children and teachers (Morrow, 1989). The physical environment contributes to teaching and learning and supports the development of literacy. Through the appropriate arrangement of the physical setting, the whole language classroom invites students to become literate, self-reliant, and lifelong readers and writers (see Figure 5.1). The physical design of the classroom is next described in detail, starting with a print-rich environment.

Print-Rich Environment

For optimal literacy development, an instructional program requires a classroom that is rich in print. If children are to learn to read by reading, they must be immersed in print and language. The classroom should be alive with print and be so inviting that children will want to read and write. A print-saturated environment not only immerses the children in language, but it also provides them with purposeful reading activities.

An abundance of books and print materials should be available to children—fiction, nonfiction, magazines, newspapers. Wall stories, which are enlarged texts separated into individual pages, are frequently hung around the room. These wall stories can be commercial products or stories the children themselves have created. Charts of every type and nature are posted around the room: word charts, brainstorming maps, class-generated rules, class-generated ideas for writing, checklists to enable students to evaluate themselves, alphabet charts. Other print sources include notices, posters, labels, children's writing, captioned pictures, duty lists, messages, reminders, murals with descriptions, words of songs, nursery rhymes, and children's names (on labels, drawings, and messages). Print is placed on the chalkboard, on the classroom walls and doors, and in the learning centers.

Teachers often label objects in their classroom or place written descriptions or directions near or on these objects or on classroom furniture. Some teachers prefer to have labels already up when the children enter the classroom at the beginning of the school year, while others would rather prepare the labels collaboratively with the children or have the children prepare the labels themselves. Some teachers label individual objects within the classroom—for example, chalkboard, Author's Chair, sink, puzzles—while others believe that labels should be in meaningful form—complete sentences for real purposes: "When we are hot, we open the window." "Please don't waste paper. Put it in the scrap box." "Our snacks are in this closet." (See Figure 5.2.)

Children are surrounded with environmental print in their homes and neighborhood, and this is true for the whole language classroom as well. Environmental print is print that is used daily in the real world to identify, label, and give directions or instructions. Environmental print relies on getting the message across in a quick and economical fashion. It differs from the language of books in that only a few words or a phrase is used. The format is intended to catch the reader's eye and to promote the product or service. Therefore the print may not be standard and may be quite colorful. Environmental print in the classroom includes labels and boxes from a variety of products, catalogs, menus, buttons with slogans, stamps, envelopes, junk mail, business cards, menus, telephone directories, T-shirts, and lunch boxes.

Once a variety of print materials have been amassed, time should be made available for children to explore, investigate, and use these materials. A print-rich environment implies that students participate in the act of literacy. Children should write the daily attendance slip and lunch or snack count, fill in library borrowers cards, and complete any other writing activities that are part of a class routine. This gives children a chance to write for real purposes and to contribute to the literacy-rich environment.

A print-rich classroom displays children's writing. Individual journals or writing sheets can be hung from the chalk tray by plastic hooks or from hooks in a pegboard. Bulletin boards can be reserved for sharing children's

Figure 5.1A Diagram of a Whole Language Classroom

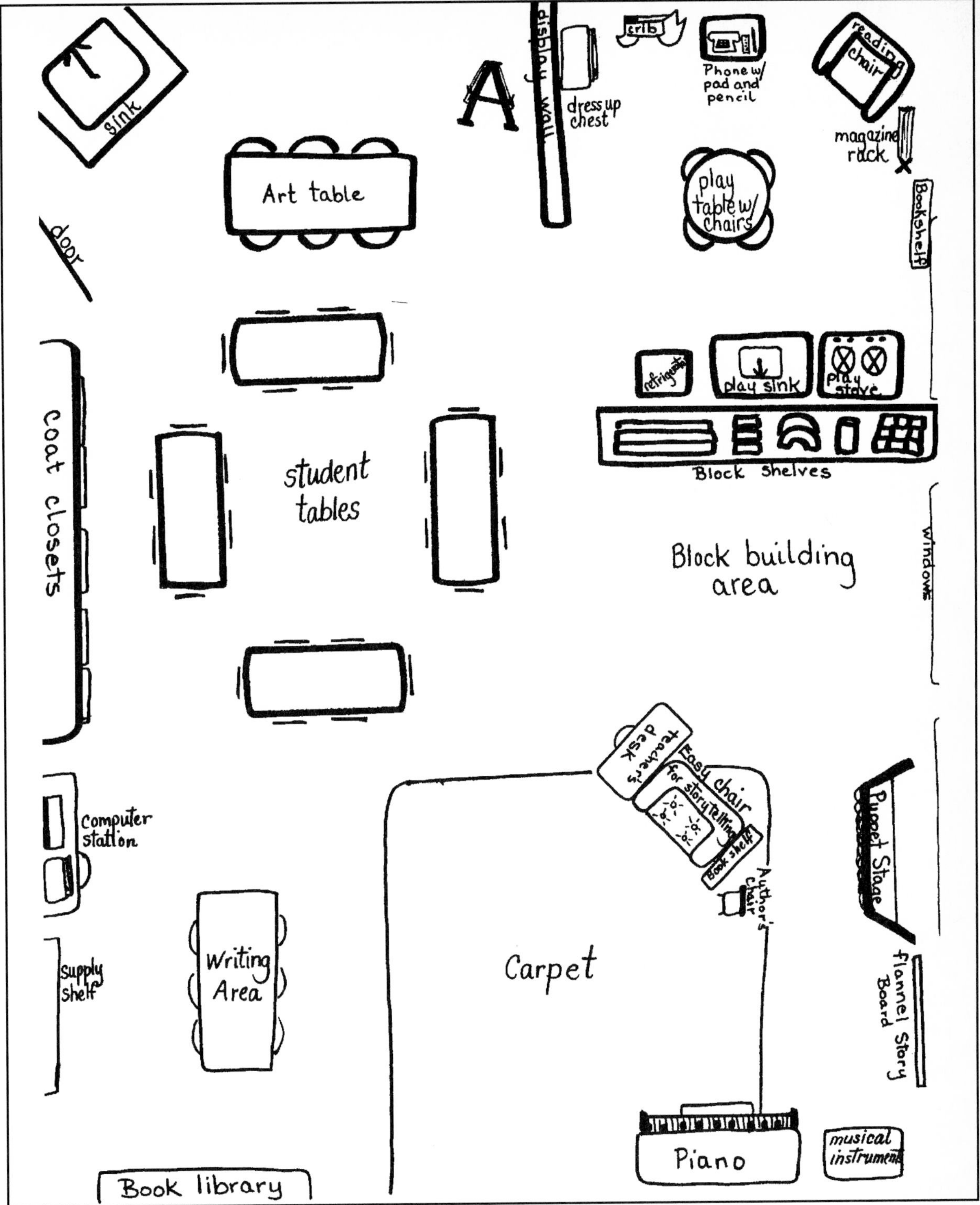

Figure 5.1B Diagram of a Whole Language Classroom (cont.)

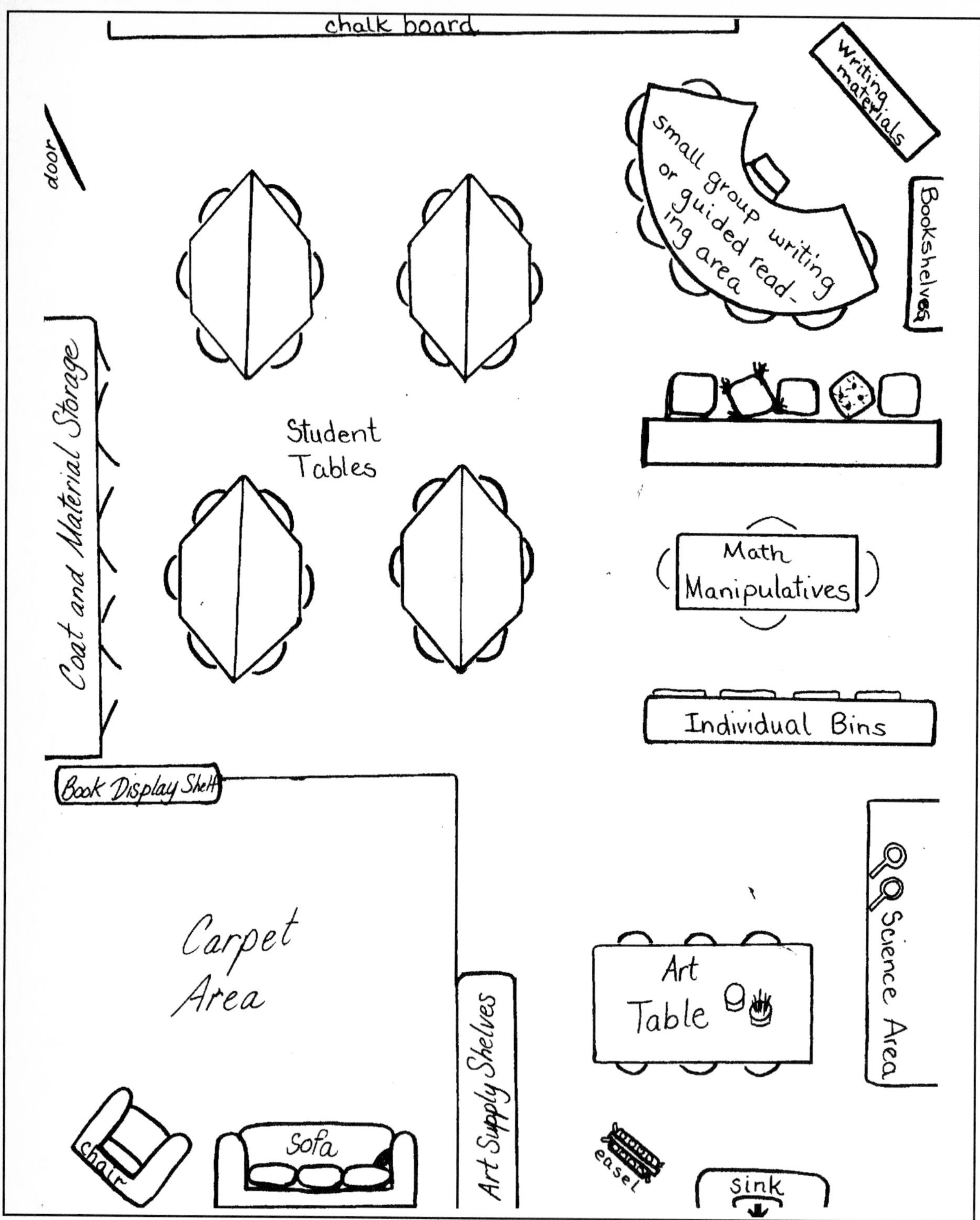

Figure 5.2 Labels in the Classroom

written pieces. Children's writing can also be hung on clotheslines. Big Books that the children have created can be displayed on easels or hung from skirt hangers and be available for borrowing (see Figure 5.3).

One purpose for having a print-saturated classroom is to expose children to a variety of different types of print and the many topics that are dealt with in print. This exposure develops an awareness of language that stimulates children to become involved with printed materials.

In addition to creating the print for the environment, children can read the walls. This activity entails children having an opportunity to go around the room and read what is available. The child may use a pointer to point to each word as it is read. Often children are paired for this activity.

A print-rich environment creates a language laboratory within the classroom. To immerse children in written language, the classroom is designed so that children will be interested, involved, and challenged. A print-rich classroom allows children to learn language, learn about language, and learn through language.

Figure 5.3 Big Book on Skirt Hanger

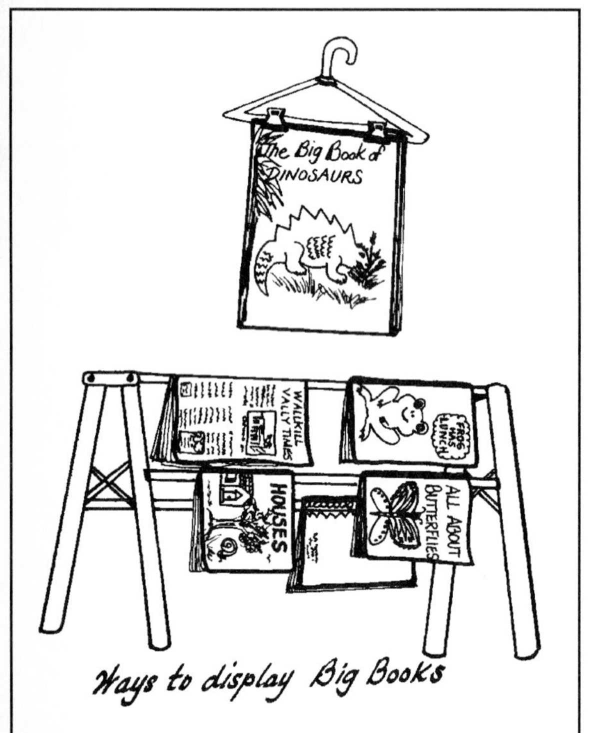

Classroom Library

The classroom library is the heart of the classroom and should be established before any other center. The purposes of the classroom library are to support instruction, facilitate independence in reading, and promote reading of all kinds. The physical setup of the library should be attractive enough to invite children to come, visit, and learn. There should be a wide variety of reading materials on a wide range of reading levels and interests. Housed in the library should be books for pleasure and books that support the curriculum. The literature should include all genres: fiction, nonfiction, plays, scripts for Readers' Theater, poetry, nursery rhymes, jokes, jingles. Strickland and Morrow (1988) suggest that there be five to eight books per child at different reading levels. About 25 books should be replaced every two weeks, either with new selections or with books used earlier in the year. It is recommended that the books be displayed (as much as possible) with the covers facing the readers. (See Figure 5.4.)

In addition to books, environmental reading materials should be provided: menus, catalogs, *TV Guide,* newspapers, magazines, logos, greeting cards, food packages (such as cereal boxes), and even perhaps business cards. Of course, student writing is of equal importance in the classroom library, for books written by classmates are much appreciated and enjoyed.

The location of the library may vary from classroom to classroom depending on the actual size and shape of the room. The library may be placed in a corner, partitioned off from the rest of the room by shelves or bookcases. Frequently there are comfortable chairs (such as rocking chairs), pillows, cushions, and rugs. Stuffed animals also may be present, representing favorite book characters, such as Clifford the Big Red Dog or Curious George, or available as "listeners" for emergent readers. Posters, student illustrations, and book projects may also be incorporated into the physical design of the library. The more personalized the library, the more children will take pride and ownership of it.

Classroom libraries may take many shapes and designs. Whereas most libraries are partitioned-off sections of the room, some teachers use motifs and alternate arrangements. Lofts or bathtubs filled with soft, comfortable cushions are sometimes provided for special reading places. Some teachers have built story-book cottages and castles for their libraries. Children's input is always desirable when planning and designing a classroom library.

Although the main function of the classroom library is to provide a place for children to get and read books, the library is also a place to practice functional reading and writing skills. (See Figure 5.5.) If books are categorized or alphabetized, students can practice locating books and returning them to their proper places. Name writing can also be practiced by having children write their names in order to take out books. Writing materials can be made accessible so that children can learn how to conduct research and record their findings. The library is not intended to be merely decorative. It should be used throughout the day for many purposes: to locate books for Sustained Silent Reading, to get information, and to get materials for enjoyment.

Figure 5.4 Book Storage in Class Library

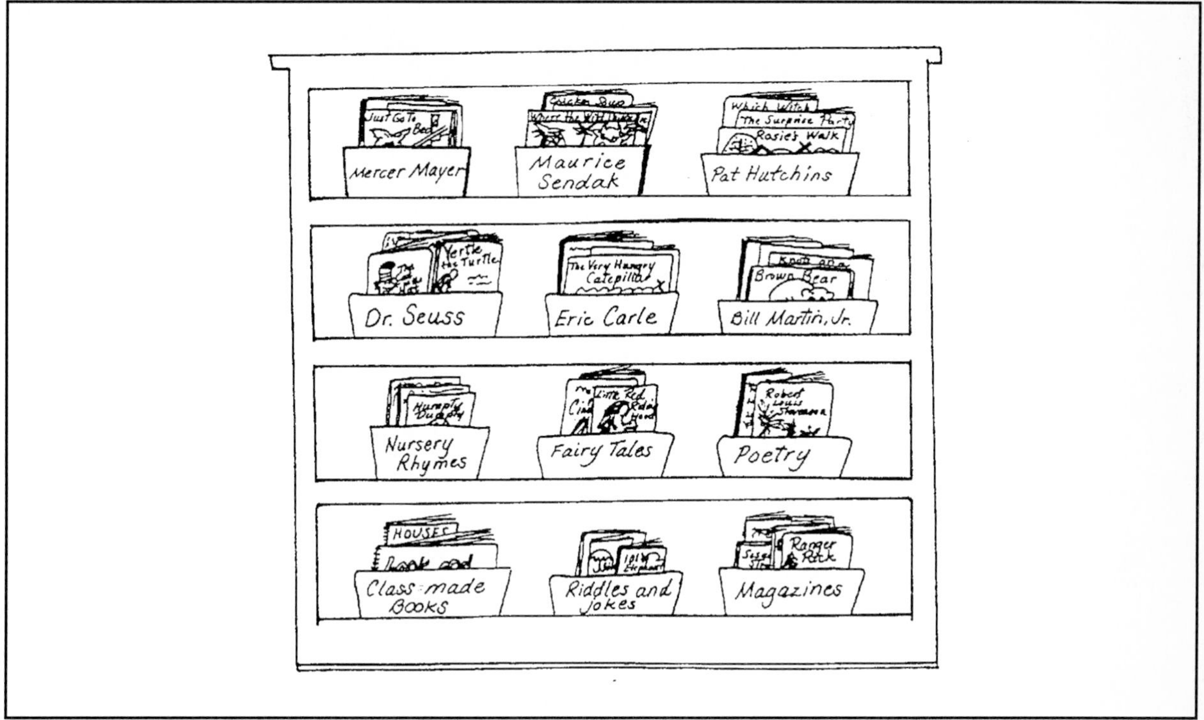

Learning Centers

An excellent way to organize space in an effort to promote learning is to establish learning centers. Learning centers are classroom areas that contain collections of materials and activities designed to reinforce, develop, and enrich skills and concepts. These activities and materials range from simple to more complex and from concrete to more abstract. Learning centers are intended to promote the goals of the curriculum and to meet children's needs to be active, to interact with others and their environment, and to make decisions (Seefeldt and Barbour, 1990). They are used as follow-up for instruction, as places to practice and perfect what was taught, and as places for interacting and sharing (Kohia Teachers Centre, 1983). Visually, learning centers should be designed so as to capture the attention, interest, and imagination of the children. The centers must both arouse and sustain interest.

Learning centers can make learning come alive, can make it more personal for the children. They help to provide for children's differing learning styles and abilities. They offer a means for teachers to create an educational, practical, and stimulating environment. By establishing centers in their classrooms and by allowing children the opportunity to participate in activities in the centers, teachers are freed to offer more individualized attention and guidance (Kohia Teachers Centre, 1983).

The arrangement of the centers within the classroom is crucial. Teachers should make classroom floor plans, using graph paper and cutout pieces of paper to represent the equipment and the furniture. By moving the pieces of paper around on the floor plan, teachers can experiment with different room arrangements. Once centers are established, teachers should observe the traffic flow to determine the effectiveness of movement among centers and within the classroom. Pathways should facilitate movement, not impede it. When arranging centers, teachers should take into consideration that some are more active and noisy than others (e.g., the block or construction centers will not

Figure 5.5 The Reading/Writing Center

The Reading/Writing Center

Include in this area:

An overstuffed chair or rocker
A rug and cushions
Flannel board and pieces
Magazine rack
Book shelf with numerous book selections
Paper, markers, crayons, pencils
A box with cards for spelling word check
Writing table
Puppets (displayed here on a boot rack)
Tape recorder and headsets
Computer station
Wooden tack strip to display student work
A chart with library pockets or fabric pockets to create a word bank.

be as quiet as the reading corner or the writing center). Putting a noisy center adjacent to a quiet one may not be advisable. Teachers should also consider the availability of private areas in the classroom. Some children need to be alone occasionally, and their needs should be met. Another consideration is the teacher's ability to supervise children as they work and move about. By experimenting, by observing centers in action and movement within the classroom, teachers can evaluate and make necessary adjustments. If the concept of centers is new to teachers, it is best that they begin slowly, introducing only one or two centers at the beginning of the school year. As both teachers and children become comfortable with centers, more can be added.

Besides making centers available, the teacher has additional roles. Teachers must be knowledgeable about their curriculum and the goals for the year so that they will know when to establish a learning center or to include specific materials and activities. Centers, whenever appropriate, should be used as part of the instructional program. Children should be shown how to use the centers and how to manage them. Materials have to be maintained and replenished. Again, learning centers must be kept interesting and stimulating (Kohia Teachers Centre, 1983).

When introducing children to centers, the teacher should begin by preparing them to use a limited number of centers. Children should know what the centers are for, how to use them, and how to care for, clean up, and return materials. A practice run with a small group of children is beneficial before actual implementation.

To help in management, the centers need to be clearly labeled, and a system should be established for choosing centers. Figure 5.6 contains pictures that may be used as labels for the centers. Of course, the children can draw and write labels for the centers as well. Picture labels can be duplicated and used when students choose the specific center in which they will be working. The number of pictures that teachers put out is determined by the number of students a center can accommodate. For example, an easel accommodates two children, so two easel cards will be made available; if the listening station can accommodate six children, six cards will be made available; and so forth. This system gives the children some choice, but the number of children in each center is manageable.

There are many types of centers: library, writing, listening, science, art, social studies, math, housekeeping, dramatic play, block, and thematic. Some centers—such as the library, Writing Center, and Listening Center—will be permanent, while others, such as thematic centers, may be temporary. These temporary centers may appear throughout the year to capitalize on the children's interests or curricular undertakings. Examples of thematic centers include the grocery store, the bakery, the doctor's office, and the circus. Whether centers are permanently established or used temporarily, the materials and activities should be varied and changed periodically so as to sustain the children's interest and curiosity.

Writing Center

To demonstrate the value of writing, teachers will have an area where writing implements and materials are available. This is the Writing Center. Writing Centers support the instructional program and allow children to engage in a variety of writing experiences, which for young children includes drawing or illustrations. Writing Centers may be incorporated into a Literacy Center (which also includes the classroom library and Listening Center) or may be in a separate section of the classroom. Inside Writing Centers are a table and chairs (usually providing for seating of four to six children at any one time), boxes or containers for storing the children's writing folders or journals, and many writing materials: lined and unlined paper, colored paper, adding machine paper, blank books, cards, envelopes, pencils, markers, crayons, pens, glue, clips, stapler, tape, cardboard, and clipboards. Some of these materials will be used in the drafting stage, some in revision, some in editing, and some in publishing. Paper, pens, crayons, and markers can be housed in such containers as clean milk cartons or juice cans. After the top has been cut off, a milk carton is perfect for small hands and will hold 12 thick crayons. Erasers tend to disappear quickly. To alleviate this, children can brand their own erasers. Rulers, cellophane tape, glue, brass fasteners, paper clips, and staplers can be housed on trays or in flat boxes, appropriately marked.

FROM THE CLASSROOM OF . . .

Jean Mumper Wallkill, New York

Materials in the Classroom

To assist students with organizational skills, cut and paste, or draw pictures on 9" × 12" oak tag, of materials needed for the day. The cards can be hung or placed on the chalk tray as needed.

Today we need a
pencil.

Today we will use

Remember your library
book.

Please get your

Figure 5.6 Picture Labels for Learning Centers

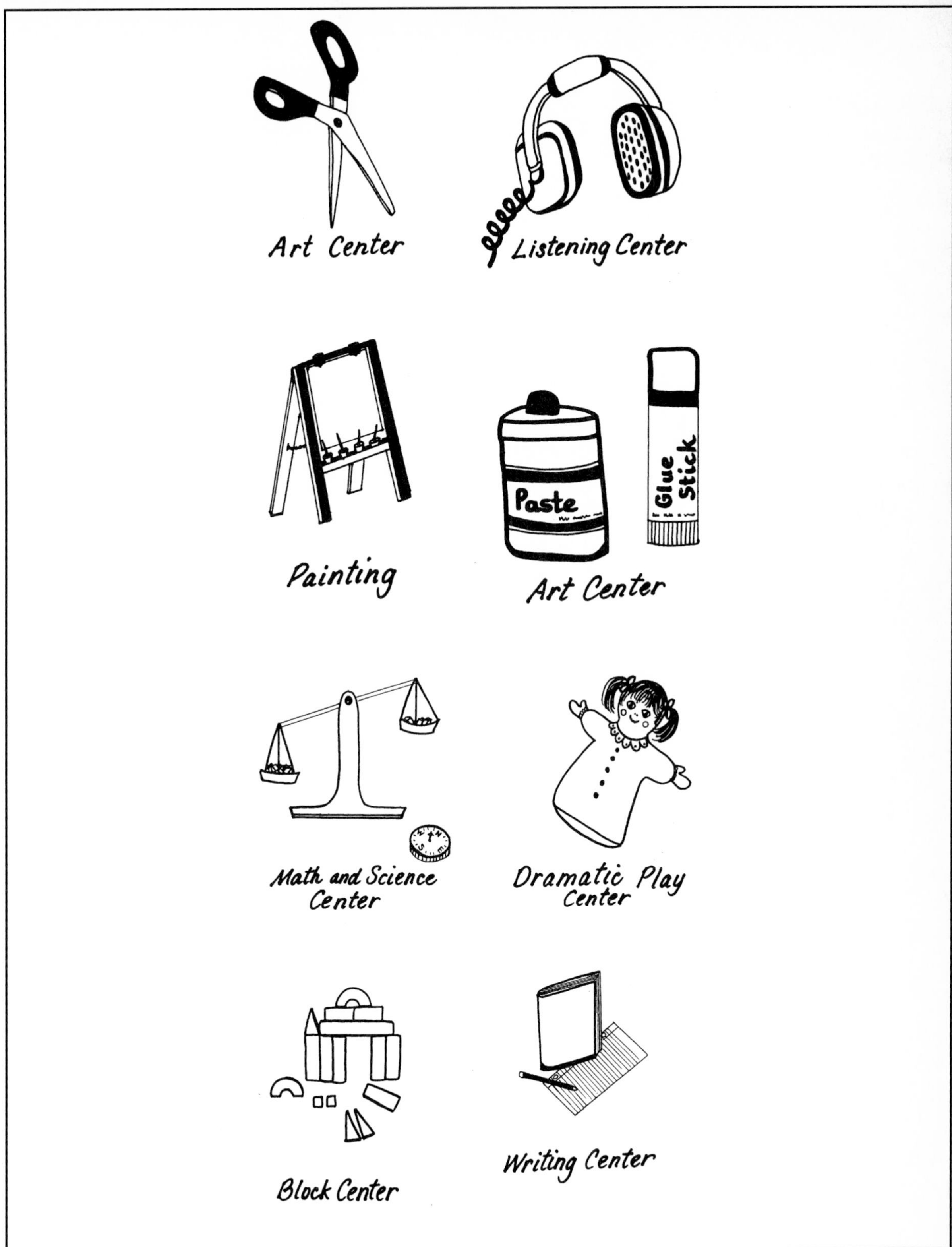

Scissors should be stored—handles up—in a container like a coffee can.

A date stamp, a stamp bearing the words "Under Construction" or "Draft," and an ink pad are also important. Children should be trained to date their writing so that a complete record of their growth as writers can be kept. Because parents are often concerned when they see papers that are not completely correct, the "Under Construction" stamp will inform them that the writing piece is not yet complete and that mechanics will be addressed at a later stage in the writing process.

If possible, the students should be involved in the design of the Writing Center and in obtaining and caring for the materials placed there. Housekeeping should be left to a rotating staff of students. Simple tasks, such as seeing that pencils are sharpened and papers are stacked, can be done by even very young children.

By having an abundance of writing materials readily accessible, children are free to create and choose how they will publish and share their writing. Although publishers now offer for purchase shape books and patterns for shape books, children—left to their own ingenuity—can come up with original designs, particularly if these designs are appreciated by the teacher and other classmates. Blank books may also be purchased but—given budget constraints—may easily be constructed. One early childhood teacher creates blank books by covering the fronts and backs of cereal boxes with wallpaper and stapling blank sheets of paper in between. Another kindergarten teacher uses two pieces of wallpaper (no cardboard) as covers, with several sheets of paper sandwiched between. At the beginning of the year, she uses just one wallpaper cover, to show children where the front of the book is. By doing this, she reinforces one of the concepts about print—differentiating between the front and back cover—and indicates that the front cover represents the beginning of a book.

In addition to the materials mentioned, writing resources may be available to help children. Picture dictionaries, word cards, children's "very own" or key words (words that have personal meaning for children), and personalized dictionaries can be provided. Word cards may be kept in decorated boxes in the Writing Center. These cards list common words according to specific categories: color words, number words, words for parts of the body, transportation words, school-related words, and so on. There may also be word cards for each letter of the alphabet. These may be kept in boxes as well, in shoe bags, or in felt wall hangings with separate pockets for each letter. Words that students may refer to are also kept on charts, particularly if the words have been generated to accompany the study of a theme or a curricular area. Young children will also go to books that have been read to them, or ones that they have read, for words to use in their writing, so the classroom library also becomes a valuable writing resource.

Teachers may also provide stimuli for writing. Pictures or objects may be displayed that could stimulate children to begin writing. One first-grade teacher has a box of photographs, collected from her family and from the children in her classroom, that are popular as writing sources. It is best not to provide story starters (sentences or paragraphs that are the beginning of a story or a situation that could be written about) or to assign writing topics. Rather, teachers should encourage children to come up with their own ideas for writing.

Let's not forget that today's children are growing up in a technological world, so many Writing Centers will also have a computer. There are computer programs to facilitate the writing process, programs to create Big Books (enlarged texts), and programs for publishing sources. In addition to computers, Writing Centers may contain a primary typewriter for the children's use.

Other additions to the Writing Center could be notice or message boards (places where messages between students and between the teacher and the students can be exchanged, as well as places for teachers to post information), mailboxes, and bulletin boards where children's writing can be shared or a classroom author-of-the-day can be featured. The Author's Chair (a special chair in which children sit while reading their writing to others) may be placed in the writing center or nearby.

Although it is important to provide an appropriate physical setting, it is equally important to provide the appropriate atmosphere and opportunity for writing. Children must have time to use the Writing Center, and it should be available for use both at designated times and at times when children are engaged in other activities. Children must have the opportunity to interact with one another. Working together is a positive experience, whether a child is asking for help with spelling or requesting comments on a piece of writing. Some students may prefer, however, to write alone, at their desks or sitting propped against a wall with a clipboard. Individual learning styles should be respected and honored. The Writing Center will be successfully implemented if children feel free to explore and experiment with all kinds of writing. Freedom to try gives children an opportunity to create, refine their writing, and develop into real writers. The center serves as another vehicle to foster self-expression and to help children reach their full potential as young authors.

Listening Center

Another center that may operate by itself or that can be incorporated into a Literacy Center is the Listening Center. Here children listen to audiotapes or records as they follow along in books. Equipment and materials needed for the Listening Center are tape recorders, record players, earphones, cassettes, and records. Although most centers use earphones so as not to disturb the rest of the class, a Listening Center can still be effective without them. If children are interested in an activity, they are not distracted by what is going on elsewhere in the room. This works the other way around as well. If children are busily engaged in another center or instructional activity, the sound of the cassette player will not disturb them.

A simple cassette player and record player will have a connection for a jack that allows hook-up for eight to ten earphones, although it is best to keep the number of children working in the center to a manageable group of about four to six children. Cassettes and records should be changed frequently, keeping in mind that certain favorite songs and stories are listened to repeatedly.

An abundance of audiotapes, records, and read-alongs are available. Suggested materials are listed in the appendices. In addition to materials purchased or borrowed from the school library, teacher-, parent-, or student-made tapes are welcome. Tapes can be made of favorite stories, poems, and songs, as well as of writing the children have produced themselves. Listening to stories and poems is another means of immersing children in print and providing practice with interesting and motivating materials.

Science Center

The current movement in the United States and in science education is hands-on science. Instead of just using textbook material, science classes in elementary schools have kits and materials that children handle, experiment with, and devise questions about and solutions to as they work through real problems. In addition to regularly scheduled science lessons, teachers also use Science Centers to allow children to manipulate and investigate alone or with their classmates. Science Centers should promote curiosity, encourage hypothesizing and observation, and provide opportunities for experimenting, discovering, and recording and sharing discoveries (Kohia Teachers Centre, 1983). The concerns of recycling, endangered species, the environment, and health issues have all been added to the traditional science curriculum. Weather, rocks and minerals, fossils, dinosaurs, electricity, living and nonliving things, space, physics, and chemistry are only some of the topics now being taught in which children are involved with projects rather than reports.

Any surface area—such as tables, window ledges, or desks—can be converted to a display and work space. Since the science topic being studied is usually featured in the center, the materials will focus on this particular curricular objective. Included will be science equipment, artifacts, books, articles, science magazines, filmstrips, transparencies, and other hands-on materials. A recycling box can be kept at the center to focus on the need to recycle discarded materials. The intent of a Science Center is to provide children with the opportunity to investigate, experiment, and explore in order to reinforce and extend the science concepts being developed. As with other centers, children should be expected to contribute articles to the center and to help with maintenance. A sample Science

Center activity—a guided investigation—is presented in Figure 5.7.

Math Center

Another type of investigative center is the Math Center. A Math Center should support the classroom mathematics program; present enriching and enjoyable activities related to the current math topic; allow for practice, skill development, and application of various math concepts; and give children opportunities to manipulate objects and to construct mathematical concepts and understandings. Children need to develop and construct math concepts for themselves through their own experiences, and Math Centers provide this hands-on exploration. Children need experiences, interactions with others, the language to accompany the experiences, and time to think about and reflect on their experiences. Children need opportunities to handle, manipulate, and explore materials as they think about mathematical ideas.

A Math Center should contain a variety of manipulatives, such as Cuisenaire rods, pocket calculators, clocks, timers, counting materials (beans, plastic disks, cereal, wooden tiles, buttons), calendars, dominoes, blocks (interlocking or free standing), playing cards, dice, scales, rulers, and cups. There should be materials for children to sort and classify, count, perform number operations, measure, graph, and estimate and to complement any of the areas of the mathematics curriculum. In addition to manipulatives, paper should be available for children to use to predict, hypothesize, graph, and write math problems and stories. These can be featured in a special display area in the Math Center. There can also be charts, posters, articles, and books dealing with mathematics. When literacy activities are incorporated into such content areas as math, children are able to see the connections between the language arts and learning in the real world.

Dramatic Play Center

This area, which includes the house corner and puppet stage, is an area for children to role-play or act out stories. Besides such equipment as child-sized refrigerators, stoves, and doll beds, this center will also have items that create a print-rich environment. A clip with a pencil and paper attached fastened to the refrigerator door encourages children to create grocery lists. The corner can be regularly stocked with empty kitchen containers that have print, such as coffee and juice cans or cereal and cracker boxes. As children play in this center, they will bring in containers from their own favorite foods to add to the grocery lists and to stock the shelves. One kindergarten teacher took actual cereal boxes, flattened them, punched three holes in each, and then placed them in a binder. This became the Cereal Book. The children took great delight in turning the heavy cardboard pages and reading the various names or enjoying the pictures. This type of book can be made using any familiar packaging that children enjoy and recognize: toothpaste boxes, soap wrappers, potato chip bags.

Telephone directories can be placed near the telephone. Children love to find their last names and telephone numbers in directories. They can highlight their names with colored markers. A small address book can also be placed there in which children can enter their own names, addresses, and telephone numbers. This is an easy way for them to learn about alphabetical order and to practice writing important information. A calendar can be hung, and children can write their appointments in the squares.

Next to an easy chair, a stack of magazines could be kept. *TV Guide* is the most widely read publication in the United States, and children could be taught to use it by reading about programs and selectively choosing what they will view. A colorful cookbook can be placed near the stove for children to refer to while pretending to cook meals.

The idea is to create a learning center that reflects the world outside school as realistically as possible. Catalogs, sales circulars, newspapers, playing cards, and junk mail all belong in this area as much as dishes, dolls, dress-up clothes, and puppets. Figure 5.8 illustrates how seriously children take their dramatic play. As you can see, the boys were barring the girls from their secret meeting place. In turn, the girls responded by stating that the boys were likewise not allowed, "not even Stanley" (guess who wrote the original note).

Figure 5.7 Guided Investigation

Investigations

private eyes:

1. ________ 3. ________

2. ________ 4. ________

Questions for the audience after presentation to see what the audience has learned:

Question: ________________________

____

Answer: ________________________

____

Q: ________________________

____

A: ________________________

____

____

To the audience:
Do you have any questions to ask the experts?

What do I want to know about ________ (Topic/Subject) that I don't know now?

Question: ________________________

____

Answer: ________________________

____

Q: ________________________

____

A: ________________________

____

Q: ________________________

____

A: ________________________

____

What I learned about ________ (Topic/Subject).
(Information for presentation of my project.)

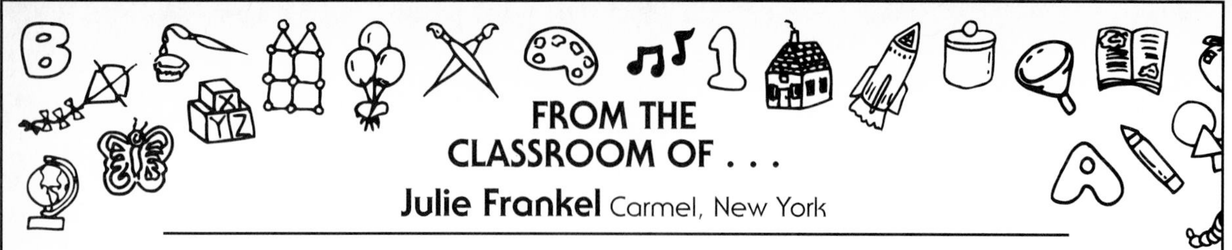

FROM THE CLASSROOM OF . . .

Julie Frankel Carmel, New York

INSTRUCTIONAL STRATEGY: WORDS ON MY SHIRT

Environmental print is an excellent way to teach concepts about print and to develop children's awareness of print in their everyday lives. Today children come to school as walking "billboards" with sayings and advertisement on their shirts. To capitalize on this natural reading material, the shirt can be read by the class during community meeting time. In addition, the students can add a page to an on-going class book, entitled *Words on My Shirt,* showcasing their shirt's message. Since it is virtually impossible for emergent readers and writers to recreate the message while wearing the shirt, the activity can be a home-school one. When children wear a shirt that they would like to share in their class book, they can take home a T-shirt shaped page with the following message.

WORDS ON MY SHIRT
Please have your child draw and write the words on the shirt that was worn to school today.
The drawing should go on the paper shaped like a shirt that was sent home with this notice.
Each "Shirt" will be a page in the book.

This book is one that is written by the children throughout the year, with pages added as needed. To add a motivating touch, the book, which is shaped like a shirt, can be covered with an actual T-shirt. Young children enjoy touching the fabric, as well as reading their own and their friend's shirts.

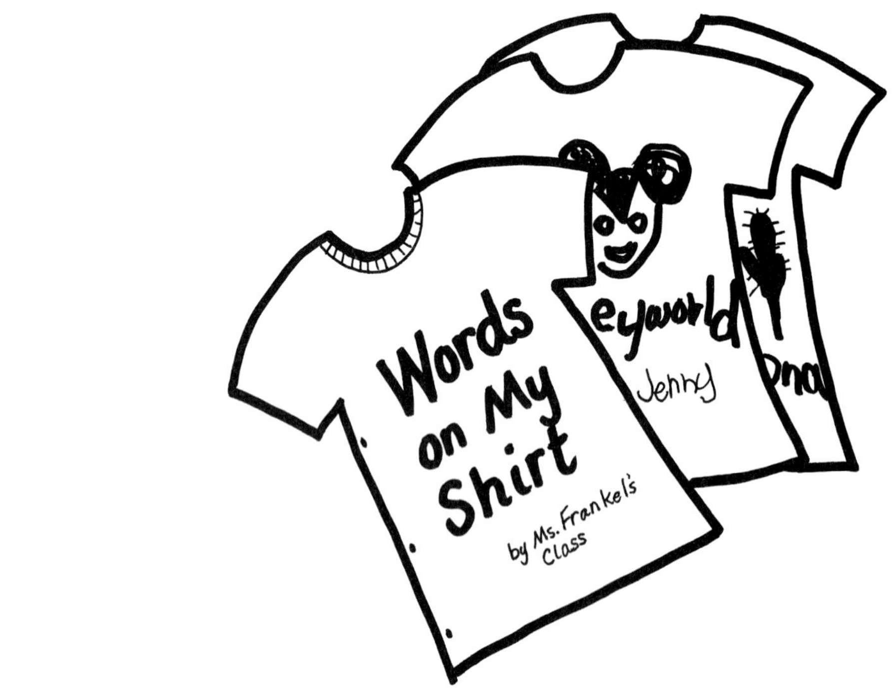

Figure 5.8 Children's Labels for Dramatic Play Area

Block Center

Blocks are essential for children of all ages. The Block Center allows children to create things that replicate the real world on a small scale. It encourages creativity and cooperative interactions with classmates. It affords a chance for children to develop their large-motor skills as well as to engage in imaginative play. In choosing a space for the Block Center, a teacher must keep several things in mind. Children will need a large enough area to create such things as houses, bridges, and castles, and construction sometimes takes several days. Therefore this center should be removed from areas with heavy traffic. Adequate storage areas for the blocks are also needed—on open shelves, in wagons, in boxes, or in bins.

In addition to blocks, school supply catalogs that illustrate block cities or buildings can be made available. Books about road signs or vehicles might be nearby as well. Car and racing magazines are popular with young children and can be included in the center. Inverted shoe boxes can be painted and cut to create doors and windows. Marking pens work well for labeling the city or town buildings, and clay and popsicle sticks can be used to create signs. If possible, the block area should be a place where a project may continue for several days and that need not be cleaned up each day. It is important to realize that play is the work of young children, and play is where reading and writing begin.

Arts and Crafts/Construction Center

Learning centers that are more informal in nature and that emphasize self-motivation and self-selection also add an important dimension to the classroom setting. Because these centers are open-ended in the types of activities chosen and the materials selected, the variations and the materials included are limitless. An Arts and Crafts/Construction Center is one such center where children can manipulate a variety of materials and produce imaginative creations.

It is suggested that this center be located near a sink, if possible. Many materials should be available: paper, scissors, paste or glue, wallpaper sample books, newspapers, paint chip samples, fabric scraps, paint, cardboard, yarn, egg cartons. Children need to explore various media to illustrate their ideas; for example, when using paint, children can use brushes, sticks, string, fingers, and sponges or blow through straws. Adults need to keep in mind that often for children the process is far more important than the product. As children develop, their play needs fewer props and materials and becomes more dependent on their imagination, ideas, and language.

Thematic Centers

Centers created around themes are ways teachers can continually provide interesting and relevant learning experiences. Possibilities include seasonal centers and centers to explore current topics in social studies. For example, when community helpers are studied, a bakery, doctor's office, post office, grocery store, fire station, or police station can become the focus of a learning center. These centers tend to be temporary and are changed according to what is occurring in the classroom. However, a center can have a concept that remains, with the content being the changeable feature.

To illustrate this, let's look at a center featuring each child that could be titled "All About Me," "Meet Our Class," or "Me Museum" (Strickland and Morrow, 1989). Every child has an opportunity to be featured throughout the school year. Displayed in this center could be current or baby pictures, favorite books or toys, information on the child, baby shoes, or any memorabilia that the child wishes to show. Figure 5.9 is an example of such a center, featuring our young reader and writer—Sarah.

There is no need to feel that a large classroom is needed in order to establish learning centers. The idea is to maximize the existing classroom space creatively and to be flexible. The space that is used for a Social Studies Center one month can be converted into a Science Center the next month. Tables, crates, extra desks, window ledges, and floor space can become a center. Centers are based on a philosophy that children learn best when they figure things out for themselves, independently or cooperatively. Through the use of centers, children are given opportunities to make choices, explore, and make decisions and judgments based on these choices.

Literacy in Centers

Centers allow and encourage children to be actively involved in experimentation, exploration, and investigation. But centers also provide innumerable opportunities for children to engage in functional reading and writing experiences. This can be accomplished relatively easily and

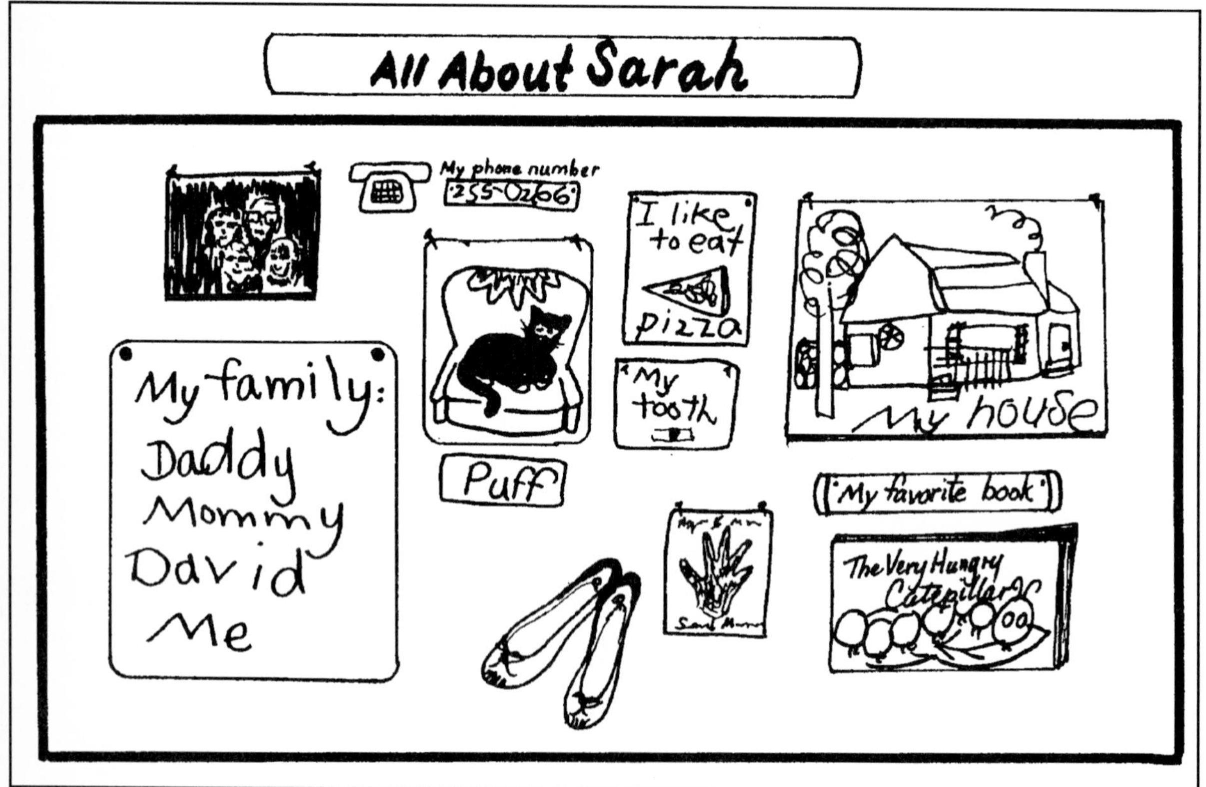

Figure 5.9 All About Me—Sarah—Thematic Center

simply. Having writing materials as integral parts of centers encourages children to incorporate writing into their activities. For example, sheets or pads of paper may be placed in the following:

- **The Dramatic Play or Housekeeping Center**—near the telephone so that children can record telephone messages or attached to the refrigerator in the play kitchen so that children can jot down grocery lists or things to do (just like at home!)
- **The Math Center**—for recording the number of items counted, graphing the number of colored jelly beans, or illustrating number stories or word problems
- **The Construction or Block Center**—so that children may label their buildings and creations and show ownership (see Figure 5.10)
- **The Science Center**—for recording observations and making illustrations

Reading materials can be placed in the center as well—including books, magazines, poetry, and an assortment of environmental print. For example, let's assume that the focus of the Math Center is the concept of time (sequencing events, days of the week, months of the year, the calendar, and duration—for example, how long is a minute? an hour?). Besides such manipulative materials as clocks, timers, and objects or pictures to sequence, there may be books on this topic, calendars, schedules, and the *TV Guide*. Specific books that might be included are:

The Very Hungry Caterpillar by Eric Carle
Cookie's Week by Cindy Ward
Chicken Soup with Rice by Maurice Sendak
The Scarecrow Clock by George Mendoze
The Grouchy Ladybug by Eric Carle
Learn to Tell the Time with the Munch Bunch by R. Giles
The True Book of Time by F. Ziner and E. Thompson

A mixture of fiction, nonfiction, and environmental print materials shows children how reading is related to the real world and to the classroom curriculum.

As an illustration of how literacy can be addressed in learning centers, let's look at the reading and writing possibilities in a center modeled after a fast-food restaurant. For reading, there would be a sign for the restaurant and logos on the sign, on workers' clothing, and on any preprinted materials or packaging. Menus of varying sizes and types (those exhibited on walls, regular-sized, and takeout) and brochures describing the restaurant, informing customers how many hamburgers have been sold, and advertising new products make excellent reading sources as well. Children could practice writing orders, making change, and writing receipts. The cooks could prepare grocery lists and create new recipes. Maps could show the locations of other restaurants in the chain. A suggestion box could be placed in a visible location for the customers to offer advice and suggestions.

Evaluation and Learning Centers

As stated in Chapter 4, teachers assess and evaluate their children throughout the entire day, across the entire curriculum. When children are busily engaged in centers, teachers may want to continue their observations, anecdotal records, and conferring with students. The suggestions provided in Chapter 4 are applicable here. Teachers need to be prepared with record-keeping devices—such as Post-its or index cards—and to be alert to observational possibilities. Teachers may want to observe and record children's preferred learning center, their interactions with others in the center, and their organizational behaviors. By constantly observing and interacting with children, teachers continue to develop a literacy profile of their students.

MATERIALS IN THE CLASSROOM

Since one goal of a whole language classroom is to provide a balanced reading program (one in which children are read to, are read with, and have the time and opportunity to read independently), it is necessary to provide a variety of different types of resources and materials. It

Figure 5.10 Child's Label for Construction Center

Can you read this kindergartner's message? After a great deal of time and effort on his construction project, this young boy got some paper and a magic marker and busily wrote this message, which he attached to his creation.

THE ULTMT GRL CTR AZ RADT

In conventional spelling, his message says, "The ultimate girl catcher is ready." When asked how it worked, he stated that it's simple, "All you do is wait for a girl to go by and put it around her neck. She's caught!"

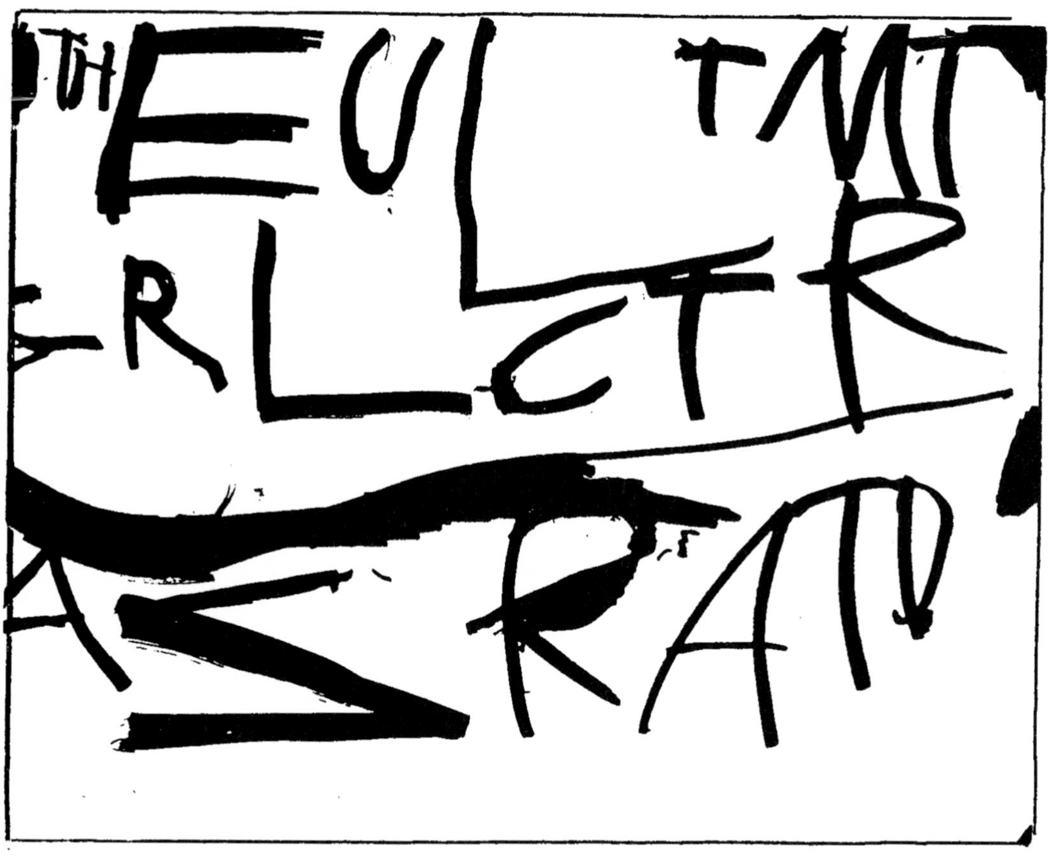

should be remembered, however, that in the past published materials have commonly been treated as if they themselves were the curriculum. Whole language is a philosophy and is not synonymous with particular resources, although many publishers would have teachers believe so. It has become tempting to believe that by switching from graded readers and workbooks and substituting more literature, whole language will result. Teachers need to be empowered to select their own materials, using their students as curricular informants, that is, using what they know about their students along with what they know about their curriculum and children's learning to make informed decisions. Selecting materials for teachers is somewhat antithetical to a whole language philosophy. Thus teachers must have a knowledge of the types of materials available, where these may be obtained, and how they can be used.

Having a variety of reading and writing materials in the classroom encourages and motivates children to read and write for a variety of purposes. The materials selected also play a key role in modeling the purposes of reading and writing. Teachers' choices also affect how often children read and write, their attitudes toward reading and writing, and even the quality of their reading and writing (Rhodes and Dudley-Marling, 1988).

Rhodes and Dudley-Marling (1988) suggest that teachers consider several questions as they select materials:

1. Are the materials representative of real communication; that is, are they materials that communicate ideas, stories, or information as opposed to teaching skills?
2. Is natural language used?
3. Do the materials have any relevancy to the students' own lives and experiences?
4. Can divergent responses to the materials be obtained?
5. What information about the real world is learned from the materials?
6. Do the materials represent print that is used outside the classroom?
7. Are the materials predictable in nature?

Mooney (1988) also presents some criteria for teachers to consider when choosing books for the classroom:

1. Do the materials have charm, magic, impact, and appeal? (Do they have the power to encourage the reader to reread?)
2. Are the ideas within the materials worthwhile? (Do they merit readers' time in getting the message?)
3. Are the shapes and the structures appropriate for the particular materials?
4. Is the language used effective?
5. Are the materials authentic?

Decisions involving instructional matters are not prescribed by published materials but are assumed by the teacher and adapted, adjusted, refined, and formed by the students and the teacher using an abundance of materials. Instructional materials should consist of whole, meaningful texts, not of isolated exercises on language fragments or paraphrased text. Having the responsibility for choosing materials may at first seem overwhelming, but resources are available to provide teachers with assistance in choosing books. Textbooks on children's literature written for university courses (by such authors as Charlotte Huck, Bernice Cullinan, and John Stewig) are excellent for gaining a background on literature genres and for specific titles and suggested grade levels. Professional journals, such as *The Reading Teacher, Language Arts, The New Advocate,* and *Book Links* review children's books, as do many newspapers. Published anthologies, such as those written by Jim Trelease and Beverly Kobrin, are likewise good sources of children's literature. Newsletters, such as *The Yellow Brick Road,* discuss children's books and even provide suggestions for activities to accompany the books.

Human resources should not be forgotten. In addition to university professors, librarians (both school and public) are quite knowledgeable about children's books and can suggest books that children enjoy and that have relevance to certain curricular topics. Children's bookstores are gaining in popularity, and these can be checked for additional suggestions.

Many publishers are making concerted efforts to provide teachers with excellent literature for classroom use. Some publishers offer packaged sets of quality literature, and these may be grouped by levels to help teachers determine appropriate selections for their students.

In times of budget constraints, teachers may have to be creative as well as economical when trying to obtain materials. When money is available, some states, such as New York, permit teachers to purchase children's literature with textbook and workbook monies. Teachers should check to see whether their own states permit this. Children and parents may donate books they no longer use, but it is best to check whether school districts have a policy for accepting gift books. Book clubs have special offers for teachers whereby teachers receive bonus points when their students purchase books. These may be exchanged for Big Books, class sets of books, reference books, or individual titles. Schools may sponsor book fairs, and a percentage of the profits earned by the school may be taken in books rather than in cash. Of course, the school librarian can supply books depending on the size of the school collection.

When considering books for the classroom, teachers should obtain a variety and a balance of literature. There should be books of all kinds for reading to children; for reading with children in shared book experiences, guided reading groups, and literature workshops; and for children to read by themselves. Books should be representative of different genres (both fiction and nonfiction) and reflect different interests and reading abilities. In addition to a variety of books, teachers should include:

- Big Books (books with enlarged texts)
- Predictable books (see following discussion)
- Cards or posters with poems and rhymes
- Children's newspapers
- Children's magazines
- Children's own published books
- Skinny books (books made from pulled-apart anthologies and the better selections from basal readers)
- Games
- Read-along book and tape sets
- Songs
- Wordless books

Predictable Books

Good literature uses language and experiences that are familiar to children. Familiar language and experiences enable children to predict what is on the page in terms of the language used and the meaning of the story. Books are predictable when they allow children to predict both quickly and easily the author's message and how the author is going to present this message.

There are several reasons for using predictable literature. Since children arrive at school quite eager to read, predictable literature provides them with the experience of real literature and makes them feel like real readers. Predictability is particularly important in choosing materials for emergent readers, for it allows them to use all three cueing systems (semantic, syntactic, and graphophonic). Predictable materials use rich language, facilitate the development of sight vocabulary, and give children the opportunity to predict and confirm what they are listening to or reading. Predictable materials aid children in reading for meaning and are highly motivational. Because of the nature of the materials, predictable books also provide a framework for children's writing since they are excellent models and can be used as springboards for innovating on text.

Sources of predictable literature include books, songs, poems, rhymes, and finger plays. The following are characteristics of predictability that the teacher can look for when choosing predictable materials:

1. **Match between the content in the text and the reader's background knowledge and experiences.** Such authors as Judy Blume, Patricia Reilly Giff, and Beverly Cleary write books that have characters and events with which the children can identify.
2. **Rhythmical, repetitive, or cumulative patterns.** The author repeats words, phrases, sentences, or themes.
   - **Rhythmical.** *Drummer Hoff, I Can't Said the Ant,* and *"Quack!" Said the Billy-Goat*
   - **Repetitive.** *The Important Book, Greedy Cat,* and *The Fat Cat*
   - **Cumulative.** *The Great Big Enormous Turnip, If You Give a Mouse a Cookie,* and *The Napping House*
3. **Familiar sequences.** Numbers, alphabet, days, months, colors, seasons
   - *Chicken Soup with Rice* by Maurice Sendak
4. **Familiar stories or story lines.**
   - "The Three Little Pigs"
5. **Good match between the text and the illustrations.**
   - *Brown Bear, Brown Bear, What Do You See?* by Bill Martin, Jr.
   - *Mrs. Wishy Washy* by Joy Cowley
6. **Series books.**
   - Berenstain Bears books
   - The *George and Martha* books
   - *Frog and Toad* books

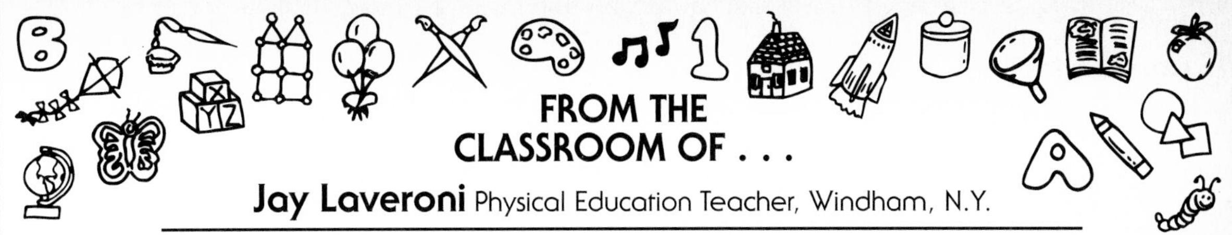

FROM THE CLASSROOM OF . . .

Jay Laveroni Physical Education Teacher, Windham, N.Y.

We're Going on a Bear Hunt

Jay Laveroni, a physical education teacher, liked to incorporate many cross-curricular activities into his physical education program. A favorite of his, and his students, is going on a Bear Hunt. Prior to the activity, he informed his kindergarten students that they were going to turn the gym into a book. He gathered the children into a circle and read the book, *We're Going on a Bear Hunt,* retold by Michael Rosen and illustrated by Helen Oxenbury. He encouraged prediction, visualization, and echo reading as he read the story.

After the reading of the story, he pointed out various stations around the gym, which would represent the areas the children in the story visited on their bear hunt, e.g., grass, river, mud, forest, snowstorm, cave, front door, and bedroom. He had some gym equipment available for the children to use to represent the places in the story. For example, the children placed cones in a row to create a forest, used jumpropes for the grass, and gym mats to make a cave. The children also brainstormed appropriate actions to use as they went through the grass, mud, river, cave, etc.

Once the logistics were planned and the story settings set up, Jay reread the story as the children acted it out. As they revisited the story, they delighted in the sploshing through the river, stumbling through the forest, and racing to escape from the bear!

Not only did the children get to enjoy a wonderful story, they were given the opportunity to playfully reenact the story. In his physical education class, Jay was able to integrate drama, sequencing, problem-solving, following directions, cooperative learning, and movement. The children were given the opportunity to interpret such delightful language as *squelch, squerch, swashy, splosh, oozy,* and *goggly.* Although this reenactment took place in the gym, it can be adapted to the classroom setting, using ordinary classroom materials as blocks, room dividers, and rugs, or can be done as a flannel board activity once the children have made the flannel board characters and settings. Older children may locate other examples of playful language in other pieces of literature, which can be acted out, made into new stories, placed on wall charts, or can serve as models for their own writing.

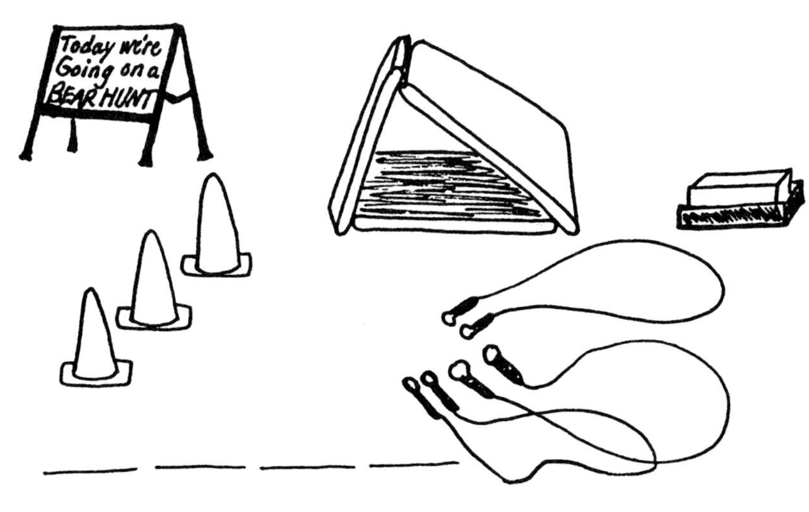

7. **Guessing Books.**
    - *Choose Your Own Adventure* books
    - *Encyclopedia Brown* series
    - *Q Is for Duck: An Alphabet Guessing Game*

(Rhodes, 1981; Bridge, Winograd, and Haley, 1983)

For a more complete listing, see Appendix A.

Predictable books can create positive feelings about reading. They foster fluency and help students overcome the habit of sounding out all the words. They are particularly beneficial for children whose oral language is nonstandard or delayed. Predictable materials are excellent for beginning implementation of an integrated language arts curriculum.

More Structured Materials

Teachers initially may need the support of more structured materials when moving from traditional programs into whole language. Again, publishers have made available such supportive materials, for example, *Journeys* (Ginn-Canada), *Bridges* (Scholastic), *Bookshelf* (Scholastic), *Impressions* (Holt, Rinehart and Winston). These are intended to provide teachers with help in their literacy program but are not to be used like a traditional basal program. Teachers are encouraged to use their professional judgment, to be flexible, and to pick and choose from the suggestions provided.

PLANNING FOR INSTRUCTION

Teacher planning is vital to the successful implementation of a whole language classroom. Both long- and short-term planning should be considered. Long-term planning will take a look at where the children presently are, what they are capable of doing, the goals for the children and how they will be achieved, the content to be covered, the resources used, and the ongoing assessment and evaluation that will occur (Davidson, 1990). One effective way of planning long term is to use a web or semantic map, as in thematic instruction, which is discussed in Chapter 9.

Short-term planning includes the schedule for the week, the content that will be covered, and the resources that will be used. There are numerous teaching styles, and even within traditional, transitional, or whole language classrooms, teachers plan instruction in many different ways. One has only to look at an educational supply catalog to see dozens of prepared planbooks for teachers. Traditionally, an elementary classroom planbook has five 2-inch squares in which to plan each day's activities. These squares are intended to provide equal space for reading, language arts, science, math, and social studies. With the movement to integrate subjects, many planbook publishers eliminated the boxes and converted to a morning/afternoon format. Since whole language teachers allot time differently, some find it easier to design their own planbook pages. See Figure 5.11 for samples of teachers' plans.

Teachers divide their days into longer blocks of time during which it is possible to integrate the curriculum. This freeing up of scheduled time allows children to practice reading and writing throughout the day, across the curriculum. It removes the artificial barriers between curricular areas and allows one instructional objective to flow naturally into another area of the curriculum. For example, Baswill and Whitman, teachers of grades 1 and 2 (1986), divide their day into large blocks of time: Shared Language, Personal Reading, Science/Social Studies, Writing, Independent Practice (Learning Center Time), Physical Education/Music, and Mathematics. Other examples of how teachers divide their school day can be seen in Figure 5.12. Suggested time allotments for the various elements present in whole language classrooms are offered in Figure 5.13. These should be helpful for allocating time when organizing the school day.

Teachers also use such management tools as schedule or agenda boards. A schedule board shows blocks of time with choices of activities. Children are to choose or are assigned certain activities during that time frame. Available activities may include going to the overhead projector and reading stories or poems on transparencies, working in the Art or Cooking Center, going to the Listening Center, reading the print on walls or books from their book boxes, writing, or working with the teacher. Teachers devise simple symbols or phrases to indicate the activities, such as a picture of a child with earphones for the Listening Center, an easel for the

Figure 5.11A Samples of Teachers' Plan Books

Traditional Plan Book

Teacher: Grade: Week of

	Subject:	Subject:	Subject:	Subject:	Subject:	Subject:
Monday						
Tuesday						
Wednesday						
Thursday						
Friday						

Art Center, and the letter *T* for working with the teacher. The activities are intended to be flexible and changeable, so the symbols are constructed so that they can be moved around (using magnetic strips, Velcro, or thumbtacks). Making a range of activities available to children enables them to develop initiative, responsibility, and the ability to cooperate with others. By having the children purposefully engaged, the teacher can work individually with certain children or group some children for help in a specific area. This time also permits teachers to do Running Records, conduct conferences, and observe children.

One function of a planbook, from an administrative perspective, is to provide plans for substitute teachers in the event of emergencies or teacher illness. An effective way to prepare for such days is to have a folder or large envelope with an overview of a typical day, a class list, and the class routines as well as several possible activities from which a substitute can select. Included in this file should be several new books, a list of songs and games the students know, a possible art activity, and a note about children with special needs or concerns.

Teacher planning is essential for successful implementation of an effective and balanced classroom program. Teachers must consider their long-term goals, their short-term objectives, and their daily planning. When children assume responsibility for their own learning, they will be aware of the structure of the in-

Figure 5.11B Samples of Teachers' Plan Books (cont.)

Daily Opening Routine:
Greet each child as they arrive. They take pencils and crayons to their seats. Open with Pledge to the Flag. Assign daily class leaders (2)(BELOW). They wear Leader Badges and deliver attendance list, any messages, etc. Each table has a leader marked by a ✱(to get materials, assist with snack, attendance, etc.

Week of 7-11 : #6 Month October

	Daily Attendance: List absentees and ✓ beside when excuse is sent.	DAILY LEADERS and SPECIAL AUTHORS:	Shared Books:
MONDAY	Butterfly hatching cont. In journals illustrate cocoons. OUT: none	(L) Mikhail + Susan; Author's chair: Angie, Melissa; Poem/fingerplay: Teddy Bear, Teddy Bear	Old favorite: The Three Bears; Act Out; New: Ask Mr. Bear
TUESDAY	Butterflies hatch? TU or WED; examine with hand lens - record observations on log; OUT: none	(L) Amy + Monique; Author's Chair: Jonathon, Chris; Poem/fingerplay: Wheels on the Bus	Old favorite: Berenstein Bears Bread and Honey: Ask; New: Teddy Bears Moving Day
WEDNESDAY	Write exp. chart story for hatching butterflies; OUT: Jonathon ✓	(L) Ashley + Laura; Author's Chair: Robert, Tim; Poem/fingerplay: Bear in my ear…	Old favorite: Brown Bear, Brown Bear; New: The Winter Bear; Bobby Bear's Red Raft
THURSDAY	✱ Emergency bus practice drill 9:15 am; OUT: Jonathon ✓	(L) Matt + Angie; Author's chair: Douglas, Heather; Poem/fingerplay:	Old favorite: Beady Bear; New: Bear Mouse; Blueberries for Sal
FRIDAY	Sharing sheets home about Patterns; out: none	(L) Heather + Robert; Author's Chair: Lauren, Brian; ✱Read to BEARS; Poem/fingerplay: Teddy Bear Picnic Song	Old favorite: A Bargain for Frances; Little Bear: Minarik; New: The Bear's Water Picnic

Buses dismiss daily at 11:25

SNACK TIME at aprox. 10am daily TABLE LEADERS ASSIST

Community Meeting Time: To begin each daily session…
On the RUG ~ Ask class leaders if they have a story to share. Use Author's Chair. Discuss CALENDAR and WEATHER. Discuss daily plans, theme in progress, do poetry, songs, and finger plays. End with a SHARED BOOK.

Activities and Centers:		
Math: Stringing Beads in 10's; Bouncing ball around a circle	Make paper bag puppets of 3 Bears; Make banana bread for FRIDAY	Monday - Letters home about Bear Picnic Friday: all children bring in own bears.
Song: Teddy Bears Picnic; TUESDAY 10:35-11:15 MUSIC (B); Make butter - shake cream in jar	Art: Cut and glue: The Big Bus w/Button Wheels; Math: Graph our bears Small - Med - Large	**Theme for the Week(s):**
Paint butterfly "blobs" fold for symmetry; Wednesday: Teacher With teacher aide Library 10:35-11:15	Create "Window Book" for Brown Bear "I look out the window and what do I see?" "I see a ___ looking at ME!"	**Bears** and butterflies
THURSDAY 10:35-11:15 P.E. (K); Investigate BUGs with handlens	Math: count and sort beans; Art: Bean mosaics; Science: plant each type of bean	Amy's new kitten to Visit
Parade with Bears; Parent Visitation Day; Mrs. O'Donnell	Illustrate our Bear Parade + Picnic; Blowing bubbles	Picnic day - in or out? weather; - honey sandwiches w P.B. + butter; - milk; - apples; ✱ Bubble Gum

Figure 5.12A Daily Schedules

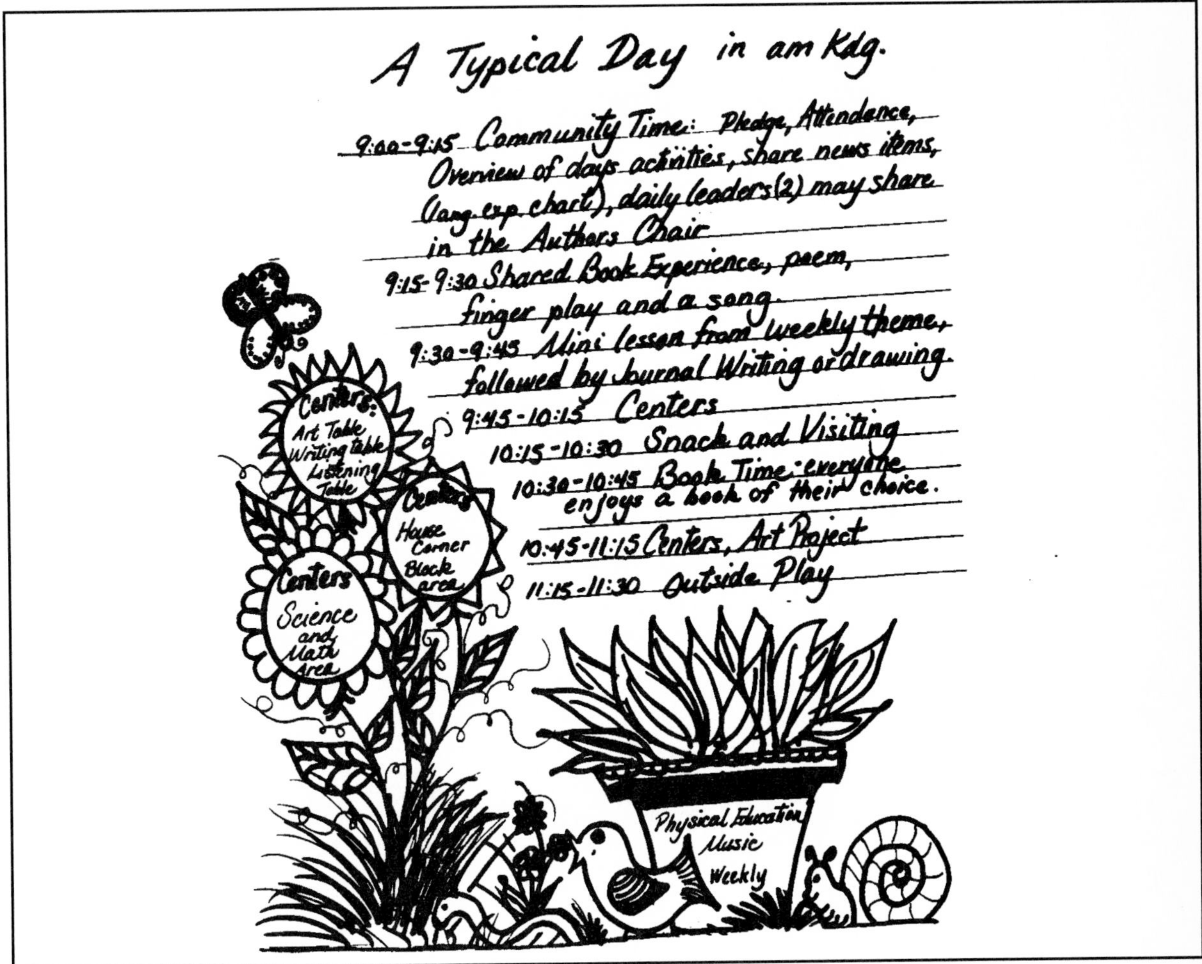

structional program, and the daily routines can run smoothly even when the teacher is absent. However, it is still necessary to have alternate plans and a description of the classroom program for substitute teachers. In educational circles, it has been joked that some teachers have their plan books laminated because they conduct the same activities at the same time each year. This cannot occur in the type of classroom that this book is espousing. Teachers and children work together as colearners, as coplanners. Each class is unique and must be respected as such. Although planning is integral to whole language, it is flexible and mindful of the strengths, needs, and interests of the children who reside there.

A Typical Day in am Kdg.
9:00-9:15 Community Time: Pledge, Attendance,
Overview of days activities, share news items,
(lang. exp. chart), daily leaders (2) may share
in the Authors Chair
9:15-9:30 Shared Book Experience, poem,
finger play and a song.
9:30-9:45 Mini lesson from weekly theme,
followed by Journal Writing or drawing.
9:45-10:15 Centers
10:15-10:30 Snack and Visiting
10:30-10:45 Book Time: everyone
enjoys a book of their choice.
10:45-11:15 Centers, Art Project
11:15-11:30 Outside Play
Centers:
Art Table
Writing table
Listening Table
Centers
House Corner
Block area
Centers
Science and Math Area
Physical Education
Music
Weekly

THE CHANGING TEACHER'S ROLE

Traditionally, teachers do most of the talking, most of the instructing, most of the decision making, and most of the evaluating in the classroom. Teachers instruct, or teach a lesson; then students are expected to demonstrate mastery by independently completing workbook pages or skill/comprehension sheets. The teacher's role is to correct the work or, in fact, to find all the errors. The teacher is essentially a critic.

Contrary to this perception of the teacher's role is an evolving awareness of the many roles teachers now play as they guide their students into literacy. No longer are teachers the only ones to dispense knowledge, to instruct, to eval-

Figure 5.12B Daily Schedules (cont.)

GRADE 1 SCHEDULE

8:45-9:10	Welcome Journal Writing Free Activity
9:10-10:00	Shared Language Session (including classroom routines, reading aloud, shared book, modeled writing, language experience, and *Math Their Way*)
10:00-10:30	Writing
10:30-11:00	Specials
11:00-12:30	Reading/Writing Workshop
12:30-1:30	Lunch
1:30-1:45	Reading Aloud
1:45-2:45	Activity Time Themes Writing Workshop
2:45-3:00	Closure for Day Dismissal

From Donna Jeffress
Mill Road School
Redhook, New York

Figure 5.12C Daily Schedules (cont.)

GRADE 2 SCHEDULE

8:45	Responsibilities (all management tasks, e.g., attendance, lunch count, obtaining materials are done by the children at this time). When these are taken care of, the next activity is then undertaken.
8:55-9:30	Writer's Workshop
9:30-10:30	Theme Study
10:30-11:00	Recess (The entire school recesses at this time so that cooperative planning can occur)
11:00-12:30	Literature Study (the number of groups vary, usually from 3 to 4 depending on the titles offered and the interests of the children)
12:30-1:30	Lunch/Recess
1:30-2:10	DEAR Time Read Aloud (usually a chapter book related to the theme)
2:10-2:50	Math
2:50-3:00	Evaluation Process (the teacher and the students meet to talk about what was learned, what they enjoyed, what they didn't care for, and how the day in general went) Dismissal

From Joan Westover
Marbletown Elementary School
Roundout Valley Central Schools

uate—and no longer are these their only roles. Teachers have expanded their roles, and they have shared the responsibility of learning with their students.

How many times has a teacher wondered why, despite a well-planned, well-taught lesson, children have not learned what was taught? The reasons are varied and involve more than the method or the materials used. Skill and drill are no competition for today's generation of children, who are brought up viewing the big screen. Children have an enormous store of knowledge when they enter school, and teachers must capitalize on this prior knowledge and expand and refine it through a meaningful curriculum.

Children learn at their own rate and when they are developmentally ready, so teachers must transfer the power of learning to the child, assume the role of facilitator, and assist the learning process. This has greater impact on

Figure 5.13 Suggested Time Allocations for the Elements of Whole Language

The Elements of Whole Language

Time Guidelines for K–2 gr.

Reading to Children	Daily 15–30 min.
Shared Book Experience	Daily 10–30 min.
Sustained Silent Reading	Daily 5–20 min.
Guided or Individualized Reading	Daily 30 min. per student or lit.group 3–5 times wk.
Language Experience	Daily 10–20 min.
Writing Process	Daily 10–40 min.
Modeled Writing	Daily 5–10 min.
Sharing Time	Daily 10–20 min.
Content Area Reading/ Writing & Themes	Daily 20–30 min.

and is far more meaningful to the learner than are the stand-up teaching techniques of the past. It is not easy to give up the power of being architect, director, and evaluator of all instruction. But teachers, as well as children, must become risk-takers.

In a whole language classroom, children are brought into the planning process. "This is the topic we are required to learn. What do we already know about this topic? What more would we like to find out? How shall we go about learning more?" With teacher guidance, children undertake responsibility for obtaining information, working cooperatively with others, and sharing or reporting on the new learning. The teacher ensures that the conditions for learning are in place and then permits the students to proceed. By involving students in planning, gathering materials, and finding information, teachers demonstrate that they value children's language and ideas.

Teachers have several critically important functions in promoting literacy and in furthering learning. These roles affect their students' attitudes and the quality of the classroom program. Teachers' encouragement and influence positively affect reading and writing. In addition to their role in facilitating the learning process, teachers demonstrate the advantages that membership in the "Literacy Club" has for the children. Teachers continually show children the importance of reading and writing, not only during language learning time but also across the curriculum and in real life.

Teachers also model aspects of the curriculum. They model effective reading and writing behaviors when they read and write in front of children; they model reading and writing strategies when they think aloud in front of the children. At any point when children demonstrate a need to be instructed, to be shown how to do something, teachers provide that instruction and modeling. Teachers in whole language classrooms do indeed provide direct instruction, and this goes for decoding and mechanics as well as meaning.

Teachers plan, observe, instruct, and facilitate. In many ways teachers are like coaches. Coaches have long-range plans for their teams, break these plans into shorter and more manageable time frames, show (or let others show) the players how to perform, allow practice time with relevant feedback, encourage, and then let players play the game for themselves as the coaches sit on the sidelines or in the dugout observing and providing guidance as needed. It is the players who play the game; it is the students who should be doing the reading and writing in real reading and writing situations. It is the teacher who facilitates the process, who guides, who listens to and observes the students. The teacher needs to provide meaningful experiences in which children can learn and discover and needs to assist them on this journey or in this discovery. In a whole language classroom, the teacher is an active participant in the discovery process.

One of the most important roles that whole language teachers play is that of a lifelong learner. The present-day knowledge explosion is not only a concern of the students but also confronts teachers with new research, new pedagogical implications, new demands from society, new developments in assessment and evaluation. Teachers must likewise avail themselves of the conditions of natural language learning as they immerse themselves in information about literacy (through professional journals, staff development, workshops, conferences, colleagues, their own students). They

Figure 5.14 The Physical Characteristics of a Whole Language Classroom

The following eight components and considerations are essential for an effective, productive classroom. The questions following each item will help an observer determine if the whole language philosophy is in use in the room.

1. Furniture Arrangement
   - ☐ Are tables used for seating or are desks arranged in groups?
   - ☐ Does the arrangement encourage interaction?
   - ☐ Does the floor plan allow smooth traffic flow?
   - ☐ Are there both public and private places, i.e., places for the whole class to meet and places where students work alone or in pairs?
2. Student Work
   - ☐ Is individuality respected in display pieces (or does every item look nearly the same)?
   - ☐ How recent is the student work?
   - ☐ Is an area available for students to display or hang their own creations?
3. Library Area
   - ☐ Are there adequate books and are they readily available to the students?
   - ☐ Are all types of books and magazines available (poetry, picture books, content area books, trade books, newspapers and periodicals)?
   - ☐ Are student-made books displayed?
4. Classroom Labels and Signs
   - ☐ Are classroom materials labeled in complete, meaningful sentences?
   - ☐ Did children make any of the signs?
   - ☐ Do signs facilitate order, learning, and independence?
5. Reading and Writing Center
   - ☐ Is an area of the classroom designed for reading and writing activities?
   - ☐ Is the area separated from other active or noisy areas?
   - ☐ Is the area inviting and appealing to students?
6. Audiovisual Materials
   - ☐ Is a Listening Center with individual headsets available for student use?
   - ☐ Are other audiovisual materials (equipment and filmstrips, videotapes, TV and VCR) available?
   - ☐ Have students been encouraged to create their own video or photo stories?
7. Dramatic Play Center
   - ☐ Is a puppet or dramatic play area available?
   - ☐ Is a flannel board available?
   - ☐ Are materials readily available to encourage creativity?
8. Record Keeping
   - ☐ Has the teacher made charts or checklists to keep track of student information and participation in the room?
   - ☐ Do students assume some responsibility for record keeping?
   - ☐ Is the format for public record keeping nonthreatening, nonjudgmental, and positive?

must see demonstrations of effective literacy teaching. They need to try things out (to practice), be allowed to take risks and make mistakes, and get positive and encouraging feedback. This can be achieved through a peer coaching model whereby teachers observe each other and discuss ways to improve instruction. Teachers continue to make a difference in the quality of school life, and as their roles expand and change, teachers will see greater differences in the quality of experiences that schools provide for students.

SUMMARY

This chapter looked at how the physical classroom design and the materials in a literacy program support children's learning. Critical to promoting literacy growth and development is the amount of print that surrounds children, the opportunities that exist for including language throughout the curriculum, and the kinds of materials that best further language learning. Figure 5.14 serves as a review of the components of a classroom rich in language as well as a checklist to guide in setting up such a classroom.

In order to provide an optimal learning environment, teachers must consider expanding and changing their roles and must engage in both long- and short-term planning. Throughout the chapter, the notion of involving children whenever possible was encouraged—in planning, in organizing, in managing, in instructing. Of equal importance was the teacher's being a colearner in the classroom. In this way, the students and the teacher grow, develop, and learn together. Each day offers new opportunities to keep learning and changing.

BIBLIOGRAPHY AND SUGGESTED REFERENCES

Baskwill, J., & Whitman, P. (1986). *Whole language sourcebook.* Ontario, Canada: Scholastic.

Bridge, C.; Winograd, P.; & Haley, D. (1983). Using predictable materials vs. preprimers to teach beginning sight words. *The Reading Teacher, 36,* 884–891.

Davidson, A. (1990). *Literacy 2000: Teachers' Resource.* Crystal Lake, Ill.: Rigby.

Jewell, M., & Zintz, M. (1990). *Learning to read naturally.* Dubuque, Iowa: Kendall/Hunt Publishing Company.

Kohia Teachers Centre. (1983). *Learning centers.* Auckland, New Zealand: Author.

Mooney, M. (1988). *Developing lifelong readers.* Katonah, N.Y.: Richard Owen Publishers.

Morrow, L. (1989). Designing the classroom to promote literacy development. In D. Strickland and L. Morrow (Eds.), *Emerging literacy: Young children learn to read and write,* pp. 135–146. Newark, Del.: International Reading Association.

Rhodes, L. (1981). I can read! Predictable books as resources for reading and writing instruction. *The Reading Teacher, 34,* 511–518.

Rhodes, L., & Dudley-Marling, C. (1988). *Readers and writers with a difference.* Portsmouth, N.H.: Heinemann.

Seefeldt, C., & Barbour, N. (1990). *Early childhood education: An introduction.* Columbus, Ohio: Merrill Publishing Company.

Strickland, D., & Morrow, L. (1988). Creating a print rich environment. *The Reading Teacher, 42,* 156–157.

Strickland, D., & Morrow, L. (1989). Environments rich in print promote literacy behavior during play. *The Reading Teacher, 43,* 178–179.

Sulzby, E.; Teale, W.; & Kamberelis, G. (1989). Emergent writing in the classroom: Home and school connections. In D. Strickland and L. Morrow (Eds.), *Emerging literacy: Young children learn to read and write,* pp. 63–79. Newark, Del.: International Reading Association.

CHILDREN'S LITERATURE CITED

Berenstain Bear books (series). New York: Random House.

Brown, M. W. (1949). *The important book.* New York: Harper and Row.

Cameron, P. (1981). *I can't, said the ant.* New York: Scholastic.

Carle, E. (1977). *The grouchy ladybug.* New York: Thomas Crowell.

Carle, E. (1987). *The very hungry caterpillar.* New York: Scholastic.

Causley, C. (1986). *"Quack!" said the billy-goat.* London: Walker Books.

Choose your own adventure books (series). New York: Bantam.

Cowley, J. (1980). *Mrs. Wishy-Washy.* San Diego: The Wright Group.

Cowley, J. (1988). *Greedy cat.* Katonah, N.Y.: Richard C. Owen.

Elting, M. (1980). *Q is for Duck: An alphabet guessing game.* Boston: Houghton Mifflin.

Emberley, B. (1967). *Drummer Hoff.* New York: Prentice Hall.

Frandsen, K. (1984). *I started school today.* Chicago: Children's Press.

Galdone, P. (1973). *The three little pigs.* New York: Seabury Press.

Giles, R. (1981). *Learn to tell time with the Munch Bunch.* Windemere, Fla.: Rourke Publishers.

Kent, J. (1971). *The fat cat.* New York: Scholastic.

Lobel, A. *Frog and Toad* books. New York: Harper and Row.

Marshall, J. *George and Martha* books. Boston: Houghton Mifflin.

Martin, B. (1970). *Brown bear, brown bear, what do you see?* New York: Holt, Rinehart, & Winston.

Numeroff, L. (1985). *If you give a mouse a cookie.* New York: Harper and Row.

Parrish, P. *Amelia Bedelia* books. New York: Harper and Row.

Sendak, M. (1986). *Chicken soup with rice.* New York: Scholastic.

Sobol, D. *Encyclopedia Brown* books. New York: Lodestar Books.

Tolstoy, A. (1968). *The great big enormous turnip.* New York: Franklin Watts.

Ward, C. (1988). *Cookie's week.* New York: G. P. Putnam's Sons.

Wood, A. (1984). *The napping house.* New York: Harcourt Brace Jovanovich.

Ziner, F., & Thompson, E. (1975). *The true book of time.* Chicago: Children's Press.

SUPPORTING EMERGENT LITERACY: IMPLEMENTATION (GRADES PRE-K–2)

HANDS

Hands can help
wash the car
or
draw a star.

Hands can help
pet the cat
or
put on a winter hat.

Hands help us
bake a pie
or
touch the sky.

Hands help us
feed the fishes
or
wash the dishes.

Hands can help us
when we draw
or
cut a tree with a saw.

Hands help us
mop the floor
or
open the door.

Hands can
clap or tickle
or
help us eat a pickle.

Hands can help us
button our shirt
or
clean up the dirt.

Hands can help us
with this book
to turn the pages
when we want
to look!

Jean Mumper's
Kindergarten Class
Wallkill, NY

Inspired by: *Hands* by Marcia Vaughan

OVERVIEW

Although whole language is based on a philosophy and is not a recipe or formula for teaching reading and writing or a prepackaged set of materials, various practices are associated with whole language classrooms. Of utmost importance is the provision of a risk-free, developmentally appropriate, print-rich environment. Within this environment can be seen such common practices as establishing routines, community meetings, language experience, reading to children, shared reading, guided reading, Sustained Silent Reading, and process writing. These are some of the practices that are explained throughout this chapter since they facilitate growth in children's reading and writing. Within each of the practices, opportunities for strategic learning will be highlighted, as the development of independent, strategic learners is a top priority for education today.

Questions to Ponder

1. How do community meetings enhance literacy development?
2. What kinds of reading experiences best meet the needs of emergent learners?
3. What is the role of phonics in the reading/writing program?
4. Can young children be expected to use the writing process?
5. How can emergent readers and writers become strategic learners?

CLASSROOM PRACTICES

A Big Book favorite of early childhood classrooms is Bill Martin's *Brown Bear, Brown Bear, What Do You See?* The classic line is, "Brown bear, brown bear, what do you see?" and this is followed by the bear's seeing a series of colorful animals: yellow duck, red bird, blue elephant. As each animal is revealed, the bear utters a repetitive line: "I see a _____ _____ looking at me," with the blanks filled in with an animal and its color. The book closes with a classroom of children "looking at me." If this scenario were moved into schools with real-life students, what would these children look like or what would they be doing? In a child-centered classroom, these children would be excited, involved, motivated, and self-directed. It is the intent of this chapter to focus on and to *look* at what we would *see*—the activities and practices that help children develop as readers and writers.

Establishing Routines

Children do not become independent learners without guidance or support from the classroom teacher. In whole language classrooms, teachers and children are involved in many productive activities simultaneously, and yet the classroom is not chaotic. Children are engaged in authentic reading and writing experiences and move about the classroom confidently and purposefully. This degree of control and responsibility does not happen without prior preparation. To manage a classroom effectively without constant direction and discipline, teachers have to establish routines early in the school year. To achieve a well-organized classroom in which teachers and students are able to find and organize materials with a minimum of stress, teachers spend a considerable amount of time at the beginning of the school year (approximately 4–6 weeks) establishing routines. Many of these routines are established cooperatively with the children, which contributes to the class's becoming a true community of learners.

Many community meetings (a whole-class gathering time) are devoted to teaching children how to find, care for, and put back materials. Rules for working, for using learning centers, and for choosing activities are discussed, cooperatively agreed on, and frequently written down for future reference by the children. Children are not inundated with these procedures but are introduced to them gradually. Practice time is provided with the teacher observing, demonstrating, and offering suggestions and advice as needed. Once children are familiar with the routines, they are given the responsibility for conducting themselves appropriately and for helping train newcomers to the classroom or classmates who need more time to learn.

Classroom rules should be worked out with the children. Acceptable behaviors should be brainstormed, with the most popular items discussed, confirmed or adjusted, and adopted as part of the class constitution. This constitution should contain rights and responsibilities of the teacher, the students, and others who may visit the class. The teacher may include some non-negotiable items, based on certain rules that are school or school district policy. See Figure 6.1 for several models of classroom rules. Children may brainstorm general guidelines for appropriate classroom behavior as is seen in the two kindergarten classrooms, or they may use a technique called a *"Y Chart."* With Y Charts, any area of concern can be explored collaboratively, using three categories which form a *Y—what it looks like, what it sounds like, and what it feels like* (Hill & Hancock, 1993). The activity can be modified to construct *T Charts,* which only use two categories—*what it looks like and what it sounds like.* The second graders in the example provided discussed *respect,* and how it related to their behavior both in and out of the classroom.

The use of different voice levels for different purposes should be demonstrated. Children should realize when it is appropriate to speak quietly or to talk more loudly. Children should speak softly to the person next to them when sharing, brainstorming, or seeking help. Noisier activities, such as blocks and housekeeping play, are acceptable at appropriate times. The use of written messages, which provides a way children can support one another, can be encouraged.

Ways of getting the children's attention should be established. Some teachers turn off the lights, design a clapping or finger-snapping rhythm, raise hands in a *V* sign, or sing a simple tune. Ways for children to get the teacher's attention should also be addressed. If the needs are along academic lines, children can be given "need help" slips that have places to write their names and their problems. A buddy system can be set up so that children can go to each other for help. When cooperative learning is established in the room, children soon know who is available for help in spelling, math, or reading.

Whereas establishing routines does not appear to be instructionally related, and there is a tendency to hasten this process to get to the heart of the curriculum, without procedures in place children will not learn as effectively as they could. Teachers will also be burdened with managerial tasks and will have to monitor be-

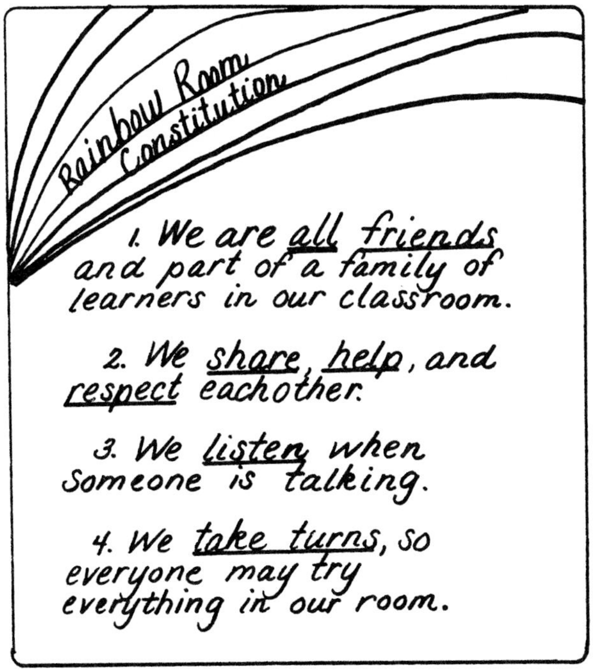

Rainbow Room Constitution

1. We are all friends and part of a family of learners in our classroom.

2. We share, help, and respect eachother.

3. We listen when Someone is talking.

4. We take turns, so everyone may try everything in our room.

Figure 6.1A

Figure 6.1B (cont.)

What can I do if someone does something I don't like?

I can talk to them.

If someone takes something from me, I can ask them to give it back.

I can share things.

I can ask them to stop.

I can't hurt them.

I can be their friend.

Mrs. Cyndi LaPierre's Kdg.
Windham, N.Y.

Figure 6.1C (cont.)

Good Cafeteria Manners

Look like	Sound like
• people standing politely to buy food	• listening to teachers
• garbage put in cans	• talking quietly to your friends
• raised hands	• saying "please" and "thank you"
• kids busy eating lunch	• waiting your turn to talk so no one shouts
• kids keeping hands and feet off others	• lots of whispering
• people being patient and waiting	• lunch boxes and trays quietly hitting the tables
• getting on line nicely	• using good language

Mrs. Constantindes' Second Grade

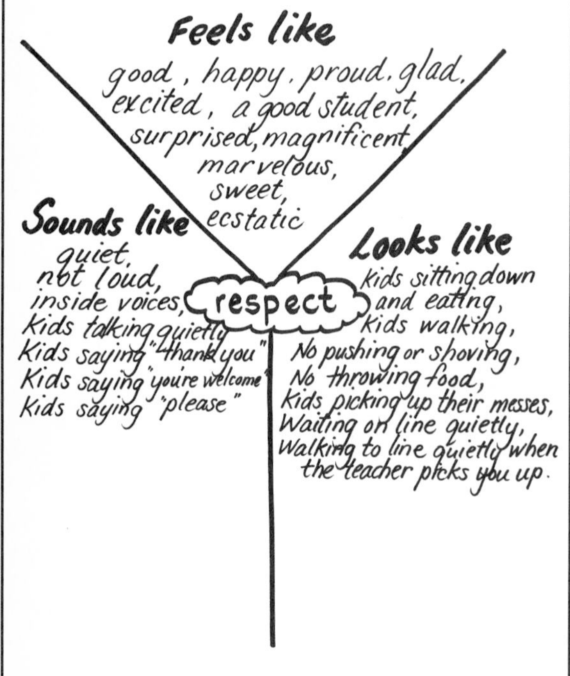

Figure 6.1D (cont.)

havior to a greater extent if routines are not in place. This ultimately takes time away from instruction and curriculum-related activities. Thus time must be devoted to ensuring that children can cope independently in various class activities and know how to utilize and care for the materials. For learning to occur, the classroom must have a sense of organization and management.

Community Meetings

One goal of whole language is to establish a community of learners. The word *community* implies a group of people living in the same place under agreed-on laws or rules. At the beginning of the school year, approximately 25–30 individuals are brought together in a room and expected to interact, grow, and learn. This experience is much more successful and rewarding when the individuals become a community. However, community building takes careful planning.

Each day begins with a community meeting or gathering time, generally on a rug or in a special area designated for whole-class meetings. Usually the children sit on the floor facing the teacher. This is a time to anticipate the day's events, share important happenings, renew acquaintance, mark milestones, and celebrate accomplishments. The community meeting begins the day, every day. It offers stability and predictability to the entire class. In today's transient and unstable culture, the school setting often provides the only stability some children have in their lives.

During the meeting time, songs are often sung, finger plays or rhymes are shared, books are read together, and the calendar, weather, and news events are discussed. If children have written something special, they may share it at this time. Photographs, drawings, lost teeth, or the birth of puppies, kittens, gerbils, or new siblings are enjoyed. It is a family time that pulls the class together and yet celebrates the children's individuality.

Often during the community meeting time, a teacher must take advantage of the teachable moment. If a child brings in something to share that sparks interest, this becomes a focus for class discussion and exploration. A child might bring in a special rock or colorful leaf, and this might spur investigations into rocks or leaves. Children may bring in favorite books that could be read or discussed. They may also bring in items that are related to what is currently being studied in the classroom, and the meeting may flow naturally into this particular curricular area.

A great deal of learning occurs during the community meeting time. Many curricular areas are integrated and incorporated into this time, which can last from 15 minutes to well over an hour:

- mathematics with the calendar, schedule of the day, counting
- science with the weather or sharing of environmental and scientific materials
- social studies with the news of the day or sharing of objects and experiences related to the curriculum
- language arts with the many opportunities to listen, speak, read, and write
- taking of the attendance

A great deal of language occurs during the community meeting time. Children listen to stories, read along during a shared book experience, sing songs, discuss events, record the weather and data for the calendar, write the news of the day. Even the taking of the attendance provides many learning opportunities for young learners. Children get to recognize and read their classmates' names, learn the letters of the alphabet in their and their friends' names, and do many playful language activities as rhyming, sorting names according to initial sounds, counting letters in names, and so on. Figure 6.2 is an example of an attendance board in a kindergarten classroom. At the beginning of the school year, the children's photographs are taken and placed alphabetically by first name in a pocket chart. Accompanying the pictures are name cards, which are initially placed in back of the picture. When the children enter into the classroom at the start of the school day, they place their name cards in front of their pictures. During community meeting time, the teacher and the children note who is absent, how many children are in attendance, whether the number of children present represent an odd or even number, and so forth.

Minilessons may be undertaken at this time as well. These could be reading related, or the teacher could model some facet of the writing process. The community meeting time provides

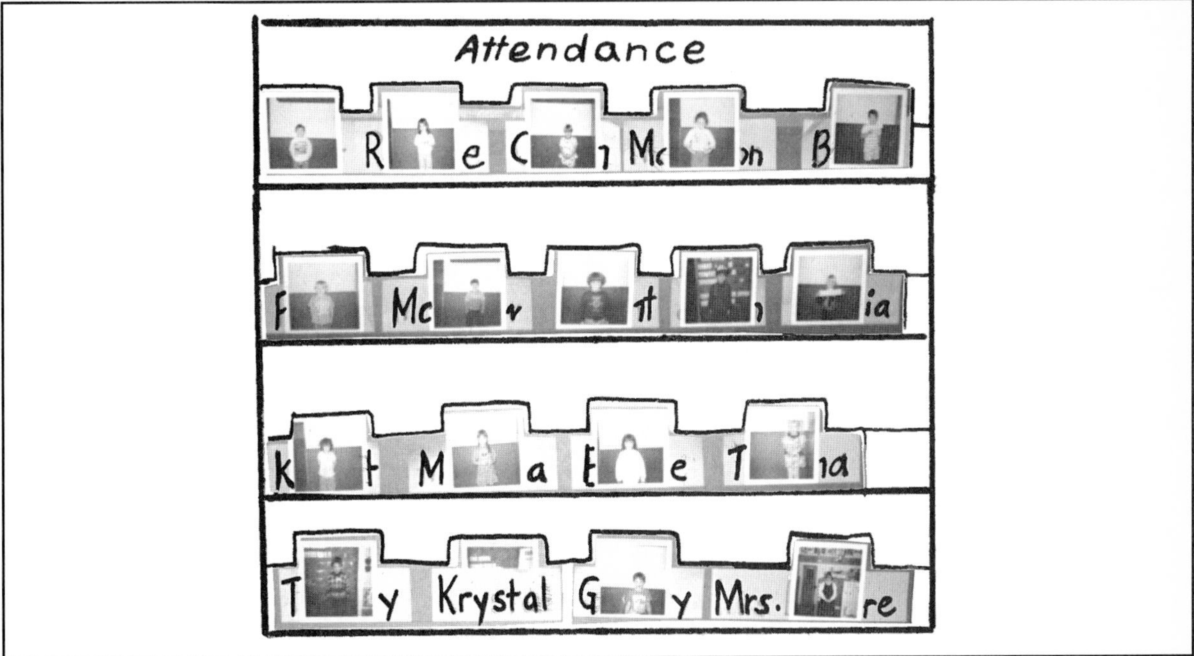

Figure 6.2

the teacher and the children with many opportunities to use language in meaningful and enjoyable ways; helps children develop positive self-esteem as their contributions are respected, shared, and acknowledged; and establishes a warm and pleasant atmosphere in which learning can occur. Although the time used for community meetings is relatively brief, the contributions these gatherings make further the development of a community of learners.

Language Experience

Language experience is an approach to teaching literacy that is based on the oral language generated by children during experiences that are either firsthand or vicarious. It is a method of teaching reading whereby children's writing is used for instructional purposes. This approach integrates the teaching of reading with all the other language arts as children listen, speak, record or have recorded, and read their personal experiences, ideas, and thoughts. Language experience uses the children's language as the reading source. As children see their speech written down, they begin to grasp the concept that the purpose of reading is communication. Thus, language experience builds on two elements of learning—experience and language.

This approach allows children to gain knowledge from the experience and becomes a means of building knowledge about the nature and functions of reading. A major benefit of this approach is its immediacy and its relevance to children because it draws on children's personal experiences, is written in the child's own language, and is highly predictable. Language experience grows out of natural, ongoing classroom activities. It fosters children's active participation in literacy activities and promotes a close contact between the teacher and the students. Children learn about the world and learn language simultaneously (Butler, 1988).

There are many advantages to making language experience a part of the whole language classroom. Because the reading material is based on the natural spoken language of children, children find this approach highly motivating and very satisfying. Children can perceive the relationship between the spoken and the printed word. Since the content of the printed text is obtained from the children, they bring meaning to that message and consequently know what the text has to say. Therefore children experience success, which enhances the development of positive self-concepts.

Language experience can be organized and implemented in several different ways: key words or "Very Own Words," dictation on a one-to-one basis, individually written stories, and group-dictated stories. Based on the work of Sylvia Ashton Warner, the concept of key words is frequently a part of the language experience approach in early childhood classrooms. This method is especially effective for second language learners.

Key words are personally selected by the student, written on an index card, and kept either on a key ring or stored in a small box. The teacher asks the students what word they would like to learn to read. Children tend to choose highly personal words and words that excite or delight them. Frequently children will choose their own names; the names of parents, caretakers, siblings, or friends; words pertaining to the holidays; or names of movie or television heroes. If children have difficulty choosing a word, they can be prompted by being asked about family members, animals, favorite foods, books, or television shows. After the students respond, the word is recorded on an index card. On the back of the card or on a separate sheet of paper, the students may draw a picture or give a sentence or two using the word. If the key ring method is chosen, the words are put on the ring and hung on a hook. A cover is made for the packet of key words with the child's name displayed on it (see Figure 6.3).

Whenever the child wants to add another word to his or her collection, or when the teacher is working on key words with individuals or a small group, the child retrieves the cards, recognizing and reading his or her own name and classmates' names. Children can use the words as a personal dictionary and can also proudly read their words to their classmates. Children should be given time to read and reread their words to themselves, their friends, and their teacher or other adults.

Words already on the ring should be reviewed before children get a new word. If the child is unable to read a word several days in a

Figure 6.3

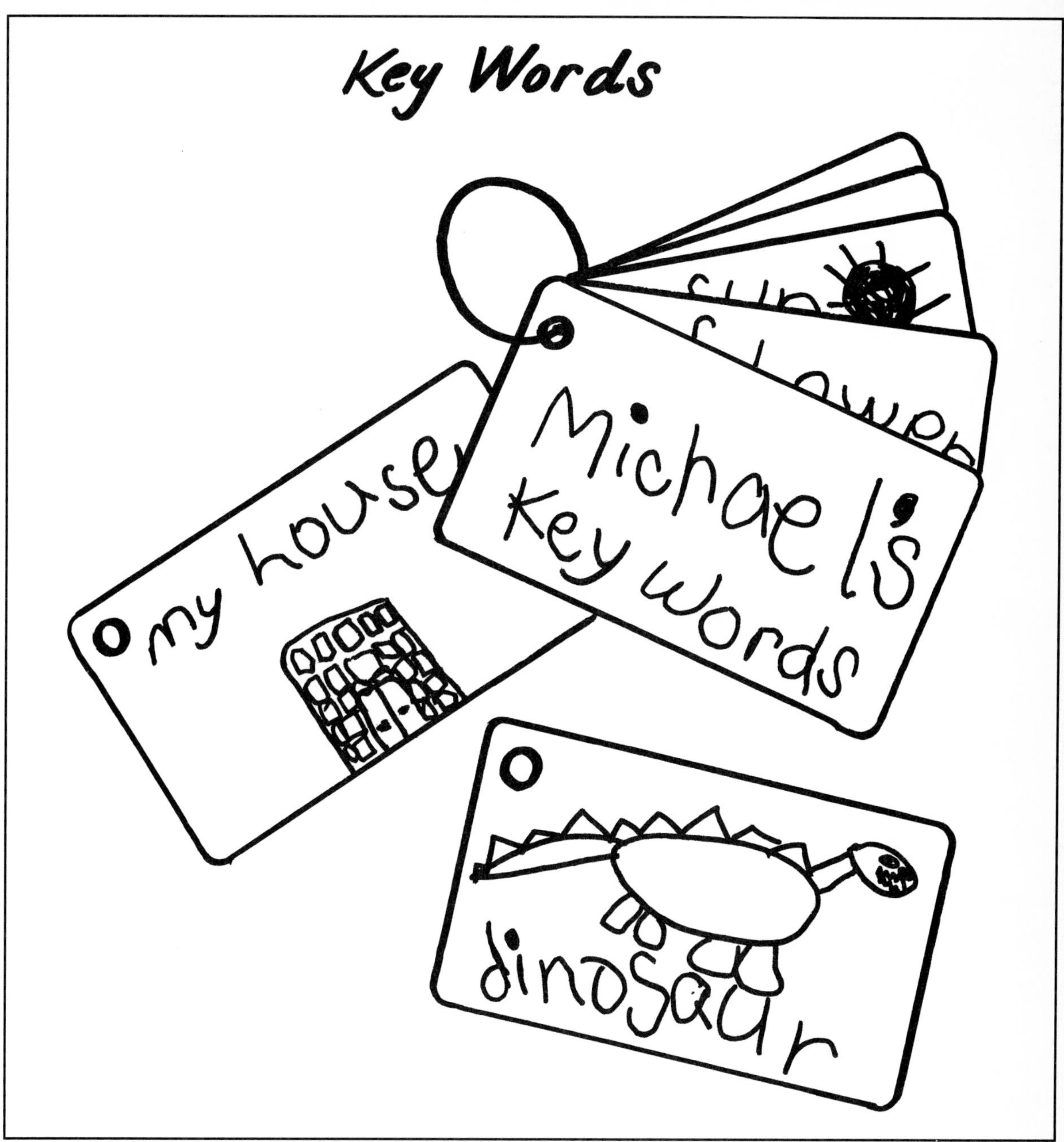

row, the child should be asked whether that word is really meaningful—and if it is a word the child really wants. If not, the word should be removed from the ring and replaced with a new word. Ownership of the word is of the utmost importance. Children feel great pride when they can read their own key words. Most teachers are surprised to find that even after a long school holiday, children remember all of their key words. It is recommended that the children's words accompany them from kindergarten to first grade and, if necessary, to second grade.

Teachers may also take dictation from the children as part of the language experience approach. These may be words to accompany a picture, a response to a book, or a journal entry.

The children's exact words should be written down since children are making connections between oral and written language. The teacher may then read the words back to the child, pointing to each word as she or he reads. On subsequent rereadings, the child reads along with the teacher. The trend today, however, is to let the child hold the pencil and write for her- or himself rather than rely on the teacher for the scribing.

The basic method of implementing language experience is the dictated or experience story. There are several steps to follow when writing experience stories with children (Hall, 1981; Jewell and Zintz, 1990; Butler, 1988b):

1. **Provide a stimulus or common experience.** The purpose of providing a stimulus or common experience is to generate language and capitalize on children's natural curiosity. The topics for discussion can be initiated by the teacher or by the children. Rich oral language can be stimulated by such items as live animals, rocks, pictures, collections, films, filmstrips, books, photographs, wordless books, or visitors. Items that generate a lot of talk are preferable. Oral language can also be stimulated by group activities or by such projects as field trips, cooking, or constructing things.

2. **Record the children's language.** Once the talking is completed, the children's actual language about the experience is recorded on chart paper or on transparencies for the overhead projector. It is important that the children's actual words be transcribed since children will now associate what they say with the printed words. If the child says "mouses" and *mice* is recorded, the child will read *mouses* for the printed word *mice*.

3. **Read the message or story.** The teacher initially reads the printed text, followed by several rereadings by the children. The teacher may use a pointer or point by hand to the words as the children read along. This procedure can be repeated for several days.

4. **Provide follow-up activities.** Involving children in follow-up work allows them to participate in many types of activities. The activities may focus on mechanics (such as capitalization and punctuation), on word identification, or on reading for fluency. Some follow-up activities that may be used include:

- **Oral cloze.** The story is read to the children with key words omitted. Children fill in the gaps.
- **Word hunt.** Children go to the experience story to find a word that
  - rhymes with *hand* (sand)
  - starts like *wall* (water)
  - means "does not sink" (float)
  - has two little words in it (sailboat)
- **Matching.** Word or phrase cards are made from words in the story. Children match the words or phrases.
- **Cut and match.** Children are given two copies of the story. They then cut one of them into sentence strips and match (or rearrange) the strips to reconstruct or match the intact text.
- **Word banks.** Children choose words of personal interest to put in their own word banks. The words may be kept on rings or stored in boxes. Children may occasionally do word-sorting activities, such as classifying words according to initial sounds, finding rhyming words, and looking for animal words. Other possibilities are naming words, action words, interesting words, science words, compound words, three-syllable words, and so on.
- **Reading the walls.** Language experience stories are sources for children to practice reading, alone or with a buddy.

Language experience is an approach to literacy that helps children grow naturally into reading and writing. Children are provided with many experiences and are encouraged to talk about them. Their comments are recorded on chart paper. Through language experience, children can make sense of their experiences and have a permanent record of them. Language experience helps make children aware of the conventions of print, the correct spelling of words, and the fact that printed text is both whole and meaningful. Samples of language experience stories are provided in Figures 6.4 and 6.5.

Interactive Writing

Another technique that involves oral discussion and collaborative writing is interactive writing. Interactive writing emphasizes both oral con-

Figure 6.4 Sample Language Experience Story—Group Story

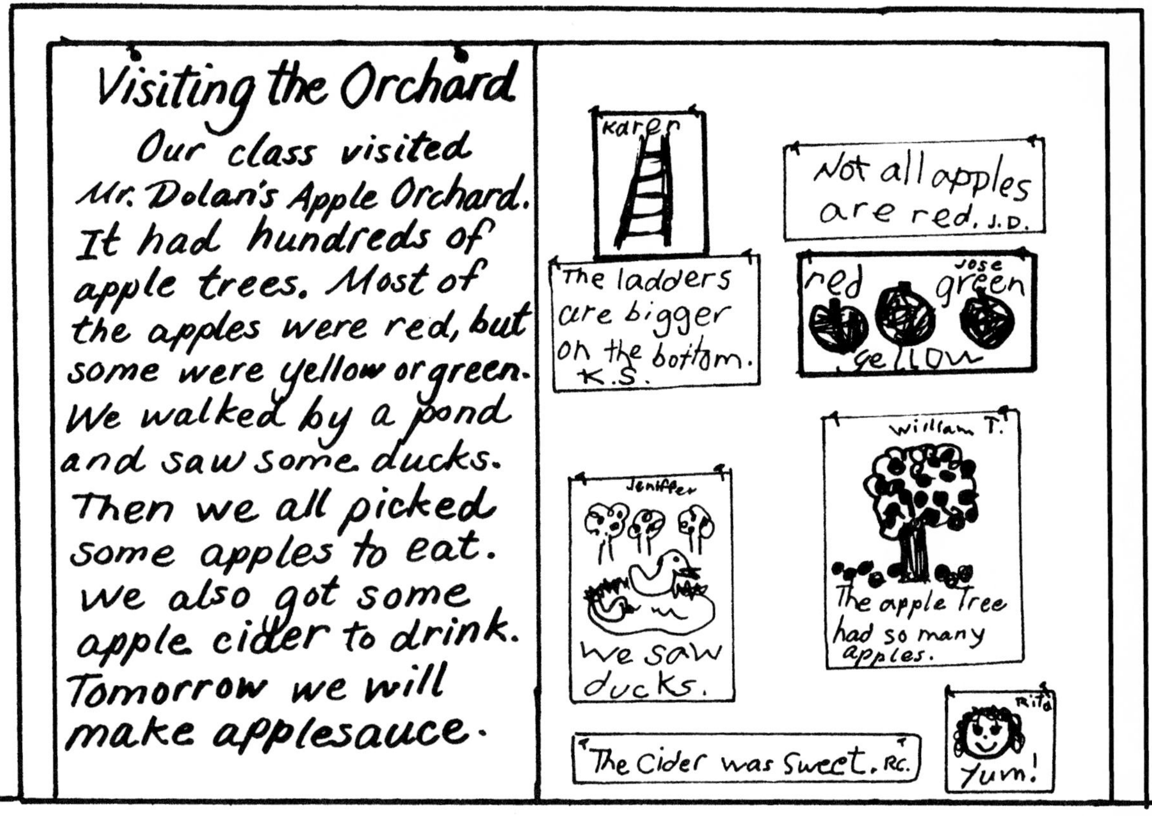

versation and the sharing of the mechanics of the writing task. It "is a dynamic process that involves teachers and children in: (1) negotiating the composition of text, either narrative or informational; (2) constructing words through analysis of sounds; (3) using the conventions of print; (4) reading and rereading texts; and (5) searching, checking, and confirming while reading and writing" (Pinnell and McCarrier, 1994, 161).

During an interactive writing session, the teacher and the students collaborate to construct a piece of written text. The stimulus for the written text can be a classroom experience or can result from the reading of a piece of children's literature. Prior to the writing, there are extensive discussions to determine the contents of the writing. Interactive writing can occur during the writing of the morning message, Daily News, a letter, a retelling, an innovation of a big book, part of a Reading Recovery session, and the like. In addition to the discussion, another key aspect of interactive writing is the sharing of the role of the scribe.

Unlike language experience where the teacher does the scribing, during interactive writing both the teacher and the students do the recording. The message can be written on chart paper if the entire class or a small group is involved in the activity, or it can be done on a single sheet of paper with only one child. As the message is negotiated, the children write down the parts of the text that they are capable of, with the teacher filling in the rest. For example, a kindergarten class was listing the reasons they go to school and a child stated, "We go to school to learn to write our name." The teacher then invited individual children to come up and write the message. Several children came up and wrote the words *we, go,* and *to* correctly.

Figure 6.5 Sample Language Experience Story—Individual Child's Story

Rosa's Pets

by Rosa Santiago

I have two mouses. One is named Tiny and one is named Grey. Grey is the big one. He is bigger 'cause he eats lots more than Tiny. Tiny hardly gets any food. But he can run faster. Sometimes he keeps me awake when he runs in the wheel.

When it came to writing the word *school,* a child wrote *skl.* The teacher validated the correct aspects of the word and then covered up the *k* with correction tape. She then wrote the letters *choo* and let the child write the final *l.* The process continued with the teacher and the students alternately writing the message until it was complete.

The benefits of interactive writing are many. As the children construct the message, they attend to the details of print and to letter-sound relationships. They constantly reread what is being written as the text is being negotiated, and when the writing is complete, they read it as a shared reading activity or independently. Interactive writing is an instructional strategy that shows children how written language works so that they can do it independently.

Reading to Children

"The Three Little Pigs," "Little Red Riding Hood," *Curious George, The Cat in the Hat, Make Way for Ducklings* . . . "Read it again! Read it again!" How many of you used these words when you were young children? Many of you had treasured childhood favorites that became companions, either at bedtime or some other special family reading time. Perhaps you can even remember details of these shared reading experiences—your father's laugh at a humorous antic in one of Bill Peet's books or Grandma's warmth as she read *Ira Sleeps Over.* Not only did these special times provide memorable experiences for you, but they helped you achieve in school as well. Research has shown that reading aloud to children improves their cognitive development and promotes an interest in reading and a love of books (Anderson, Hiebert, Scott, and Wilkinson, 1985). The United States Department of Education, in their publication *A Nation at Risk* (1987), stated that children were more successful in school if their parents or caretakers read to them on a regular basis, made plenty of books available, and encouraged the exploration of literature.

Many youngsters, like most people, come to school having heard and discussed stories—but many do not. Many have not had the pleasure of bedtime story reading with their parents. Many will not have favorites to share. Many have not had the opportunity to tell what happens next in a story. As stated earlier, when parents read to their preschoolers, generally their purpose is to share a special time together and to provide a warm, caring setting for reading books. However, the activity of reading and discussing books has many additional benefits. Reading to children:

- influences academic achievement
- familiarizes children with the language of books
- aids in story retelling and in developing a sense of story
- enhances language development
- increases vocabulary and adds to children's background knowledge

- provides information
- introduces a variety of genres, text structures, authors, and illustrators
- offers a model of good oral reading when teachers read aloud
- stimulates children's imaginations
- provides opportunities for children to hear stories they are unable to read by themselves
- provides models for writing and opportunities to learn how authors structure text
- fosters a love of and an enthusiasm for books and reading

(Strickland, 1987; Butler, 1988b; Trelease, 1989; Mason, Peterman, and Kerr, 1989; Cullinan, 1989; Davidson, 1990; Cullinan & Galda, 1994)

Jim Trelease, whose *Read-Aloud Handbook* has sold millions of copies throughout the world, states, "The benefits that come from reading aloud help the entire curriculum, especially since reading is the curriculum. The principal ingredient of all learning and teaching is language" (1989, 34). Exposing children to good literature on a regular basis enables reading habits to develop naturally and enthusiastically (Routman, 1988). Therefore one feature of a whole language classroom is for teachers to read to children as frequently as possible. *Becoming a Nation of Readers* proposes that there are no substitutes for teachers who read to their students. Reading aloud whets children's appetites for reading and models skillful oral reading. It is suggested that reading aloud continue throughout a child's schooling.

It should be noted that children should be exposed to all types of reading material, not just fiction. Children should be exposed to nonfiction, poetry, rhymes, jingles, plays, and songs as well. There should be a balance of genres because children need successful experiences with all types of text.

There are some general guidelines to use when reading aloud to children:

1. **Choose books and a focus for the reading.** Several features to consider when choosing books to read aloud are a well-developed story, humor, warmth, characters and situations that children can identify with, illustrations that support the text, and language that is rich and memorable. The books need to be varied, and there should be a balance of genres. A book may be chosen for a particular reason—because it is related to a theme, as an introduction to an author or illustrator, to have children experience a variety of genres—or for pure enjoyment.

The book should first be read by the teacher. It is suggested that teachers read books that they themselves enjoy, for it is difficult to give children the message that reading is pleasurable when a teacher is reading a book that she or he does not like.

2. **Read the book.** Initially the cover, title, illustrator, and possible story structure or genre should be discussed with the children. The children should also be asked to make predictions about the story or information to be read. The book could be related to other books the author has written or to books of a similar genre.

Teachers may discuss the type of text to be read, for example, identifying *It Could Be Worse* as a folktale or *The Reason for a Flower: Plants That Never Ever Bloom* as an information book. Teachers may also provide relevant background information. For example, before reading *The Reason for a Flower: Plants That Never Ever Bloom,* teachers may discuss flowering plants and why their flowers are essential. The discussion can be broadened to point out that although flowers are necessary for most plants to reproduce, not all plants bloom. By providing information on the genre and background knowledge, the teacher facilitates an understanding of the text. In addition, this helps develop an awareness of the various writing formats authors use (Mason et al., 1989).

The book should be read with expression. During the reading the teacher may provide relevant information to stress important points or exciting parts. At times, the teacher will stop to elaborate on a point the author is making. The children will also be checking their predictions and offering new ones. However, to avoid interrupting the flow of the story, there should not be too many pauses, questions, or explanations.

3. **Respond to the story.** After reading, there should be time for student comments and opinions. Students may ask questions to extend the story or relate the story or information to their own lives and experiences.

The book should then be placed in an accessible location—for example, the library corner—for future rereading or browsing. Books that are read aloud frequently become classroom favorites. For instance, *Stone Fox,* which was read aloud in a third-grade classroom, was subsequently read again by every member of the class.

Throughout the practice of reading aloud, teachers and children interact. Discussions are held prior to reading. During reading, teachers respond to their students' reactions and questions and elaborate on the story events. After the reading, the story may be reviewed, discussed, and related to personal experiences, and follow-up activities may be undertaken. Reading to children is a wonderful way for teachers to influence their students' reading achievement, support literacy development, and foster a love of reading.

Teachers sometimes find it difficult to remember what titles they have read to children, especially when teachers have two half-day kindergarten sessions and read the same titles year after year. Teachers also have favorites—books as well as genres—and may neglect some titles and types of books. For example, if teachers do not particularly enjoy science fiction, they may never or infrequently read science fiction to their students. In order to help teachers keep track of what was read and to provide a balanced reading diet, a Literature Genre Sheet can be kept. Teachers can use this sheet to list the titles and genres of specific books read.

Shared Book Experience or Shared Reading

Let's go back to that warm, comfortable environment in which parents and their offspring shared special times with books. Books were read and reread, and children were provided with rich literacy experiences even before they entered school. In order to help children continue to grow as readers and writers, the shared book experience was developed to help welcome children into the "Literacy Club" (Smith, 1988) in the school setting. The shared book experience is an approach to reading that is based on the bedtime reading experience. In shared reading, the teacher and the entire class or a group of children sit close to one another while sharing the reading and rereading of a variety of texts. It is a cooperative, interactive, nonthreatening, enjoyable learning experience.

Don Holdaway (1977) is credited with developing the shared book experience. He observed what occurred during bedtime reading and what good teachers do to construct meaning while they read. To facilitate the process, he introduced the concept of Big Books, which are books with enlarged text. Although Big Books are the preferred reading material for shared reading, any text may be used. It is the importance of the shared space that is significant, not the large print.

There are many reasons for the advantages of the shared book experience. Through this experience, children learn about reading. They learn what a book is, what a skilled reader does with text as it is read, story structure, the conventions and language of books, and that reading is a meaningful and pleasurable experience. Shared reading encourages active participation and involvement on the part of the children. All children participate with confidence in shared reading because they can reconstruct meaning through the predictable nature of the text, the illustrations, and the support of the teacher and other children. It is a supportive approach that respects children as contributing members of the community of learners.

Strategies and skills are taught in the context of real reading activities, not in isolation. Shared reading allows teachers to demonstrate reading strategies and print conventions. The texts provide models for writing and are sources for innovating on text. Shared reading provides opportunities for children to respond to the stories through writing, related reading, art, and drama. Through the variety of books available, shared reading gives children time to have fun with language. The shared book experience is a way of helping children learn about reading. It is an excellent means of introducing children to reading, for children learn to read by reading.

Procedures to follow when implementing shared reading include:

1. **Choose a book.** A book is chosen because it is enjoyable and memorable and will

help children become involved in reading and learning how to read. Books should be chosen for their language, their story line, and their potential to contribute to the children's literacy development. Publishers are producing a great number of Big Books to capitalize on the growing popularity of whole language. Therefore teachers should be wary. Just because books are big does not mean they are good. A book could be chosen for a specific purpose: to illustrate certain conventions, introduce an author or illustrator, for prediction, for enjoyment, or as a model for innovation of text. The story lines are well developed or the language is enchanting. Many publishers—including Rigby, the Wright Group, and Richard Owen—have books available for the shared reading experience. A complete listing of publishers and available materials is in the appendix.

2. **Set the stage.** An easel or some form of book holder is used for ease of handling Big Books. Teachers often use a pointer to touch the words as they are read and to call attention to key points in the text. The children gather around the teacher in front of the easel, usually sitting on the floor while the teacher sits on a low chair. The teacher then prepares the children for reading by discussing the cover, illustrations on the front and back covers, the author, the illustrator, and the probable theme. Children may be asked to make predictions regarding the story's content.

3. **Read the book.** The pace of the first reading is lively, and there are relatively few stops. Teachers may pause to have children confirm their prediction and make new ones. Usually teachers will point to each word as it is read (voice pointing). In this way children can make the connection between the spoken word and the written word.

4. **Reread the text.** Rereading the text is essential and gives children the opportunity to participate in the reading, recall the story, and observe reading strategies and language conventions. The more rereadings there are, the more confident the children will become.

5. **Make key teaching points.** Rereading and revisiting the text allow teachers to make key teaching points. It is preferred that teaching points not be made in the first reading in order to allow the children to enjoy the language and the story. Teachers may demonstrate print conventions during rereadings. These conventions include:

- front and back covers
- directionality (books are read from top to bottom and from left to right)
- the fact that print (the words) carries the message, not the pictures
- one-to-one correspondence between the spoken and written words
- letter-sound associations
- the fact that punctuation aids understanding
- spacing between words

Teachers may use masking devices, tools that use a sliding bar or a cut-out space to highlight a word or phrase. The text is highlighted by placing the mask over what is to be read and sliding the bar to reveal only what the teacher wishes to highlight. This enhances the development of sound-symbol relationships and helps build sight vocabularies. Instead of a mask, an overhead projector can be used, with portions of the text covered by cardboard strips. The cardboard is moved along, revealing the text underneath. Figure 6.6 provides an example of a masking device. Teachers may also place Post-its on words and have children predict the miss-

Figure 6.6 Masking Device

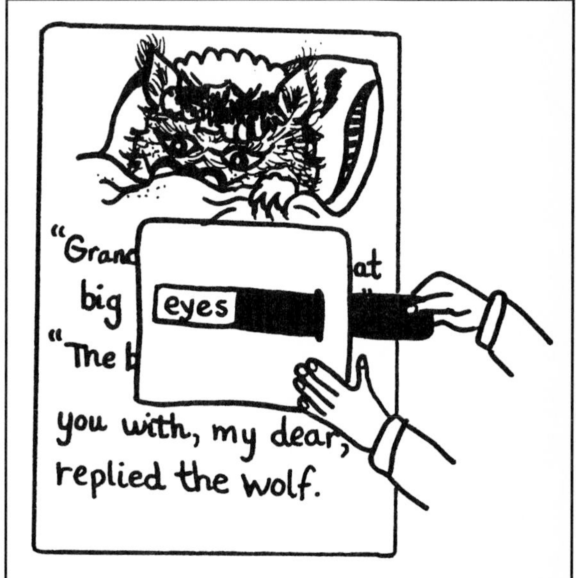

ing word based on the meaning of the text and even perhaps the initial letter.

Reading strategies may be addressed as well. Such reading strategies as the following can be the focus of rereading sessions (Butler, 1988a).

- discovering reading as a meaning-making process
- predicting and self-correcting using all the cueing systems (graphophonic, syntactic, and semantic)
- handling unknown words (skipping them or making a good guess and reading to the end of the sentence or phrase)
- reading fluently and with expression

6. **Respond to books with appropriate sharing by children.** Children should have many opportunities and many ways to respond to books and to extend the shared reading experience. If enlarged texts are used, smaller versions should be available as well so that children may be free to reread and enjoy the stories at any time. Children may also use the books as springboards and respond using art, drama, music, research, discussion, writing, retelling, and innovating on the text. Figure 6.7 shows the many possibilities for responding to Big Books. Some examples of these response modes applied to particular books are shown in Figure 6.8.

Even though Big Books are available from many publishers, it is not necessary that they be purchased. Big Books can be created by the children and the teacher as well. Children's language experiences can be compiled and made

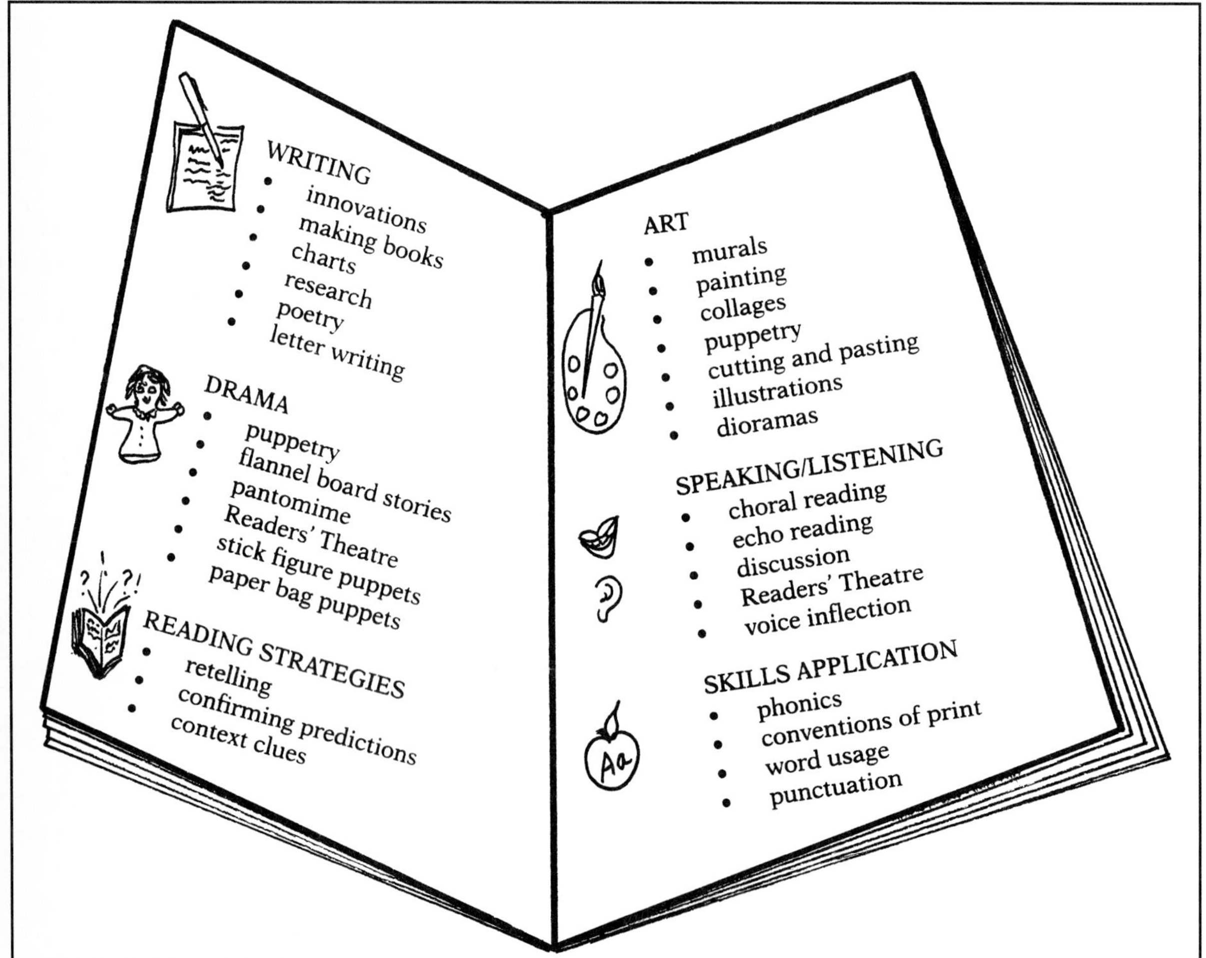

Figure 6.7 Book of Ideas

Figure 6.8

Response Mode: ART
Book: *Mrs. Wishy-Washy*
Activity: Mural of Mrs. Wishy-Washy and the animals in the story. Brown paint may be spattered on the mural to indicate the animals are covered with mud and are in need of baths.

Response Mode: DRAMA and COOKING
Book: *The Gingerbread Man*
Activity: Children can create flannel board characters for this story. The story can be retold using the characters with appropriate scenery. Children can also make gingerbread men and act out the story with the grand finale being that they can be the fox that gets to eat the gingerbread man.

Response Mode: MUSIC and INNOVATION ON TEXT
Book: *Down by the Bay*
Activity: Children can sing the lyrics of the book and create new lyrics that can be compiled in a class book.

Pattern writing: a big book made by children after reading Brown Bear, Brown Bear, What do You See?

Response Mode: RESEARCH and INNOVATION ON TEXT
Book: *I Spy*
Activity: The book *I Spy* provides a series of clues describing some creature (e.g., a vulture, an owl). Children could research other creatures and create a class version of *I Spy.*

Response Mode: WRITING
Book: *The Enormous Watermelon*
Activity: *The Enormous Watermelon* is a takeoff on many different fairy tales. Children could write their own version of a popular fairy tale or folktale.

Response Mode: INNOVATION ON TEXT and ART
Book: *Brown Bear, Brown Bear, What Do You See?*
Activity: After reading *Brown Bear, Brown Bear, What Do You See?* children could write their own personalized versions. The things seen could be a result of walks in the environment, other animals, toys, and the like. The objects could be color coded as well. Children could construct their own "What I See" books. These books could have paint swatch samples on one side and be graduated in nature. The blue page, for example, could be filled with blue objects the children saw, such as blueberries, a ball, a house. These could be drawn or cut from magazines.

into Big Books. Big Books can be created from pictures on calendars, photographs, or song lyrics. The fronts and backs of cereal boxes can be made into Big Books with children providing the print to accompany the cereals selected. Books can be made in various shapes. For example, a Tyrannosaurus-shaped book can house information on dinosaurs, a bear-shaped book can be used for the children's innovations on *Brown Bear, Brown Bear, What Do You See?*, and a bus-shaped book can tell about different means of transportation. Children can make pocket books, using Ziploc bags for the pockets. The children's original writing can be placed in the pockets for easy removal (Thornell, 1991; Kettenring and Graybill, 1991).

During the shared book experience, children learn two important aspects of reading: the process of making sense of what they read and the concepts and conventions of print. Children learn about word attack skills, phonics, and high-frequency (sight) words while they are engaged in the process of real reading, not in isolation. Shared reading provides many opportunities to show what fluent reading sounds like, how language works, and how to integrate the three cueing systems to construct meaning. More important, shared reading gives children the opportunity to behave like real readers and to learn how to read in an enjoyable, memorable fashion.

Interactive Charts

Interactive charts are child-centered and visually appealing learning materials that provide children with the opportunity to manipulate print in concrete ways and to translate their knowledge about oral language to written form. Young children are active, concrete learners. Therefore, being able to manipulate print provides support for the development of their emergent reading behaviors. Charts allow children to engage in meaningful literacy experiences at varying developmental stages of reading. They foster the development of literacy through social interaction with teachers and classmates. Such skills and strategies that can be taught using interactive charts include:

- directionality
- differentiation between letters, words, and sentences
- the concept of space between words
- letter and word recognition
- mechanics such as punctuation and capitalization
- letter-sound relationships
- rhyming words
- compound words, contractions, endings, root words
- rereading or reading beyond to figure unknown words
- cross-checking, for example, using several sources to determine an unknown word

Any poems, nursery rhymes, songs, finger plays, or language experience stories can be made into interactive charts. The chosen text should be printed neatly onto strips, which are then attached to poster board. Some element in the text that can be manipulated is chosen, for example, rhyming words, number words, children's names, and sentences, and written on cards or strips of cardboard. Illustrations can be added to facilitate the reading of the chart and to enhance the chart aesthetically. Paper fasteners, magnetic tape, and Velcro are excellent materials to attach the manipulable components to the poster board. Clear pockets made from remnants of laminating paper can be attached to the poster board to store the extra components.

When children read the charts, they can change the words of the text by deleting or covering those on the initial chart, and adding others of their own choosing. For example, think about the rhyme about the peanut sitting on the railroad track.

> A *peanut* sat on a railroad track,
> *Its heart was all a flutter*
> A choo-choo train came rushing by.
> Toot, toot, *peanut butter.*

The children could change the food that sat on the track and the resulting change after the train came rushing by.

> A banana sat on a railroad track,
> *Feeling so fine and fit;*
> A choo-choo train came rushing by.
> Toot, toot, *banana split!*

Using charts appeals to young children since they are attractive, easily accessible, and contain rich, memorable text.

Charts enhance children's development in the affective domain as well since they are motivational, help improve self-confidence, and provide children with successful experiences with print. Children associate reading with pleasure and view themselves as readers. Using charts appeals to children since they are attractive, easily accessible, contain rich, memorable text, allow children to be successful, and are enjoyable (Schlosser and Phillips, no date). An excellent resource with many fine examples of interactive charts can be found in *Building Literacy with Interactive Charts* by Kristin Schlosser and Vicki Phillips. Some examples of interactive charts can be seen in Figure 6.9. Interactive charts are powerful and enjoyable learning materials that contribute to any class literacy program.

Guided Reading

Once children can read independently, silent reading assumes a significant role in the reading program. However, it is not enough for

Figure 6.9A Interactive Chart

teachers merely to assign activities and pages to be read with minimal support; teachers must guide children as they are learning and trying to use and apply developing strategies and skills (Johnson and Louis, 1990). During guided or supported reading is the time when teachers instruct students in areas that will enable them to grow as readers (Butler, 1988b). Guided reading is an approach to reading instruction where teachers and their students, "talk, think, and read through a text which offers manageable challenges" (Mooney, 1995, p. 55). During guided reading teachers have the opportunity to help children gain deeper understanding of texts and appreciate the author's style and techniques, challenge children to think beyond the text, and demonstrate

Figure 6.9B Five Little Monkeys Spinner (cont.)

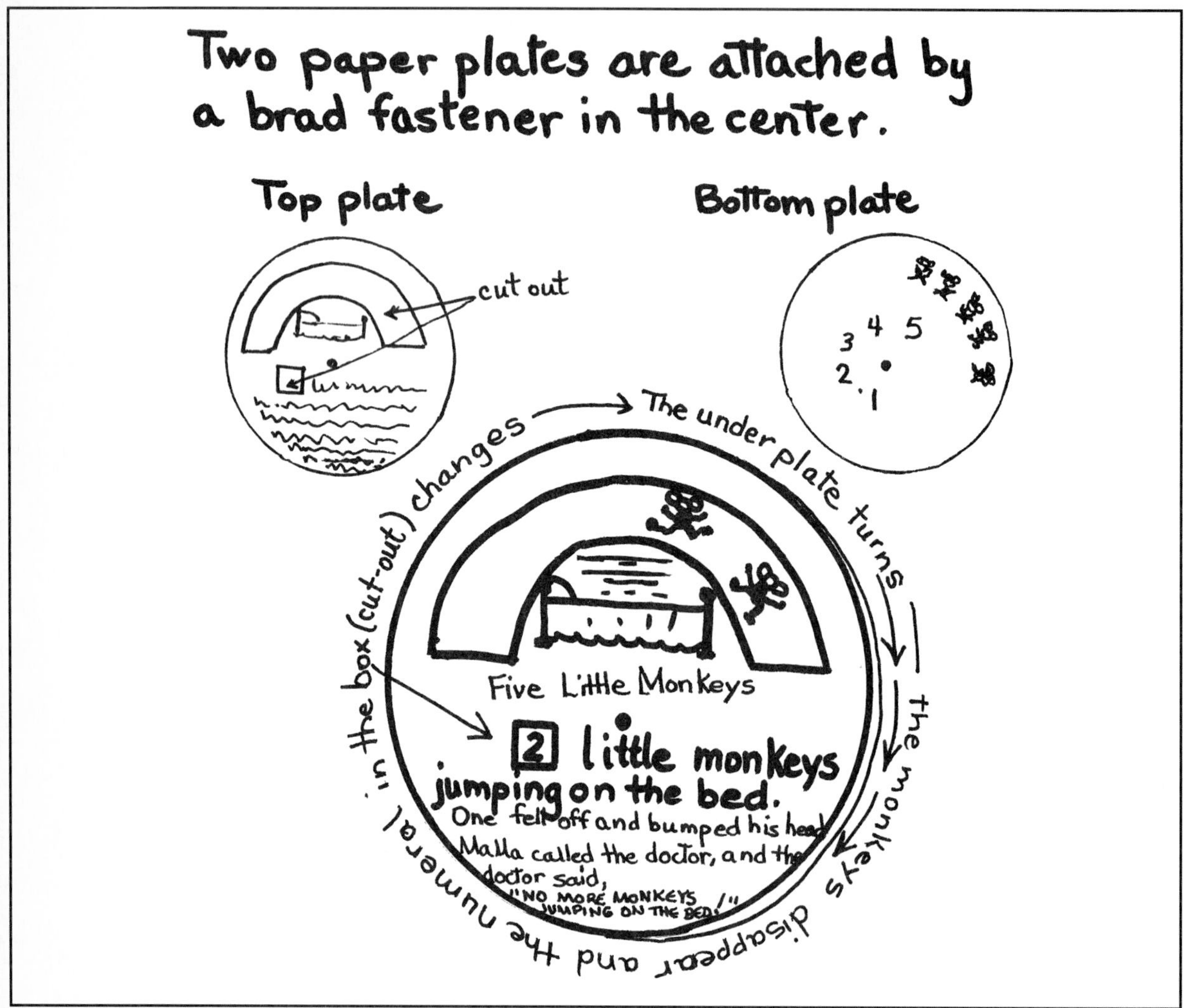

reading strategies and language conventions in context (Butler and Gamack, 1988).

It is necessary that children be given instruction, support, and practice in reading silently, since most of the reading done throughout a person's life is silent. By becoming competent silent readers, children can become self-reliant learners. Silent reading enables children to realize what real reading is—an interaction between the author and the reader whereby the reader constructs meaning from the text.

Guided reading is an aspect of the reading program in which the teacher works with a small group of children (generally six to eight students) in order to help them delve deeper into what they read. Understanding is facilitated through the ongoing interactions among the readers, the text, and the teacher.

When choosing materials for guided reading, there are several features to keep in mind. Just as Goldilocks chose to eat the porridge that was "just right" and to sleep in the bed that was "just right," teachers need to choose books that are "just right" for their students. The materials should be supportive of the readers, be closely matched to their abilities, needs, and interests, and provide reasonable challenges (Mooney, 1995). In addition, topic familiarity, the form and style of the text, the literacy language, the pictorial support, the size, amount, and the placement of the print on the page should also be considered (Peter-

FROM THE CLASSROOM OF . . .

Jean Mumper Wallkill, New York

Guess My Book

Cut and paste the small pictures of books from catalogs on 3"×5" index cards, along with the title. Students can draw a card and act out a part of the story for the class to guess or they can search for objects to give clues. This may be done individually or with partners.

son, 1991; Weaver, 1992; Depree and Iversen, 1994; Fisher, 1995).

As children progress from being emergent readers to early readers to fluent readers, the instructional materials change in complexity in the number of words and lines on the page, the placement of the text on the page, the size of the print, and the spacing between words. The role of the illustrations also changes, with the pictures in the materials for emergent and early readers being more supportive of the text. The language structures increase in sophistication and difficulty from the extensive use of oral language patterns to various forms of written language. The texts move from highly predictable events and repetitive language to include a wide range of genre, for example, nonfiction, myths, legends, and plays.

Many publishers level their books to help teachers select the most appropriate reading materials, for example, the Wright Group, Rigby, Ready to Read, and Story House Corporation. In addition, some teachers design their own categories. For example, Fisher (1995) uses an eight-level scheme with the beginning levels having only two to eight words on a page. More advanced levels increase in complexity in story structure, vocabulary, genre, and the amount, size, and placement of the text. By categorizing the books intended for guided reading, either using those provided by publishers or their own designs, teachers can provide the best reading instruction to help their students move toward independence in their literacy learning.

Guided reading has many advantages and benefits. Children and books are matched during this procedure, which allows teachers to work on specific aspects of the reading process that children need at this time. When working with youngsters in guided reading, teachers have additional opportunities to observe the reading strategies the children are using. During guided reading, teachers can make relevant demonstrations of reading strategies and print conventions as the children are involved in real reading activities. Guided reading develops children's competence and confidence in using these strategies.

The focus of guided reading is to help children develop as readers. When teachers engage their students in guided reading, they are teaching them how to read by and for themselves. Guided reading is not a haphazard occurrence; rather it takes careful planning. To ensure that guided reading will be an effective component of the literacy program, there are some steps teachers should consider:

1. **Prepare for guided reading.** A focus (objective) for the lesson should first be determined. The purpose may be to introduce an author or a particular genre, to explore the differences between stories on the same topic, to look at literary devices, or to focus on reading strategies, word identification, or language conventions. Perhaps the objective will be to have children identify words in context, expand their vocabulary, or develop conceptual understandings. With the focus established, teachers then select appropriate materials, keeping in mind the children's needs, interests, and developing reading abilities. The materials should be chosen for enjoyment, the opportunities for teaching and learning they present, and their relevance to the children's experiences and background knowledge. Teaching and learning opportunities include interesting beginnings, a well-developed story line, word attack skills, and good endings.

There are many sources of suitable material for use in guided silent reading. Many publishers, such as the Wright Group, Rigby, and Richard Owen, offer sets of books that lend themselves well to guided reading. Many of these are graded, which helps the teacher choose appropriate titles. Other sources include poems, multiple copies of trade books, children's newspapers or magazines, and even stories from basal reading programs.

2. **Set the stage.** This step includes providing the background information the children need to understand the selection, setting a purpose, and motivating the students. Clay (1991) proposes that if the goal of a literacy program is to get children to read new texts independently, then teachers can facilitate this by providing a rich introduction to the selection. Good introductions make unfamiliar texts more accessible to young readers since additional support is needed for unfamiliar or somewhat challenging texts. Rich introductions create scaffolds within which children can complete the first reading of a story.

It is exceedingly important that children have the necessary background information for what they read. This could be accomplished by discussing the children's experiences (those that are relevant to the selection), talking about the ideas in the selection and asking questions about these ideas, or showing pictures, illustrations, or objects related to the selection and discussing them. Teachers can also discuss text features that might pose problems for the children (Clay, 1991). These features could be related to the author's language (to familiarize children with the language of the text) or to the meaning of the text.

Setting a purpose for reading is related to the objective(s) and can originate with either the teacher or the student. Children should know why they are reading, how much they have to read, and what they should do when they finish reading. For example, children may read several pages in a book to confirm or alter their predictions about the story events.

The book should be introduced by discussing the title and cover illustration. Children should venture opinions on the topic of the book. Before children read the text silently, they should be reminded what to do when they meet a word they do not know (Butler, 1988b):

- Read on to the end of the sentence or paragraph.
- Reread to see if there are any clues to the meaning of the word.
- Think about what the word might mean and guess words that make sense and sound right.
- Check the letters in the word to see if they match the guesses.
- Omit the word and continue reading.
- Ask someone for help with the word.

Although it is important for children to have strategies to call on when meeting unfamiliar words, occasionally it may be better to provide the word for very young children.

3. **Read the book.** Frequently teachers will talk young emerging readers through the text, focusing on details that will help the children to be successful. Children will read samples of the text in order to confirm their predictions. The degree of support given will vary, depending on the readers' competency. After having been guided through the text, children read the book independently, with the teacher nearby observing in order to provide support as needed. Enough time should be allotted so that all children can finish. Children should be allowed to read the text by themselves before being expected to read it orally or to discuss or respond to it. Some books may be read in a single sitting, as is the case in most early childhood classrooms, while others may be enjoyed over several days. Some teachers allow children to work in pairs.

Each child should have a copy of the book that is to be read. Until the children have firmly established one-to-one correspondence, they should be asked to read with a finger to aid in the reading. Once one-to-one matching is secure, they should be encouraged to read with their eyes, and only resort to using their finger when they are in need of extra support on challenging material.

During the emergent and early stages of reading, the children are not expected to read silently first. Frequently, teachers read the book aloud on the first reading, with the children following along with their finger. However, once children have developed a clear understanding of one-to-one correspondence, they can be asked to read each page "in their minds" (Williams, 1990).

Children should be expected to read for meaning, but teachers need to assist their students in their quest for constructing meaning. Young readers need to be encouraged to look at the illustrations to obtain information about the story, check to see if the text makes sense, verify if the words used match those of the author, and self-correct when necessary. Teachers can provide questions or prompts such as those in Figure 6.8 in order to help the children develop their ability to cross-check while reading.

4. **Return to the book.** Following silent reading, children are given opportunities to return to or revisit the text to

- discuss what has been read to offer different opinions and interpretations (documenting their points of view with relevant references in the text)
- clarify points by rereading portions of the text
- address problem areas in word identification
- read the story in pairs
- respond creatively to the text
- respond in literature logs

Guided reading occurs with both trade books and basal reading programs. It presents an opportunity for teachers to provide worthwhile reading and writing experiences with both types of material. Figure 6.10 is an example of written response following guided reading.

It is not always necessary to follow up a story with an activity other than rereading. Some stories are read many times, with each successful reading generating more success as children become skilled at anticipating the text. Routman (1988) points out that stories may be read six or more times in order to develop fluency and competence.

Guided silent reading is an approach that permits teachers and small groups of students to read and talk their way through a piece of text. The purpose is to read books in a supportive environment in order to develop reading strategies and to build competence and confidence.

Sustained Silent Reading (SSR) or Drop Everything and Read (DEAR) Time

A balanced reading program includes reading *to* children, reading *with* children, and reading *by*

Figure 6.10

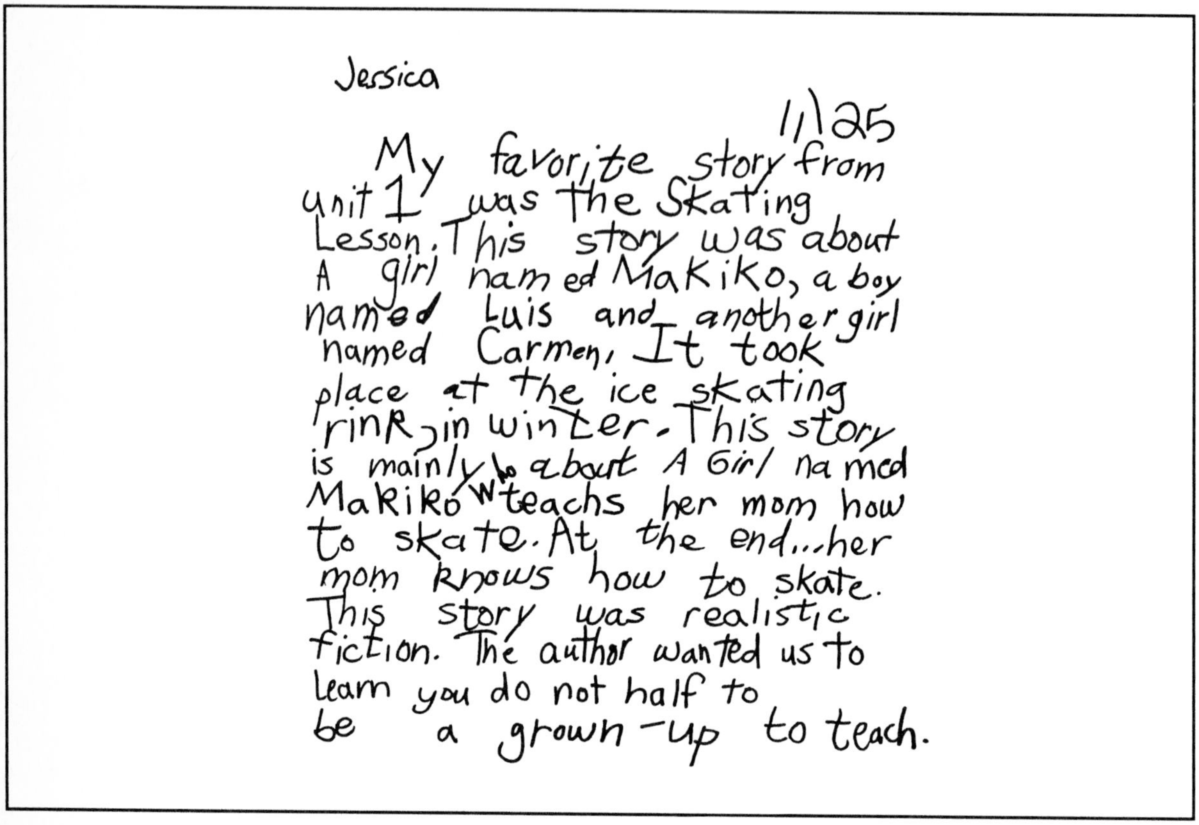

Jessica

1\25

My favorite story from
unit 1 was the Skating
Lesson. This story was about
A girl named Makiko, a boy
named Luis and another girl
named Carmen, It took
place at the ice skating
rink, in winter. This story
is mainly about A Girl named
Makiko who teachs her mom how
to skate. At the end...her
mom knows how to skate.
This story was realistic
fiction. The author wanted us to
learn you do not half to
be a grown-up to teach.

children. Children must be given demonstrations of what an expert does when reading, must be supported in their quest for attaining literacy, and must be allowed to practice. Reading to children and reading with children (language experience, shared reading, and guided reading) have already been discussed. Now it is time to allow children to practice reading. Sustained Silent Reading (SSR) or Drop Everything and Read (DEAR) time is an activity in which everyone in the classroom—the students, the teacher, the aides, visitors—reads for a designated period of time. SSR is an approach to reading that allows children to practice reading while simultaneously observing an adult (or adults). SSR operates on the idea that the more children (or anyone) do something, the better they become because of the practice. Therefore the more students read, the more they learn about the act and the process of reading, and the better readers they become.

The major emphasis of SSR is on enjoyment, with children and teachers reading self-selected materials for pleasure. In addition to time to practice reading, SSR has other advantages. Reading ability is enhanced and attitudes toward reading are improved. An interest is created in books, and children are provided with excellent practice in using their developing reading skills. Children also see an adult model reading, which demonstrates reading as an enjoyable and worthwhile pastime. Since teachers read as well, they have a chance to catch up on current literature. By noting what their students choose, teachers have the opportunity to see students' reading tastes and performances. SSR develops the habit of reading and builds a love of reading.

The procedure for implementing SSR is relatively straightforward:

1. **Designate a specific time for reading.** A time for SSR should be scheduled on a daily

basis. Although teachers vary in their choice of times, two time slots work very well: right after the children return from lunch or right before they go home for the day. The duration will vary according to the children's age and past experiences with SSR. Generally the time range is 5–15 minutes. Initially sessions for very young children will be brief, but as children become familiar with the procedure, the time can be lengthened. A timer is recommended so that no one has to become a clock watcher. Since the emphasis is on enjoyment, prolonged sessions should be avoided—it is best to leave the children wanting more!

2. **Set the stage.** The rules for SSR are taught or reviewed with the children. They should have their reading materials at hand and be prepared for each session. Changing books during SSR is discouraged, so some advance preparation is necessary. Children may choose a place to read—at their desks, in the reading corner, or in any other comfortable spot in the room—so long as they do not disturb others.

3. **Everyone reads.** The timer should now be started, and everyone should be happily engaged with a book. It is important that the teacher not be tempted to use this time to correct papers or catch up on management tasks. Teachers are serving as role models when they read, and this is a necessary component of SSR. If teachers detect restlessness on the part of the students, they can conclude the session. A comment such as "Well done, you were such good readers today," ends the session on a positive note.

4. **Responding to the books.** No required book reports or responses are connected with this approach. This is the time to show children that literature is a source of enjoyment. However, teachers may want to provide a brief sharing time or time for children to give a short book talk. In this way children become acquainted with other books and reading materials that their friends are enjoying. Teachers may also ask children to "say something" to a classmate. This is an opportunity for children to share something from the story, to react, to critique. But the best follow-up to reading is actually more reading.

Although the emphasis of this approach is on children reading individually and silently, teachers may make adjustments according to the needs and abilities of their students. Instead of reading alone, young children may read with a buddy, and instead of reading silently, they may talk quietly. Because young children may not be able to read the text yet, they may look at the illustrations and talk their way through a story. As children gain more fluency and competence, vocalizations during reading ultimately disappear. Gutkin (1990) describes sustained ______ reading in her kindergarten classroom. After several unsuccessful attempts with the silent part of this program, she permitted the children to continue their energetic and frequently noisy sessions. She found the children still thoroughly enjoyed books and the sustained reading time, but they wanted to share, to talk about the books they were reading. She goes on to describe the enthusiasm and the subsequent fascination her students had when one boy was reading a furniture/toy catalog and discovered that his classroom had one of the pictured items (a kidney-shaped table). The children then went on a search of the classroom to find other items pictured in the catalog. Sustained ______ reading added to both the children's intellectual lives and their social lives. Sustained ______ reading became sustained loud reading in this particular classroom.

SSR convinces children of the value of reading and gives them valuable practice time. Beginning SSR in kindergarten sets the stage for the development of a lifelong reading habit.

Graphophonics: Phonemic Awareness and Phonics

Phonemic Awareness

As stated in the discussion on the reading process, effective readers use three different sources of information when constructing the meaning of print, for example, the graphophonic, syntactic, and semantic cueing systems. Readers coordinate and integrate these cueing systems when attempting to understand what they are reading. The process can be likened to swimming, an activity that demands coordination of proper breathing along with leg and arm movements. Real swimming does not occur on the shore of a lake or alongside a swimming pool, but rather occurs in the water. Likewise, real reading occurs with connected text, not with isolated skills and drills. However, in swimming, instructors may direct the swimmer's attention to arm or leg movements or improved breathing techniques in order to enhance the swimmer's ability. In reading, instructors can demonstrate how graphophonic cues support literacy since no reading can take place without using the graphophonic cueing system (Newman and Church, 1990).

As children attempt to read more challenging texts, they will encounter words that they do not automatically recognize. They will need assistance in acquiring strategies for figuring out unknown words and therefore need to be taught strategies for analyzing words. This includes phonemic awareness and phonics.

Most children enter school with an adequate vocabulary and the ability to pronounce most of the sounds in their language clearly. However, many young children lack an aspect of language known as *phonemic awareness* (Yopp, 1992; Griffith and Olson, 1992). Spoken words are comprised of sounds or phonemes, and phonemic awareness is the ability to examine language independently of meaning and to be able to manipulate its component sounds (Cunningham, 1995). Phonemic awareness allows children to use letter/sound correspondences to read and spell words and is a precursor to the learning of phonics. Therefore it plays a major role in those skills that require the manipulation of sounds, for example, word recognition and spelling (Griffith and Olson, 1992).

Phonemic awareness can be developed through instruction and practice (Adams, 1990; Griffith and Olson, 1992; Yopp, 1992, 1995). The primary goals of any activities involving phonemic awareness are to facilitate children's ability to perceive that speech is made up of a series of sounds and to depict what good readers and writers actually do when they read or spell unfamiliar words.

There are many techniques and activities that might be used to develop phonemic awareness. The activities are designed to simulate the learning that took place during more than 1,000 hours of informal literacy experiences that children have before entering school (Cunningham, 1995). These include activities using sounds, invented spelling during writing activities, rhyming and playful language activities, matrix boxes, and children's literature.

Activities Using Sounds

There are a variety of activities that involve the manipulation of sounds that teachers might do to develop their students' phonemic awareness. There are sound-matching activities during which children have to determine which words begin with certain sounds or have to generate words beginning with certain sounds. Figure 6.11 depicts a chart that a kindergarten class generated for the letter *p*. They initially brainstormed words that they knew beginning with the letter *p* and then added other words to the chart as they came across them during other class activities.

Sound isolation activities can also be utilized. Children can be provided with a word and asked to tell what sound occurs at the beginning, middle, or end of the word. To make these sound activities more playful, Yopp (1992) utilizes familiar tunes such as "Old MacDonald Had a Farm," "Twinkle, Twinkle Little Star," and "Jimmy Crack Corn and I Don't Care." For example, to help children isolate sounds, the song "Old MacDonald Had a Farm" might be sung as follows:

> What's the sound that starts these words?
> *Dog, dig,* and *dance?*
> /d/ is the sound that starts these words:
> *Dog, dig,* and *dance.*
> With a /d/ here, and a /d/ there,
> Here a /d/, there a /d/, everywhere a /d/, /d/,
> /d/ is the sound that starts these words:
> *Dog, dig,* and *dance.*

Other sound activities include blending sounds to form words (e.g., /c/ /a/ /t/ for *cat,* substituting sounds at the beginning of words, (e.g., *hall* becomes *call*), and segmenting words into their component sounds, which is the most challenging activity of all.

Writing Experiences and Invented Spelling

Children practice many reading skills when they write (Clay, 1985), and phonemic awareness is enhanced when children engage in daily writing

Figure 6.11

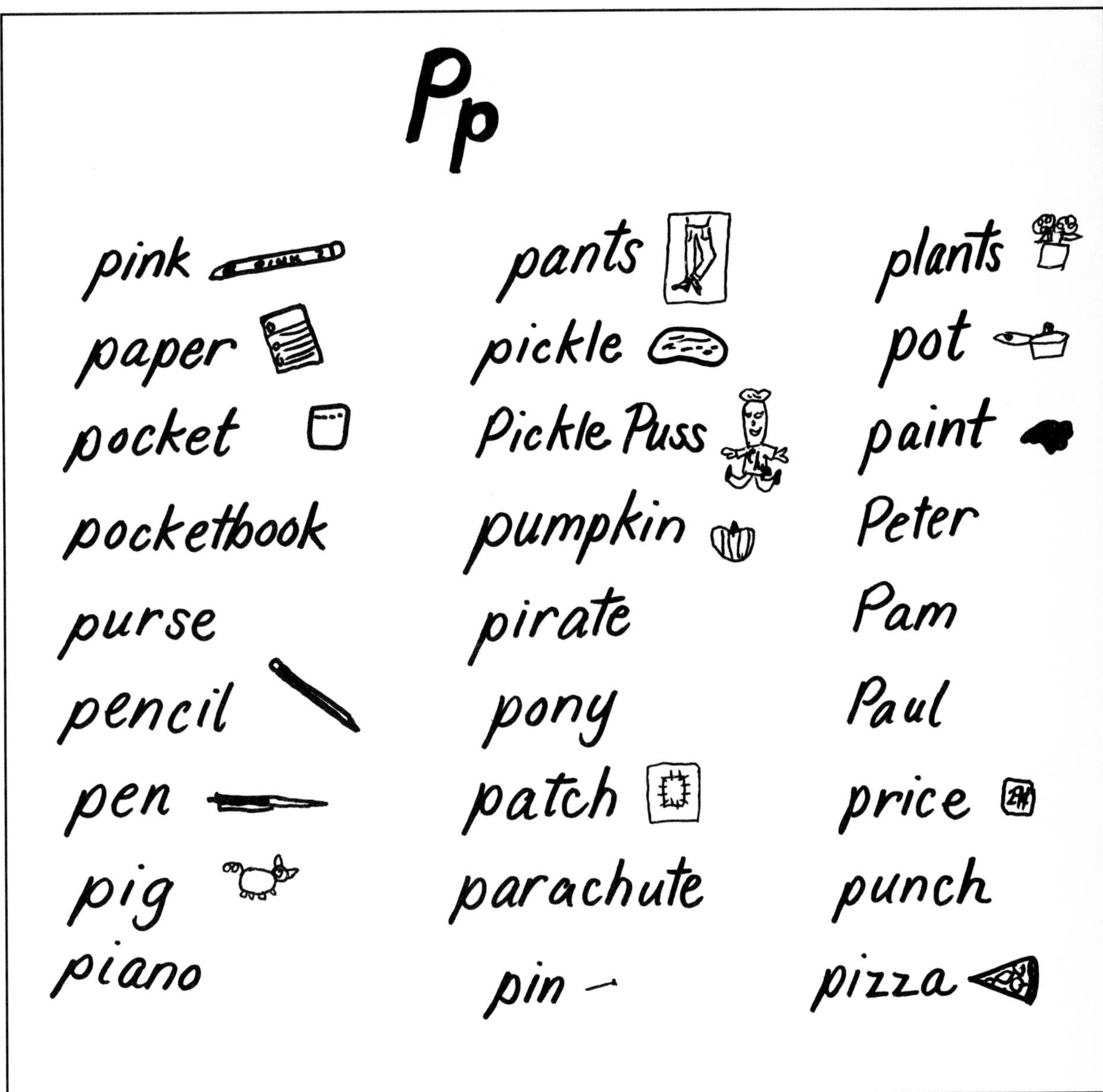

experiences. When children spell words, they have to map the spoken language into its written form. The more children write, the better they become at segmenting the individual sounds into words. Children are developing their ability in phonemic awareness when they use their "ear," spelling as they compose, e.g., spelling words by listening to the individual sounds in the words (Fisher, 1995). Children who are allowed and encouraged to invent spelling develop a strong sense of phonemic awareness.

Rhyming and Other Playful Language Activities

Nursery rhymes, chants, street and jump rope rhymes, alphabet books, riddles, storytelling, and authors such as Dr. Seuss usually play a large role in the development of phonemic awareness (Mattingly, 1984; Adams, 1990; Yopp, 1992; Cunningham, 1995). Teachers should take advantage of children's natural propensity and curiosity to experiment with sounds and design activities that stimulate language play.

Matrix or Elkonian Boxes

Matrix boxes, developed by a Russian psychologist named Daniel Elkonian, have become a widely used procedure to help children think about the order of sounds in spoken words. They are used in Reading Recovery (see Chapter 12) to help children learn how to segment words into their individual phonemes. As children segment a word into its component sounds, they write the letter or letters that represent that sound into a separate box. For example, the word *cake* would have three boxes, one for /c/, one for /a/, and the last for /k/, representing the three phonemes in the word. Figure 6.12 illustrates some examples of the use of matrix boxes.

Children's Literature

Probably the most accessible vehicles to develop children's ability to segment words into sounds are children's books that deal playfully with sounds through alliteration, rhyme, and other phoneme manipulations (Griffith and Olson, 1992). There are many excellent examples of children's literature that draw attention to the sounds of language that can be used to facilitate the acquisition of phonemic awareness. Figure 6.13 provides a sampling of children's literature for this purpose.

When using books to develop such skills as phonemic awareness, the books should be read first for enjoyment. After hearing the story, the children should discuss the story, especially what made the book enjoyable, for example, the word play.

It must be remembered that the main objective of addressing phonemic awareness is to give children a strategy for constructing meaning. Activities to develop the graphophonic cueing system are not intended to replace meaningful interactions with print. The activities are intended to supplement such meaningful activities as reading aloud, shared reading, and language experience, and to provide a way to draw attention to the phonemic base of language.

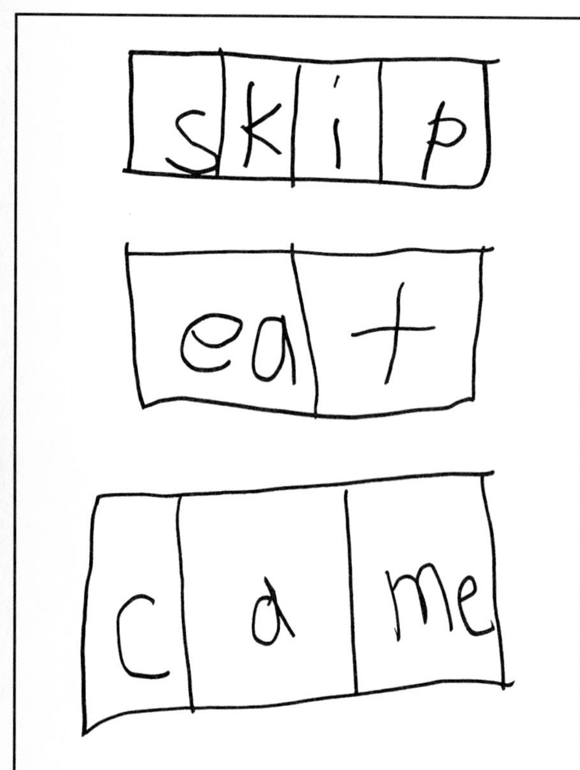

Figure 6.12

Phonics

Despite the ongoing debate as to whether phonics should be taught, there is general agreement that children need to use and learn the graphophonic cueing system. The issue is not whether phonics should be taught, but rather *how* children can learn and profit from phonics instruction and *what* contexts are most appropriate for teaching phonics (Powell and Hornsby, 1993).

Phonics "refers to various approaches that are designed to teach children about the orthographic code of the language and the relationships of spelling patterns to sound patterns," (Stahl, 1992, 618). The purpose of phonics is to help children develop an understanding of the alphabetic principle so that they can: form an approximate pronunciation when reading, which is then checked against knowledge of words and the context of the text; and form an approximate spelling of a word when writing (Ministry of Education, B.C. Canada, 1991).

Quality phonics instruction should be an essential part of reading instruction, integrated and relevant to the reading and writing of real texts (Stahl, 1992). There are several techniques that are promising for enhancing children's decoding

Figure 6.13

Barrett, J. (1983). **A Snake is Totally Tail.** *N.Y.: Atheneum.*

Bayer, J. (1984). **A, My Name is Alice.** *N.Y.: Dial.*

Bernstein, J. (1979). **Fiddle with a Riddle: Write Your Own Riddles.** *N.Y.: Dutton.*

Crews, D. (1986). **Ten Black Dots.** *N.Y.: Scholastic.*

Cummings, P. (1989). **Goodness Gracious!** *Norwood, South Australia: Omnibus Books.*

Degen, B. (1983). **Jamberry.** *N.Y.: Harper & Row.*

Elting, M. & Folsom, M. (1980). **Q is for Duck: An Alphabet Guessing Game.** *N.Y.: Clarion.*

Folsom, M. (1985). **Easy as Pie: A Guessing Game of Sayings.** *N.Y.: Clarion.*

Hepworth, C. (1992). **ANTics!** *N.Y.: G. P. Putnam's Sons.*

Hoban, T. (1987). **26 Letters and 99 Cents.** *N.Y.: Scholastic.*

Houget, S. (1983). **I Unpacked My Grandmother's Trunk: A Picture Book Game.** *N.Y.: Dutton.*

Merriam, E. (1989). **Chortles: New and Selected Wordplay Poems.** *N.Y.: Morrow.*

Most, B. (1980). **There's an ANT in ANThony.** *N.Y.: Mulberry Books.*

Noll, S. (1987). **Jiggle Wiggle Prance.** *N.Y.: Puffin Books.*

Parish, P. **Amelia Bedelia.** *Various titles.*

Shaw, N. (1986). **Sheep in a jeep.** *Boston: Houghton Mifflin.*

Slepian, J. & Seidler, A. (1986). **The Hungry Thing.** *N.Y.: Scholastic.*

Slepian, J. & Seidler, A. (1990). **The Hungry Thing Returns.** *N.Y.: Scholastic.*

Yolen, J. (1992). **Street Rhymes Around the World.** *Honesdale, PA.: Boyds Mills Press.*

Yolen, J. (1993). **Sleep Rhymes Around the World.** *Honesdale, PA.: Boyds Mills Press.*

Zolotow, C. (1965). **Someday.** *N.Y.: HarperTrophy.*

abilities: authentic reading and writing, children's literature, word sorts, and word play.

Authentic Reading and Writing

In the past, phonics was taught almost exclusively through the use of worksheets and workbooks. However, more meaningful phonics instruction can be undertaken during such regular reading and writing activities as the writing and discussing of the Morning Message, modeled writing, interactive writing, chart reading and writing, and during shared reading. During any of these reading and writing opportunities, teachers and children have to use phonics and phonic lessons can result from the ongoing use of such instructional activities.

In addition to the above techniques, teachers can choose poems or songs that highlight certain sounds. After the children have had the opportunity to enjoy the text, the teacher may then address key teaching points. They might point out words that begin with certain sounds, have the same vowel sounds, or belong to the same word family. The children could circle the sound being featured and then spend time locating that sound in other materials. Class charts could be constructed listing the words that were located.

When looking for sources for materials that feature certain letters or sounds, poetry anthologies are highly useful. Teachers can collect songs, poems, and chants and store them where they can be readily retrieved. In addition, there are publishers that produce materials just for that purpose. Figure 6.14 is an example from *Pathways to Literacy,* a program that provides examples of many chants and poems that can be used for phonics instruction.

Writing provides a wealth of opportunities for addressing phonics. When children write, they naturally record their thoughts using words. Encouraging invented spelling of these words helps children develop their decoding ability. As they write, children say the word slowly and try to listen to the sounds that they hear. Writing becomes a natural medium for applying letter-sound knowledge (Cunningham, 1995).

Any classroom activity can be utilized to enhance children's literacy abilities, and teachers should capitalize on the ongoing class offerings to promote the teaching of phonics. Phonics is

Figure 6.14

CONVERSATION

Aletha M. Bonner

Cackle, gobble, quack, and crow,
Neigh and bray and bleat and low,
Twitter, chirrup, cheep, and coo,
Bark and growl and purr and mew.

Humming, buzzing, hiss, and sting,
Hoot and cuckoo, caw and sing,
Squeal and grunt and snort and squawk;
Who said, "only people talk"?

not the learning of rules and the filling in of worksheets, and teachers must ensure that reading and writing form the core of their phonics instructional program.

Using Children's Literature For Phonics Instruction

Children's literature is an excellent resource for phonics instruction. Any piece of literature can provide a forum for the discussion of various aspects of language. Teaching phonics in association with children's literature maximizes children's learning opportunities. A sampling of books to teach specific phonic elements includes:

- Kent, Jack. (1971). *The Fat Cat.* New York: Scholastic. (short *a*)
- Henkes, Kevin. (1987). *Sheila Rae, the Brave.* New York: Greenwillow. (long *a*)
- Galdone, Paul. (1973). *The Little Red Hen.* New York: Scholastic. (short *e*)
- Keller, Holly. (1983). *Ten Sleepy Sheep.* New York: Greenwillow. (long *e*)
- McPhail, David. (1984). *Fix-It.* New York: E. P. Dutton. (short *i*)
- Berenstain, Stan and Jan. (1964). *The Bike Lesson.* New York: Random House. (long *i*)
- McKissack, Patricia. (1986). *Flossie and the Fox.* New York: Dial. (short *o*)
- Cole, Brock. (1986). *The Giant's Toe.* New York: Farrar, Straus, & Giroux. (long *o*)
- Marshall, James. (1984). *The Cut-Ups.* New York: Viking Kestrel. (short *u*)
- Lobel, Anita. (1966). *The Troll Music.* New York: Harper & Row. (long *u*)

(Trachenburg, 1990)

These are but a sampling of literature available to make the teaching of phonics a meaningful activity. Teachers should be alert to the language teaching possibilities of any book, keeping a listing of these titles or adding to their own classroom libraries.

Word Sorts

Another excellent activity to develop the habit of analyzing words by looking for patterns is the use of word sorts (Gillet and Temple, 1994; Cunningham, 1995). For a word-sorting activity, children look at a group of words and sort them into categories based on sound or spelling patterns. Word sorts may be used with any collections of words that are available, for example, key words, word banks, or words on the wall, with the purpose of the activity being to focus students' attention on the various features of words. The children study and compare the words and determine the features that several words share in common. Some sorting activities include sorting for: (Gillet and Temple, 1994)

- initial sounds
- rhymes
- silent letters
- consonant blends or digraphs
- vowel digraphs, for example, *ee, oa, ea, ay*
- number of syllables
- shared grammatical features, for example, adjectives or nouns
- words with similar meanings

In many classrooms, word sorts are accompanied by word hunts. Teachers post the categories to use and the children are encouraged to locate other examples that then are recorded on chart paper or placed in a pocket chart. Hunting for words is an important transfer step since it draws children's attention to word features and spelling patterns in real reading materials (Cunningham, 1995).

Word Play

"Just as lion cubs gambol and tumble to develop the ability they need as predators, human children invent kinds of play that exercise their mind" (Moffett and Wagner, 1993, 35). Very young children delight in nursery rhymes and songs, frequently manipulating the sounds and words to create their own versions. Children also enjoy jokes, puns, riddles, tongue twisters, and expressions that produce images they find amusing. Books with riddles, jokes, rhymes, and unusual use of words and expressions draw children into the delight of language, and sharpen their literacy skills. A listing of books that engage children into playing with words can be seen in Figure 6.15.

Including instruction in the graphophonic cueing system is a necessary part of a balanced literacy program. However, teachers should assume a major role in how this instruction is provided. The kind of phonics instruction needed is not the kind associated with the memorization of rules and the utilization of workbooks, but rather the kind of phonics instruction that reflects current understanding of how young children learn to read and write. Authentic reading and writing experiences should form the core of the phonics instructional program. Educators must reject the either/or debates of the past, and promote a balanced literacy program in which phonics instruction is a means to help children become successful as literacy learners (Cunningham, 1995).

Cameron, P. (1961). **"I Can't," Said the Ant.** New York: Cowar McCann.

Carter, D. (1990). **More Bugs in Boxes.** New York: Simon & Schuster.

Deming, A. (1994). **Who is Tapping at My Window?** New York: Penguin.

Galdone, P. (1968). **Henny Penny.** New York: Scholastic.

Gordon, J. (1991). **Six Sleepy Sheep**. New York: Puffin Books.

Hague, K. (1984). **Alphabears.** New York: Henry Holt.

Krauss, R. (1985). **I Can Fly.** New York: Golden Press.

Prelutsky, J. (1989). **Poems of A. Nonny Mouse.** New York: Alfred A. Knopf.

Raffi. (1987). **Down by the Bay.** New York: Crown.

Sendak, M. (1990). **Alligators All Around: An Alphabet.** New York: HarperTrophy.

Shaw, N. (1989). **Sheep on a Ship.** Boston: Houghton Mifflin.

Seuss, Dr. (1974). **There's a Wocket in My Pocket.** New York: Random House.

Winthrop, E. (1986). **Shoes.** New York: HarperTrophy.

Figure 6.15

Writing in Emergent Literacy Classrooms

Traditionally it was thought that children had to read before they could write; therefore writing was not considered as important as reading instruction. Yet children were given writing assignments, usually on a topic the teacher chose, for example, "My life as a pencil" or "A funny thing happened . . .". Children were expected to produce perfect copies, complete with the proper heading (name, date, subject, title). Frequently, writing was assigned as seatwork, so the teacher was not even available to help the stumped writer, to encourage, or to support.

Writing in today's emergent literacy classrooms is quite unlike this—in opportunity, in emphasis, and in support. Today children are provided with a balanced writing program, just as they are provided with a balanced reading program. Writing occurs during a designated writing time, as well as throughout the day and across the curriculum. A balanced writing program in an emergent literacy classroom includes:

- language experience stories
- pattern writing (modeling the writing after certain books, such as *Brown Bear, Brown Bear, What Do You See?* or *Smarty Pants*)
- writing during dramatic play and activity center time (learning centers)
- functional writing (writing for real-life purposes, such as in sign-ins for attendance, sign-ups for activities, writing class notices, labeling, invitations, greeting cards, rules, recipes, notes)
- journal writing
- process writing
- writing across the curriculum

Several of these aspects of a balanced writing program have been discussed previously—language experience stories, pattern writing (during the shared book experience), writing during dramatic play and activity center time, and functional writing. Other writing opportunities are discussed in the following sections.

Journal Writing

Many emergent literacy instructional programs include journal writing as an integral part of the balanced writing program. Journal writing can be reserved for personal expressive writing, which is a type of nonfiction in which children express their feelings or opinions (Heller, 1991). Although journal topics are usually child-generated, they can also be teacher directed: "Write in your journal about today's science lesson when we went outside to look at our class tree," or "What did you learn during our math lesson?"

Generally teachers set aside a designated time for children to write in their journals, allowing perhaps 5–15 minutes daily. Some teachers have their students write when they arrive for the day. In this way the children can expound on some significant event that happened since the class was together last. Writing at this time also sets a positive tone for the rest of the day. Other teachers choose a time later in the day, sometimes during learning center time.

Some teachers use commercially prepared journals, blank books, or notebooks, which come in a variety of attractive packaging. Other teachers, as stated previously, construct their own journals using available materials.

Journal writing should not be graded, but rather can serve as evidence of student progress over the year. By keeping dated sample journal entries, teachers can note a student's growth over time. In this way the students themselves, their parents, and the teacher can trace the developing writers' progress.

Journal writing time is not necessarily a quiet time. Rather, social interaction should be encouraged. Children should be permitted to talk as they write and to ask their peers for assistance in spelling or for information. Collaborative talk supports the writing process.

It should be remembered that journal writing, like any aspect of the writing process, is developmental and all stages will appear within an emergent literacy classroom. Very young children will initially scribble, draw, or use random letters, invented spelling, or conventional spelling. Journal entries may consist of drawings (which are writing for young children), drawings accompanied by letterlike forms, or drawings accompanied by invented spelling. Young children generally draw first (using drawing as a form of rehearsal) and write later. After a while they may reverse the process and write first and then illustrate their text. Figure 6.16 provides samples of children's journal writing in grades K–2.

It is important to remember that children will move in and out of these stages. Even if they usually use invented spelling, children occasionally will revert and just draw. This is a normal part of the process.

The content of children's journals tends to vary, although some children will have favorite, recurring topics. Manning, Manning, and Hughes (1987), in examining the content of journals in first grade, found that the writing fell into ten categories:

- pictures only
- scribble or random letters
- labels or descriptions of pictures
- lists
- copies of texts
- retelling of texts
- personal content
- imaginative content
- informative content
- other writing forms, such as puzzles

These topics can be sources for additional writing or explorations, as in process writing, which is discussed in the next section.

When introducing journals to young children, teachers may be greeted with "I can't write." To show children that it is acceptable to start with pictures, teachers may introduce writing by discussing pictures of cave writing or Native American pictographs (Friedman, 1986). They may also show the writing of former students and keep these samples on display for

FROM THE CLASSROOM OF . . .

Joan Westover Rondout Valley, New York

GENERAL LITERATURE STUDY GROUP PLAN

Day One

1. The teacher familarizes the group with the language of the book by reading the story orally. The book is held so that all group members can see as the teacher points to the words.
2. Students are given individual copies of the book, and the group is invited to take part in a shared-reading session.
3. The group engages in a literal discussion about the book.
4. Students are encouraged to discuss similar events from their own lives.
5. Students listen to the story on tape in the listening station.
6. Students are encouraged to react to the story in their literature logs.

Day Two

1. Before meeting as a group, the students are directed to read the book to a partner.
2. When the group meets, reactions in literature logs are shared and discussed.
3. The group takes part in a shared-reading session with minimal participation by the teacher.
4. Students engage in a discussion by means of critical, interpretive, and/or divergent thinking.
5. Author's style is examined in terms of one or more of the following aspects: characterization, setting, lead sentences/endings, conflict/conflict resolutions, description, qualities of that particular genre, etc. (Children are encouraged to use such elements within their own writing.)
6. Literature within the same schema is made available.
7. Children are encouraged to describe within their logs a past experience related to the story.

Day Three

1. Before meeting as a group, students are directed to "partner-read" the book.
2. Within the group meeting, logs are shared and discussed.
3. The story is read in one of a variety of ways, such as choral reading, Reader's Theatre, actual dramatization, etc.
4. Word hunts or phrase hunts are conducted and the three cueing systems (semantics, syntax, grapheme/phoneme) are stressed and modeled within the context of the book.
5. Other language games (such as cloze activities, sequencing of story events, finding causes for and/or effects of story events, word referent searches, contraction hunts and rewrites, possessive possession, etc.) are played within the content of the story.
6. Literature extension projects are discussed and planned by the children. The type of project, the method/media used to complete the project, creative problem solving, and effective use of time are among the students' responsibilities. (For project ideas, see Literature Study Projects list included in this packet.)
7. Children discuss their project plans in their literature logs.

(continued)

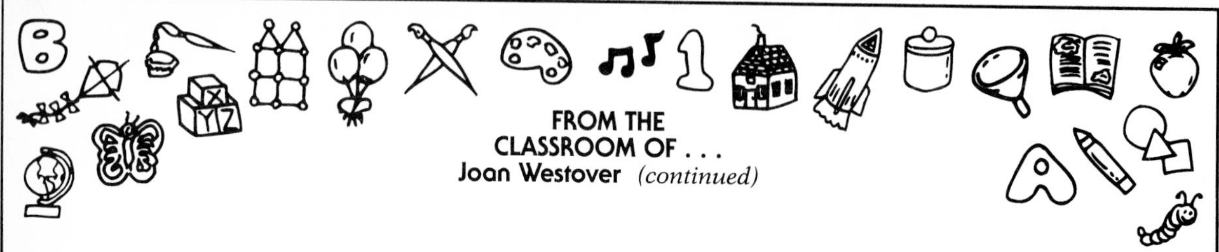

FROM THE CLASSROOM OF . . .
Joan Westover *(continued)*

Day Four

1. Children are directed to read their books to friends who are not within their literature groups.
2. Children work on literature extension projects, beginning in a structured setting but primarily in independent group settings.
3. The teacher conducts small group guided-reading sessions.

Day Five

1. Children read their books in situations that they prefer.
2. Literature projects are completed.
3. Literature within the same schema is shared.
4. Literature study projects are presented to an audience.
6. Encourage children/parents to order books from book clubs.
7. Schedule Book Talk Days when other classes and parents may come in and listen to children read, tell, or dramatize stories.

Activities for Parents Related to School Literature Programs

1. Provide a newsletter periodically about book-related activities in school.
2. Ask parents to participate in some literature-related activity at school. (For example, reading to children, helping with book bindings and covers, fund-raisers to purchase books.)
3. Have a workshop for parents that describes the important purpose and activities of the classroom's literature program.
4. Have a workshop for parents describing how they can participate in home recreational reading.
5. Make available readings for parents, such as the *Read Aloud Handbook*. Set up a loan system for such materials so that interested parents may borrow them.

children to refer to throughout the year. Young children have to be reassured that their writing does not have to resemble grown-up writing. They should be encouraged to do it their way (Sulzby, 1988).

Some teachers prefer just to have children write in personal journals. There may be opportunities for sharing the students' entries, or the entries may be kept private. Some teachers use journals to dialogue with their students—they read their students' entries and respond briefly. In this way they model correct spelling and sentence structure and serve as an audience for the children. Children appreciate the special attention and recognition from the teacher. Still other teachers incorporate some dictation into journal writing. For the most part the children use invented spelling, but once in a while (perhaps once a week), teachers will become secretaries for their students. These teachers feel they are expanding their students' writing repertoires and are offering children an opportunity to write more complex stories (Hipple, 1985).

Process Writing

In some emergent literacy classrooms, writing is not encouraged or considered significant except for copying exercises or practice-writing the alphabet, while in others there is an abundance of writing. In classrooms where children's original composing is valued, children's

Figure 6.16A Samples of Journal Writing

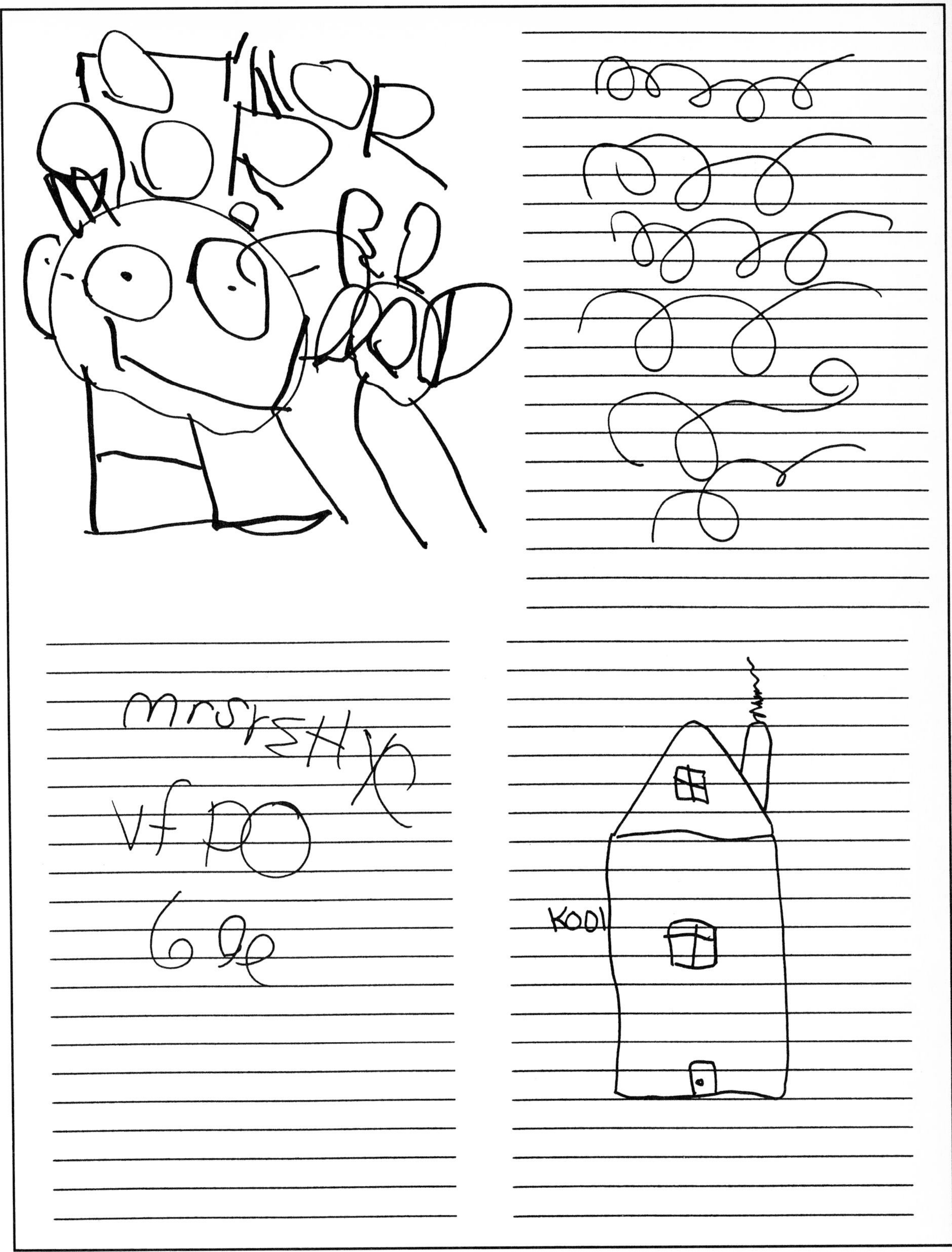

Figure 6.16B Samples of Journal Writing (cont.)

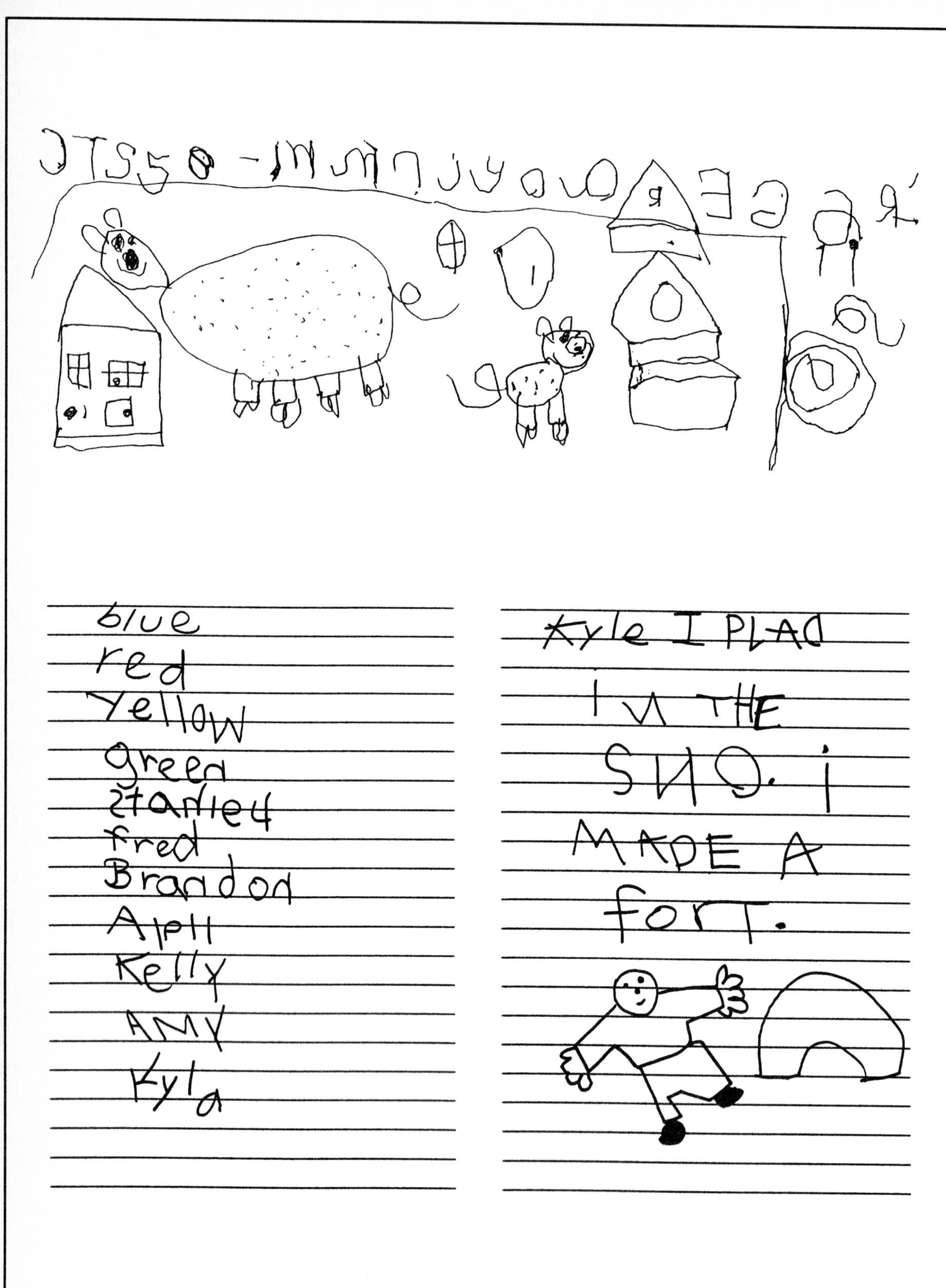

blue
red
Yellow
green
fred
Brandon
Kelly
AMY
Kyla
Kyle I PLAD
IN THE
SNO. i
MADE A
fort.

Figure 6.16C Samples of Journal Writing (cont.)

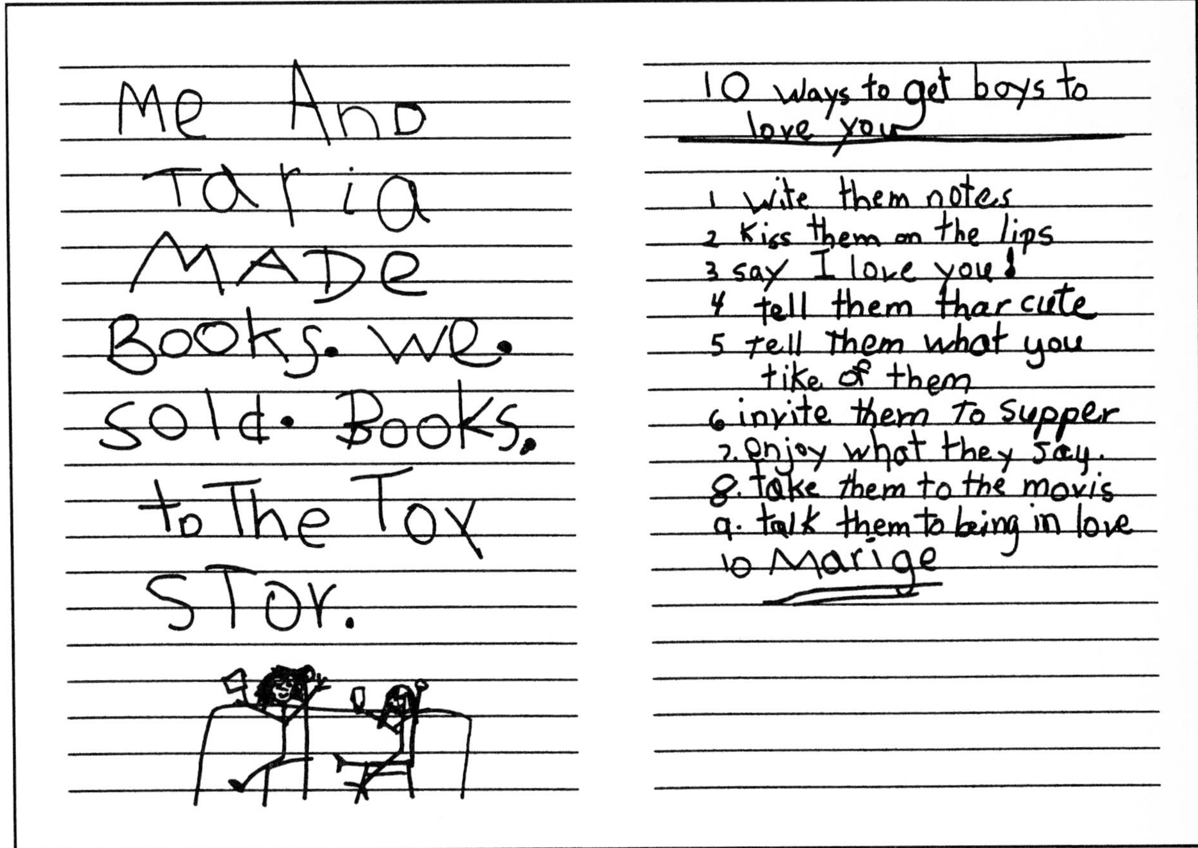

emergent writing is both encouraged and accepted.

The current thought about writing in the case of young children is that it is destructive to think that children are unable to write until they have mastered the mechanics of writing; it is destructive to think that young children come to school knowing nothing about writing. Many educators have proposed that young children can write before they can read (Chomsky, 1971; Clay, 1975). Young children can write and will write if they are given the opportunity to do so. In fact, young children, when questioned as to whether they were able to read or write, responded that they could write but acknowledged their inability to read (Graves, 1983). Children perceive themselves as writers and should be provided with many writing opportunities.

Teachers who integrate writing throughout their instructional programs are attempting to capitalize on what actually occurs in literacy-rich homes (Sulzby, Teale, and Kamberelis, 1989). Yet because school is a different setting from the home, the literacy program must be organized in a different fashion. Using a process approach to writing is an effective way to capitalize on children's desire to write, to help them grow and develop as writers, and to organize the writing program.

In Chapter 2, the writing process is presented as an ongoing, recursive process that consists of five steps or stages:

- prewriting
- drafting
- revision
- editing
- sharing or publishing

These principles are applicable for very young writers. Children must have ownership of and responsibility for their writing, choosing topics, deciding whether to publish, and determining the format for publishing. They must be given time to write and appropriate feedback and support. They must be provided with models for writing—through literature, observing the teacher write, and seeing and hearing the works of other young authors. However, being inexperienced, they must be given adequate demonstrations of the writing process, and these may have to be repeated many times.

Children should write from the very first day of school. To show children that they are indeed writers, many teachers demonstrate that even if someone is unable to read what is written, it is still writing. By putting a message on the chalkboard, the teacher can show the children that even though they can't read it as yet, it is still writing and can be read by others. This is likened to the fact that although other children may not be able to read their classmates' writing pieces, the young authors themselves can read their own writing for their classmates.

Modeled writing is an integral part of the writing process in an emergent literacy classroom. Many teachers model for a brief portion of the writing period on a regular basis. They may model topic generation, from listing possible topics to discarding several topics before choosing one that they will then write about as the children observe. An overhead projector is ideal for such modeling, or chart paper may be used instead. When the teacher is writing, she or he talks aloud, letting the child witness the teacher thinking while writing. Children can see that writing is not continual. The teacher stops to reflect, cross out, and occasionally asks for advice and assistance from the children. At another time, the teacher may take the same piece and model revision, followed by editing and publishing sessions in subsequent meetings.

Young children may write in a variety of ways, and most writing for kindergartners and first graders will involve drawing. Children view their drawings as forms of writing, so teachers, when discussing the children's pieces, should refer to them as writing, not drawings. "Tell me what you wrote about" is preferred to "What did you draw?" By constantly immersing children in print, demonstrating all aspects of the writing process, discussing authors' styles and techniques when reading literature, and having children share their writing with their classmates, teachers will enable children to grow in their writing ability gradually. Scribbles will be replaced with drawings that are labeled with letterlike figures, which will be replaced with the use of invented spelling, and so forth. Young children's attempts should be respected, and with appropriate feedback in a risk-free environment, children should develop as writers.

Oral language plays a dominant role in the writing program in the early grades. Children solve tasks with the help of speech, as well as with their eyes and their hands. Therefore, they need to talk about possible writing topics, to talk as they write, and to present their finished pieces in the Author's Chair. Calkins (1986) notes that young children have difficulty remembering what they want their stories to say while attending to writing. Children solve this by talking and drawing. These serve as reminders of how their stories should go.

Regarding the content of young children's writing, Calkins (1986) found that children's stories do not really qualify as such. Rather, the writing is more "I know something about . . ." pieces. They are more inventories of information than stories with all the elements of story structure. Children's writing tends to lack the form of stories, an identifiable sequence of events, and real endings. Talking with children about stories and asking pertinent questions to help children discover these elements help children become better writers.

Children know even less about expository forms of writing. For young children, expository writing tends to be "All About . . ." pieces. They are primarily improvising or listing when undertaking expository writing (McGee and Richgels, 1990). Again, children have to be read nonfiction pieces, discuss how nonfiction is structured, and see teachers demonstrate the writing of an expository piece. Both comprehension in reading and composing in writing are hindered by inadequate background knowledge and inadequate knowledge about how texts are structured. Young readers and writers cannot construct meaning without having both print and nonprint experiences.

Frequently teachers conduct minilessons at the beginning of Writers' Workshop, and this goes for emergent learners as well as for older, more accomplished writers. Minilessons should be simple, brief, focused, and grow out of observations of the children. Minilessons may be categorized into four areas (Giacobbe, 1991, cited in Avery, 1993):

- procedures, having to do with the operation and management of the writing session
  - establishing rules for the workshop
  - using writing folders
  - putting dates on the writing
  - procedures for proofreading
- strategies that writers use
  - rereading for meaning and clarity
  - strategies to correct spelling
  - inserting information using a caret
  - crossing out to make changes rather than erasing
- qualities of good writing
  - using words that make pictures
  - writing effective leads and endings
  - eliminating overuse of "and" or "then"
  - adding information to make the piece clearer
- writing skills
  - using capital letters appropriately
  - using proper punctuation
  - leaving spaces between words
  - using commas to separate words in a series

(Avery, 1993)

An effective minilesson that can be used to introduce young authors to the writing process is demonstrating the developmental ways that young children write. Fisher (1995) demonstrates to her first graders how she might have written as a young girl. She might say, "When I was little, I might have":

- scribbled as I wrote
- written some different letters that I knew
- written the first sound I could hear in a word
- put down the first and the last sounds that I could hear
- put down some of the letters and left spaces for those I didn't know
- used book spelling.

As she talks about each stage, she provides an example of the developmental stage. By doing this, she shows the children that however they write is acceptable for them at this particular time. Children need support and guidance during each stage of the writing process. In prewriting, the teacher can talk about ideas for writing, and the children can generate both a class list and individual lists. These ideas may be placed on charts or in the children's own writing folders. Heller (1991) offers several suggestions for topic generation:

1. **Expert list.** For this activity, the teacher first lists several things that she or he can do well (e.g., baking, running, drawing). Then the children can talk about things they do well and have an interest in.

Kindergarten	Grade 1	Grade 2
running	dressing dolls	playing ball
coloring	tying shoes	riding bikes
pumping on swings	video games	writing on lines

2. **Curiosity list.** On this list would be topics that the teacher or the children know little about but always wanted to learn about. Some children may want to know more about dinosaurs, snakes, or what Native Americans ate during the time of the Pilgrims. Teachers may want to model what they are curious about, such as sketching, calligraphy, Australia.

3. **Literature-inspired topics.** After a piece of literature is shared, children may want to write about the topic that was presented. They may want to write an alternate version of a fairy tale or additional adventures for a favorite character (such as Curious George or Clifford). They may become fascinated by certain ideas and want to research and write about them.

4. **Content area ideas.** Any area of the curriculum can be inspirational for writing—science, social studies, mathematics.

These writing explorations should not be limited to summaries of information but can take alternate forms. For example, children may write poetry or personal narratives after undertaking a study of the environment. They may record science observations, such as of growing plants or chicks hatching. Math problems and math stories can be written. Alphabet books in curricular areas (e.g., *The ABC Book of Volcanoes* or *The ABC Book of the Sea*) help children develop both concepts and a sense of the style of expository writing.

During the composing stage or drafting, children need to concentrate on getting their ideas down without concern for mechanics. Many young children draw first and then write the accompanying text. The drawings may be free expression, or the teacher may provide some structure. Teachers can give children a sheet of paper with a circle divided into pie-shaped wedges. On each wedge, the child can draw an event from the intended story (Heller, 1991). This will help the child think the story through as well as remember it.

In order to free children from mechanics, teachers must encourage them to use invented spelling. "Spell it as it sounds," "Use your ear spelling," or "Spell it like a 5- (or 6- or 7-) year-old" can be said when children request a word's spelling. Children can be provided with "Try" cards or "Have-a-Go" cards for which they spell a word two or three times and then choose what they think is the best spelling. When teachers see these cards as they circulate around the room, they can supply the correct spelling. Figure 6.17 is an example of a "Have-a-Go" card, and Figure 6.18 shows a sign in a classroom that announces that invented spelling is used there.

Spelling resources should be readily available, and children should be shown how to use them. Such resources as personal dictionaries, class word lists and charts, picture dictionaries, and literature can help children as they are writing. Since writing in emergent literacy classrooms is a social experience as well, young children should turn to their classmates for help when needed.

During the drafting stage, teachers can provide support and encouragement as they circulate and by asking, "How is it going?" "What else could you say about . . . ?" "How many stories do you have here?" Having children listen to each other's stories both informally and in the Author's Chair can help children while drafting or revising.

Once children have selected a piece for publication, they are ready to revise and edit. Teachers can model revision using a story of their own written on chart paper. They can cut and paste, insert words, and delete phrases. This story can be posted, and later the teachers can model how they proofread and edit their piece.

Not everything children write needs to be revised, and younger children are less likely to do much revision. For young children, the piece chosen for publication should be as perfect as a child can make it; that is, goals for publication should be developmentally appropriate. Some realistic goals for revision are (Heller, 1991):

- **Grade 1.** After writing a variety of pieces, children choose one piece from their writing folder to revise each term.
- **Grade 2.** Students choose at least one fictional piece, one nonfiction piece, and a poem each term.

Children can also be taught to confer with one another regarding their writing. This can be done in pairs at any convenient spot in the room. Children need to be shown what happens during such peer conferences and be helped with the types of questions to ask. When first introduced to peer conferences, children can merely state what they liked about their classmate's piece and ask questions for clarification. Later the following questions can be placed on chart paper or in the children's writing folders to guide them during conferences:

THE AUTHOR MIGHT ASK

1. How does my writing sound to you?
2. Can you help me with the beginning (middle, end)?
3. What word(s) can I use for . . . ?
4. Do I need to add anything?
5. Do I need to leave something out?
6. Do you have any other suggestions?

THE LISTENER MIGHT ASK OR SAY

1. What do you mean by . . . ?
2. I don't really understand . . .
3. I really liked the part . . .
4. I would like to hear more about . . .
5. Why did you . . . ?
6. What do you think about your writing?

When children are ready to edit their own stories on their journey to publishing, they can make a list of the things they can do independently. For instance, in their writing folders can be a list of editing skills appropriate for young children. These can include checking for initial capital letters, final punctuation marks, and paragraph indents. Children can circle any words they think do not look like conventional spelling. They can then be responsible for correcting a certain number of the misspellings—for example, two or three—and the final editor (the teacher, a volunteer, or a parent) can correct the rest. Children should not be overwhelmed, but they should

FROM THE CLASSROOM OF . . .

Kathy Pike and Jean Mumper New Paltz, New York

SPELLING TIPS FOR WRITERS—BY STUDENT WRITERS

Instead of posting charts around the room that are teacher-made or commercially made, spelling hints and tips can be generated by the children themselves. These can be collected and put on a chart, or they can be individually collected and written on a pencil shape. The name of the child who gave the spelling tip would appear on the chart or pencil shape, and if possible a picture of the child could also be attached.

you can put a dash — for sounds you don't know. Michael

You can put a dash for sounds you don't know how to write. (Michael)

Look for the word in a book about what you are writing about. Heidi

Use a book. Take a book on the topic you are writing about, and you look for the word in the book. (Heidi)

I make each sound in my mind and my friend tells me. Kyle

I make each sound in my mind, and my friend tells me the letter. (Kyle)

Try sounding out the word. Listen to what the words say to you in you mind. Listen slowly. Alicia

Try sounding out the word. Listen to what the words say to you in your mind. Listen slowly. (Alicia)

Close yours eyes and think how the word looks. Amanda

Close your eyes and think how the word looks. (Amanda)

Figure 6.17 Have-A-Go! Spelling Card

HAVE-A-GO!

First try	Second try	Teacher
frm	frum	from
rit	rite	write
drariring	draring	drawing
reed	read✓	
Skol	skoll	school

1. Write the word as you think it is spelled—sound it out.
2. Try several spellings.
3. Which looks right?
4. Check with the teacher, another student, or a dictionary.

realize that conventional spelling and correct grammar and punctuation are ultimate goals.

Coping with the amount of work young children want to publish may be overwhelming because they often want to publish everything. One possible solution is to hold a conference with each child once a week at which the child can tell about a piece she or he wishes to publish. In this way, each child will have the opportunity to publish once a week and grow to understand that not everything should be published.

To help teachers manage and organize a writing program, there needs to be some record keeping on the part of both the teacher and the young writers. Children can keep their own writing folders, which can be envelopes, file folders, folded sheets of paper or cardboard, or commercially produced writing folders. Inside the folder are kept drafts, a child's own topic list, a list of the child's publications (noting topic and date, and perhaps form of publication), and an "I Can Use" checklist denoting the skills the child has learned and is capable of using. This "I Can Use" list can be a prepared checklist that students merely mark, or it can be done in a creative format, for example:

- petals on a flower
- apples or leaves on a tree
- balloons in the hands of a clown

The possibilities are endless. On each petal (apple, balloon, etc.) are written the skills the child can do independently. In this way the child can see at a quick glance what writing skills he or she has and can also watch the flower (and progress) grow. (See Figure 6.19.)

Other items can be kept in writing folders as well, such as the children's own spelling words. However, it is difficult for young children to manage lots of individual pieces of paper, and it is best to keep the folder as uncluttered as possible.

When children are ready to publish, many options are available. They can post their published pieces on a special bulletin board reserved for classroom writing, make a book for the class or school library, audiotape their story, create a pamphlet, or have the story typed on the computer. Children may do the actual publication by themselves or with the assistance of a volunteer helper. Sharing writing in the Author's Chair is generally an integral part of the writing period and serves as an additional means of publication.

In addition to the children's record keeping, teachers may want to keep writing samples obtained throughout the year in a portfolio; keep anecdotal records on the children's strengths, needs, and progress; and maintain whatever

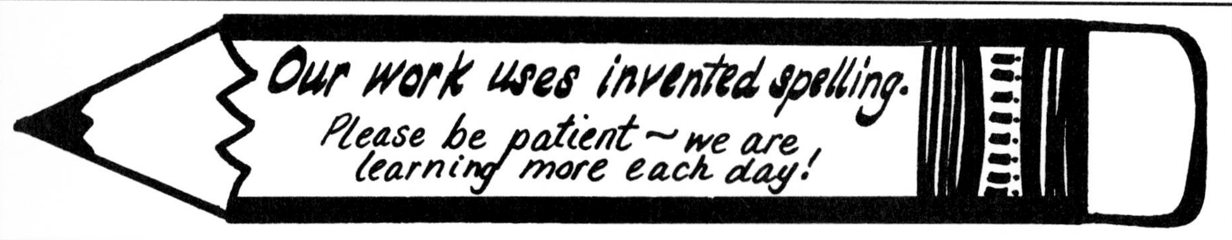

Figure 6.18 Invented Spelling Sign

Figure 6.19 Watch Our Garden Grow

else is essential to help guide the instructional program.

The following format for a typical writing session illustrates how process writing is implemented:

1. **Getting started.** The children may be gathered together on the mat for the initial part of the writing period. A piece of student writing or a piece of literature may be shared.
2. **Modeling.** For perhaps five to seven minutes, the teacher may model some aspect of the writing process or give a minilesson on an area that has been identified as something the children need (e.g., the use of capital letters in names or of commas in a list of items).
3. **Think time.** The children are then asked to think about a story to make a picture in their heads. Teachers can suggest that children think of the "Five *W*'s" (who, what, where, why, and when) and the "*H* question" (how). Several children can share ideas, or children can talk to a buddy.

4. **Writing.** Those children who are ready can move off and start writing. Those who need more help can remain with the teacher.
5. **Roving conference.** The teacher then moves around the room checking to see whether the children are on task, who needs help, and where children are in the writing process. At this time teachers have available their record-keeping devices to note special needs and topics for modeling sessions.
6. **Individual group conferences.** Children can sign up for a conference with the teacher or with a small group of classmates. These conferences initially deal with the content of the writing pieces and later with editing and proofreading.
7. **Self-evaluation.** Children should be expected to check their work for both content and mechanics. This can be done alone or with a peer.
8. **Sharing.** Toward the end of the session (which generally lasts from 30 to 45 minutes), children may want to share their stories in pairs, in small groups, or with the whole class.

Making a chart outlining what authors do during writing and displaying it in a prominent place may be helpful for children as they work through the writing process. Figure 6.20 is a sample of such a chart.

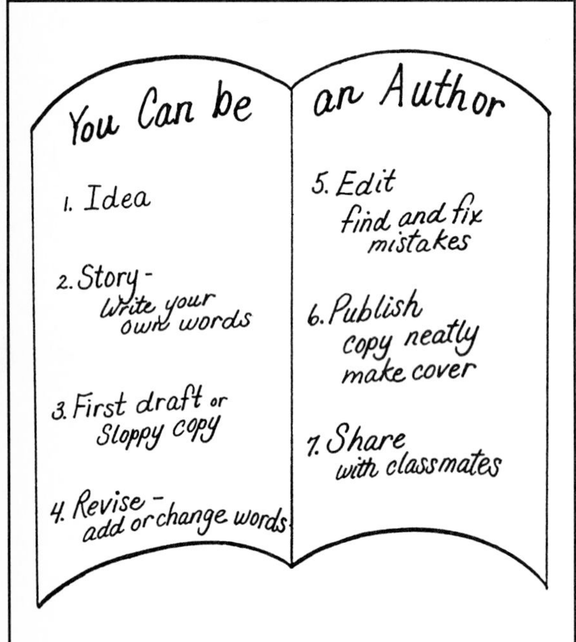

Figure 6.20 I'm An Author Chart

Spelling

Along with the crafting of writing, attention must be paid to the mechanics, and this includes spelling. When teachers plan for spelling, they must take into consideration the developmental nature of children's language acquisition. Spelling is a cognitive process, with children progressing through the various developmental stages. Teachers should facilitate this natural progression through the developmental stages by helping children learn more about the nature of the English orthography and by helping them develop strategies to learn how to spell (Bolton & Snowball, 1993). A spelling program must be flexible and must cater to children's individual learning rates and styles. Children need to be provided with correct models of language to allow them to grow in their ability to communicate. Appropriate demonstrations of correct spelling and explanations of how to identify and correct misspelled words should be provided as needed.

In a spelling program, "the emphasis must be on the purpose and function of words to express or gain meaning using a written text" (Wing Jan, 1991, 9). Spelling programs should include:

- graphophonic information
- morphographic information (information on word structure and word meanings)
- visual memory activities
- resource skills (ability to use resources to check for correct spellings)

(Wing Jan, 1991)

Spelling programs should allow children to develop independently and to assume responsibility for their own learning. Spelling activities should be designed to provide practice and reinforcement of words.

Among the goals of a spelling program are these (Wing Jan, 1991; Bouffler and Bean, 1989):

- to develop the children's interest, motivation, and competence in spelling accurately
- to demonstrate the reasons for accurate spelling
- to provide personalized spelling programs related to the children's individual spelling needs
- to give children strategies that will enable them to learn how to spell words

- to give children opportunities to practice their knowledge about spelling
- to generate interest in language
- to provide an environment conducive to developing competent spellers and writers
- to foster children's concern for correct spelling

Given the goals for an effective spelling program, spelling instruction can be enhanced through a variety of practices:

- daily writing experiences, such as the Daily News, Morning Message, story writing, letter exchange
- modeling of conventional spelling through such writing instructional activities as interactive writing, wall stories, charts, language experience stories, and so on
- the encouraging of risk taking and the use of inventive spelling
- many opportunities to talk about and play with language
- the provision of spelling resources
- class explorations into particular features of language, for example, locating words with consonant digraphs, the use of the suffix "ed"
- the use of minilessons

(Bolton & Snowball, 1993; Routman, 1993)

Spelling is considered to be an aspect of written language, and it is best addressed within the context of writing. The emphasis should be on developing skills that are related to word use, word meaning, and word structure as opposed to merely developing skills in reproducing letters correctly.

Some teachers prefer to present words in lists, and perhaps even give spelling tests, along with observing their students' writing. However, instead of allowing a commercial program to dictate the exact words and generalizations to be learned, these teachers encourage their students to assume some responsibility for the selection and learning of words. When implementing a spelling program, teachers can decide how many words are appropriate for each child to learn. Children then identify the specified number of words from their daily writing. These are recorded in their spelling notebooks. Teachers can also suggest certain words, such as words commonly used in writing. The children then practice these words throughout the week in a variety of activities. Figure 6.21 is an example of a chart that can be displayed to help children learn correct spellings.

Children are encouraged to practice their words both in school and at home, alone and with

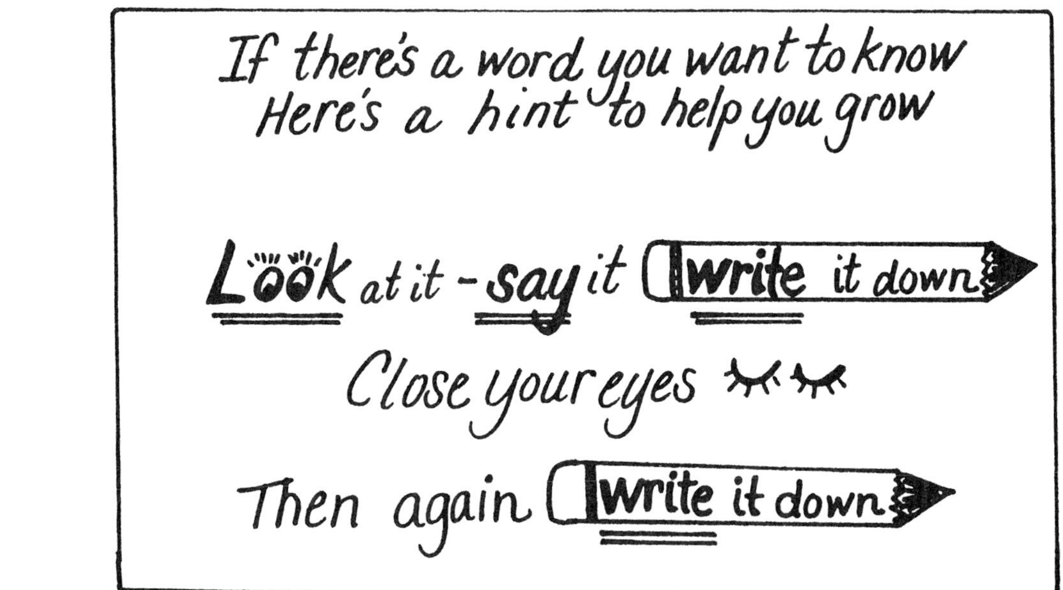

Figure 6.21A Chart to Help Children Learn Spelling Words

Figure 6.21B Alphabet Card (cont.)

a partner. Toward the end of the week, children test one another, and misspelled words become part of next week's lesson and word study.

Many teachers feel that spelling awareness and development cannot be left to chance. They are aware that spelling development will profit from all the language activities undertaken in the classroom but feel that this immersion may be insufficient. Some teachers want to provide consistent effective strategies that deal with spelling. Figure 6.22 provides some effective practices that help develop spelling. These take into consideration the children's developmental spelling level.

Handwriting

Handwriting is likewise addressed in a balanced literacy program. Again, teachers do not want children to practice incorrect letter formation; they want them to develop fluency in their handwriting. Therefore teachers take time to provide some modeling of letter formation, cor-

Precommunicative Stage

(Stage when children first use symbols to represent words.)

- Develop children's interest in print by reading aloud, creating a print-rich environment, taking environmental word walks, and the like.
- Teach the names of the letters of the alphabet.
- Develop letter-sound correspondence through shared reading, language experience, modeled writing, and so on.
- Read daily.
- Encourage children to read a variety of reading materials.
- Discuss directionality, concepts of words, rhyming.
- Encourage writing, e.g., language experience, children's writing, teacher modeling.
- Talk about spelling to children and parents.
- Introduce such terms as *letter, word, sentence,* and *sounds.*
- Encourage children to listen for and distinguish sounds at beginnings and ends of words and in rhyming words.
- Encourage correct pronunciation of words.

Semiphonetic Stage

(Stage that represents children's first attempts to apply letter-sound correspondence.)

- Encourage and demonstrate interest in children's attempts at writing.
- Provide quality writing experiences.
- Continue to develop sound-symbol correspondence.
- Continue language experience, asking for help with spelling.
- Continue to read daily and discuss concepts about print.
- Brainstorm words, categorize them, and place on charts or cards.
- Discuss invented spelling with children and parents.
- Compile lists or charts of words used frequently in writing.
- Encourage children to write by representing sounds in the order they hear them.

(*continued*)

Figure 6.22 Classroom Practices to Promote Spelling Development

Phonetic Stage

(Stage when the entire sound structure of words is represented.)

- Continue to read daily.
- Continue to provide quality writing experiences.
- Develop awareness of correct spelling, emphasizing the visual features of words.
- Expose children to word families, spelling patterns, and word structure.
- Explore sound-symbol associations.
- Provide opportunities for children to group words.
- Introduce "Have-a-Go" cards.

Transitional Stage

(Stage when children start to assimilate the basic conventions of standard English orthography.)

- Provide the correct model of spelling.
- Help children to identify misspelled words by circling or underlining them.
- Provide children with writing resources.
- Provide a spelling program using words from children's writing, word banks, class themes, and words commonly used in writing.
- Conduct word studies, e.g., affixes, root words, comparisons, homonyms.
- Provide children with word-sorting activities, e.g., grouping words based on similarities, such as similar meanings, word families, same vowel sounds.
- Continue to read daily.
- Continue to provide quality writing experiences.
- Develop children's resource skills.
- Extend use of personal word banks.
- Encourage use of mnemonics.
- Develop repertoire of strategies to remember words.
- Emphasize the importance of correct spelling for an audience.

Correct Stage

(Stage when children are aware of the English orthographic system.)

- Continue to conduct word studies and word sorts.
- Provide some systematic spelling instruction to increase spelling awareness and to correct misspelled words.
- Provide quality writing experiences.
- Have children keep spelling notebooks or personal dictionaries.
- Develop skills in proofreading.
- Develop children's responsibility for identifying and correcting their own spelling.
- Encourage children to use a variety of strategies when spelling words.
- Further develop use of references.
- Continue to provide quality reading experiences.

(Buchanan, 1989; Coate and Castle, 1989; Wing Jan, 1991)

rect spacing, and the like. Generally, this is done on chart paper or on an overhead projector during a minilesson. Teachers choose letters that help make young learners independent or letters they have observed that children need to learn.

One helpful way to keep track of students' handwriting progress is to prepare an index card for each letter of the alphabet (see Figure 6.23). As teachers observe improper letter formation while students are writing, they can jot down the student's name on the proper alphabet card for demonstrations and practice at a later time. Teachers do not want to neglect mistakes that later can become habits. But it is important not to interrupt the thinking process as children are writing.

Another way of providing help on letter formation is to pair a student who is having difficulty with a peer who has mastered letter formation. The children can practice together on the chalkboard using chalk or water; on paper with a pencil, markers, or paint; or in a tray of sand or salt.

Handwriting cards can be prepared by the teacher or a volunteer, demonstrating proper letter formation and providing some words for practicing the letters. These cards can be kept in a box and used by the children when practice is needed. (See Figure 6.24.) Frequently, children will have handwriting notebooks for practicing letters. Such notebooks also serve as a means of documenting student growth in handwriting.

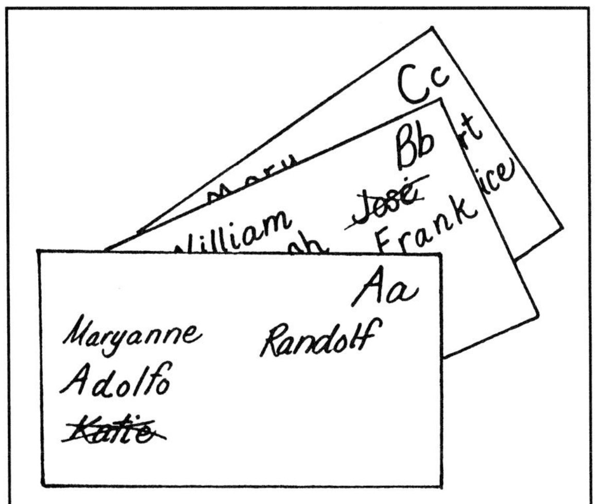

Figure 6.23 Cards to Identify Children with Handwriting Difficulties

Figure 6.24 Handwriting Cards

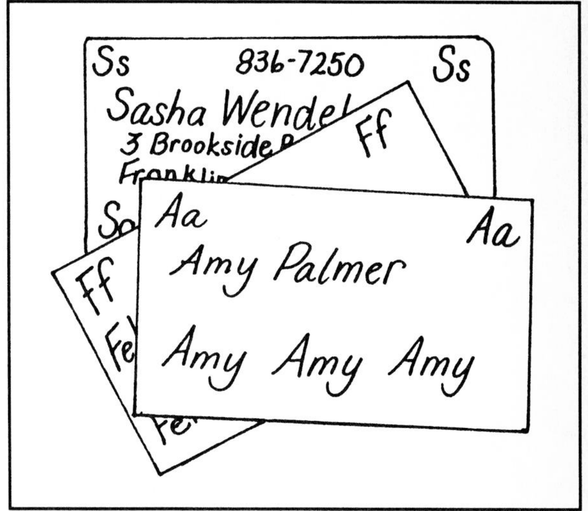

Writing Across the Curriculum

Generally, school districts or individual states provide guidelines or syllabi for generating the curriculum for each grade level. By looking over the specified curricular areas, teachers can note opportunities to include meaningful reading and writing experiences. Figure 6.25 describes the typical curriculum for grades K–2, which can serve as a framework for incorporating reading and writing across the curriculum.

It is exceedingly important to connect writing to other parts of the curriculum, and there are many occasions throughout the school day to do so. Each and every subject area affords opportunities for writing, whether these are recordings of observations (such as in science), research on topics currently being studied, journal reactions to literature or a viewing of a television show or videotape, preparing lists of materials to use in an activity, and so on. The many writing forms listed in Chapter 2 can be used across the curriculum.

Conclusion of Emergent Writing

Writing is an important aspect of the literacy development of young children. Writing helps chil-

Figure 6.25A Curriculums for Grades K–2

Curriculum for Grade K

Reading, Writing Speaking, Listening/ Language Arts	listening to stories and books read aloud listening to others improving speech, and word usage speaking in complete sentences following a simple text as teacher voice points recognizing rhyme repeating patterns sequencing stories and events
Math	one-to-one correspondence counting/number-numeral relationship recognizing shapes: △, ○, □, ▭ concept of clock, calendar, and passage of time recognizing coins and value simple measurement
Science	observing weather, seasons, and change the sun: source of heat, life, and energy living/nonliving things plants—how they grow animals—farm, zoo, wild, care of pets difference in earth, moon, and stars sink/float
Social Studies	relationships: home and family home address different types of jobs comparing/contrasting children of other countries how/why things change social relationships
Health	dental hygiene eating habits and manners fire/bus safety appropriate seasonal clothing

Figure 6.25B Curriculums for Grades K–2 (cont.)

Curriculum for Grade 1	
Reading, Writing Speaking, Listening/ Language Arts	recognizing environmental print use of inventive spelling establishing a sight vocabulary enunciation and pronunciation creating stories and poems retelling favorite stories literature response activities participating in group discussions beginning to identify story grammar
Math	use of numberline counting and writing to 99 understanding place value based on unit of 10 comparing quantity and size value and exchange of coins measurement: inch, foot, yard, and metric using clock to tell time on hour and half hour beginning word-problem solving
Science	grouping and classifying plants and animals air/water and ecology parts of a plant day and night/sun, moon, and stars weather and seasons how simple machines work
Social Studies	community helpers how jobs are related homes around the world reading and constructing simple maps understanding reasons for holidays
Health	how to avoid germs and viruses personal hygiene need for exercise and rest healthy eating habits/food groups clothing and weather drug, alcohol, tobacco awareness

Figure 6.25C Curriculums for Grades K–2 (cont.)

Curriculum for Grade 2	
Reading, Writing Speaking, Listening/ Language Arts	self-monitoring for understanding developing strategies for word identification beginning to proofread reading silently for specific purposes alphabetizing through second letter using guide words in a primary dictionary using the table of contents and index of a book literature response journals refining invented spelling
Math	addition and subtraction facts through 18 counting and writing to 999 introduction to division and multiplication using clock for telling time to the minute measurement: length, weight (solid and liquid) word-problem solving—one step using money in daily routine
Science	earth/moon/gravity magnetism space exploration animals, reproduction, and animal babies how seasons affect plants, animals, and people stars and constellations effects of weather
Social Studies	multicultural holiday celebrations American patriotic holidays comparing/contrasting families around the world food sources and distribution Abraham Lincoln and George Washington Martin Luther King, Jr.
Health	dangers of drug and substance abuse classifying foods by basic food groups preventing diseases

Figure 6.26 I Think I Can Bulletin Board

dren develop in their ability to segment words phonemically, to make appropriate sound-symbol associations, to compose, and to comprehend. An atmosphere must be created in the classroom that not only promotes writing but also makes it desirable and worthwhile for children to become writers. Through writing, children maintain their continued membership in the community of learners and in the "Literacy Club."

SUMMARY

The bulletin board that Jean Mumper creates with her children, "I think I can. I think I Can . . . I Know I Can . . ." (see Figure 6.26) perhaps sums up best what this chapter is about—all the literacy experiences that children *can* do in a whole language classroom. If the cars on this literacy railroad were to be filled with the activities that abound in child-centered, print-rich classrooms, they would overflow with authentic reading and writing experiences. Aboard would be reading and writing to, with, and by children. This chapter explained the why and the how of including such practices as reading aloud, shared reading, guided reading, Sustained Silent Reading, process writing, journal writing, modeled writing, and writing across the curriculum.

In addition, this chapter stressed the setting up of a positive reading and writing environment where children are respected, given choices, and encouraged to take risks. "I think I can" truly evolves into "I know I can" as children continue to grow as readers and writers.

BIBLIOGRAPHY AND SUGGESTED REFERENCES

Adams, M. (1990). *Beginning to read: Thinking and learning about print.* Cambridge, Mass.: MIT Press.

Anderson, R.; Hiebert, E.; Scott, J.; & Wilkinson, I. (1985). *Becoming a nation of readers: The report of the commission on reading.* Champaign, Ill.: Center for the Study of Reading.

Avery, C. (1993). . . . *And with a light touch: Learning about reading, writing, and teaching with first graders.* Portsmouth, N.H.: Heinemann.

Bolton, F., & Snowball, D. (1993). *Ideas for spelling.* Portsmouth, N.H.: Heinemann.

Bouffler, C., & Bean, W. (1987). *Spell by writing.* Rozelle, NSW, Australia: Primary English Teaching Association.

Bouffler, C., & Bean, W. (1989). *Spelling: A writer's resource.* Sydney: Rigby Education.

Buchanan, E. (1989). *Spelling for whole language classrooms.* Winnipeg, Manitoba, Canada: Whole Language Classroom.

Butler, A. (1988a). *Shared book experience.* Crystal Lake, Ill.: Rigby.

Butler, A. (1988b). *The elements of whole language.* Crystal Lake, Ill.: Rigby.

Butler, A., & Gamack, J. (1988). *The story chest in the classroom: Stages 8 and 9.* Crystal Lake, Ill.: Rigby.

Calkins, L. (1986). *The art of teaching writing.* Portsmouth, N.H.: Heinemann.

Chomsky, C. (1971). Write first, read later. *Childhood Education, 47,* 296–297.

Clay, M. (1975). *What did I write?* Portsmouth, N.H.: Heinemann.

Clay, M. (1985). *The early detection of reading difficulties.* Portsmouth, N.H.: Heinemann.

Clay, M. (1991). Introducing a new storybook to young readers. *The Reading Teacher, 45,* 264–273.

Coate, S., & Castle, M. (1989). Integrating LEA and invented spelling in kindergarten. *The Reading Teacher, 42,* 516–519.

Cullinan, B. (1989). Literature for young children. In D. Strickland and L. Morrow (Eds.), *Emerging literacy: Young children learn to read and write,* pp. 35–51. Newark, Del.: International Reading Association.

Cullinan, B., & Galda, L. (1994). *Literature and the child.* Orlando, Fla.: Harcourt Brace.

Cunningham, P. (1995). *Phonics they use.* New York: HarperCollins.

Davidson, A. (1990). *Literacy 2000—Teachers' Resource.* Crystal Lake, Ill.: Rigby.

Depree, H., & Iversen, S. (1994). *Early literacy in the classroom.* Bothell, Wash: The Wright Group.

Fisher, B. (1995). *Thinking and learning together: Curriculum and community in a primary classroom.* Portsmouth, N.H.: Heinemann.

Fraser, J., & Skolnick, D. (1994). *On their way: Celebrating second graders as they read and write.* Portsmouth, N.H.: Heinemann.

Friedman, S. (1986). How well can children write? *The Reading Teacher, 40,* 162–167.

Griffith, P., & Olson, M. (1992). Phonemic awareness helps beginning readers break the code. *The Reading Teacher, 45,* 516–523.

Gillet, J., & Temple, C. (1994). *Understanding reading problems: Assessment and instruction.* New York: HarperCollins.

Graves, D. (1983). *Writing: Teachers and children at work.* Portsmouth, N.H.: Heinemann.

Gutkin, R. (1990). Sustained ________ reading. *Language Arts, 67,* 490–491.

Hall, M. (1981). *Teaching reading as a language experience,* 2nd ed. Columbus, Ohio: Charles E. Merrill.

Heald-Taylor, G. (1985). *Making and using big books.* Toronto, Ontario, Canada: Shirley Lewis Information Service.

Heller, R. (1991). *Reading-writing connections: From theory to practice.* New York: Longman.

Hill, S., & Hancock, J. (1993). *Reading and writing communities: Co-operative literacy learning in the classroom.* Armadale, Australia: Eleanor Curtain Publishing.

Hipple, M. (1985). Journal writing in kindergarten. *Language Arts, 62,* 255–261.

Holdaway, D. (1979). *Foundations of literacy.* Portsmouth, N.H.: Heinemann.

Jewell, M., & Zintz, M. (1986). *Learning to read naturally.* Dubuque, Iowa: Kendall/Hunt.

Johnson, T., & Louis, D. (1990). *Bringing it all together: A program for literacy.* Portsmouth, N.H.: Heinemann.

Jones, M., & Nessel, D. (1985). Enhancing the curriculum with experience stories. *The Reading Teacher, 39,* 18–22.

Kettenring, L., & Graybill, N. (1991). Cereal boxes foster emergent literacy. *The Reading Teacher, 44,* 522–523.

Kintisch, L. (1986). Journal writing: Stages of development. *The Reading Teacher, 40,* 168–172.

Manning, M.; Manning, G.; & Hughes, J. (1987). Journals in first grade: What children write. *The Reading Teacher, 41,* 311–315.

Martinez, M., & Teale, W. (1987). The ins and outs of a kindergarten writing program. *The Reading Teacher, 40,* 444–451.

Mason, J.; Peterman, C.; & Kerr, B. (1989). Reading to kindergarten children. In D. Strickland and L. Morrow (Eds.), *Emerging literacy: Young children learn to read and write,* pp. 52–62. Newark, Del.: International Reading Association.

Mattingly, I. (1984). Reading, linguistic awareness, and language acquisition. In J. Downing and R.

Valatin (Eds.), *Language awareness and learning to read,* pp. 9–25. New York: Springer-Verlag.
Mavrogenes, N. (1986). What every teacher should know about emergent literacy. *The Reading Teacher, 40,* 174–178.
McGee, L., & Richgels, D. (1990). *Literacy's beginnings: Supporting young readers and writers.* Boston: Allyn and Bacon.
Ministry of Education. (1991). *Primary program foundation document.* British Columbia.
Moffett, J., & Wagner, B. (1993). What works is play. *Language Arts, 70,* 32–36.
Mooney, M. (1995). Guided reading—The reader in control. *Teaching K–8, 25,* 54–58.
National Commission on Excellence in Education. (1983). *A nation at risk: The imperative for educational reform.* A Report to the Nation and the Secretary of Education. Washington, D.C.: U.S. Government Printing Office.
Newman, J., & Church, S. (1990). Commentary: Myths of whole language. *The Reading Teacher, 44,* 20–27.
Peterson, B. (1991). Selecting books for beginning readers. In D. Deford; C. Lyons; and G.S. Pinnell (Eds.), *Bridges to literacy: Learning from Reading Recovery,* pp. 119–147. Portsmouth, N.H.: Heinemann.
Pinnell, G., & McCarrier. (1994). Interactive writing: A transition tool for assisting children in learning to read and write. In E. Hiebert & B. Taylor (Eds.), *Getting reading right from the start: Effective early literacy interventions,* pp. 149–170. Boston: Allyn & Bacon.
Powell, D., & Hornsby, D. (1993). *Learning phonics and spelling in a whole language classroom.* New York: Scholastic.
Routman, R. (1988). *Transitions: From literature to literacy.* Portsmouth, N.H.: Heinemann.
Routman, R. (1993). The uses and abuses of invented spelling. *Instructor, 102,* 36–39.
Smith, F. (1988). Joining the literacy club. In F. Smith (Ed.), *Joining the literacy club: Further essays into education,* pp. 1–16. Portsmouth, N.H.: Heinemann.
Snowball, D. (1993). A sensible approach to teaching spelling. *Teaching K–8, 23,* 49–53.
Stahl, S. (1992). Saying the "p" word: Nine guidelines for exemplary phonics instruction. *The Reading Teacher, 45,* 618–625.
Strickland, D., & Morrow, L. (Eds.) (1989). *Emerging literacy: Young children learn to read and write.* Newark, Del.: International Reading Association.
Strickland, D., & Taylor, D. (1989). Family storybook reading: Implications for children, families, and curriculum. In D. Strickland and L. Morrow (Eds.), *Emerging literacy: Young children learn to read and write,* pp. 27–34. Newark, Del.: International Reading Association.
Sulzby, E. (1988). *Emergent literacy: Kindergartners write and read, including Sulzby coding system.* Ann Arbor, Mich.: University of Michigan and North Central Regional Educational Laboratory.
Sulzby, E.; Teale, W.; & Kamberelis, G. (1989). Emergent writing in the classroom: Home and school connections. In D. Strickland and L. Morrow (Eds.), *Emerging literacy: Young children learn to read and write,* pp. 63–79. Newark, Del.: International Reading Association.
Thornell, C. (1991). Creating big books and predictable books. *The Reading Teacher, 44,* 521–522.
Trachtenburg, P. (1990). Using children's literature to enhance phonics instruction. *The Reading Teacher, 43,* 648–654.
Trelease, J. (1995). *The new read-aloud handbook.* New York: Penguin.
Wagstaff, J. (1995). *Phonics that work: New strategies for the reading/writing classroom.* New York: Scholastic.
Weaver, B. (1992). *Defining story levels.* Charlotteville, New York: Story House Corporation.
Williams, R. (1990). *Integrated learning workshops: The balanced language program.* Bothell, Wash: The Wright Group.
Wing Jan, L. (1991). *Spelling and grammar.* Sydney, Australia: Ashton Scholastic.
Yopp, H. (1992). Developing phonemic awareness in young children. *The Reading Teacher, 45,* 696–703.
Yopp, H. (1995). Read-aloud books for developing phonemic awareness: An annotated bibliography. *The Reading Teacher, 48,* 538–542.

CHILDREN'S LITERATURE CITED

Bridwell, N. *Clifford* books (series). New York: Scholastic.
Cowley, J. (1980a). *Mrs. Wishy Washy.* San Diego: The Wright Group.
Cowley, J. (1980b). *Smarty Pants.* San Diego: The Wright Group.
Drew, D., (1990). *I spy.* Crystal Lake, Ill.: Rigby.
Galdone, P. (1970). *The three little pigs.* Boston: Houghton Mifflin.
Gardiner, J. (1980). *Stone Fox.* New York: Crowell.
Heller, R. (1983). *The reason for a flower: Plants that never ever bloom.* New York: Grosset.
Hyman, T. (1983). *Little Red Riding Hood.* New York: Holiday House.

Martin, B. (1970). *Brown bear, brown bear, what do you see?* New York: Holt, Rinehart, and Winston.

McCloskey, R. (1941). *Make way for ducklings.* New York: Viking.

Parkes, B., and Smith, J. (1986). *The enormous watermelon.* Crystal Lake, Ill.: Rigby.

Raffi. (1987). *Down by the bay.* New York: Crown Publishers.

Rey, H. A. (1941). *Curious George.* Boston: Houghton Mifflin.

Schmidt, K. (1967). *The gingerbread man.* New York: Scholastic.

Seuss, Dr. (1957). *Cat in the hat.* New York: Beginner Books.

Vaughan, M. (1986). *Hands.* New York: Scholastic.

Waber, B. (1972). *Ira sleeps over.* Boston: Houghton Mifflin.

Zemach, M. (1976). *It could always be worse.* New York: Scholastic.

BEYOND EMERGENT LITERACY: ORGANIZATION AND CLASSROOM MANAGEMENT (GRADES 3–6)

San Francisco Earthquake
by Kelli Kanvin and Alana Schultz

Earthquake	Earthquake
Earthquake cracks open	
	Shaking violently
chairs and tables	chairs and tables
Fly all over	
	just missing you
As they pass by	As they pass by.
The first thought	
	is death
As you sit	
	waiting for it
To end.	to end.

Kelli Kanvin, Grade 5
Alana Schultz, Grade 6
Bennett School
Onteora Central Schools
Boiceville, New York

Inspired by: *Joyful Noise: Poems for Two Voices* by Paul Fleischman
and *Earthquakes* by Seymour Simon

OVERVIEW

It is now time to make new literacy connections for students in grade 3 and beyond. Whole language with older readers and writers has some similarities to and some differences from emergent literacy classrooms. In order to demonstrate the commonalities and the uniquenesses, this chapter and the next visit transitional and whole language classrooms in grades 3 through 6 and show how the classrooms are arranged, organized, and managed and ways in which reading and writing are addressed in these grades. This chapter specifically addresses the physical design of the classroom, resources for organizing and managing the whole language classroom, scheduling, and alternatives to worksheets and workbooks.

Questions to Ponder

1. How can the classroom be arranged to facilitate implementing whole language in grades 3–6?
2. How are learning centers used in grades 3–6?
3. What can be done to help students become more self-directed and self-reliant?
4. How can the day be organized in order to cover all the needed content?
5. What purposeful activities can replace traditional seatwork?

ORGANIZATION AND MANAGEMENT OF THE CLASSROOM

Physical Design of the Classroom

As with the home in fostering learning to talk and emergent literacy classrooms that immerse children in a print-rich environment in fostering learning to read and write, the organization and management of classrooms for older students are likewise important in furthering literacy development. If we were to visit whole language classrooms in grade 3 and above, we would see many of the same features that are discussed in Chapter 5. The physical arrangement of the classroom would permit spaces for private investigation and reflection, for cooperative efforts (either peer or small group), and for whole-class activities and sharing. The rooms would be divided using similar devices, such as movable shelves and chalkboards, pieces of furniture (such as desks and couches), and file cabinets.

Although many classrooms still have individual student desks, many schools have replaced desks with tables, necessitating setting up storage areas for the students' personal supplies and books. The use of tables permits more flexible grouping arrangements and offers excellent work areas for projects. Tables also take up less floor space than do individual desks, thereby freeing space for centers and community meetings. When teachers inherit desks and budgets make ordering tables unrealistic, teachers frequently cluster the desks. The tops of the desks are considered public property (therefore available for general class use), while the insides remain the students' private property. Desks can be rearranged as needed.

Learning centers (or stations) are still visible in the upper grades, although they may be fewer in number and have less space devoted to them. Still crucial to any literacy program is the library corner. As in the emergent literacy classroom, this is an attractive, inviting section of the room littered with books, comfortable furniture (couches, beanbag chairs, rocking chairs), posters, and display areas for projects and author studies. The library corner may be designed around a theme—such as a tropical island with palm trees and beach chairs—or may be set up using such unusual equipment and furniture as lofts and bathtubs.

Listening and writing centers may be incorporated into the library corner, thereby turning it into a Literacy Center, or may be located in separate areas. Housed in these centers are equipment for listening and writing supplies. Other centers may include a computer center, a math manipulatives center, or a thematic center. Thematic centers change in focus and design as areas of study change and reflect the integration of various curricular areas.

The room itself is alive with print—on bulletin boards, message boards, charts and checklists, in areas designated to showcase student writing and projects. Student writing resulting from both Writers' Workshops and other curricular areas is evident and prominently displayed,

FROM THE CLASSROOM OF . . .

Curt Fulton Wallkill, N.Y.

DOODLE BOOKS

Children, like adults, just love to doodle whenever possible, wherever possible. So why not in the classroom? The students in Curt Fulton's sixth grade classroom not only get the opportunity to doodle on the back of their worksheets and on extra recycled paper, but their teacher responds to their doodles by creating cartoons out of them. When Curt's students have finished their work, they are permitted to doodle. When Curt sees the doodles, he adds cartoon-like speech bubbles, often using a play of words, humor, a personal message to the doodler, etc. As captions, comments, and dialogue are added to the students' doodles, the resulting products are compiled into a class Doodle Book. As the year progresses, the students not only contribute doodles, but add their own meaningful text as well. The doodles become excellent vehicles for teacher-student communication and enhance the students' growing vocabularies as they explore and play with language. Doodle Books are yet another kind of dialogue journal where teachers, students, and their classmates can engage in written conversations and have fun with their written language. Below is an example of an entry into the Doodle Book.

as are books pertaining to classroom investigations and explorations (see Figure 7.1).

The whole language classroom is purposefully arranged to encourage student responsibility, to permit flexible grouping options, and to immerse students in a variety of forms of language. A whole language classroom promotes students' ownership of their own learning, celebrates process as well as product, and values the students' input in their quest to become readers and writers. Students are consulted in arranging the room, and it is their work that is celebrated and displayed.

Materials in the Classroom

The same considerations regarding selection and use of materials discussed in Chapter 5 for the emergent literacy classroom apply to the upper grades as well. An abundance of resources—which include books, writing materials, manipulatives, and artifacts—must be available. Students must have ample opportunities to explore and investigate using different resources, and the emphasis must be on discovery and investigation as opposed to answering prepared comprehension questions or constantly engaging in convergent-type activities. Materials must not become the curriculum but rather must be used to support the learning that is to occur.

When choosing books for literature study or to accompany a thematic unit or particular curricular area, teachers must be aware that a variety of literature—both fiction and nonfiction—is needed on many different reading levels. In selecting books, teachers need to take into consideration student interest, the type of language used, the kind of information presented, the authenticity of the materials, and the applicability of the literature to the content and processes that are to be learned.

Many titles will be needed for the various reading activities—for example, Sustained Silent Reading, reading aloud, shared reading, guided reading, individualized reading, and reading across the curriculum. Fortunately, today publishers provide excellent listings of literature in their catalogs, and many even arrange literature into topics or themes and provide suggested grade levels. To find interesting and effective titles, teachers may consult the many textbooks on children's literature, professional anthologies, school and public libraries, colleagues, and students. They may discuss books with their colleagues, attend conferences and make a note of books suggested by the speakers, and read newsletters and book reviews.

Teachers need to become familiar with the literature available. It is essential that the teacher preread the books and be thoroughly knowledgeable about the selections.

Some suggested titles that have proved effective for grades 3–6 include:

GRADE 3

Amelia Bedelia by Peggy Parrish
Bedtime for Francis by Russell Hoban
Freckle Juice by Judy Blume
I Was a Second Grade Werewolf by Daniel Pinkwater
Magic School Bus by Joanna Cole and Bruce Deegan
Pippi Longstocking by Astrid Lindgren
Ramona Quimby, Age 8 by Beverly Cleary
Socks by Beverly Cleary
The Velveteen Rabbit by Marjorie Williams

BEYOND GRADE 3

Anastasia Krupnik by Lois Lowry
Charlotte's Web by E. B. White
Fantastic Mr. Fox by Roald Dahl
Island of the Blue Dolphins by Scott O'Dell
My Side of the Mountain by Jean Craighead George
My Teacher Is an Alien by Bruce Coville
Tales of a Fourth Grade Nothing by Judy Blume
The Celery Stalks at Midnight by James Howe
Hatchet by Gary Paulsen

This listing is just suggestive and has proven to work well with students of this age. For publication information about these books, see Appendix E.

Books should not really be relegated to particular grade levels, but in many instances schools make decisions about the use of particular books at certain grade levels for motivational

Figure 7.1A Physical Design of the Classroom

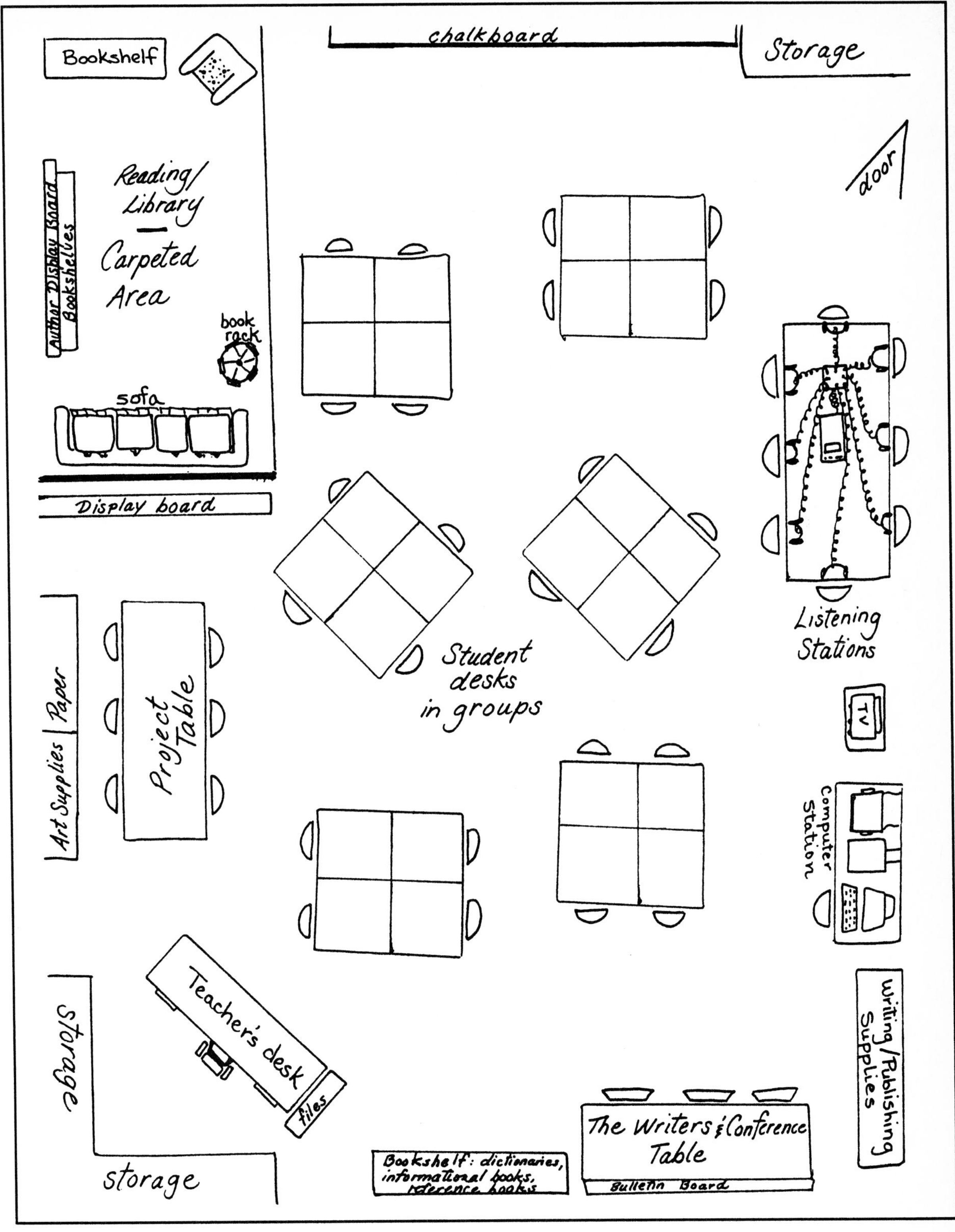

Figure 7.1B Physical Design of the Classroom (cont.)

and instructional purposes (e.g., reserving certain titles for literature workshop in grade 5). These decisions should be negotiated among all the teachers involved.

The materials need to be organized in some fashion to permit easy access and practical storage. Individual titles may be housed in the class library for use at DEAR time, for research, and as sources for writing models. Multiple copies may be kept in storage areas in teachers' individual classrooms or in a central storage area in the school building to allow for maximum use among the faculty.

Books that are to be used for thematic studies or curricular investigations or referred to periodically throughout the year need only be listed somewhere by category. A list of books for teaching about trees, for example, may be kept in a file box with notations as to where the books were formerly obtained. Whatever management system works best for teachers—whether file boxes or three-ring binders—a record needs to be kept of titles to use and their whereabouts. Using a wealth of resources on a daily basis throughout the school year can be overwhelming if teachers do not document their past efforts or their planning.

Of course, books are not the only resources. Other print sources need to be used as well, and these include primary sources (such as deeds, documents, and journals), magazines, reference materials, and newspapers. Besides print resources, there must be ample writing and publishing materials and materials for exploration and investigation, especially in the areas of mathematics and science. Without adequate, easily accessible resources, teachers will have difficulty moving beyond prepackaged teaching programs like basals and into more child-centered, literature-based literacy programs.

Time Tables/Schedules

Another important aspect of setting up whole language classrooms is an arrangement of the school day that no longer fragments the curriculum and that provides adequate time for real learning to occur using authentic literacy tasks

FROM THE CLASSROOM OF . . .

Joyce Valenti Science Teacher, Windham, N.Y.
New York State Teacher of the Year 1994–1995

What are Scientists?

At the beginning of the school year in order to get to know her students and to assess their knowledge and attitudes about science, Joyce asks them to bring in artifacts that represent what science means to them. The students amass a variety of collections, representing many scientific endeavors and explorations. For example, some students bring in rocks, plants, and living animal specimens, while others may bring in simple machines, rocket models, and kits from scientific supply stores. The students provide a brief oral and written description of their collection. This gives Joyce added information as to their communication skills.

Later in the year, and frequently as a culminating activity for the year, Joyce has her students design lab coats to represent a scientist from a particular field of their choosing. The students are limited to using white garbage bags as the material for their lab coats. The creations are displayed during a science fashion show. For example, a budding botanist decorated her lab coat with pictures of flowers, seed packets, and the like. An entomologist illustrated a variety of insects, designing some using fabric, pom-poms, pipe cleaners, etc. On his back were some cardboard wings, completing the lab coat.

An adaptation of this activity might be to share the book, *What are Scientists?* by Rita Gelman and Susan Busbaum. This book is a rhyming tribute to the people who enter the field of science. Some outer space creatures go to earth to find out what scientists are and what they do. Word origins are provided, e.g., *astron* in Greek means *star* and *physica* in Latin means *natural things*. Even though the book depicts all types of scientists, it leaves a message to aspiring scientists—that to be a scientist means to be curious, ask lots of questions, and try to find solutions to the questions. It admonishes that scientists are not from outer space, rather they are ordinary people just like the readers of the book!

FROM THE CLASSROOM OF . . .

Jim McIntyre Pine Bush, N.Y.

BODY MAPS

Need a way to have your students become acquainted with each other, or to develop a character in a book, then why not introduce your students to *Body Maps?* Jim McIntyre, a sixth grade teacher, has his students construct body maps at the beginning of the year. Each student is given a generic body shape, and collects pictures, words, and phrases that are representative of his or her hobbies, interests, families, talents, and the like. These are laminated and displayed around the room. Identities can be kept secret for awhile as classmates try to figure out who the body map represents, or they can be shared at a community meeting. Naturally, they make excellent displays for Open Houses and wonderful additions to student portfolios.

A variation of this technique is to use the body map to represent a character from a book. For example, let's look at Brian, the main character in the book *Hatchet* by Gary Paulsen. Brian is a survivor of a divorce, of a plane crash, and of spending months in the wilderness of Canada. He has encounters with such wild animals as a moose, fish, bears, and birds, all of which contribute to the story. In addition, fire, a tornado, a survival pack, a spear, and a bow and arrow all have significance to his survival. Pictures and words could be collected to represent these events and objects. These body map characters could be displayed on a bulletin board featuring favorite books or characters.

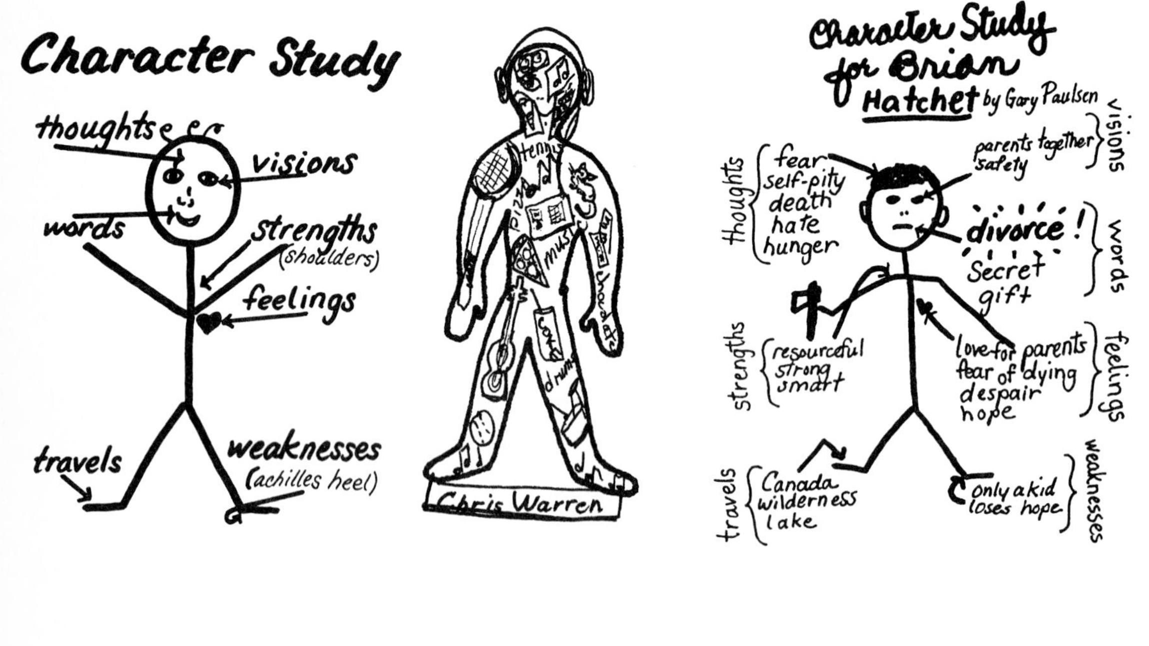

and activities. Every teacher has unique constraints owing to the school's master scheduling, so classroom schedules must take into account special area teachers, compensatory education teachers in both mathematics and reading, speech teachers, and so on. Thus no one schedule will work for everyone. Following is a generic schedule for one day in a process reading and writing classroom (i.e., a whole language classroom):

A DAY IN THE LIFE OF A PROCESS READING AND WRITING CLASSROOM

8:50–9:00	Journal Writing
9:00–9:15	Community Meeting
9:15–9:40	Shared Reading/Poetry
9:40–10:40	Readers' Workshop
10:40–10:50	Snack
10:50–11:20	Specials
11:20–12:05	Writers' Workshop
12:05–12:50	Lunch
12:50–1:05	DEAR Time
1:05–1:45	Math
1:45–2:50	Thematic Study Science Social Studies
2:50–3:00	Clean Up/Dismissal

In order to help teachers plan their day, suggested time allocations for the elements of whole language are provided in Figure 7.2. Several other examples of schedules are outlined in Figure 7.3. Although there are variations, all schedules allot a great deal of time to reading and writing and to integrating the curriculum. A more in-depth look at a typical day in a process reading and writing classroom is given in Figure 7.4.

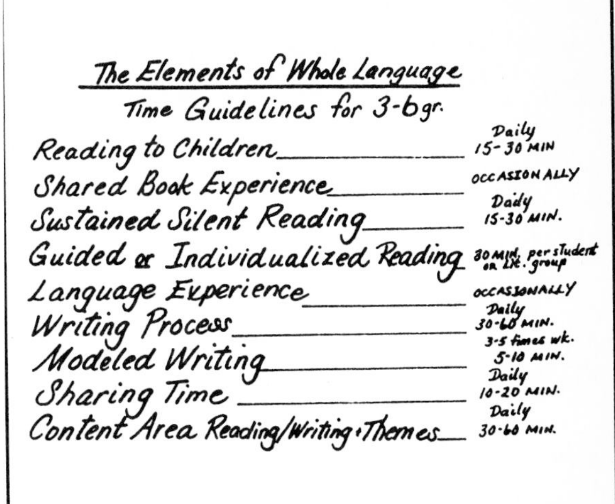

Figure 7.2 The Allocations for the Elements of Whole Language

CLASSROOM ROUTINES IN THE UPPER GRADES

If classrooms are to be organized to encourage student choice and independence, then there must be some system to ensure that students develop self-reliance. Just as with younger learners, in the beginning of the school year students in the upper grades must have training in classroom routines and management. They have to be involved in developing rules regarding movement around the room and for working with others. They have to be apprised of what to do when they have completed their work and what to do if they are working independently and don't understand how to do something.

Cooperatively developing rules for appropriate classroom behavior can be part of community meetings held at the beginning of the school year. Desired behaviors (behaviors that can be accepted by the students and the teacher) can be brainstormed and listed on charts. These can be reviewed for a few days, amended, and revised. The final product can be posted in the classroom and, if need be, modified at any time throughout the year. In addition to being involved in establishing an effective classroom management system, students gain valuable knowledge of participation in government and work together for a common goal.

Since there will be many opportunities throughout the day, throughout the curriculum, and throughout the year for students to assume responsibility for their own learning, they need to be aware of the possibilities and opportunities present in the classroom if they should be confused about something or have finished their work and need something else to do.

Figure 7.3 Daily Class Schedules

From Joe Gasparini:

SAMPLE SCHEDULE

Joe Gasparini, Grade 6—Self-contained Integrated Day (I.D.) at Hyde Park Elementary School

8:30–8:45	The A.M. Routine (preparation for the day)
8:45–8:55	Journal Writing (free-write)
8:55–9:15	Class Meeting —Journal sharing —outline work of the day —general discussion —announcements
9:15–10:30	Language (generally I.D. theme related) —literature groups —reading conferences —process writing —author's circle —individual and/or whole or small group conferences or lessons on spelling, grammar, etc. —independent & I.D. theme related work

(Note: Not all of the above is done in one class session. On a given day, for example, literature groups may meet followed by small group lessons. Independent and I.D. work occur daily.)

10:30–11:00	Special Classes (Art, Music, Library, P.E. x 2 weekly)
11:00–11:45	Mathematics (generally I.D. theme related) —problem solving pairs & groups —individual and/or whole or small group conferences
11:45–12:45	Lunch/Recess
12:45–1:00	Story/Read-aloud
1:00–1:15	DEAR (Drop Everything And Read)
1:15–2:15	I.D. (Integrated Day) Theme Work —research and project work on Social Studies and Science related themes into which Language and Math and sometimes Special Classes are integrated —individual and/or whole or small group planning sessions and conferences
2:15–2:35	Band/Chorus or additional theme work
2:35–2:50	The P.M. Routine (preparation for the end of the day)
2:50	Dismissal

(Note: This is an example of a flexible, rotating schedule that centers around the school-wide master scheduling of special classes that meet at different times every day. So, for example, on another given day, I.D. theme work and math may occur in the morning, and language may occur in the afternoon, etc.)

Teachers should establish, along with student input, a system whereby students can seek help from a classmate or from the teacher without disrupting the rest of the class. A "Need Help" sign can be placed on the student's desk, a sign-up list can be made available for students seeking help, or specific students can be designated as class helpers.

Responsibility for helping others can be rotated among the class members. Teachers can also encourage students to help one another at all times without a formal help system in place.

Since students work at different rates and will be at varying points in their Writers' or Readers' Workshop, some will finish writing, reading, and activity projects before others. To avoid having nothing to do—with resulting possible misbehavior—students should be aware of activities they may choose once their class assignment is completed. A chart listing such pos-

Figure 7.4 A Typical Day in the Integrated Classroom Program

Monday, December 9, 1991

(Please Note: The activities for major content areas as outlined on this day do not occur at the same time daily. Whereas language is scheduled for the morning on this day, it may be scheduled in the afternoon on another day. One may think of the schedule as a flexible and floating one whose only bounds are the scheduling of special classes, i.e., art, and lunch and recess periods.)

8:30–8:45 A.M. ROUTINE
Upon their arrival the students go into an A.M. routine, which basically is a preparation time for the day. In this time they organize their materials, hand in assignments, sign up for lunch choices, etc.

8:45 OFFICIAL START OF THE SCHOOL DAY
Salute to the flag.

8:45–8:55 JOURNAL WRITING
This is a free-writing time in which the students are invited to record in their personal journals anything that they wish, i.e., stories, poetry, reflections, etc.

8:55–9:00 ATTENDANCE AND MISCELLANEOUS BUSINESS

9:00–9:15 (variable time) MORNING MEETING
This is the time to officially greet one another. Those students who wish to do so may share something from their journal writing. After each sharing there is time for other students to comment. I next outline the day from the Today Board (a plan for the day is presented and discussed briefly). Then miscellaneous announcements are made. In closing, the students then may bring up any concerns, questions, etc. that they may have.

9:15–10:30 LANGUAGE
Many different language activities occur during this time period that may or may not directly relate to our integrated theme, which at this time is "The Human Body." These activities consist primarily of literature groups, writing process, author circles, and individual, small-group or whole-class lessons. On this particular day, two of the three literature groups (Caldecott, Newbery, and Wilder) will meet separately with me to continue our discussion about the nutritional and survival needs of the main character Sam from *My Side of the Mountain.* This literature selection supports our theme of "The Human Body." The students who are not presently participating in the literature group will work independently in Writers' Workshop. On this particular day, these students will be involved in peer revision and editing of a writing piece with the multicultural theme "Me, My Family, My Holiday." Upon completion of this assignment, the students will then work on their individual component to the human body theme. Students are researching and preparing presentations on topics related to the human body that are of particular interest to them.

10:30–11:00 I.D. THEME WORK
The students will continue to study and evaluate nutritional information from food packaging. They are to pay particular attention to the caloric, protein, carbohydrate, fat, and sodium content of the food products. They will make decisions about which foods are more nutritious and less nutritious and present their thinking in the form of a nutrition chart for comparison and discussion.

(*continued*)

Figure 7.4 A Typical Day in the Integrated Classroom Program (cont.)

11:00–11:45 MATH PROBLEM SOLVING
The students were given information on the caloric content of such nutrients as fats and carbohydrates (1g fat = 9 calories; 1 g carbohydrate = 4 calories). Students will use manipulatives to construct an algorithm by which they can figure out the calories of these nutrients as they are found in different food products selected from the nutrition charts. Concepts of decimals, percentages, and fractional parts will be reviewed and further developed in this and subsequent lessons.

11:45–12:45 LUNCH & RECESS

12:45–1:00 DEAR (Drop Everything and Read)
This is a daily quiet time when the students and I select reading material for no other purpose than to take time and to read for ENJOYMENT!

1:00–1:15 READ ALOUD
I will continue to read aloud to the students from James Howe's *A Night Without Stars.* Synopsis: A sixth-grade girl faces the trials, tribulations, and triumphs of her open-heart surgery. This is a literature selection that fits nicely with our human body theme.

1:15–1:45 PHYSICAL EDUCATION

1:45–2:35 I.D. THEME WORK
The students will continue to make oral and visual presentations of the individual components to the human body theme. On this day, Cathleen is presenting her research on taste in the form of an oral report and a taste demonstration of different foods. David will be presenting his research on smoking and its adverse effects on the lungs leading to lung cancer. He will also demonstrate the accumulation of tar and nicotene on cotton in a "cigarette-smoking machine." If time permits, Krista will present her research on substance abuse.

2:35–2:50 P.M. ROUTINE
Students do classroom maintenance chores—clean chalkboards, organize classroom supplies, etc. Then they tend to their personal needs—assignments, packing belongings, etc.

2:50 DISMISSAL

sibilities can be developed for student reference (see Figure 7.5).

Offering students choices helps develop their sense of responsibility. Involving students in cooperatively arranging and designing the classroom and in developing a system where all may function productively fosters students' ownership of their learning and prepares them for life outside school.

INSTEAD OF SEATWORK

When considering activities for students to do throughout the day in any given curricular area, teachers must consider the purpose and worthiness of any of the assigned or optional activities. For years students have spent large portions of the school day filling in blanks, coloring ditto sheets, or working on fragmented worksheet exercises, most of which were used to keep them busy and quiet while the teacher worked with other children, generally in a basal reading group. These types of activities are no longer desirable—so what do teachers give their students *instead of seatwork?*

The possibilities are endless, although initially the idea of abandoning seatwork activities—which may represent years of idea collection by the teachers—seems frightening. One teacher, when told of the move in her school away from ditto sheets and workbooks,

FROM THE CLASSROOM OF . . .

Donna Howell Cairo, N.Y.

IF YOU HAD TO CHOOSE ONE BOOK

Think about having to leave the Planet Earth with the strong possibility of never being able to return and being allowed to take only one book with you. This dilemma is addressed in the book *The Green Book* by Jill Paton Walsh. The inhabitants fleeing catastrophic conditions on Earth must resettle on a faraway planet, and personal belongings are limited. The students in Donna Howell's sixth grade class relive this adventure. They too plan what to take in the form of food, supplies, clothing, equipment, and the one book allowed each person. Donna's class anguishes over the perfect book to take, and the reasons for their choice. What one book would you take along on this lifetime venture?

stored her collection in her home just in case she needed it. After several years of success with other types of activities, she ended up casting away her traditional seatwork ditto sheets with no remorse or looking back.

Because the classroom is a process classroom—that is, innumerable activities are going on in various stages at all times—activities and projects are always available for the students. Both Readers' and Writers' Workshops provide ample opportunities for students to pick up where they left off and continue with their reading, writing, responding to literature in journals, research, and projects. Science, social studies, and thematic studies encourage students to delve further into the area of study, to explore, and to investigate, either alone, with a buddy, or with a small group. Students are no longer constrained by a mountainous load of paperwork but have time to pursue interests and class topics in greater depth. Figure 7.6 suggests specific activities that can replace seatwork, but it is best to keep in mind that the replacements should be purposeful and permit

Figure 7.5 What To Do Charts

WHAT TO DO

If I don't know *what* to do
or
how to do it:

- Ask a classmate.
- Read the directions again very carefully.
- Sign up on the "I need help" list.
- Ask the teacher if she's free.
- Work on something else until I get help.

WHAT TO DO

When my work is done

- Add to my writing topics list.
- Continue writing on my latest piece.
- Write in my journal.
- Read a book from the library or for Literature Workshop.
- Read a magazine article.
- Help a classmate.
- Research an area for our class theme study.
- Work on my book-sharing project.
- Share my writing with a friend.
- Organize the class library.
- Clean up or organize a learning center.
- Work on the computer.
- Refill supplies (e.g., in Writing or Publishing Center).
- Continue working on my guided investigation alone or with a buddy.
- Read with a buddy.
- Work on an activity in a learning center (station).
- Prepare a book talk.
- Find a poem for Poetry Sharing Time.

the students to broaden their knowledge and apply what they have learned, not just serve as substitutes for seatwork to keep students quiet.

SUMMARY

This chapter discussed the organization and management of the whole language classroom. Just as houses need foundations on which to build the rest of the structure, literacy programs need to be grounded in a sound support system. Integral to the success of any literacy program is how the classroom is arranged, what management techniques are necessary to encourage student choice, input, and independence, and the choice, availability, and use of materials to support the learning. As in the case of emergent literacy classrooms, the physical environment is designed to permit flexibility among student groupings and to immerse students in a variety of print resources. Students need to be involved

Figure 7.6 Instead of Seatwork

LANGUAGE ARTS ACTIVITIES

LISTENING/SPEAKING

- Listen to a taped version of a book.
- Make a tape of your writing and listen to it.
- Listen to some classical music and write about the mood it portrays.
- Tape-record a speech, oral report, or book talk.
- Tape-record stories for read-alongs for classmates or for younger readers.
- Tape-record your parents reading a story aloud and bring it to class for others to hear.
- Listen to your classmates' writing.

READING

- Read your book for Readers' Workshop or from DEAR time.
- Read your latest writing piece aloud to a friend.
- Read through drafts in your writing folder to find one you can develop.
- Read extra material for our class theme.
- Read some poems and select one to share during Poetry Sharing Time.
- Read a play or a script for Readers' Theatre.
- Read a newspaper or a magazine from the Library Corner.
- Contribute to the class card file of books our class has read.
- Read the entries in the Class Journal.
- Read the calendar for upcoming events.
- Read the messages on the Message Board.
- Read any letters or news in your class mailbox.
- Look through the dictionary for interesting words, word origins, multiple meanings.
- Use the encyclopedia to find information for your guided investigation.
- Read editions of our class newspaper and literary anthology.
- Read with a buddy.

WRITING

- Continue working on your draft.
- Write in your literature response log.
- Write a "Dear Reader" book talk.
- Write in the Class Journal.
- Write in your personal journal
- Add to your "I Can Write About" List.
- Write a poem, story, or article to go with what we are studying in science, social studies, or our theme.
- Write letters to friends or to companies to obtain information for a class project.
- Write a piece for the class newspaper.
- Write a piece for the weekly Parent Newsletter.
- Write a script for a wordless book.
- Take part in a written conversation with a friend.
- Write about a famous historical figure.
- Compare two books, characters, events.
- Pretend you are a character in a book and write to another storybook character.

(*continued*)

Figure 7.6 Instead of Seatwork (cont.)

- Write a letter to a favorite author.
- Write a letter to the principal, janitor, secretary expressing thanks for all they do.
- Write a request to the PTA.
- Write invitations to parents, guest speakers, other school members to a special event.
- Construct a time line for a period in history.
- Write greeting cards for special occasions.
- Transform a poem into a story, a story into a poem, a nonfiction piece into a narrative, a narrative into nonfiction.
- Write a script for a play or Readers' Theatre.
- Prepare speeches for yourself or be a ghostwriter for famous people.
- Write a letter or journal entry as if you were a famous historical figure or a character in a novel.
- Put together a travel brochure for a country or state that the class is studying.
- Make a story map of the book you are reading.
- Write stories for younger readers.
- Interview real-life people, other teachers or students, community members.
- "Interview" a character in a book.

EXPRESSIVE ARTS ACTIVITIES

- Make a mural of books read or to accompany class investigations.
- Make scenery, props, costumes for a book-sharing activity or a play.
- Illustrate a time line with historical figures and pictures of significant events.
- Construct collages to accompany poems or areas of class study.
- Draw, paint, or color illustrations for your writing, book-sharing activities, or thematic study.
- Make puppets for dramatic interpretations.
- Mold characters or scenery from clay or papier-mâché to accompany stories.
- Make flannel board characters for storytelling.
- Construct roll stories.
- Prepare a chalk talk for a favorite story.
- Fingerpaint feelings and reactions to mood music.
- Make a silhouette of yourself or a storybook character and then write a poem, song, or character study on it.
- Collect "junk" found around the schoolyard and make a collage.
- Create illustrations for the class newspaper.
- Plan a videotaped production for a book-sharing activity.
- Make a cartoon strip for a book.

ACROSS THE CURRICULUM

- Conduct a survey and graph the results.
- Keep records of daily temperatures, rainfall.
- Keep a weather calendar.
- Chart the growth of class plants.
- Observe and record observations of class pets.
- Collect mathematics, social studies, or science terms and make a glossary.

(*continued*)

Figure 7.6 Instead of Seatwork (cont.)

- Work with math manipulatives in the Math Center.
- Use the calculator to solve problems or do thinking activities and exercises with it.
- Keep a time line of significant events in history or occurring at the present time.
- Label maps of the United States or the world.
- Make a map of the places you have visited.
- Practice your multiplication and division facts.
- Use a computer program for math, science, or social studies.
- Make a map of our town, school, or classroom.
- Make models of the solar system, an underwater laboratory, a house in the future, a community on the moon.
- Create a culture—design homes, clothing, a flag, write patriotic songs, construct a map, write a history of the culture, choose some ethnic foods.
- Keep a list of how mathematics is used in our daily lives.
- Map the settings for books read this year.
- Make a glossary of geographic terms and illustrate it.
- Make alphabet books or All About ___ Books on topics in science, social studies, and mathematics.
- Write biographies about people who have made significant contributions in science, mathematics, social studies, art, music, etc.

in designing the physical facility and in cooperatively determining rules for living and working together. Students need to be knowledgeable about what to do if they are confused or are having difficulty, and about activities to engage in that are purposeful and have relevance to their curriculum or to the real world. Chapter 8 presents the types of learning that occur in a literacy program—a balanced reading and writing program—in grade 3 and beyond.

BIBLIOGRAPHY AND SUGGESTED RESOURCES

Barchers, S. (1990). *Creating and managing the literate classroom.* Englewood, Colo.: Teacher Ideas Press.

Bauer, K., & Drew, R. (1991). *Lesson plan book for the whole language and literature-based classroom.* Cypress, Calif.: Creative Teaching Press.

Butler, A., & Turbill, J. (1984). *Towards a reading-writing classroom.* Primary English Teachers Association, Rozelle, Australia.

Cambourne, B., & Turbill, J., (1987). *Coping with chaos.* Portsmouth, N.H.: Heinemann.

Eisele, B. (1991). *Managing the whole language classroom.* Cypress Calif.: Creative Teaching Press.

CHILDREN'S LITERATURE CITED

Fleischman, P. (1989). *Joyful noise: Poems for two voices.* New York: Harper & Row.

George, J. Craighead (1959). *My side of the mountain.* New York: Viking.

Howe, J. (1983). *A night without stars.* New York: Avon.

Simon, S. (1991). *Earthquakes.* New York: Morrow Junior Books.

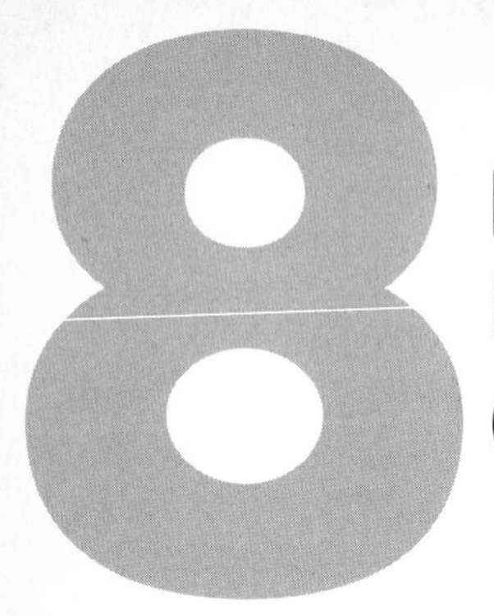

BEYOND EMERGENT LITERACY: IMPLEMENTATION (GRADES 3–6)

The First Journey to Freedom

Quiet. I must be quiet.
Tiptoe northwards
Carefully.
North star
Up above,
shining bright,
Guiding me,
With promises
Of freedom's sweet taste.
The wind
Is cold and chills.
My ragged clothes
are no comfort.
One shoe is left
Full of holes.
Pebbles are sharp,
But I must go on.
Deserted
By kin
Who traveled with me.
They are gone.
Lost to die owned
By another.
I am alone
But yet I continue
The journey.
I must go on to freedom.
I cannot live hiding
From the sun's warm rays
Behind trees quickly
At every sound
Fearful
Of the world.
God shall aid
Those who trust.
I shall not belong
To someone,
Like a goat or an ox.
I must go on,
Following freedom's scent
That wavers through
The night.

Shana Katz
Grade 6
Rondout Valley Intermediate School
Rondout Valley
New York

Inspired by: *Steal Away* by Jennifer Armstrong

OVERVIEW

Now that the organization and management of classrooms that are beyond the emergent literacy stage have been addressed, it is time to look at the instructional practices. This chapter explores balanced reading and writing programs, which include reading and writing *to* students, *with* students, and *by* students. In addition, ways of using the basal reading program in a more holistic manner are presented in order to provide teachers with the support they need on their journey into whole language.

Questions to Ponder

1. How can literature be used instead of a basal program and still incorporate some skills and strategies into the instructional lessons?
2. What can teachers do during guided reading to replace comprehension questions?
3. How can writing be used purposefully throughout the day in all areas of the curriculum?
4. How can teachers provide direct instruction and still be considered whole language teachers?
5. How can teachers evaluate their students' reading and writing progress and achievement if they don't test for skills and comprehension?

A BALANCED READING PROGRAM

Frequently when children are able to read for themselves, teachers focus their attention on particular aspects of the reading program (especially guided reading with the accompanying emphasis on skills and comprehension questions) and abandon other areas, such as shared reading and reading aloud to children. However, reading *to* children, reading *with* children, and reading *by* children are as important in the upper grades as in emergent literacy classrooms.

Reading to Children

Teachers need to continue to read aloud to students on a daily basis and perhaps more than once a day. Students need to have their reading repertoires stretched, and teachers can do this by reading and sharing a variety of genres. Some students may not be capable of reading certain books by themselves but are capable of learning the material if it is read to them. So another advantage of reading aloud to older children is the resultant increase in knowledge. Students may become interested in a topic or an author, which motivates them to delve deeper into the area that was shared or to find additional books by that author. Reading aloud to children on a regular basis demonstrates that reading is a pleasurable activity. These sessions may also become welcome respites in the students' busy lives. If schools include among their goals creating lifelong readers, then the students' appetites for reading must be whetted while they are still young.

Teachers may question what to read aloud and how to find the time for reading aloud in an already full schedule. In answer to the first question, any piece of literature can be shared during read-aloud time: picture books, novels, newspaper excerpts, magazine articles, poetry. Children's books are listed in the appendices, but remember that both schools and communities have excellent librarians who delight in matching books with children. At this stage, students need to be exposed to nonfiction. If teachers schedule several read-aloud sessions, one can deal with informational writing. Many upper-grade teachers read aloud twice a day, using a picture book (and there are many excellent nonfiction picture books) or a newspaper or magazine article during one session and a novel during the other.

Finding time for reading aloud is possible because much ~~of~~ the curriculum is integrated. Sharing a poem at the beginning of the day, welcoming the children back from lunch with a story, and reading a chapter from an interesting novel before sending them home are just a few possibilities.

Reading with Children

Occasionally whole language is criticized because of misconceptions about the teacher's role in a whole language classroom. Some critics object that there is no direct instruction in whole language classrooms—that is far from the truth. In addition to being facilitators, whole language teachers do indeed instruct their students. This is most evident in the reading with children aspect of the reading program—shared reading and guided reading.

Shared reading tends to be synonymous with Big Books, thereby reinforcing the belief that once children outgrow the need for enlarged texts they no longer need shared reading. Not true! Shared reading continues as a valued practice throughout the school years. Gradually Big Books are no longer used in upper-grade classrooms, but teachers still implement the philosophy that accompanies shared reading. It should be noted, however, that publishers are now offering enlarged texts with excellent photographs or illustrations in content areas studied in the upper grades, so more and more Big Books are finding their way into grades 3–6. Shared reading implies that an expert is sharing reading knowledge with a novice, and there is much children need to know and can profit from when a teacher shares a text with them.

Shared reading can use an enlarged text with an accompanying discussion of the content or organization of the text—for example, typical text structures in the content areas—or of the processes and strategies needed to read that particular text. But most often, shared reading is done using an overhead projector with any classroom material while the teacher models how to read the text or the use of reading strategies. Shared reading may not occur on a daily basis as in the lower grades but is used when introducing something new or when the students demonstrate a need for the instruction.

Reading with children also takes the form of guided reading. Here teachers assume various roles—facilitator, instructor, and audience for book discussions and for sharing projects that evolve from a particular book. This approach to guided reading is discussed under the heading "Readers' Workshop."

Reading by Children

In addition to reading aloud to students and reading with students, teachers need to give students time to practice reading silently. Therefore setting aside 20–30 minutes or more daily for DEAR time or Sustained Silent Reading is exceedingly important. The emphasis of this practice is on enjoyment, not book reports. Students can record which books they have read and even rate them, with ratings serving as a selection guide for classmates, but they should not be made to answer questions about their reading or do involved literature projects. DEAR time is the beginning of the students' journey toward becoming lifelong readers.

As Peterson and Eeds (1990) point out, children must have time to read without having to do anything afterward. This is the "time for the reader to become one with the character, to be embedded in the action of the story, to live intensively within the imaginary world created by the author. This is the time readers compile personal literary histories, exploring literary worlds beyond the borders of their lived experience. Students just read!" (Peterson and Eeds, 1990, 12).

Besides reading self-selected books for enjoyment, students may be reading other literature for other reasons as well. Teachers may choose to implement an individualized reading program whereby everyone in the room is reading a book of his or her choice. There will also be conferences with teachers, responding to literature through reading response logs, and follow-up activities. In contrast to DEAR time, there is accountability, and teachers may accompany the individualized reading with instructional lessons (either individual or group) and perhaps group discussions on such topics as characterization, plot development, author's style, and theme.

Reading also occurs at various times throughout the day in other curricular areas. Books are a source of information for research that may evolve from a science or social studies topic. Whenever themes are being implemented, students will be surrounded by books for further exploration into the theme, for necessary data for a project, for enrichment. There are numerous opportunities to put literature into students' hands and allow them to read for different purposes. It must be remembered that all three aspects of a reading program (reading to, with, and by children) are important, and teachers must ensure that their students have ample opportunities to interact with literature by hearing stories, working through texts with teachers, and reading by themselves. A balanced reading program should be at the heart of the elementary school curriculum.

Readers' Workshop

"Once upon a time . . ." How many of you remember those treasured days of childhood when you were entranced by the magic of books? How many of you had favorites you wanted read over and over again, with not a word omitted? Many of us grew up cherishing such beloved books as *Make Way for Ducklings, Caps for Sale,* and *Katy No Pocket.* These days continue for many lucky people who first grew to love books through hearing them read aloud and then became readers themselves, establishing a lifelong habit and love of recreational reading.

Think of the preschooler saying, "Read it again!" Think of the teenager who, given money by his grandparents, went to the mall and spent most of his time and most of his money in the bookstore. Think of the adult who made sure she had a book to read during her vacation. *Then* think of the classroom. How much time is spent reading literature as opposed to basal readers? How many children fall in love with their basal readers? How many children say, "Read it again!"? How many children spend vacations with beloved basals?

Fortunately, classrooms and reading instruction are changing, and many teachers are choosing literature-based reading programs instead of traditional basal reading programs. Literature or Readers' Workshop has replaced or is supplementing the basal program. Readers' Workshop is a means of structuring reading instruction by forming small, temporary groups of students who have elected to read, discuss, and interpret the same reading material. Readers' Workshop welcomes, celebrates, and builds on the students' responses to what they have read (Daniels, 1994). Because a major portion of the balanced reading program is devoted to Readers' Workshop, also referred to as Book Clubs or Literature Circles, a major portion of the discussion of a balanced reading program is devoted to this topic. A rationale for using literature in the classroom is provided first, followed by an explanation of how a literature-based reading program might be implemented.

Although it is preferable to use literature exclusively as the basis of reading instruction, it is also possible to use literature productively along with the basal reading program. Many of the implementation strategies for Readers' Workshop may be used with a basal program as well, and a separate section on using the basal in a more productive manner follows later in this chapter.

It is important to remember that the term *literature* encompasses both fiction and nonfiction. Literature includes stories and novels, poetry, magazines, plays, and informational material.

Why Literature in the Classroom?

There are several reasons for the current popularity of literature-based reading programs. First, recent reports on U.S. reading instruction—such as *Becoming a Nation of Readers* (Anderson, Hiebert, Scott, and Wilkinson, 1985), *First Lessons: A Report Card on Elementary Education in America* (Bennett, 1986), and *Report Card on Basal Readers* (Goodman, Shannon, Freeman, and Murphy, 1988)—call for an increased role for literature in the elementary school curriculum. In order for children to become proficient readers, they must be provided with many opportunities to read quality literature.

Alongside the reports on U.S. education is the growth and popularity of the whole language approach. Whole language advocates realize that children learn to read by reading, and therefore children's literature provides the framework for reading instruction in whole language classrooms (Newman, 1985; Goodman, 1986; Altweiger, Edelsky, and Flores, 1987). Instead of being dictated to by basal publishers, teachers are turning to children's literature because they recognize the inherent value of using literature.

Interestingly, basal reading publishers have altered their programs to reflect the interest in literature. Reading selections incorporate more unadapted literature, and many publishers offer supplemental libraries. Unfortunately, many basals still emphasize skills while using litera-

FROM THE
CLASSROOM OF . . .
Kathy Pike and Jean Mumper New Paltz, New York

Expanding Vocabulary Word Books

In order to expose children to a wider vocabulary and to help them get rid of "tired" and overused words, individual word charts or books can be compiled by the class. This activity can be introduced during a writing or reading mini-lesson and continued throughout the course of the year. Words for *said, went,* or *asked* provide excellent opportunities for illustrating the variety of words that may be used instead. Special praise may be given to students who incorporate the new vocabulary into their writing.

Words for **Went**

hurried	came
slid	ambled
rushed	scurried
CRAWLED	stamped
scampered	
drove	

ture, and this may impact the goal of having children use literature as a source of pleasure. If literature is associated with questions and worksheets, children will not turn to reading for enjoyment and relaxation.

Many in the field of education have long advocated using children's books in the classroom (Huck, 1990; Cullinan, 1989; Stewig, 1988; Galda, Cullinan, and Strickland, 1993; Eeds and Hudelson, 1995). As Huck states, "Literature not only has the power to change a reader, but it contains the power to help children become readers" (Huck, 1990, 3). Literature has both educational and personal-social values.

EDUCATIONAL VALUES

- promotes reading achievement and school success
- provides opportunities for students to develop an increased awareness of reading strategies
- fosters young children's knowledge of concepts about print (top-to-bottom, left-to-right reading; concept of words; and so on)

- enhances language development because literature contains meaningful and memorable written language
- develops a sense of story (narratives) and familiarizes children with expository writing styles
- serves as a model for writing
- enhances the depth and breadth of literary response
- increases world knowledge
- enhances and elaborates on other curricular areas
- provides opportunities for children to become competent readers

(Kiefer, 1988; Huck, 1990; Galda, Cullinan, and Strickland, 1993; Eeds and Hudelson, 1995)

Research has shown that reading achievement, language development, growth in vocabulary, and reading comprehension have been enhanced by using literature (Heath and Branscombe, 1986; Wells, 1986; Eldridge and Butterfield, 1986; Anderson et al., 1985; Nagy, Herman, and Anderson, 1985). Young children who have been read to and who have developed a sense of story and book language tend to be more successful in school than do children who have not had literature experiences.

Hearing good literature read aloud "anchors the sounds of the language of literature in the minds of the students" (Peterson and Eeds, 1990, 9). Children come to experience and appreciate the beauty of language and the possibilities it presents to tell stories and provide information. Literature also allows children to experience pleasure—literature essentially brings joy to life in a classroom (Peterson and Eeds, 1990).

Children continue to profit from being read to and from their own reading as they progress through school. As students approach the end of their high school careers, thoughts turn to the SATs. Two high school juniors were overheard discussing their scores and subsequent training to improve these scores. One boy thanked the other for his excellent advice on how to improve his verbal score. He had followed his friend's advice with much success. Curious, one of the authors asked the student who had given the advice exactly what he had said. The reply: "That's easy. I told him to *read!* That's how come I did so well, because I read a lot."

Reading achievement and language growth aren't the only areas that are affected by the use of literature. Writing improves as well. By being exposed to a variety of writing styles and stylistic devices, children can use these as models for their own writing endeavors. Examining how authors provide good story leads and effective conclusions demonstrates various aspects of writing for aspiring young writers.

Much of what people learn is gained through reading. By being read to and by reading selections independently, children gain a great deal of knowledge. Comprehension is facilitated as children add to their experiences and knowledge base. The more knowledge children possess, the more successful they will be in school. One of the authors recently hosted a visiting professor from New Zealand. This was a first-time visit to the United States for the professor. While touring Boston, the New Zealander saw her first fire hydrant, saw her first squirrel, and visited Boston Common, which is featured in Robert McCloskey's *Make Way for Ducklings*. Toward the end of the day, she remarked how amazed she was to realize how much she had learned throughout her life by reading children's literature.

Besides providing educational advantages, literature also contributes to a reader's personal and social growth. Literature is concerned with feeling and educates the heart as well as the mind (Huck, 1989). Following are some of the personal-social values attributed to exposure to literature.

PERSONAL-SOCIAL VALUES

- broadens a child's personal experiences
- presents the universality of the human experience, such as survival, success, interactions with others, and the like
- develops insights into human behavior
- fosters and develops compassion and humaneness
- kindles and stretches the imagination
- provides vicarious experiences
- helps children develop an appreciation of literature
- provides multicultural understandings
- provides opportunities for self-reflection
- adds richness to the readers' lives

- offers enjoyment and relaxation
- provides a lens through which people can examine their own lives, experiences, cultural realities, and worldviews
- enables children to become "hooked on books"

(Nova Scotia Department of Education, 1978; Kiefer, 1988; Huck, 1989, 1990; Galda, Cullinan, and Strickland, 1993; Eeds and Hudelson, 1995)

Literature should be an integral part of the classroom reading program because "literature nurtures the imagination, stimulates emotional and intellectual growth, promotes insight into human behavior, and fosters awareness of the universality of human experience. Through literature, students can learn to appreciate their own heritage, respect the heritage of others, and become sensitive to stereotypes based on race, religion, ethnicity, physical or emotional handicap, and gender" (New York State Education Department, 1989, 54). Children gain both academically and personally, for literature both entertains and educates. Of great significance is the fact that children will be given a true gift—that of being someone who not only is able to read but who also chooses reading as a pleasurable activity.

Planning for Readers' Workshop

Now that a rationale for using literature has been provided and teachers have decided to use literature as the basis for reading instruction, some planning is necessary before actual implementation can take place. When considering undertaking a Readers' Workshop approach the teacher must first obtain suitable reading materials, which of course means books. Since the students will meet in small groups, multiple copies of books are necessary. Teachers must decide for themselves what books to choose or make decisions collaboratively with other faculty members.

There are many sources of books for classroom use. First, teachers should consider the books they personally enjoy and incorporate them whenever possible. There is nothing like an enthusiastic book lover, for this enthusiasm is frequently contagious. Of course, the same could be said for sharing the children's personal favorites as well. Following is a list of sources of information about books:

- Professional books
  - *Read-Aloud Handbook* by J. Trelease
  - The New York Times *Parent's Guide to the Best Books for Children* by E. Lipson
  - *For Reading Out Loud* by M. Kimmel and E. Segal
  - *Eyeopeners* by B. Kobrin
  - *Literature and the Child* by B. Cullinan & L. Galda
  - *Adventuring with Books* (book-length bibliographies published by the National Council of Teachers of English)
- Professional journals
  - *The New Advocate*
  - *The Horn Book Magazine*
  - *School Library Journal*
  - *Booklist*
  - *Booklinks*
  - *The W.E.B.*
- Reviews in:
  - *The Reading Teacher*
  - *Language Arts*
  - *Learning*
  - *Instructor*
  - newspapers (such as *The New York Times Book Review*)
- Surveys
  - *Children's Choices* (IRA publication)
  - *Teacher's Choices* (IRA publication)
  - by local reading councils, state reading organizations, public libraries, schools
- Newsletters about books
  - *Yellow Brick Road*
- Exhibits at conferences, bookstores
- *Reading Rainbow*
- Award winners: Newbery, Caldecott, American Library Association, NCTE
- Recommendations
  - other teachers
  - students
  - parents
  - personal taste
  - librarians
- Catalogs from publishing companies
- Book clubs
  - *Trumpet*
  - *Scholastic*

Once the books have been ordered and obtained, teachers should familiarize themselves with the books by reading them, if they have not done so already. It would be helpful for teachers to jot down notes about the books to refer to during book talks or for future reference. If teachers keep a book file, they can also note key teaching points they plan to make or have made, projects undertaken, difficulties they may have encountered, and any other relevant observations.

A planning sheet or literature guide may be used. This sheet is divided into several sections: an overview with such information as the title, author, a brief summary of the book, the teacher's goals for the book, and key teaching points or concepts to be developed; a prereading section; a during-reading section; and a postreading section. This planning sheet is used as a guide for the literature study, always allowing for flexibility and student input. A sample literature planning guide appears in Figure 8.1.

Readers' Workshop: Structure and Format

Ideally, 45 minutes to 1 hour should be allocated for the workshop. A workshop format should be predictable, although teachers may first experiment with several possibilities before deciding on the format that works best for them. A possible format might include:

Minilesson (5–15 minutes)
Literature Study Groups (rest of allocated time)

Teachers may opt to begin or end each session by reading aloud or having students share interesting passages. Rather than beginning each session with a minilesson, teachers may wish to conclude with a minilesson or with everyone, including the teacher, reading silently. Teachers generally do not meet with each group on a daily basis. On the days that the students do not meet with the teacher, they are engaged in silent reading, responding to reading in their response logs, reading with a buddy, or working on a book-sharing project.

It is recommended that three or four titles be introduced to the students. However, at the beginning of the school year, teachers may start off a literature workshop by having the entire class read the same book. By reading and responding to a single title, students become familiar with the workshop format. On a designated day (Fridays work particularly well), book talks are given on each book. The students then have an opportunity to visit with each book and indicate their choices. Over the weekend, the teacher looks over the choices and attempts whenever possible to give children their first choice. The class is divided into three literature groups, and announcement of the group placements is done on Monday morning.

Minilessons

Teachers may structure the literature workshop by beginning or sometimes ending the workshop with a minilesson. Various kinds of minilessons may be demonstrated. Lamont and MacKenzie (1989) discuss three types:

1. **Procedures**
   - discussing where materials are kept and how to use them
   - showing students how to set up their response logs
   - modeling how to write entries in response logs
   - modeling how to discuss literature
   - other organizational concerns
2. **Literature**
   - introducing students to different genres
   - illustrating story grammar (story structure)
   - discussing the key elements of literature (e.g., elements of fiction, such as point of view, suspense, mood, word choice, symbolism, flashback, foreshadowing, and exaggeration, and elements of nonfiction, such as topic, subtopics, main ideas and supporting details)
   - author studies
   - sharing books by both the teacher and the students
3. **Strategy/skills**
   - showing students how to choose books
   - providing strategies to use when encountering unknown words
   - providing strategies to use when encountering difficulty in making meaning
   - fostering prediction while reading
   - helping students learn how to self-monitor while they read (metacognition)

It is important that students be thoroughly aware of and comfortable with the procedures and strategies to call on if their read-

Figure 8.1 Literature Planning Guide

TITLE: *The True Story of the Three Little Pigs*
AUTHOR: Jon Scieszka

SUMMARY: The traditional tale of "The Three Little Pigs" is told from the perspective of the wolf, who tries to convince the reader that he was framed and was really a victim of circumstances.

GOALS AND OBJECTIVES

- to review elements of fiction
- to introduce point of view
- to provide opportunity to respond to a familiar fairy tale or folktale from the perspective of another character
- to develop the theme of "Wolves: Fact and Fiction"
- to extend point of view into persuasive writing

CONCEPTS FROM BOOK

- literary elements
  - story parts
  - point of view
- skills
  - cause and effect
  - sequence
  - compare/contrast
  - elements of persuasive writing

BEFORE READING

- Introduce the book:
  - Discuss prior knowledge of the story "The Three Little Pigs."
  - Look at book jacket and title and discuss meaning of word *true.*
  - Discuss roles of wolves in literature.
  - Predict what the story will be about.

DURING READING

- Continue predicting, confirming, or refining predictions.
- Retell events in story.
- Discuss story elements and put data on story map.
- Compare wolf's role in this story with other known stories that feature wolves.
- Discuss how the wolf's point of view changes the message of the story.
- Analyze cause/effect relationships.
- Address reading strategies as needed (e.g., what to do with unknown vocabulary words, self-monitoring, predicting, self-questioning).

AFTER READING

- Continue retelling story.
- Complete story map.
- Put significant cause-effect relationships on chart.
- Discuss point of view and how this could relate to students' lives.
- Complete Author/You statements:
  - "Wolves are tricky animals that can't be trusted."
  - "There are different ways of looking at things."
- Discuss open-ended questions (either orally or in response logs):
  - Are wolves treated unfairly in literature?
  - How is this wolf character similar to the portrayal of wolves in other pieces of literature?
  - How does the author use humor?
  - Does writing this story from the wolf's point of view affect the interpretation?
  - What do you think the author is trying to tell us?
  - Why do you think the book is titled *The True Story of the Three Little Pigs?*
- Discuss ways the author tried to convince readers to believe the teller of the story.
- Discuss other ways people try to persuade others to believe or do something.
- Response forms:
  - Respond to questions in literature log.
  - Write another story from a different character's point of view.
  - Collect samples of persuasive writing and place on a bulletin board.
  - Make story map of student version of familiar fairy tale as told from another perspective.
  - Research wolves and their roles in the balance of nature.
  - Do Readers' Theatre of the book.
  - Write a letter of recommendation for the wolf to get him out of jail.

ing should break down. Figure 8.2 outlines some useful strategies for students, which can be discussed, modeled, and placed on a chart for reference.

The time devoted to minilessons should be no more than 15 minutes since it is best to use the majority of the time for reading and responding to the texts. Minilessons may be undertaken with the whole group or with small groups of children on an as-needed basis. Some minilessons, such as procedural ones, may take more time at the beginning of the year when the literature workshop is being initiated. For teachers who have transitional classrooms, minilessons provide an opportunity to do some skills work, but this should not take priority over real reading.

During the time scheduled for minilessons, teachers or students may do book talks or "Have You Read This?" sessions in order to talk about books they have recently read and enjoyed. This may take the form of a brief oral review or a "Dear Reader" letter. "Dear Reader" letters may be addressed to the entire class, to the teacher from a student, or to a specific student. Examples of "Dear Reader" letters are provided in Figure 8.3. Books that are shared may be logged onto file cards or kept in a "Have You Read This?" book. The students can write either a brief recommendation or a longer review.

The rest of the workshop is devoted to reading, responding to what has been read, and sharing the book through a project activity. Literature groups do not have to meet daily, for students need time to read, reflect, and respond. If teachers stagger group sessions without meeting on a daily basis, there is then time for conferences, observing students, and focusing on other assessment issues. The workshop can be conceived of as having three stages: prereading, during reading, and postreading. In order to provide a complete picture of a literature workshop, each stage is discussed separately.

1. Ask yourself, "Does this make sense?" It should always make sense to you.
2. Think about what you can do if the material doesn't make sense.
   - If a word doesn't make sense:
     - Use the first letter and context to make a guess.
     - Skip it and come back later if it seems important.
     - Read on to get the general idea.
     - Check the dictionary.
     - Ask for help.
   - If the whole material doesn't make sense:
     - Reread earlier parts to see if you missed something.
     - Read on.
     - Ask for help from a teacher, parent, or friend.
     - Get an easier book.
3. Be a risk taker. Don't be afraid to take a chance in reading.
4. Ask yourself questions as you read: "What does that mean?" "I wonder if ___ will happen next?"
5. Remember: It's better to read a skinny book all the way through than to read very little of a thick, hard one.
6. Read some material more carefully than others, depending on the information you want to get.
7. Try to make connections to other information or stories you know.
8. Visualize a story or material as you are reading it.
9. Reread a book if you love it.
10. Write like your favorite author does if you want to.
11. Don't be afraid to make up a song for a character, draw a scene, or write "the next chapter" just for the pleasure of it.
12. If you love a book, tell a friend.

(Courtesy of Dr. Kathleen Scholl, Assistant Professor, Westminster College, Pa.)

Figure 8.2 Strategies to Watch For and Encourage with Readers

Dear Readers,

Want to read a "WRETCHED" book? If you do—or even if you don't—Chris Van Allsburg's The Wretched Stone is a fascinating story.

Imagine a sea captain telling you his story about a very, very strange voyage. When the ship first left port, the crew was enthusiastic, worked diligently, and played and sang together. This all changed, however, after a brief stop on a lush island where they went searching for fresh fruit. No fruit was to be found—no animals were to be found—no wildlife at all, just forest and a very intriguing stone. This stone fascinated the crew, and with some difficulty they hoisted the stone aboard the ship.

Then things started to happen. The crew became mesmerized by the glowing stone. They no longer worked; in fact they no longer resembled men. Slowly they became transformed into hairy beasts. The captain became concerned, especially as a storm brewed and no one was available to help man the ship. How could they survive? Would the stone be their undoing?

Miraculously they did survive and the book ends happily—sort of—with the crew transformed back to being human. BUT despite becoming men again, the crew developed a strange longing for a particular type of fruit, a fruit that their bestial form readily enjoyed!

Using a diary format to tell this story, the author made me THINK, made me QUESTION, made me WONDER. Would the men remain as men? Is the longing for that certain fruit a warning of future bestial behavior? Will the rock, with its mysterious glow and power, resurface and claim other victims?

I like books that make me THINK, QUESTION, and WONDER!

See for yourself. Read Chris Van Allsburg's

THE WRETCHED STONE!

Fondly,

Your Teacher

Dear Jade,

I reccomend a fun packed book called "There is a Boy in the Girl's Bathroom!" It is very interesting book about how 2 boys totally different can be friends. It also gives us secrets of what boys may do to us girls. So Beware! Keep up your reading. Please read this cool book!

Yours Truly,

Jess

P.S. Books up!

Prereading

This is the time for teachers to introduce the book in more detail than in the book talk, provide activities to activate prior knowledge, and invite prediction of the text. Some teachers may want to address key vocabulary prior to the students' reading of the book. However, whenever possible, students should be allowed to encounter words in context and apply their strategies for handling unknown words. If vocabulary is to be introduced during prereading, a webbing activity is beneficial, with the students supplying relevant background information and the teacher perhaps adding the vocabulary when needed (Bromley, 1995). Of course, the words could be elicited or volunteered during prereading discussions as well.

Activities to activate prior knowledge include:

- brainstorming
- webbing
- writing information known about the topic
- filling in a knowledge chart
- relating personal experiences
- marking agree/disagree statements
- asking questions
- researching an aspect students think may be addressed by the author

Naturally, only a few of these activities would actually be done. Students would also make predictions based on such things as the title, book jacket or cover, chapter titles or subheadings, author's known style, known information about the elements of the particular genre, and their own background information.

Then it is time for students to read the text. Students have traditionally been assigned whatever has to be read, but literature workshops encourage student choice whenever possible. First, students were able to choose a book to read (within a range provided by the teacher); now they can choose how much to read. The students together decide on how many pages or chapters to read by the next literature circle time (as the small groups may be called). If the students are too ambitious and assign themselves an unrealistic goal, the teacher may step in and make a suggestion to reduce the number of pages. Likewise, if the students do not assign enough pages, the teacher can make suggestions. It is important that the students read the assigned pages in preparation for the next meeting. It is also important that they not go ahead since this could affect discussions and predictions.

Of course, decisions about pages are made for chapter books only. If literature workshops use picture books that can be read at one sitting, then the workshop format will vary somewhat. The students may reread the book each day, focusing on different aspects of the book. Generally, picture books are used with younger readers or with children experiencing reading difficulties. Using picture books provides the support needed by these students at this particular time in their school career and development as readers. Repeated readings with accompanying literature conversations become opportunities for student growth both academically and in their self-esteem.

During Reading

Once students are immersed in their books, certain activities occur. The students are mostly reading during this stage, either alone or with others, aloud or silently. They may also be writing in response journals, discussing in literature circles, conferencing with the teacher, or working on a book-sharing activity.

After reading the assigned number of pages or chapters, students may react to their reading by writing in their response journals or logs. What frequently happens initially is that children will either summarize what they have read or talk about what they like or don't like about the text so far. To avoid this, the role of the teacher is crucial. Teachers need to model various ways to respond to text. This should be done throughout the year with different types of texts. Sometimes teachers could model by relating what was read to a personal experience. At other times, they could comment on the author's style, the characters' actions, things they found incongruent with the story, and so forth. For example, while reading *Sounder,* a story about a poor southern family in the early 1940s, Sister Mary Joseph modeled her own literature response to her fifth-grade students. This was shared with her students after they had read that the father in the story had been arrested, leaving his wife to care for their three small children in very difficult times. She wrote the literature response as if she were the wife.

> I stood stunned by the forceful intrusion of the sheriff and his men. They grabbed my husband and accused him of stealing ham; it was a necessary thievery. We were starving and a man has to do what he has to do.
>
> None were gentle, but each man tugged and pulled in opposite directions, my frightend husband pale with fear. I knew well his fears. I believe they were as mine. What would happen to each of us? How now could we survive without the head of our household? Where would they take him? Would he be killed, beaten or starved? Why? Where? When? Would? So many questions raced through my mind, not waiting for the one before to be pronounced or answered. My fears. My worries. Mine to endure. One ham stolen, but all of our lives drastically changed and we are only beginning to understand its impact. Would we ever be together again? When? For how long? I tremble with fears and worries that run my body numb and cold, my voice dumb.
>
> (Sister Mary Joseph—Kingston, New York)

As a result of Sister Mary Joseph's modeling, one of her students, David, likewise responded as the mother in *Sounder* and confided that he chose to portray the wife because she had lots of worries just like his father who was widowed and was left alone to raise his family.

Character Portral—Mother in Sounder

> I was so worried and fearful. Just to see my husband arrested was too much. My mind was flowing with pictures of begging on the side of a dirt road, my children not knowing where I was, how they would get food to feed the family. I was fearing the day when a crumb would be all they had. And then—Sounder. How can we feed him? How can we keep him? The Biggy was, how can we survive?
>
> We were married for a long time and now we have to part.
>
> (David—Grade 5)

Other examples of some types of responses teachers could model for their students are provided in Figure 8.4. Teachers can also have students like David share their responses with the entire class to serve as models.

To help with an occasional writer's block, teachers can brainstorm with students and list possible topics to be considered when responding in the literature logs. Some possibilities include:

- If I were (choose a character from the book), I would have . . .
- I think that . . . will happen next.
- I wonder if . . .
- I don't really understand why . . .
- This made me think of . . .
- It was not fair that . . .
- Perhaps the author could have . . .
- This story is like . . .
- The beginning of the story was . . .
- The author's use of . . . made me feel . . .
- I was surprised by . . .
- What impressed me was . . .

Teachers could also keep a file of open-ended questions available to use as prompts. Such questions as are listed in Figure 8.5 have proven to be helpful for both books read in an entire setting and chapter books.

Students could also comment on the author's use of setting, stylistic devices (such as flashbacks), the point of view, language used, the characters' development throughout the story, the author's use of humor or suspense, and their feelings about the story or the characters. Students could write "Dear Reader" letters to the teacher, their classmates, school officials, or their parents or engage in a dialogue about the book with either the teacher or their peers. Dean Witham, a fifth-grade teacher, and Brenda Myers, a sixth-grade teacher, provide alternatives to what students may or may not write about in their response logs. (See "From the Classroom.") Samples of students' literature log responses are provided in Figure 8.6.

In conducting literature circles, Routman (1991) concludes the group sharing and text discussion by writing the next session's assignment and the requested response on portable chalkboards, with each group having its own chalkboard. The students copy the question directly

Figure 8.4 Teacher Modeling of Literature Response Entries

TITLE: *How Many Days to America* by Eve Bunting
SUMMARY: A young family seeks to emigrate to America. First they flee from their homeland with few personal possessions, make their escape by sea, and undergo several hardships before being welcomed to America's shores.

TEACHER RESPONSE

This story reminded me of my own family as they sought the welcoming arms of America when they escaped from the tyranny of their homeland, lost their few meager possessions, and trudged bravely across Russia seeking the land "that had streets paved with gold." Like the family in Eve Bunting's book, my family likewise sought freedom first by foot and eventually by boat. This book represents the hope and fulfilled promises that America has come to mean—to the families who are currently emigrating and to families like mine who have found happiness and opportunity in a free land.

TITLE: *The Pinballs* by Betsy Byars
SUMMARY: This story is the tale of several children who are placed in a foster home and how they adjust, adapt, and even find friendship and some happiness.

TEACHER RESPONSE

The Pinballs made me wonder about what it would be like to be placed in a foster home, what kind of person takes in foster children, and how might the placement be made easier for both the foster children and the families who will be caring for them. Because these children have endured many hardships and have become masters at survival, it is difficult to greet them with the usual warmth that generally accompanies family membership. I puzzled over what could be done to make them welcome, give them a sense of security, and offer some hope for the future. Perhaps a letter beforehand telling what their future family is like, pictures of family members, the house, and pets. Perhaps foster siblings could write as well, and when they arrive respect the privacy and possible slow rate of adjustment they may have. The book did leave the reader with a hopeful sense that foster children can be given better lives and can be better people because of the care and concern their foster parents gave.

TITLE: *My Side of the Mountain* by Jean Craighead George
SUMMARY: A young boy leaves his family to live in the wilds of the Catskill Mountains.

TEACHER RESPONSE

Even though I enjoyed *My Side of the Mountain,* particularly for the amount of knowledge the author and main character possessed regarding survival in nature, I still was somewhat disturbed by the fact that parents could allow a young boy to run away from home and live in the mountains for a winter all by himself. The father even visited his son for Christmas and still left him there alone with no companions and no schooling. It was also somewhat distressing that several townsfolk knew of his whereabouts and supported his decision to live alone at too young an age. Despite this concern, I had to marvel at how much the author knew about nature, how adept at survival the main character was, and the use of a journal by the main character to chronicle his life in the wilderness.

(*continued*)

Figure 8.4 Teacher Modeling of Literature Response Entries (cont.)

TITLES: *James and the Giant Peach* by Roald Dahl
Fantastic Flying Journey by Gerald Durrell

SUMMARIES: *James and the Giant Peach* describes a boy's escape from his hateful aunts, his incredible voyage in a giant peach with enlarged animal companions who can speak, and his ultimate happiness in his new peachstone house in New York City.

Fantastic Flying Journey chronicles the balloon journey of an uncle and his niece and nephews around the world seeking a missing relative. Along the way the travelers encounter many adventures and even talking animals.

TEACHER RESPONSE

These two books reminded me of each other because both detailed fantastic flying journeys, had talking animals, and had relatives who ultimately were responsible for the voyages. The close calls suffered by the travelers had many parallels. The animals had unique personality traits that were revealed in their conversations with the main characters. *The Fantastic Flying Journey* provided many more details about the fauna and flora of areas visited and was therefore somewhat more realistic than *James and the Giant Peach.* Of course there was a difference in the mode of travel as well—a somewhat believable hot-air balloon fully equipped as opposed to a peach lit only by a glowworm's light. Both were delightful fantasy tales, ones that would spark anyone's imagination.

into their journals and respond after they have read the predetermined pages or chapters. At times Routman uses a question she has planned, but frequently she uses one that has arisen from the group discussion.

In order to help her third-grade students write responses, Kelly (1990) uses a procedure that includes the following prompts:

- What did you notice in the book?
- What are your feelings about the book?
- What does this story remind you of in your own life?

To introduce this approach, Kelly first reads stories aloud and uses the prompts in whole-group activities. The students respond orally, and Kelly writes the responses on a chart so that they can be reread by the class. This structure allows her students to respond orally and to hear others' interpretations, and demonstrates that all responses are appropriate and valued. These sessions then become a framework for future literature response activities.

Later on in the year, around January, Kelly continues to read stories aloud, and the students begin responding in writing. Initially, the students are given a five-minute time limit to respond, but gradually the time is increased.

Teachers could also model this procedure by writing their own responses to the prompts on an overhead projector or on chart paper. Following is an example of teacher modeling for *Wilfred Gordon McDonald Partridge* by Mem Fox. This book is about a young boy with four names who befriends the elderly residents of a retirement home. One resident, who likewise has four names—Nancy Alison Delacourt Cooper—loses her memory. Wilfred Gordon McDonald Partridge learns about memories and helps Miss Nancy find her lost memories.

1. **What did you notice about the book?** I noticed that young children and old people can be friends and can help each other. Sometimes the elderly and the very young don't share common experiences and ideas, so they don't appreciate one another. But through reading *Wilfred Gordon McDonald Partridge,* you can see that the young and old can develop meaningful relationships and can have happy times together.

2. **How did this book make you feel?** Because I read about so many lonely elderly peo-

Figure 8.5 Questions for Literature Response Logs

- Describe the setting in the story. Does it make a difference to the story or could the story occur elsewhere?
- What kind of person is the main character?
- What is the incident that the author uses to get the story going (i.e., what is the problem)?
- How does the author use suspense? humor? exaggeration?
- Do any of the characters change during the story? What made them change?
- Who is telling the story? Would the story change if someone else told the story?
- Does the story convey some feeling or mood? How does the author accomplish this?
- Does this story resemble any other story you have read?
- What is the main idea behind this story?
- What information did you learn from the writing?
- Is there anything that makes this author's work different from that of other authors?
- Were there any clues that the author used to help you predict the ending? If so, what were they?
- Do the language and style of writing fit the book?
- Is the story realistic?
- What questions would you ask the author if you could interview him/her? How do you think the author would answer your questions?
- What question would you like to have answered as you read more in the next section of the book?
- In what ways would you like the real world or people you know to be more like the world and characters in the book?
- Do you agree or disagree with the ways the main character thinks and acts?
- What was the most interesting (surprising, unusual) thing you learned from the book?
- Why do you think the author ended the book the way he/she did?
- Is the author's writing style similar to that of other authors you have read?
- What is your favorite part of the book?
- If you were to illustrate the book (or parts of the book) what would your illustrations look like?
- What interesting or unusual words or phrases did you find?
- Was the title appropriate? Why do you think the author chose this title?
- What was the author showing about life in the story?
- Would you recommend this book? Why or why not?

(Atwell, 1987; Harste, Short, and Burke, 1988; Parsons, 1990; Routman, 1991)

ple, this book made me feel warm inside. It was heartening to see a young boy care enough to bring some pleasure to a woman who, through growing old, was losing her memories. Also, it put a value on simple things that ultimately triggered Miss Nancy's memory instead of the notion of having to spend a great deal of money on expensive items. If one thinks about it, it is the element of time and sharing that can bring happiness and demonstrate caring.

3. **What did this story remind you of in your own life?** This story reminded me of my own grandmother, who lived to be 98 years old. She never lost her memories, however, but rather regained some as she aged. These long-forgotten memories took place during her youth in her native country of Russia. One particularly significant memory was her being chosen from all the girls in her village to give flowers to the czar. Like Miss Nancy, my grandmother remembered and shared these memories with the very young.

Students generally bring their response logs to the literature circle. Their responses serve as the basis for the conversations that take place during the literature circle time. Not only does responding to the literature facilitate the discussions in the group sessions, but it also fosters an increased understanding of the text, enhances writing skills, and promotes emotional involve-

Figure 8.6A Samples of Student Response Log Entries

Readers' Workshop Journal Entries
from Dean Witham's fifth-grade students

These students range in ability from very literate to dedicated nonreader.

Number the Stars by Lois Lowry
Marybeth Saunders: I am on page 60. Kristie almost told a soldier that Ellen was celebrating New Year's Eve. I said to myself, "No, Kristy!" Luckily the author decided to listen to me!

I am on page 67. So far Annmarie and Ellen are enjoying their stay at the Henriks'. If I were them I would be very bored because there are no books, no Nintendo, and no t.v. I am glad Annmarie has a sister and a friend along with her because it would be like having to sit with grownups all day and listen to them talk. Sometimes that gets boring.

There's a Boy in the Girls' Bathroom by Louis Sachar
Emily Katt: Jeff doesn't really like Bradley, but he is pretending to. I think that is very rude. If he doesn't like him then why doesn't he tell Bradley? I mean, it's the sensible thing to do. Even if Bradley is a bully he has the right to know.
Brenda Mereness: I think this book is really good so far. I was surprised when I started to read it and my mom asked me to do something. Usually I go right away. But I said, "Yeah, in a minute!" I think I was really tied up in the story! After a while I finally went to see what she wanted.

Blubber by Judy Blume
Kristy Glassen: (summary for book) This book was great, until the ending. It just left off with a nonexciting thing. It wasn't interesting at all. If I were the author, I would end it with something catching, that makes the reader want to read the next book.

Ramona the Brave by Beverly Cleary
Karen Jablonsky: I don't think that Ramona should have hidden her progress report because even though there weren't pleasant comments on it, that still wasn't the right thing to do.

The Minden Curse by Willo Davis Roberts
Kelly Wohlgemuth: When I was reading today I liked it when it said, "Leroy went *bounding* up to Mrs. Fowler." I thought the word "bounding" was descriptive because a lot of times people just write things like "He ran over to Mrs. Fowler."

From the Mixed-Up Files of Mrs. Basil E. Frankweiler by E. L. Konigsburg
Shane Holbert: I'm glad that Claudia and Jamie are going home but it must be a really unhappy moment for both of them. Even if they both want to go home it is probably worse for Claudia because it was like she loved the statue called Angel.

Memorable sentences found by students in their novels this year:

From the Mixed-Up Files of Mrs. Basil E. Frankweiler by E. L. Konigsburg
Ideas drift like clouds in an undecided breeze.
Claudia and Jamie were so hungry that their stomachs felt like tubes of toothpaste that had been all squeezed out.

Bones on Black Spruce Mountain by David Budbill
A hermit thrush, startled awake, sang a short, interrupted song in the night and then was silent again.
He saw his arms and hands begin flowing back and forth like slow fish through water.
Seth watched the beautiful, lithe, red and yellow and black and purple and orange speckled fish shiver its sudden way to death.

My Teacher Is an Alien by Bruce Coville
My hands were trembling like a pair of gerbils that had just been dropped into a snake pit.

Figure 8.6B Samples of Student Response Log Entries (cont.)

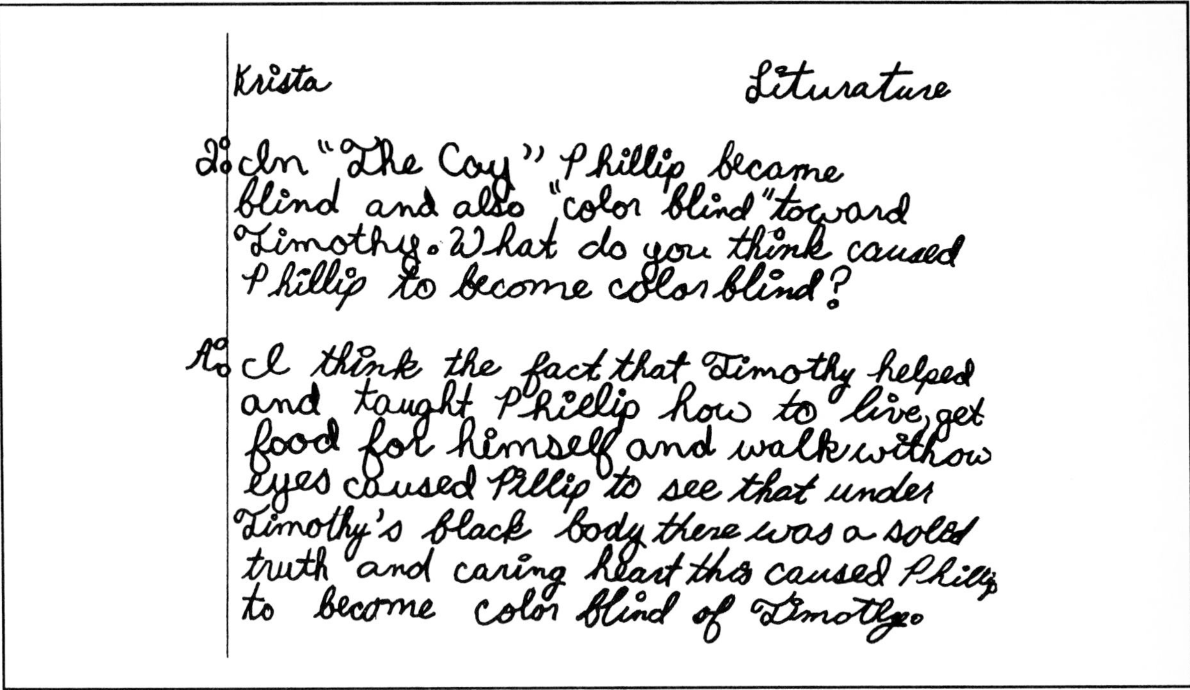

Krista Literature

Q. In "The Cay" Phillip became blind and also "color blind" toward Timothy. What do you think caused Phillip to become color blind?

A. I think the fact that Timothy helped and taught Phillip how to live, get food for himself and walk withow eyes caused Pillip to see that under Timothy's black body there was a soled truth and caring heart this caused Phillip to become color blind of Timothy.

ment with and an appreciation of all types of literature (Kelly, 1990).

How often students write in response logs and how frequently they meet for literature circle vary from teacher to teacher. Many teachers have children respond to each assigned number of pages; others, like Atwell (1987), have the children respond on a limited basis. Atwell runs an individualized reading program, and she herself undertakes a dialogue through journal writing with the students about what they are reading. Young children may need the structure of writing frequently, but again this is an individual decision by the teacher.

Another way of approaching the implementation of literature circles is to have the students assume different roles while participating in discussion groups. Literature circles embrace the spirit of true collaboration, for example, student-initiated inquiry, student choice, self-direction, mutual interdependence, personal interactions, and self- and group assessment (Daniels, 1994). Students may need to acquire the social skills of collaboration, which can be attained by assigning structured roles that are used during the process. Instead of everyone responding in journals, either through open-ended responses or responses to teacher prompts, various task roles are assigned to the students, which vary from day to day. The goals are to help children to read and discuss books more effectively and to help spark and sustain natural conversations about literature. The roles include:

Discussion Director The discussion director has the responsibility to think up good discussion questions, to convene the meetings, and to solicit contributions from other members.

Literary Luminary/Passage Master The literary luminary takes the members back to memorable, important sections of the text and reads them or has them read aloud.

Connector The connector takes the members from the text world into the real world, where the readers' experiences are connected to the literature.

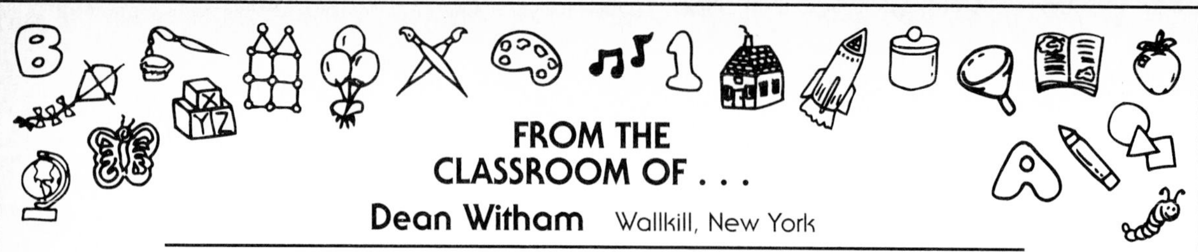

FROM THE CLASSROOM OF . . .

Dean Witham Wallkill, New York

WHAT I CAN WRITE ABOUT

I can write about:

- how I feel in general about what I read
- something I would change about this section if I were the author
- something that a character did that I did or didn't like, and why
- something that the author did that I didn't expect
- how I would have acted if I had been in this section as myself
- how I would have acted if I were one of the characters in this section
- what I would do next as myself, or as one of the characters
- a character that I like, and why
- a character that I'd get rid of, or a new one I'd add
- the emotion in the section—what the characters are feeling
- something that made me feel happy, sad, or angry or made me laugh
- what I think might happen next; then I can write next time if I was right or not
- who is telling the story, and if they should be
- what a character looks like; then I can draw the picture
- a really descriptive word or sentence that I liked a lot
- a word that I've never seen before—I can guess what it means, then check to see if I was right
- if the section was confusing or boring, and why
- a simile that I found (like/as comparison)
- a metaphor that I found (direct comparison)
- where the setting is, and describe it (is it important to the story?)

What I should NOT do when I am writing in my journal

I should avoid:

- writing "it was good/great/funny" without telling WHY
- writing "I just can't wait to read more!" each time
- just retelling the story in my own words without adding any of my feelings
- writing about the same thing each time
- forgetting to write—I should make entries about every 10 to 15 pages

FROM THE CLASSROOM OF . . .

Brenda Myers Bainbridge, New York

IDEAS FOR THE QUESTION

"What Should I Write in My Reading Log?"

Chapter Title:

Book Title:

Pages Read _______

Here are some ideas to write about:

- Some words you didn't know (list them with page numbers)
- The story so far seems to be about . . .
- I now predict that this will happen . . .
- I especially like the part when . . .
- I didn't understand the part when . . .
- I was right when I predicted that . . .
- There was something in this story that reminded me of . . .
- A scene I read that seemed like I was watching a movie was (page number) . . .
- Something new I learned was . . .

Illustrator The illustrator invites graphic, nonlinguistic responses to the text. The job of the illustrator is to draw some kind of picture related to the reading, for example, a sketch, cartoon, diagram, flow chart, stick figure, and so on.

(Daniels, 1994)

These particular roles are required for all meetings of the literature circles. In addition, there can be more roles assigned, depending on the number of participants in the literature circle and the desired purpose. These include: summarizer (who prepares a brief summary of the reading); vocabulary enricher (who is on the lookout for important words); travel tracer (who tracks where the action takes place in the reading); and investigator (who digs up background information on any topic related to the book). These various roles encourage diverse ways to construct meaning: visualization (the illustrator); associative thinking (the connector); analytical thinking (discussion director and vocabulary enhancer); and dramatization (literary luminary). All of the task roles are designed to support collaborative learning by offering students clearly defined, interlocking responsibilities.

The students are given role sheets, which are temporary support devices that help the students construct their own responses, ideas, and questions. There are individual role sheets for each of the assigned roles. See Figure 8.7 for an example of a role sheet for the discussion director. Each sheet briefly describes the task and provides prompts for helping the students discover and record the desired information. For example, following the description of the role of the literary luminary (whose task is to locate special sections of the text to share with the group), there are three columns entitled *location* (page and paragraph where the sections that are to be shared are located), *reason for picking,* and *the plan for reading.* The students are to fill in the information that they then bring to the literature circle. The task sheets are meant to be

Figure 8.7

DISCUSSION DIRECTOR

Name ______________________________

Group ______________________________

Book ______________________________

Assignment p_____–p_____

Discussion Director: Your job is to develop a list of questions that your group might want to discuss about this part of the book. Don't worry about the small details: your task is to help people talk over the big ideas in the reading and share their reactions. Usually the best discussion questions come from your own thoughts, feelings, and concerns as you read, which you can list below, during or after your reading. Or you may use some of the general questions below to develop topics for you group.

Possible discussion questions or topics for today:

1. ______________________________
2. ______________________________
3. ______________________________
4. ______________________________
5. ______________________________

Samples questions:

What was going through your mind while you read this?
How did you feel while reading this part of the book?
What was discussed in this section of the book?
Can someone summarize briefly?
Did today's reading remind you of any real-life experiences?
What questions did you have when you finished this section?
Did anything in this section of the book surprise you?
What are the one or two most important ideas?
Predict some things you think will be talked about next.

Topic to be carried over to tomorrow ______________________________

Assignment for tomorrow p_____–p_____

temporary devices and ultimately should become obsolete when the students are capable of conducting lively, multifaceted book discussions, sparked from open-ended entries in response logs.

Integral to the success of learning from and through literature is the need to discuss and share the literary experiences. All children need an opportunity to converse about books, self-reflect, and analyze. Genuine book conversations are not interrogations or "gentle inquisitions" (Eeds and Wells, 1989) led by teachers who only use questions to engage their students in talk. Rather they are lively exchanges that encourage children to explore literature responses and to participate in jointly constructing rich interpretations of literature (McGee, 1995). During these "grand conversations" (Peterson and Eeds, 1990: Raphael et al., 1995; McGee, 1995; Wells, 1995) about books, the students share their own interpretations based on their own experiences, attitudes, and purposes and help their classmates see what they might otherwise have overlooked. Conversations about literature captivate and challenge readers and are powerful tools for expanding children's responses to literature (McGee, 1995).

The teacher's role is different from that of the traditional basal reading program teacher armed with a teacher's manual and a prescribed reading curriculum. In a Readers' Workshop, the teacher acts as a collaborator, as a facilitator, as an audience for student interpretation, and as one who encourages and helps students with the observations that can be obtained from books (Short and Kauffman, 1995; Wells, 1995). Teachers create a community of learners—a community that allows children to demonstrate their involvement with literature and to locate meaningful ways to use language for learning about themselves and the world of books (Wells, 1995). The teacher models possible responses for books, helps students make connections to their own lives and to other pieces of literature, and is available for support and instruction if word recognition breaks down. Teachers are responsible for determining those teachable moments that invite their students to learn about and to share knowledge about authors, illustrators, and their craft. As in the past, teachers also observe and evaluate their students during this guided reading time. However, instead of book tests, more authentic measures of assessing and evaluating the students are used (e.g., anecdotal records, Running Records or miscue analysis on oral reading samples, checklists, and analysis of response logs). During workshop time, teachers note and observe whether the students were prepared for the session, that is, brought the book and response log, read the assigned pages, participated in the dialogues, and listened to others. Figure 8.8 is an example of a checklist that might be used to document student growth and progress.

While in the process of assessing their students during Readers' Workshop, teachers may want to analyze the responses that the students provided in their literature logs. Since it is preferable that students respond in a variety of ways, teachers may want to document the particular kinds of responding their students are offering. Fries (1994) categorizes her students' responses under the following attributes:

I. COMPREHENSION
   A. Summarization (retelling)
   B. Characterization
      - simple character maps or webs
      - compares him-/herself to characters
      - analyzes the actions and motives of the characters
      - records the development of the character(s)
   C. Predictions
      - makes acceptable predictions
      - documents predictions with evidence
   D. Questioning
      - asks literal questions
      - wonders about questions that go beyond the text
      - offers answers to questions

II. PERSONAL RESPONSE
   A. Relates text to own experiences
   B. Describes emotions felt while reading the text
   C. Explains how s/he would have acted in similar situation

III. LITERARY ELEMENTS
   A. Makes comments or suggestions to the author

Figure 8.8 Response to Literature Checklist

(Petersen and Eeds, 1990, 68–69)

RESPONSE TO LITERATURE CHECKLIST

I. Enjoyment/Involvement	**often**	**occasionally**	**rarely**
• Is aware of a variety of reading materials and can select those s/he enjoys reading.	_____	_____	_____
• Enjoys looking at pictures in picture story books.	_____	_____	_____
• Responds with emotion to text: laughs, cries, smiles.	_____	_____	_____
• Can get "lost" in a book.	_____	_____	_____
• Chooses to read during free time.	_____	_____	_____
• Wants to go on reading when time is up.	_____	_____	_____
• Shares reading experiences with classmates.	_____	_____	_____
• Has books on hand to read.	_____	_____	_____
• Chooses books in different genres.	_____	_____	_____
II. Making Personal Connections			
• Seeks meaning in both pictures and the text in picture story books.	_____	_____	_____
• Can identify the work of authors that s/he enjoys.	_____	_____	_____
• Sees literature as a way of knowing about the world.	_____	_____	_____
• Draws on personal experiences in constructing meaning.	_____	_____	_____
• Draws on earlier reading experiences in making meaning from a text.	_____	_____	_____
III. Interpretation/Making Meaning			
• Gets beyond "I like" in talking about story.	_____	_____	_____
• Makes comparisons between the works of individual authors and compares the work of different authors.	_____	_____	_____
• Appreciates the value of pictures in picture story books and uses them to interpret story meaning.	_____	_____	_____
• Asks questions and seeks out the help of others to clarify meaning.	_____	_____	_____
• Makes reasonable predictions about what will happen in story.	_____	_____	_____

(continued)

Figure 8.8 Response to Literature Checklist (cont.)
(Petersen and Eeds, 1990, 68–69)

	often	occasionally	rarely
• Can disagree without disrupting the dialogue.	____	____	____
• Can follow information important to getting the meaning of the story.	____	____	____
• Attends to multiple levels of meaning.	____	____	____
• Is willing to think and search out alternative points of view.	____	____	____
• Values other perspectives as a means for increasing interpretative possibilities.	____	____	____
• Turns to text to verify and clarify ideas.	____	____	____
• Can modify interpretations in light of "new evidence."	____	____	____
• Can make implied relationships not stated in the text.	____	____	____
• Can make statements about author's intent drawn from the total work.	____	____	____
• Is secure enough to put forward half-baked ideas to benefit from others' responses.	____	____	____
IV. Insight into Elements Authors Control in Making Story			
• Is growing in awareness of how elements function in story.	____	____	____
• Can talk meaningfully about:			
characters	____	____	____
setting	____	____	____
mood	____	____	____
incident	____	____	____
structure	____	____	____
symbol	____	____	____
time	____	____	____
tensions	____	____	____
• Draws on elements when interpreting text/constructing meaning with others.	____	____	____
• Uses elements of literature in working to improve upon stories written.	____	____	____
• Makes use of elements in making comparisons.	____	____	____

B. Identifies author's purpose for writing the text
C. Compares text with other pieces of literature
D. Identifies important events in the text

A grid can be prepared listing the above attributes, and the students' responses can be recorded. Students may have more than one area checked off if their responses contain a variety of perspectives. By analyzing the responses over time, teachers can see whether they need to nudge their students to expand their literature response repertoires or whether they need to continue modeling a variety of responses.

Naturally, there will be occasions when students will read ahead, being so captivated by a story. At these times, students are still expected to respond in journals (if this is the procedure established by the teacher and the rest of the class) and can participate in conversations as long as they do not reveal the rest of the text. While the others are still reading the workshop selection, these students now read another self-selected book until the rest of the class finishes the first book.

The preceding discussion is based on the use of multiple copies of books with small groups of students. However, some teachers prefer individualized reading programs in which all the children read books of their own choosing. Some elements are similar to those discussed previously, but there are some major differences for both the children and the teacher. In setting up an individualized reading program, teachers need to provide and be familiar with a wide range of books in order to help their students make appropriate selections. There should be reading materials of every genre with a variety of subject matter and reading levels. Some key components of individualized reading programs include student self-selection and independence in monitoring, evaluating, and sharing (Carter, 1990). After students select their books, they read silently, respond in literature response logs, confer with the teacher, and may complete an after-reading project.

An important aspect of such a program is the reading conference, which is the cornerstone of an effective individualized reading program. The reading conference is the time for students to share their reading experiences, usually with the teacher but also with peers, parent helpers, or paraprofessionals. An effective conference gives students opportunities to:

- share their pleasure in their reading
- further their ability to respond to literature
- demonstrate their ability to learn independently and to self-evaluate
- relate what they are reading to their previous experiences
- develop their abilities to make and express opinions

An effective reading conference also provides teachers with opportunities to:

- monitor their students' reading progress
- extend their students' abilities to respond to literature
- identify the strengths and needs of their students and plan accordingly
- monitor their language program
- share their students' enthusiasm for and enjoyment of books

(Nicol and Silvestri, 1992)

Certain activities may occur during reading conferences. First, the teacher ensures that the child feels comfortable. Teachers then invite the children to share their thoughts and feelings about the chosen text. After this sharing, the children select a section of the book that they would like to read aloud to the teacher. This oral reading is followed by discussion and careful questioning. The children are encouraged to make critical comments and relate the book to their experiences. The conference concludes with the teacher and the child negotiating follow-up activities and discussing other possible reading selections (Nicol and Silvestri, 1992).

After Reading

Once a book is nearly finished or after it is finished, students can plan one book-sharing activity. Occasionally it is welcome to do nothing but savor the book through dialogue or conversation, but book-sharing activities can be planned by the group and then shared with the rest of the class. These activities can be elaborate (e.g., a mock wedding for Sarah and Jacob in *Sarah Plain and Tall*), involve further research (e.g., investigating wedding customs after reading *Julie of the Wolves* or homelessness after reading *Maniac Magee*), or can just be part of a general class discussion on the books that were read. Possibilities for literature response activities are presented in Chapter 10.

In addition to projects and book extensions, other types of analyses and activities are possible:

1. **Agree/Disagree Statements (done orally or in writing).** Students are given statements to which they may agree or disagree. They must provide reasons why they chose the answer they did.

- Book: *The Indian in the Cupboard* by Lynne Banks
- Statements:
  - Omri was being selfish when he didn't share the Indian.
  - Keeping an Indian gave Omri more problems than pleasure.

2. **Levels of Excitement Plot Profiles.** This activity can be done individually or with the entire class. First, students list the significant events that occurred in the story. Then they assign a level of excitement (from a rating of 1, which indicates little or no excitement, to a rating of 10, which is indicative of lots of excitement). The events are listed on the horizontal axis of a graph and the excitement or tension levels on the vertical axis. The events and levels are then plotted. A typical story tends to begin with little or no excitement and builds up to a peak toward the end. The level tends to go down after the exciting climax. An example of a Plot Profile can be seen in "From the Classroom" of fifth-grade teacher Bob Barnes.

3. **Story Maps.** Story maps are visual representations of the essential elements of the parts of a story, that is, characters, setting, problem, main events, resolution, and theme. They may take many forms such as those seen in Figure 8.9. Two excellent resources that have a wealth of story map ideas are: *Story Maps and More* (Norwood and Abromitis, 1992) and *Literature Circles* (Paziotopoulos and Kroll, 1992).

4. **Yes/No Statements.** Students respond to a yes/no question by documenting why they responded as they did.

Figure 8.9A

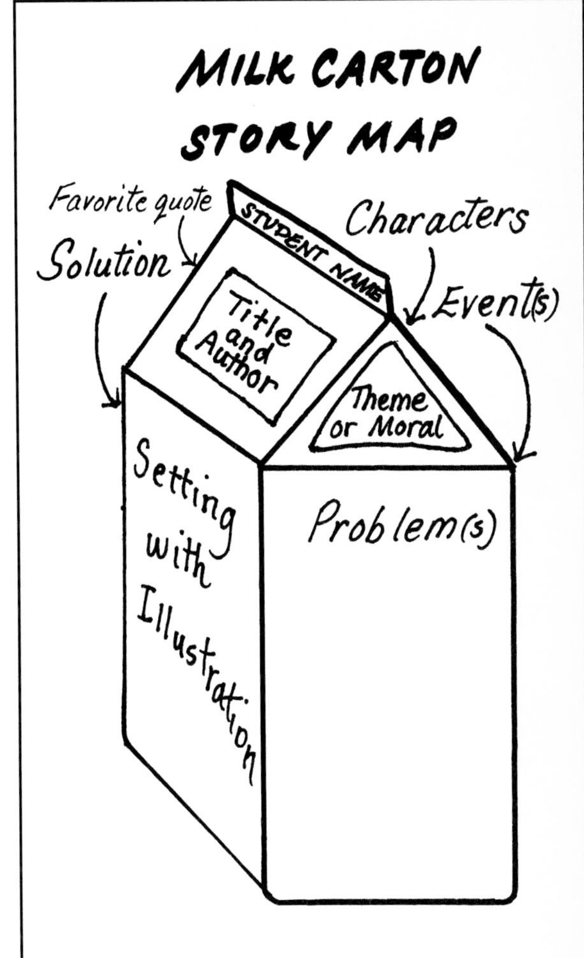

- Book: *Stone Fox* by John Gardiner
- Question: Did young Willy deserve to win the dog sled race?

5. **Author/Me Statements.** Students respond to a statement that can be attributed to the author. They find evidence in the story as to why the author would support that statement or refute it if they disagree and then offer their own opinions.

- Book: *The True Story of the Three Little Pigs* by Jon Scieszka
- Statement: Wolves are tricky animals that cannot be trusted.

Figure 8.9B (cont.)

Figure 8.9C (cont.)

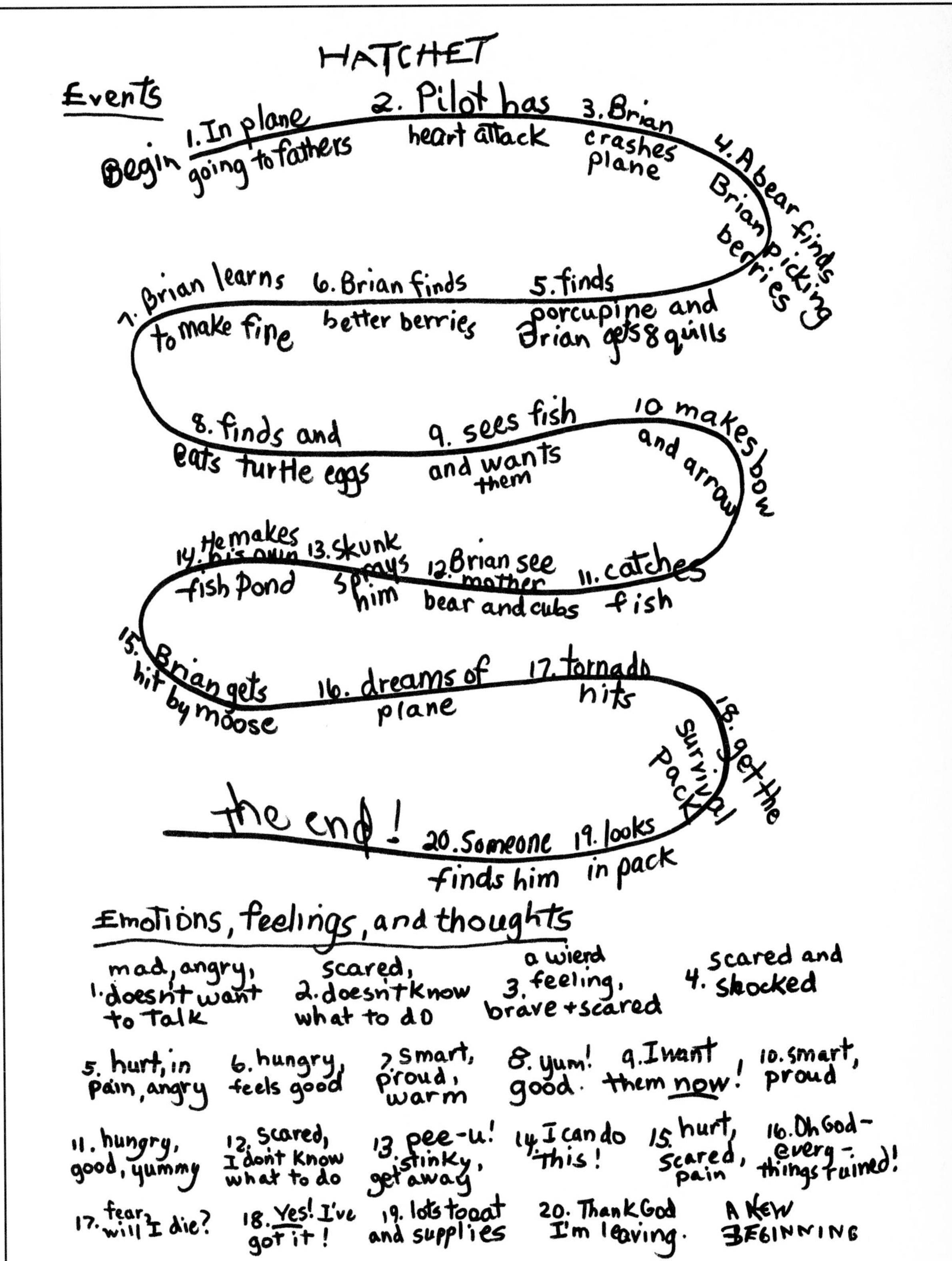
HATCHET
Events
Begin
1. In plane going to fathers
2. Pilot has heart attack
3. Brian crashes plane
4. A bear finds Brian picking berries
5. finds porcupine and Brian gets 8 quills
6. Brian finds better berries
7. Brian learns to make fire
8. finds and eats turtle eggs
9. sees fish and wants them
10 makes bow and arrow
11. catches fish
12. Brian see mother bear and cubs
13. skunk sprays him
14. He makes his own fish pond
15. Brian gets hit by moose
16. dreams of plane
17. tornado hits
18. get the survival pack
19. looks in pack
20. Someone finds him
the end!
Emotions, feelings, and thoughts
1. mad, angry, doesn't want to talk
2. scared, doesn't know what to do
3. a wierd feeling, brave + scared
4. scared and shocked
5. hurt, in pain, angry
6. hungry, feels good
7. smart, proud, warm
8. yum! good.
9. I want them now!
10. smart, proud
11. hungry, good, yummy
12. scared, I don't know what to do
13. pee-u! stinky, get away
14. I can do this!
15. hurt, scared, pain
16. Oh God - every-things ruined!
17. fear, will I die?
18. Yes! I've got it!
19. lots to eat and supplies
20. Thank God I'm leaving.
A NEW BEGINNING

Figure 8.9D (cont.)

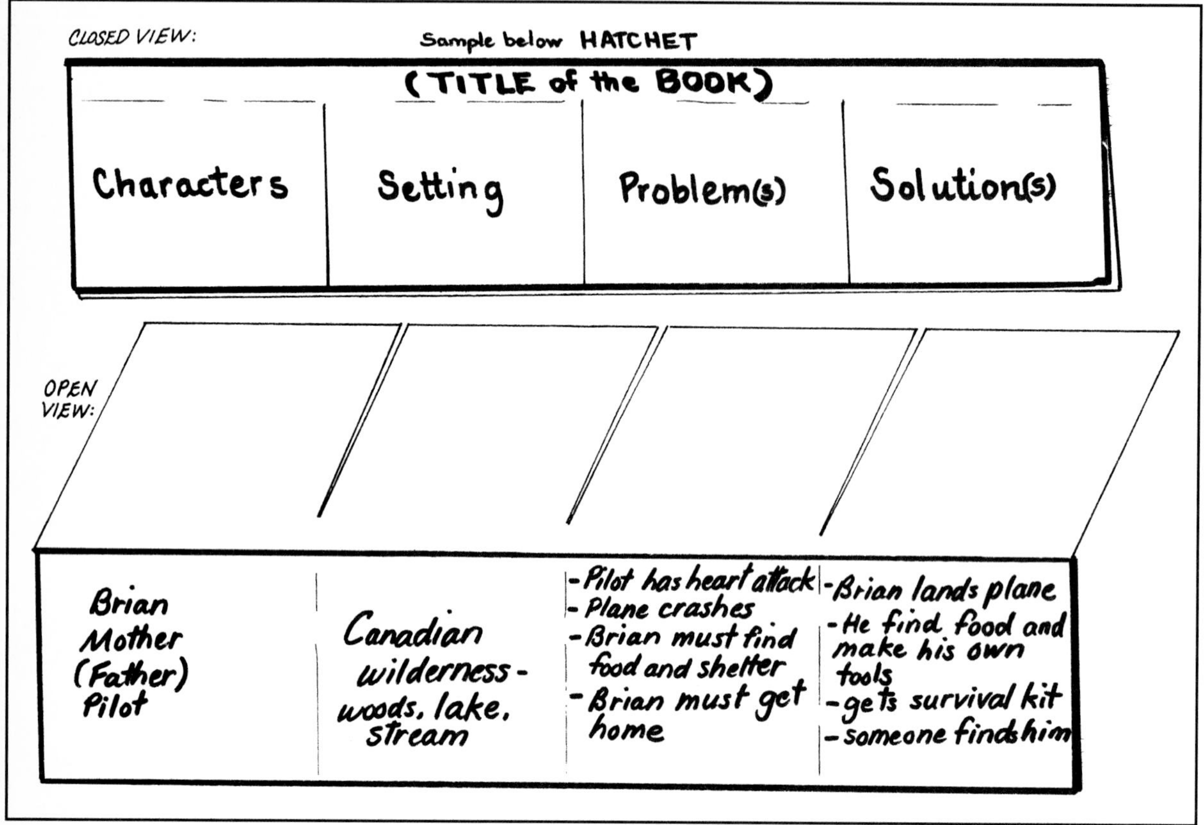

6. **Rating Scales.** Students can rate statements or books. A typical rating scale can go from 1 (not at all) to 5 (all).

- Book: *Sign of the Beaver* by Elizabeth Speare
- Statements:
  - Native Americans show respect for their environment.
  - Knowing the ways of the Native Americans can aid survival in the forest.
  - Friends should share common beliefs.

A scale for rating books is used in Dean Witham's fifth-grade classroom. In addition to a rating, books that receive a score of 5 also have a gold star placed on their cover to indicate a strong recommendation. The scale and explanation of the ratings is as follows:

5—Excellent. The best of its kind. I would strongly recommend it. Very well written.

4—Very Good. Worth reading. Interesting, with many really great sections. I would recommend it.

3—Good. The story held my interest most of the time. I would probably recommend it.

2—Fair. Some good spots, but overall I would probably not recommend this book.

1—Poor. Boring or poorly written. I would not recommend this book.

7. **"Dear Reader" Letters.** These are written book talks, which were explained previously. They can be written by the teacher to the class or to a certain student or by a student to the teacher or to a classmate.

8. **Student Reviews.** To accompany the ratings used in Dean Witham's class, students can write reviews or report on books orally. This can be likened to TV commentaries on new

Figure 8.9E (cont.)

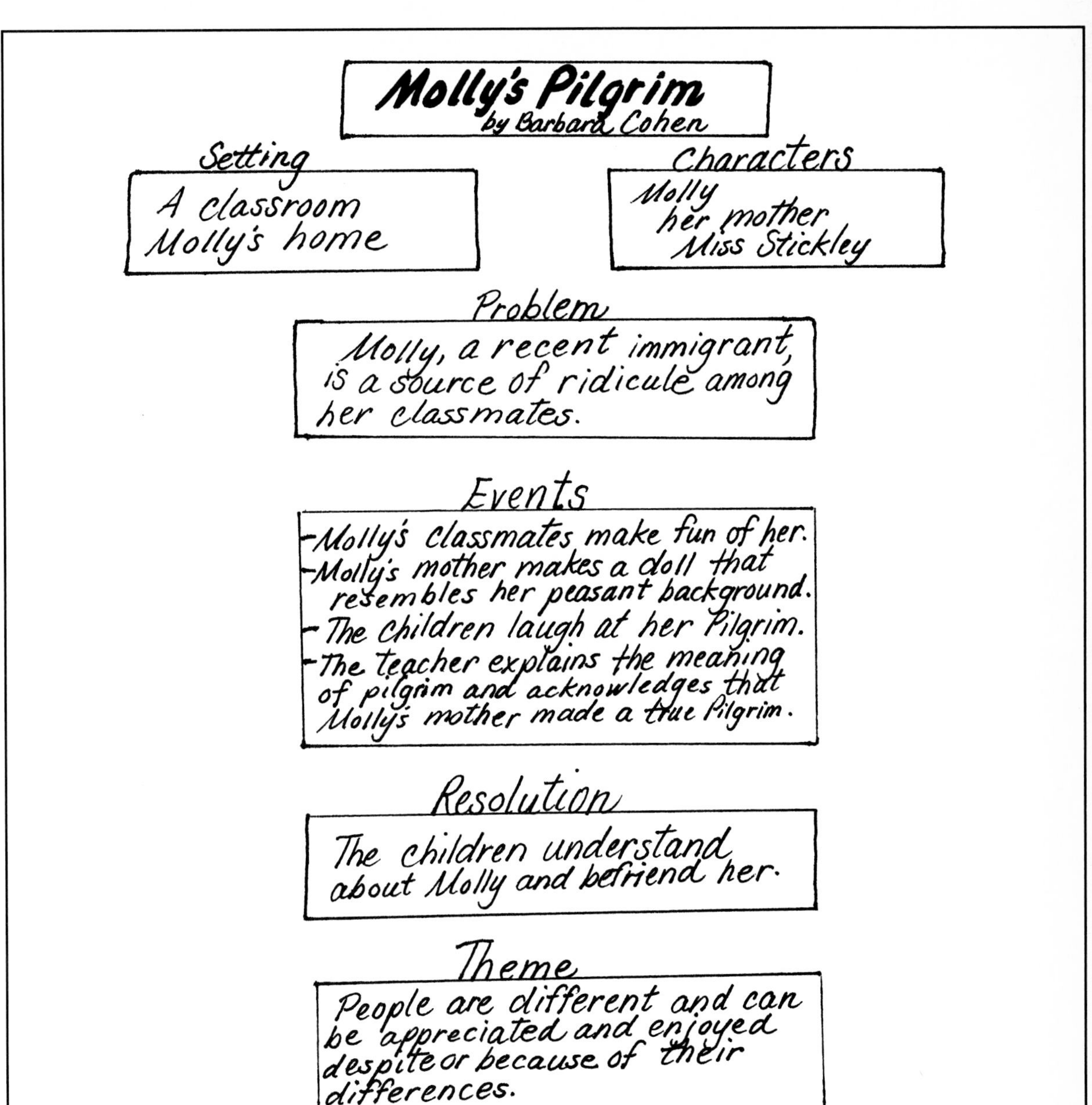

movies or plays. Student reviews can begin or end a workshop session, be included in a class newspaper, or be posted on the class message board for all to read.

9. **Character Maps/Webs.** Character maps or webs are examples of graphic organizers that help students with characterization. They are excellent tools for examining actions, personality traits, and motives of characters in literature. Several variations of character webs may be seen in Figure 8.10.

To give an example of one teacher's journey into whole language, let's look at Angeletti (1991), who made the transition from a basal program to a literature-based reading program. In making the change, Angeletti had several goals:

Figure 8.9F (cont.)

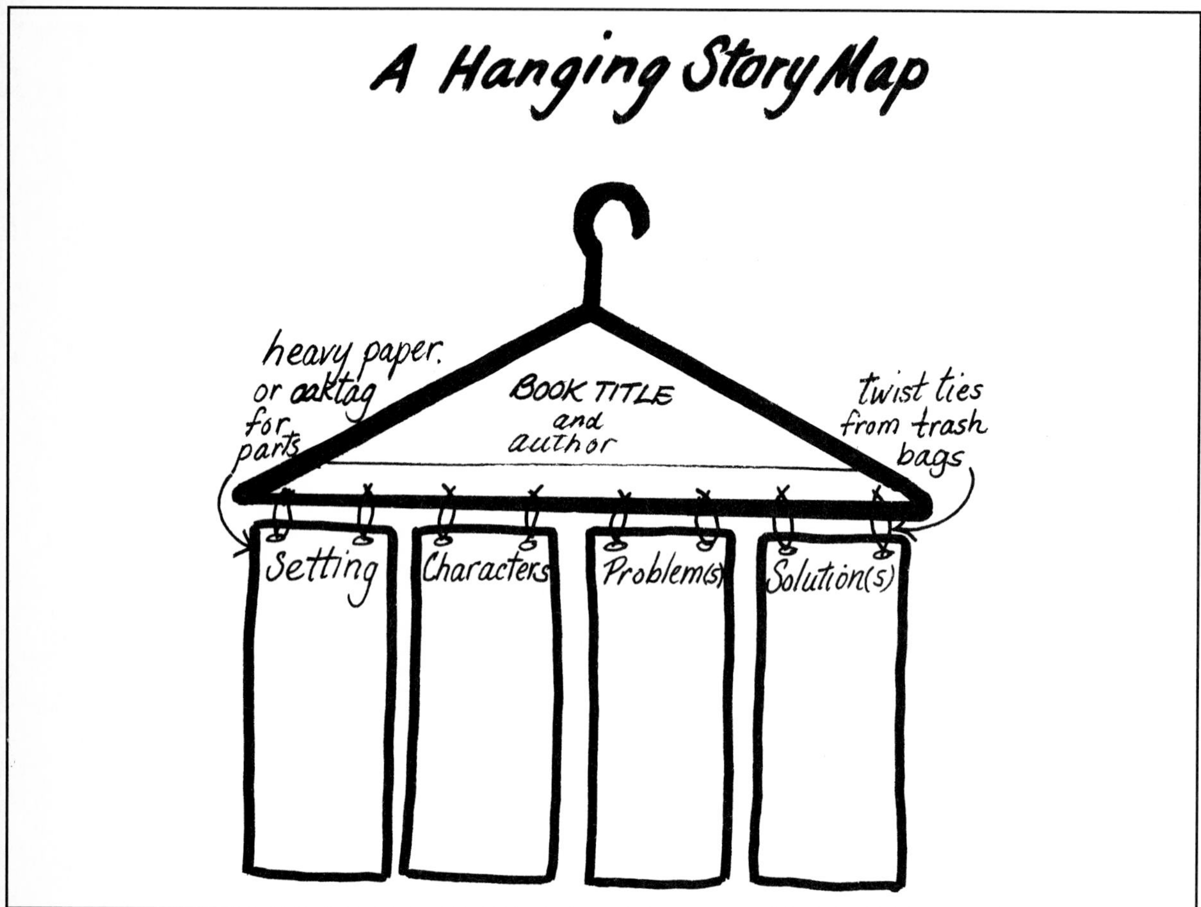

- to promote a love of reading and writing
- to have her students respond to literature through discussions and writing by evaluating the story, the characters, the author's purpose, and the author's writing style
- to develop comprehension strategies while still focusing on the whole story
- to develop independent, confident readers and writers who can share their reading and ask thoughtful questions

In order to accomplish her goals, Angeletti implemented some questioning techniques to encourage her students to think about their reading and to share their responses both orally and in writing. Question cards were prepared for several categories: opinion, comparison-contrast, drawing conclusions, characters, author's style, author's purpose, and type of literature. (See Figure 8.11.) Each category of questions was first modeled by the teacher, followed by whole-class and small group practice. The beginning of each language arts session (the literature workshop) was begun with a minilesson that included modeling responses to questions on a card. Following silent reading, the students met in small groups to respond to the questions introduced at the beginning of the session. After the group sessions, the students then responded in writing. Once students were comfortable with each card, they were encouraged to choose any card when responding to their books.

In evaluating the procedure, Angeletti noted that the children progressed from a retelling stage (when they merely restated the

Figure 8.9G (cont.)

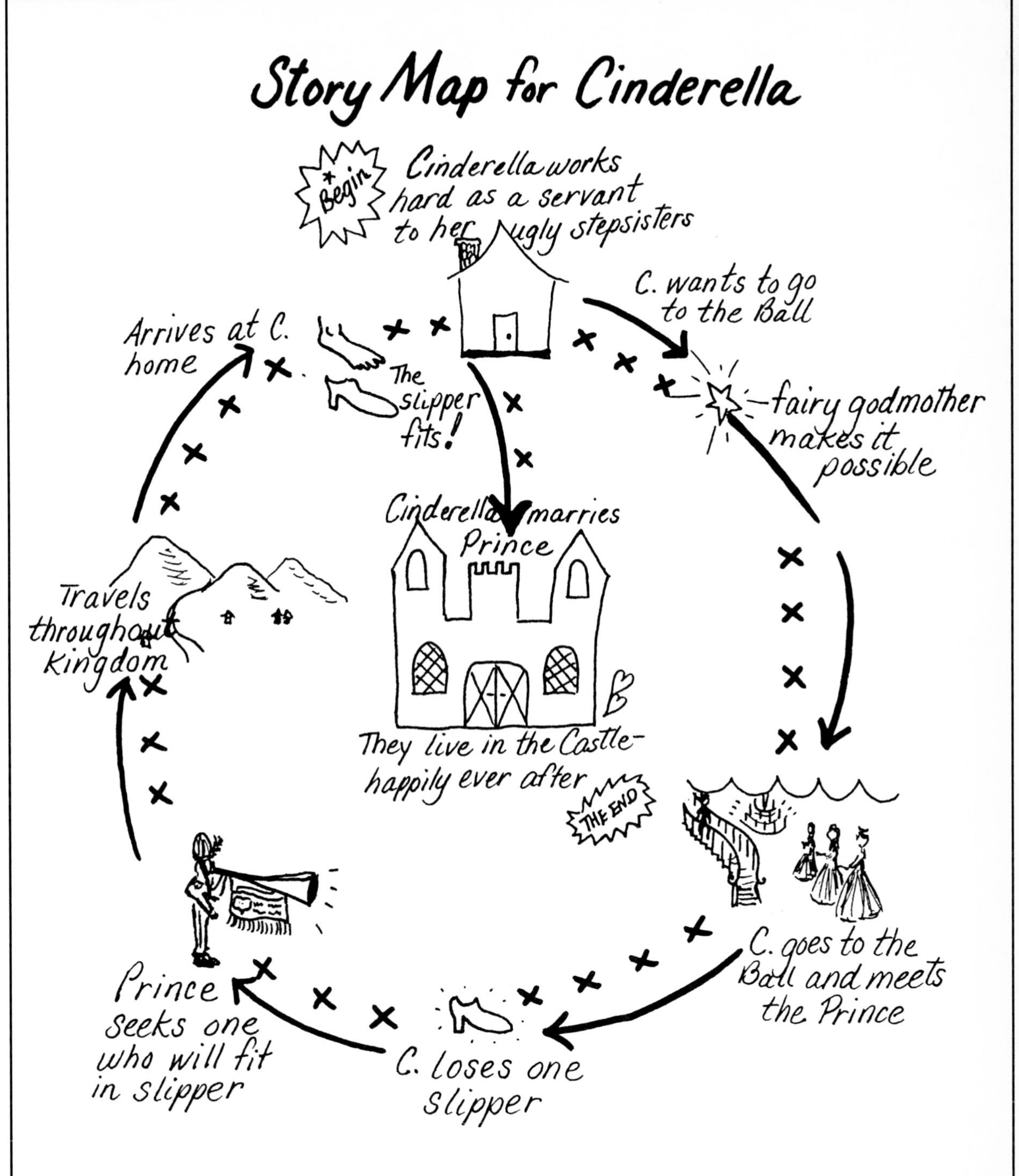

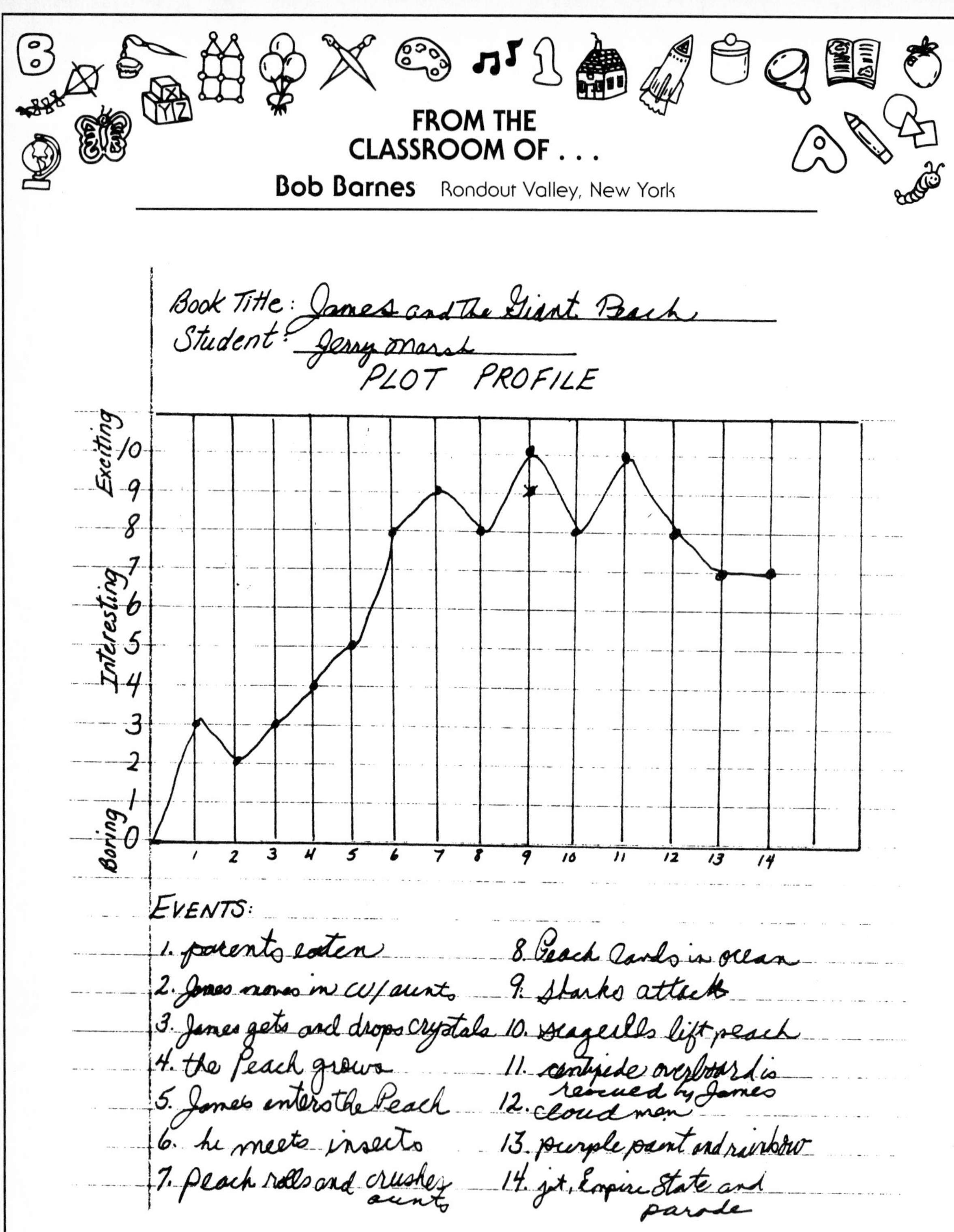

FROM THE CLASSROOM OF . . .

Bob Barnes Rondout Valley, New York

Book Title: James and the Giant Peach

Student: Jerry Marsh

PLOT PROFILE

EVENTS:

1. parents eaten
2. James moves in w/aunts
3. James gets and drops crystals
4. the Peach grows
5. James enters the Peach
6. he meets insects
7. peach rolls and crushes aunts
8. Peach lands in ocean
9. Sharks attack
10. seagulls lift peach
11. centipede overboard is rescued by James
12. cloud men
13. purple paint and rainbow
14. jet, Empire State and parade

Figure 8.10A

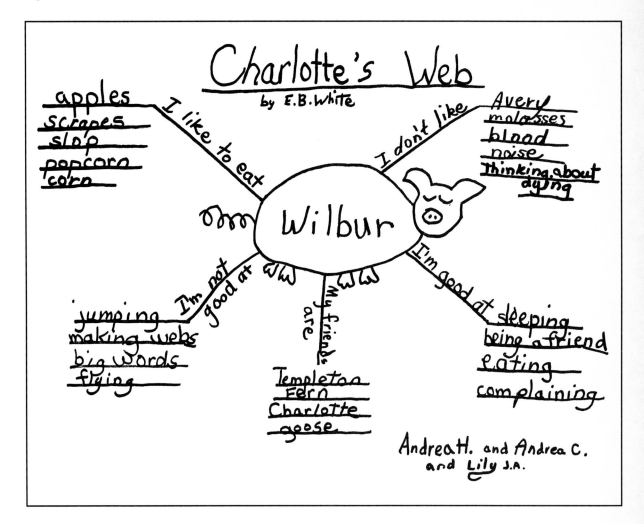

stories in their own words) to a responding stage (when they included many statements about what they were thinking or liked) to an evaluation stage (when they made inferences, drew conclusions, and discussed the author's purpose and characterization). Angeletti is not alone in her observations of student growth in a literature-based reading program. Samway (1991) likewise reported dramatic changes. She noted that students naturally compared books and authors, initiated fruitful conversations about what they read, and made relevant associations between events and characters in the literature and their own lives. Moreover, the students became enthusiastic, motivated learners.

Literature circles, Readers' Workshops, or Book Clubs are not just terms for any kind of small-group reading lessons. They stand for a sophisticated blending of collaborative learning along with independent reading in the framework of reader response theory (Daniels, 1994). To be genuine, literature circles should contain several distinctive features:

- student choice of reading material
- the formation of small, temporary groups by book choice, not by reading level or ability
- the reading of and responding to different books by different groups of children
- regularly scheduled meetings of the groups to discuss their reading

Figure 8.10B (cont.)

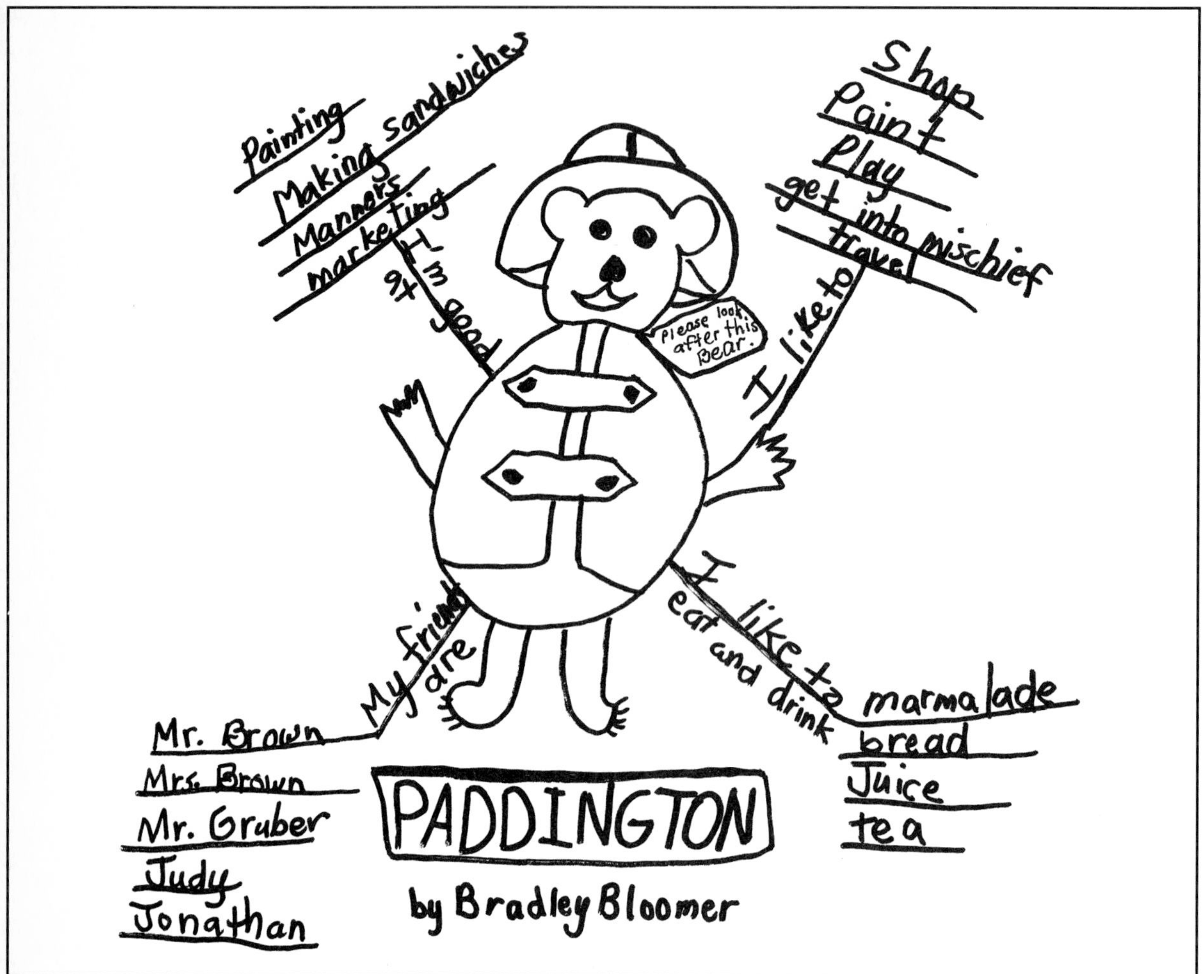

- student generation of discussion topics
- open-ended conversations about books, with the encouragement of personal connections, digressions, and the asking of open-ended questions
- the teacher serving as facilitator
- evaluation consisting of teacher observation and student self-evaluation
- the sharing with classmates once the books have been finished

(Daniels, 1994; Raphael and McMahon, 1994; Raphael, Goatley, McMahon, and Woodman, 1995; Wells, 1995; Short and Kauffman, 1995).

Although this approach to teaching reading is new and challenging, teachers—through their own immersion in this technique, through practice, and with feedback—will come to trust themselves and their students to grow in their abilities to read and converse about literature with both clarity and insight. They will recognize the possibilities for both student and teacher growth that can occur through the conversations and dialogues about literature. Literature provides a means of understanding the world and illuminating the lives of all it reaches. Readers' Workshop provides a means of putting books in the hands of students for

Figure 8.10C (cont.)

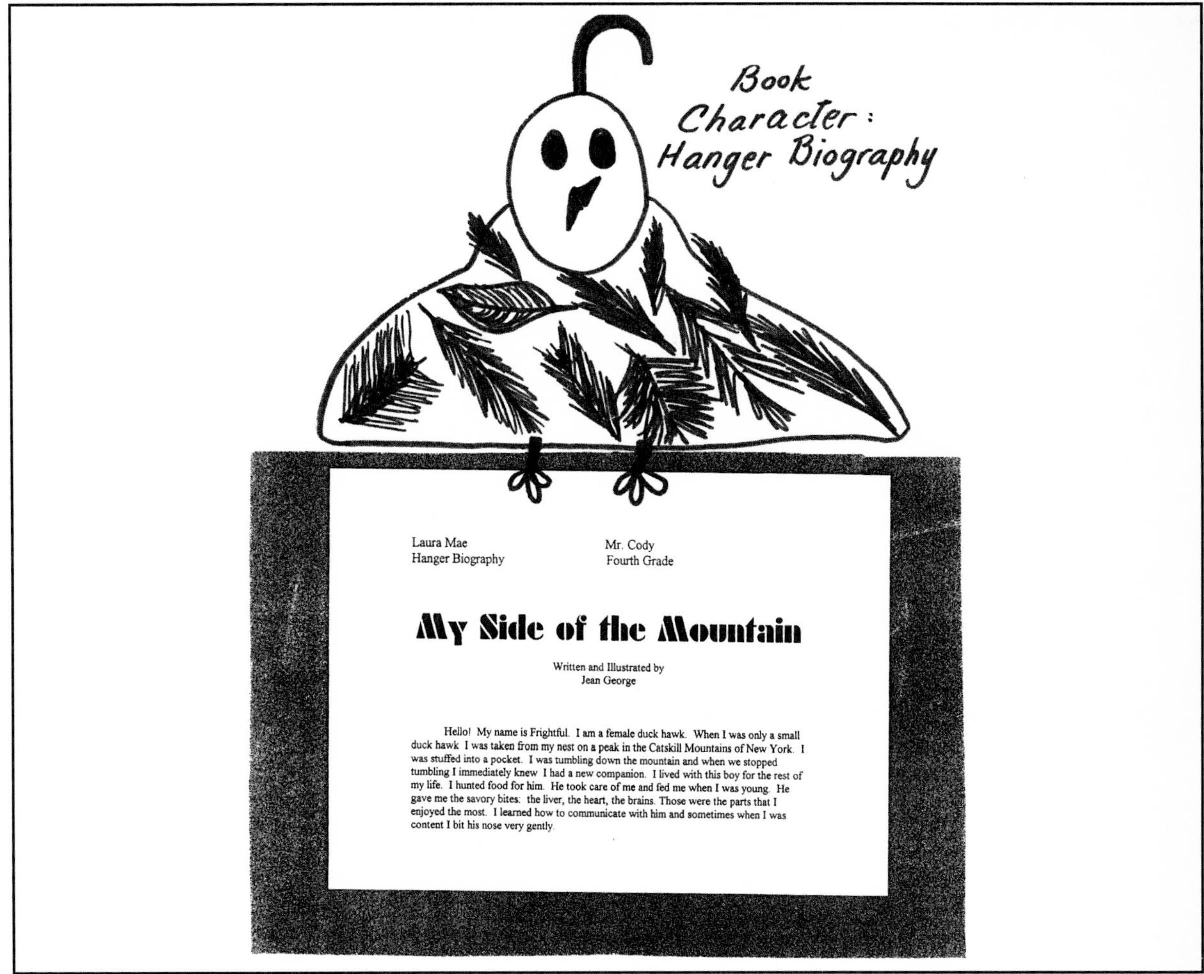

learning and for enjoyment. The students in Figure 8.12 say it all!

Book Character: Hanger Biography
Laura Mae
Hanger Biography
Mr. Cody
Fourth Grade
My Side of the Mountain
Written and Illustrated by
Jean George
Hello! My name is Frightful. I am a female duck hawk. When I was only a small duck hawk I was taken from my nest on a peak in the Catskill Mountains of New York. I was stuffed into a pocket. I was tumbling down the mountain and when we stopped tumbling I immediately knew I had a new companion. I lived with this boy for the rest of my life. I hunted food for him. He took care of me and fed me when I was young. He gave me the savory bites: the liver, the heart, the brains. Those were the parts that I enjoyed the most. I learned how to communicate with him and sometimes when I was content I bit his nose very gently.

A BALANCED WRITING PROGRAM

Just as students need a balanced reading program, they likewise need a balanced writing program. The purpose of a Writers' Workshop is to help children develop their abilities as writers (Atwell, 1987). In grade 3 and above, children should be given ample opportunities to write, to see demonstrations of the various stages of the writing process, and to use writing across the curriculum. The same considerations for establishing a writing program described in Chapter 2 are applicable here: time, process, ownership, climate, resources, expectation, and demonstration (Graves, 1994). These key elements are addressed in the discussions of Writers' Workshop, journal writing, and writing across the curriculum.

Writers' Workshop

One way of structuring the writing program is to use a workshop approach. First, the teacher needs to set aside a significant portion of the

Figure 8.10D (cont.)

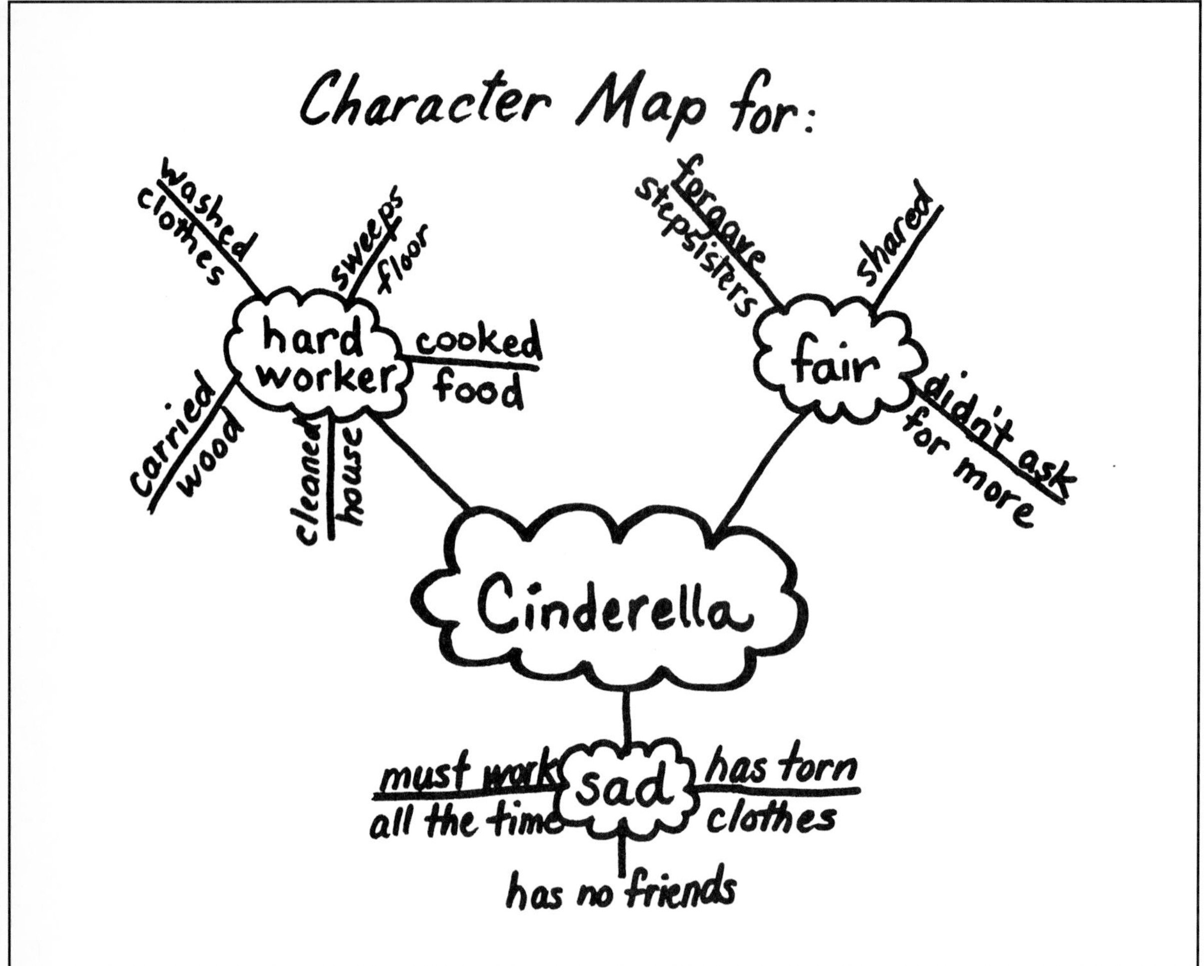

school day for the workshop. A regularly scheduled time each day (or as many days as possible) is necessary for children to be able to anticipate the writing, prepare for it mentally and physically, and participate in the writing process. Ample time should be scheduled (approximately 45–60 minutes in the upper grades) to allow children to become immersed in their writing and for minilessons, conferences, and sharing. The workshop can be structured in several ways, but after experimenting with the possible structures it is advisable to settle on one so that the students can expect certain features to occur on a regular basis. (That is not to say that teachers cannot be flexible and alter the format as needed or as other opportunities arise.) A possible format for a 45-minute workshop is as follows:

Minilesson (5–10 minutes)
Writing time/conference time (25–30 minutes)
Sharing (10 minutes)

Atwell (1987) adds another component to her Writers' Workshop—Status of the Class—which occurs after the minilesson. If an hour is allocated, then additional time can be added to any of the three aforementioned areas. Each element of the workshop is presented separately, with suggestions and activities offered for implementing them.

Figure 8.11 Question Cards

APPENDIX
Question Cards

Comparison and contrast card 1

Choose two characters from one story. Do the characters look alike? How are they alike? How are they different? What problems do the two characters have that are the same? How are the feelings of the characters different?

Comparison and contrast card 2

Choose two stories. Were the places alike? How were the stories the same? How were they different? How were the story endings different? Which story do you like better? Why? Which character did you like better? Why?

Opinions

What did you like about the main character? What did the character do that made you like him or her? What did you think about the ending? Was anything surprising to you in the story? What was it? Why were you surprised?

Inference

Look at the pictures and at the title. What do you know about the story before you begin to read it? Read the story. Think about the ending. If the story had continued, what might have happened? Why?

Drawing conclusions

Draw a picture of your favorite character. Tell as much as you can about what kind of person your character is. Tell things he or she did in the story. Is this a nice person? Why or why not? Would you like to have this person for a friend? Why or why not?

Characters

As you read a story you learn about the characters by what they say and do. Choose a character from your story. What kind of person is your character? Do you like him or her? Why? How would they act if you were with him or her?

Author's style

Every writer has his or her own style of writing. When we learn the author's style, we know what to expect from that writer. We often know whether books written by a particular author will be easy picture books or chapter books. We know what kind of characters are typical of the writer—animals that talk, or people like us. We might know whether there will be a happy ending. We know whether we would enjoy reading another book by the same author. Choose an author whose style you know and tell what you know about the author's style of writing. Give examples from books you have read by that author.

Author's purpose

Sometimes authors write a story to teach you something. Sometimes they tell a story about something that happened to them. Sometimes they just want to entertain you, or they may have another reason for writing. Tell in one sentence why the author wrote the story you read. Then tell how you knew the author's reason for writing the story.

Type of literature

Tell what kind of book you are reading. Look for clues that let you know. If it is fantasy or fiction, for example, there may be animals that talk, or magic things may happen. If it is realistic fiction, there may be real people in the story, and the story could have happened, but the author made it up, perhaps using ideas from his or her own life. If you find rhyming words, short lines, and writing that makes every word count, you are reading poetry. Or you may be reading facts from a book like an encyclopedia. If so, the book is factual. Think about what section of the library you would go to in order to find the book. Then put your book into one group and tell what clues let you know which type of book it is.

MiniLessons/Focused Lessons

Teachers frequently begin the workshop with a minilesson. These lessons cover many areas of the writing curriculum and can be done with the entire class, a small group of students, or individuals. The content of the lesson is determined by careful teacher observation of the students' needs, not by a predetermined scope and sequence in a language arts textbook. However, there is no need to throw out those textbooks, for some make excellent resources to use in planning minilessons.

At the beginning of the school year, minilessons may focus on such procedures as locating and using the writing resources, setting up writing folders, and helping students start per-

Figure 8.12 Student Reactions to Readers Workshop

(Third Graders in Susan Friedland's Class)

Reading Clubs are very fun! We go in groups to help each other read better, to think deeper, and to talk more interestingly. When we go in our clubs we think, act, and talk like adults because this is an adult program. I feel that this program makes us act more mature. I also think that this program makes us get along better. I also think that when we read a chapter together as a class we get to learn more about each other. My last thought is I think that this is the best program that I ever did!!! (Cory)

Reading Clubs help us get smarter and get better at our vocabulary. We learn about other people's interpretations of the book. When you get to do reading, you get into groups and discuss your books. You work together like a family. (Lee)

In our groups, we think deeper. We also work together as a community. (Erik)

In our Reading Club, we talk about how we feel, think, and what we would like to know. We try very hard to think deeper. In our Reading Club, we help each other with reading. When someone gets stuck, they say they need help and we help them. (Jessica)

In our reading groups we talk about a lot of things. Some things that we talk about are personal connections, characters, settings, and the main idea. When we ask questions we ask **why** so we think more deeply. We work as a community and always help one another. (Ashley)

I think the reading clubs are fun! My favorite part of the reading clubs is when we discuss what we wrote. Other classes should try it too! (Kerry)

sonalized topic lists. As time goes on, teachers use the minilesson time to model all aspects of the writing process: topic selection, narrowing topics, drafting, revision, editing, and publishing. Teachers demonstrate to students how to conference with each other and help them devise checklists or charts on peer conferences and peer or self-editing. The mechanics of writing are addressed during minilessons as well. Students may need help with sentence structure, determining paragraphs, other grammatical areas, spelling, and punctuation. Therefore minilessons can focus on procedural issues, writers' craft, or mechanics. Although minilessons are generally conducted at the beginning of a workshop, lessons on identified needs can occur during the actual writing time as well. Figure 8.13 lists types of minilessons that may be presented.

Teacher modeling is an exceedingly important aspect of a classroom writing program. Students have had very little opportunity to see others write and generally have very unrealistic expectations about their own writing abilities and about the writing process itself. Writing is a craft and needs to be demonstrated to students. As Graves (1994) points out, children have to see teachers struggle to match their intentions with the words that reach the page.

Hodgson (1995) describes a modeling session on using more exciting words in writing. To begin the session, she read from a piece of literature that the class was currently reading and asked her students to name some interesting words the author used. These words were recorded on chart paper. Next, she shared a draft of her own, containing such overused words as *nice* and *good*. She asked the children, "What do you notice about this piece of writing?" "Is it interesting?" "Could it be improved?" "How can I make it better?" To help children find a variety of words, she distributed copies of a thesaurus and

Figure 8.13 Types of Minilessons in Writing

PROCEDURAL
- Workshop procedures
- Writing folders (use and storage)
- Storage of materials
- Status of the class
- Choosing topics for writing
- How to use the publishing center
- Rules for using the computer
- Conferencing techniques
- Publishing

AUTHORS' CRAFT
- Function, form, and audience
- Writing process
- Expository writing
- Narrative writing
- Expressive writing
- Persuasive writing
- Notetaking
- Showing, not telling
- Plot
- Setting
- Leads
- Endings
- Characterization
- Point of view
- Theme
- Use of dialogue
- Author styles
- Doing research

WRITERS' TOOLS/SKILLS
- Spacing between words
- Indenting
- Capitalization
- Punctuation
- Grammar
- Spelling
- Proofreading
- Sentence combining
- Sentence expansion
- Overused words
- Run-on sentences
- Word usage
- Effective vocabulary

showed them how to use it. After they had helped her with her writing, they took out their latest draft and replaced two words with more interesting ones. At the beginning of the year, teachers need to ensure that all their students are taught the basic writing process and accompanying skills. Throughout the year, small groups of children may be gathered according to need and further modeling provided.

Occasionally it may be necessary for teachers to spend a large amount or perhaps even all of the scheduled writing time on some aspect of the writing process. Thus, instead of a minilesson, which is brief, students are given focused lessons. Focused lessons can appear periodically through the year, dealing with such issues as writing leads, organizing writing, choosing or narrowing topics, using words to show rather than tell, characterization, editing, and endings (Nathan, Temple, Juntunen, and Temple, 1989). Again, like minilessons, focused lessons arise out of demonstrated needs and are not the outgrowth of traditional language arts textbook activities. Ideas for both minilessons and focused lessons come from the teacher's understanding of how writing is learned and from observing the students in all phases of the writing process. (See Figure 8.14 for a sample focused lesson on apostrophes.)

Writing/Conference Time

In order to provide a complete picture of the writing/conference time, each of the components will be addressed separately. Applicable minilessons dealing with each phase are presented then as well. However, it must be remembered that individual students will be at various phases of the writing process at any given time. Therefore the classroom must be structured so that students have space to move around to conference with one another, space where small groups of students can meet in Writers' Circle, and space where the authors can ultimately share their pieces with the entire class. Students must know where the resources are and must be trained to use them so that the teacher is free to circulate, conference with students, and give minilessons.

Figure 8.14 Focused Lesson on Apostrophes

OBJECTIVES

- The students will be able to identify possessive nouns in their reading.
- The students will be able to use apostrophes to make nouns show possession (both singular and plural).
- The students will collect samples of possessive nouns and place them on a class chart.

MATERIALS

chart paper, overhead projector, trade books, Post-its, witch's hat

MOTIVATION

Put on the witch's hat and pretend you are a witch attending the annual Witches' Convention on the night before Halloween. Tell the students about last year's convention and the HORRIBLE thing that occurred. Explain that at the convention the witches are required to place all their personal belongings outside the cave where the meeting takes place. After last year's meeting ended, all the witches went to get their brooms, owls, cats, demons, and other witch items, but lo and behold, some evil spirit had mixed everything up and no one could figure out which objects belonged to which witch. What were they to do?

STRATEGIES

Ask the children to brainstorm possible solutions the witches could have used to solve the problem. How could the witches show which objects belonged to them? Extend the discussion to real life, and ask students how they and their parents show that things belong to them (e.g., marking items, name tags, deeds, and so on). Give each student some Post-its and have them label some items in their desks or backpacks or items in the classroom. Choose some labels and place them on the chalkboard, chart paper, or overhead projector.

Amanda's backpack
Jared's pencil
Jillian's pencil case
the boys' bathroom
the students' library

Ask which punctuation mark appears in all the phrases listed. Liken the apostrophe to a deed. Take each phrase and discuss what the owner possesses. Talk about whether there is one owner or more than one owner and where the apostrophe occurs. As a class, come up with rules for using apostrophes to show possession.

To practice identifying possessives and making nouns show possession, the students can continue to put Post-its on items. The following paragraphs could be placed on the overhead projector, one at a time. In the first paragraph, the students are to identify the possessives, and in the second paragraph, they are to make some nouns show possession. In the case of the second paragraph, the students are getting some practice in proofreading for correct punctuation.

> Paragraph 1: Mousekin was following a path to one of his homes in the chestnut log. Right in the middle of the path was a jack-o-lantern that someone had thrown away after Halloween. The jack-o-lantern's eyes were bright and the size of a shoe button. Suddenly an owl swooped down, and the owl's tallons grabbed for Mousekin. Mousekin jumped straight into the jack-o-lantern's mouth.

(*continued*)

Figure 8.14 Focused Lesson on Apostrophes (cont.)

> Paragraph 2: Inside the pumpkin, Mousekin looked about. He was in a beautiful golden room. From the room windows, Mousekin could see the owl sulking in the evergreen tree. Since it was morning and time for him to go to sleep, Mousekin eyes closed and he slept for the day. Later Mousekin heard a cat paws as he rustled in the leaves outside. The jack-o-lantern terrible teeth and very scary face frightened the cat away. As autumn changed into winter, something happened to the jack-o-lantern shape. The pumpkin eyes closed in the frosty air, and its mouth shut against the cold wind. Mousekin house was now cozy, so he curled into a tiny fur ball and fell fast asleep.

Variation: Use a current piece of literature and find items the characters possess. Label these items and place them on a chart. For instance, students could list and label items that belong to Mrs. Frisby or items that the rats would want to take to their new home in the valley as they read *Mrs. Frisby and the Rats of NIMH.* Or they could pack the items that belong to Maniac Magee as he moves from place to place in *Maniac Magee* by Jerry Spinelli. The students could collect possessive nouns they encounter in their daily reading. These could be placed on a class chart, or the class could make a book on apostrophes.

EVALUATION

- Observation, discussion, and teacher questioning
- Participation in chart writing activity
- Use of possessives in daily writing

Status of the Class. Prior to beginning the actual writing time, teachers may want to check exactly what their students are working on and where the students are in the process. Therefore a few minutes several times a week (or daily) are spent surveying the class and noting each student's activity on a "Status of the Class" recording sheet (see Figure 8.15). By glancing over this sheet periodically, teachers can note which students may need extra support and encouragement, which students are ready to publish, and where teachers should focus their attention and efforts during the writing/conference time.

Freewriting. After a minilesson and after surveying the students' writing progress, the teacher and class move into the writing session. This can be done by having everyone—including the teacher—freewrite for five minutes. After the freewriting or sustained silent writing, the teacher then circulates while the children continue writing. Children can continue to write on their freewriting topics or can select any piece in their writing folder for further drafting, revision, or preparation for publication.

Writing/Conferencing. The majority of the Writers' Workshop time will be spent writing and conferencing. When first introducing the workshop, teachers may wish to establish some guidelines, which may include (Atwell, 1987):

- no erasing—draw lines through writing that is to be changed
- write on one side of the paper only
- date and label all pieces
- save everything
- speak in quiet voices
- work really hard

These guidelines may be introduced during a minilesson as effective techniques that enhance writing. Teachers may save samples of student work from prior years to illustrate some of the guidelines.

When first implementing the writing process, teachers may have to model each stage. Because children may have been accustomed to a writing program in which drafts became final copies in a single setting and the teacher has selected the topics, the children will need teacher assistance in choosing topics and in getting

Figure 8.15 Status of the Class Sheet

Writing - Status of the Class

Student	Monday 2/3	Tuesday 2/4	Wednesday 2/5	Thursday 2/6	Friday 2/7
Tony	finish final copy - "Spaghetti"	D_1 Book review	D_1 cont.	R_1 Bk. review	PC Bk review
Aileen	Pr research sonnet	D_1 "The Garden"	D_1 cont. "The Garden"	TC / R_1 The Garden / adjectives	R_2 "The Garden"
Chang	PC poem "snow"	R_1 "Snow"	TC "Snow" work on the meter	R_2 "Snow"	E "Snow"
David	E "Sailing"	P "Sailing" - computer	S "Sailing" w/ slides	D_1 Poem or story ?	D_1 Short story: mystery
Patty	D_1 "Feathers in the Snow"	D_2 "Feathers...	PC — R_1 conf then revision	Abs.	R_2 Self revision "Feathers...
José	D_1 "Class Play w/ Melinda	D_1 - con't Play "Free Lunch"	GC w/ Chang and Aileen R_1 "Free Lunch"	R_2 "Free Lunch"	TC Play - flow
Karen	Abs.	Abs.	Pr - outline: "The Sleepover"	D_1 "The Sleepover"	PC "The Sleepover"
Melinda	D_1 Play w/ José →	w/ José →	w/ José →	w/ José →	w/ José
Jennifer	S "Cross Country Skiing"	D_1 response to newspaper article	D_2 editorial letter	GC w/ Patty and Karen Newspaper ed. letter R_1	TC on R_2 letter to Editor

KEY

Pr — prewriting
D — drafting D_1=draft 1
D_2=draft 2
TC — Teacher conference
GC — group conference
PC — peer conference
R — revising R_1=1st revision
R_2=2nd revision
E — editing
P — publishing
S — sharing

started. Teachers should be instrumental in helping students find writing topics. Much of writing comes from the events that occur in our daily lives, from what appears to be trivial (Graves, 1994). Writers need to listen and observe the details of living—they need to learn to read the world. Graves (1994) suggests that teachers model how to obtain writing topics that grow out of ordinary experiences. For example, as their students watch, teachers list all the details of their lives during the last 24 hours. Once this is accomplished, they jot down some quick questions about themselves and their world. One of the elements from the list is chosen and a ten minute piece is written from it. Graves admonishes that teachers write quickly, changing nothing. They should allow any thoughts and questions to enter their writing even though they may be unrelated to the topic. Finally, teachers should lower their standards and not try to sound too literary. This process may be repeated over time because writers need practice in seeing, observing, questioning, and in reading the world—students and teachers alike.

Opportunities may also arise throughout the day as the class discusses issues, stories, memories, and events. Teachers should be on the lookout for ideas that emerge from their students. Experiences that can become the focus for writing can also be created in the classroom, such as guest speakers, hatching chicks or caterpillars, or experiments. By brainstorming with the students and pointing out writing possibilities as they occur, teachers help students discover topics and generate ideas for future writing.

Throughout the school year students should be keeping an "I Can Write About . . ." topics listing. This sheet can be kept in the students' writing folders for future reference and additions. Initially students can record several areas in which they have expertise or an interest. Whenever an interesting or possible topic is unearthed—during another curricular area, a teachable moment, from reading a story, or the like—the teacher can point out the writing possibility and encourage the student to add it to the list.

Students can be issued writing invitations as well. Graves (1983; 1994) occasionally uses a "Nudge Paper," which is given to students to give them a slight push in the right direction. "Nudges are based on sound observation, on listening to children, and on a careful reading of their texts" (Graves, 1994, 93). This nudge sheet can be used to help children avoid overuse of a word, find other descriptive words, or add additional information. Other invitations include:

- collections of photographs that can serve as stimuli for writing
- newspaper or magazine articles to which the students can respond
- picture settings, an activity in which students locate magazine pictures depicting a setting that becomes the background for a story that the student writes (Harste, Short, and Burke, 1988)
- wordless books for which the students can write the text
- choose-your-own-adventure books for which students write new adventures
- cartoons with the words deleted

The teacher actually needs to write in front of the students, modeling each phase of the writing process and thinking aloud while writing. When first initiating a Writers' Workshop, the teacher must model topic selection and development. During this modeling session, the teacher explains that there are several possible topics, lists them, and perhaps even lists some words or thoughts related to each topic. Then the teacher selects one topic and explains why it was chosen. Depending on the nature of the topic and the form of the writing, the teacher may create a semantic map or web for the topic or conduct relevant research. After the prewriting activities and think-alouds, the teacher begins to write.

Through such modeling and minilessons, students are exposed to various prewriting techniques, such as brainstorming, webbing, researching, thinking, and drawing. But it is not enough just to generate ideas for writing. Students need to see and hear how to shape and develop a piece of writing. Discussions and modeling sessions need to be held on how to write about a certain topic, ideas for good opening lines, possibilities for organizing the piece, and effective endings. Students need help in moving from idea generation to text production.

The activities throughout the main portion of the workshop vary. While some children may

Figure 8.16 What to Do Checklist

What to Do During Writing Time

- Choose a topic from your "I Can Write About" List.
- Brainstorm new topics for writing.
- Begin a new draft.
- Add to or revise your writing piece.
- Research information for your writing.
- Make a semantic map or web about your topic.
- Look through books for writing ideas.
- Read your writing with a buddy.
- Look for and circle misspelled words.
- Check your piece for capitalization and punctuation.
- Take part in a group conference.
- Sign up for a conference with the teacher.
- Illustrate your article or book.
- Listen to your classmates' writing pieces.
- Read over your pieces and choose one to publish.

What to Do If You Are Stuck

- Look through books for ideas.
- Talk to a buddy.
- Ask others for suggestions.
- Sign up for a conference.
- Freewrite on any topic or idea.

What to Do If You Can't Spell a Word

- Spell it the way you think it looks.
- Write the word three different ways and choose the one that looks right.
- Spell the word the way it sounds.
- Use the dictionary.
- Look at books or charts where the word may be.
- Ask a buddy to help.
- Spell it the best way you can, circle it, and correct the spelling later.

(Adapted from Nathan, Temple, Juntunen, and Temple, 1989.)

be deciding on topics, gathering information on their chosen topic, or talking to others about ideas for writing, other students will be writing or conferencing with their peers or the teacher. Still others will be meeting in the Writers' Circle or publishing their pieces.

Throughout the writing time, the teacher moves among the students conducting brief conferences, sometimes referred to as roving conferences. At this time, teachers can note how much writing the students have done since the last writing session and check on those who are having difficulty. By conducting roving conferences, teachers can get an idea of how everyone in the class is doing. Teachers generally ask such open-ended questions as, "How's it going?" "What is your writing about?" "What will you do next?"

It is suggested that the teacher use a small chair or wheeled stool while conducting roving conferences. It is less intimidating for children and much more personal when teachers are at the same eye level while encouraging, guiding, prodding, and supporting young authors.

Roving conferences tend to be brief, since the intent is to keep the students' momentum

[ ] Did I circle misspelled words?
[ ] Did I correct the words that weren't spelled correctly?
[ ] Did I use complete thoughts when I wrote each sentence?
[ ] Are any of my sentences run-ons?
[ ] Did I use correct punctuation?
[ ] Did I begin my sentences with capital letters?
[ ] Did I use capital letters correctly in other parts of my writing?
[ ] Did I indent?
[ ] Did I have a buddy check my piece?

(Adapted from Nathan, Temple, Juntunen, and Temple, 1989.)

Figure 8.17 Proofreading Checklist

flowing. Students who need more time and support can sign up for more extended conference sessions with the teacher or may meet with their peers. However, some teachers, like Atwell (1987), prefer to use only roving conferences because more extended conferences are too time consuming and during longer conferences the ownership frequently reverts to the teacher.

There may be times when children do not wish to be disturbed while they are writing. This need for quiet writing time should be respected. Many teachers set aside an area where children can go to solitude. Atwell (1987) has an area referred to as "No Man's Land" where her students can go when they want to signal to both the teacher and their peers that they want some uninterrupted time for writing.

While the students are working, they may refer to checklists or charts that are the result of discussions held during mini- or focused lessons. Although there are many books pertaining to the teaching of writing that include sample checklists and charts, it is preferable that the students devise their own with the help of the teacher. It may be helpful for the teacher to refer to commercial checklists in order to guide students to discover what they want to include and what would be meaningful to them. Checklists such as those presented in Figures 8.16 and 8.17 foster student independence, self-reliance, and self-evaluation because they help students focus on what they can do and what they might do.

In addition to working alone, students are encouraged to support one another in all phases of the writing process. Frequently students will meet to plan writing, to provide ideas and suggestions during writing, to review each other's writing, and to help proofread. Discussions about what should occur during peer conferences should take place at the beginning of the

1. **LISTEN:** Listen to your buddy's draft.
2. **PRAISE:** Tell what you liked or thought was interesting about the piece.
   - I enjoyed the part where you . . .
   - You used some interesting words like . . .
   - Your story made me feel . . .
   - Your characters were realistic because . . .
   - The piece reminded me of . . .
   - Your story has lots of action that makes it interesting.
   - You use conversation quite well.
3. **ASK:** Ask any questions you may have about the draft or topic.
   - I am a little confused about . . .
   - Are there any parts you are having trouble with?
   - Could you add (delete, change) . . . ?
   - What are your plans for this piece?
   - Where did you get your ideas for this piece?
   - How come you know so much about . . . ?
   - What happened after . . . ?
   - What do you like best about your piece?
4. **SUGGEST:** Offer helpful suggestions for improving the draft.

(Nathan, Juntunen, and Temple, 1989; Tompkins, 1990.)

Figure 8.18 Guidelines for Peer Writing Conferences

1. Does my lead make you want to read my piece?
2. Do you think I need to add any more information to my topic?
3. Do you think I should delete some information?
4. Should I combine some sentences?
5. Do I need to change some words?
6. Is my writing piece focused? Did I stick to my topic?
7. Do I have a good ending?
8. What suggestions do you have for improving my writing?
9. Could you tell what the main idea of my piece was?
10. What are you most pleased with in my piece?
11. Did you learn anything from my writing?

(Nathan, Temple, Juntunen, Temple, 1989; Tompkins, 1990)

Figure 8.19 Questions Young Authors May Ask During Conference Time

Figure 8.20 Writing Conference Questions

THE PROCESS CONFERENCE

In the process conference, the focus is on the writing process. Teachers ask questions to help students get started, develop their writing pieces, sequence their writing, revise and proofread, and see their own progress. These questions are used throughout the entire writing process and may be used in both roving conferences and more formal conferences.

Questions:

How is your writing going?
Where are you now in your draft?
Where do you think you'll begin?
What do you think you'll do next?
Why did you choose this lead? this ending?
What's your favorite part of your piece?
What made you write about this subject?
Tell me about your writing.
If you put that idea in, what could you do with it?
When you aren't sure how to spell a word, what can you do?
Are you having any problems?
What was the easiest (hardest) thing for you in this piece?
What did you learn from your writing?
Would you do anything differently if you were going to write this again?
How does this piece of writing compare with others you have written?
What have you tried that was new in your writing?

THE CONTENT CONFERENCE

In the content conference, the focus is on the meaning of a piece of writing. The author reads the draft aloud to a peer or to the teacher. The listener then questions or responds to the content of the writing. The writer chooses whether to add or delete information.

Questions:

Who is your intended audience?
Tell me more about . . .
Do you have enough information?
Do you want to add (or delete) any information?
How does it sound to you?
Do you like your lead? your ending?
Where did you get your information for this piece?
Does your ending go with your beginning?
Do you have too much information?
What can you do to make this better?
Tell me what you think about it.
Can you think of a different way to say this?
Have you tried cutting it up and moving pieces around?
Do you know any more about the topic?
How many stories do you have here?
Can you tell me what you mean when you say . . .?
What is the most important thing you are trying to say?
Could you be more specific here?
What are you going to do now?

(*continued*)

Figure 8.20 Writing Conference Questions (cont.)

EDITING, PUBLISHING, OR SKILL CONFERENCES

In the editing, publishing, or skill conferences, the teacher works on punctuation, capitalization, spelling, grammar, format, and other writing conventions. Frequently, these types of conferences take place at the end of the writing process when the piece is ready for publication. It is important that the teacher not work on too many skills at once but rather on the one or two skills that are significant to the author's progress in learning to write.

Questions:

Have you spelled all the words correctly?
Have you used the proper punctuation?
Have you used paragraphs and indented those paragraphs?
How can I help you find and correct your errors?
Are you ready for a final copy?
Who will you share your piece with?
What publication form will your writing take?

school year. Together as a class, students should develop procedures, checklists, or charts on the proper conduct and dialogue that will ensure effective peer conferences. Figures 8.18 and 8.19 are examples of guidelines for peer writing conferences and questions both young authors and their reviewers may ask during peer conferences.

Students may conference in pairs for peer conferences, or they may meet in a small group, which they might want to call the Writers' Circle. Here the authors share their pieces and invite feedback from their classmates. By sharing in a group, students engage in purposeful dialogue and hear a wide range of perspectives. Group sharing allows students to gain varied perspectives on a problem, try out something different, share effective writing techniques, and run ideas past an audience (Atwell, 1987). The goal ultimately is to help children achieve independence. Through these oral interactions, children discover meaning and gain new skills.

Again, the teacher needs to hold demonstrations and discuss with students about how to conduct themselves during Writers' Circle. It is not helpful for classmates merely to state that they liked the piece without offering support for their statement. In addition to giving the young author praise, classmates should also ask questions about unclear portions of the writing piece and make suggestions for improvement. It is important for all participants to realize that the input received is welcome, but it is the author's sole decision to incorporate or reject the suggestions.

After teachers have finished with roving conferences, they may either continue their own personal writing or meet with students who have signed up for conferences. Such conferences tend to be lengthy and may focus on the content of the student's writing piece, writing mechanics, or publishing possibilities. The teacher should keep logs or records of these meetings, noting the purpose of the conference and suggestions made to the young author. Figure 8.20 describes the types of conferences and possible questions that may be asked during the conferences.

Conferences are the keys to better writing. Conference time is the time for actual teaching, listening to young authors, and responding to students' ideas and needs. It is the time for sharing, reacting, and reflecting (Turbill, 1983). Conference sessions need not be lengthy; in fact, if they are longer than 10 minutes per student, the time may not be being used as effectively as possible. It is important that the teacher not dominate the conference but rather let the student be the main talker. The teacher should be positive, demonstrate an interest in what the young author is trying to express, and become aware of the student's strengths, interests, and needs. The teacher needs to develop questioning techniques that foster students' solutions to their own problems.

Teachers confer with students to help them consider what is working, what may need more

Figure 8.21 Samples of Process Writing

Lauren Huggins December 18, 1991
Writing 6-G

"Amy, get ready to go to grandma's and grandpa's, we can't be late for dinner" said my mother. So I ran down stairs and got my coat on. I had to wait for my mother and father and sister and brothers to get their coats on. After that we were off and we hopped in our car.

When we arrived, we all got out and went inside. The first thing ~~we~~ ~~et~~ my grandma did was pinch our cheeks and gave us a big wet kiss. I hate it when my grandma does that. We had to wait about 30 minutes to eat dinner. Then my grandma said come and get it. We had chicken, potatos, corn, and rice plus more. As we were eating all of the sudden my grandpa's dentures fell out! "Yuck" everyone was saying. How gross I thought. Good thing none of my friends were over. So my grandpa just put them back in and continued to eat. After dinner I went and ~~to~~ ~~get~~ got a magazine and started to read. Then my grandma sat down behind me and read over my shoulder at the same thing,

Figure 8.21 Samples of Process Writing (cont.)

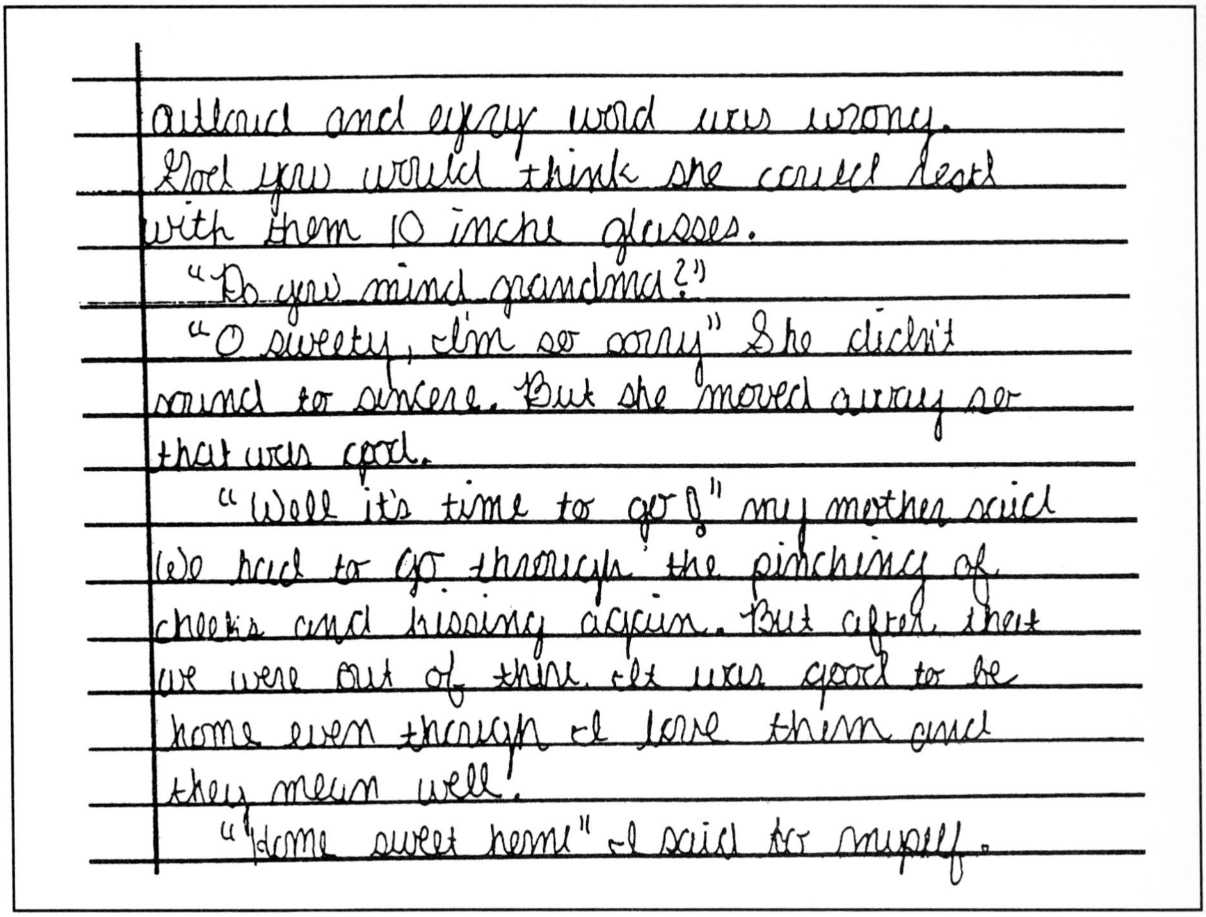

outloud and every word was wrong.
God you would think she could read
with them 10 inche glasses.
"Do you mind grandma?"
"O sweety, I'm so sorry" She didn't
sound to sincere. But she moved away so
that was good.
"Well it's time to go!" my mother said
We had to go through the pinching of
cheeks and kissing again. But after that
we were out of there. It was good to be
home even though I love them and
they mean well.
"Home sweet home" I said to myself.

attention, and what direction they may pursue next (Atwell, 1987). During conferences, teachers allow time for deliberation and reflection. They listen attentively and give writers the opportunity to talk about and try out their options for continued work on their pieces. If students' attempts are unsuccessful, teachers may provide several solutions. Teachers should not withhold information that will help writers solve problems (Murray, 1983). Writers want to know how to improve, how to move forward. "A writer wants response that is courteous and gentle, that gives help without threatening the writer's dignity" (Atwell, 1987, 66).

After students have met with peers, the teacher, or both and have revised and proofread their pieces to their satisfaction, they are ready to publish or share their writing. As Turbill (1982) notes, the essence of publishing is not just producing a book or published piece, but rather getting the pieces of writing to readers. Authors need to take their intended audience into consideration and then choose a form of publication that will best meet the needs of and attract the desired audience. Publishing possibilities are many, as listed in Chapter 2.

Sharing. In addition to publishing their works, young authors enjoy sharing them. The last portion of the writing/conference time is reserved for class sharing. Authors may bring their published pieces to the Author's Chair (Graves and Hansen, 1982) or to a group share circle (Atwell, 1987) and share their writing. At this time the feedback from the audience is appreciation and enjoyment. Young authors may also share their writing over the loudspeaker, with other classes, or in school publications. Samples of student process writing appear in Figure 8.21.

Figure 8.21 Samples of Process Writing (cont.)

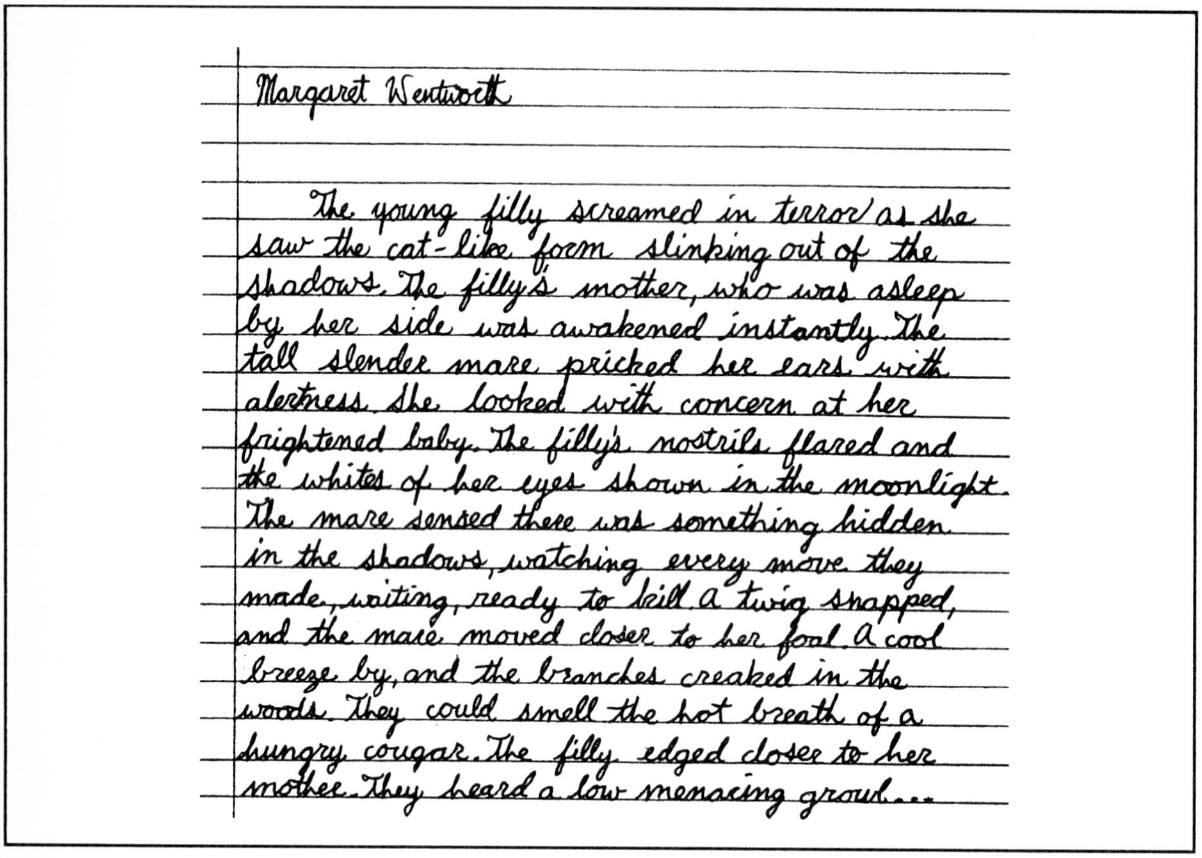

Margaret Wentworth

The young filly screamed in terror as she saw the cat-like form slinking out of the shadows. The filly's mother, who was asleep by her side was awakened instantly. The tall slender mare pricked her ears with alertness. She looked with concern at her frightened baby. The filly's nostrils flared and the whites of her eyes shown in the moonlight. The mare sensed there was something hidden in the shadows, watching every move they made, waiting, ready to kill. A twig snapped, and the mare moved closer to her foal. A cool breeze by, and the branches creaked in the woods. They could smell the hot breath of a hungry cougar. The filly edged closer to her mother. They heard a low menacing growl...

Writing Folders

A system is needed to organize the amount of writing produced throughout the year. Writing folders help authors manage and organize their writing. At the beginning of the year, students are given a file folder, three-ring binder, or cardboard box in which to collect their writing. Some teachers prefer to use file folders with pockets and center clips to aid in separating and managing the writing. Students should place in the folders only writing they consider publishable, not such informal writing as messages or letters. Pieces will be in various stages of the writing process. If teachers use folders that have pockets, one pocket may be used to hold topics and brainstorming sheets and the other, the student's drafts (Nathan et al., 1989). The center of the folder holds all the writing the student produces.

Writing folders can also include the following items:

- students' personal topic sheets ("I Can Write About" sheets)
- sheets proclaiming what students have learned from their writing
- listing of all writing undertaken by the students, with some system to indicate published pieces, for example, an asterisk or a column for noting whether the piece was published
- checklists ("Things to Do During Writing Time," "Things to Do During Conference Time," "Proofreading Checklist")
- guideline sheets ("Guidelines for Peer Conferences," "Questions to Ask in Conferences")
- proofreading symbols

The folders are stored in a cardboard box or a plastic crate in a convenient place, such as in the Writing Center, on an accessible shelf, or on a library cart. Students are free to get their writing folders any time they have an opportunity to write. Folders are returned to the storage area when writing is finished for the day.

Although most teachers use manila folders for writing folders, commercially produced folders are available. These are often highly decorated and come with preprinted information on such topics as commonly misspelled words, stages in the writing process, and editing and proofreading marks. They may have multiple pockets for prewriting activities, drafts, and completed pieces.

Journal Writing

"Dear Diary"—how many of you kept diaries at one time in your life? How many of you have read diaries, journals, or excerpts from logs written by other people? In the school setting, journals are documents of academic and personal growth, records of developing insights, and tools used to gain those insights (Fulwiler, 1980). Using journals in the classroom presents an opportunity to incorporate writing on a regular, if not daily, basis (Tompkins, 1990). Journals are regarded quite favorably in educational settings because they serve a variety of purposes—self-expression, thinking through issues, solving problems in content area subjects.

Journals have been around since the invention of paper and were even found among the ruins of Pompeii and in Egyptian tombs. Many famous people have kept diaries or journals, including Leonardo da Vinci, Fyodor Dostoyevski, Louisa May Alcott, and Anne Frank (Steiner and Phillips, 1991). People have used journals to express their thoughts, share their experiences, and try out ideas. Now teachers are incorporating journal writing into their instructional programs as they recognize the benefits of journal writing. Journals serve the following purposes:

- provide a forum for students to reflect, learn, and gain an understanding of the curriculum
- help students make personal connections to the subject matter being studied
- provide a place for students to document observations, responses, and data
- provide writing practice
- promote fluency in writing and reading
- provide a means to explore personal responses
- offer a way to guide small-group discussions and student-teacher conferences
- encourage risk taking as students write freely, exploring and experimenting with ideas and writing conventions
- validate students' personal experiences and feelings
- promote thinking
- help students prepare for class discussions, study for tests, and understand reading assignments
- provide a vehicle for evaluation (both self-evaluation and a means for teachers to note growth and progress)
- assist students in becoming independent learners
- permit students to undertake more active roles in the learning process and assume more responsibility for their own learning

(Fulwiler, 1987; Allen, 1989; Parsons, 1990; Routman, 1991)

A journal can provide an opportunity for students to use writing to explore their learning, feelings, experiences, and written language. "A journal can appreciate and enjoy the present, but it can also recall the past, explore the future, enrich relationships, help solve problems. It can provide a catharsis for strong emotion, or be a place for reflection and introspection. It can be used to build a rich fantasy life" (Steiner and Phillips, 1991, xi).

Without much difficulty, journals can become an integral part of the curriculum. The possibilities for incorporating journal writing into the school day and throughout the curriculum are many. Journals can take many forms: personal journals or diaries, dialogue journals, written conversations, reading response logs, learning logs, simulated journals, writing notebooks, and class journals. Each of these journal possibilities is discussed separately.

1. **Personal journals.** The purpose of personal journals is for students to record or recount events in their own lives and to write about self-chosen topics. The writing is infor-

mal and private. To help students who may have difficulty deciding what to write, a list of possible topics for journal writing can be brainstormed and placed on a chart or sheet to be inserted in a student's writing folder. A list of possible topics is provided in Figure 8.22, and samples of students' personal journals are included in Figure 8.23.

2. **Dialogue journals.** Dialogue journals are defined as written conversations between two individuals. Here students and teachers (or students and other students) converse with one another through writing on a meaningful, continued basis. The student writes to the teacher about something of interest or something that concerns him or her at that time, and the teacher responds and frequently asks questions. Dialogue journals present opportunities for true interactions and communication between teacher and students. They are conversational in tone and, like a personal journal, may be private. Through dialogue journals both teachers and students are empowered because the interactions that occur enhance the dynamic exchange of information. Mutual understanding can develop and education can be personalized (Bode, 1989).

To help in the management of response to students' entries, teachers often respond on a rotating basis. Staton (1987) suggests that when responding to journal entries, teachers acknowledge what was written and encourage further writing, provide additional information on the topic, write less than the student, and avoid asking too many questions. It is important to remember that teachers' responses need not be lengthy and should not be a question-and-answer session. Rather, the interchange is built on trust and respect. Teacher comments are intended to affirm the author and to encourage further writing. Teachers' responses should say to the students that their experiences are valued and that the teacher appreciates that the student is sharing them (Schubert, 1987). These written conversations are a bridge between talking and writing and provide opportunities for strong bonds to develop between teachers and students.

Dialogue journals need not be used only between teachers and students but can also be undertaken between students. These buddy journals are similar to diaries that students keep together in which they converse in writing with one another (Bromley, 1989). Students generate their own topics when writing in buddy journals. Buddies for journal writing may be selected randomly for a designated period of time—for example, two weeks, one month, one semester—or students may choose writing partners.

Some advantages of buddy journals are that students are helped to see the connections between reading and writing, are given opportunities to practice reading and writing in meaningful ways, and are able to capitalize on their natural inclinations to converse. In addition, buddy journals provide real audiences and authentic reasons for writing, build interest and

Figure 8.22 Topics for Journals

- my family
- things I like to do
- pets
- friends
- holiday happenings
- personal events
- movie or sports stars
- make-believe events
- superheroes
- travel (real or imaginary)
- early memories
- Today I did . . .
- I feel . . .
- a talk with . . .
- I used to think (believe) . . .
- what I like best (least) about . . .
- the best (worst) thing that happened to me
- looking back
- looking ahead
- the way I would change my (life, school, the country) . . .
- People place too much importance in . . .
- I felt really proud when . . .
- I'm different from everyone else because. . .
- Let me tell you about (how to) . . .
- If I could trade places with . . . , I . . .

Figure 8.23A Sample of Students' Personal Journals

WELL I FINALLY GOT TO MEET PAPA POLARIS. I WISH I DIDN'T. HE'S OLD AND HE'S LIVED ALL HIS LIFE FOR SNOWMOBILING. BUT NOW I DON'T KNOW, I JUST FEEL SO SAD. HE'S SO DEPRESSED AND HE CAN BARELY WALK. HE SAID, "SO HOW CAN I RIDE IF I CAN BARELY WALK." HE'S BEEN SNOWMOBILING FOR MORE THAN 20 YEARS (PAUL SAYS EVEN MORE). NOW I FEEL EMPTINESS BECAUSE I CAN'T HELP HIM. YESTERDAY HE STOPPED IN THE SHOP. PAUL PULLED ME OVER TO THE SIDE AND SAID, "HE'S REALLY SAD, TRY TO CHEER HIM UP, TALK ABOUT SNOWMOBILES."

confidence in writing, offer students opportunities to share concerns and insights, and promote student cooperation and collaboration (Bromley, 1989). Dialogue journals, whether used between teacher and student or student and student, involve purposeful, personalized communication that can enhance literacy. (See Figure 8.24.)

3. **Written conversations.** Written conversations are similar to dialogue journals in that two or more individuals are involved in writing or responding to one another. Written conversations may take on a more instructional focus because they are frequently used in conversing about a curricular area. For ex-

Figure 8.23B Sample of Students' Personal Journals (cont.)

A Special Toy

One of my favorite toys is my Cabbage Patch Kid. Her name is Emilina Gaylene. My Grandmother Me Ma gave her to me. I got her on my Mothers birthday. Me Ma tricked me by saying it was a present for my Mother. Then she asked if I would like to help open it. When I opened it, I saw it was really for me! Emilina was my Christmas gift. I got her early because our family was going on a year long trip.

Figure 8.24 Sample of Students' Dialogue Journals

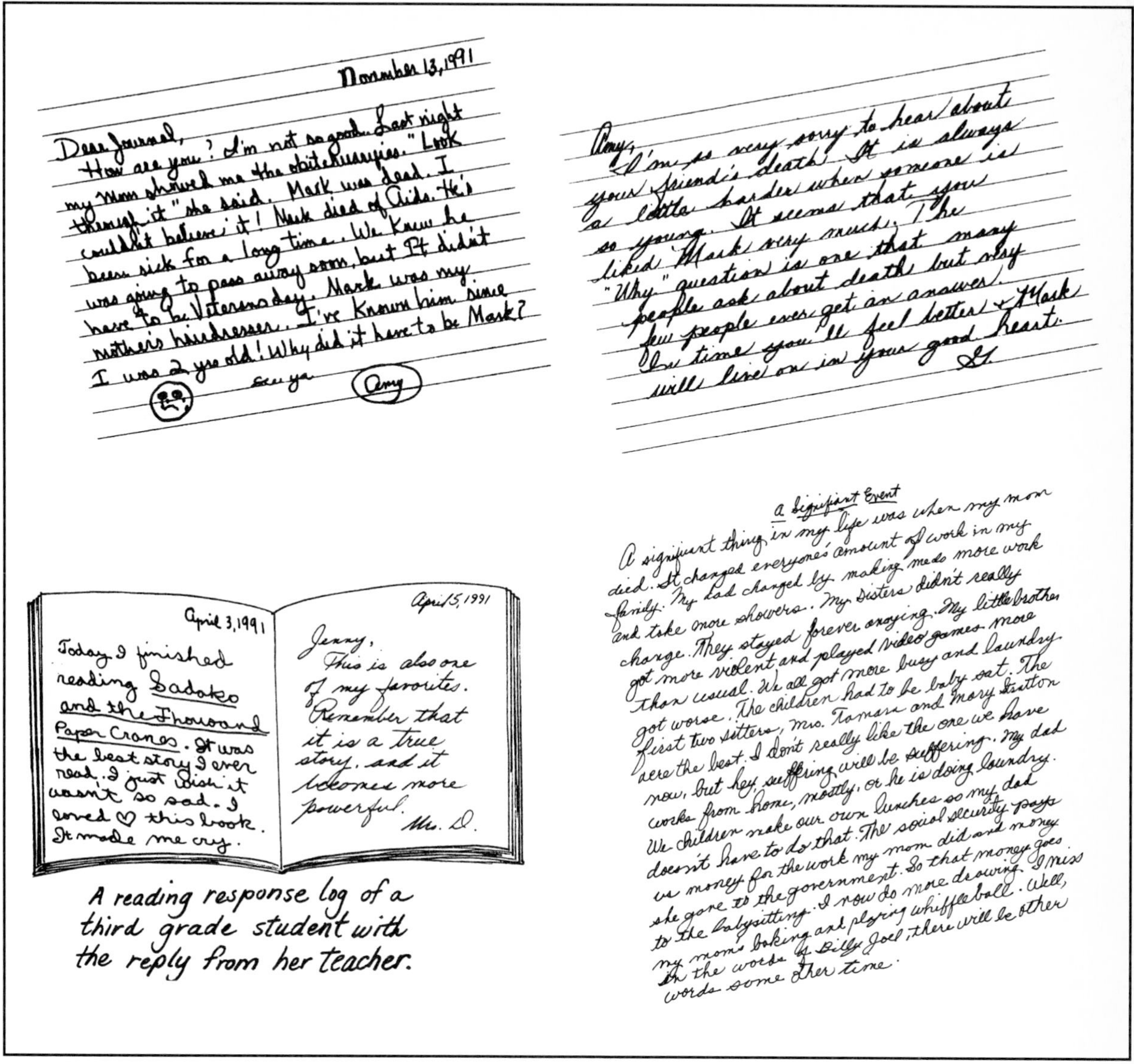

November 13, 1991

Dear Journal,
How are you? I'm not so good. Last night
my Mom showed me the obitchuaryies. "Look
through it" she said. Mark was dead. I
couldn't believe it! Mark died of Aids. He's
been sick for a long time. We knew he
was going to pass away soon, but it didn't
have to be Veterans day. Mark was my
mother's hairdresser. I've known him since
I was 2 yrs old! Why did it have to be Mark?
See ya
Amy

Amy,
I'm so very sorry to hear about
your friend's death. It is always
a little harder when someone is
so young. It seems that you
liked Mark very much. The
"Why" question is one that many
people ask about death but very
few people ever get an answer.
In time you'll feel better & Mark
will live on in your good heart.
G.

April 3, 1991
Today I finished
reading Sadako
and the Thousand
Paper Cranes. It was
the best story I ever
read. I just wish it
wasn't so sad. I
loved ♡ this book.
It made me cry.

April 5, 1991
Jenny,
This is also one
of my favorites.
Remember that
it is a true
story, and it
becomes more
powerful.
Ms. D.

A reading response log of a third grade student with the reply from her teacher.

A Signifiant Event
A signifiant thing in my life was when my mom
died. It changed everyone's amount of work in my
family. My dad changed by making me do more work
and take more showers. My sisters didn't really
change. They stayed forever anoying. My little brother
got more violent and played video games more
than usual. We all got more busy and laundry
got worse. The children had to be baby sat. The
first two sitters, Mrs. Tamara and Mary Stratton
were the best. I don't really like the one we have
now, but hey, suffring will be suffering. My dad
works from home, mostly, or he is doing laundry.
We children make our own lunches so my dad
doesn't have to do that. The social security pays
us money for the work my mom did and money
she gave to the government. So that money goes
to the babysitting. I now do more drawing. I miss
my mom's baking and playing whiffleball. Well,
in the words of Billy Joel, there will be other
words some other time.

ample, students may discuss the content they are learning about in a thematic study, a world crisis in current events, or a topic in science or social studies. They may go beyond writing about the content and may reflect on their learning, note difficulties, or make connections to their own lives.

4. **Reading response logs.** Reading response logs are an integral part of the literature workshop, as discussed in this chapter. Students react to books they are reading or respond to open-ended questions. Frequently response logs are used as the basis for discussion in literature groups. Sample student response log entries are provided in Figure 8.25.

5. **Learning logs.** Learning logs are places where students can record and react to what they are learning in subject areas. Writing is used to reflect on the learning, to note gaps in students' knowledge, and to explore relationships between what is being learned and students' prior experiences and knowledge. Learn-

Figure 8.25 Student Response Log Entries

Mark L.

Q. In "a night without stars," do you think Donald had good reasons to act in a hostile way to people? Why or why not? How would you handle the situation if you were in Donald's place?

A. Donald had some good reasons to act in a hostile way. Alot of kids were calling him monster man and stuff. But he overdid it. Because when people were nice to him he was still mean and cruel. If I was in Don's place I would have ignored the kids that were making fun of him and be nice to other people.

My Side Of The Moutain
Movie vs Book

vs

Movie	Book
1. tooka bus to the mountains	1. hitchhiked on a truck + walked the rest of the way.
2 he brought his raccon from home	2. found raccon on mountain
3 he sleeps in a tree because of a bear	3 sleeps in his home-made tent, no bear ever comes
4 started fire without help or hesitation	4 went to man who taught him how to keep and make fire.
5 a hellecopter comes because he saw some smoke	5 hellecopter doesn't come

ing logs can be used in all subject areas. Students can explain how to do a math problem or science experiment, record observations, or react to a word or slogan before beginning a social studies topic. The purpose is to help students clarify their own thinking about what they are learning.

6. **Simulated journals.** In a simulated journal, students assume the role of another person, writing from that person's point of view. For instance, they may pretend they are Christopher Columbus on his first voyage to the Americas or write log entries as if they were astronauts. Written conversations between historical figures can also be included in simulated journals. Simulated journal entries need not be reserved for historical figures. Characters in books can "write" as well, for example, James in *James and the Giant Peach* can detail the events as he crossed the ocean on his memorable voyage, or Maggie in *Muggie Maggie* can write about her feelings as she is forced to learn cursive writing in school.

7. **Writing notebooks.** These are likened to authors' notebooks in which students can keep lists of ideas for future writing, interesting words or quotes, or even drafts of stories, poems, and articles. Recently one student took a notebook to a beach that had been wracked by a winter storm. His purpose was to record any inspiration he might capture on his walk that could be developed at a later time.

8. **Class journals.** Class journals present opportunities for the entire class to write and reflect on a topic or issue. These journals are kept in a central place and circulated when students are ready to record their own entries. Students can react to a recent class event, respond to a piece of literature or poetry, contribute to project planning, or record observations and reactions about field trips, guests, or experiments. The idea is for the students and teacher to write on a common topic that is of interest or concern to all. Class journals can become memory books for the class during a school year.

To introduce any of these forms of journal writing, teachers need to explain the purpose of the activity and to model a sample entry. Teachers can record actual classroom happenings; present a written sketch of a character or person of interest; generate lists of words, ideas, or plans; examine personal experiences and thoughts; and experiment with ideas (Steiner and Phillips, 1991). Teachers can also read interesting excerpts from published diaries and journals, read entries from characters who use journal writing in chapter books, and share actual student entries (with permission, of course). It is essential that teachers prepare students by taking the time to talk about possible topics, demonstrate the process of journal writing, and show the value of journal writing activities (Routman, 1991).

Writing Across the Curriculum

"I didn't have time for writing today," is a statement heard frequently as teachers have to assume more and more responsibility for areas other than teaching or when an interruption alters the day's schedule. However, writing can be extended beyond Writers' Workshop into other areas of the curriculum.

Writing is a powerful learning tool. Students can use writing both to learn subject matter and to demonstrate or apply what they have learned. There are many benefits of using writing across the curriculum (Myers, 1984; Hembrow, 1986; Tompkins, 1990):

- Writing facilitates learning of information in the content areas and about oneself as a learner.
- Students develop language skills, writing ability, and writing fluency.
- Critical thinking is enhanced.

By using writing in content area lessons, students develop and further their knowledge base while practicing language skills. As students write, they organize, classify, and evaluate what they are learning and what they have learned. While writing expressively, students are thinking on paper (Collins, 1985) and are becoming actively involved with the content, thereby establishing ownership (Allen, 1989). While students are writing, they make discoveries and connections with prior experiences and across disciplines. Moreover, responding to content is not entirely intellectual, since it operates "in conjunction with the affective mode, relating learning to beliefs, attitudes, and interests" (Allen, 1989, 2). Writing fits into daily routines and into any aspect of the curriculum. Let's examine the possibilities. First, teachers have to realize that their students can assume some responsibility for organizing and managing the class. They can take attendance, take lunch counts, and record book orders—all of which involve functional writing. Letter writing to obtain information for class projects and investigations, to invite or thank speakers, and to express opinions can be undertaken by the students. Students can assume responsibility when signs or labels are needed to identify areas of the room, to explain exhibits from a curricular study, to illustrate a concept being developed on a bulletin board, or to show classmates how to use or do a particular activity. Any classroom routine, organizational activity, or management issue should be considered as writing possibilities for the students.

Now let's go beyond the classroom routines and look at the curriculum. Each and every curricular area can involve writing at some point in the lesson. (See Figure 8.26 for suggested curriculum for grades 3–6.) Prior to beginning an area of study or a lesson, students can write what they know about the topic, what they expect to learn, or make predictions. Their knowledge and expectations can be shared with a classmate through a written conversation about the topic. During a lesson, students can record what they are learning, add information to a semantic map about the topic, and engage in another written dialogue with a peer. After the lesson, further research may be involved that necessitates notetaking and writing what is learned. Writing in a learning log allows the student to reflect on the lesson's content and to state what she or he has learned or may still find confusing. A sampling of writing activities across some curriculum areas is provided in Figure 8.27, and examples of how reading and writing can be incorporated into content area teaching appear in "From the Classroom" of Mary Ellen Bafumo.

One goal of school is to help students become independent, reflective learners. Writing can help students achieve this goal and can help teachers see where students are on their quest for independence. Having students reflect in writing on what is to be learned and determine a strategy (or strategies) for achieving the learning can help them gain knowledge. Students can think aloud through any problem-solving activity in any curricular area, and if this introspection is done in writing, it can be used to monitor students' growth over time and help students see the problem being confronted. Writing remains as a permanent reminder and a permanent record for subsequent analysis and discussion.

Writing across the curriculum reinforces the functional and purposeful role that writing has both in school and in the real world. If we believe, as we state earlier in this book, that students learn to read by reading and learn to write by writing, then using any opportunity to involve writing benefits students, both in the short term in their learning of current subject areas and in the long run, throughout life. Samples of student writing across the curriculum are provided in Figure 8.28.

USING THE BASAL PRODUCTIVELY

Many teachers and administrators are still reluctant to replace their basal programs. Many teachers need the support of a somewhat structured program, and many districts have invested considerable money in purchasing basal programs. Although we are promoting the use of literature as the means of delivering reading instruction, we are aware of the constraints many educators face and the possibilities of basal programs in implementing a balanced reading program.

Basals have changed considerably over the past years. Much of the change is the result of the whole language movement. Publishers fear a loss of business and recognize that whole language practices and activities are educationally sound. Thus, they have altered their programs to include more unadapted literature. Teachers' manuals are less prescriptive, allowing for some teacher choice and decision making. Fewer skills are offered, and those that are included generally have some relevance to the reading selection. Because of such changes, combined with flexible use by teachers, the basal may be considered as a vehicle for delivering the

Figure 8.26A Curriculum for Grades 3–6

Curriculum for Grade 3

Reading, Writing Speaking, Listening/ Language Arts	increasing time for silent reading reporting experiences orally with accuracy writing of various genres reading more nonfiction developing dictionary skills using reference resources in thematic projects refining editing and proofreading skills using paragraphs in writing beginning cursive writing
Math	problem-solving analysis (one- and two-step problems) creating and reading graphs and charts 55 addition and inverse subtraction facts basic multiplication and division facts through the sixes Roman numerals through XII writing and reading numbers up to five places understanding simple fractions and equivalents counting by twos, threes, and fours to 100 basic metric measurement use of computers
Science	the changing surface of the earth earth's atmosphere and motions stars and earth's moon sources of energy life cycles of animals/birds/trees/flowers conservation of natural resources/recycling magnets and electricity how sound is produced climate and weather
Social Studies	career choices local community development Native Americans and pioneers shelters/homes of animals and people transportation and how it has changed communication technology reading maps and globes holiday celebrations and customs
Health	sources of food and clothing simple first aid disease control and prevention community safety need for exercise knowing the correct names for body parts

Figure 8.26B Curriculum for Grades 3–6 (cont.)

Curriculum for Grade 4

Reading, Writing Speaking, Listening/ Language Arts	developing a spelling consciousness silent and oral reading listening skills/note taking creative and informative writing research writing/locating information/encyclopedia skills developing strategies for content area reading/writing readers/writers workshop writing good lead sentences/peer conferencing readers' response journals
Math	multiplication and division facts through nines long division with one-digit divisor concept of mixed numbers numeration systems/metric measurement finding simple averages/use of a calculator/computer problem solving using multi-steps simple geometry Roman numerals through L understanding subsets
Science	environment of local area ecosystem: plants/animals/insects; balance of nature recycling/air and water pollution solar system/universe/living in space minerals and rocks history of planet Earth and influences of weather famous scientists
Social Studies	local history study of own state and its resources and history regions of the world: climate, geography, resources, government how local community operates why we need laws using the globe map studies
Health	body functions digestive, circulatory, respiratory systems basic food groups care of the body/dangers of drugs, alcohol, tobacco mental and personal hygiene

Figure 8.26C Curriculum for Grades 3–6 (cont.)

Curriculum for Grade 5

Reading, Writing Speaking, Listening/ Language Arts	oral and silent reading in larger blocks of time/content area reading presenting original play/Readers' Theatre combining sentences homonyms, synonyms, antonyms strategies for revising own writing: letters/stories/reports/plays/poems dictionary use for word meaning, analysis, and spelling use of study material: index, table of contents/legends/keys/graphs webbing/clustering identifying types of literature using a thesaurus
Math	multi-step problem solving—verbal and written decimals/fractions/percents distributive and associative properties numeration system/Roman numerals to C long division with multiple-digit divisor metric measurement reading and creating graphs, tables, and scale drawings use of calculator and computer algorithm/geometric concepts extended
Science	space exploration/sun/Milky Way/stars adaptation of plants and animals/food chain properties of water and air trees/conservation/recycling biotic communities bacteria, molds latitude and longitude/magnetic fields electrical/chemical/force systems
Social Studies	exploration and discovery of America colonial and pioneer life in America westward movement natural resources/industrial and cultural growth in United States geography and presidents of the United States comparison of United States and Canada: culture, resources, gov't. map skills environmental issues
Health	basic first aid local health resources/hospitals water and air pollution sewage disposal bicycle safety care of eyes and teeth/nutrition and diet sexual education

Figure 8.26D Curriculum for Grades 3–6 (cont.)

Curriculum for Grade 6

Reading, Writing Speaking, Listening/ Language Arts	semantic feature analysis writing: letters, factual material, verse, prose, poetry webbing/clustering extending dictionary skills/building vocabulary identifying types of literature semantics and propaganda varying reading rates/reading for different purposes/skimming bibliography building organization of a book
Math	using decimals and relationships between decimals and fractions Roman numerals to M/other ancient numeration systems dividing and multiplying fractions and mixed numbers operations of powers/exponents/factoring/percent area, perimeter, volume reading line, bar, and picture graphs problem solving, oral and written, multiple steps calculator and computer
Science	classification of living organisms microbes/algae/fungi energy: atomic and nuclear simple machines/motors/engines/electricity astronomy/space and space travel elements of sound, light, and heat discoveries and inventions/famous scientists recycling/conservation/earth's future fundamental geology
Social Studies	cultures and countries of Western Hemisphere/Canada and Mexico peoples of Central America/West Indies/South America/Australia history and organization of the United Nations world trade and economy map-reading skills transportation and communication daily current world and local events/politics
Health	cure and prevention of disease health research sex education and sexual diseases tobacco, alcohol, and narcotics awareness nutrition and the heart basic first aid personal hygiene and appearance

guided reading portion of the balanced reading program.

When reviewing the basal program for particular grade levels, teachers should read each selection carefully along with the information in the teachers' manuals. Then teachers should decide which selections and activities are meaningful for their class. Teachers should be decision-makers, not follow the basal program rigidly. We advocate skipping stories or activities associated with particular selections or using stories out of order when they fit into the theme being studied or because they are interesting.

WRITING IN MATHEMATICS

- learning logs (e.g., what students know about fractions, what they learned about fractions, what they are still confused about, how fractions are used in real life)
- writing story problems
- thinking through writing (e.g., writing steps or explanations of how to solve a particular problem)
- writing up an analysis of data from a graph
- "All About _______" books (e.g., informational books about such math concepts as *calculators* or *currency*
- songs, raps, or poems about math concepts

WRITING IN SOCIAL STUDIES

- learning logs (e.g., what they know about the Bill of Rights, what they learned about the Bill of Rights, further information or clarification needed, how the Bill of Rights affects their daily lives)
- simulated journals
- writing biographies
- constructing time lines or flow charts
- writing summaries of information learned
- notetaking or outlining
- written scripts for dramatic interpretation of a historical event
- simulated newspapers (e.g., a newspaper from a particular period in history or a culture being studied)
- "If You Were There" books
- "A Day in the Life of _______" books (a famous person, a typical day in a country, on the job for various occupations)

WRITING IN SCIENCE

- learning logs (e.g., what students know about electricity, what they learned about electricity, what still confuses them, how electricity is used in their lives, how it can be conserved)
- observations
- writing up experiments (e.g., expectations, predictions, observations, results)
- reports on a science topic
- writing up results of guided investigations
- science newsletter
- "All About _______" books (trees, pollution, eagles)

Figure 8.27 Writing Across the Curriculum

Figure 8.28A Samples of Student Writing Across the Curriculum

asthma
By: Dan + Chris

Astma consists of weezing, coughing and being hard to breath. Pollen can cause asthma attacks. You can get asthma from genes but just because some one in your family has asthma, it does not mean you do. I is hard to find out if someone has asthma and they need to take lots of tests. Reversible obstructive ~~are~~ airway disease ROAD! ~~It~~ is another name for asthma. You can get asthma from being alerject ~~from~~ to animal hair.

Basal programs can be used as anthologies, since publishers have made concerted efforts to include worthwhile selections in all types of genre. Workbooks do not have to be ordered or used, and the money saved can be allocated for purchasing classroom libraries supplementing basal programs or trade books. Many techniques described in the discussion of Readers' Workshop can be used with basal readers: response logs, dialogues, and sharing activities.

If teachers feel they need the support of a teachers' manual, again the teacher should be selective. This goes for prereading activities, vocabulary instruction, comprehension questions,

Figure 8.28B Samples of Student Writing Across the Curriculum (cont.)

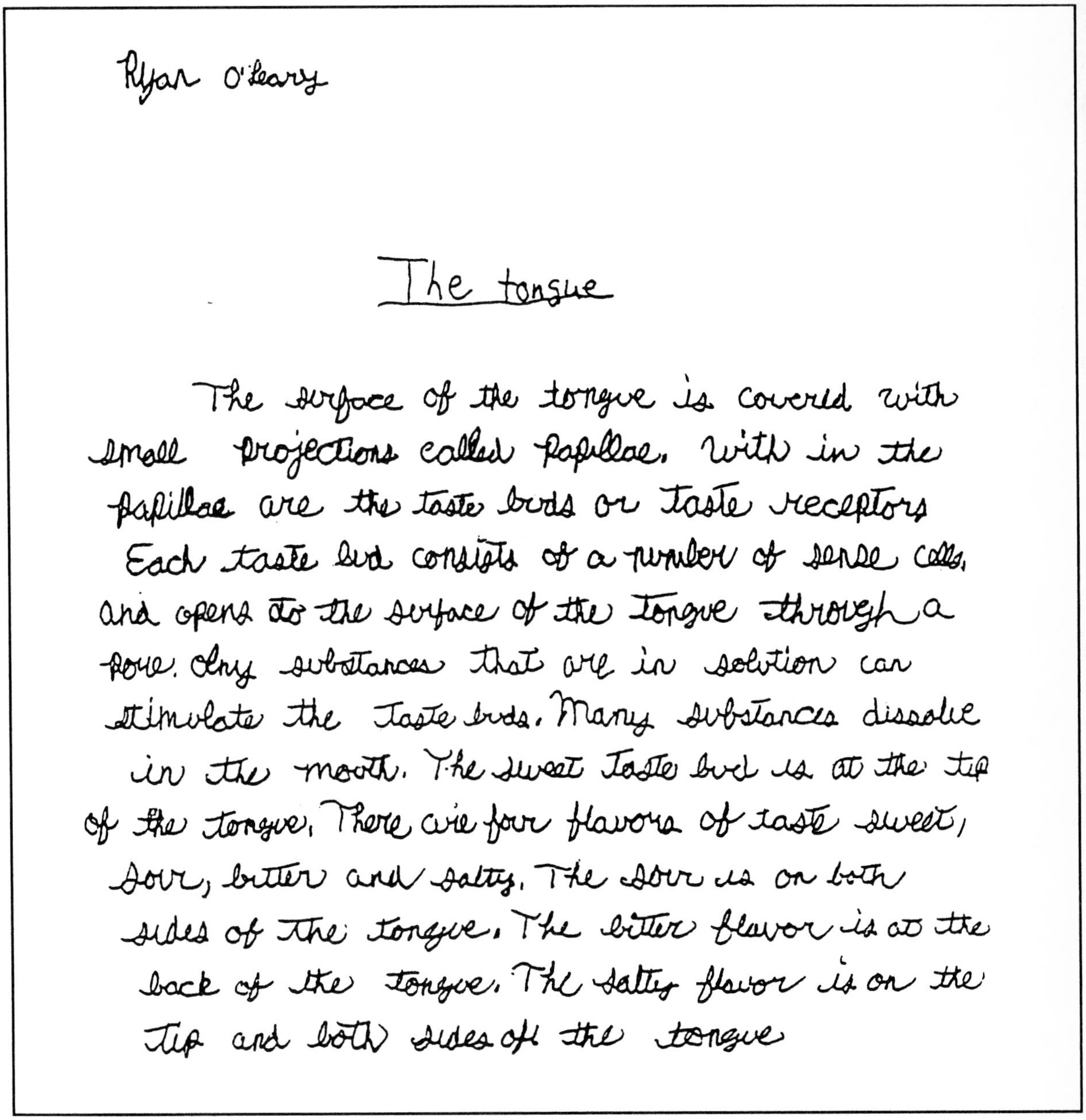

Ryan O'Leary

The tongue

The surface of the tongue is covered with small projections called papillae. With in the papillae are the taste buds or Taste receptors Each taste bud consists of a number of sense cells, and opens to the surface of the Tongue through a pore. Only substances that are in solution can stimulate the Taste buds. Many substances dissolve in the mouth. The sweet Taste bud is at the tip of the tongue. There are four flavors of taste sweet, sour, bitter and salty. The sour is on both sides of The tongue. The bitter flavor is at the back of the tongue. The salty flavor is on the Tip and both sides of the tongue

postreading activities, and skill development. Teachers can emphasize practices that promote student independence and a love of literature instead of the skill-and-drill practices formerly associated with basal programs. This may mean that little formal vocabulary instruction is undertaken prior to reading, and subsequently addressing vocabulary and strategies to unlock unknown words. Teachers may address only a few selected skills that have relevance to real-life learning and make sure that some of the suggested follow-up activities are incorporated into the teaching sessions. These follow-up sessions usually involve activities that are meaningful for

FROM THE CLASSROOM OF . . .

Mary Ellen Bafumo New Paltz, New York

CREATING A CULTURE

To apply what was learned in social studies and geography, students can create their own culture. Students may pick an area in which to design their culture, or the coordinates of the location may be provided by the teacher, which allows practice in map reading as well.

When designing this culture, teachers and students should agree on the particular aspects that should be included. For instance, students could locate a specific area in the world, noting the physical features, waterways, weather, and the like. These would naturally influence the types of clothing, activities, recreational facilities, etc. that the culture study would include. Some suggested activities are:

- making a map of the area selected or provided, making sure to note several physical features, waterways, cities
- describing the weather (could have seasonal variations or could remain the same for the entire year)
- designing clothing and costumes (for special events, patriotic occurrences, and for everyday use)
- writing a song and designing a flag for the culture
- writing a history for the culture, or presenting significant events on a timeline
- creating folk heroes with biographical information
- determining a constitution for the community
- planning and preparing ethnic foods for the culture
- creating games and sports activities that are popular
- noting businesses and manufactured products that may be indicative of the inhabitants' special skills and talents

The number of activities and the depth of the investigations and planning naturally will vary depending on the amount of time allocated for the culture study, the resources available, and the age and sophistication of the students. In an in-depth study, students can create a literature for the culture, writing their own folktales, trickster stories, history. A class newspaper can be written, featuring the various cultures the students have created. Of course, the topics of world peace, saving their environments, and pollution could grow out of this particular study. An excellent culminating experience is to have the students present their cultures to each other or to other members of the school community.

students and offer students opportunities to apply what they have learned, use writing and the expressive arts, and seek out related literature selections.

Some basal programs organize their basal readers around themes; these themes can be expanded into longer units of study, thus becoming springboards for more in-depth classroom study. Selections in basal readers can be incorporated into other curricular areas or into a theme currently being explored. The resources listed in the teachers' manual may be helpful for planning a unit of study, and some of the activities may be worthwhile as well. A literature planning guide for a basal story and ways to balance trade books and basal readers are given in Figures 8.29 and 8.30.

With careful planning and thoughtful analysis of the various offerings of basal programs, teachers may make judicious use of the basal readers and suggestions in the teachers' manual. With the freedom to experiment and to adapt and modify the basal program, teachers may use basal readers as a part of a balanced reading program. However, it should be remembered that use of the basal must be accom-

Figure 8.29 Literature Planning Guide for a Basal Reader

TITLE: **Sleeping Ugly**
from **Don't Wake the Princess**
(Theme—Hopes and Dreams)
(Celebrate Reading, ScottForesman, Grade 4)

AUTHOR: Jane Yolen

STORY SUMMARY: In this variation of **Sleeping Beauty**, there was a beautiful but mean princess named Miserella and a poor but kind orphan named Plain Jane. One day Miserella gets lost in the woods and finds an old fairy who takes her to Jane's house. Because of her kindness, the fairy grants Jane three wishes. Miserella angers the fairy so much that she turns her feet into stone and makes frogs come out of her mouth. Being considerate, Jane wastes two of her wishes on restoring the wretched princess back to her former state. Miserella continues to annoy the fairy, so that the fairy accidentally puts all of them to sleep for 100 years, before Jane can be granted her final wish. One hundred years pass, and a prince passes by and kisses Plain Jane. Jane wishes that he would fall in love with her and he does. The two marry and live happily ever after. The miserable Miserella remains asleep and serves as a decorative piece in their home.

GOALS AND OBJECTIVES

- to compare and contrast characters and fairy tales
- to recognize humor as one aspect of an author's craft
- to predict using prior knowledge
- to retell a fairy tale using the elements of story grammar
- to connect this fairy tale with other texts
- to respond to the story creatively, personally, and critically

BEFORE READING

The students can be asked to brainstorm different fairy tales such as **Snow White, Cinderella, Rapunzel** and so forth. Students can retell the story as it was written, or from the perspective of another character, e.g., the queen in **Snow White.** Before reading **Sleeping Ugly,** the class could construct a chart showing the point of view in some familiar fairy tales, as well as a list of other characters who could retell the tale.

Once the book is shown, the students could be given time to preview the text and to discuss why this book resembles a fairy tale. The students could relate the story to other fairy tales. After previewing, the students could generate a list of questions they would like answered and make predictions as to the contents of the story.

DURING READING

The students could:

- continue predicting, confirming, or refining predictions
- discuss the elements of story grammar
- note the aspects of the story that place it in the fairy tale genre
- answer the questions that they had raised during pre-reading
- address reading strategies as needed, e.g., using context to discover meaning of words or passage, self-monitoring, predicting, self-questioning

AFTER READING

Since this story is a parody of **Sleeping Beauty,** the students could construct a Venn diagram comparing and contrasting the two stories. They could look for other parodies of traditional fairy tales, such as the ones listed in the **Cinderella** theme in Chapter 9. A chart listing the traditional tales and the spin-offs could be constructed, and the tales compared and contrasted.

After reading a variety of the spin-offs of the fairy tales, the students could write their own original versions. The stories could be compiled in a class anthology, **Once Upon a Time.** Scripts could be written so that the students could perform their original version or the published ones. Other writing possibilities include:

- responding to the prompt, "If I had three wishes . . ."
- writing a sequel to the story
- writing to the authors of the parodies to ask why they wrote the spin-offs and where they got their ideas
- designing character sketches
- constructing time lines for events that could occur in the next 100 years if they, the students, should fall asleep or for events that might have occurred when Plain Jane and Miserella fell asleep.

Another idea for writing is to give the students a quote from the story: **"Gently, gently," said the old fairy, shaking her head. "If you are not gentle with magic, none of us will go anywhere."** They could then respond in their literature logs as to the benefits and possible dangers of magic. They could locate examples from children's literature to substantiate their claims.

Since the story is intended to be part of a theme, **Hopes, Dreams, and Wishes,** the characters in the theme all seek to fulfill a hope, dream, or a wish. The children could discuss how Plain Jane fulfilled her wish, and relate her experience to other stories in the anthology.

Figure 8.30 Balancing Trade Books and Basal Readers

- Students can compare trade book versions with selections that were adapted or abridged in the basal program and discuss possible reasons for the differences.
- Trade book versions can be used instead of basal selections.
- After reading a selection from the basal on a particular topic, topics may be extended by using other trade books on the topic or trade books can be substituted for some of the basal selections.
- Trade books can be read to the students, or the students can read for themselves books by authors of basal selections.
- Thematic units can be developed, or existing thematic units in the basal program can be extended by using trade books, newspapers, magazines, or poetry.
- Treatments of literary elements—such as theme, characterization, and point of view—and the language used may be compared in the trade books and basal selections.
- Instead of being asked traditional comprehension questions, students may respond in writing in their literature logs, followed by conversations about the books read or issues raised.
- Story maps may be constructed after the reading of a narrative selection in lieu of answering comprehension questions.
- Prereading vocabulary exercises can be replaced by webbing or writing activities to elicit background knowledge.
- When reading nonfiction, the students may engage in a KWL activity (what the know, what they want to know, and what they have learned).

(Adapted from New York State Education Department, 1989.)

panied by reading aloud, shared reading, Sustained Silent Reading, reading across the curriculum, and reading and talking about books.

SUMMARY

This chapter focused on the instructional activities that take place in grades 3–6. The emphasis was on providing students with a balanced reading and writing program—reading and writing to, with, and by children. A balanced reading program includes reading aloud, shared reading, guided reading, Sustained Silent Reading, and individualized reading. A balanced writing program includes Writers' Workshop, journal writing, and writing across the curriculum. In addition, ways of using the basal in a productive manner, particularly as part of guided reading, were presented.

Throughout the chapter, the role of students in assuming more responsibility for their own learning was stressed. The instructional activities described are not mere ends in themselves, but rather are means for students to achieve independence and to become reflective learners. As a result of such an instructional program, students should become effective readers and writers, not only knowing how to read and write, but also how to evaluate their progress. Moreover, students—as a result of being immersed in reading and writing, having opportunities to see and hear good reading and writing, and having taken part in many rewarding reading and writing experiences—enjoy reading and writing and choose to become readers and writers outside the classroom.

BIBLIOGRAPHY AND SUGGESTED REFERENCES

Allen, S. (1989). Writing to learn: The use of the journal. *Reading Around Series.* Carlton, Victoria, Australia: Australian Reading Association.

Altweiger, B.; Edelsky, C.; & Flores, B. (1987). Whole language: What's new? *The Reading Teacher, 41,* 147–155.

Anderson, R.; Hiebert, E.; Scott, J.; & Wilkinson, I. (1985). *Becoming a nation of readers: The report of the Commission on Reading.* Champaign, Ill.: Center for the Study of Reading.

Angeletti, S. (1991). Encouraging students to think about what they read. *The Reading Teacher, 45,* 288–296.

Atwell, N. (1987). *In the middle.* Portsmouth, N.H.: Heinemann.

Atwell, N. (1991). *Side by side.* Portsmouth, N.H.: Heinemann.

Bennett, W. (1986). *First lessons: A report card on elementary education in America.* Washington, D.C.: U.S. Department of Education.

Bode, B. (1989). Dialogue journal writing. *The Reading Teacher, 42,* 568–571.

Bromley, K. (1989). Buddy journals make the reading-writing connection. *The Reading Teacher, 43,* 122–129.

Bromley, K. (1995). Enriching response to literature with webbing. In N. Roser and M. Martinez (Eds.), *Book talk and beyond: Children and teachers respond to literature,* pp. 90–101.

Butler, A., & Turbill, J. (1987). *Towards a reading-writing classroom.* Portsmouth, N.H.: Heinemann.

California State Department of Education. (1987). *English-language arts framework.* Sacramento, Calif.: Author.

Calkins, L. (1986). *The art of teaching writing.* Portsmouth, N.H.: Heinemann.

Carter, G. (1990). *Individualized reading.* Auckland, New Zealand: Waiatarua Publishing.

Collins, C. (1985). The power of expressive writing in reading comprehension. *Language Arts, 62,* 48–54.

Cullinan, B., & Galda, L. (1994). *Literature and the child.* Orlando, Fla.: Harcourt Brace Jovanovich.

Daniels, H. (1994). *Literature circles: Voice and choice in the student-centered classroom.* York, Maine: Stenhouse Publishers.

Eeds, M., & Hudelson, S. (1995). Literature as foundation for personal and classroom life. *Primary Voices K–6, 3,* 2–7.

Eeds, M., & Wells, D. (1989). Grand conversations: An exploration of meaning construction in literature study groups. *Research in the Teaching of English, 23,* 4–29.

Eldridge, J., & Butterfield, D. (1986). Alternatives to traditional reading instruction. *The Reading Teacher, 43,* 33–37.

Fries, S. (1994). *Ownership through literature response logs.* Pre-Conference Institute, International Reading Association, Toronto, Canada.

Fuhler, C. (1990). Let's move toward literature-based reading instruction. *The Reading Teacher, 43,* 312–315.

Fulwiler, T. (1980). Journals across the disciplines. *English Journal, 69,* 14–19.

Fulwiler, T. (1987). *The journal book.* Portsmouth, N.H.: Boynton/Cook.

Galda, L.; Cullinan, B.; & Strickland, D. (1993). *Language, literacy, and the child.* Orlando, Fla.: Harcourt Brace Jovanovich.

Gambrell, L. (1985). Dialogue journals: Reading-writing interaction. *The Reading Teacher, 38,* 512–515.

Goodman, K. (1986). *What's whole in whole language.* Portsmouth, N.H.: Heinemann.

Goodman, K.; Shannon, P.; Freeman, Y.; & Murphy, S. (1988). *Report card on basal readers.* New York: McGraw-Hill.

Graves, D. (1983). *Writing: Teachers and children at work.* Portsmouth, N.H.: Heinemann.

Graves, D. (1994). *A fresh look at writing.* Portsmouth, N.H.: Heinemann.

Graves, D., & Hansen, J. (1983). The author's chair. *Language Arts, 60,* 176–183.

Harste, J.; Short, K.; & Burke, C. (1988). *Creating classrooms for authors.* Portsmouth, N.H.: Heinemann.

Heath, S., & Branscombe, A. (1986). The book as narrative prop in language acquisition. In B. Schieffelin and P. Gilmore (Eds.), *The acquisition of literacy: Ethnographic perspectives.* New York: Ablex.

Hembrow, V. (1986). A heuristic approach across the curriculum. *Language Arts, 63,* 674–679.

Hodgson, M. (1995). *Show them how to write.* Bothell, Wash.: The Wright Group.

Huck, C. (1989). Literature as the content of reading. In G. Manning and M. Manning (Eds.), *Whole language: Beliefs and practices, K–8,* pp. 124–136. Washington, D.C.: National Education Association.

Huck, C. (1990). The power of children's literature in the classroom. In K. Short and K. Pierce (Eds.), *Talking about books,* pp. 3–15. Portsmouth, N.H.: Heinemann.

Jackson, N., & Pillow, P. (1992). *The reading-writing workshop: Getting started.* New York: Scholastic.

Johnson, T., & Louis, D. (1987). *Literacy through literature.* Portsmouth, N.H.: Heinemann.

Keegan, S., & Shrake, K. (1991). Literature study groups: An alternative to ability grouping. *The Reading Teacher, 44,* 542–547.

Kiefer, B. (1988). *Children's literature: Lighting up the reading program. In The leadership letters.* Columbus, Ohio: Silver Burdett & Ginn.

Kelly, P. (1990). Guiding young students' response to literature. *The Reading Teacher, 43,* 464–470.

Kimmel, M., & Segel, E. (1983). *For reading out loud! A guide for sharing books with children.* New York: Delacorte.

Kobrin, B. (1988). *Eyeopeners.* New York: Penguin Books.

Lamont, B., & MacKenzie, T. (1989). Literature workshops: Empowering students in a whole language classroom. Microworkshop presented at International Reading Association, 34th annual convention, New Orleans.

Lipson, E. (1991). The New York Times *parents' guide to the best books for children.* New York: Times Books.

McGee, L. (1995). Talking about books with young children. In N. Roser and M. Martinez (Eds.), *Book talk and beyond: Children and teachers respond to literature,* 105–115.

Murray, D. (1983). First silence, then paper. In P. Stock (Ed.), *Forum: Essays on theory and practice in the teaching of writing.* Upper Montclair, N.J.: Boynton/Cook.

Myers, J. (1984). *Writing to learn across the curriculum* (Fastback #209). Bloomington, Ind.: Phi Delta Kappa Educational Foundation.

Nagy, W.; Herman, P.; & Anderson, R. (1985). Learning words from context. *Reading Research Quarterly, 20,* 233–253.

Nathan, R.; Temple, F.; Juntunen, K.; & Temple, C. (1989). *Classroom strategies that work.* Portsmouth, N.H.: Heinemann.

Newman, J. (1985). *Whole language: Theory into use.* Porstmouth, N.H.: Heinemann.

New York State Education Department. (1989). *Reading and literature in the English language arts curriculum K–12.* Albany, N.Y.: New York State Education Department.

Nicol, A., & Silvestri, L. (1992). *Reading conferences that work.* Sydney, Australia: Primary English Teaching Association.

Norwood, M., & Abromitis, B. (1992). *Story maps and more.* Rolling Meadows, Ill.: Blue Ribbon Press.

Nova Scotia Department of Education. (1978). *Literature in the elementary school.* Halifax: Author.

Parsons, L. (1990). *Response journals.* Portsmouth, N.H.: Heinemann.

Paziotopoulos, A., & Kroll, M. (1992). *Literature circles.* Darien, Ill.: M. Kroll.

Peterson, R., & Eeds, M. (1990). *Grand conversations.* New York: Scholastic.

Raphael, T., Goatley, V., McMahon, S., & Woodman, D. (1995). Promoting meaningful conversations in student book clubs. In N. Roser and M. Martinez (Eds.), *Book talk and beyond: Children and teachers respond to literature,* pp. 66–79. Newark, Del.: International Reading Association.

Raphael, T., & McMahon, S. (1994). Book Club: An alternative framework for reading instruction. *The Reading Teacher, 48,* 102–116.

Reutzel, D. R., & Cooter, R. (1991). Organizing for effective instruction: The reading workshop. *The Reading Teacher, 44,* 548–554.

Routman, R. (1991). *Invitations: Changing as teachers and learners, K–12.* Portsmouth, N.H.: Heinemann.

Samway, K. (1991). Reading the skeleton, the heart, and the brain of a book: Students' perspectives on literature study circles. *The Reading Teacher, 45,* 196–205.

Schubert, B. (1987). Mathematics journals: Fourth grade. In T. Fulwiler (Ed.), *The journal book,* pp. 348–358. Portsmouth, N.H.: Boynton/Cook.

Short, K., & Kauffman, G. (1995). "So what do I do?": The role of the teacher in literature circles. In N. Roser and M. Martinez (Eds.), *Book talk and beyond: Children and teachers respond to literature,* 140–149. Newark, Del: International Reading Association.

Staton, J. (1987). The power of responding in dialogue journals. In T. Fulwiler (Ed.), *The journal book,* pp. 47–63. Portsmouth, N.H.: Boynton/Cook.

Steiner, B., & Phillips, K. (1991). *Journal keeping with young people.* Englewood, Colo.: Teacher Ideas Press.

Stewig, J. (1988). *Children and literature.* Boston: Houghton Mifflin.

Sunflower, C. (1993). *75 Creative ways to publish students' writing.* N.Y.: Scholastic.

Tompkins, G. (1990). *Teaching writing: Balancing process and product.* Columbus, Ohio: Merrill Publishing Company.

Trelease, J. (1995). *The new read-aloud handbook.* New York: Penguin.

Turbill, J. (1982). *No better way to teach writing!* Sydney, Australia: Primary English Teaching Association.

Turbill, J. (1983). *Now we want to write!* Sydney, Australia: Primary English Teaching Association.

Wells, D. (1995). Leading grand conversations. In N. Roser and M. Martinez (Eds.), *Book talk and beyond: Children and teachers respond to literature,* 132–139. Newark, Del.: International Reading Association.

Wells, G. (1986). *The meaning makers.* Portsmouth, N.H.: Heinemann.

Whitehead, D. (1992). *Language across the curriculum.* Hamilton, New Zealand: Berkley Publishing.

Zarillo, J. (1989). Teachers' interpretations of literature-based reading. *The Reading Teacher, 43,* 22–28.

CHILDREN'S LITERATURE CITED

Armstrong, J. (1992). *Steal away.* New York: Orchard Books.

Armstrong, W. (1969). *Sounder.* New York: Harper.

Banks, L. (1981). *Indian in the cupboard.* New York: Doubleday.

Byars, B. (1987). *The pinballs.* New York: Harper and Row.

Bunting, E. (1988). *How many days to America?* New York: Harper and Row.

Cleary, B. (1990). *Muggie Maggie.* New York: William Morrow.

Cohen, B. (1983). *Molly's Pilgrim.* New York: William Morrow.

Dahl, R. (1961). *James and the giant peach.* New York: Knopf.

Durrell, G. (1987). *The fantastic flying journey.* New York: Simon and Schuster.

Fox, Mem. (1984). *Wilfred Gordon McDonald Partridge.* New York: Viking Penguin.

Galdone, P. (1970). *The three little pigs.* Boston: Houghton Mifflin.

Galdone, P. (1974). *Little Red Riding Hood.* New York: McGraw-Hill.

Gardiner, J. (1980). *Stone Fox.* New York: Crowell.

George, J. (1959). *My side of the mountain.* New York: Dutton.

George, J. (1972). *Julie of the wolves.* New York: Dutton.

MacLachlan, P. (1985). *Sarah, plain and tall.* Boston: Harper and Row.

McCloskey, R. (1941). *Make way for ducklings.* New York: Viking.

Payne, E. (1944). *Katy no pocket.* Boston: Houghton Mifflin.

Scieszka, J. (1989). *The true story of the three little pigs.* New York: Viking.

Slobodkina, E. (1949). *Caps for sale.* Reading, Mass.: Addison-Wesley.

Speare, E. (1984). *Sign of the beaver.* Boston: Houghton Mifflin.

Spinelli, J. (1990). *Maniac Magee.* New York: Scholastic.

Van Allsburg, C. (1991). *The wretched stone.* Boston: Houghton Mifflin.

9 THEMATIC INSTRUCTION

The Great Wall – Sandals – Rice – Chop Sticks – Statues – fountains – music – tiny trees – fancy costumes – birds –

CHINA

Imagine
if I was in China
with all the roofs like canoes
and people all different from me.
Flowers blooming, incense burning,
bells ringing, birds singing,
fancy costumes, tiny trees –
It would be so much for me to see!

by Jamie

CHINA

From the classroom of
Jean Mumper
Grade 3
Wallkill, N.Y.

OVERVIEW

It is the beginning of a new school year, and you are faced with a blank lesson plan book, each page having 2-inch boxes waiting to be filled in with notations about the various curricular areas—reading, mathematics, English, spelling, handwriting, social studies, science—with programs for drug and alcohol abuse, gifted and talented children, computers, and so forth. How does a teacher fill those boxes and still provide a cohesive, meaningful instructional program for the students?

Traditionally each box represented a distinct subject, and each subject was treated as if it existed in isolation from the rest of the curriculum. With the school day being just so many hours long, and with the demands placed on the teacher, not all curricular areas received equal attention. In fact, many times instruction in certain disciplines, such as science and social studies, was postponed or forgotten in order to cover the other areas.

Today, teachers are questioning this fragmentation of the curriculum and are seeking ways to make learning more meaningful and valuable for their students. This is being accomplished through the use of themes to integrate the curriculum. By integrating all the curricular areas and relating them to a central topic or theme, teachers are able to present opportunities for learning in a systematic and organized way. This chapter presents reasons for an integrated curriculum, guidelines for planning and implementing thematic instruction, and sample themes.

Questions to Ponder

1. Why is it beneficial to integrate the curriculum?
2. Why use themes?
3. What are appropriate topics for themes?
4. How do teachers plan thematic instruction?
5. How do teachers implement a theme?

RATIONALE FOR USING THEMES

Thematic instruction is not new; teachers have been using thematic units for years. Typically, the primary grades have used a thematic approach when teaching such topics as holidays, transportation, and community helpers. However, themes occupied a relatively small portion of the school day and school year, and much of the curriculum was still segmented. Children went from subject to subject, never seeing any connections among the disciplines, never seeing the function of the language arts in learning other content areas.

Now the movement is toward using language (listening, speaking, reading, and writing) for authentic purposes across all areas of the curriculum: social studies, science, mathematics, and the expressive arts of music, art, and drama. A thematic approach provides an organizational framework for students to learn language as well as to learn through language.

There are many reasons thematic instruction is being used in whole language classrooms today. Thematic units link the content of the various curricular areas and depict connections among the disciplines. Using a thematic framework, students can learn language while constructing knowledge (Pappas, Keifer, and Levstik, 1990; Walmsley, 1994).

Through thematic instruction, teachers can provide their students with a variety of reading and writing experiences. Heretofore there has been a domination of the reading and writing of narrative text in elementary classrooms, but thematic explorations encourage and demand the reading of a wide range of materials and writing for different purposes and audiences on a variety of topics (Walmsley, 1994). Students can learn new ways to deepen their learning experiences and their responses to literature and to reflect on their personal interpretations and responses (Moss, 1994). Themes provide a context in which students are exposed to a variety of genres, topics, and authors and are given an opportunity for in-depth literary study while increasing their knowledge of the world. Integrating the curriculum with themes provides an experience-based, meaningful environment in which students continue to grow and learn. The topics used in thematic instruction tend to be broadly based so as to take advantage of students' individual differences and to provide students with choices while pursuing their learning. Themes become a vehicle for delivering the curriculum.

The advantages of using themes are many. The following is a summary of the positive results of an integrated curriculum:

- The language arts are integrated with the rest of the curriculum, and therefore authentic purposes and real audiences are used for language learning.

- Reading and writing are treated and utilized as functional skills.
- Through themes, students are involved in language arts activities that are purposeful, meaningful, and creative.
- Reading and writing development and academic achievement are enhanced through the wide curricular focus in thematic instruction.
- Teachers are provided with opportunities to assemble a wide variety of instructional materials when integrating the curriculum.
- Themes provide teachers with an abundance of opportunities to integrate literature into all aspects of the curriculum and school day.
- Themes give students a focus for their learning in an interesting and challenging environment.
- Themes provide opportunities for students to gain knowledge through means that are best suited to their own learning styles, since a variety of teaching and learning strategies and activities are used.
- Student motivation, interest, and self-esteem are enhanced as students become more actively involved in their learning.
- Themes provide teachers with a structure for planning, instructing, and evaluating.
- Themes give teachers a means to stop fragmenting the curriculum and to start integrating it.
- Group cohesiveness is developed through students' working cooperatively and collaboratively.
- Themes give parents an opportunity to be involved in their children's learning and to become classroom resources.
- Thematic instruction allows teachers to present a topic with enough breadth and depth to give all students opportunities to learn something about it.
- Problem solving, creative thinking, and critical thinking processes can be developed within all aspects of the thematic study.
- Themes stimulate self-directed discovery and investigation both within and outside the classroom.
- Themes promote metacognitive awareness by providing reflective opportunities.
- Themes allow teachers to use the amount of time in a busy school day in an efficient and effective manner.
- Students have sustained time and the opportunity to investigate topics in depth and to engage in reflective inquiry.

(Pappas et al., 1990; Kostelnik et al., 1991; Walmsley, 1994; Meinbach, Rothlein, and Fredericks, 1995)

The remainder of this chapter focuses on the process of thematic instruction—from choosing topics to planning to implementing. Several examples of themes on different grade levels are also provided.

IDEAS FOR THEMES

There is no one recommended way to plan thematic instruction. But there are several things to keep in mind when contemplating integrating the curriculum. First, the goals and objectives of the state, district, and grade level should provide guidelines for determining the instructional focus. Themes must have as their focus the attainment of the curriculum. "Only when themes have clearly articulate central ideas and related goals and outcomes will the many potential advantages be realized," (Lipson, Valencia, Wixson, and Peters, 1993, 260). Remember that themes are vehicles for delivering instruction, and teachers should always be mindful of what they want their students to learn. Of course, there are some goals and objectives that underlie all themes. These include:

- to provide students with meaningful and enjoyable experiences with literature
- to provide students with a context for exploring literature both independently and in groups
- to have students experience meaningful reading, writing, listening, and speaking activities in authentic situations with real audiences
- to have students explore a topic thoroughly and to engage in reflective inquiry
- to provide students with opportunities to connect the various disciplines
- to stimulate the learning of important concepts through firsthand, self-directed, and self-initiated experiences

Another consideration is for teachers to ensure that children are partners in learning and that when planning themes, children's interests and enthusiasm should be kept in mind (Pappas et al., 1990; Walmsley, 1994). Teachers could initially take full responsibility for choosing and organizing themes and then allow their students to assume a more active role as the teacher becomes more comfortable with curriculum integration and as the year progresses.

A theme topic should be broad enough to incorporate a variety of instructional materials and activities, but not so broad that the students cannot make the connections among the areas that are explored. It has been criticized that many themes seen in classrooms today lack substance. Although the theme claims to be about a subject or topic, for example, bears, the topic in reality is treated superficially. Routman (1991) considers these themes "correlational" as they may use activities from the various disciplines, but they do not integrate them in a meaningful manner. What is missing is the developing of important concepts and skills. Teachers need to invest their time "in conscious, deliberate, thoughtful topics and themes" (Routman, 1991, 227). Keeping this in mind, teachers should give careful thought in selecting topics. Meaningful topics for thematic units can come from many sources. A few possibilities are:

- Content related topics
  - science (life cycles, magnetism, electricity)
  - social studies (American Revolution, immigration, ancient cultures)
  - mathematics (counting, measurement, time)
  - health (caring for the body, nutrition, AIDS)
  - art (artists, impressionism, sculpting)
  - music (jazz, patriotic music, history)
- Special events and calendar-related topics (holidays, Olympics, circus, local or national celebrations, elections)
- Current hot topics and issues (natural disasters, local concerns that affect the community or state, environmental issues)
- Student generated topics and interests (topics that result from student interests, hobbies, leisure activities)
- Biographical topics (historical figures, politicians, community members, scientists)
- Literary topics (literature genres, author studies, exploration of a single book)
- Conceptual themes (survival, friendship, courage, intergenerational relationships)

(Walmsley, 1994; Meinbach et al., 1995)

Figure 9.1 lists other ideas for themes.

Of course, children may provide the idea for a thematic exploration. In one first-grade classroom the children were discussing the Constitution. The discussion ultimately led to the eagle as the symbol of the United States. The children became so interested in this bird that a minitheme ensued. The children researched eagles—types, habitats, diet and habits, the fact that they are endangered, sizes, and so on. Charts with facts about eagles were written and displayed, children wrote about eagles during writing time, and their study culminated in a book about eagles. In another class, the teacher had obtained cocoons that hatched in the classroom. When the children wanted to know more about cocoons, a unit on moths and butterflies was undertaken. Sometimes children will go somewhere or bring something into the classroom to share, and these teachable moments can develop into integrated units.

Contemporary basal readers connect stories and activities by themes, and thus basals can be a source of ideas for integrated instruction. But teachers should go beyond the basal and bring in other literature and educational experiences. In fact, many manuals suggest other books and activities that can extend the theme being addressed.

There are many resources to help teachers in all aspects of curricular integration. These include publishers which provide already prepared units, such as 21st Century Education, Troll, and Scholastic. Other publishers, such as Permabound, provide thematically arranged booklists. Professional journals, for example, *Science and Children, Learning, The Web: Wonderfully Exciting Books, Book Links,* and *Teaching Pre-K through 8,* to name a few, publish articles on themes and provide booklists to use in the designing and implementing of themes.

PLANNING FOR INTEGRATION

After a topic has been decided on, it is time to plan and collect resources. Initially, everything

Figure 9.1 Proposed Thematic Units (Grades K–6)

Grade Level	Student Interests	Across the Curriculum	Seasonal or Holidays	Literary Genres	Author Studies	Book Studies
K	Me! Houses/ Streets/ Neighborhoods	All About Me Unit Shelters Colors	Months/ Seasons Adopt a Tree— Follow Changes Halloween/ Valentines Day	Nursery Rhymes Fairy Tales Mother Goose	H.A. Rey Lois Ehlert Ezra Jack Keats	Over in the Meadow Clifford the Big Red Dog The Snowy Day
1	Dinosaurs Bears	Families Animals Fire Safety— Smokey	Hibernation Extinction Presidents Holidays	Fantasy/Fiction Poetry Plays	Eric Carle Leo Leoni Peggy Parish	Cloudy with a Chance of Meatballs Ira Sleeps Over
2	Insects/Bugs Super Heros	Families Around the World Trees Ecology/ Recycling	Johnny Appleseed Weather Holidays Around the World	Tall Tales Cartoons/Jokes/ Riddles Dictionary	Shel Silverstein Chris Van Allsburg William Steig	Stone Soup Amelia Bedelia Caps for Sale
3	Giants Oceans	Native Americans U.S. Geography Habitats	Native Americans/ Thanksgiving Chinese New Year	Folktales Diaries Science Magazines for Children	Beverly Cleary Roald Dahl E. B. White	Sadako Ramona Charlotte's Web
4	Sports Heros Rocks and Minerals	Local/State History Olympics/ Greek History Geology	Women's History Water Cycles Weather and Physical Earth	Informational Books Atlas Sports Biographies	Judy Blume Patricia Reilly Giff Sid Fleishman	Stone Fox James and the Giant Peach How to Eat Fried Worms
5	Universe Telephones	Revolutionary War Space Exploration Communication	Adaptation of Life Forms Veterans/ Memorial Day	Autobiographies Encyclopedias Historical Fiction Thesaurus	Beatrice Gormley Jean Fritz Katherine Paterson	Sarah Plain and Tall Island of the Blue Dophins Maniac Magee
6	Computers Opposite Sex	Inventions/ Inventors Our Neighbors in Africa Body Language & Cultural	Life: Then & Now Study of Pioneers St. Patrick's Day/Ireland	Newspaper Young Adult Novels Technical Journals— i.e., Computers	Christopher Collier Mary Calhoun Lloyd Alexander	Julie of the Wolves My Teacher Is an Alien

that is known about a topic should be written down. All ideas that come to mind should be listed because one idea can lead to another. As the list grows, relationships among ideas will begin to emerge and ideas can be categorized under different headings. At all times, the goals of the state, the district, and the grade level should be kept in mind. In addition, the teacher should be aware of what the students already know about the topic and how to build on this prior knowledge. As one teacher states, "There should be reading, writing, listening, speaking, and problem solving for a real purpose in the real world."

The next step is to think of activities and possible resources that could be used in implementing the theme. Brainstorming allows the theme to be extended in many meaningful directions. Teachers may use several organizational schemes for planning thematic instruction. These are depicted in Figures 9.2 and 9.3. Both blank examples and written samples are provided as models and for your own use in planning themes.

One planning form uses a semantic map or web, which some teachers prefer since it can grow as ideas are amassed. A semantic map is a diagram that presents information in a graphic form (Heimlich and Pittleman, 1986). It is worthwhile for colleagues to brainstorm, for ideas seem to be triggered when several people are involved in this activity. There is no one format for a semantic map. Activities may be listed under the various curricular areas, which is perhaps easier if the procedure is unfamiliar. Or they may be listed under teacher-designated categories; for example, for a theme on "Incredible Edibles" one category could be "Food Geography," and various foods and their origins could be explored. Another category could be "World Hunger," with the focus on discovering where hunger is a major problem in the world. Whereas using a semantic map is the preferred planning activity, some teachers like to use separate boxes or circles for each curricular area. Whichever approach is chosen should work for the individual teacher and be helpful in theme development. Semantic maps are included in the sample themes that follow later in this chapter. Figure 9.4 presents suggested activities for themes.

LOCATING RESOURCES AND DEVELOPING A BIBLIOGRAPHY

The selection of the materials for themes depends on a number of factors such as the curricular concerns, instructional goals, student interests, and the experiential levels of the students. Themes are built around materials that are age-appropriate and meaningful, ones that will be used to foster personal involvement and the discovery of real-life connections (Moss, 1994). Whereas it is the teacher's ultimate responsibility to locate resources for the topic, students, librarians, parents, and colleagues can also be involved. Once a topic has been determined, it is beneficial to let others know about it so that resources can be obtained from many sources. Resources to consider include trade books; magazines; newspapers; textbooks; encyclopedias; primary sources, such as journals, letters, diaries, logs, and deeds; audiovisual materials; and people in the community and within the school.

A bibliography of suggested books should be developed. This list should be extensive and include different genres so as to broaden the children's literary experiences. The teacher should be familiar with all books used. Besides the local or school libraries as sources for obtaining books, annotated bibliographies are available, as are such publications as *The New Read-Aloud Handbook* (Trelease, 1995), and *Eye-openers* (Kobrin, 1988). Professional journals and book review sections of various newspapers review children's literature. Professional books available to teachers on curricular integration and thematic instruction are included in the bibliography. These include sample themes and units, as well as practical suggestions for implementation.

After generating a bibliography, the purposes of the books should be identified. There should be books for reading aloud (as an introduction to the unit or during the unit), guided reading (which means multiple copies), independent reading, and research. (The term *books* refers to any print resource.)

In addition to being highly motivational, read-aloud books are chosen to introduce students to different works of literature, to illustrate key concepts or ideas, or because they may be too difficult for students to read by themselves even in a guided reading situation. These books likewise provide students with opportunities to hear good oral reading modeled by the teacher. Depending on the children's age, the number of read-alouds will vary. In the lower grades, there may be a different read-aloud book or books for each day of the unit. In the upper grades, the majority of read-alouds may be full-length books; thus only one book will be chosen. Teachers may also read aloud short extracts or excerpts of stories, articles, journals, and other print sources. Note that thematic instruction is undertaken in kindergarten as well. Therefore the purposes of the books chosen for the integrated unit will differ somewhat. Books still are used to introduce units, to motivate children, and to provide relevant background information. However, they will also be used to

Thematic Unit Plan

Theme Title Houses Aproximate duration 2 wks.

Learner Outcomes students will: realize the NEED for homes / learn our addresses / learn about our community / make maps / observe construction / become aware of change / write and expand vocab. / enjoy books related / incorporate safety rules / build a town

Books - Trade and Textbook chapters for reading	Related Language Arts Activities: Speaking, Listening, Writing
Home. Emberly, E. Ten, Nine, Eight. Bang, Molly Houses. Adler, Irving The Little House. Burton, V. My House-Mi Casa in Two Languages. Emberly, E. Houses of Snow, Skin, and Bone. Shemie. B. Annabel's House. Messenger. N. Fly Away Home (about homelessness) How a House Happens. Adkins, J. Little Turtle. Lindsay. V. Itsy-Bitsy Spider A House is a House for Me Busy Street, Rat-a-Tat-Tat > Rigby My Home, Who Lives Here > Wright Story Box	- Compare and contrast · homes of old and now · town and country homes · homes around the world · animal homes - labeling: · room · parts of buildings · streets in town - write about various animal homes - orally describe ones own home or room - write about / describe / illustrate the view from a window - practice giving directions to get to ones home - practice · address · phone numbers

Figure 9.2B Thematic Unit Plan (cont.)

Thematic Unit Plan Title Houses

Social Studies	Math
- Compare homes in America over past 200 years - Explore Native American homes - Take a neighborhood walk ↔ - Notice architecture: sketch ↔ - Discuss homes away from home motels/hotels/travel homes tents/campers - Discuss homelessness/shelters - Visit the Vanderbilt Mansion - Visit Washington's Headquarters	- counting rooms/windows - study a builders blueprint Make map of our town identify shapes in buildings - sequencing the steps of building - Visit a building site under construction
Science	**Related Music and Art**
- Climate - how homes are different - Physical structures and the environment: shapes building mat'ls - Observe and record the activity of an ant farm hermit crab turtle - Explore how bricks are made - Visit the saw mill	- create our own version of Busy Street (Rigby) with a street for matchbox cars - rinse sm. milk cartons and use pattern to create a house - on mural paper draw roads and set up our neighborhood - Farm Homes - tune of Farmer in the Dell - Little Turtle - song/poem - create popup
Health/Safety	**Learning Centers**
- homes and insulation - home security/locked doors/strangers - Community buildings/helpers -fire House -rescue squad phone #'s -hospital	- Set up "construction site" in block center - various shape boxes to create buildings - "Out My Window" add-a-page book at the writing center - Put an address book in house corner for students to record home address - science center - ant farm

Figure 9.3A Theme Map

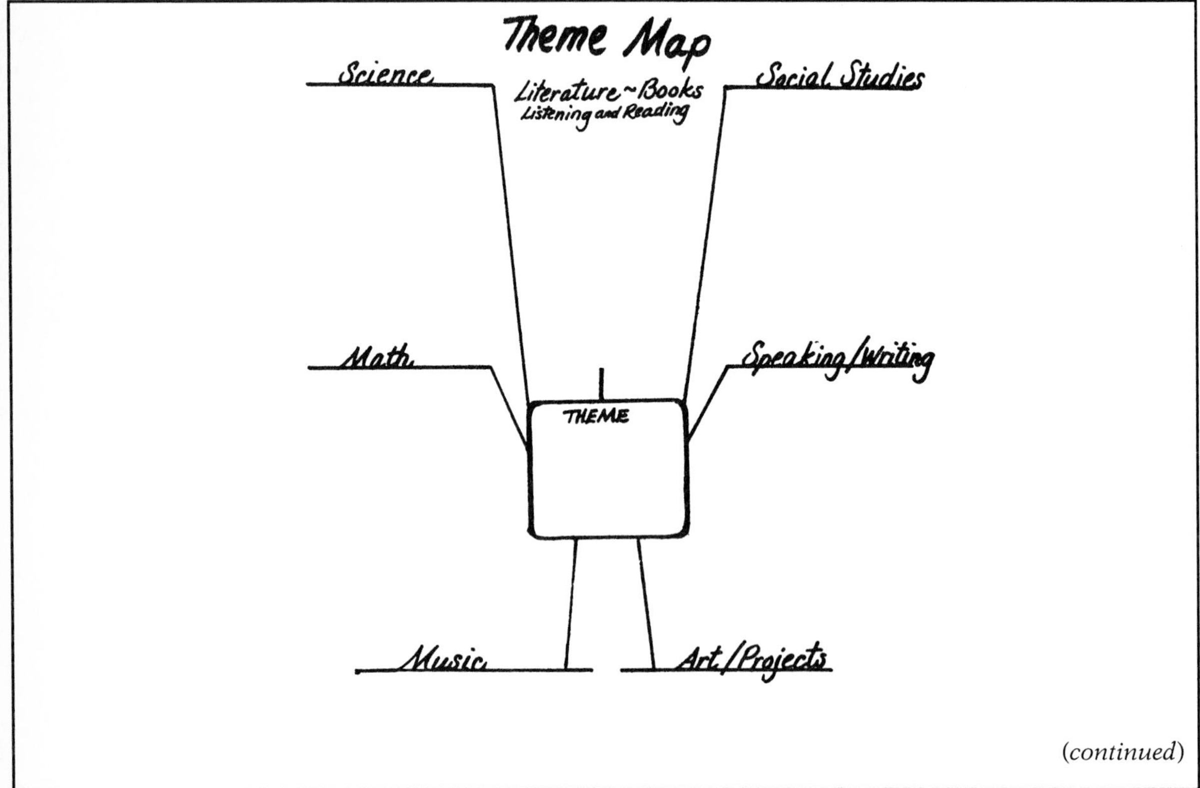

(*continued*)

develop the basic concepts of print (left-to-right and top-to-bottom reading, punctuation, and concepts of a word), to provide opportunities for students to use oral language in discussing and sharing books, to foster language ability, and to provide a firm foundation for further reading instruction.

Books chosen for guided reading should be relevant to the theme and sufficiently challenging and complex that the students can apply any reading skills and strategies they may possess or the teacher wants them to learn. This is the time when reading instruction occurs. These are books that children may not choose on their own because they appear too difficult. Since guided reading involves assistance from the teacher, the books should be a little more challenging than those used for independent reading. For each theme, again depending on the duration of the theme, several books should be selected for guided reading. Students will choose which book to read with the teacher. The groups then are determined by the students' choice. Generally, students do not choose books that are beyond their ability. Rather, they look over the choices to find a selection that appeals to them and they are capable of reading.

Besides whole texts, shorter pieces may also be used in guided reading. Newspaper and magazine articles, poetry, journals and diaries, and selections from longer works might be used.

Books chosen for independent reading should take into consideration students' interests, students' reading abilities, and applicability to the theme (Walmsley and Walp, 1990). There should be a balance between more challenging selections and easier to read books to provide for the wide range of reading abilities that exist in any classroom. However, books should not be assigned based on ability levels, and children should have the opportunity to self-select books.

Another group of books should be selected so that students may conduct independent research. These again should range from easy to more challenging. There should be magazines,

Figure 9.3B Theme Map (cont.)

LISTENING/SPEAKING

reading stories aloud
taped stories
retelling stories
storytelling
interviews
sharing student writing
Readers' Theatre
reading sections of stories
book talks
videos
filmstrips
selecting appropriate music to accompany books/themes
guest speaker presentations

WRITING

creative stories
plays
captions
informational pieces
interview questions
invitations
poems
articles
charts
book reviews
book making
school newspaper
narrative for wordless books
research a topic

THEMATIC INSTRUCTION

READING

books of all kinds
poetry
reading for enjoyment
reading for information
Readers' Theatre
magazines or periodicals

DRAMA

puppet plays
movement
shadow plays
plays
improvisation
mime
Readers' Theatre
videotape children's productions
dress-in-character day
relive-an-era day

ART

murals
posters
books
illustrations
painting (brush, string, finger)
origami
three-dimensional projects
papier-mâché
drawing
clay
puppets (hand, bag, stick, marionettes)
book jackets
linoleum/vegetable/sponge printing

primary documents, charts, pictures, and encyclopedias. Placing these in a center designated for research is advisable.

Since it is probable that the theme will be repeated again in the future, it is helpful to put a notation beside the resource telling where it was obtained. This procedure should be continued with all the books in the bibliography and for all other resources. When it comes time to collect all the resources, a quick perusal of the list will provide the desired information. After a book has been read to the class, it is suggested that the date the book was read be lightly penciled in a noticeable place. This becomes increasingly important when themes are repeated yearly or kindergarten teachers have two sessions. Sometimes it is difficult to remember when or even if a book was shared with the children. By noting the date, teachers can remember which year and with which class the book was used.

In addition to print materials, there are many audiovisual resources. Look into what

Figure 9.4 Suggested Activities for Themes

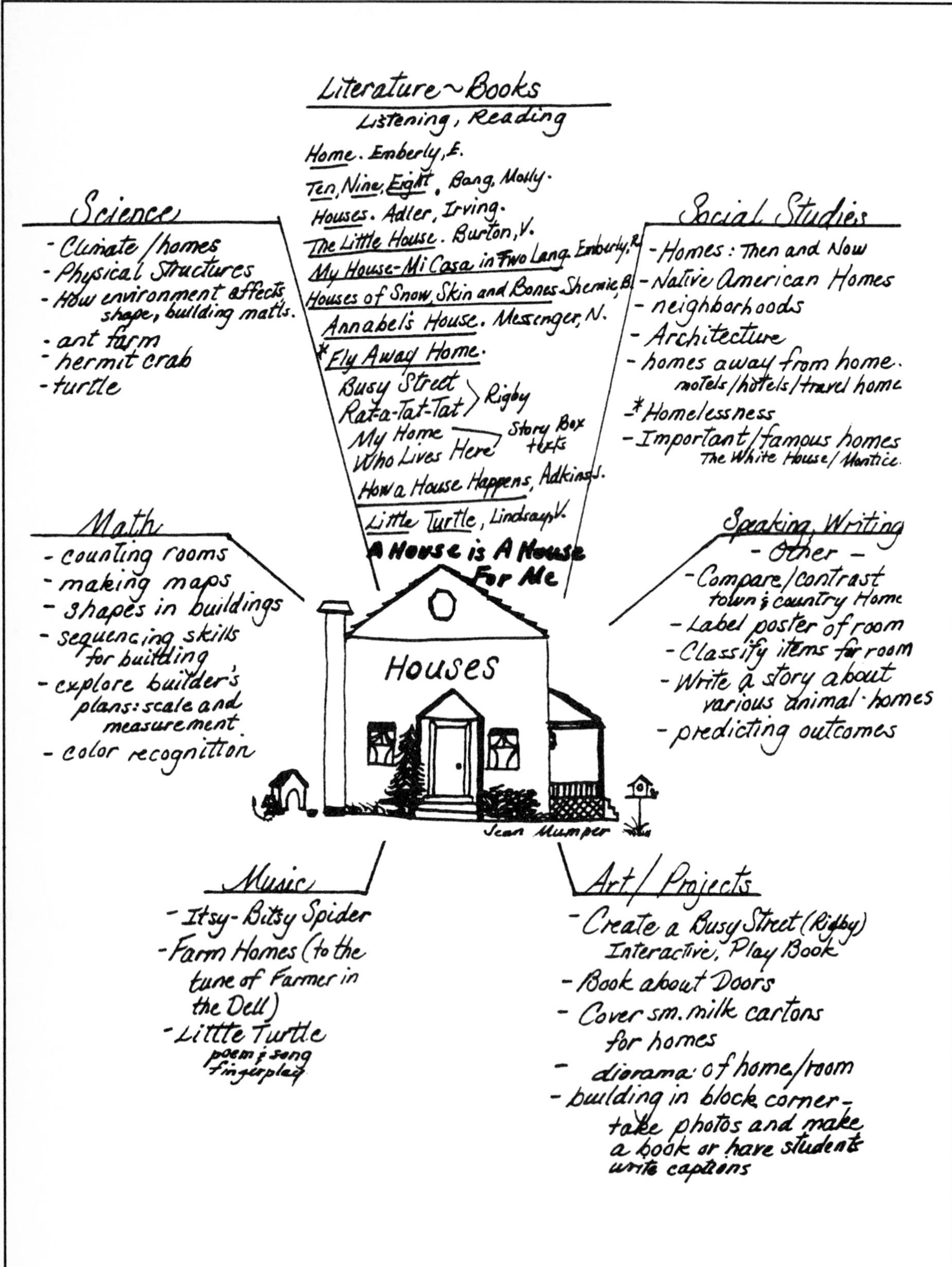
Literature ~ Books
Listening, Reading
Home. Emberly, E.
Ten, Nine, Eight. Bang, Molly.
Houses. Adler, Irving.
The Little House. Burton, V.
My House-Mi Casa in Two Lang. Emberly, R.
Houses of Snow, Skin and Bones-Shemie, B.
Annabel's House. Messenger, N.
*Fly Away Home.
Busy Street
Rat-a-Tat-Tat
Rigby
My Home
Who Lives Here
Story Box texts
How a House Happens, Adkins, J.
Little Turtle, Lindsay, V.
A House is A House For Me
Science
- Climate / homes
- Physical Structures
- How environment affects shape, building matls.
- ant farm
- hermit crab
- turtle
Social Studies
- Homes: Then and Now
- Native American Homes
- neighborhoods
- Architecture
- homes away from home. motels/hotels/travel home
-* Homelessness
- Important/famous homes The White House/Montice.
Math
- counting rooms
- making maps
- shapes in buildings
- sequencing skills for building
- explore builder's plans: scale and measurement
- color recognition
Speaking, Writing - Other -
- Compare/contrast town & country Home
- Label poster of room
- Classify items for room
- Write a story about various animal homes
- predicting outcomes
Houses
Jean Mumper
Music
- Itsy-Bitsy Spider
- Farm Homes (to the tune of Farmer in the Dell)
- Little Turtle poem & song fingerplay
Art / Projects
- Create a Busy Street (Rigby) Interactive, Play Book
- Book about Doors
- Cover sm. milk cartons for homes
- diorama of home/room
- building in block corner - take photos and make a book or have students write captions

filmstrips, videotapes, movies, and computer programs are available and should be included in the list of resources. You may also need artifacts, which could include rocks, models, shells, costumes, and any other objects that may be used to motivate the students, illustrate concepts, or be part of learning centers.

As teachers undertake theme planning, they will need to organize the materials, notes, and background readings in some systematic way. Some teachers organize their materials in three-ring binders, which keeps them neat and enables them to be rearranged easily but limits teachers to items that fit in the binder. Other teachers prefer to use file folders (especially legal size) or boxes that are labeled and kept in storage closets. As materials are amassed, there are additions, changes, and even deletions to the collection. These result from new discoveries and from trying things out with the children and seeing what does and does not work.

To illustrate what types of materials should be filed, let's consider a thematic unit on "Incredible Edibles." Newspaper and magazine articles on foods, nutrition, and food additives can be filed for background knowledge for the teacher or for possible research sources for the children. As activities are found in teaching magazines, provided by colleagues, or created as a result of reading children's literature, these ideas can be written up and placed in the folder. Sample packages of incredible foods found in grocery stores can be collected for future use (e.g., dinosaur-shaped macaroni, gummy bear candy, and shark-shaped fruit snacks). Other things to keep are the growing bibliography, sample menus from fast-food restaurants, newspaper ads, and any ideas for cross-curricular activities. This file will continue to grow even after the unit is completed.

LESSONS AND ACTIVITIES

The next stage in preparing for thematic instruction is designing lessons and activities, which are developed after teachers become familiar with the possible resources that will be used. Reading the literature and gaining knowledge about the topic will result in further additions to the semantic map. Once the theme is researched, an introductory lesson should be decided on and a tentative sequence of lessons and activities should be planned. These lessons and activities should be considered as points of departure. As the students and teacher work through the theme, many new ideas and lessons will evolve.

During the planning of lessons and activities, opportunities should exist for integrating curricular areas, the language arts, and the expressive arts. Meaningful opportunities for functional reading and writing experiences should be an integral part of the activities undertaken.

Suggestions for activities to extend books are provided in Chapter 10. Various writing forms are discussed in Chapter 2. These may be referred to when planning themes.

THEMATIC INSTRUCTION IN A BUSY SCHOOL DAY

Organizing the day for thematic instruction is another piece of the curriculum integration process. Some teachers who are not restricted to basal group reading may use a theme throughout the school day, filling in most of the day with integrated instruction. Most teachers, however, would find this overwhelming to do at first and may be unable to owing to administrative constraints on their time and curriculum. These teachers would set aside a block of time—generally 1 hour to 90 minutes—in which to undertake the theme. Of course, the theme may spill over to other time slots, but this occurs naturally and should be welcomed.

THE PLAN BOOK

Now back to the plan book. Those 2-inch boxes with their artificial boundaries still remain a puzzle. No longer can all the 2-inch pieces be joined to form a complete picture. As with the various disciplines, the discrete boundaries tend to fade and disappear ultimately. They are replaced by large chunks of time devoted to language learning (e.g., Readers' and Writers' Workshop) and thematic instruction. Teachers find themselves abandoning traditional plan books and creating their own management systems. Because the children are ultimately responsible and are quite self-sufficient in

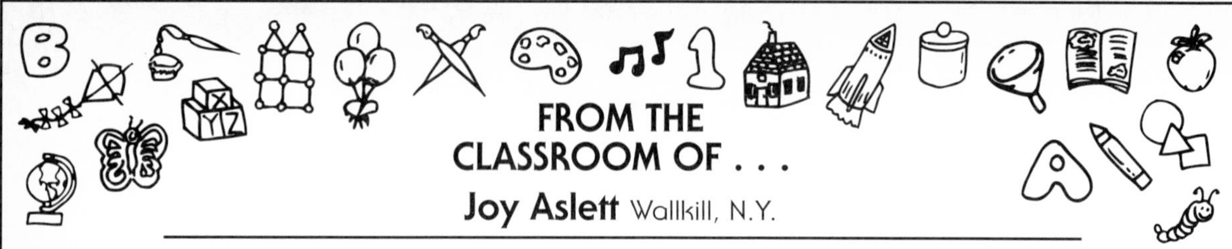

FROM THE CLASSROOM OF . . .

Joy Aslett Wallkill, N.Y.

ACCORDIAN BOOK

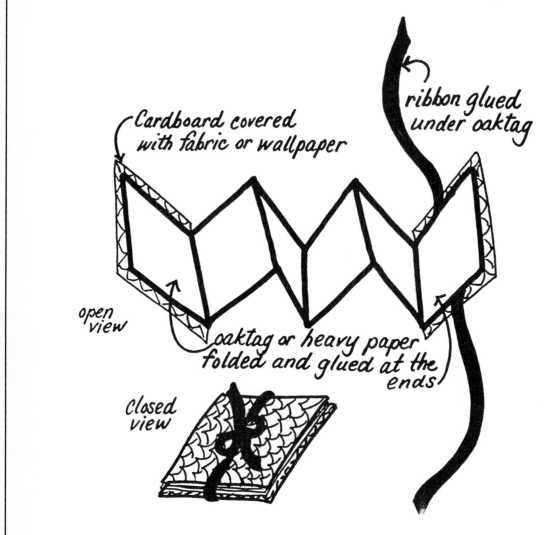

Books make wonderful GIFTS and what better way to give a present than to give a homemade book—whose decorated covers serve as the gift wrappings! Joy Aslett has her students construct small, accordian books to record special events, messages, and a student's own writing. Other uses for the book include generating time lines, recording story events, creating memory books, or making greeting cards, These folded paper books are covered with fabric or wallpaper, with a satin ribbon attached so the book can be tied and given as a gift or kept as a keepsake. Used for curriculum tie-ins, diaries, storehouses for memories, or as gifts, these books will be cherished for years.

directing their own learning, substitute teachers are informed by the children themselves.

Now that the *process* of thematic instruction has been presented, the *products* of thematic instruction (the themes themselves) are provided to illustrate what can be done when integrating the curriculum. Several types of themes are included: sample themes for both the primary and intermediate grades, versions of a folktale, an author's study, and a single piece of literature.

CHILDREN AROUND THE WORLD: A MULTICULTURAL STUDY

To begin our exploration into thematic instruction, we chose the global theme of *Children Around the World.* This particular theme was selected because of its wide applicability and relevance. Studies involving cultural diversity have assumed prominence in educational programming and can be implemented with young learners as well as with older students. Undertaking themes that promote an awareness and celebration of cultural diversity increases cultural understanding and respect. Research suggests that it is appropriate to introduce global studies during the elementary school years since elementary school children are more receptive to accepting different cultures and develop more positive attitudes to people from different lands (Diakiw, 1990). Moreover, the possibilities for whole class and individual exploration are numerous, and the literature plentiful. The theme presented is but a springboard for more in-depth study of different cultures around the world.

This unit is designed to help students discover similarities and differences between themselves and other children around the world. By studying various cultures, the students will be able to see the world through another's eyes. As the students "travel" the world, they will visit children in other parts of the world. They will have the opportunity to read, write, research, and utilize the creative and expressive arts as they take their journey. The literature and activities used in this unit will help students develop an understanding and appreciation of other cultures and ways of life. This literature enables complex, global issues to be dealt with sensitively and honestly. As students explore this theme, they will learn that it is "a small world after all."

As with any thematic unit, it is necessary for teachers to think about what they want their students to learn, using themes as the vehicle. Teachers are held accountable for a given curriculum with specified knowledge and understandings and these must be given priority when thinking about developing themes. A listing of some of the learner outcomes in this sample unit, "Children Around the World" follows:

Learner Outcomes: Children Around the World

- will become familiar with a variety of cultures
- recognize the similarities and differences among cultures throughout the world
- respect and value the customs, traditions, and values of other cultures
- relate the similarities and differences among cultures as depicted in literature
- use map skills to locate the countries studied in the unit
- gain an appreciation for a variety of literary genre

In addition to the above learner outcomes, this unit is a way of implementing the language arts curriculum and giving children opportunities to be engaged in expressive arts activities. The literature is extensive, as are the writing opportunities. Therefore children will read a wide selection of books during shared reading, guided reading, and Sustained Silent Reading. Students working cooperatively and collaboratively on projects and research can establish a group cohesiveness in the classroom. Prior to implementing any theme, learner outcomes and objectives must be considered. On completion of any theme, teachers and students should evaluate the learning that took place based on the intended goals.

Introducing the Unit

Students can be launched into a world of literature and adventure by embarking on a voyage around the world without even leaving the classroom. The means of travel for these armchair adventures is through oral language and through the world of print. The imaginary trip begins in the students' hometown and takes the students to various countries around the world. Prior to embarking on this extraordinary adventure, certain classroom preparations have to be undertaken. Since the mode of transportation chosen for the trip is a hot air balloon, the children need to design a balloon and equip it with needed supplies such as food, clothing, tools, recording instruments, and maps. Therefore research on hot air balloons needs to be conducted by the classroom "crew." Students can brainstorm items that are essential for the trip, how the items should be stored, and other issues that need to be considered before departing.

After designing and equipping the balloons, the class can meet as a whole. Class meetings can be held prior to landing at each new destination. At this time the country or area to be visited can be introduced and located on a map. The children could also be given travel diaries at this time. The travel diaries become their passports to learning about the areas visited. These diaries become special places for keeping track of the events on the tour, the books read, and students' responses and thoughts about the literature and their armchair adventures. See Figure 9.5 for a sample of a travel diary.

Prior to beginning study of any particular country or geographic area, a chart could be developed detailing, "What We Know About _______." A parallel chart could be entitled, "What We Would Like to Know About _______." These charts allow the teacher to tap into the students' prior knowledge about the areas to be visited and helps them set their own purposes. Since this study will take the children around the world, a chart of every country visited could be constructed using such categories as the name of the country, location, climate, foods, clothing, holidays, famous people, entertainment, and significant sites.

Some of the charts could be done as whole class activities for those countries that the class visits together. It might be beneficial for individual or small groups of children to investigate other countries as well, and this would involve independent research. A Research Planning Guide is depicted in Figure 9.6 to help children focus their research efforts and to support fledgling researchers.

An excellent book for introducing the journey is *The Fantastic Flying Journey* by Gerald Durrell. This book, subtitled, "An Adventure in Natural History" provides an account of the travel adventures of the eccentric Uncle Lancelot and his great niece and nephew. The world travelers undertake an epic voyage to many exotic places in a hot air balloon. During their stopovers they are able to communicate with the animals due to some magical powers given to them at the beginning of the trip. *The Fantastic Flying Journey* provides an account of natural history, embedded in a delightful tale of danger and excitement. While the class follows the world adventures of Uncle Lancelot and his crew, the classroom journey can now begin!

Implementing the Unit

Along with the daily reading of *The Fantastic Flying Journey,* teachers might like to share several other books while preparing for the voyage around the world—*This Is the Way We Go to School* and *We Are Alike . . . We Are Different.* Both of these books give the students an opportunity to discuss, reflect, and compare ways people are alike and different throughout the world.

After the children are prepared to embark on their journey, books from the unit can be displayed. Some of the titles can be used for independent reading and research, for read-alouds, and for guided reading. The class should be encouraged to bring in other books and artifacts from the countries to be visited. These could be kept in a special section of the classroom, or the classroom itself can evolve into a living museum. There are a variety of activities that can occur during this thematic study and Figure 9.7 is a semantic map outlining the possibilities. For purposes of this thematic study, the description of the activities will be categorized under reading, writing, the creative and expressive arts, and other curricular areas.

Reading

Culturally diverse literature portrays the uniqueness of individual cultures and the universality of all cultures (Sims Bishop, 1992). They depict that all of humankind share common experiences but retain distinctive cultural traditions. For each of the countries visited, students can compare their own community and traditions with those around the world. Venn di-

Figure 9.5

TRAVEL DIARY / PASSPORT

TRAVELER'S NAME: DATE(S):

Country Visited:

Country's Flag

Create a national symbol

Latitude and Longitude of the capital city:

Related reading or sources:

What I learned about ______:

Figure 9.6

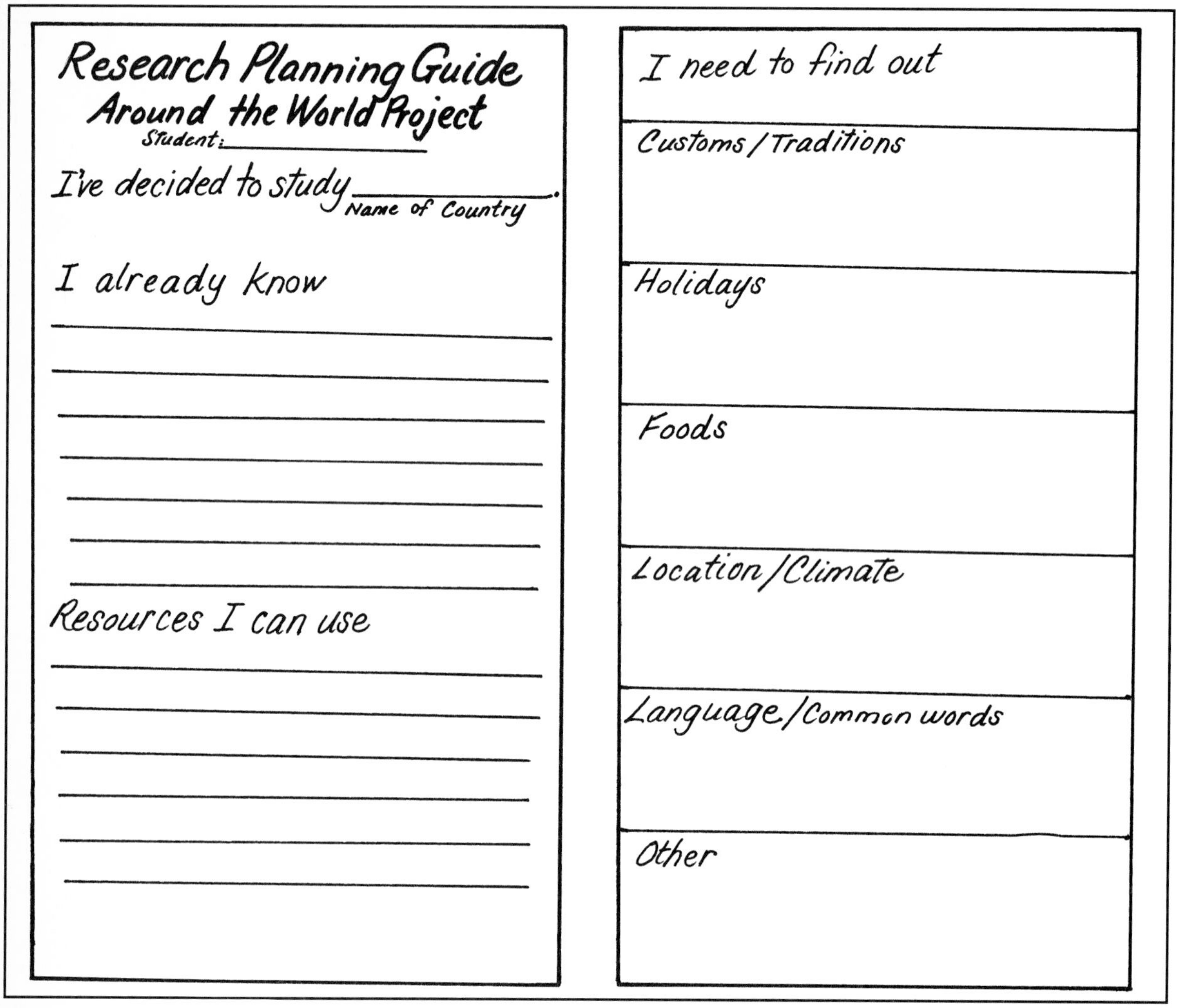

Research Planning Guide
Around the World Project
Student: ______________
I've decided to study ______________.
Name of Country

I already know

Resources I can use

I need to find out

Customs/Traditions

Holidays

Foods

Location/Climate

Language/Common words

Other

agrams similar to the one depicted in Figure 9.8 can be constructed and discussed. When books present authentic images from other cultures, children learn that although all cultures are distinct and different, people share such universal needs as love, acceptance, belonging, family, friends, food, shelter, and clothing (Cullinan and Galda, 1994).

In addition to reading books about the people and their environment, a nation's folklore should be explored. "Folktales provide a window on the collective experiences, dreams, and values of a cultural group. Called a *mirror of a people* they reflect the beliefs, rituals, and songs of a group's heritage" (Cullinan & Galda, 1994, 346–347). For each destination, the class can listen to and read some of the wondrous literature that belongs to each culture—from the Anansi stories of Africa to the Baba Yaga tales of Russia.

Literature naturally will be utilized in the researching and learning about each of the countries and regions visited. So in addition to fictional stories, folklore, poetry, and the like, there should be nonfiction books, magazines, encyclopedias, atlases, CD ROMS, and so on, available for the students to obtain factual information. Students can collect or send away for brochures, publications, and travel guides, which also become part of the reading materials

Figure 9.7

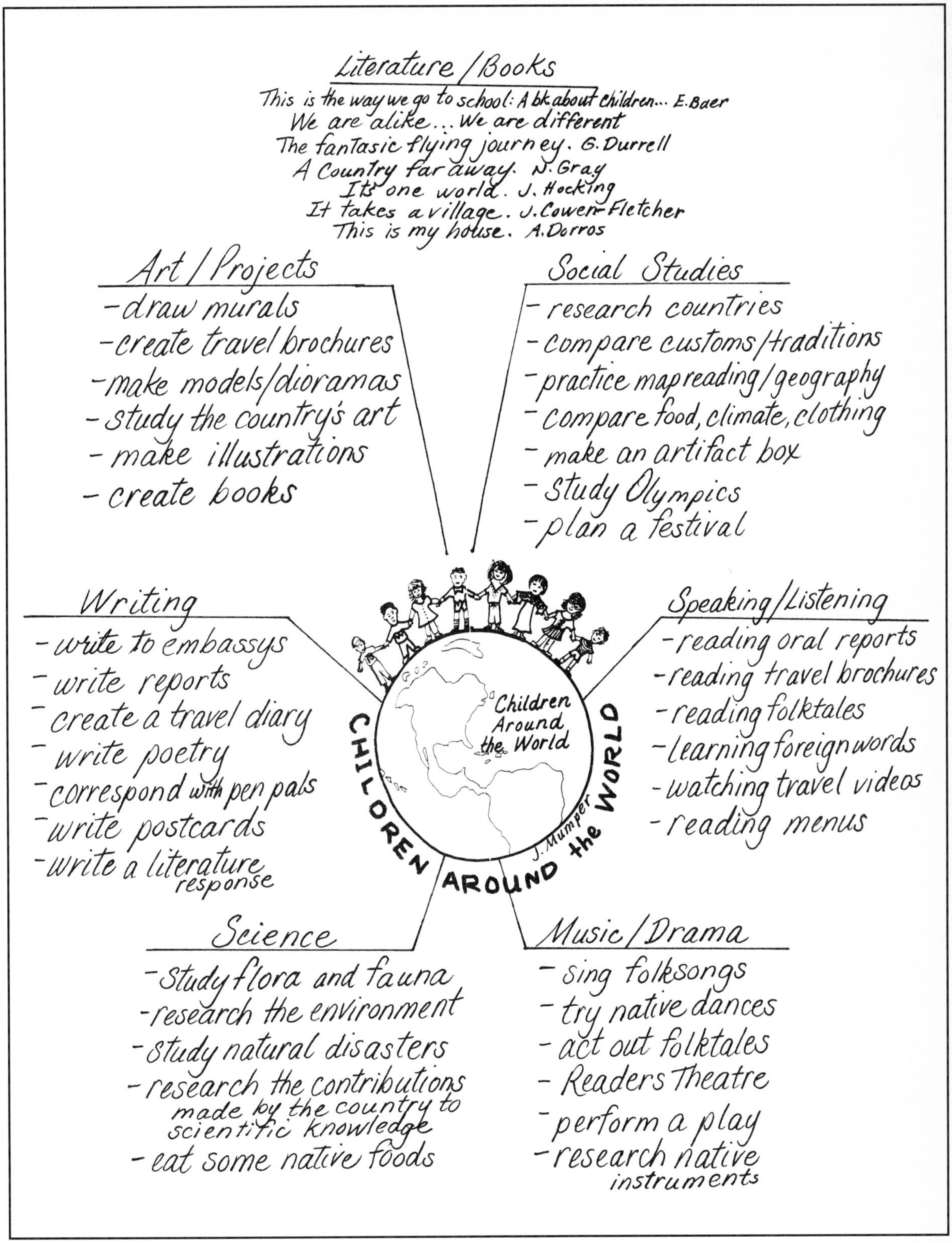

Literature/Books

This is the way we go to school: A bk about children... E. Baer
We are alike... We are different
The fantasic flying journey. G. Durrell
A Country far away. N. Gray
Its one world. J. Hocking
It takes a village. J. Cowen-Fletcher
This is my house. A. Dorros

Art/Projects

- draw murals
- create travel brochures
- make models/dioramas
- study the country's art
- make illustrations
- create books

Social Studies

- research countries
- compare customs/traditions
- practice mapreading/geography
- compare food, climate, clothing
- make an artifact box
- Study Olympics
- plan a festival

Writing

- write to embassys
- write reports
- create a travel diary
- write poetry
- correspond with pen pals
- write postcards
- write a literature response

CHILDREN AROUND the WORLD

Children Around the World

J. Mumper

Speaking/Listening

- reading oral reports
- reading travel brochures
- reading folktales
- learning foreign words
- watching travel videos
- reading menus

Science

- Study flora and fauna
- research the environment
- study natural disasters
- research the contributions made by the country to scientific knowledge
- eat some native foods

Music/Drama

- sing folksongs
- try native dances
- act out folktales
- Readers Theatre
- perform a play
- research native instruments

Figure 9.8

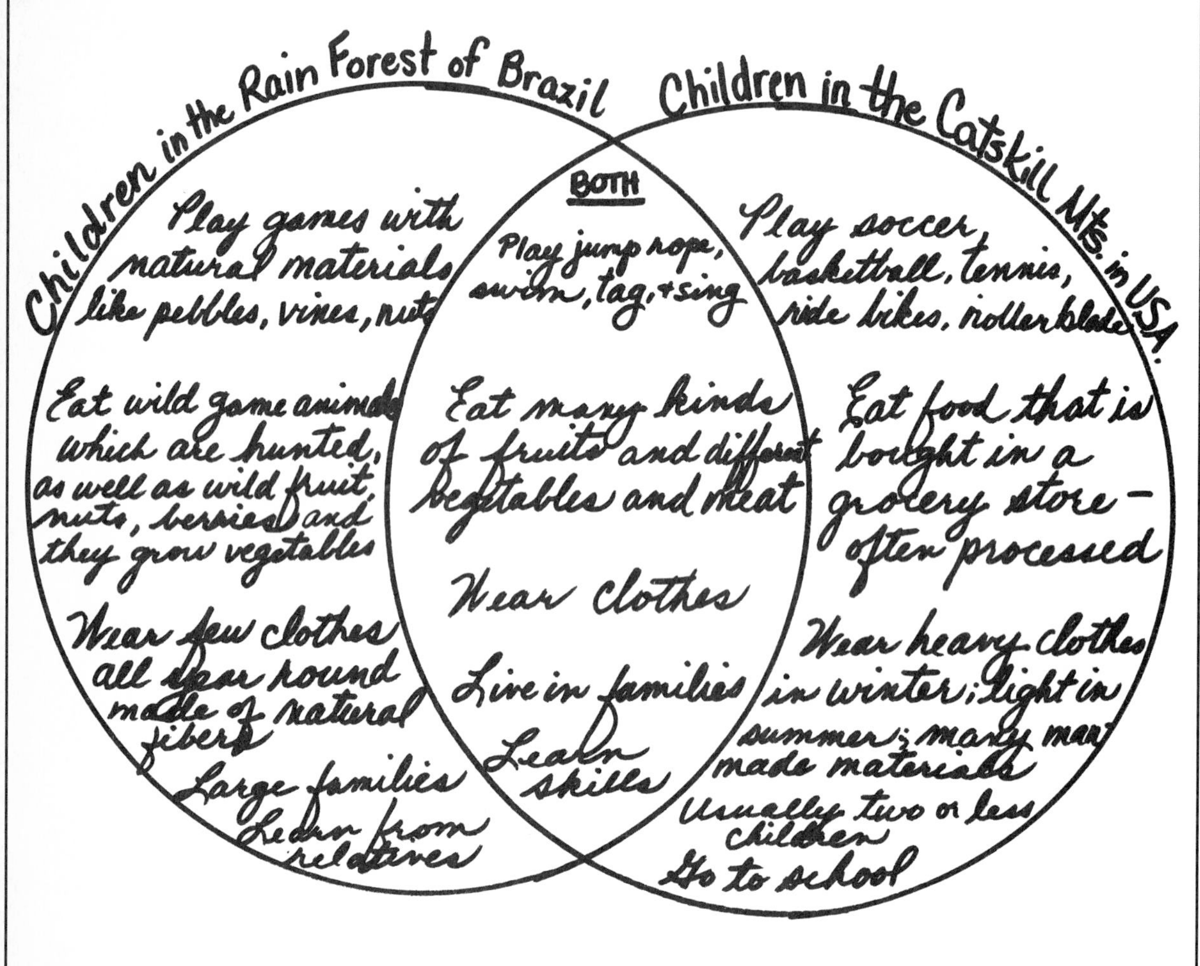

for this theme. Some books that might be used are found in the bibliography.

Writing

Writing activities can be inspired by the books in the bibliography, current events, or the interests of the children themselves. A sampling of writing activities includes:

- Writing a diary while pretending to be one of the characters in the literature.
- writing original poems or stories, patterned after the literature of the country, for example, Anansi stories from Africa or haiku poetry from Japan
- writing a newspaper or travel magazine for the countries visited, with the articles varying from descriptions of scenic spots, adventure stories, advertisements for native products, and so forth
- Conducting research and writing reports about the stopovers or the contributions of people who live or lived in the countries visited.
- Introducing a penpal program, which can be conducted through the regular mail or by computer.

Another way to incorporate writing and geography is to introduce *Travelmates*. This is a program where a class chooses a traveling animal or item that represents the class to accompany a journal on worldwide adventures. Whenever someone is traveling, he or she packs the critter along. The critter "writes" in the journal with the help of the traveler, or the traveler describes the critter's adventures. Mag Scarey's third-grade class in Windham, New York, sent their mascot—a small, stuffed dog named Snoopy—on a year-long adventure. Snoopy sent them postcards from all his travels, and the children eagerly plotted his travels on a world map. Occasionally, he returned, and the journal was shared. Along with descriptions of places he visited were postcards, coins, ticket admissions, brochures, and photographs. During that school year, Snoopy visited Australia (twice), Germany, Spain, Israel, France, Italy, Greece, and Turkey, among other countries, and logged 60,000 miles!

The Creative and Expressive Arts

As with any visit to a foreign land, no trip would be complete without being exposed to the music, dance, and theater of the country. During the children's "visit" to each of the countries, they might attend performances of the ballet, folk dances, and circuses, and view museum exhibits, and so on—with the help of technology of course! Each country would have its unique cultural offerings that the students should be able to experience and enjoy.

To incorporate art into the destinations, the students can illustrate their books, brochures, and reports, make murals, and undertake projects. In addition, they can be exposed to the art of particular countries and can try their hands at such artistic endeavors as *Pysanky* (Ukrainian egg-decorating), *Shkatulki* (Russian lacquered boxes), calligraphy (Japan), carving (the Maori in New Zealand), and kite making (China). Each country has a cultural heritage that will widen the artistic horizons of the children.

There are also many opportunities for drama and creative dramatics while traveling throughout the world. Students can choose their favorite folktales to dramatize or can create flannel board stories from the literature. Children can also rewrite one of the tales and present it as a Readers' Theater. Many countries and regions, such as China and Africa, have traditions of storytelling, which can enrich this theme study.

Other Curricular Areas

For each stopover, there are other cross-curricular possibilities depending on the time, interests of the students, and the destinations themselves. Similar to the travelers in *The Fantastic Flying Journey*, the class can explore the natural history aspects of each country and region, learning about the fauna and flora, the climate, and the environment. The unique contributions that the countries have given to humanity can be explored, for example, the invention of paper by the Chinese. The class could discuss the implications of these contributions and the role they play in their own lives. For example, the children could undertake a "No Paper Day" or note in their journals each time they use paper (and how much) during the day.

Let's not forget physical education. Each country enjoys its own games and sporting events, and children should be introduced and exposed to the physical activities that children engage in around the world. Just take the country of China. Some popular activities include Ping-Pong, gymnastics, skipping rope, soccer, marbles, and "kick bag."

Culminating Activity

There are several possibilities that can conclude *Children Around the World*. The class can create a museum to display all their creations and products that resulted from the thematic study. They can become museum curators and invite others to the opening of a special exhibit. Foods from around the world can be served as refreshments, with accompanying music from other lands playing in the background. If the study is undertaken during a year of the Olympics, an Olympic festival and games can be the culminating project.

Many of the above activities and much of the discussion were modified from several sources: *Children Around the World* (Carpenter, Mumper, and Pike, 1994); *Communities Around the World* (Pike, Carpenter, and Mumper, 1995); and *A Fantastic Flying Journey* (Pike, 1991). The possibilities for global studies are endless. There is a wealth of literature available, and with a little imagination, children can experience armchair adventures around the world. So take out your passports and take your class on a Fantastic Flying Journey!

CINDERELLA

Themes can be implemented using the many versions of an individual story. Since folktales and fairy tales have been part of the oral tradition of cultures worldwide, they make excellent resources for this thematic approach. To illustrate how this can be done, a thematic approach to the story "Cinderella" is demonstrated. A bibliography at the end of the chapter lists many versions of this tale. As new versions are discovered, they can be added to the list. A thematic map that was used to plan the unit is provided in Figure 9.9.

Cinderella is perhaps the best-loved and most widely recorded fairy tale in the world. Cinderella stories are found in more parts of the world, told in more languages, and in more different ways than any other tale. In China, she is known as Yeh-Shen, in Vietnam, she is called Cam, and in Germany her name is Ashenputtel. The Algonquian Native Americans call her Little Burnt Face or Rough Face, whereas to the Egyptians, she is Rhodopis. No matter what she is called, she tends to be a young person (most often a female) who is mistreated by her family but receives magical help so that she can be recognized for the virtuous and beautiful person that she is (Sierra, 1992).

Now considered stories for children, Cinderella stories were once told by adults for all members of the community. The events were often frightening and gruesome, but Cinderella survived unharmed and triumphant with the help of strange and magical beings. There are at least 1,500 different versions throughout the world, with the first complete Cinderella story to be written down over one thousand years ago in China—Yeh-Shen. Prior to that, a Greek historian, Strabo, recorded a story told in Egypt about Rhodopis, a slave who ultimately became the wife of a pharaoh. In this retelling, Rhodopis had one of her sandals stolen by an eagle as she was bathing. The eagle dropped it into the lap of the king, who was so fascinated with the sandal that he sent messengers throughout the country to locate the sandal's owner. Rhodopis was discovered, brought to the king, and became his wife. The story was told as history, and it is not known if Rhodopis was a Cinderellalike figure. This version is, however, the earliest written record of one of the motifs of a Cinderella story, the slipper test for the choosing of a bride.

The most familiar Western version of Cinderella is credited to Charles Perrault, a Frenchman who lived during the seventeenth century when fairy tales were very popular at the court of King Louis XIV. His version introduced the fairy godmother as the magical helper, and he is also responsible for the use of a glass slipper as the identify test. It has been debated as to whether Perrault intended the slipper to be made of glass (*verre* in French) or fur (*vair*). Perrault's version, which provides the basis for the well-known Disney adaptation, promotes the moral that people should be judged by their inner beauty, as opposed to outward appearances or fancy clothing.

Cinderella stories are easily recognizable by having similar structure, theme, and even some common details. However, there are variations. See Figure 9.10 for an example of a Comparison/Contrast Chart for some Cinderella stories. Some Cinderellas are portrayed as stronger heroines, who are more in control of their destiny. The magical helpers may differ in the stories—fairy godmothers, animals, kind elderly women, and even dolls provide magical support in Cinderella stories. Identity tests can likewise change from story to story. In many versions, the slipper test is used to discover the true Cinderella, but there are other tests as well, from completing a series of seemingly impossible tasks to being able to visualize invisible heroes. Just exploring the history of such a fairy tale and the changes that are apparent from version to version and from place of origin can be a fascinating endeavor for students and their teachers.

As stated previously, thematic instruction should fulfill purposeful curricular objectives. Using a fairy tale such as Cinderella can provide teachers with opportunities to incorporate many areas of the curriculum—language arts, social studies, art, music—and to address instructional objectives such as:

Figure 9.9

Semantic Map for Cinderella Theme

Reading-other versions
Prince Cinders
Moss Gown
Princess Furball
Tatter coats
The Egyptian Cinderella
The Talking Eggs
Mufaro's Beautiful Daughters
Yen-Shen: Cinderella from China
Paper Bag Princess

Princesses in literature
- collect other tales with a princess or prince
- research present day monarchies (ex. England, Thailand, Moraco)
- research pharaohs
- explore the history of fairy tales

Art
- make mural versions
- illustrate original versions by students
- make puppets
- design scenery for play
- make costumes
- create a story on roll paper for a round container
- make dioramas

Compare/Contrast
- read many versions
- make a semantic feature analysis chart
- create a Venn diagram
- draw or paint a mural with illustrations and events from different versions

Step-families
- discuss varying relationships within families
- brainstorm ways Cinderella could have responded to situations in the story

J. MUMPER

Drama
- act out the story
- perform a puppet show
- do a Readers Theatre performance
- retell the story using flannel board pieces

Multicultural
- compare/contrast many versions
- locate the country of origin on a map

Writing
- write an original version
- write a version from another characters point of view
- compose a thank you note to the fairy godmother
- write a play script

Figure 9.10

Title-Author/ Origin-Setting	Main Characters	Cause of lowly position	Quest or desire	How wish is granted	Where/how hero is met	Test	Ending
Cinderella translated by Diane Goode/ French version	Cinderella 2 stepsisters Fairy godmother Prince	Father remarried and she became a servant	To go to the ball	Fairy godmother uses magic wand	At the palace	If glass slipper fits	Cinderella marries prince
Egyptian Cinderella by Shirley Climo/ Egypt	Rhodopis Servant girls Master Pharaoh	Stolen into slavery by pirates	To go to see Pharaoh's court	Falcon steals slipper and gives it to Pharaoh	By the Nile River	If red slipper fits	Rhodopis marries Pharaoh
Princess Furball by Charlotte Huck/ German	Princess Furball Father Nurse King Cook	Escapes from an arranged marriage to an ogre	Freedom	She runs away and is captured in a forest	At three royal balls	Is found wearing golden ring	Furball marries King
The Talking Eggs by Robert O. San Souci/ American South	Blanche Mother Mean sister, Rose Old Woman	Unloved daughter	Acceptance	Old woman gives her magical talking eggs	At a well	No laughing at strange sights Making soup Selecting eggs	Blanche becomes wealthy Mom and sister remain poor
Mufaro's Beautiful Daughters by John Steptoe/ African	Nyasha Manyara Father King	Belittled by sister	To be chosen as Queen	Treats the disguised King with kindness	On the road in the woods in the city	Who would be generous and kind	Nyasha marries King Manyara becomes a servant
Yeh-Shen retold by Ai-Ling Louie/ China	Yeh-Shen Stepmother Stepsister	Father dies	To go to the festival	Magic fish bones	At the pavilion during the search for the owner of a lost slipper	If slipper fits	Yeh-Shen marries King
The Rough-Face Girl by Rafe Martin/ Algonquian Native American	Rough-Face Girl 2 sisters Poor father Invisible Being (father's wise sister)	Poor and mistreated by sisters	To marry the Invisible Being	By the wise sister who sees beyond the physical	At a lakeshore	Seeing an Invisible Being	Rough-Face Girl marries Invisible Being
Vasilissa the Beautiful adapted by Elizabeth Winthrop/ Russian	Vasilissa Father Stepmother 2 stepsisters Baba Yaga Old Woman Tsar	Poorly treated by stepmother and stepsisters	Survival	Magic from a little doll	At the palace	She weaves shirts from flax	Vasillissa marries the Tsar

- to expand children's understanding of folklore, especially the way that tales can vary yet remain constant
- to provide opportunities for students to read both extensively and intensively
- to use one tale as the springboard for projects in reading, writing, art, drama, and comparative literature
- to explore and compare the cultural elements in one folktale and its variants
- to provide meaningful opportunities for explorations in geography, map reading, and research as it pertains to one folktale
- to provide, enjoyable, stimulating and meaningful experiences with literature

Fairy tales can be used with both very young children and with older students. There are many reasons for children to listen to and read fairy tales (Wartenberg, 1995). Fairy tales provide a link between generations, as many years ago people sat around fires telling stories of heroic and magical deeds. They can relieve the listener from the strain of everyday life as they provide examples of problem solving in a fanciful setting. As Bettelheim states (1975), fairy tales contain many truths, for example, that people are not always good and that life is full of obstacles that can be overcome. Most important, fairy tales attract and hold children's attention, stimulate curiosity and imagination, and encourage growth (Wartenberg, 1995). "Each fairy tale is a magic mirror which reflects some aspects of our inner world, and of the steps required by our evolution from immaturity to maturity" (Bettelheim, 1975, 309).

Introducing the Theme

Most themes are introduced in whole group sessions in which students are encouraged to share their personal knowledge and thoughts about a topic. As a means of introducing the theme of Cinderella, an artifact box can be shared with the students (see Figure 9.11). The outside of the box could be decorated with words and phrases from the folktale, while inside there could be objects related to the theme. Objects could be used that would be representative of the most well-known version, that of Charles Perrault: a broom, cinders, tattered clothing, a pumpkin, a slipper, a clock, a magic wand. Or to make the task more challenging, objects could be added that are representative of several versions: red slippers (*The Egyptian Cinderella*); a gold ring (*Princess Furball*); an egg (*The Talking Eggs*); or a fish (*Yeh-Shen*). The students can guess which folktale is represented. Once the folktale is revealed, the objects and their relevance to the story can be discussed. The stu-

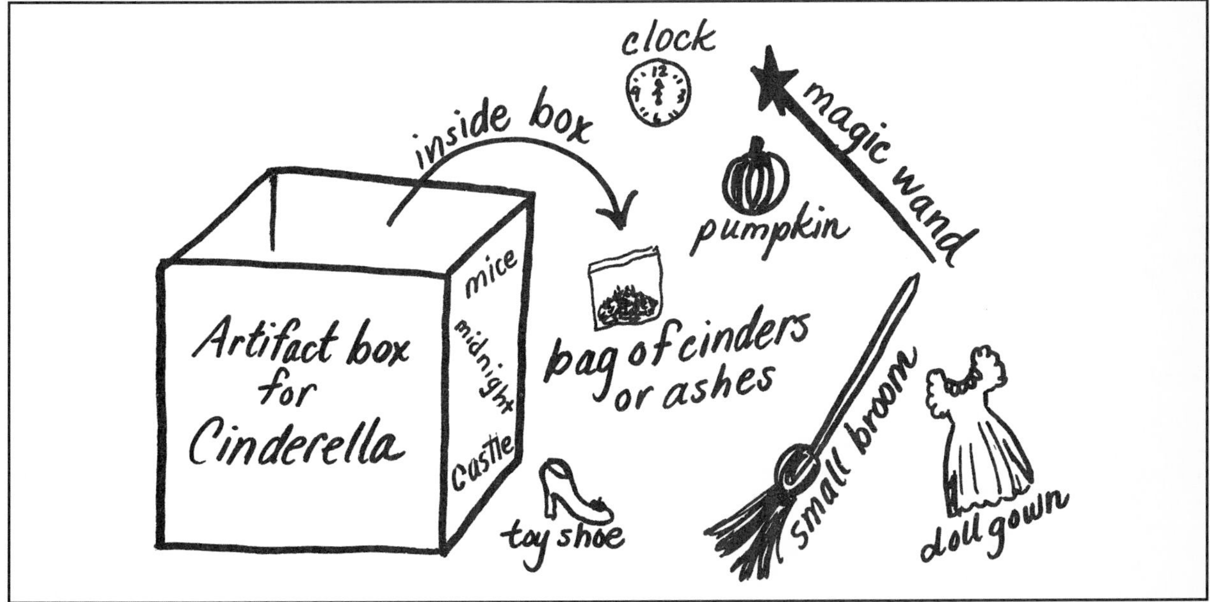

Figure 9.11A

Figure 9.11B (cont.)

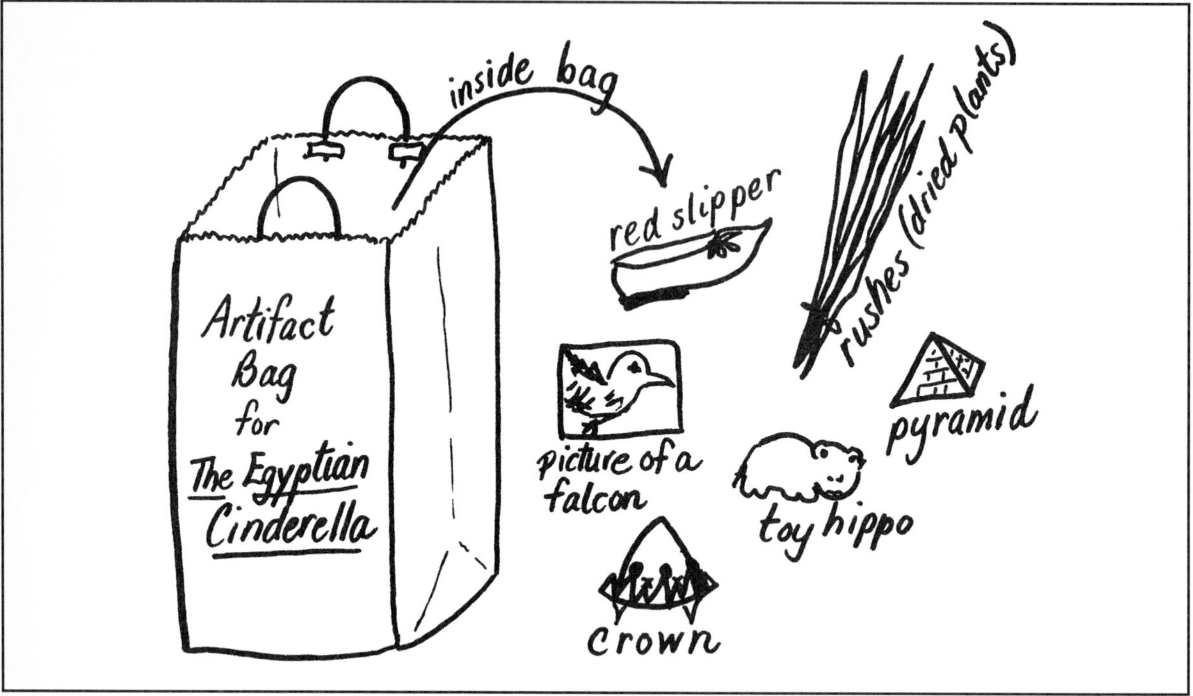

dents can then be informed that they will be studying various versions of Cinderella, and that the significance of the unknown objects (if they are used) will become apparent as they become involved in the study.

Prior to reading one of the versions of the fairy tale, the children can be asked to write a retelling of the Cinderella story or, if they are very young children, to retell the story orally. The children can share their versions, which more than likely will be similar to the Walt Disney adaptation. Common elements in the students' versions can be recorded on chart paper, and kept for reference throughout the study of Cinderella. At this point, one variant of Cinderella can then be shared and discussed. It is recommended that one of the Charles Perrault versions be chosen to initiate the theme as this version will be the most familiar to the students. There are many retellers of Perrault's Cinderella: Marcia Brown, Amy Erlich, Fiona French, Paul Galdone, Diane Goode, and Barbara Karlin, among others. Later in the same day, a different version can be brought out and read. This could be another Perrault version or one of the other Cinderella stories listed in the bibliography. Immediately the children can begin to compare and contrast the two versions. Some children will state that they have Cinderella books or the video at home, and they should be encouraged to bring them to school.

Implementing the Study

On the second day of this literature study, the full collection of Cinderella books can be displayed. As the children bring in their own versions, these are added to the collection. Time is provided for the children to study the different types of illustrations. If a coloring book version is available, some pages may be placed in the art center for children to enjoy. Appropriate puppets or character dolls can be placed in the creative/drama center for the children to use in re-creating the story.

Investigations

Editions in which the text is in a language other than English can also be shared. However, many of the non-English versions can be quite gruesome. For example, the German version has the stepsisters cutting off their toes and heels to fit into the slipper, and their eyes pecked out by

FROM THE CLASSROOM OF . . .

Richard Tabor Marcellus, N.Y.

STORYCASES

As a means of involving his students' parents in their child's education, Richard Tabor created *Storycases.* These are child-initiated parental involvement packets that contain a book, and some related props such as games, puzzles, and puppets, as well as teaching and learning suggestions and activities. Richard utilizes a variety of containers as holders for his parental involvement project: briefcases; backpacks; gym bags; camera bags; wooden boxes; cookie tins; fabric and vinyl bags; tie envelopes; suitcases; purses; and pet carriers to name a few. Garage sales and parent donations have proven to be valuable sources for obtaining containers.

Some of his book and storycase ideas with some of the props utilized include:

- *The Doorbell Rang* (felt cookies and paper plates in an empty cookie mix box)
- *Frog and Toad Together* (stick puppets)
- *Grouchy Ladybug* (matching time and animal game in a pizza box)
- *If You Give a Mouse a Cookie* (sequence picture cards in a paper bag shaped like a cookie)
- *The Three Bears* (alphabet board game)
- *Mouse Count* (plastic or felt mice and a sock snake stored in a plastic jar)

At the beginning of the school year, a letter is sent home to each parent, explaining the *Storycases.* A laminated note also accompanies each Storycase as a reminder to the parents as to the procedure and purpose for the Storycase. To help keep track of the contents, each Storycase has a sheet of paper that lists the book and the other items that accompany it. Parents and children alike have enjoyed this experience, and it becomes a highlight of the school year.

NOTE: This teaching idea has been transformed into a book by Richard Tabor and Suzanne Ryan, *Storycase—Surprises to Take Home,* published by Teachers Ideas Press.

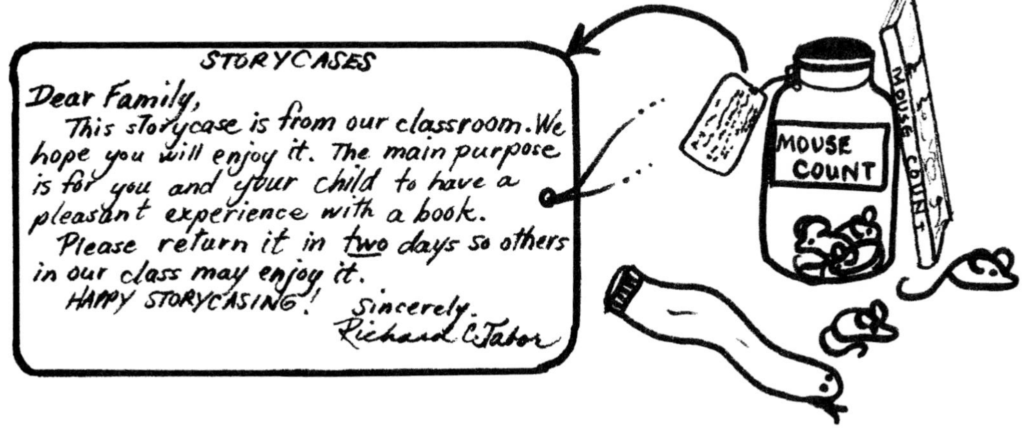

STORYCASES

Dear Family,
This storycase is from our classroom. We hope you will enjoy it. The main purpose is for you and your child to have a pleasant experience with a book.
Please return it in two days so others in our class may enjoy it.
HAPPY STORYCASING!
Sincerely,
Richard C. Tabor

birds because of their unkind behavior. If there are children or parents in the classroom able to read these non-English versions, they can be invited to share them. The children can examine the writing and illustrations. This provides an opportunity for a minilesson on multicultural awareness. Children can look to see how the pictures and story line vary across cultures and discuss the reasons for the differences.

A discussion of the major characteristics of fairy tales can be another focus for a minilesson (or lessons). Fairy tales are usually about animals and humans, include magic or supernatural powers or knowledge, and most often have happy endings. Frequently they begin with "Once upon a time . . ." and end with "happily ever after." Children can discover these elements for themselves and check to see whether they occur in other fairy tales.

Comparing/Contrasting Versions

After reading several versions, the children will begin to realize that the story lines differ. In some versions, there are mean stepmothers and stepsisters, while in others there are only fathers in the story. The magic in the story differs in the various versions as well. Whereas the fairy godmother will be the most familiar to the children, in other versions there are kindly old women, magic fish, and even a magic doll in the Russian version. Some versions have the prince or king fall in love with Cinderella on first sight, while in others, the king falls in love just by seeing the slipper. The treatment of the evil characters changes in the various stories. In many, the stepmothers and stepsisters are punished, while occasionally they are forgiven and the sisters even given spouses. Some Cinderellas, such as Princess Furball and Blanche in *The Talking Eggs,* are strong heroines, whereas the Perrault Cinderella is more accepting of her plight in life. See Figure 9.12 for other ways of comparing and contrasting Cinderella stories: a Semantic Feature Analysis Grid and an example of a Venn Diagram comparing and contrasting two versions of this fairy tale.

In addition to the many different cultural versions of Cinderella, there are innumerable parodies or spoofs about the Cinderella story. Some authors create humor by playing with traditional literature. They play with the plot, patterns, motifs, characters, and the settings found in the traditional stories and they generate humor with surprising twists, reversals, and contemporary touches (Moss, 1994). Students

Semantic Feature Analysis for Cinderella

Book Character	has sisters or stepsisters	has a magical person, animal, or object	slipper	evil characters are punished	has a party or ball	marriage to royalty
Rhodopis (Egyptian Cinderella)	−	+	+	−	+	+
Cinderella (Perrault)	+	+	+	+	+	+
Vasillissa	+	+	−	+	−	+
Rough Faced Girl	+	+	−	−	−	+
Furball	−	+	−	−	+	+
Yeh-Shen	+	+	+	+	+	+

Figure 9.12A

Figure 9.12B (cont.)

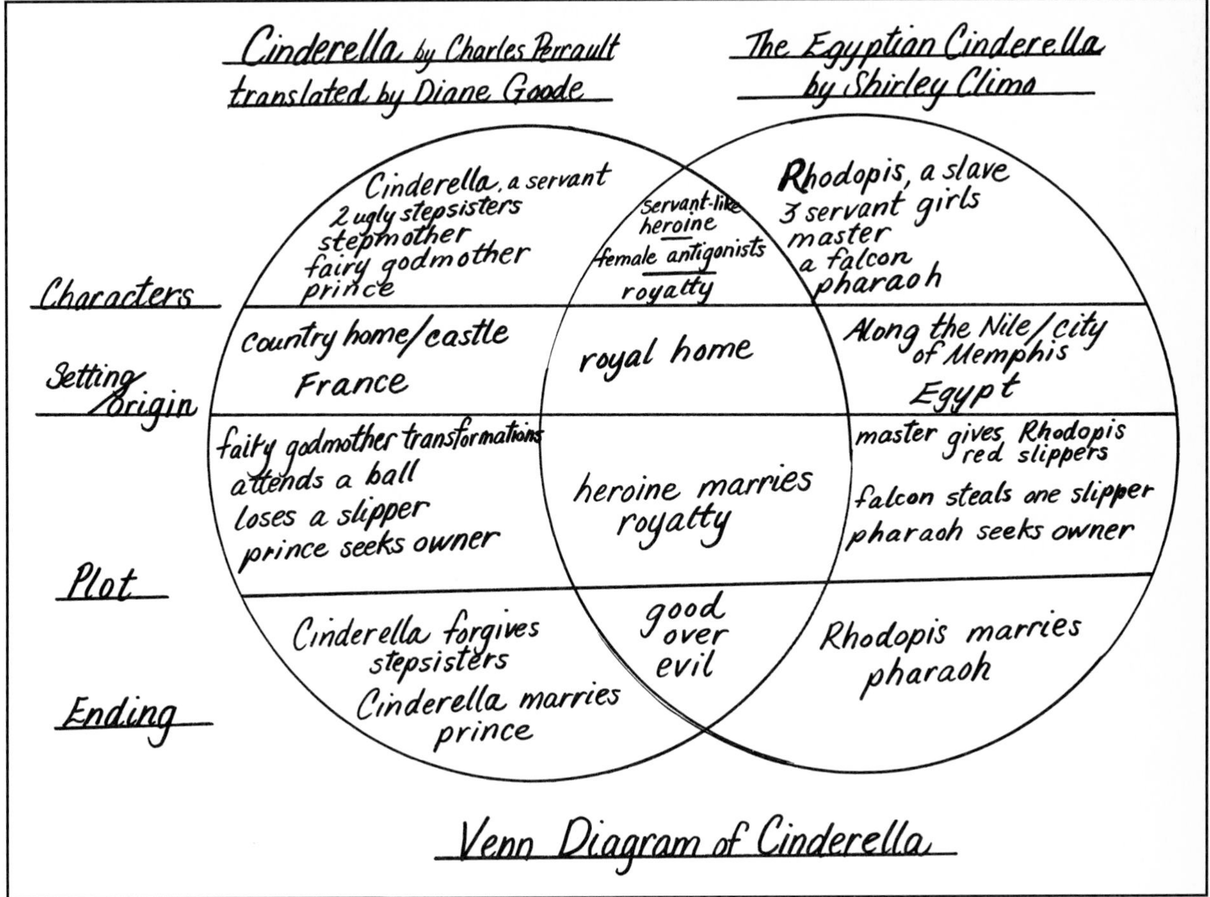

can identify the connections and the changes between these modern versions and the traditional ones. They can also identify the literary devices that the authors use such as shift in viewpoint and flashbacks. Several examples of modern Cinderella stories include: *Prince Cinders, Ugh,* and *Sydney Rella and the Glass Sneaker.* Others can be found in the bibliography.

Drama

Children can act out the story or create their own versions using the puppets or flannel board characters in the creative/drama center. Stick puppet versions of the characters can be made by the children with shoe boxes used as stages. Figure 9.13 shows a story glove that the teacher and the children can use for storytelling. Children can act out the stories themselves using simple props and costumes, such as a broom, tattered clothing, cinders, a wand, or other props that are suggestive of the different versions. These plays can be improvised, or scripts can be written. They can be repeated as many times as necessary to include all students who wish to participate.

Writing

Many writing opportunities are available during this literature study. In addition to creating the comparison/contrast chart and writing scripts for plays, children can write their own versions of the tale. These can be retellings or the children's own creative versions. The story might be written from the point of view of a different character, such as the stepsisters, stepmother, or the prince. *The Coachman Rat* which is a first-person account of the rat who was transformed

Figure 9.13 Story Glove

into a coachman by the fairy godmother could serve as a model, as could *Cinderella: The Untold Story* and *That Awful Cinderella.* Other writing possibilities include:

- journal entries from a character in a Cinderella story
- an invitation to the ball
- announcement of the wedding
- the constructing of time lines to depict the various versions of Cinderella.
- creating of a feminist version of the story
- writing the story in a first-person narrative
- intertwining other familiar folktale or fairy tale characters into the story
- writing biographies or autobiographies for the key characters
- recreating the story as it might be told by a key character to his or her grandchildren
- directions: to Baba Yaga's hut in the forest (*Vasilissa the Beautiful*)
- instructions: how to make soup (*Princess Furball*) or how to spin flax (*Vasilissa the Beautiful*)
- newspaper articles: about any part of this newsworthy event
- captions: for illustrations in books, on murals
- dialogue: for cartoon versions of the story, Readers' Theater scripts, plays

Teachers or the students could compose "What if . . ." questions to help in the creation of new versions. For example:

- What if Cinderella refused to try on the slipper?
- What if Cinderella didn't like the prince?
- What if she stayed until the end of the ball or didn't lose her slipper?

Some versions provide unique settings for the familiar version of the tale, for example, *Cinderella* by San Jose and Santini unfolds against the backdrop of turn of the century Manhattan and *Cinderella* by Delamare occurs in a Venetian setting. Children could rewrite their own version in a setting of their own choosing. This could fit in well with the study of local or state history, history of the United States, or even global studies.

Art

Children can publish their own illustrated versions of this classic folktale, make puppets, make costumes and scenery for a play, and create a mural showing events from several versions of the story. Children can create shoe box dioramas depicting scenes from the story. The events could also be reproduced on a long strip of paper, rolled, and shown in oatmeal-container viewers. Since Baba Yaga appears in the Russian version of Cinderella, students can create her unique surroundings, for example, a miserable hut standing on chicken legs, surrounded by a wall decorated with human skulls. The depicting of Baba Yaga's domain in *Vasilissa the Beautiful* can be compared with illustrations from other Baba Yaga stories.

In addition to offering exciting reading experiences for the students, the books on the Cinderella theme expose the students to the work of a variety of gifted artists. As the students explore the relationship of the text to the illustrations, they can discover and appreciate the techniques the artists use to create meaning. Picture books allow students to enjoy the books aesthetically, as well as provide opportunities for students to become aware of different artists and their use of such artistic elements as color, line, shape, and texture. An exceptional resource for examining different artistic styles and media can be found in Cooper Edens's *The Three Princesses—Cinderella, Sleeping Beauty, and Snow White* (1991). This book is a compilation of 25 illustrators who have interpreted these tales for the last 125 years.

Other Curricular Areas

This story has many possibilities for exploration into other curricular areas. As mentioned previously, multicultural investigations can be conducted while studying Cinderella stories. A large world map can be placed on a bulletin board, and as a version is shared, children can locate its country of origin on the map and place a character from the story on or near the source.

Because the story promotes the virtue of kindness, discussions on helping others and being considerate of others can be entertained. This particular theme can evolve into other literature studies as well—another folktale or fairy tale perhaps—or even a study of stereotypes in literature (e.g., stepmothers and stepsisters are usually portrayed as evil in stories as are such animals as wolves). The children may want to look at the role that magic plays in other works, and construct a chart of other examples of magical events, for example, the beans in *Jack and the Beanstalk.* In at least one version of Cinderella—*Vasilissa the Beautiful*—a witchlike creature, Baba Yaga, is central to the story. Other fairy tales involving witches could be collected, or even stories that feature Baba Yaga.

Culminating Activity

After the children have completed the theme, they can revisit their original information and retelling of the story that they generated on the initiation of the theme. They now can discuss the variations of the tale, the cultural connections, and the values espoused in the tales. They might want to share what they have learned with others—their parents, other classes, senior citizens. A Cinderella ball or festival may be planned. The children would plan the event, write invitations, and prepare refreshments. Possible activities that could occur during the event include:

- retellings of Cinderella
- performing a play or a Readers' Theater production of the story
- conducting a tour of the classroom, sharing the many versions of the story, showing the products from the study (art, writing, and so on)

Developing a theme around a folktale presents an opportunity for children to explore the mystery of how stories can vary as they are told in different cultures and in different times. The potential for interpretations and explorations are endless. Beyond the academic learning that can take place, children can discover or rediscover stories that excite and have excited people from all over the world (Wartenberg, 1995).

AUTHOR STUDY

Author studies provide young children with an opportunity to study the body of work of one author. Children learn about style, plot, characterization, and book language through reading, discussing, and responding to books written by one author. Many begin to see the author as a mentor for their own writing. Author studies are an easy medium for bringing children into the "Literacy Club."

Beginning an Author Study

An author should be chosen who appeals to the teacher and whom most children will enjoy reading. The entire body of the author's works should be read by the teacher. Depending on the number of books the author has written, their availability, their complexity, the grade level, and the time teachers wish to allocate for author studies, the length of the theme can vary from one week to three or four weeks. An area in the classroom should be established to display the books and biographical information about the author. Author studies may be ongoing, and authors featured on a regular basis. If so, a permanent area in the library corner may be designated for featured authors.

Getting Resources for the Author Study

One of the first tasks in undertaking author studies is to obtain as many of the author's works as possible. There are many sources for teachers to call on when seeking materials: the school library, the public library, parents, children, and colleagues. School library media specialists not only may have copies of desired titles in the school library but may also be able to obtain copies from other libraries in the school district or from interlibrary loan. It is recommended that teachers, when planning any thematic unit, have a means of alerting other faculty members, perhaps through a bulletin board in the faculty room or a notice outside the classroom door announcing a future theme. (See Figure 9.14.)

Many book clubs feature authors and provide author study packages. For example, The Trumpet Club has tapes on authors and suggested activities to accompany the authors' books. Publishers frequently have biographical information about their authors. Various professional books feature authors and provide relevant biographical information, including *Famous Children's Authors* (Norby and Ryan, 1988), *An Author a Month (for Pennies)* (McElmeel, 1990), *An Author a Month (for Nickels)* (McElmeel, 1991), and *An Author a Month (for Dimes)* (McElmeel, 1993).

By being given personal information about an author, children become more motivated and get to know the author as a person. Many au-

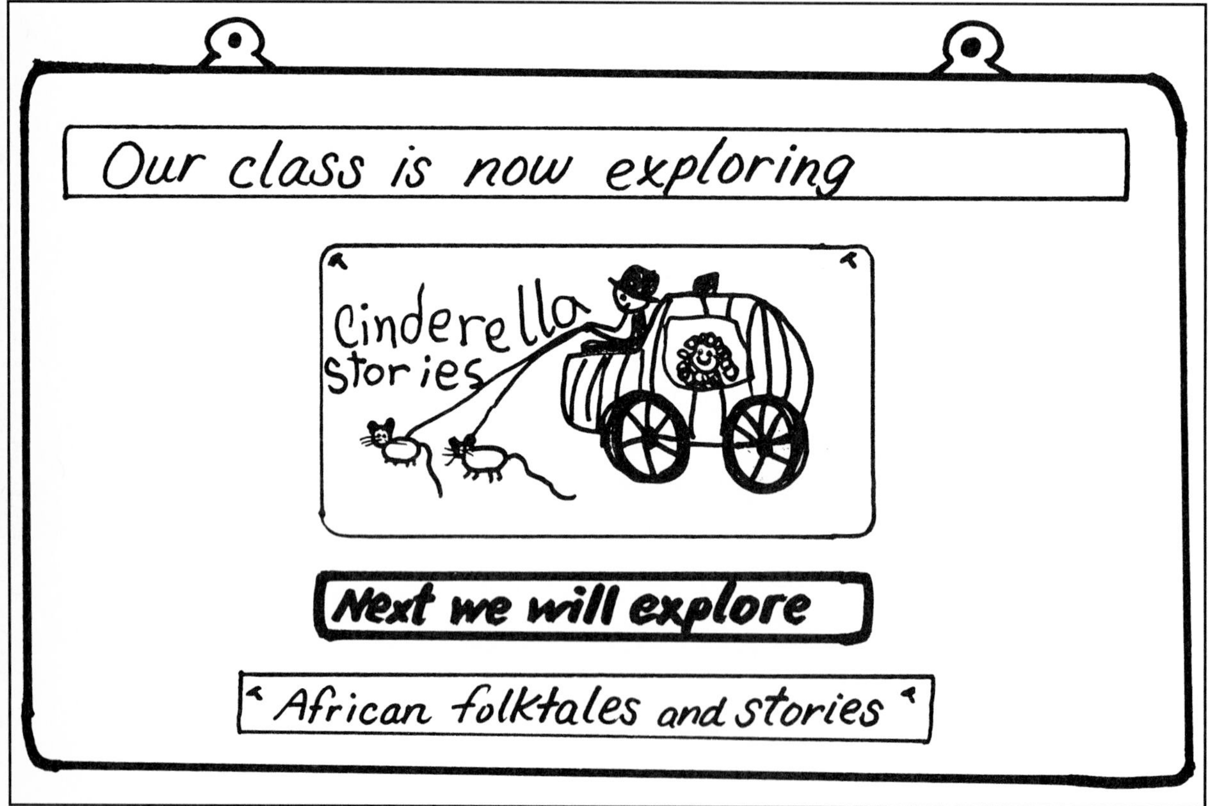

Figure 9.14

thors write about themselves or provide autobiographical information in their books. For instance, Joy Cowley, the New Zealand author of numerous children's books, has written several books (including *Joy Cowley Writes*) in which she discusses her writing process, provides personal background information, and answers children's questions. Tomie dePaola puts a little of himself into his books—for example, his cats—and has written *The Art Lesson,* a fictionalized autobiography about becoming an artist and illustrator.

If possible, it is recommended that multiple copies of the author's works be obtained to allow for grouping by interest. Having children read the same text encourages lively discussions and creative literature response activities.

Implementing the Study

Throughout the year many authors may be featured. In the lower grades, Eric Carle, Leo Lionni, Dr. Seuss, Lois Ehlert, and Chris Van Allsburg quickly become favorites. Older children thoroughly enjoy such authors as Beverly Cleary, Patricia Reilly Giff, Bruce Coville, Gary Paulsen, and Jean Craighead George. There is no end to the number of authors suitable for author studies.

To model an author study, Jan Brett was chosen. Jan Brett is both an author and an illustrator and has created and illustrated more than two dozen books. She lives in a seacoast town in Massachusetts, close to where she grew up. As a child, she decided to become an illustrator and spent many hours reading and drawing. She often read books about and illustrated the many animals she had as pets. She says, "I remember the special quiet of rainy days when I felt that I could enter the pages of my beautiful picture books. Now I try to recreate that feeling of believing that the imaginary place I'm drawing really exists. The detail in my work helps to convince me, and I hope others as well, that such places might be real."

Children will be interested in how Jan Brett gets ideas for her books and her illustrations. As a student at the Boston Museum School, she spent many hours in the Museum of Fine Arts. The landscapes, sculptures, porcelain—all the beautiful images from her experiences come back to her in her painting. Personal experiences enhance any author's or illustrator's creations, and Jan Brett continues to seek ideas for her books through enriching and taking advantage of her own personal experiences. Brett's *Annie and the Wild Animals* was inspired by her daughter's wish to have a wolf or moose for a pet. On meeting a little girl, Miriam, whose sense of adventure intrigued her, Brett decided to put her into a book. Miriam was used as a model for both the personality and physical features of *Goldilocks and the Three Bears.* Brett's pet mouse, Little Pearl II, was used for the model for the mice in *Goldilocks and the Three Bears* and for *The Mitten.*

She also uses travel as a means of constant inspiration. Together with her husband, who is a musician with the Boston Symphony Orchestra, she visits many countries throughout the world. While traveling, she researches the architecture and costumes that appear in her books. "From cave paintings, to Norwegian sleighs, to Japanese gardens, I study the traditions of the many countries I visit, and use them as a starting point for my children's books."

What is unique about Jan Brett is that she is a frequent correspondent to lovers of her work and has prepared brochures on several of her books. In these brochures, she reveals how she got the idea for the book, background information on the topic of the book, and insights on how she illustrated the book. Children will be fascinated to see how Jan Brett transforms family members, neighbors, pets, and friends into book characters. Seeing pictures of the models along with the final outcome brings the illustrations to life and serves as inspiration for budding authors and illustrators.

Throughout these brochures are chatty descriptions and information, and frequently there is an opportunity for the reader to try his or her hand at some illustrating. Interestingly, Jan Brett depicts herself as a bear character in these brochures. Jan Brett's readers will delight in getting to know her through her "All About . . ." brochures and her love for her household menagerie, including a husky named Perky Pumpkin, a quarterhorse named Westy, and Little Pearl, a mouse. She has also given a home to a hedgehog, a character that frequently appears in her books. Brochures are available for *Trouble with Trolls, The Wild Christmas Reindeer, The Mitten, Berlioz the Bear, and The Owl and the Pussycat.* They are welcome additions to any school or classroom library. Figure 9.15 is a sample of Jan Brett's brochure.

A suggested bibliography of her works include:

- *The Wild Christmas Reindeer*
- *Berlioz the Bear*
- *The Trouble with Trolls*
- *The Owl and the Pussycat*
- *The Mitten: A Ukrainian Folktale*
- *Goldilocks and the Three Bears*
- *The Twelve Days of Christmas*
- *The Christmas Trolls*
- *Fritz and the Beautiful Horses*
- *Annie and the Wild Animals*
- *The First Dog*

Once the author's books and biographical information are displayed, the children should be encouraged to explore and investigate the materials. A class discussion on the author and her books can be held to determine how much information the children have about the author and how many have enjoyed her books. To introduce the author study, the teacher may read aloud one book—*The Mitten,* for example—encouraging predictions as the book is read. Book talks may be given about Brett's other books, with time provided for the children to browse through the collection. If multiple copies are available, children then select a title. Those choosing the same title become a literature study group.

Students can participate in a variety of reading, writing, listening, speaking, and expressive arts activities:

- Listen to the teacher read aloud one of the titles.
- Read the titles independently.
- Read the books as a shared reading or guided reading experience.
- Discuss the books.
- Dramatize one of the books.
- Perform a Readers' Theater with one of the selections.
- Make a Jan Brett bulletin board, with literature log responses, biographical information about the author, and children's drawings capturing significant events or characters in the stories (see Figure 9.16).
- Write one of the books from the point of view of a particular character, for example, Berlioz the Bear. Since Berlioz is a musician, inspired by the Boston Symphony Orchestra, a travel diary of the bear's performances could be kept.
- Share student writing about Brett's books.
- Write a sequel to *Fritz and the Beautiful Horses,* now that he has been accepted into the walled city.
- Since *Fritz and the Beautiful Horses* is about acceptance and inner beauty, as opposed to outward appearances, entertain a discussion on this concept. Find other examples in literature where people or animals have been scorned because of their differences. Talk about ways that people can value differences.
- Keep a reading journal or response log.
- Write another folktale or version of *The Mitten.* Locate other books written about this folktale and compare the other versions.
- Have the students write their own troll stories. The students can also conduct research on trolls and bring in some trolls that may be in family collections. As an art project, the children can construct their own trolls, either using paper or sculpting materials.
- Make flannel board renditions of one of Brett's books.
- Listen to classmates share ideas and reactions to Brett's books.
- Write a book talk or "Dear Reader" letter for a book.
- Make a poster featuring the author or one of her books.
- Collect and read other folktales or illustrated poems, similar to *The Owl and the Pussycat.*
- Have the children write to Jan Brett and pose questions they may have. Jan Brett likes to receive photographs of children and hangs them up in her studio. The children could send along class photographs, per-

Figure 9.15

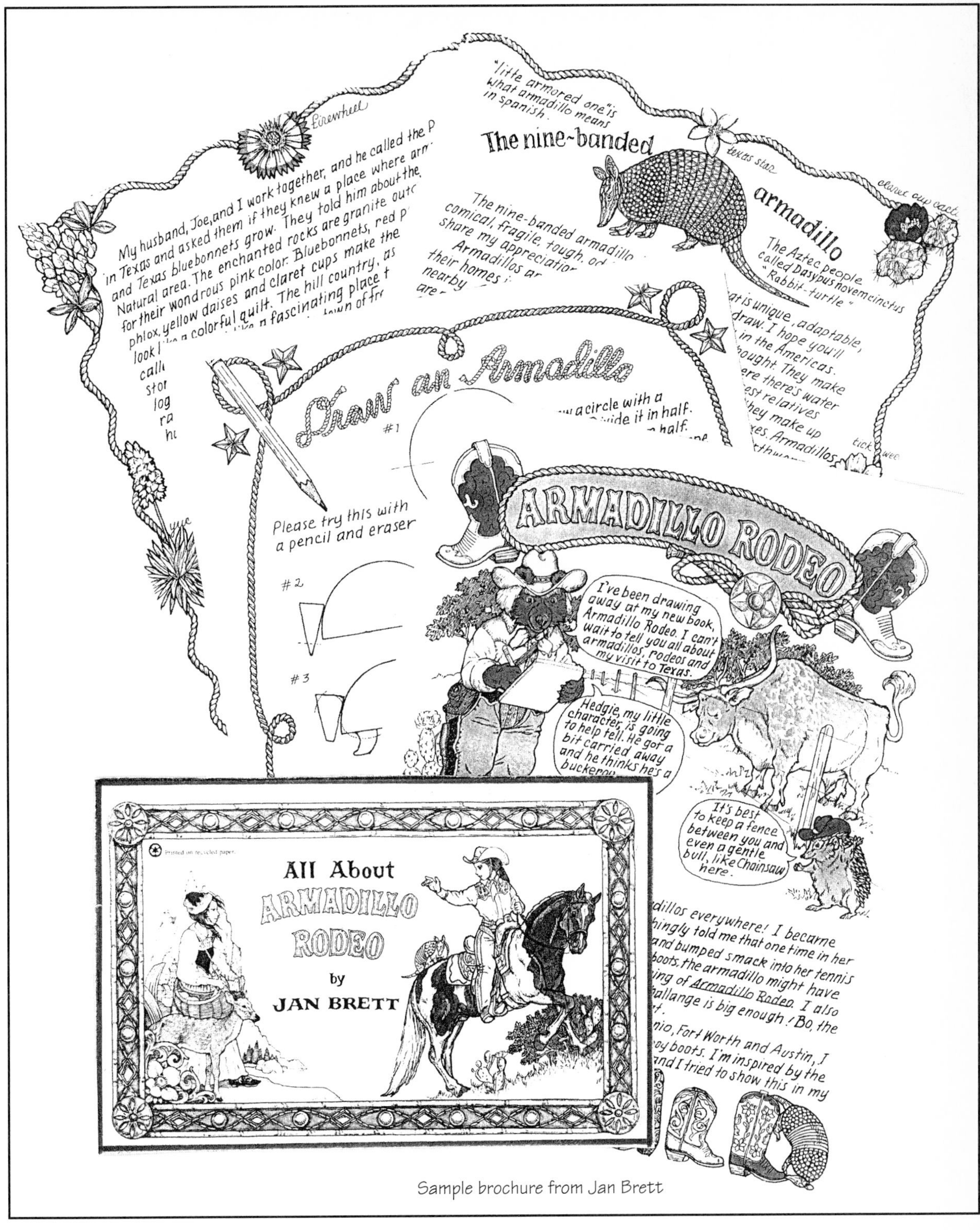

Sample brochure from Jan Brett

Figure 9.16 Sample Bulletin Board

An Author Study of
Jan Brett

Jan Brett decided she wanted to illustrate books when she grew up. As a child she spent many, many hours reading and drawing. Many of Jan Brett's ideas for books come from her childhood memories.

She also travels around the world to research the architecture and costumes that appear in her pictures.

Who is Jan Brett?

K	W	L
"Her books have beautiful edges." Siobhan	"Where does she live?" Jade	-We learned that the bear sneezed!" Jamie
"She's an author." Bradley	"How many books did she write?" Andrea	-She adopted a hedgehog.
"I read one with a white mitten." Lauren	"Does she have any kids?" David	-She lives in MA.
"Yes, and a mouse sneezed and the mitten blew up!" Jon	"How old was she when she wrote her first book?" Jamie	-She travels a lot with her husband.
"I think she made a book about an owl." Joshua	Did she take art lessons? Siobhan	-Many of her ideas come from childhood memories.
	Could she come for a visit?	

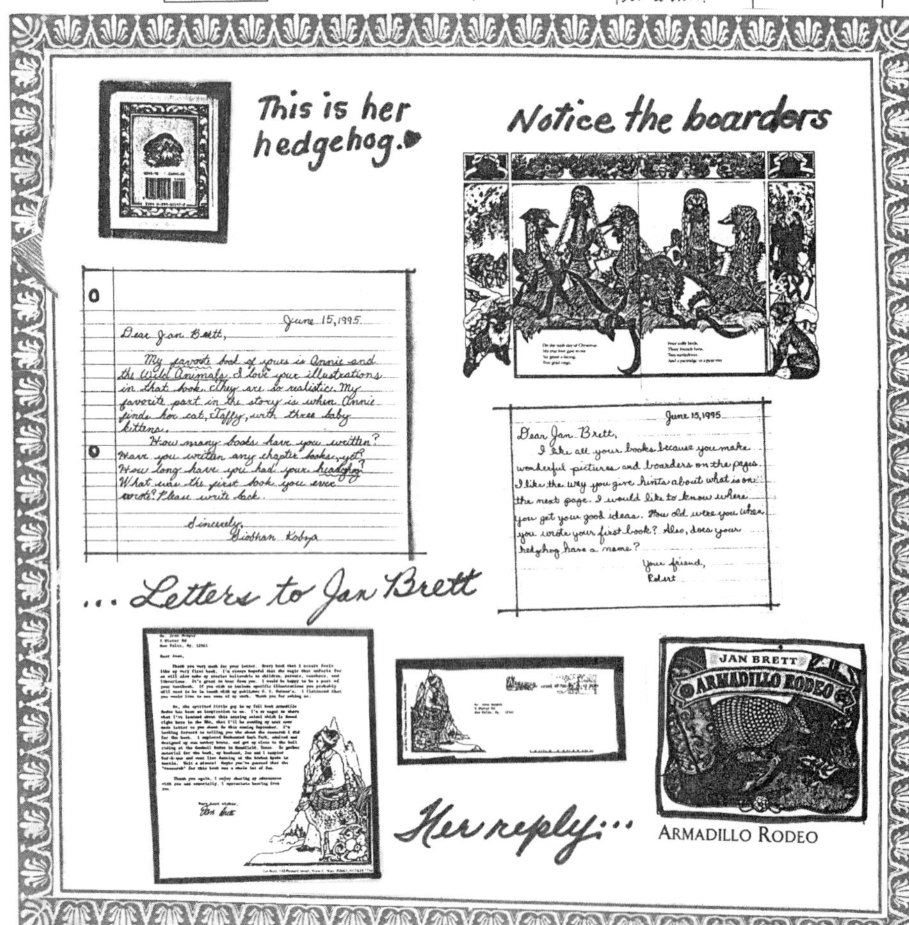

June 15, 1995

Dear Jan Brett,

My favorite book of yours is Annie and the Wild Animals. I love your illustrations in that book. They are so realistic. My favorite part in the story is when Annie finds her cat, Taffy, with three baby kittens.

How many books have you written? Have you written any chapter books, yet? How long have you had your hedgehog? What was the first book you ever wrote? Please write back.

Sincerely,
Siobhan Kobza

June 15, 1995

Dear Jan Brett,

I like all your books because you make wonderful pictures and boarders on the pages. I like the way you give hints about what is on the next page. I would like to know where you get your good ideas. How old were you when you wrote your first book? Also, does your hedgehog have a name?

Your friend,
Robert

FROM THE CLASSROOM OF . . .

Kathy Pike Windham, N.Y.

MY LITTLE FRIEND

Every classroom and all children need a little friend and there's a perfect solution in the *My Little Friend* series created by Evelyn Finnegan, which is published by Little Friend Press in Boston, Massachusetts. My Little Friend is a doll-like creature who snuggles into the pockets of children. As he accompanies his "big friends" to such places as the ballpark and to the dentist, My Little Friend has his own share of adventures.

The possibilities for using My Little Friend are innumerable. First of all, the publisher has created a My Little Friend three-dimensional bookmark and also a sweater which has a secret pocket for housing My Little Friend. The bookmark, itself a doll-like creature, can accompany the students in the classroom to their homes, on field trips, vacations, and sleep-overs. The children can create their own My Little Friends by constructing them out of cardboard or felt. A pocket can be constructed out of cardboard and placed on the outside or on the inside cover of a journal. The journal can record the special memories that My Little Friend gets as a result from his travels with his big friends.

The sweater and My Little Friend that are available from the publisher can become part of the Library Corner. A doll or stuffed animal can wear the sweater and sit with a child as he or she reads the adventures of My Little Friend or any other book of interest. Naturally, new adventures of My Little Friend can be created by the children and made into individual books or compiled into a class big book.

My Little Friend—a class traveler, a springboard for writing, and a new friend to be loved!

haps drawing borders around them in a style similar to hers.

- Music plays an important part in Jan Brett's life, and in her brochures she even suggests pieces that can accompany her books, for example, "Flight of the Bumblebee" for *Berlioz the Bear.* Find appropriate pieces of music for her other books.
- Keep a simulated journal of one of the characters in *Goldilocks and the Three Bears.*
- After enjoying the enchanting illustrations in any of her books, students can create

their own illustrations of a folktale or poem of their choosing. These drawings can be displayed in the classroom, the cafeteria, or in the library. The library corner can be transformed into a Jan Brett Museum at this time.

Culminating Activity

This theme may be concluded in several ways. Students may wish to have a "Meet the Author" afternoon, when someone can role play the author while classmates interview her. Brett can be asked such questions as these:

- How do you come up with ideas for a book?
- What kind of training did you have in order to illustrate in so many different ways?
- What kinds of models do you use for the characters and animals in your books?
- Since you travel so much, what has been your favorite place you have seen? Where do you plan to go next?
- Will the hedgehog appear in any more of your books?
- If you were to pick a favorite book that you wrote or illustrated, which one would you pick?

At this event, which can be an Author's Tea, students can read portions of Brett's books, dramatize one, and share their own literature extension activities.

Instead of a presentation, the students may choose to publish a literary newsletter or magazine, perhaps titled *Author Studies*. A publication can be undertaken for each author studied. Featured in the publication could be biographical information, excerpts from the author's books, book reviews, response log entries, and any other book-sharing activity the class may have undertaken.

Another possibility is to feature the author in a school showcase, which may be placed outside the main office, outside the library, or in the classroom. Many schools have permanent display areas that make excellent vehicles for sharing thematic studies. Again, the author's books, photograph, and the activities the class completed during the study may be displayed.

LITERATURE STUDY

Yet another means of implementing thematic instruction is through the use of a single selection and there are many appropriate titles available which encompass all interest and ability levels. When considering this approach, teachers should be careful not to dissect the book or make curricular connections that are irrelevant. The objective is to use a piece of literature as an enjoyable reading and learning experience so as not to discourage children from discovering the joys of reading. Many titles are worthwhile exploring thematically, for example *Hatchet, The Pinballs, The Lottery Rose,* and *Sadako and the Thousand Paper Cranes.* To illustrate how one piece of literature can be used as a means to implement a theme, one of the Cinderella stories, *The Egyptian Cinderella,* was chosen. See Figure 9.17 for a semantic map for *The Egyptian Cinderella.*

The Egyptian Cinderella
by Shirley Climo
Thomas Y. Crowell, 1989

Story Summary

In this version of Cinderella, set in Egypt in the sixth century B.C., Rhodophis, a slave girl, is chosen by the pharaoh to be his queen.

Prereading Activities

There are several possibilities for introducing this literature study. The word *Cinderella* could be placed on the board or on an overhead, and the students could respond to it, telling what they know about Cinderella, or they could do a written or oral retelling of a familiar version of the tale. If the book is already part of a study of the theme of Cinderella, they could then predict what an Egyptian version might be like. Egypt could be located on the map, and information known about the country could be brainstormed and listed on a chart.

To help in the prediction of the story, key words from the story could be given to the students as an aid in constructing the story. For example:

Egypt	slave	servants	animals
master	riverbank	slippers	pharaoh
feast	dirty clothes	falcon	talons
queen	search	barge	reeds

Figure 9.17

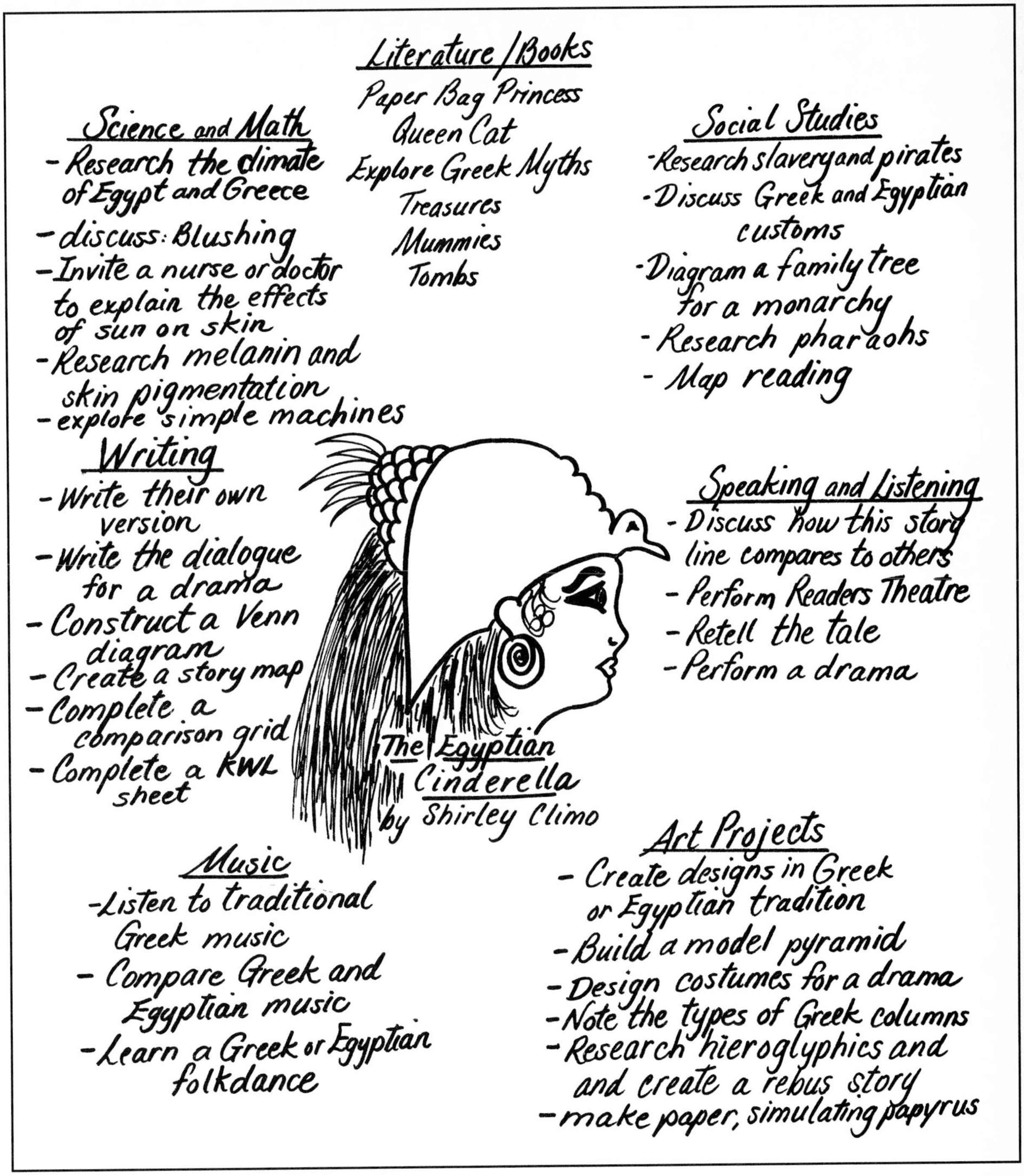

Literature / Books
Paper Bag Princess
Queen Cat
Explore Greek Myths
Treasures
Mummies
Tombs

Science and Math
- Research the climate of Egypt and Greece
- discuss: Blushing
- Invite a nurse or doctor to explain the effects of sun on skin
- Research melanin and skin pigmentation
- explore simple machines

Social Studies
- Research slavery and pirates
- Discuss Greek and Egyptian customs
- Diagram a family tree for a monarchy
- Research pharaohs
- Map reading

Writing
- Write their own version
- Write the dialogue for a drama
- Construct a Venn diagram
- Create a story map
- Complete a comparison grid
- Complete a KWL sheet

Speaking and Listening
- Discuss how this story line compares to others
- Perform Readers Theatre
- Retell the tale
- Perform a drama

The Egyptian Cinderella
by Shirley Climo

Music
- Listen to traditional Greek music
- Compare Greek and Egyptian music
- Learn a Greek or Egyptian folkdance

Art Projects
- Create designs in Greek or Egyptian tradition
- Build a model pyramid
- Design costumes for a drama
- Note the types of Greek columns
- Research hieroglyphics and and create a rebus story
- make paper, simulating papyrus

The students could then write or retell their own version of *The Egyptian Cinderella.*

The students could also generate questions prior to the reading of the book. For example, they might want to know about any magic that might occur in the story or whether the Nile River or pyramids might be featured. They might wonder about the test that will be given to the Cinderella character to prove she is worthy of becoming the queen. Of course, they will want to note the similarities and differences of this version to the one they are most familiar with.

Teachers might also construct an anticipation/reaction guide for the book. Anticipation/reaction guides alert the reader to some of the major concepts and ideas in the book before it is to be read. They are also helpful in determining the extent of the students' prior knowledge about a topic to be addressed in a piece of text. For *The Egyptian Cinderella,* the students might respond to the following statements. Their task is to fill in the Before column with a "yes" or a "no" prior to reading the book. On finishing the book, they would revisit the statements, again indicating their agreement or disagreement.

The Egyptian Cinderella

Before	After	
______	______	1. The Egyptian Cinderella would have mean stepsisters.
______	______	2. She would lose one precious slipper at a ball or festival.
______	______	3. A search would be made for the owner of a slipper.
______	______	4. The Egyptian Cinderella would be befriended by animals near the Nile River.
______	______	5. The Pharaoh would fall in love with the Egyptian Cinderella upon seeing her at a festival in his royal court.

Any piece of literature chosen for literature study may be shared in a variety of ways, such as silent reading, guided reading, or reading aloud. The sharing depends on the teacher's objective and the availability of multiple copies. Depending on how the book is to be shared, the students would now listen to or read the story. Their version could be compared with that of the version written by Shirley Climo.

During Reading

During the reading of the book, the students could continue to make and confirm their predictions. They could note the characteristics and qualities in the text that contribute to the Egyptian setting. If they have generated their own questions, they could respond to them orally or in their literature logs.

After Reading

If any of the prereading activities were undertaken, the student responses could be compared with their postreading responses and reactions. Rhodopis, the Egyptian Cinderella, could be compared with other Cinderellas. Is Rhodopis a strong or a passive Cinderella? Is she accepting of her plight in life or does she try to take control of her destiny? Were there any magical elements in the story? How is the pharaoh similar to or different from the princes in the other versions?

At this time, the students' versions of their Egyptian Cinderella stories could be compared, and the students could complete their anticipation/reaction guides. The students could write and respond to some "What if" questions such as:

- What if the hippo hadn't splashed mud on Rhodopis's slippers?
- What if a crocodile had snatched her slipper instead of the falcon?
- What if her master hadn't given her dancing slippers?
- What if Rhodopis had a fairy godmother?
- What if the pharaoh hadn't seen Rhodopis hiding in the rushes? How else could he have found her?

Other postreading activities could include:

- researching Egypt, its culture, traditions, climate
- investigating Egyptian gods and the role they played in the daily lives of the people
- comparing Egyptian and Greek gods

- exploring simple machines, for example, the lever, inclined plane, and the pulley, and the roles they played in Egyptian life
- comparing this version of Cinderella with other versions
- constructing Venn diagrams, semantic feature analysis grids, or comparison/contrast charts to compare different versions of Cinderella
- rewriting *The Egyptian Cinderella* using some hieroglyphics instead of traditional print. The children could consult the book *Croco'nile,* which uses hieroglyphics to help tell the story.
- make paper, simulating papyrus
- read other books, both fiction and nonfiction, about Egypt.

A sampling of literature can be found in the bibliography.

Culminating Activity

The culmination of this literature study could revolve around a Cinderella theme in general or around this particular version of the story. A Cinderella museum could be constructed, with the students acting as the museum curators. Guests could be invited to the opening of the Cinderella exhibit. Or if the book was not part of a general study, an Egyptian exhibit could be featured instead. The children could be responsible for setting up an environment that represents Egyptian life and display the many projects that resulted from the study. Invitations could be written on papyrus like paper, using some hieroglyphics to create authenticity. The students could dress up in Egyptian costumes and listen to some Mid-Eastern music. If many Cinderella versions were studied, the students could come as their favorite Cinderellalike character (male or female).

Literature studies can be very enjoyable, educational experiences. It is hoped that this example will serve as an inspiration. Naturally there are many ways to approach a literature study. Rather than having the book shared as a read-aloud, the children can read the book themselves, alone, or with a friend and can respond in literature logs. Other activities can vary as well, depending on the students' interests and the resources available.

After a unit has been completed, both the teacher and the students need to evaluate the theme. Teachers need to consider whether their curricular objectives were fulfilled, the activities were meaningful, and the students were able to connect the new learning to their personal lives and what future changes and adaptations need to be made. Students can evaluate themes by noting what they learned, the most enjoyable activities, areas that caused them difficulty, and how they worked, whether alone or in a cooperative group. A sample student evaluation form is shown in Figure 9.18.

SUMMARY

The focus of this chapter was integrating the curriculum through thematic instruction. Themes offer teachers efficient ways of organizing the language arts curriculum and integrating other disciplines with language arts instruction. Moreover, "themes represent a fundamentally different way of approaching the elementary curriculum in which enlarging children's knowledge of their world is the primary aim, with the development of literacy and other skills subsumed within the content" (Walmsley, 1994, 10–11). Through themes, students increase their knowledge of the world by becoming involved in meaningful projects on topics that are both challenging and interesting. Skills and strategies are learned as they are needed in the thematic explorations and investigations, not as separate or isolated subjects.

This chapter presented a rationale for using themes and ideas and suggestions for implementing a thematic approach. To help with thematic instruction, a review of the process of planning and implementing themes is provided in Figure 9.19. Several types of themes were included: a cross-curricular study of "Children Around the World," an in-depth study of a single folktale (Cinderella), an author study (Jan Brett), and a theme evolving from a single piece of literature (*The Egyptian Cinderella*). Themes are intended to be vehicles for integrating the curriculum and fulfilling the objectives of the

Figure 9.18

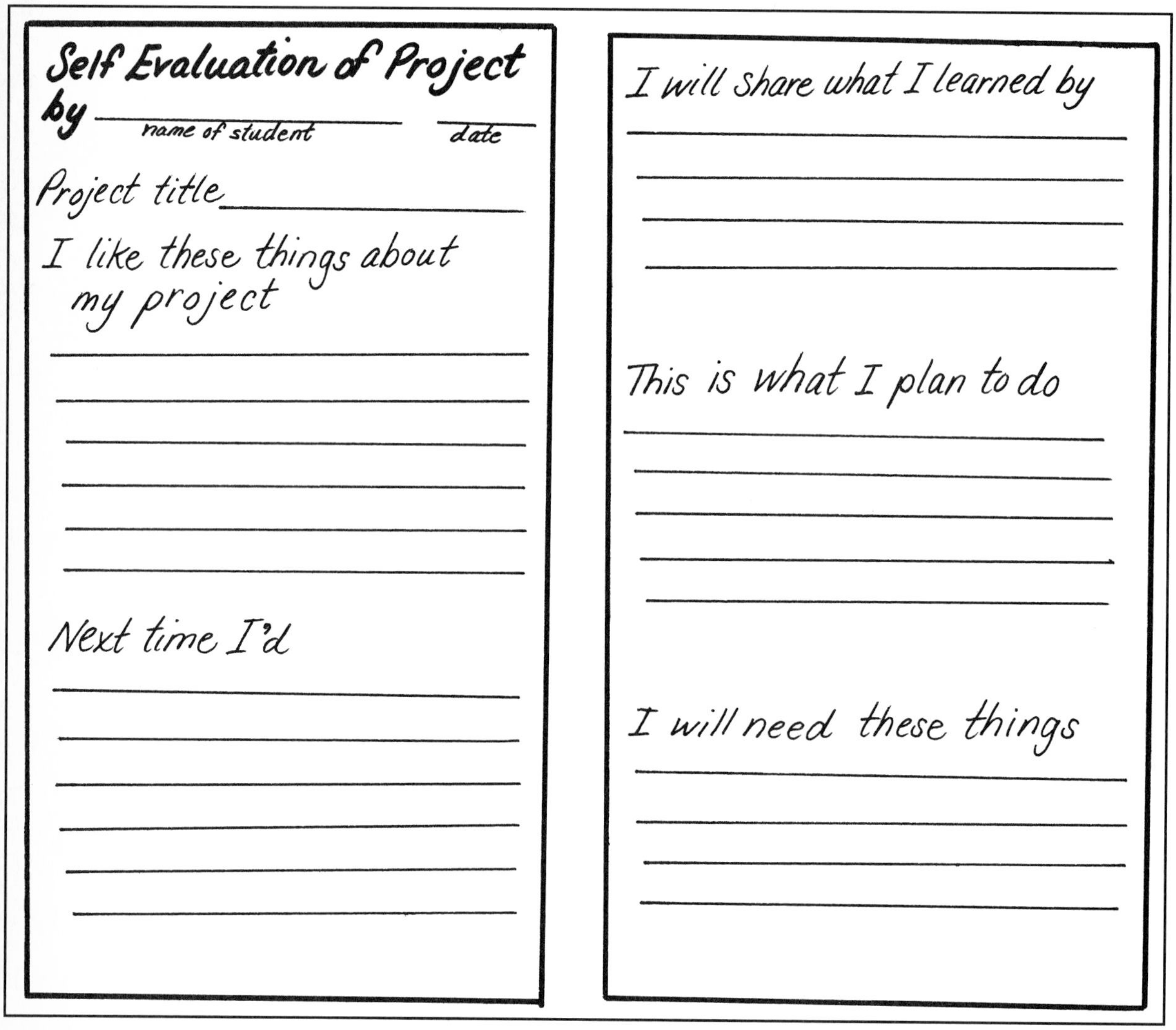

Self Evaluation of Project
by ______________ ______
name of student date

Project title ______________

I like these things about my project

Next time I'd

I will share what I learned by

This is what I plan to do

I will need these things

instructional program. Whereas we presented many interesting and creative extension activities and projects, the focus should not be on the creation of these projects, but rather on their meaningfulness and relevance to the curriculum and to the literature being used.

Children learn best when they are actively involved in their learning. Thematic instruction provides teachers and students with opportunities to integrate learning, explore a topic, and engage in authentic language arts activities at the same time. All the activities undertaken during thematic instruction must help children connect their learning with their own worlds. In addition, themes help teachers organize and manage their curriculum while allowing children to learn at their own pace—individually, in cooperative groups, or as an entire class. Another compelling reason for incorporating themes into the instructional program is the enjoyment that both teachers and children derive from thematic studies. Hopefully this chapter provided enough information and inspiration to motivate you to attempt themes as yet another way to help children make *New Connections* to literacy.

Figure 9.19 Steps in Designing and Developing a Thematic Unit

I. SELECTING A THEME
   A. Consider the needs and interests of your students.
   B. Consider your curricular goals and objectives.
   C. Look at the syllabi in the content areas (science, social studies) for thematic possibilities.
   D. Look at other areas of the curriculum that can be developed thematically (self-esteem programs, thematically arranged stories in basal readers, environmental awareness, holidays).
   E. Undertake an author study (Chris Van Allsburg, Tomie dePaola, Beverly Cleary).
   F. Introduce a unit on a particular fairy tale or folktale, such as "Cinderella" or "Three Little Pigs."
   G. Use a particular genre as the focus of the unit (mystery stories, humorous literature, science fiction).
   H. Choose a unit based on characters in literature, such as grandparents, wolves, or foxes.
   I. Use themes in literature to develop such themes as survival, courage, and memories.
   J. Commercially prepared units are available for adaptation or suggestions.
   K. Don't forget teachable moments.

II. CHOOSING RESOURCES AND DEVELOPING A BIBLIOGRAPHY
   A. Alert others to the unit you are considering to allow them to contribute to the bibliography and resources (students, colleagues, other teachers, friends, librarians, parents).
   B. Check professional journals, books with book lists, promotional materials from publishers, newspaper reviews, and book clubs for possible books.
   C. Read each book and evaluate it: Will the material contribute to the students' knowledge? Does the material match the needs and interests of my students? Does the book have literary value?

III. PLANNING FOR THEMATIC INSTRUCTION
   A. Consider how the books and materials can be connected with the theme and your goals.
   B. Identify the purpose(s) of the books (for reading aloud, independent reading, guided reading, literature circles, springboards for writing or the expressive arts, research).
   C. Plan lessons and activities for the theme, but remember that these should only be a point of departure. Allow students input as the theme develops.
   D. When planning, consider how the other content areas might be incorporated.
   E. Plan a tentative sequence of lessons and activities.

IV. IMPLEMENTING THE UNIT
   A. Prepare students for the theme by using an activity that will activate prior knowledge and will be motivational.
   B. Continue the unit, either throughout the day and across the curriculum or during the designated time for thematic instruction.
   C. Plan a culminating activity with the children that will help celebrate and showcase all that has been learned and enjoyed throughout the experience.
   D. Keep notes on how the theme is progressing, adding new books and activities as needed or introduced.

(continued)

Figure 9.19 Steps in Designing and Developing a Thematic Unit (cont.)

V. EVALUATING THE UNIT
   A. Student evaluation can be done by contract (students and teachers design a list of activities that must be fulfilled for a particular grade), observation (of participation, initiative, group interactions, and completed products and projects), conferencing and self-evaluation.
   B. Evaluate how you would teach the unit in the future.

CHILDREN AROUND THE WORLD

Baer, E. (1990). *This is the way we go to school: A book about children around the world.* New York: Scholastic.

Cheltenham Elementary School Kindergartners. (1991). *We are alike . . . We are all different.* New York: Scholastic.

Choi, S. (1991). *Year of impossible goodbyes.* Boston; Houghton Mifflin.

Cowen-Fletcher, J. (1994). *It takes a village.* New York: Scholastic.

Daly, N. (1985). *Not so fast Songololo.* New York: Puffin Books.

Dooley, N. (1991). *Everybody cooks rice.* Minneapolis: Carolrhoda Books.

Dorros, A. (1992). *This is my house.* New York: Scholastic.

Durrell, G. (1987). *The fantastic flying journey.* New York: Simon & Schuster.

Fernandez, M. (1995). *Rainbow kids.* Miami, Fla.: DDl Books.

Gerberg, M. (1991). *Geographunny: A book of global riddles.* New York: Clarion.

Gray, N. (1988). *A country far away.* New York: Orchard Books.

Grifalconi, A. (1986). *The village of round and square houses.* Boston: Little, Brown and Company.

Haskins, J. (1990). *Count your way through Germany.* Minneapolis: Carolrhoda Books.

Heide, F., & Gilliland, J. (1990). *The day of Ahmed's secret.* New York: Lothrop, Lee, & Shepard.

Heide, F., & Gilliland, J. (1992). *Sami and the time of the troubles.* New York: Clarion.

Hocking, J. (1989). *It's one world.* Victoria, Australia: Five Mile Press.

Hru, D. (1993). *Joshua's Masai mask.* New York: Lee & Low Books.

Joosee, B. (1991). *Mama, do you love me?* New York: Scholastic.

Kendall, R. (1992). *Eskimo boy: Life in an Inuqiaq Eskimo Village.* New York: Scholastic.

Klamath County YMCA Family Preschool. (1993). *The land of many colors.* New York: Scholastic.

Kroll, V. (1992). *Masai and I.* New York: Four Winds Press.

Krupp, R. (1992). *Let's go traveling.* New York: Morrow Junior Books.

Lankford, M. (1992). *Hopscotch around the world.* New York: Morrow.

Lewin, T. (1993). *Amazon boy.* New York: Macmillan.

Morris, A. (1989). *Bread, bread, bread.* New York: A Mulberry Paperback Book.

Morris, A. (1990). *On the go.* New York: Scholastic.

Naidoo, B. (1988). *Journey to Jo'burg.* New York: HarperCollins.

Pellegrini, N. (1991). *Families are different.* New York: Scholastic.

Cinderella Stories

Brown, M. (1954). *Cinderella.* New York: Aladdin Books.

Climo, S. (1989). *The Egyptian Cinderella.* New York: Thomas Y. Crowell.

Climo, S. (1993). *The Korean Cinderella.* New York: HarperCollins.

Cohlene, T. (1990). *Little Firefly: An Algonquian legend.* Mahwah, N.J: Watermill Press.

Cole, B. (1986). *Princess Smartypants.* New York: G. P. Putnam's Sons.

Cole, B. (1987). *Prince Cinders.* New York: G. P. Putnam's Sons.

Compton, J. (1994). *Ashpet: An Appalachian tale.* New York: Holiday House.

Cox, M. (1893). *Cinderella. Three hundred and forty-five variants of Cinderella, Catskin, and Cap o'Rushes, abstracted and tabulated.* London: David Nutt.

Delamare, D. (1993). *Cinderella.* New York: Simon & Schuster.

Disney, W. (1987). *Cinderella.* New York: Scholastic.

Edens, C. (1991). *The three princesses—Cinderella, Sleeping Beauty, and Snow White.* New York: Atheneum.

Edwards, H. (1992). *Computerella.* Crystal Lake, Ill.: Rigby Education.

Ehrlich, A. (1985). *Cinderella.* New York: Dial.

Elwell, P. (1988). *Cinderella.* Chicago: A Calico Book.

Evans, C. (1972). *Cinderella.* London: Chancellor Press.

Galdone, P. (1978). *Cinderella.* New York: McGraw-Hill.
Granowsky, A. (1993). *Cinderella: A classic tale* and *That awful Cinderella.* Austin, Texas: Steck-Vaughn Point of View Series.
Goode, D. (1988). *Cinderella.* New York: Alfred A. Knopf.
Hooks, W. (1987). *Moss gown.* Boston: Houghton Mifflin.
Huck, C. (1989). *Princess Furball.* New York: Greenwillow Books.
Jacobs, J. (1989). *Tattercoats.* New York: G. P. Putnam's Sons.
Karlin, B. (1989). *Cinderella.* New York: Trumpet.
Jackson, E. (1994). *Cinder-Edna.* New York: Lothrop.
Louie, Ai-Long. (1982). *Yeh-Shen: A Cinderella story from China.* New York: Philomel.
Martin, R., & Shannon, D. (1992). *The rough-face girl.* New York: G. P. Putnam's Sons.
McKissack, P., & McKissack, F. (1985). *Cinderella.* Chicago: Children's Press.
Mehta, L. (1985). *The enchanted anklet.* Toronto, Canada: Lilmur Publishing.
Melmed, L. (1994). *Prince Nautilus.* New York: Lothrop, Lee & Shepard.
Minters, F. (1994). *Cinder-Elly.* New York: Viking.
Myers, B. (1985). *Sidney Rella and the glass sneaker.* New York: Macmillan.
Onyefulu, O. (1994). *Chinye.* New York: Viking.
Perlman, J. (1992). *Cinderella penguin.* New York: Puffin Books.
Perrault, C. (1985). *Cinderella.* New York: Dial Books for Young Readers.
San Jose, C., & Santini, D. (1994). *Cinderella.* Honesdale, Pennsylvania: Boyds Mills Press.
San Souci, R. (1989). *The talking eggs.* New York: Dial Books for Young Readers.
San Souci, R. (1994). *Sootface.* New York: Doubleday.
Shorto, R. (1990). *Cinderella* and *Cinderella: The untold story.* New York: Carol Publishing Company.
Sierra, J. (1992). *Cinderella.* Phoenix, Arizona: The Oryx Press.
Steptoe, J. (1987). *Mufaro's beautiful daughters: An African tale.* New York: Lothrop, Lee & Shepard.
Winthrop, E. (1991). *Vasilissa the beautiful.* New York: HarperCollins.
Wright, K. (1994). *Tigerella.* New York: Scholastic.
Yorinks, A. (1990). *Ugh.* New York: Farrar, Straus, & Giroux.

Egyptian Literature

Aliki. (1979). *Mummies made in Egypt.* New York: HarperCollins.
dePaola, T. (1987). *Bill and Pete go down the Nile.* New York: Putnam.
Der Manuelian, P. (1993). *Hieroglyphs from A to Z.* New York: Rizzoli.
Gerrard, R. (1994). *Croco'nile.* New York: Farrar, Straus, & Giroux.
Harris, G. (1992). *Gods and Pharaohs from Egyptian mythology.* New York: Peter Bedrick.
Hart, G. (1994). *Tales from Ancient Egypt.* Washington, D.C.: AMIDEAST.
Heide, F., & Gilliland, J. (1990). *The day of Ahmed's Secret.* New York: Lothrop.
Johnson.Davies, D. (1993). *Folk tales of Egypt.* Washington, D.C.: AMIDEAST.
Macaulay, D. (1975). *Pyramid.* Boston: Houghton Mifflin.
Morley, J. (1991). *An Egyptian pyramid.* New York: Peter Bedrick.
Sabuda, R. (1994). *Tutankhamen's Gift.* New York: Atheneum.
Snyder, Z. (1967). *The Egypt game.* New York: Atheneum.
Stokes, W., & Stokes, W. (1980). *Messages on stone.* Salt Lake City: Starstone.
Stolz, M. (1978). *The cat in the mirror.* New York: Dell.
Walsh, J. (1995). *Pepi and the secret names.* New York: Lothrop.

BIBLIOGRAPHY AND SUGGESTED REFERENCES

Baskwill, J., & Whitman, P. (1986). *Whole language sourcebook.* Richmond Hill, Ontario, Canada: Scholastic-TAB Publications.
Baskwill, J., & Whitman, P. (1988). *Moving on: Whole language sourcebook.* Richmond Hill, Ontario, Canada: Scholastic-TAB Publications.
Bettelheim, B. (1975). *The uses of enchantment: The meaning and importance of fairy tales.* New York: Knopf.
Carpenter, M.; Mumper, J.; & Pike, K. (1994). *Children around the world.* Kingston, N.Y.: Twenty-first Century Education, Inc.
Cullinan, B., & Galda, L. (1994). *Literature and the child.* Orlando, Fla.: Harcourt Brace.
Diakiw, J. (1990). Children's literature and global education: Understanding the developing world. *The Reading Teacher, 43,* 296–301.
Gamberg, R.; Kwak, W.; Hutchings, M.; & Altheim, J.; with Edwards, G. (1988). *Learning and loving it: Theme studies in the classroom.* Portsmouth, N.H.: Heinemann.
Heimlich, J., & Pittelman, S. (1986). *Semantic mapping: Classroom applications.* Newark, Del.: International Reading Association.

Katz, L., & Chard, S. (1989). *Engaging children's minds: The project approach.* Norwood, N.J.: Ablex Publishing Company.

Kobrin, B. (1988). *Eyeopeners—How to choose and use children's books about real people, places, and things.* New York: Penguin.

Kostelnik, M.; Howe, D.; Payne, K.; Rohde, B.; Spalding, G.; Stein, L.; & Whitbeck, D. (1991). *Teaching young children using themes.* Glenview, Ill.: Good Year Books.

Lipson, M.; Valencia, S.; Wixson, K.; & Peters, C. (1993). Integration and thematic teaching: Integration to improve teaching and learning. *Language Arts, 70,* 252–263.

McCarthy, D. (1993). Travelmates: Geography for kids (and stuffed pets). *Teaching K–8, 24,* 32–35.

McElmeel, S. (1990). *An author a month (for pennies).* Englewood, Colo.: Teacher Ideas Press.

McElmeel, S. (1991). *An author a month (for nickels).* Englewood, Colo.: Teacher Ideas Press.

McElmeel, S. (1993). *An author a month (for dimes).* Englewood, Colo.: Teacher Ideas Press.

Meinbach, A.; Rothlein, L.; & Fredericks, A. (1995). *The complete guide to thematic units: Creating the integrated curriculum.* Norwood, Mass.: Christoper-Gordon Publishers.

Moss, J. (1984). *Focus units in literature: A handbook for elementary school teachers.* Urbana, Ill.: National Council of Teachers of English.

Moss, J. (1990). *Focus on literature: A context for literacy learning.* Katonah, N.Y.: Richard C. Owen Publishers.

Moss, J. (1994). *Using literature in the middle grades: A thematic approach.* Norwood, Mass.: Christopher-Gordon Publishers.

Norby, S., & Ryan, G. (1988). *Famous children's authors.* Minneapolis: T. S. Denison and Co.

Pappas, C.; Keifer, B.; & Levstik, L. (1990). *An integrated language perspective in the elementary school: Theory into action.* New York: Longman.

Pike, K. (1991). A fantastic flying journey-through literature. *Language Arts, 68,* 568–576.

Pike, K.; Carpenter, M.; & Mumper, J. (1995). *Building early understanding: Communities around the world.* Lake Katrine, N.Y.: Twenty-first Century Education, Inc.

Routman, R. (1991). *Invitations: Changing as teachers and learners K–12.* Portsmouth, N.H.: Heinemann.

Sierra, J. (1992). *The Oryx multicultural folktale series: Cinderella.* Phoenix: The Oryx Press.

Sims Bishop, R. (1992). Multicultural literature for children: Making informed choices. In V. Harris (Ed.), *Teaching multicultural literature in grades K–8,* p. 41. Norwood, Mass.: Christopher-Gordon.

Thompson, G. (1991). *Teaching through themes.* New York: Scholastic.

Trelease, J. (1989). *The new read-aloud handbook.* New York: Penguin.

Walmsley, S., & Walp, T. (1990). Integrating literature and composing into the language arts curriculum: Philosophy and practice. *The Elementary School Journal, 90,* 251–274.

Walmsley, S. (1994). *Children exploring their world.* Portsmouth, N.H.: Heinemann.

Wartenberg, A. (1995). Using fairy tales with older children. *Reading Today, 12,* 26.

Worthy, M., & Bloodgood, J. (1992-1993). Enhancing reading instruction through Cinderella tales. *The Reading Teacher, 46,* 290–301.

CHILDREN'S LITERATURE CITED

Brett, J. (1981). *Fritz and the beautiful horses.* Boston: Houghton Mifflin.

Brett, J. (1985). *Annie and the wild animals.* Boston: Houghton Mifflin.

Brett, J. (1987). *Goldilocks and the three bears.* New York: G. P. Putnam's Sons.

Brett, J. (1988). *The first dog.* Orlando: Harcourt Brace Jovanovich.

Brett, J. (1989). *The mitten.* New York: G. P. Putnam's Sons.

Brett, J. (1990). *The wild Christmas reindeer.* New York: G. P. Putnam's Sons.

Brett, J. (1991). *Berlioz the bear.* New York: G. P. Putnam's Sons.

Brett, J. (1991). *The owl and the pussycat.* New York: G. P. Putnam's Sons.

Brett, J. (1992). *Trouble with trolls.* New York: G. P. Putnam's Sons.

Brett, J. (1993). *Christmas trolls.* New York: G. P. Putnam's Sons.

Brett, J. (1994). *Town mouse, country mouse.* New York: G. P. Putnam's Sons.

Byars, B. (1977). *The pinballs.* New York: Scholastic.

Cowley, J. (1989). *Joy Cowley writes.* Brisbane, Australia: Rigby Education.

DePaola, T. (1989). *The art lesson.* New York: G. P. Putnam's Sons.

Friedman, I. (1984). *How my parents learned to eat.* Boston: Houghton Mifflin.

Hunt, I. (1976). *The lottery rose.* New York: Berkley Books.

Lester, A. (1989). *Imagine.* New South Wales, Australia: Allen & Unwin Pty Ltd.

Paulsen, G. (1987). *Hatchet.* New York: Puffin Books.

10 EXPRESSIVE/CREATIVE ARTS IN READING AND THE OTHER LANGUAGE ARTS

Ten Black Dots
Hiding in the Rain Forest

1 dot can make Jennie's hummingbird flying in the sun
or the eye of Colby's iguana when day is done.
2 dots can make the feet of Mike's frog
or Dana Lee's spider monkey by a log.
3 dots can make Jesse's jaguar's face
or Shawn's iguana waiting for a race.
4 dots can make seeds from Jordan's rafflesia flower grow
or the feathers on Andrew V.'s toucan glow.
5 dots can make Mike's termite run
or Patrick's harpy eagle looking to have fun.
6 dots can make Joe's pitcher plant in pink
or Jordan's butterfly searching for nectar to drink.
7 dots can make Dana's rosy periwinkle bloom
or give Andrew P.'s jaguar lots of room.
8 dots can make Dana Lee's forest fish
or Patrick's ocelot as wild as he could wish.
9 dots can make Vanessa's Honduran milk snake slither
or Elisa's lichen on a tree by the great river.
10 dots can make Taylor's tiger growl
or Ari's frog on the prowl.
Count them. Are there really ten?
Now we can begin again, counting dots from one to ten.

by the Second Graders in Mrs. Constantinides' Class
Windham, N.Y.

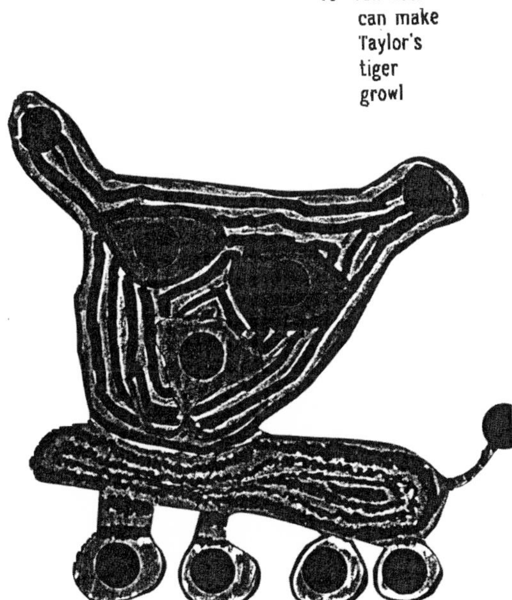

10 Ten dots
can make
Taylor's
tiger
growl

Inspired by *Ten Black Dots* by Donald Crews.

OVERVIEW

By responding to literature in a variety of ways, students deepen and extend their interpretations of what they read. Involving learners in response activities permits readers to savor literature and gives them time for application and reflection. Responding to literature should involve both verbal and nonverbal activities. This chapter presents the many possibilities for involving the expressive and creative arts in the literacy program. Explored are literature response activities using writing, art, music, cooking, drama, and puppetry. Various ways of making and sharing books are offered. In addition, the use of oral language in the literacy program is explained by bringing Readers' Theater and storytelling into the classroom. Participation in the expressive arts stimulates creative thinking, fosters the exploration and expression of personal interpretation, and helps develop a sense of satisfaction and self-worth.

Questions to Ponder

1. What contributions can art, music, and drama make to a literacy program?
2. What types of book sharing and publishing activities are possible in the classroom?
3. How can teachers facilitate the development of oral language?
4. How can oral reading be used purposefully in the reading program?
5. In what ways can storytelling be used throughout the curriculum?

LITERATURE RESPONSE ACTIVITIES

As mentioned in Chapter 9, responding to literature is an integral part of the balanced reading program and is a way writing may be used purposefully as well. Although at times teachers and students may wish to share books only through discussion and dialogue, frequently they want to pursue additional activities. Extending literature through writing, art, music, cooking, drama, and puppetry allows students to return to the text many times for enjoyment as well as for additional information. For young children, revisiting the text builds sight vocabulary, reading fluency, and background knowledge. For more experienced readers, reinspection of the text reveals additional insights and appreciation of the author's craft. By extending who was learned from or appreciated in the literature, children are given additional time to enjoy the books, to reflect on the author's message, or to make personal connections with the literature. Students need the time and opportunity to respond to literature in a variety of ways throughout the school year. Literature response activities using writing, art, music, cooking, drama, and puppetry are presented here along with resources that may be used for additional information and inspiration.

Teachers should be acquainted with various methods and activities to extend students' responses to literature. These response activities should foster students' imagination and creativity as well as promote understanding. Responses to literature may take many forms. It is important to remember that we are providing a menu of creative possibilities, not recipes to be followed verbatim. The type of literary response should be appealing to the children and depends to a large extent on their interests, creative abilities, and developing talents. Since responding to literature should be individual, no two responses should be exactly alike. We will now discuss how teachers and their children make *New Connections* by using literature creatively.

Sharing Literature Through Writing

The use of writing to share books is discussed in Chapters 5, 6, and 7. Literature selections can serve as models for future writing efforts. Books with repetitive patterns can motivate students to create adaptations on the book or write additional verses or events. Excellent books for this purpose include *Brown Bear, Brown Bear, What Do You See?* and *If You Give a Mouse a Cookie.* The authors of these books have themselves written other versions: *Polar Bear, Polar Bear, What Do You Hear?* and *If You Give a Moose a Muffin.* Books with certain themes, examples of specific uses of author's craft, and books using interesting and unusual techniques frequently serve as models for student writing. To illustrate, some authors have incorporated writing itself into the fabric of the story as the characters use writing (letters, journals, diaries) to tell or help tell the story. Students can read these and write original stories using the writing technique inspired by the author. The following are examples of books that use writing in such a manner:

LETTER WRITING
Sarah Plain and Tall
Your Best Friend, Kate
Taking Jason to Grandma's
Arthur's Pen Pal
The Jolly Postman
The Jolly Christmas Postman
The Postcard Pest
Letters from Rifka

DIARY OR JOURNAL WRITING
My Side of the Mountain
Harriet the Spy
Dear Mr. Henshaw
The Diary of a Church Mouse
The Diary of Neil Aitken
Antarctic Diary
Only Opal: The Diary of a Young Girl
Mostly Michael
Nettie's Trip South
My Prairie Year
So Much to Tell You
An Owl in the House: A Naturalist's Diary

Books written from the character's point of view can offer insights and inspiration into students' writing from particular perspectives. Books that can serve as models include *Ben and Me, Mr. Revere and I,* and *The True Story of the Three Little Pigs*.

A sampling of writing activities includes:

1. **Letter writing.** Students can write letters to authors, to classmates about the book, or from one book character to another.

2. **Newspaper reporting.** Using a newspaper format is an interesting way to share books. Headlines may be written, a character might write to "Dear Abby," an event from the book might be written for a certain section of the newspaper, author interviews may be conducted, and so on. For example, the marriage of Mistress Mouse to Frog in *Frog Went A-courtin'* might appear on the society page, or Sarah in *Sarah Plain and Tall* might describe her journey from New England to the Midwest in a travel column. A "Dear Abby" letter might be written by Peter, the older brother in Judy Blume's *Tales of a Fourth Grade Nothing, Superfudge,* and *Fudge-A-Mania.*

> Dear Abby,
>
> My problem is my brother Fudge. First he pretends he is a bird and tries to fly and breaks his teeth. Now he has swallowed my pet turtle Dribble. What can I do?
>
> Your friend,
> Peter
>
> Dear Peter,
>
> Be patient. It'll all come out in the end.
>
> Abby

3. **Alphabetical book reports.** These can be written with an activity or events from the book told in alphabetical form. Information books can also be written using the ABC format (e.g., *The Ocean Alphabet Book* or *The Icky Bug Book*). Appendix B lists alphabet books.

BOOK: *Curious George Rides a Bike*
A accident with his bike
B bike that he got for his birthday
C curious
D did tricks on his bike
E elephant in the show

An example of an alphabet informational book by a first-grade class is provided in "From the Classroom" of Elizabeth Kimiecik.

4. **Personality reports.** This is a version of the alphabetical book report, with the letters from the character's name being used to describe personality traits.

*A*musing
*M*ixed-up
*E*njoyable
*L*ively
*I*diotic
*A*stonishing
*B*ewildered
*E*xcited
*D*izzy
*E*nthusiastic
*L*ikable
*I*nteresting
*A*ppealing

5. **Shaped book reports.** Book summaries or reviews can be written on shapes suggested by the content of the story. For example, bear shapes can house stories dealing with bears, a door can hold the answer to what lurks behind it, as in *There's a Nightmare in My Closet,* or a suitcase can tell the travels of *Ira Sleeps Over* or *Your Best Friend, Kate.* For older readers, an outline of the country where the story took place, of an object that plays a significant role in the story, or of a building where the story occurred can be drawn with information from the story or reactions to the story written inside the outline. For instance, the outline of China may be drawn with the titles of Chinese fairy tales or folktales written inside, and a peach may be the ideal shape to detail James's adventures in *James and the Giant Peach.*

6. **Personality reports.** Several quotations from a book can be selected that are representative of the personality, the attitudes, or the motives of a character in the story. The quotations can be accompanied by an explanation as to why these quotes represent the character. A personality cube may also be constructed for characters in the story.

7. **Silhouette biographies.** Silhouettes may be drawn for story characters, and the character's personality or life may be portrayed inside.

8. **Booked for travel.** The children describe the people, events, climate, dress, and customs of places visited via books. These observations may be recorded on individual passports to good reading.

Sharing Literature Through Art

Art activities for responding to literature can be as extensive as the teachers' and students' creativity and creative energy permit. Having a well-stocked art center can lead to many innovative projects and literature response activities. Materials that should be readily available include construction paper, poster board, paints, crayons, markers, fabric and wallpaper samples, cardboard tubes, egg cartons, pipe cleaners, toothpicks, dowels, plastic meat trays, small boxes of various shapes, buttons, socks, paper plates, and yarn. The possible art forms are numerous and can include collage, painting, murals, dioramas, three-dimensional creations, puppets, bookmaking, origami, drawing, illustrating, photography, mosaics, wall hangings, and so on. Some specific art activities are as follows:

1. **Hung up on books.** Sharing books using ordinary hangers can be an unusual and motivating way to do a literature response activity. Mobiles can be made depicting objects in the book (e.g., the items that the caterpillar eats in *The Very Hungry Caterpillar*) or characters can be created from hangers with a paper-covered hanger serving as the body of the character, a head pasted on the neck of the hanger, and hands extending from the two ends. On the body of the hanger can be descriptions of the character or a significant event in the character's life.

2. **Costume designing.** For historical figures, characters who have unique styles of dress (such as science fiction characters), or characters from other lands and cultures, costumes can be designed and constructed from fabric, yarn, fur, beads, lace, wallpaper, and fringe. Actual dolls, paper dolls, pipe cleaner characters, or clothespin dolls may be used. A humorous variation would be to design clothing for animals. The book *Animals Should Definitely* Not *Wear Clothing* can be read to provide ideas for the students.

3. **Listen and sketch.** Occasionally books can be read aloud while students sketch the scenes or the settings as they listen. *The Judge* is an excellent read-aloud to accompany student illustrations. As the book progresses, hints at what the monster in the story looks like are provided, and only at the end is the actual monster depicted. Students could compare their illustrations with their classmates' and the author's versions.

4. **T-shirts, quilts, and tapestries.** These can be created depicting reading slogans, scenes from the books, or favorite characters. Fabric crayons or liquid embroidery can be used as well as actual stitchery.

5. **Literary maps.** Maps may take many forms and may feature such things as book characters the world over, animals in books and where they live, and biography maps.

6. **Lifelines.** A lifeline can be drawn for a character showing the important events in his

FROM THE CLASSROOM OF . . .

Elizabeth Kimiecik Warwick, New York

A SCIENCE ALPHABET BOOK

When Elizabeth's first-grade class was studying about the earth, the culminating experience became a class book on the earth. Each of the children chose a letter of the alphabet from an envelope. Science and library books were also available as references for children. Below are some of the entries, with the students' invented spellings intact. The conventional spellings follow.

A

A is for air. Air is all uround the earth. And air hupps us breeth and if we did not have air we would die. (A is for air. Air is all around the earth. And air helps us breathe and if we did not have air we would die.)

B

B is for brook. A brook is like a strem. The water runs bon fast. Fish live in a brook. You can stap on rooks all the way acast. (B is for brook. A brook is like a stream. The water runs by fast. Fish live in a brook. You can step on rocks all the way across.)

C

C is for cave. A cave is made of rack. Suam bears hiebrnanaet in the cave. A cave is deaek. You can naet see in it. (C is for cave. A cave is made of rock. Some bears hibernate in the cave. A cave is dark. You cannot see in it.)

D

D is for desert. A desert is a pees of land that go's on an on. A desert is made of nuthing but sand. A desert is veri dry becas it is very hot thar. A cautus lives in the desert. (D is for desert. A desert is a piece of land that goes on and on. A desert is made of nothing but sand. A desert is very dry because it is very hot there. A cactus lives in the desert.)

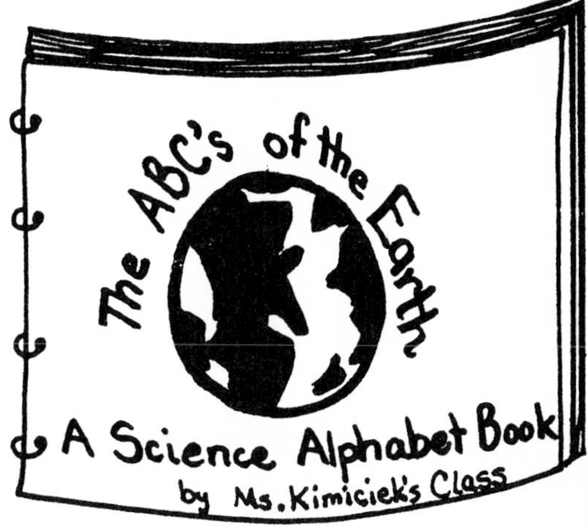

L

L is for lava. Lava is from volcanos. Lava is very very hot. Lava is so strog. So strog it will wipe your house cler awaye. When lava gets hard it becums land. (L is for lava. Lava is from volcanos. Lava is very very hot. Lava is so strong. So strong it will wipe your house clear away. When lava gets hard it becomes land.)

Y

Y is for you. You are erportin to the world. You take good care of the earth. You make the earth purfict and buodefel. You help take care of the earth. (Y is for you. You are important to the world. You take care of the earth. You make the earth perfect and beautiful. You help take care of the earth.)

or her life. Rolls of adding machine paper are excellent for this purpose.

7. **Box bottom movies.** Movies can be constructed using the bottom of a box, paper clips, and magnets. Story characters are drawn and paper clips pasted onto their backs. The characters are then placed on the upper side of a box bottom and moved by a magnet held underneath the box.

8. **Flip movies.** A series of scenes from a story are bound together and then thumbed through quickly to simulate action.

Sharing Literature Through Music

The joy of learning to read and write can be extended through music. Music is, in fact, a form of language—a medium for personal expression and communication. When children hear and repeat chants and songs over and over, they are internalizing the concepts that are basic to literacy development. Through music, children move from the familiarity and comfortable patterns of speech to the language used in books. Music should not be reserved only for a 30-minute pullout time slot with a music specialist. Classroom teachers should work hand-in-hand with music teachers, not only to explore and enjoy music in its own right, but also to use music as a means to enhance reading and writing. Teachers should also incorporate music whenever possible into the regular classroom program. Students can learn songs, meet the lyrics in print, write original lyrics, practice using some of the concepts of print (e.g., one-to-one correspondence), learn vocabulary, and enjoy music for the expressive, emotional qualities it can release. Even if teachers are not particularly musical, many resources are available for classroom use. The following are some activities that can work for sharing literature through music or using music to extend and enrich the curriculum:

1. **Meeting lyrics in print.** When children learn the words to music, frequently they do not see the words in print. The easiest language for children to learn to read is the language with which they have some familiarity. Therefore reading words with musical accompaniment is an aid to building sight word recognition while participating in an enjoyable reading-musical experience. The words of songs can be printed on charts or on large pieces of cardboard to be filed in a box of songs available for independent reading (Harp and Brewer, 1991).

2. **Musical books.** An abundance of poems and stories have been set to music and published as books (e.g., *Down by the Bay, Over in the Meadow, There Was an Old Woman Who Swallowed a Fly*). Children can listen to both an oral reading of the story and the musical version. Picture songbooks and music resources are listed at the end of this chapter.

3. **Musical accompaniment.** Children can choose music to accompany the reading of stories or poems. For example, during the reading of *Rondo in C,* Beethoven's rendition can be played. For *The Snowy Day,* soft classical music can be chosen to create the feeling of a snowfall.

4. **Music, literature, and art.** Sometimes students can demonstrate understanding and show appreciation of music and literature through art activities. Some possibilities (Harp and Brower, 1991) are:

- drawing or painting a picture of a song
- finger painting the mood the song conveys
- molding clay figures to depict characters in songs
- making puppets to accompany songs
- making posters to advertise musical sharing sessions
- illustrating songs for class books

5. **Songs for patterning.** Many familiar songs can be patterned for different occasions. The children can learn the words of both the original version and their adapted one. Some songs that lend themselves to this activity include "Row, Row, Row Your Boat," "If You're Happy and You Know It," "Old MacDonald," and "Twinkle, Twinkle, Little Star." An example of students' extending "Down by the Bay" is seen in "From the Classroom" by Jean Mumper.

6. **Responding to songs.** Songs can readily be incorporated into the language arts program and can serve as springboards for reading, writing, and expressive arts activities. For example, such songs as "Everything Grows" by Raffi can be extended doing the following activities:

- planting seeds and keeping a journal of their progress

- locating pictures of things that grow and making growing books
- engaging in movement activities, for example, moving as if they were people in the various stages of life from baby to teenager to elderly

7. **Music and the content areas.** A pleasurable way to motivate content area learning is to begin, extend, or enrich a curricular area using music. For instance, if a particular culture or historical period were being studied in social studies, music of that culture or era could be played and enjoyed. Science topics, such as the ocean or flight, also provide opportunities for incorporating music.

8. **Music response journals.** To help children develop an appreciation for all types of music, particularly classical music, children can keep music response journals. They can be invited to respond in written form to music. As they listen to the songs, they should pay attention to the lyrics, the instruments chosen, the rhythms, and the mood that the music conveys. They can jot down any images, feelings, thoughts, or impressions that come to them as they listen. The music might even inspire the writing of poetry, as poetry is a natural way to express feelings and reactions to pieces of music. Initially, teachers can begin with songs that are familiar to the students and then present more unfamiliar music. Younger children can respond using illustrations and later can discuss with their classmates how the music made them feel (Cecil and Lauritzen, 1994).

Music, both through singing of songs and the listening and appreciation of musical pieces, should be an integral part of the lives of children. The integration of music and other curricular areas, especially literacy oriented activities, can unite children's hearts and minds (Cecil and Lauritzen, 1994).

Sharing Literature Through Cooking

Literature can lend itself to cooking experiences. Such books as *Rain Makes Applesauce, The Popcorn Book, The Pancake,* and *Stone Soup* naturally suggest the making of the featured foods. Students can plan menus to accompany *George Washington's Breakfast,* write their own recipes for blueberry creations after they read *Blueberries for Sal,* and compile recipe books from either their own original recipes or recipes collected from parents, grandparents, or other community members. A variety of books for children to savor and use as inspiration for classroom cooking activities are listed at the end of this chapter.

Sharing Literature Through Drama

The development of literacy and the use of drama in the classroom are natural partners. "Drama and reading have in common the creation of meaning from words, the use of language to express language, and the requirement that the participant bring his or her own experience to the material in order to interpret it" (Harp and Brewer, 1991, 452). Drama is a powerful tool for helping children learn. Through drama, children work cooperatively, develop their self-expression and thinking abilities, and foster their creative imaginations (Cecil and Lauritzen, 1994). Drama can be a springboard for many language experiences. "It provides opportunities for children not only to talk as they take on roles in the central dramatic event, but also to read, write, and reflect, individually, in groups, and as a community, as they ponder problems posed by the drama and come to recognize the power of the art form" (Booth, 1994). Its role in the classroom is described in detail in a following section. The many forms of drama provide meaningful contexts in which children can share, extend, and apply what they have learned and enjoyed through literature. Here is a series of dramatic activities that combine reading, writing, literature, and drama:

1. **Living books.** Living books, books that come alive through pantomime and improvisation, can be presented. Students can dress up like book characters and act out events and scenes from the stories.

2. **How-to demonstrations.** If a book is read that teaches its audience how to do or make something, a demonstration showing others how to do it or showing how a character did or made it can be given.

3. **Mirroring.** Mirroring is an excellent activity for developing observation and concentration. After observing themselves in a mirror, two

FROM THE CLASSROOM OF . . .

Jean Mumper Wallkill, New York

Down by the Bay Lyrics and Illustrations

Other verses for *Down by the Bay* written by children include:

— Did you ever see a goat
Riding in a boat?

— Did you ever see a snail
Splashing in a pail?

— Did you ever see a bear
In purple underwear?

— Did you ever see a bug
Sleeping on a rug?

— Did you ever see some trees
Surrounded by fleas?

— Did you ever see a frog
Dancing on a log?

— Did you ever see a worm
Getting a perm?

— Did you ever see a duck
Splashing in the muck?

— Did you ever see a fox
Wearing red socks?

A classroom big book made as an extension activity after learning the song *Down by the Bay* by Raffi.

children face one another. One child acts as a mirror and imitates the other. The player who is the mirror reflects the other child's facial expressions, gestures, and movements (Lundsteen, 1989).

4. **Freeze play.** As children improvise a book and act out the story for their classmates, occasionally the teacher or person designated for the role calls out "Freeze Play" and the actors freeze in position. While the actors are frozen, the audience is asked, "What do you think the characters will do next?" The actors then follow the suggestions, followed by a discussion about whether the suggestions made sense in the context of the story (Thompson, 1988).

5. **Role-playing.** Children may role-play story characters. A script may be written to accompany the role-playing or the students may improvise the dialogue as they perform.

6. **Movement vocabulary.** To encourage physical warm-up, children can compile a list of words to act out. Some of the movements can be done in place (e.g., swaying, rocking, shaking) while others may be done moving from place to place (stalking, slinking, hobbling). Some movements involve leg and foot movements (skipping, kicking, tiptoeing) and others, the arms and hands (digging, clenching, kneading). Still others involve facial movements (chewing, pouting, winking) or demonstrate emotions (shrugging the shoulders to show depression and shaking the fists to show anger) (Lundsteen, 1989).

7. **Mock trials.** A mock trial may be undertaken, especially for suspenseful or mystery stories. Students create the roles of defendants, prosecutors, defense lawyers, the judge, witnesses, and jury. Student reporters can also be on the scene to record the information for the class literary newspaper (Temple and Gillet, 1989).

Other activities for incorporating drama in the instructional program are described in the sections on puppetry, drama, Readers' Theater, and storytelling.

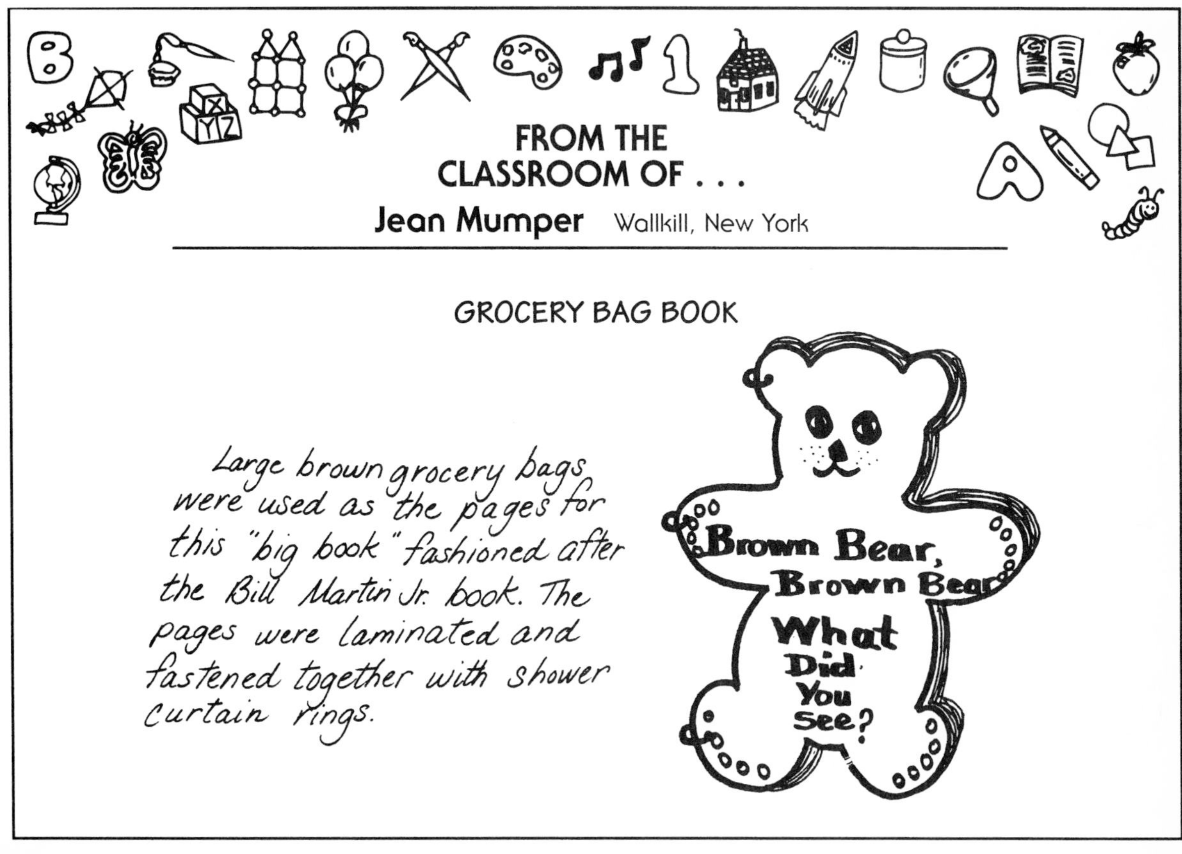

FROM THE
CLASSROOM OF . . .
Jean Mumper Wallkill, New York
GROCERY BAG BOOK
Large brown grocery bags were used as the pages for this "big book" fashioned after the Bill Martin Jr. book. The pages were laminated and fastened together with shower curtain rings.
Brown Bear,
Brown Bear
What
Did
You
See?

Sharing Literature Through Puppetry

Puppetry is a wonderful means of encouraging oral communication and sharing literature. Children enjoy puppetry and frequently use puppets with much pleasure and enthusiasm. However, teachers should ensure that making the puppets does not overshadow their use. Puppets are a means to an end—to enhance growth in oral language and to provide students with opportunities to experiment and create. Classroom energy should be spent on attaining these goals, not on puppet construction.

Puppets are an excellent medium for creative expression. Puppets can be used for dramatic play or in more formal presentations. Not only can children interpret literature through puppets, but they can also act out and express emotions without seeming to be personally responsible. Puppets give shy or self-conscious children chances to contribute and take part in dramatic activities because the puppets, not the children themselves, perform the actions. Children can be hidden by puppet stages or can focus on the actions of the puppets rather than the audience's reactions. The dialogue can be tape-recorded so that children can concentrate on the puppets' movements, not the dialogue.

Puppetry should be considered a performing art, not a craft to be perfected (Temple and Gillet, 1989). However, students can create puppets using a variety of materials, limited only by their imaginations, ability to construct the puppets, and the materials available. Puppets that can be constructed relatively easily in the classroom include:

- stick puppets
- paper bag puppets
- sock puppets
- marionettes
- cylinder puppets
- paper plate puppets
- rod puppets
- hand or finger puppets
- glove or mitten puppets

Figure 10.1 shows a variety of puppet types based on "Little Red Riding Hood." Puppetry books that may prove useful when incorporating puppetry in the classroom are listed at the end of this chapter.

Bookmaking

When responding to books, children may create their own versions of the book, adapt the book, or otherwise re-create the book in an original representation. Bookmaking makes use of children's imaginations and interests and is dependent on the materials available, the time allowed, and the use of the student-authored books themselves. The process of creating books is what should be valued, not the final product. Children's books must reach an audience, whether that audience consists of classmates, parents, or other school community members.

Some possible bookmaking activities with explicit directions for constructing the books are provided in Figure 10.2. These include:

- bag books
- paper plate books
- books using commercial products and environmental print (business cards, cereal boxes, and product wrappers)
- box books
- roll stories

Sources for bookmaking and for extending literature are listed at the end of this chapter.

DRAMA

Because drama tends to be associated with polished performances, many teachers tend to shy away from using drama in the classroom. However, drama is really midway between children's informal play and what is traditionally considered as theater. Young children at play are continually acting out roles, pretending that they are animals, a mommy or daddy, or a firefighter. Using drama in the classroom capitalizes on children's natural interests and ability to pretend. Drama is informal and process oriented, while children's theater is formal and product oriented. Drama is not only appropriate for the classroom, but it also belongs in the classroom.

Drama is both useful and interesting to children. The emphasis is on the growth of students, not on finished products. Drama promotes children's development, teamwork among classmates, problem solving, and communication. The educational, social, and emotional values of drama include the following:

Figure 10.1 Puppet Types for Use with "Little Red Riding Hood"

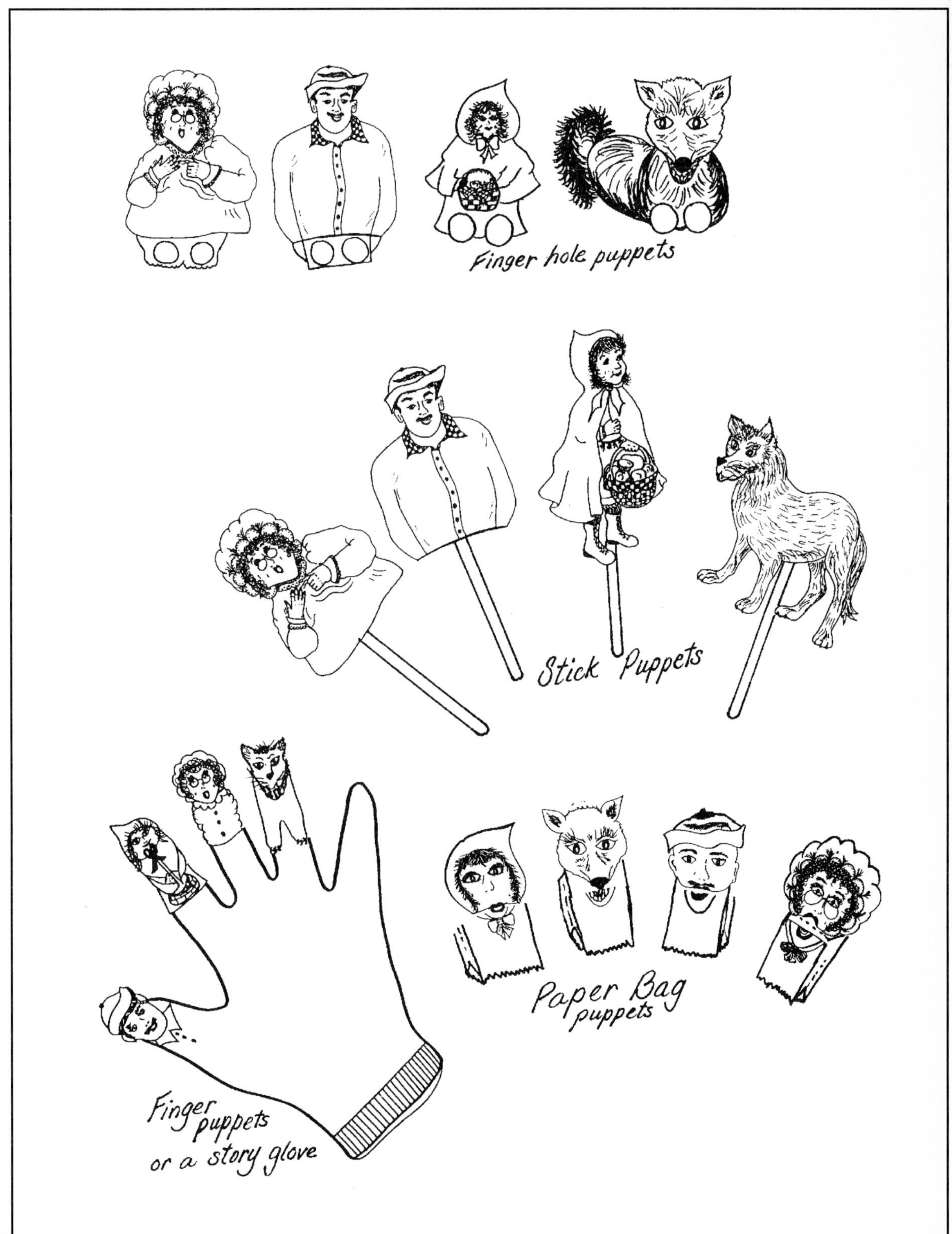

Figure 10.2A Bookmaking Activities and Projects

Frogs
Shape Books
Alphabet books
Finger Puppets
Use stick-on notes to write the text for wordless books.
Make stick puppet characters
Come to the Zoo
Theme books
Sarah's key words
A key chain with cards for an individual student word collection
Mikey and the Crayon
Rewrite and personalize a favorite book
The Little Red Hen
Story in a bag with objects for clues
Story Map: LRRH Little Red Riding Hood
Make a story map
What Makes my Heart Happy
Sheets are stored in a Valentine candy box
Create a book with loose pages to be added at any time, by anyone
house printed on top
mouse
cat
log
far
Make a Rhyme
A folded page book of rhymes
James and the Giant Peach
by Roald Dahl
Posters for book promotions
Jese's Journal
Cut wallpaper to make covers for personal journals
Indian in the Cupboard
dioramas to reflect settings
Folded paper crane
for Sadako's Peace Memorial
Projects as literature extension activities
Dizzy dogs danced daily down town
Alliteration Pop-Up Books
Bunnicula
by James Howe
Corine Miller
Student designed pocket folder for book studies
Island of the Blue Dolphins
Students design their own book jackets
Sadako and the Thousand Paper Cranes
Story Map
Beverly Cleary
Author Studies
Book Talk Videos - students record promotional talks for favorite books
Readers' Theatre Response activity
WALLKILL TIMES
Book Review
Student book reviews printed in local newspaper

Alternative Activities
Grades K–3

These alternative activities and projects encourage a child's creative participation in reading, speaking, listening, and writing.

Alternative Activities
Grades 4–6

These alternative activities and projects are *suggestions*–if students have their own ideas, encourage and support them.

Figure 10.2B Bookmaking Activities and Projects (cont.)

BOOKS DON'T HAVE TO BE FLAT, AND THEY DON'T HAVE TO SIT ON A BOOKSHELF

After visiting a school where I had taught my first workshop on creative bookmaking for elementary students, I was delighted to see many of my ideas on display in the front of a second-grade classroom. What caught my eye was the way they were displayed, on *plastic laundry hooks*.

The delightful covers the students had made were a colorful addition to the room, and the books were easily accessible to the children.

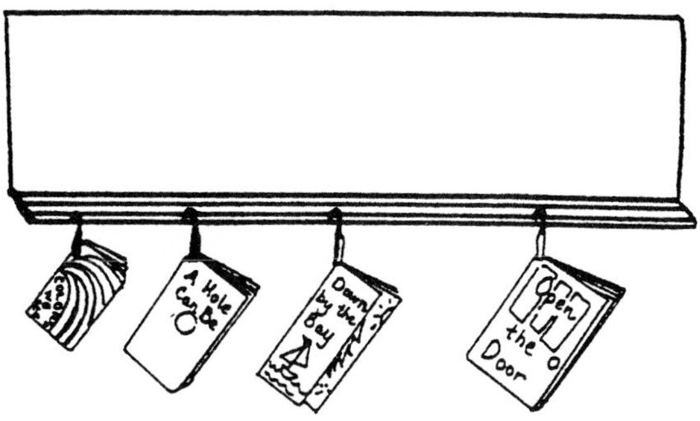

LUNCH BAG

Use the attractive, printed lunch bags or the ordinary brown bags to provide a novel writing experience. Students can cut pictures from magazines to illustrate basic food groups, then write a menu and put them all in the bag.

Alternate bag writing activities might include labeling one bag "nutritious food" and another "junk food." Students could write, draw, or cut out pictures to fill the bags.

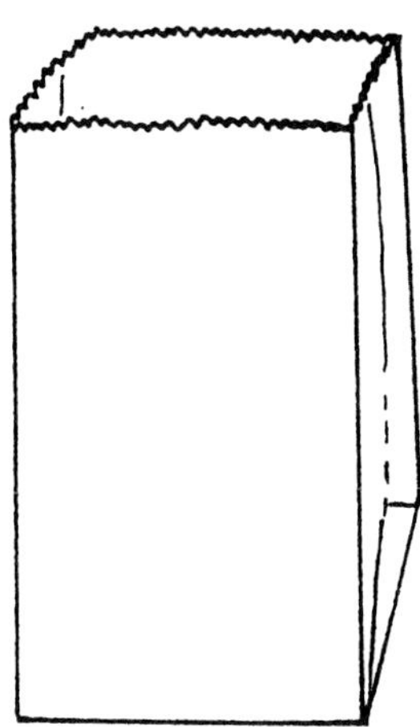

PAPER PLATE WRITING

Do a brainstorm activity with students to list as many things as possible that are round, or begin as a total group to list a few and have students continue alone or in pairs.

Use the paper plate to plan a nutritious meal. Students can cut and paste or draw pictures of the meal and write about it on the reverse side.

Create a Round Book by punching two holes in each plate and tie or fasten several together to be read as pages.

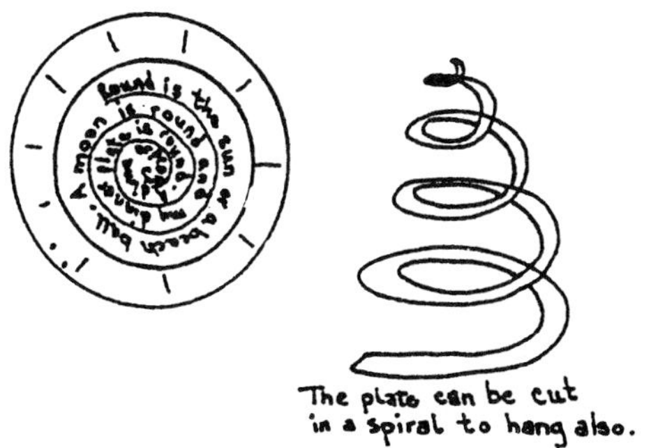

The plate can be cut
in a spiral to hang also.

BUSINESS CARDS

Have students collect the cards for a week or more. Then read, discuss, and critique the ads or messages. In pairs or small groups, students can create their own cards. 3 × 5-inch cards work well for this activity. Fasten the cards together with a shower or key ring to create a book.

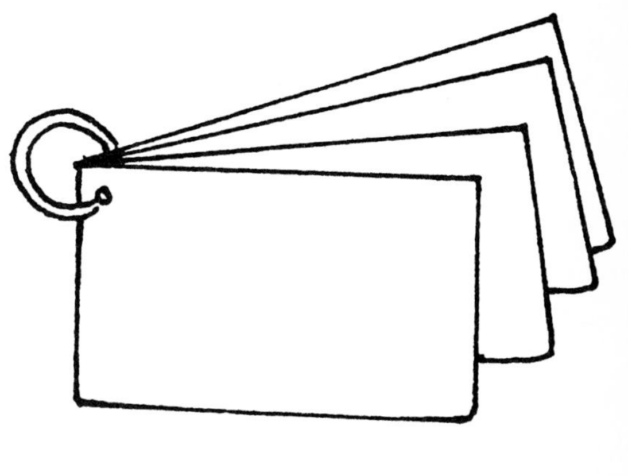

MAGIC WINDOW

Turn a plain piece of colored tag board into a pretend window. Use fabric or printed wallpaper for the curtains. Behind the window, place a picture that is drawn or cut out of a magazine.

Hang the window on the wall beside the chalkboard. Write descriptive clues on the board and allow students to guess what is behind the magic window.

After modeling this activity many times, encourage students to hide pictures and write clues.

SHOE BOX CLUE WRITING

Put an item inside the box and give five clues; begin with general clues and work up to more specific ones.

Students write their guess after each clue.

After several tries, have the students give the clues (be sure they write the clues).

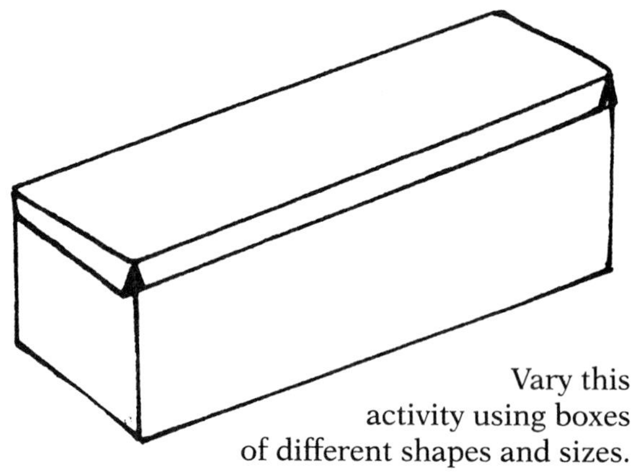

Vary this activity using boxes of different shapes and sizes.

TV "BOX" FOR A SET

With the teacher's guidance use the *TV Guide* as a reading source to select appropriate programs to evaluate. The fall preview issue is especially appropriate.

Students then select one program and write a critique.

The TV reviews are put in our TV set.

Our channel selector can be moved.

JIGSAW PUZZLE BOX

Students can write stories on various colored paper or oak tag.

We suggest the teacher cut them and purposely cut words apart to encourage kids to read to fit the pieces together (when we do puzzles, we use both shape clues and color or picture clues).

If the puzzles are of different colors, several can be stored in one box.

Figure 10.2D Bookmaking Activities and Projects (cont.)

AN OLD-FASHIONED RECIPE BOX

Here is a book from long ago that is not flat.

Have students ask their parents or grandparents to help them write down the recipe for a favorite dish.

This can be the start of a lifetime collection.

We purchased a box of printed recipe cards from "Current" for less than $2 for 100 cards. Students were excited to write their final copies on them.

SUITCASE BOOKS

We have a great time with this! Collect many travel brochures—they make great reading.

Allow students to select a country they would like to visit/learn more about/take a fantasy trip to. They then research the spot.

They can make a packing list and pack for one day, or create their own travel poster to complement the brochure, or write what they learned about the place.

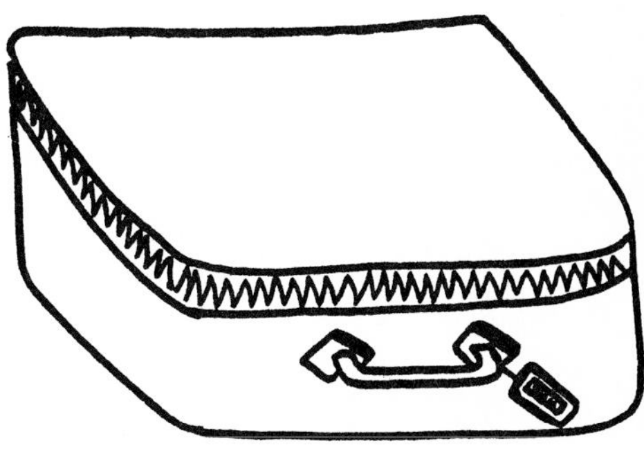

STORY IN AN EGG

After sharing many stories about eggs and what comes from them—both factual and fantasy stories—encourage students to take their own egg (a plastic pull-apart type) and write on a piece of paper what they would like to see come out of their egg.

When students are writing their pieces, encourage them to tell what their creation would do or what they would do with it.

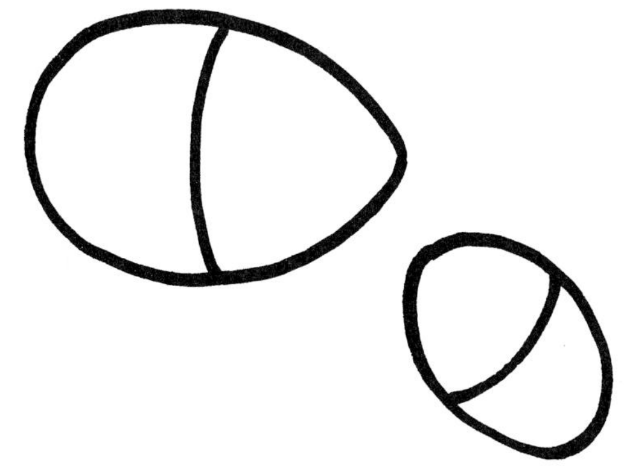

LOOK AND TELL ME WHAT YOU SEE

Repeat a design in different areas on separate pieces of paper. With no predetermined ideas, encourage students to imagine what the design might be.

After incorporating the design into their artwork, they can write about it.

GRADUATED PAGE EDGES

Often the way pages are cut or folded can create an interesting book. A clever book of colors is born using paint sample strips.

Expose the students to many of the wonderful books about colors as models.

STORY IN A SHOE

Ask students to complete this sentence on a piece of adding machine tape: "This shoe took me to . . ."

Depending on students' ability level, the writing may include location, climate, or a physical description.

A BASKETFUL OF . . .

dreams (concerns, joys, qualities, adjectives, etc.)

Use a basket with clay in the bottom into which popsicle sticks or straws can be pushed.

Students are asked to write their contributions on flowers that are taped or glued to the sticks or straws.

Each child writes on his or her own paper flower.

ROOM DESCRIPTIONS

Using oak tag folded into thirds, children draw their room (classroom, bedroom, etc.).

Place their written descriptions on the floor.

POEM POCKET

"I always kept a poem in my pocket . . . ," my grandmother used to say. Sure enough, in her apron pocket she'd have one! She read and wrote poetry on any old envelope or scrap. It gave me the idea for my poem pocket.

Short poems can be copied, cut out, or written by the students or teacher and placed in the poem pocket for brief reading times.

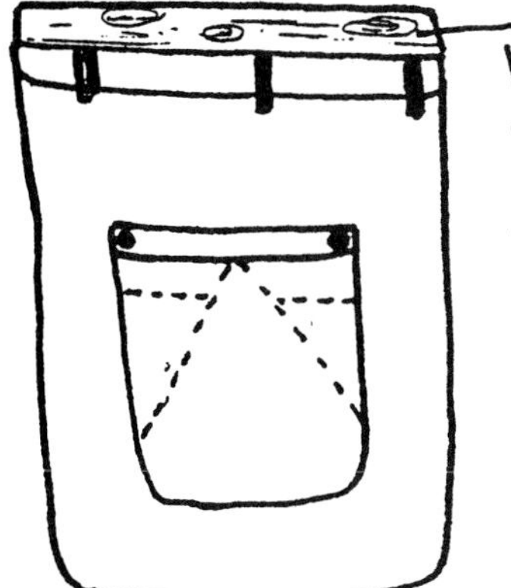

COAT HANGER BIOGRAPHY

Using lined paper to fit a clothes hanger, have students write about themselves or a favorite T-shirt. Hang the finished writing as a wall or hall display.

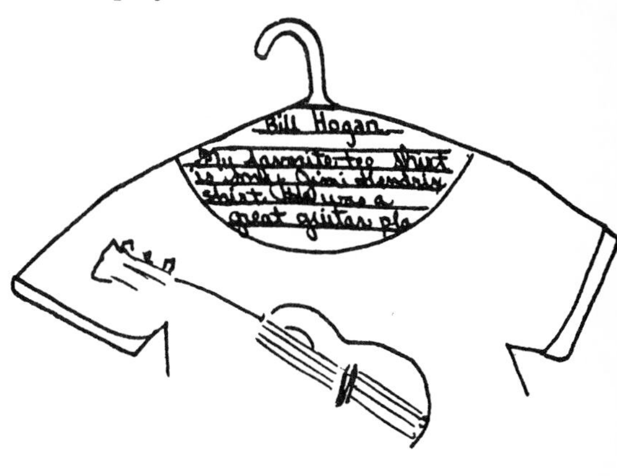

ACCORDION BOOKS

Instead of binding all left page edges together, alternate left and right so the book can stand up or be held in a circle with a paper clip. Use heavy tag board or cardboard. The drawing and writing can be done directly on the board for a permanent book, or sheets can be clipped as drafts or displays during process writing.

Hold the pages together with paper clips to change to a circle.

BOOK POSTERS

After reading an award-winning book, invite students to design a poster to encourage others to read it. (The award should appear on the poster.) This activity works well with partners also.

BOOK JACKETS

After reading a favorite book, cut plain paper to make a book jacket (this would be done after looking at publishers' jackets as models).

Students can then create their own jackets for books they have read.

FABRIC-COVERED COMPOSITION BOOK

1. Cut two pieces of heavy paper or tag board *slightly smaller* than the inside front and back covers of the composition book. Set these aside.
2. Lay the fabric print side down and place the open composition book on it. Cut the fabric $1\frac{1}{2}$ inches larger than the open book on all four sides. Clip off the corners.
3. Cut two diagonal slits, toward the spine, at the top and bottom of the book.

Put glue on the two small pieces, *fold them inward,* and run a thin strip of glue between them where the spine rests.

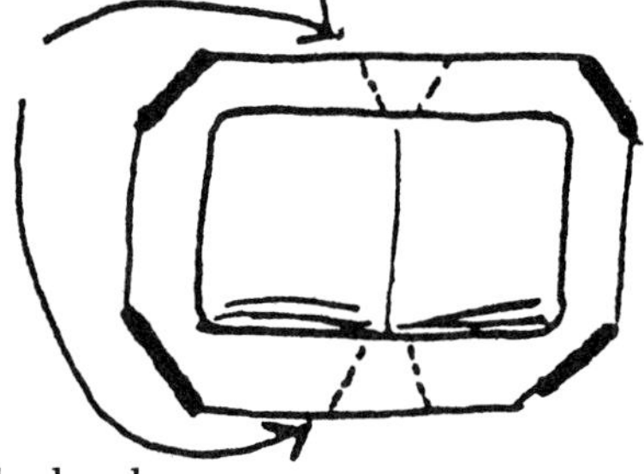

4. At each corner cut slits at right angles to the book.

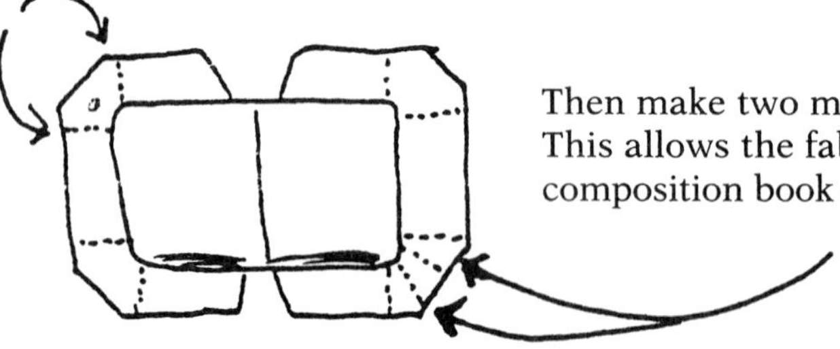

Then make two more slits between them at each corner. This allows the fabric to cover the curved corners of the composition book smoothly.

Put a small amount of glue on all corner pieces and fold them over the book.

5. Put glue on remaining pieces of fabric and fold them over the edges.
6. Run a *small* bead of glue around the edge of the tag board pieces (see step 1) and place them over the inside fabric edges to finish the job.

"FOLD AND CUT" PAPER BOOK

To make a simple cut paper-bound book, use four sheets of 81/2"× 11" paper. Fold two sheets together for top illustration and twosheets together for bottom illustration. The **heavy** black lines represent cuts made in the papers with scissors. After the cuts are made, slip the left side of the top two sheets into the slit and under the left side of the bottom 2 sheets. Fold them all in the center to make a book.

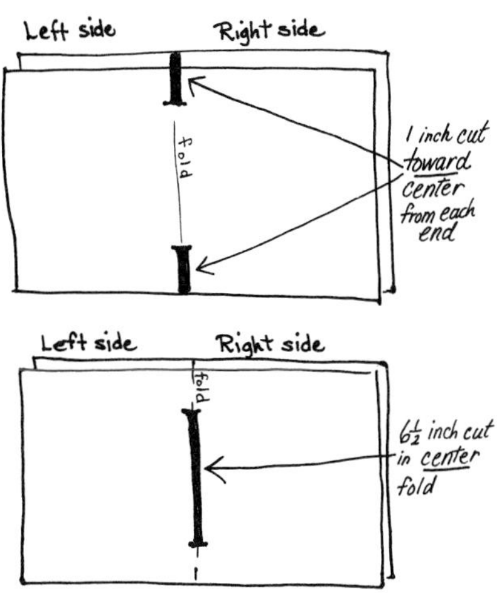

STANDUP OAKTAG BIOGRAPHY

Students research a famous person and write a brief summary on 3 × 5 index cards, which are then stapled to an oaktag cutout of the upper torso. They can stand up on a shelf or window sill.

THE "MATCHBOOK" BOOK

This book may vary in size. Since it is called a matchbook book, the size is usually about as large as the palm of an adult hand.

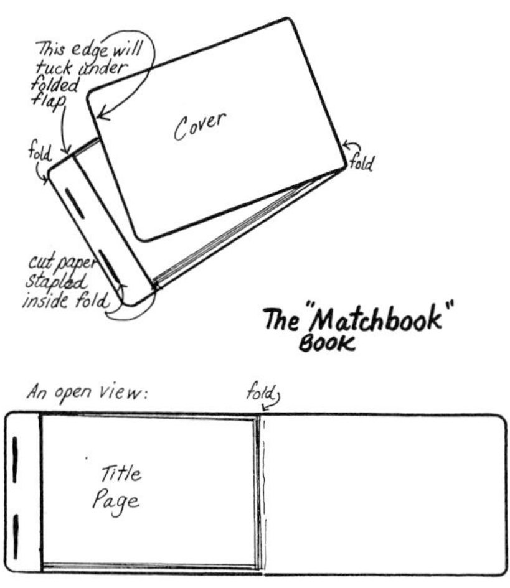

- Language ability is enhanced (oral, written, and nonverbal).
- Creativity is developed.
- Participants are given a channel to express their emotions.
- Children grow in ability to compose spontaneously orally.
- Students are given opportunities to explore life by assuming various roles and acquiring drama skills.
- Students acquire knowledge about themselves and about others from their reflections in dramatic situations.
- Students develop competence in communication skills.
- Drama encourages effective development in the language arts.
- Students' verbal abilities are improved.
- Drama offers a balance to more academic instruction.
- The reflective discussion that accompanies or follows drama activities provides opportunities for children to rethink and revisit the issues raised in the drama.

(Lundsteen, 1989; Booth, 1994; Cecil and Lauritzen, 1994)

Drama is both an art form and a powerful tool for learning and teaching. Through drama, children become better at communication, are able to explore thoughts and feelings not easily expressed orally or in writing, and experience many different interpretations of literature. They learn that their own opinions are worth expressing and are valued. Perhaps most important, children experience joy and pleasure in their learning (Thompson, 1988).

The rest of the discussion on drama explores the various dramatic forms that can be used in the elementary classroom and that can be easily integrated into all aspects of the curriculum. The following means of using drama are discussed: dramatic play, pantomime, movement, dramatization, finger plays, role-playing, and oral interpretation. As Thompson says (1988, 7), "All the world's a stage . . . and so on with the show!"

Dramatic Play

Dramatic play is common to young children. This natural, make-believe activity tends to be spontaneous, has no plot, no set sequence, and needs no real audiences. Young children reenact familiar, everyday activities when they assume the feelings, actions, and attitudes of things (e.g., airplanes, cars, toy animals, or soldiers) or people. Learning centers with dress-up clothes, playhouses, housekeeping corners, construction areas, and activities enhance children's natural ability to engage in playlike behaviors.

Tompkins and Hoskisson (1995) describe the use of prop kits, which can be assembled to promote children's dramatic play behaviors. These kits contain actual artifacts or objects, plus materials that encourage functional reading and writing activities. The props are collected, stored in boxes or plastic crates, and used for dramatic play as well as in social studies, math, and literature activities. Examples of prop kits include Post Office Kit, Medical Kit, Travel Agency Kit, Grocery Store Kit, Restaurant Kit, and Office Kit.

To demonstrate the actual articles and reading and writing materials that might be included in a prop kit, let's look at a

DEPARTMENT STORE KIT:

cash register
play money
credit cards
catalogs
ads
price stickers
bags
sales slips
clothing items (dolls' clothes or pictures of clothing might be substituted)
coupons
markers

Children have the opportunity to read or construct ads, put on sales for holidays or between seasons, price items for sale, talk to customers, make change, give credit, and the like. Not only are they involved in dramatic play activities and using talk in meaningful contexts, but they are also given opportunities to see and engage in authentic writing and reading activities.

Pantomime

Pantomime is the act of conveying ideas wordlessly through facial expressions, gestures, and other forms of body language. It is a silent art form that uses the body as a means of communication to express actions, feelings, and reactions through movement and gestures. In the classroom, pantomime can be introduced with everyday activities, such as reading a book, tying shoes, or making a sandwich. Children may pantomime animals, eating various foods, or acting out or reacting to something that has occurred in their lives. Children can also act out nursery rhymes, folktales, or stories in their basal readers. In addition to total wordless interpretations of stories, children can pantomime stories or poems that are being read by another classmate. Some stories that make excellent material for pantomime are *The Legend of the Bluebonnet, The Three Bears, The Pied Piper of Hamelin,* and *Where the Wild Things Are.*

Movement

Dramatic movement is a type of physical communication that coordinates the imagination, the mind, and the body. Through movement, children can explore and express their inner feelings and reactions to sensory experiences. They can explore ways they can use their bodies (swaying, bending, creeping, twisting, shaking). Movements can be combined with music or rhythm instruments. Children can close their eyes, listen to the music, and create movements to accompany the sounds. Movements can also accompany books or poems, such as *The Jigaree* or *The Little Old Lady Who Was Not Afraid of Anything.* Movement is an easy, nonthreatening use of drama.

Dramatization

Dramatization is an activity in which children improvise a story or poem. The children create the scenes and scenarios while improvising the dialogue and actions. The emphasis is not on the product or the art form, but rather on the process and the communication skills the children are using. While improvising, classmates are working together to invent and act spontaneously. Examples of books that can be used for dramatization are *Mrs. Wishy-Washy, The Three Billy Goats Gruff,* and *It Could Be Worse.* Early literacy development is fostered by the use of play, including dramatic story reenactments (DSR) (Martinez, 1993). In DSR, the children informally re-create or play familiar stories by either acting them out themselves or by using puppets. DSR foster children's sense of how a story "works," that is, how stories are organized. Dramatic story reenactments do not have to be teacher initiated or even teacher guided. By establishing literature-rich environments, teachers are setting the scene to motivating their students to participate in a valuable and enjoyable activity—dramatic story reenactments.

Finger Plays

Finger plays are especially suitable for young children. Finger plays involve the dramatization of simple rhyming stories. Because they invite whole-class participation, they are particularly effective with shy children or children who have speech difficulties. Examples of poems that lend themselves to finger plays are "Eensy, Weensy Spider," "Hickory Dickory Dock," and "Ten Little Indians." Marc Brown has two collections of poems to be used as hand games, *Finger Rhymes* and *Hand Rhymes.*

Role-Playing

Through role-playing, children are able to perceive situations through the eyes of others. Role-playing is an educational experience designed to help students gain insights into how others handle real-life problems and into historical and current events. Students become immersed in an event by reliving it and in doing so are learning more than mere facts. Role-playing may be used throughout the language arts or in any curricular area. Nearly every story contains episodes and characters that lend themselves to role-playing activities. History provides many suitable figures for role-playing models. Through role-playing, children can empathize with others who are less fortunate and can gain an understanding of members of other cultures or persons who have different life problems. Stories that are appropriate for role-playing include *The Island of the Skog, Deep in the Forest, The Man Who Kept House,* and *And Then What Happened, Paul Revere?*

Oral Interpretation

Oral interpretation is a technique that allows voices to re-create stories or poems with subsequent dramatic effects. Oral interpretation activities include choral speaking and Readers' Theater. Readers' Theater is discussed in the next section of this chapter.

Choral speaking is a form of oral interpretation that involves a group of readers reciting either prose or poetry. Choral speaking helps children improve their speech, appreciate and understand good literature and poetry, and gain confidence in their ability to speak before an audience. In order to provide an effective rendition of a poem or narrative, the students must be able to interpret the mood of the selection. Almost any poem lends itself to this activity, and many books are suitable as well, particularly stories that have repetitive patterns or language (e.g., *There Was an Old Woman Who Swallowed a Fly* or *The Napping House*). Several variations are possible:

- line-a-child (each child reads a line with several lines possibly read by the entire group)
- antiphonal (alternate speaking between two groups; for example, high voices can be balanced with low voices, or boys' voices can be contrasted with girls' voices)
- unison (entire group recites all the lines together)

Drama in the classroom is not likened to polished performances associated with the theater but is rather more process oriented, with the emphasis on student growth and enjoyment. When planning and evaluating the role of drama, teachers should ask themselves: Is the form of drama being considered appropriate to meet the desired objectives in language arts and across the curriculum? Is the material of high quality? Are the instructional methods appropriate for the students and can they help achieve the desired goals?

Through drama, children grow in their ability to use language, to listen more critically and effectively, and to present themselves before an audience more confidently. Self-confidence and self-esteem are by-products of positive drama experiences. By participating in the various dramatic experiences presented in this chapter, children develop socially, personally, cognitively, and effectively.

READERS' THEATER

The use of oral reading in the literacy program has come into question with the age-old practice of round-robin reading being challenged. Although knowledge about the disadvantages of round-robin reading has altered teachers' use of reading aloud, there are ways to use oral reading purposefully, indeed pleasurably, in the reading program. One way is to use Readers' Theatre as a means of responding to literature.

Readers' Theater is a dramatic activity in which readers present and interpret a piece of literature primarily using their voices, with minimal body movement. "Readers' Theater is a presentation of text that is expressively and dramatically read aloud by two or more readers" (Young and Vardell, 1993, 398). Readers' Theater can create images by suggestion that never could be realistically portrayed on the stage (Shepard, 1994). Readers' Theater is essentially a re-creation of stories through vocal expression, the primary purpose of which is to bring literature to life. When participating in Readers' Theater, students read aloud from scripts that are based on literary selections. The lines are not memorized, and the performances are not formal. Although Readers' Theater is part theater and part oral interpretation, it does not require special training in drama, elaborate props, or costumes. There is a script, but all the information is revealed by the speaking parts of both characters and narrator. Enough narration is included to provide a context for the dialogue and to keep the story line flowing.

The procedure is relatively simple. The major steps are as follows (Swanson, 1988; Lundsteen, 1989; Shepard, 1994):

1. **Selection or writing of scripts.** When considering sources for Readers' Theater (books, plays, poems, songs), it is important to keep several criteria in mind. Books chosen should have sufficient dialogue; language that is rich, colorful, and rhythmic; and a story line that is interesting and well developed. In addition, there should be plausible and natural language, a distinct writing style, and characters that are recog-

nizable and believable (Manna, 1984; Mallan, 1991). The piece should be relatively easy to read and not be too long or involved. There should be enough characters to give variety and to involve a number of students, but not too many to be confusing. Three to six characters with one or two narrators work well. Selections need not be entire books; excerpts or sections of books may be used as well. Books and sources for Readers' Theater are listed at the end of this chapter.

Particularly when initiating Readers' Theater, it may be useful to use prepared scripts. Scripts are available from the Readers Theatre Script Service (P.O. Box 178333, San Diego, CA 92117), in such professional magazines as *The Instructor,* in children's magazines, in basal readers, and in such publications as *Scholastic Big Book Magazine.* In addition, many trade books contain collections of plays. These scripts come already divided into speaking parts with minimal stage directions provided.

Ultimately, teachers and students will want to write their own scripts for Readers' Theater. When choosing possible books, songs, or poems to be used, again it is important to look for ones that have a great deal of dialogue or possibilities for dialogue. Several narrator roles may be written to help explain the story and to give additional opportunities for children to participate. Books may have to be adapted in order to condense or tighten the action and to make the script a manageable length (all the while retaining the essential actions and characters necessary to understand the interpretation). Books do not have to be rewritten but can be used verbatim. For example, *Doctor Desoto, The Ghost-Eye Tree,* and *Alexander and the Terrible, Horrible, No Good, Very Bad Day* make wonderful Readers' Theater scripts without any adaptation or further writing. Readers merely read their assigned parts, with the narrator(s) reading the descriptions and other narration.

Once the scripts have been chosen or written, they should be reproduced for every participant. It is helpful to put a cover sheet on the script with the specific character's role noted. Then the speaking parts for that character can be highlighted or color coded for ease of reading.

2. **Assigning parts.** If the book chosen is to be used as part of a literature response group, then each member of the group is assigned a part. If there are not enough parts for every child, then the students can take turns sharing a part or an extra narrator can be added.

3. **Rehearsing the script.** The rehearsal is the true essence of the Readers' Theater experience. Students have the opportunity to practice becoming fluent readers. However, they must understand the story before they can really use their voices to interpret the story for others. To help in the understanding of the story, Busching (1981) recommends using the "5W's plus one question" technique. The questions who, what, when, where, why, and how are used to probe and help students interpret the selection. Reading stories several times is not tedious for the children but rather is a pleasurable activity.

The scripts are practiced individually and with the entire group. Readers are reminded to read their parts as if they were the characters. They are also reminded to follow along as their classmates read so they will be prepared when their turn comes.

After the first reading, the story and the interpretation should be discussed as a group. Areas to focus on are the feelings of the characters in the various situations and the possible ways to show those feelings using voices. Both oral interpretation and voice quality can be addressed during group discussions. The practices may be videotaped or audiotaped for further analysis. Parts may be reassigned to allow other students to participate or to assume different roles.

4. **Planning a performance.** When students enjoy a particular script, they may wish to perform for other class members or for different audiences. The group should decide whether to make simple props or costumes. Colorful folders for the scripts can be made to use in the performance or binders can be substituted. The space for the performance has to be determined, whether this is the classroom itself, the auditorium, or the library. If the performance is to be held in a space larger than the usual practice area, students must be sure their voices are loud enough to project or must obtain microphones. If participants in Readers' Theater wish to sit during the performance, then stools should be provided.

5. **Performing the script.** During the actual performance, the students sit or stand in front of the audience holding their scripts and wearing simple costumes or holding props. They then read their lines with expression and with pleasure.

Shepard (1993) describes a variation of the traditional Readers' Theater, one that adds mime and movement to the performance. If movement is to be incorporated, then it is important to plan where the readers will start and where they will go. Shepard suggests drawing a series of movement diagrams to help spot problems and to serve as reminders for the performance. Whenever actions are described in the scripts, the readers should either try to do it or else suggest the actions through mime. Mime techniques add polish to a performance.

The benefits of Readers' Theater are many, for it is an extremely useful instructional activity. A major benefit is that students are involved in meaningful and purposeful reading and listening activities. Students are motivated to return to scripts over and over, thereby enhancing the development of sight vocabulary and reading fluency. All ability levels may participate in this activity, which negates the stigma of ability grouping. It includes other benefits (Swanson, 1988; Lundsteen, 1989; Johnson and Louis, 1990; Moffett and Wagner, 1992). Readers' Theater also:

- develops language appreciation
- promotes visual imagery
- facilitates the development of reading fluency and reading rate
- places comprehension at the heart of the reading process
- provides a context for meaningful oral reading
- demonstrates the effective use of oral language as a means to communicate an interpretation of text
- fosters understanding of the structure of stories and literary conventions
- provides worthwhile vicarious experiences
- develops discussion skills
- develops presentation skills
- is enjoyable

Readers' Theater has primarily been utilized with narrative text. However, it can also be an innovative, exciting approach to content area reading and study (Young & Vardell, 1993). By combining nonfiction trade books with Readers' Theater, teachers can incorporate content area instruction with the dynamic and interactive process of Readers' Theater.

Both teachers and students can select nonfiction books or parts of these books to adapt for Readers' Theater. Some books lend themselves more to this activity than do others. Nonfiction books that contain dialogue, for example, *The Magic Schoolbus Series* and nonfiction books dealing with social studies concepts, work wonderfully. Shorter informational books can likewise be effective across the grades due to their simplicity and focus, for example, the science books by Seymour Simon. Some examples for the various curricular areas can be found in the bibliography. The process for writing the scripts is similar to that for narrative text with the students either simply breaking the text into parts or elaborating on the original text to create their own versions. An introduction might be included, as well as a postscript to bring closure to the activity.

When students participate in developing scripts for Readers' Theater, they become involved in critical reading and revising. When they have completed the process, they frequently are motivated to read the entire text, read other books by the author, or explore the topic even further.

Experiencing nonfiction books through Readers' Theater "gives the words on the page a voice, and the students in the classroom an active role in internalizing and interpreting new knowledge" (Young and Wardell, 1993, 405). Participating in the process and in the performance of Readers' Theater is an effective vehicle for content area learning and also becomes a source of personal pride and accomplishment for the students.

STORYTELLING

Once Upon a Classroom

Once upon a classroom
So they say,
A happy teacher arrived one day,

To share a story, a smile, and a wink,
And to entice all little children to think.
She cast her spell
And wonders began,
At once there were no mortal men.
Emperors, queens, kings, and knights,
Wondrous creatures born for flight,
Laughing families holding hands,
Tumbling tots and big brass bands,
They came from long ago and far away
And everyone knew they couldn't stay.
But for moments few their tales were spun
And all enjoyed tremendous fun.
When she was through she flew away,
But hearts held her tales for many a day.
On and on and on it goes,
Jolly friends and battling foes,
Creatures captured from another place,
New friends found in outer space.
Tales to share from near and far,
Simply because from one small star,
A teacher came from far away,
To spin a yarn and warm a day
Once upon a classroom. . . .
So they say.

Karen Pillsworth (Kindergarten Teacher and Storyteller)

Another way of incorporating drama and oral interpretation in the classroom is to use storytelling. This section is largely the result of the efforts and enthusiasm of Karen Pillsworth, who is both a kindergarten teacher and a storyteller. Over the years Karen has dedicated herself to using storytelling in the classroom and to helping teachers use storytelling as part of their instructional programs.

Why Tell Stories?

Storytelling has its roots in the oral tradition. Stories have been told since the beginning of humankind to entertain, explain, inform, share experiences, and pass culture and traditions from one generation to another. Ideals and values, methods of survival, and entertainment on long winter nights were transmitted around fires, handed down from the very old to the very young. The world's best teachers used stories or parables to teach concepts in a way that was readily understood. Today the ancient art of storytelling is being revived to assist children in rediscovering their imaginations and developing their verbal and expressive skills.

Bringing storytelling into the classroom adds a new dimension to the learning process. The rewards that can be won or can accompany storytelling are many (Mallan, 1991; The National Storytelling Association). Children have been gifted with wonderful imaginations; through storytelling they can use their imaginations to visualize the details and characters in stories. When listening to stories, children actively participate, responding to the mood and anticipation the storyteller has created.

Through listening to stories, children can gain an understanding of themselves and the interactions among people. Through storytelling, the actions of people—how they show affection, jealousy, fear, friendship, competition—are revealed. Through storytelling, children are introduced to the values and literary traditions of other cultures. Stories likewise give examples of the contexts in which children can see real-life implications. They can analyze motives and actions, and these reflections can serve as reference points for their own lives and experiences. Storytelling permits children to shape their experiences by comparing them with similar experiences heard in stories.

In addition to helping children learn about themselves and others, storytelling also develops skills in listening, speaking, reading, and writing. Through exposure to stories, children internalize story structure and are exposed to such literary conventions as theme, characterization, setting, and mood. Children can draw on their prior experiences with stories when predicting or comprehending story events or when writing narratives. Effective listening skills are also developed, which are necessary prerequisites for reading comprehension. Through listening to and telling stories, children develop their ability to communicate, which not only helps in the school environment but also is essential to success in life and the work world.

Rudyard Kipling once stated, "If history were taught in the form of stories it would never be forgotten." To help make history more memorable, teachers have the opportunity to use stories for the exploration of social studies issues; that is, the social studies curriculum could become a collection of stories about many cultures

(Combs and Beach, 1994). Listening to and sharing stories as part of the social studies curriculum has many benefits. Many of the learning processes that are vital to the understanding of social studies concepts are supported by storytelling: listening; speaking; communicating ideas with classmates, accepting their reactions, and compiling these ideas and stories to address certain issues, topics, or problems. Storytelling increases the possibility of providing a dynamic and meaningful social studies curriculum. The challenge for teachers "is to look differently at what is essential to social education for the twenty-first century and to use techniques that engage children in thinking about social issues while they come to see the significance of the stories in their own lives, as well as in the lives of people around them" (Combs and Beach, 1994, 470).

When children become storytellers, they see the effects of their words on their audiences and become aware of the power of language. A significant by-product of storytelling is the accompanying level of increased self-confidence and self-esteem. Children develop confidence in themselves and in their ability to share stories with others.

In storytelling, students assume the roles of both listener and teller, thereby benefiting in several dimensions. Storytelling, as an art form and as an educational tool, is truly entertaining and motivates students to read (the stories on which the storytelling was based and pieces of literature as possible sources for storytelling). And, as Karen Pillsworth points out, it is easy to befriend children through storytelling. Storytelling brings the child closer to the teller and to the story.

Stories for Storytelling

When looking for stories to tell, Mallan (1991) suggests that the following points be kept in mind:

1. **Quick beginnings.** Quick beginnings are designed to grab the audience's attention. Children prefer to listen to stories that begin with action. Frequently, beginnings of stories are the most difficult part of storytelling, so the teller must be sure that the beginning is told clearly and confidently.

2. **Straightforward action.** The action should be direct and straightforward, flowing easily from event to event. Stories with too many subplots should be avoided.

3. **Clear climax.** The story should have a definite climax, which can be heightened by the teller's skills and delivery of the story.

4. **Limited number of characters.** Stories should have few characters, possibly not more than four. The beginning storyteller should avoid using different voices for each character, since this is difficult.

5. **Repetitive pattern.** Stories with repetitive patterns are easier to tell, the patterns serving as reminders of the story events and opportunities for audience participation.

6. **Satisfying conclusion.** Children appreciate stories with good endings.

7. **Different versions.** When looking for stories, it is helpful to look for several versions to find one that appeals most to the teller. Stories that sound like they would make excellent stories to listen to are preferred as opposed to those that are dependent on illustrations.

Possible storytelling sources are listed at the end of this chapter.

Now that the criteria have been outlined, what types of stories or experiences lend themselves to storytelling?

Everyday Experiences

An ideal place to begin storytelling is with children's (or the teacher's) everyday experiences. Anecdotes or retellings of personal events about family, pets, friends, and special happenings can serve as the basis for storytelling. Of course, let's not forget the rich traditions and different cultural backgrounds that exist in family histories. Children's personal stories can cross continents and cultures.

Folktales

Folktales, the easiest stories to tell, are stories that originated from the oral tradition, that is, stories that are passed down from generation to generation. The language used in folktales is relatively simple and strong. Because of their familiar structure (setting-problem-events-resolution-conclusion), folktales are generally enjoyed and easily understood. Folktales are stories of the personal desires, ambitions, fears, and insecurities of common, everyday folk. Characters may be stereotyped by gender or by character; that is, the characters that are good are very good and the characters that are bad are evil. Folktales appeal to both the intellect and the emotions of the listeners.

Myths

"Myths are narratives which give explanations about the origins of natural and social phenomena, or accounts of interactions between humans and supernatural beings" (Mallan, 1991, 28). These stories often use more formal language than other types of folklore and may be quite demanding to tell.

Fables

Fables are short stories, generally with a moral or a lesson that is the focal point of the story. Fables are ideal for the novice storyteller, since they are short, have few characters (predominately animals), and have a single incident. Because of the abstract nature of the moral that must be determined from the story itself, fables appeal most to children in the intermediate grades and beyond.

Tall Tales

These are folktales that combine history, myth, and fact. Characteristic of tall tales are regional settings, dialect, all-powerful heroes, heroic themes, and exaggerated humor and deeds. Paul Bunyan, Pecos Bill, and John Henry are some popular tall-tale heroes.

Stories with That Something Extra

For storytellers who feel somewhat insecure about facing an audience with empty hands, or for storytellers who want to add variety to their programs, a variety of stories use props or audience participation. These include:

Prop Stories. These stories use items or props in the storytelling. Any story that revolves around a particular object may be used. For example, a carrot can be used in the telling of *The Carrot Seed* or an apple for the story of *The Little Red House.* The latter story details a quest for a little red house, with no doors or windows, a chimney, and a star inside. Of course the search can take the listener all over the neighborhood, the United States, or the world until the house is found. The house turns out to be an apple—which has no windows or doors. It has a chimney (the stem) and a star (the seeds and seed casings), which are revealed when the apple is cut in half horizontally. There are many versions of this story, and the teller can be as creative in the retelling as desired.

Participation Stories. These stories get the audience physically involved in the telling and allow them to share ownership in the story. Participation can be as simple as repeating a phrase from the story or as involved as having members of the audience participate physically in the telling. For example, in the story *The Old Lady Who Swallowed a Fly,* the phrase "I don't know why she swallowed the fly, I guess she'll die" is easily learned and repeated naturally as the story progresses. Pausing before the phrase and making eye contact with the listeners invite them to participate on cue. Other stories that invite participation are *The Little Old Lady Who Was Not Afraid of Anything* and *The Fat Cat.* The former invites children to perform the actions of the pieces of clothing encountered by the old lady as she travels through the woods—shaking like the shirt, wiggling like the pants, clapping like the gloves, and shouting, "Boo, hoo," like the pumpkin head. In *The Fat Cat* a cat eats a series of items and people—a pot, a lady with a pink parasol, a parson. A simple prop—a sheet—is held over the cat's head, and as the cat eats each item, a child takes a place in the cat's "stomach." The class chimes in with the repetitive list of things eaten. When the woodcutter releases the "morsels eaten," the children return to their seats or places one at a time.

Puppet Stories. Puppets can add variety to a storytelling program. A special puppet can be used at the beginning of the session to signal the start of storytelling time. The appearance of the puppet lets the audience know it is time to settle down and get ready to listen. Puppet stories are always enjoyable, and an elaborate puppet stage is not necessary to make the stories come alive. Two well-made hand puppets and a well-presented story can make the audience forget the presence of the storyteller. An easy story to use is the African folktale *The Gunniwolf.*

Flannel Board Stories. Flannel board stories are a delightful way to present stories, especially to young children. Simple flannel boards are easy to make by covering sturdy cardboard or a piece of wood with felt. The size of the flannel board can vary to accommodate whole-class or individual presentations. Characters can be cut from different colors of felt or may be made from pellon. The advantage of pellon (available at stores that sell cloth and sewing supplies) is that it is colorless and also somewhat transparent, so patterns can be placed beneath it. Children can draw directly on pellon, thereby personalizing stories. See "From the Classroom" for one teacher's use of flannel board stories.

"Share a Story" Stories. "Share a story" stories are an excellent way to involve the entire audience in the storytelling activity. A familiar object or a wrapped package is used as a key. The holder of the object begins the story and then passes the object to the next person, who finishes telling a part of the story. A ball of yarn with knots spaced throughout can also be used, with the teller talking until a knot is reached. At this point the next teller continues the story. This type of storytelling is relatively nonthreatening because it can be as silly or serious as the group wishes.

Paper Folding/Paper Tearing Stories. During the telling of these stories, the teller tears or folds paper while talking to the audience. The final product is revealed just as the story is completed. Excellent stories for this activity include "The Rainhat" (which appears in *The Family Storytelling Handbook*)—in which a piece of paper becomes, among other things, a rainhat, a firefighter's helmet, a boat, and a life jacket—and *The Paper Crane,* during the telling of which paper cranes can be constructed.

Tell-and-Draw Stories/Cut-and-Tell Stories. Tell-and-draw stories combine oral telling with simple illustrations. The teller merely draws during the telling of the story. The same procedure is followed for cut-and-tell stories, with the storyteller cutting out shapes as the story is told.

With the addition of such sources as photographs, pictures, jokes and riddles, superstitions, and the like, many kinds of stories are available for telling. Once storytellers are aware of all the possibilities that exist, both in real life and in literature, they never run out of rich material to share.

Pocket Tales. Children can pocket valuable prereading and social skills thanks to an innovative method of storytelling—pocket tales—developed by Mary Lynne McGrath for her first-grade children (described by Moxley, 1994). After telling her students a story, McGrath gives each child a sheet of paper that is divided into eight squares. In each square are two words, which are significant to the telling of the story. The children then illustrate the boxes with pictures that represent the words. The children's assignment is to *pocket* the paper, take it home, and use it as a guide to help them tell the story to their friends and families. Besides being an enjoyable activity for the children, pocket tales helps them both educationally and socially. It teaches or reinforces such skills as listening, visualizing, imaging, and learning the elements of story grammar. Equally important is the sense of self-esteem the children gain from telling the stories to others. Figure 10.3 gives an example of a pocket tale sheet.

Steps to Storytelling

The steps to storytelling are easy to follow and can be done at a pace that is comfortable for the individual.

1. **Be a reader and a lover of words.** Immerse yourself in quality children's literature. Tap every resource available: colleagues, librarians, bookstores, college courses, and children.

2. **Choose stories that appeal to you and you are comfortable with.** Your joy in sharing the story will reach the audience and add to the mood you set. Remember that stories with dramatic elements will incorporate suspense into your telling and keep interest high.

Figure 10.3

Pocket Tales to go - Little Red Riding Hood

A HOME-SCHOOL CONNECTION

Red Riding Hood Grandma	ill basket	woods wolf	cottage closet
cap bed	eyes see	teeth eat	woodsman axe

1. Fold a paper into eighths
2. Brainstorm words to sequence the story
3. Write 1 or 2 words in each box to represent parts of the story
4. Students then draw a picture clue to help in retelling the story at home

3. **Know your story well and tell it in your own words.** Remember to learn the plot first. Do not try to memorize the story word for word. If you stumble and forget a word, you may panic and lose your audience.

4. **Develop voice skills.** It is usually best to begin your story in a low, soft voice. This will settle the children and cue them in that it is time to listen. As you continue, modulate your voice to the actions of the story, increasing your volume as you build to the climax. Use a tape recorder or videotape your performance to critique your voice, checking on quality and projection. It is usually best to avoid character voices unless you are working with a character script. It is easy to become confused and mix up the voices. This will take away from the credibility of your story.

5. **Learn how to pace your story.** Timing is essential in storytelling. You hold your audience by the pace you set. It is best to start at a walking pace; then you can slow down for emphasis or speed up for excitement. Repetitive phrases and pauses will add to the rhythm of your story and keep your audience ready to listen.

The most common mistake a teller makes is to rush through a story. This can happen for a variety of reasons, the most common being that the teller did not spend enough time working on the story. The stories you choose must be the ones you believe in and want to spend time on.

FROM THE CLASSROOM OF . . .

Dolores McFadden Lakeside, California

FLANNEL BOARDS IN THE CLASSROOM

Flannel boards have many uses in the whole language classroom because they offer children opportunities to extend literature, to tell stories, to stretch their imaginations. Through the use of flannel boards, children can display illustrations of original stories, books they have read, or stories or poems read by the teacher, or they can retell stories. Flannel boards may also introduce creative storytelling, demonstrate sequence of events, depict scenes in history, or illustrate a science activity.

Flannel boards can be made from felt or flannel stretched over cardboard, pressboard, or wood. Another type of flannel board is a magnetic felt board constructed from a stove pad painted white with felt glued on the flame retardent side of the pad. This dual type of flannel board is particularly valuable because it is portable and sturdy, and a variety of activities can take place on the multipurpose board.

Many materials will adhere to a flannel board: felt, yarn, sponges, foam, pipe cleaners, sandpaper, fake fur, terry cloth, and interfacing (pellon). **Pellon** is particularly useful because it is inexpensive and easy for children to use when creating their own illustrations for books, creating their own stories, or for storytelling. Any illustration can be traced on pellon and colored with fabric markers or regular crayons. Magnetic tape or small magnets can be glued on the back of the pellon to be used on the magnetic felt boards. Pellon for midweight to heavy fabrics is recommended.

Flannel board kits can be constructed using pocket folders and pellon. In one pocket is placed a book or a story, while the other pocket houses the pellon pieces. These can be kept in the library corner for students to read and act out. Folktales such as "The Three Little Pigs," "The Little Red Hen," and "The Gingerbread Boy" are excellent sources for these kits. Teachers do not have to be responsible for the pellon figures, since children love to work with pellon and having their own creations is highly motivating as well. Patterns for trying this activity can be found with the "Little Red Riding Hood" theme. Patterns for *The Little Old Lady Who Was Not Afraid of Anything* are provided in the illustration on this page.

Time and effort will pay off in confidence, and your stories will reflect this.

6. **Eye contact with your audience is essential.** When you really know your story, it will flow naturally, and you will be able to engage your audience with your eyes as well as your voice. Remember to move your focus around the group so that you do not make any one individual uncomfortable.

7. **Remember to choose stories that are age/group appropriate.** Your favorite story may not be right for every group, although many stories can be adapted for various audiences.

8. **Finally, storytellers, like all other artists, must practice to perfect their talents.** Practice in front of the mirror, in the shower, while driving to work, in front of an audience. The more you practice, the better your presentation will be and the more poised you will appear.

When evaluating storytelling, there are several questions the teller (or the listener) may ask:

- Was the beginning of the story strong and effective?
- Was the story line clear?
- Were the characterizations distinct?
- Was the ending appropriate?
- Was the eye contact with the audience effective?
- Were the facial expressions animated and appropriate?
- Were the actions appropriate to the story?
- Was the use of voice effective (e.g., rate, stress, and use of pauses)?
- What was the overall effectiveness of the presentation?

Storytelling is enjoying a renaissance, as evidenced by the growing number of professional storytellers, the appearance of articles about storytelling in professional journals, and the number of storytelling resources now available to teachers. Storytelling is an effective instructional tool to develop skills, attitudes, and concepts. Combining the story and the language used by the storyteller establishes a rapport that enables students to connect with literature. By utilizing more storytelling in the classroom, teachers help students develop and extend their use of language and their confidence in using oral language. The broad and diverse range of storytelling experiences offered to children can also help to extend their view of the world. As Karen concludes her message to future storytellers, "Happy telling!"

SUMMARY

This chapter discussed the various ways teachers and students can respond to literature. Responding to literature extends students' enjoyment of texts and offers students opportunities to deepen their insights and reflect on the content of the piece. Through writing, art, music, cooking, drama, puppetry, and bookmaking, books can be revisited, reinspected, and savored. This chapter also discussed the power of drama—a frequently neglected aspect of the curriculum. Used purposefully and regularly throughout the day and across the curriculum, drama contributes to the students' growth in communication skills in all areas of the language arts—listening, speaking, reading, and writing. Creative and aesthetic experiences are welcome additions to classroom routines and, used wisely and purposefully, can contribute to children's becoming readers and writers.

BIBLIOGRAPHY AND SUGGESTED REFERENCES

Booth, D. (1994). *Classroom voices: Language-based learning in the elementary school.* Toronto, Canada: Harcourt Brace.

Busching, B. (1981). Readers theatre: An education for language and life. *Language Arts, 58,* 330–338.

Cecil, N., & Lauritzen, P. (1994). *Literacy and the arts for the integrated classroom.* New York: Longman.

Combs, M., & Beach, J. (1994). Stories and storytelling: Personalizing the social studies. *The Reading Teacher, 47,* 464–471.

Criscuolo, N. (1985). Creative approaches to teaching reading through art. *Art Education, 38,* 13–16.

Cullinan, B. (1989). *Literature and the child.* San Diego: Harcourt Brace Jovanovich.

Cunningham, P. (1982). The clip sheet: Drawing them into reading. *The Reading Teacher, 35,* 960–962.

Harp, B., & Brewer, J. (1991). *Reading and writing: Teaching for the connections.* San Diego: Harcourt Brace Jovanovich.

Hurst, C. (1994). Diaries that aren't under lock and key. *Teaching K–8, 25,* 80–82.

Johnson, T. (1987). *Language through literature.* Portsmouth, N.H.: Heinemann.

Johnson, T., & Louis, D. (1990). *Bringing it all together: A program for literacy.* Portsmouth, N.H.: Heinemann.

Kingore, B. (1982). Storytelling: A bridge from the university to the elementary school to the home. *Language Arts, 59,* 28–32.

Lundsteen, S. (1989). *Language arts: A problem-solving approach.* New York: Harper & Row.

Mallan, K. (1991). *Children as storytellers.* Newtown, N.S.W., Australia: Primary English Teaching Association.

Manna, A. (1984). Making language come alive through reading plays. *The Reading Teacher, 37,* 712–717.

Martinez, M. (1993). Motivating dramatic story reenactments. *The Reading Teacher, 46,* 682–688.

McGuire, G. (1984). How arts instruction affects reading and language: Theory and research. *The Reading Teacher, 37,* 835–839.

Miccinati, J., & Phelps, S. (1980). Classroom drama from children's reading: From page to stage. *The Reading Teacher, 34,* 260–272.

Moffett, J., & Wagner, B. (1992). *Student centered language arts, K–12.* Portsmouth, N.H.: Boynton/Cook.

Moxley, C. (1994). Pocket tales to go. In The National Storytelling Association (Ed.) *Tales as tools: The power of story in the classroom,* 65. Jonesborough, Tenn.: The National Storytelling Press.

Nelson, O. (1989). Storytelling: Language experience for meaning making. *The Reading Teacher, 42,* 386–390.

Roney, R. C. (1989). Back to the basics with storytelling. *The Reading Teacher, 42,* 520–523.

Roskos, K. (1988). Literacy at work in play. *The Reading Teacher, 41,* 562–566.

Shepard, A. (1993). From script to stage: Tips for Readers Theatre. *The Reading Teacher, 48,* 184–186.

Temple, C., & Gillet, J. (1989). *Language arts: Learning processes and teaching practices.* Glenview, Ill.: Scott, Foresman.

Thompson, G. (1988). *Classroom drama: Act it out.* New York: Scholastic.

Thompson, G. (1989). *52 ways to use paperbacks in the classroom.* New York: Scholastic.

Tompkins, G., & Hoskisson, K. (1995). *Language arts: Content and teaching strategies.* Columbus, Ohio: Merrill.

Verriour, P. (1990). Storying and storytelling in drama. *Language Arts, 67,* 144–150.

Young, T., & Vardell, S. (1993). Weaving Readers Theatre and nonfiction into the curriculum. *The Reading Teacher, 46,* 396–406.

CHILDREN'S LITERATURE CITED

Adams, P. (1975). *There was an old woman who swallowed a fly.* New York: Grosset & Dunlap.

Ahlberg, J., & Ahlberg, A. (1986). *The jolly postman.* Boston: Little, Brown.

Ahlberg, J., & Ahlberg, A. (1991). *The jolly Christmas postman.* Boston: Little, Brown.

Bang, M. (1985). *The paper crane.* New York: Greenwillow.

Barrett, J. (1970). *Animals should definitely* not *wear clothing.* New York: Atheneum.

Blume, J. (1972). *Tales of a fourth-grade nothing.* New York: Dell.

Blume, J. (1980). *Superfudge.* New York: Dell.

Blume, J. (1990). *Fudge-a-mania.* New York: Dell.

Brisson, P. (1989). *Your best friend, Kate.* New York: Bradbury Press.

Carle, E. (1970). *The very hungry caterpillar.* Cleveland: Collins-World.

Cartwright, P. (1991). *The diary of Neil Aitken.* Austin, Tex.: Steck-Vaughn.

Cleary, B. (1983). *Dear Mr. Henshaw.* New York: Dell.

Cooney, B. (1994). *Only Opal: The diary of a young girl.* New York: Philomel.

Cowley, J. (1980). *Mrs. Wishy-Washy.* San Diego: The Wright Group.

Cowley, J. (1983). *The jigaree.* San Diego: The Wright Group.

Crews, D. (1986). *Ten Black Dots.* New York: Greenwillow.

Dahl, R. (1961). *James and the giant peach.* New York: Puffin Books.

DePaola, T. (1983). *The legend of the bluebonnet.* New York: G. P. Putnam's Sons.

Fitzhugh, L. (1964). *Harriet the spy.* New York: Harper & Row.

Fleshman, P. (1988). *Rondo in C.* New York: Harper & Row.

Fritz, J. (1969). *George Washington's breakfast.* New York: G. P. Putnam's Sons.

Fritz, J. (1973). *And then what happened, Paul Revere?* New York: Coward, McCann & Geoghegan.

Galdone, P. (1973). *The three billy goats gruff.* New York: Seabury Press.

Giff, P. (1993). *The postcard pest.* New York: Dell Yearling.

Hague, K., & Hague, M. (1981). *The man who kept house.* San Diego: Harcourt Brace Jovanovich.
Harper, W. (1989). *The gunniwolf.* New York: The Trumpet Club.
Hart, T. (1994). *Antarctic Diary.* New York: SRA Division of Macmillan/McGraw HIll.
Harvey, B. (1986). *My prairie year.* New York: Holiday.
Heinrich, B. (1990). *An owl in the house: A naturalist's diary.* New York: Little Brown.
Hesse, K. (1992). *Letters from Rifka.* New York: Trumpet.
Hyman, T. (1983). *Little Red Riding Hood.* New York: Holiday House.
Keats, E. J. (1962). *The snowy day.* New York: Scholastic.
Keats, E. J. (1972). *Over in the meadow.* New York: Scholastic.
Kellogg, S. (1973). *The island of the Skog.* New York: Dial.
Kent, J. (1971). *The fat cat.* New York: Scholastic.
Krauss, R. (1945). *The carrot seed.* New York: Scholastic.
Langstaff, J. (1956). *Frog went a-courtin'.* San Diego: Harcourt Brace Jovanovich.
Langstaff, J. (1957). *Over in the meadow.* New York: Harcourt Brace Jovanovich.
Lawson, R. (1939). *Ben and me.* Boston: Little, Brown.
Lawson, R. (1953). *Mr. Revere and I.* New York: Dell.
MacLachlan, P. (1985). *Sarah plain and tall.* New York: Harper & Row.
Marsden, J. (1987). *So much to tell you.* Boston: Little, Brown.
Martin, Jr., B. (1970). *Brown bear, brown bear, what do you see?* New York: Holt, Rinehart & Winston.
Martin, Jr., B. (1991). *Polar bear, polar bear, what do you hear?* New York: Holt, Rinehart & Winston.
Martin, Jr., B., & Archambault, J. (1985). *The ghost-eye tree.* New York: Holt, Rinehart & Winston.
Mayer, M. (1968). *There's a nightmare in my closet.* New York: Dial.
Mayer, M. (1987). *The pied piper of Hamelin.* New York: Macmillan.
McCloskey, R. (1948). *Blueberries for Sal.* New York: Viking.
McQueen, L. (1985). *The little red hen.* New York: Scholastic.
Mooney, M. (1991). *Taking Jason to Grandma's.* Bothell, Wash.: The Wright Group.
Mowat, F. (1961). *Owls in the family.* New York: Bantam.
Numeroff, L. (1985). *If you give a mouse a cookie.* New York: Harper & Row.
Numeroff, L. (1991). *If you give a mouse a muffin.* New York: Harper & Row.
Pallotta, J. (1991). *The underwater alphabet book.* Watertown, Mass.: Charlesbridge.
Other titles by Pallotta:
The icky bug alphabet book
The bird alphabet book
The ocean alphabet book
The yucky reptile alphabet book
The flower alphabet book
The frog alphabet book
The dinosaur alphabet book
The furry alphabet book
Paulsen, G. (1987). *Hatchet.* New York: Puffin Books.
Rey, H. A. (1952). *Curious George rides a bike.* Boston: Houghton Mifflin.
Scheer, J., & Bileck, M. (1964). *Rain makes applesauce.* New York: Holiday House.
Sendak, M. (1962). *Chicken soup with rice.* New York: Harper & Row.
Sendak, M. (1963). *Where the wild things are.* New York: Harper & Row.
Smith, R. (1987). *Mostly Michael.* New York: Dell.
Steig, W. (1984). *Dr. DeSoto.* New York: Scholastic.
Turkle, B. (1976). *Deep in the forest.* New York: Dutton.
Turner, A. (1987). *Nettie's trip south.* New York: Macmillan.
Viorst, J. (1972). *Alexander and the terrible, horrible, no good, very bad day.* New York: Atheneum.
Waber, B. (1972). *Ira sleeps over.* Boston: Houghton Mifflin.
Williams, L. (1986). *The little old lady who was not afraid of anything.* New York: Crowell.
Wood, A. (1984). *The napping house.* San Diego: Harcourt Brace Jovanovich.
Zemach, M. (1969). *The judge.* New York: Farrar, Straus & Giroux.
Zemach, M. (1976). *It could always be worse.* New York: Scholastic.
Zemach, M. (1988). *The three little pigs.* New York: Farrar, Straus & Giroux.

PICTURE SONGBOOKS AND MUSIC RESOURCES

Adams, P. (1975). *There was an old lady who swallowed a fly.* New York: Grosset & Dunlap.
Aliki. (1974). *Go tell Aunt Rhody.* New York: Macmillan.
Bierhorst, J. (1979). *A cry from the earth: Music of the North American Indians.* New York: Four Winds Press.

Bonne, R. (1976). *I know an old lady.* New York: Rand McNally.

Bryan, A. (1982). *I'm going to sing.* New York: Atheneum.

Child, L. (1975). *Over the river and through the wood.* New York: Scholastic.

Cloonan, Kathryn. (1991). *Sing me a story, read me a song, book I.* Beverly Hills, Fla.: Rhythm and Reading Resources.

Cloonan, Kathryn. (1991). *Sing me a story, read me a song, book II.* Beverly Hills, Fla.: Rhythm and Reading Resources.

Fleshman, P. (1988). *Rondo in C.* New York: Harper & Row.

Gag, W. (1975). *The sorcerer's apprentice.* New York: Coward, McCann & Geoghegan.

Glazer, T. (1982). *On top of spaghetti.* New York: Doubleday.

Grahame, K. (1985). *Wind in the willows.* New York: Derrydale Books.

Ivimey, J. (1990). *Three blind mice.* Boston: Little, Brown/Joy Street.

Jones, C. (1990). *This old man.* Boston: Houghton Mifflin.

Keats, E. J. (1972). *Over in the meadow.* New York: Scholastic.

Lamont, P. (1990). *Ring-a-round-a-rosy.* Boston: Little, Brown/Joy Street.

Langstaff, J. (1973). *Frog went a-courtin'.* New York: Scholastic.

Langstaff, J. (1974). *Oh, a-hunting we will go.* New York: Atheneum.

Larrick, N. (1989). *Songs from Mother Goose with traditional melody for each.* New York: Harper & Row.

Milne, A. A. (1958). *The Pooh song book.* New York: Harper & Row.

Perfection Form Company. *Story songs.* Logan, Iowa: Author. (These are teacher guides, audiotapes of songs, and song-based activities to extend children's literature themes. Individual titles are available.)

Poelker, K. (1990). *Rhythms to reading series.* Wheeling, Ill.: Hawthorne Publishers. (Individual titles are available in the series.)

Quackenbush, R. (1972). *Old MacDonald had a farm.* New York: J. B. Lippincott.

Raffi. *Songs to read.* New York: Crown Books for Young Readers.

Rigby. *Talk to me music.* (P.O. Box 797, Crystal Lake, IL 60014)
Individual titles available:
The circus is in town
Talk to me
I wear my hat
I like the rain
My dog
The T-shirt song

Spier, P. (1961). *The fox went out on a chilly night.* New York: Doubleday.

Williams, S. (1989). *Pudding and pie: Favorite nursery rhymes.* New York: Oxford University Press. (Accompanied by musical versions on audiotapes.)

Wright Group. *The Song Box.* (19201 120th Ave. NE, Bothell, VA 98011)
Individual titles available:
Down by the bay
The eensy weensy spider
Monster party
The animal fair
She'll be comin' round the mountain
The more we get together
Old MacDonald had a farm
The ants go marching
Fee-fie-foe-fum
Yankee doodle

Note: There are many performers who have prepared tapes for children. The lyrics may be transcribed onto chart paper, placed on overhead projectors, or written on individual sheets for the children to read as they sing. Several of these artists include Raffi; Tom Glazer; Sharon, Lois, and Bram; Carol King; Rosenshontz; and Peter, Paul, and Mary.

BOOKS FOR COOKING ACTIVITIES

Alki. (1976). *Corn is maize.* New York: Harper & Row.

Barchers, S., & Marden, P. (1991). *Cooking up U.S. history.* Englewood, Colo.: Teacher Ideas Press.

Barrett, J. (1978). *Cloudy with a chance of meatballs.* New York: Macmillan.

Bolton, E., & Snowball, D. (1986). *Growing radishes and carrots.* New York: Scholastic.

Cowley, J. (1983). *The biggest cake in the world.* Katonah, N.Y.: Richard C. Owen Publishers.

Cowley, J. (1986). *Yuk soup.* San Diego: The Wright Group.

DePaola, T. (1978). *Pancakes for breakfast.* San Diego: Harcourt Brace Jovanovich.

DePaola, T. (1978). *The popcorn book.* New York: Holiday House.

Ehlert, L. (1987). *Growing vegetable soup.* San Diego: Harcourt Brace Jovanovich.

Ehlert, L. (1990). *Feathers for lunch.* San Diego: Harcourt Brace Jovanovich.

Fann, C. (1989). *Vegetable soup.* San Diego: The Wright Group.
Gelman, R. (1977). *More spaghetti I say.* New York: Scholastic.
Gibbons, G. (1984). *The seasons of Arnold's apple tree.* San Diego: Harcourt Brace Jovanovich.
Gross, R. (1990). *What's on my plate?* New York: Macmillan.
Irving, J., & Currie, R. (1986). *Mudluscious: Stories and activities featuring food for preschool children.* Littleton, Colo.: Libraries Unlimited.
Krauss, R. (1945). *The carrot seed.* New York: Scholastic.
Lord, J. (1972). *The giant jam sandwich.* Boston: Houghton Mifflin.
McCloskey, R. (1948). *Blueberries for Sal.* New York: Scholastic.
McGovern, A. (1968). *Stone soup.* New York: Scholastic.
Numeroff, L. (1985). *If you give a mouse a cookie.* New York: Harper & Row.
Shaw, C. (1947). *It looked like spilt milk.* New York: Harper & Row.
Thayer, J. (1953). *The popcorn dragon.* New York: Scholastic.
Titherington, J. (1986). *Pumpkin, pumpkin.* New York: Scholastic.
Vaughn, M. (1989). *The sandwich that Max made.* Crystal Lake, Ill.: Rigby.

RESOURCES FOR PUPPETRY

Adair, M. (1964). *Do it in a day puppets for beginners.* New York: Dutton.
Baumann, H. (1967). *Casper and his friends.* New York: Walck.
Champlin, C., & Renfro, N. (1985). *Storytelling with puppets.* Chicago: American Library Association.
Coudron, J. (1983). *Alphabet puppets.* Belmont, Calif.: Fearon Teacher Aids.
Easterday, D. (undated). *Bag puppets.* Greensboro, N.C.: The Education Center.
Ficken, B. (1935). *Handbook of fist puppets.* Philadelphia: J. B. Lippincott.
Hopper, G. (1966). *Puppet making through the grades.* Worcester, Mass.: Davis Publications.
Jagendorf, M. (1952). *First book of puppets.* New York: Franklin Watts.
Krisvoy, J. (1981). *The Good Apple puppet book.* Carthage, Ill.: Good Apple, Inc.
Lewis, S. (1967). *Making easy puppets.* New York: Dutton.
Martin, S., & Macmillan, D. (1986). *Puppets and costumes.* Carthage, Ill.: Good Apple, Inc.
Mehrens, G., & Wick, K. (1988). *Bagging it with puppets.* Belmont, Calif.: Fearon Teacher Aids.
Oldfield, M. (1982). *Finger puppets and finger plays.* Minneapolis: Creative Storytime Press.
Pels, G. (1957). *Easy puppets.* New York: Crowell.
Philpott, V., & McNeil, M. (1975). *The know how book of puppets.* London, England: Usborne Publishing Co.
Punch and Judy. (1965). *Punch and Judy: A play for puppets.* Boston: Little, Brown.
Renfro, N. (1984). *Puppet shows made easy!* Austin, Texas: Nancy Renfro Studios.
Richmond, A. (1950). *Remo Befano's book of puppetry.* New York: Macmillan.
Roberts, L. (1986). *Mitt magic, fingerplays for finger puppets.* Mt. Ranier, Md.: Gryphon House.
Ross, L. (1970). *Puppet shows.* New York: Lothrop, Lee & Shepard.
Schramm, T. (1993). *Puppet plays: From workshop to performance.* Englewood, Colorado: Teachers Ideas Press.
Supraner, R., & Supraner, L. (1981). *Plenty of puppets to make.* Mahwah, N.J.: Troll Associates.
Yerian, C. (1974). *Puppets and shadow plays.* New York: Children's Press.

SOURCES FOR BOOKMAKING AND EXTENDING LITERATURE

Aliki. (1986). *How a book is made.* New York: Crowell.
Brady, M., & Gleason, P. (1994). *Artstarts: Drama, music, movement, puppetry, and storytelling activities.* Englewood, Colorado: Teacher Idea Press.
Considine, D.; Haley, G.; & Lacy; L. (1994). *Imagine that: Developing critical thinking and critical viewing through children's literature.* Englewood, Colorado: Teacher Idea Press.
Heald-Taylor, G. (1985). *Making and using big books: Unit A.* Toronto: Shirley Lewis Information Services.
Heald-Taylor, G. (1986). *Making and using big books: Unit B.* Toronto: Shirley Lewis Information Services.
Irvine, J. (1987). *Make your own pop-ups.* North Ryde, Australia: Angus and Robertson Publishers.
Irvine, J. (1993). *Straw into gold: Books and activities about folktales.* Englewood, Colorado: Teacher Idea Press.
Massam, J., & Kulik, A. (1986). *And what else?* San Diego: The Wright Group.

Moen, C. (1991). *Teaching with Caldecott Books.* New York: Scholastic.

Sattler, H. (1987). *Recipes for art and craft materials.* New York: Lothrop, Lee & Shepard.

Sheehan, K., & Waidner, M. (1994). *Earth child: Games, stories, activities, experiments & ideas about living lightly on planet Earth.* Tulsa, Oklahoma: Council Oak Books.

Staton, H., & McCarthy, T. (1994). *Science & stories: Integrating science and literature K–3.* Glenview, IL.: GoodYear Books.

Staton, H., & McCarthy, T. (1994). *Science & stories: Integrating science and literature 4–6.* Glenview, IL.: GoodYear Books.

Stowell, C. (1994). *Step-by-step making books.* New York: Kingfisher.

Sunflower, C. (1993). *Seventy-five creative ways to publish students' writing.* New York: Scholastic.

Walsh, N. (1994). *Making books across the curriculum.* New York: Scholastic.

Wendelin, K., & Greenlaw, M. J. (1986). *Storybook classrooms.* Atlanta: Humanics Limited.

BOOKS AND SOURCES FOR READERS' THEATER

Anderson, J. (1991). *Christopher Columbus: From vision to voyage.* New York: Dial.

Anno, M., & Anno M. (1983). *Anno's mysterious multiplying jar.* New York: Philomel.

Chang, I. (1991). *A separate battle: Women and the Civil War.* New York: Lodestar.

Cleary, B. (1950). *Henry Huggins.* New York: Morrow.

Cleary, B. (1983). *Dear Mr. Henshaw.* New York: Morrow.

Cole, J. (1990). *The magic school bus inside the solar system.* New York: Scholastic.

Collier, J., & Collier, C. (1974). *My brother Sam is dead.* New York: Four Winds Press.

Duke, K. (1992). *Aunt Isabel tells a good one.* New York: A Puffin Unicorn.

Freedman, R. (1990). *Lincoln: A photobiography.* New York: Clarion.

Fritz, J. (1973). *And then what happened, Paul Revere?* New York: Crowell.

Galdone, P. (1973). *The three billy goats gruff.* New York: Seabury Press.

Grimm, J., & Grimm, W. (1982). "The Bremen Town musicians." In *Favorite Tales from Grimm.* New York: Four Winds Press.

Hooks, W. (1987). *Moss gown.* New York: Clarion.

Hunt, I. (1964). *Across five Aprils.* Chicago: Follett.

Hutchins, P. (1972). *Goodnight owl.* New York: Macmillan.

Kellogg, S. (1984). *Paul Bunyan.* New York: Morrow.

Kellogg, S. (1985). *Chicken Little.* New York: Morrow.

Konigsberg, E. (1967). *From the mixed-up files of Mrs. Basil E. Frankweiler.* New York: Atheneum.

Lauber, P. (1989). *The news about dinosaurs.* New York: Bradbury.

Levine, E. (1988). *If you traveled on the underground railroad.* New York: Scholastic.

L'Engle, M. (1963). *A wrinkle in time.* New York: Farrar, Straus & Giroux.

MacLachlan, P. (1985). *A wrinkle in time.* New York: Harper & Row.

Martin, B., & Archambault, J. (1985). *The ghost-eye tree.* New York: Holt, Rinehart & Winston.

Parrish, P. (1963). *Amelia Bedelia.* New York: Harper & Row.

Perrault, C. (1985). *Cinderella.* New York: Dial.

Simon, S. (1990). *Oceans.* New York: Morrow.

Slobodkina, E. (1947). *Caps for sale.* Boston: Addison-Wesley.

Steig, W. (1976). *The amazing bone.* New York: Farrar, Straus & Giroux.

Steig, W. (1984). *Doctor DeSoto.* New York: Scholastic.

Van Allsburg, C. (1981). *Jumanji.* Boston: Houghton Mifflin.

Waber, B. (1972). *Ira sleeps over.* Boston: Houghton Mifflin.

White, E. B. (1952). *Charlotte's web.* New York: Harper & Row.

Yolen, J. (1988) *The Devil's arithmetic.* New York: Puffin.

PREPARED SCRIPTS

Bauer, C. (1987). *Presenting Readers Theatre.* New York: Wilson. This book contains brief scripts that are adapted from favorite children's books, as well as suggestions for getting started using Readers' Theater.

Laughlin, M.; Black, P.; & Loberg, M. (1991). *Social studies Readers' Theatre for children: Scripts and script development.* Englewood, Colo.: Teacher Ideas Press. This book incorporates Readers' Theater into the social studies curriculum. Both completed scripts and books to use for preparing scripts are included. Some of the completed scripts include *Pecos Bill, Mike Fink,* and *Little House on the Prairie.* Some of the suggested scripts include *Amos Fortune: Free Man, The Drinking Gourd,* and *Mr. Revere and I.*

Laughlin, M., & Latrobe, K. (1990). *Readers Theatre for children.* Englewood, Colo.: Teacher Ideas Press. This book consists of prepared scripts and books and suggestions for script development.

Some of the completed scripts are *The Secret Garden, How the Camel Got Its Hump,* and *The Wonderful Wizard of Oz.* Some of the book titles for suggested scripts (these come complete with suggested staging, narrator's opening and closing lines, and scripting suggestions) include *How to Eat Fried Worms, The Borrowers,* and *The Sign of the Beaver.*

Sloyer, S. (1982). *Readers Theatre: Story dramatization in the classroom.* Urbana, Ill.: National Council of Teachers of English. The book contains guidelines for choosing and adapting materials for Readers' Theater.

SOURCES FOR STORYTELLING

Bauer, C. (1983). *Make way for books.* New York: H. W. Wilson Company.

Bauer, C. (1993). *New Handbook for storytellers.* Chicago: American Library Association.

Bauer, C. (1985). *Celebrations.* New York: H. W. Wilson Company.

Blatt, G. (Ed.). (1993). *Once upon a folktale: Capturing the folklore process with children.* New York: Teachers College Press.

Breneman, L., & Breneman, B. (1983). *Once upon a time.* Chicago: Nelson-Hall.

Catron, C., & Parks, B. (1986). *Super story telling.* Minneapolis, Minn.: T. S. Denison and Company, Inc.

Champlin, C., & Renfro, N. (1985). *Storytelling with puppets.* Chicago: American Library Association.

Farrell, C. (1993). *Storytelling: A Guide for Teachers.* New York: Scholastic.

Farrell, C., & Nessel, D. (1983). *Word weaving: A storytelling guide.* San Francisco: San Francisco Study Center.

Hamilton, M., & Weiss, M. (1990). *Children tell stories: A teaching guide.* Katonah, N.Y: Richard C. Owen Publishers.

Hart, M. (1987). *Fold-and-cut stories and fingerplays.* Belmont, Calif.: Fearon Teacher Aids.

Hutchinson, D. (1985). *Storytelling tips: How to love, learn, and relate a story.* Boston: Foundation Books.

Irving, J. (1987). *Glad rags: Stories and activities featuring clothes for children.* Englewood, Colo.: Libraries Unlimited.

Kinghorn, H., & Pelton, M. (1991). *Every child a storyteller.* Englewood, Colo.: Teacher Ideas Press.

Livo, N., & Rietz, S. (1986). *Storytelling process and practice.* Englewood, Colo.: Libraries Unlimited.

Livo, N., & Rietz, S. (1987). *Storytelling activities.* Englewood, Colo.: Libraries Unlimited.

Livo, N., & Rietz, S. (1991). *Storytelling folklore sourcebook.* Englewood, Colo.: Libraries Unlimited.

Maguire, J. (1985). *Creative storytelling: Choosing, inventing, and sharing tales for children.* New York: McGraw-Hill.

National Storytelling Association. (1994). *Tales as tools: The power of story in the classroom.* Jonesborough, Tenn.: The National Storytelling Press.

Oldfield, M. (1973). *Lots more tell and draw stories.* Minneapolis: Creative Storytime Press.

Pellowski, A. (1984). *The story vine.* New York: Collier/Alladdin Macmillan Publishing Co.

Pellowski, A. (1987). *The family storytelling handbook.* New York: Macmillan.

Rosen, B. (1988). *And none of it was nonsense.* New York: Scholastic.

Schimmel, N. (1982). *Just enough to make a story: A sourcebook for storytelling.* Berkeley, Calif.: Sisters' Choice Press.

Shedd, C., & Shedd, M. (1984). *Tell me a story.* Garden City, N.Y.: Doubleday.

Shepard, A. (1993). *Stories on stage: Scripts for Reader's Theater.* New York: H. W. Wilson.

Stangl, J. (1988). *Is your storytale dragging?* Belmont, Calif.: Fearon Teacher Aids.

Warren, J. (1984). *Cut and tell: Scissor stories for winter.* Everett, Wash.: Warren Publishing House, Inc.

Wason-Ellam, L. (1987). *Sharing stories with children: Reading aloud and storytelling.* Calgary, Alberta, Canada: Warren West.

Note: The National Association for the Preservation and Perpetuation of Storytelling has a variety of storytelling resources. Their address is NAPPS, P.O. Box 309, Jonesborough, TN 37659.

11 COMPUTERS IN THE WHOLE LANGUAGE CLASSROOM

AND IN THAT UNIVERSE . . .

Once there was 1 Universe.
In that Universe there were 2 Galaxies.
In those Galaxies there were 3 Star Systems.
In those three Star Systems there were 4 beautiful Planets.
On those 4 beautiful Planets there were 5 odd continents.
On those 5 odd Continents there were 6 weird Countries.
In each country there were 7 States
In each State there were 8 counties.
In each County there were 9 sparsely populated Villages.
Now you will find out why.
In each of those 9 Villages there were 10 Volcanoes.
On each of those 10 Volcanoes there were 11 Cooled Chunks of Lava.
On each of those 11 Cooled Chunks of Lava there were 12 unique Flower Pots.
In each of those 12 unique Flower Pots there were 13 Plants.
Along with those 13 Plants there were 14 twisty Roots.
In each of those 14 twisty Roots there were 15 Waterways.
In those 15 Waterways there were 16 Drops of Water.
In all of those 16 Drops of Water there were 17 Micro-organisms
On each of those 17 Micro-organisms there were 18 Cilia.
Each of those 18 Cilia contained 19 Viruses.
Each of those 19 Viruses had 20 Ugly Bumps.
As to how many Bumps on each of those Viruses the answer is surprising. It is 20! 20! is 20 Factorial. 20 Factorial or 20! is equal to
2, 432, 902, 008, 176, 604, 000!
One day all of the volcanoes erupted. That is how the dinosaurs became extinct. Millions of years from now the same thing is going to happen to the Universe again!!

by Laura Constantinides
Grade 4
Windham, N.Y.

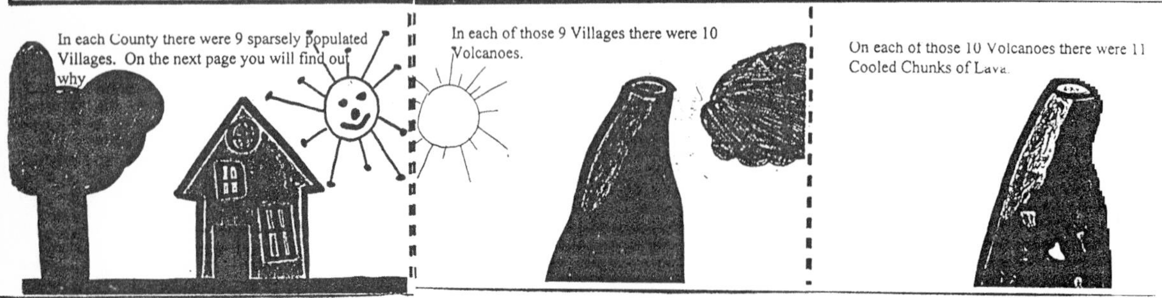

In each County there were 9 sparsely populated Villages. On the next page you will find out why
In each of those 9 Villages there were 10 Volcanoes.
On each of those 10 Volcanoes there were 11 Cooled Chunks of Lava.

Inspired by: *Anno's Mysterious Multiplying Jar*

OVERVIEW

This chapter explores the use of computers in a whole language classroom by examining research in the areas of computers and reading, computers and writing, and computers and social interactions. Whole language teachers share the belief that children learn language naturally through social interactions and by reading and writing real, meaningful texts. To support this belief about language learning and thus literacy acquisition, whole language classrooms are process oriented, and risk taking is encouraged. This extends not only to the more usual activities generally associated with reading and writing programs, but also to the use of technology in the classroom, particularly computers. As this chapter will attest, computers have earned a place in the whole language classroom. Not only is relevant information on the use of computers in whole language classrooms provided but also some practical implications. This chapter takes you into the classroom of one whole language teacher—Joan Cavagnaro—who also assisted in the writing of this chapter. We thank Joan for sharing her experiences and expertise as we make new connections for using the computer in a whole language classroom.

Questions to Ponder

1. What is the role of computers in a whole language classroom?
2. How does one choose effective computer programs that go beyond skill and drill practice and involve students in meaningful reading and writing activities?
3. What kinds of meaningful reading and writing activities can be enhanced by using the computer?
4. How can cooperative learning be enhanced when students use the computer?
5. Can parents become involved in computer-assisted instruction?

INTRODUCTION

Two important movements in U.S. schools today may well have an impact on each other. These are the whole language approach to reading and the use of computers in classrooms. "Whole language" has become a label for a grass-roots teacher movement that is making worldwide curricular changes (Watson, 1989). According to Goodman (1986), "Whole language is an attempt to get back to basics in the real sense of the word—to set aside the basal, workbooks, and the tests, and to return to inviting kids to learn to read and write by reading and writing real stuff" (38). As this movement infiltrates elementary schools across the United States, it is meeting another strong movement, the use of computer technology. Computers are becoming necessary instructional tools for the classroom. The focus of this chapter is on presenting these two movements in conjunction with one another. Smith (1985) best describes the necessity of considering this issue, stating that "electronic technology cannot be ignored in the classroom, and teachers must not leave decisions about how computers should be employed to outsiders" (161).

COMPUTERS IN THE SCHOOLS

In recent years many books have been written, articles published, workshops given, and lectures attended on the subject of whole language. College professors, parents, administrators, and teachers are embracing this philosophy with varying degrees of commitment. At the same time an entirely different faction is encouraging, if not pushing, technology into these same classrooms. Studies have found that children are drawn to technology and are intrinsically motivated to using computers (Guthrie and Richardson, 1995). This affects all areas of the curriculum—from the language arts to science to mathematics.

Schools have been moving from teaching computer applications as a separate subject, to using computers to facilitate learning in many disciplines (Bradsher and Hagan, 1995). Computer instruction has evolved from simple skill and drill activities to more thought-provoking applications, thereby enabling students to delve into complex problems in ways that promote reflection and understanding (Becker and Hativa, 1994). By having access to the Internet and being exposed to such techniques as image processing (a process that translates a picture into a matrix of dots or digits that can then be displayed on a computer screen as a photographic quality image), students can explore science by doing what scientists do—participating in a scientific community devoted to learning about the world (Raphael and Greenberg, 1995; Van Dusen and Worthen, 1995).

This use of technology is by no means limited to scientific endeavors. In language arts, students not only are highly motivated to write, but they also write more. Thanks to telecommunications, students can communicate with other students throughout the world, bringing the world into the classrooms (McCarty, 1995; Copen, 1995). Computer technology can enhance an individualized approach to learning by letting students learn and progress at their own pace, with teachers acting like facilitators who tailor their support to the needs of the individual student (Guthrie and Richardson, 1995). It is up to teachers to determine what kinds of technology assisted learning tasks can support their curriculum and then figure out how to use technology to supplement their curriculum and their instruction.

It is the intent of this chapter to discuss some of the computer applications that can enhance student learning in settings that promote a constructivist approach to learning. Some insight may be gained by looking at studies of computer use, focusing on three important aspects of a whole language approach: reading, writing, and the social milieu in which learning takes place. Although it is difficult to separate these three aspects, it is necessary to reach a clearer understanding of the possibilities of computer use in a whole language classroom.

Computers and Reading

Early developments in technology have not always been used to the best advantage in the primary grades. This is evidenced by the abundance of drill and practice type software that is currently available. The emphasis of whole language is in direct contrast to this approach. Instead of "resorting to the 'electronic workbooks' that publishers are desperately pushing, we need to explore the great potential that computers offer us" (Doyle, 1988, 239). Whole language focuses on the integration of listening, speaking, reading, and writing in meaningful ways. Shaver and Wise (1990) state that computers can be valuable tools for immersing children in print-rich environments. They reported successful results using International Business Machines' (IBM) *Writing to Read* program, a program designed to enhance writing and reading skills through the use of computers and learning centers. These centers focused on sounds, words, and sentence structure. As a result of the increase of microcomputers in kindergarten and first-grade classrooms, the teachers reported that more kindergarten students were ready for formal first-grade reading instruction. In addition, there were fewer retentions, reading and writing scores were improved, and students showed increased motivation and self-confidence.

The whole language approach to reading and writing formed the basis for the Computer Pals Across the World Project (Beazely, 1989). Computer Pals Across the World provides students with opportunities to experience language in a global classroom. Using a word processor to write messages, students send their messages through an electronic mail system to their Computer Pals in another country. The aims of the project were to offer a real context to improve communication skills, provide cultural exchanges, provide motivation for less interested students, and develop keyboarding skills. Students began by writing letters of introduction. From then on, they exchanged reports on a wide range of topics using many forms of writing, including poetry and a script that depicted a local myth or legend. They also exchanged a dialogue on social issues. Several benefits resulted from this project. Student motivation was enhanced, and students read more with increased interest and enjoyment. Reading no longer was an isolated classroom activity; rather, it was done in a meaningful context. Students scan text on the screen, read the hard copy, and share it with friends. Therefore the student is engaged in a minimum of three reading activities with each written exchange. Since students work in pairs at the screen and read the messages being sent as well as received, active interaction with the text is encouraged.

Recently, IBM introduced *Stories and More,* a voice-supported, literature-based reading comprehension program. It is designed for emergent readers in first grade as well as certain kindergarten and second-grade students. It presents traditional, contemporary, and original children's literature to be read with or without digitized speech assistance. *Stories and More* is intended to help children enjoy reading by exposing them to the rich vocabulary and illustrations found in high-quality children's literature. The program provides four on-line activities that enrich the experiences children can have with literature. The Starting Off Activity introduces each story and prepares the student for reading. These activities include building vocabulary and introducing characters and setting. During the Story Time Activity, students have an opportunity to have the story read to them while they follow along in the text. The Thinking About Activity encourages students to remember what has been read and extends their understanding of story elements and structure. The final activity is called the Going Beyond Activity, in which students are encouraged to write about what has been read. Once the students have entered their responses, thoughts, or comments, these can be printed out or read back via computer-synthesized speech. *Stories and More* offers a flexible program that can be adapted to any teaching style (IBM, 1991).

Computers and Writing

Student motivation is enhanced when students know that their writing pieces and illustrations will be printed out and published for others to see (Guthrie and Richardson, 1995). Student motivation is not the only aspect having to do with student writing that is affected by the use of computers. Using the computer results in students spending much longer on their writing. They therefore write more when using technology—they add more detail, make more revisions, and self-evaluate. In essence, they gain a better understanding of what is involved in the writing process. The computer allows students to take risks because they can easily revise their writing (Phenix and Hannan, 1984). For students who have difficulty with letter formation, the computer eliminates the burden of copying writing over and over and gives students readable, high-quality products. In this sense, using computers serves as an equalizer because the final products all have the same letter quality despite individual differences in fine-motor or writing skills (Katzer and Crnkovich, 1991). Students learn that writing involves more than one draft and that revision is a natural part of the writing process. The use of word processing can enhance the teaching of written composition and can be learned quickly, with minimum practice. The use of computer word processing in writing has a motivational value, facilitates group discussions about writing, and helps to foster peer editing (Kurth, 1987).

The computer becomes a tool in facilitating the students' use of the writing process. Once the text has been entered into the computer, it is available to be restructured and edited. As students mill around the computer, waiting for their turns, they read and discuss each other's writing (Bruce, Michaels, and Watson-Gegeo, 1985). This interaction affects the content and form of what is written. At the same time, this interaction sets a purpose for writing and identifies the audience. Since the readers are most likely the members of the class, the intended audience is well defined. When using computers to enhance student writing, language learning seems to evolve naturally through "delighted experiences of discovery" (Moore, 1989, 611).

Computers and Social Interactions

The computer is a means for children to learn both socially and cognitively, as well as a way to provide encouragement for social interactions (Clements, 1987). The research further suggests that the computer experience extends to classroom group activities where attitudes toward learning are positively affected (Clements, 1987). Children have been observed commenting positively about their computer work. They verbalize curiosity, interest, and enthusiasm, and a sense of personal control after direct involvement with computers.

Social interactions during computer use are similar to interactions in other areas of the classroom. Over time, without teacher intervention, computers facilitate cooperation, friendship formation, and interactive problem solving (Clements, 1987; Guthrie and Richardson, 1995; Bradsher and Hagan, 1994). Sometimes, pairing children is necessary when access to computers is limited; at other times, pairs are voluntary and self-selected. When children work in pairs at the computer, learning through interaction seems inevitable (DeGroff, 1989). The upright and sometimes colorful computer screen encourages this interaction. As children and teachers pass by the screen or wait for turns, discussions about the writing or graphics that are displayed become spontaneous (Bruce et al., 1985). Balajthy (1988) surveyed research on computer-based learning that suggested that the new learning environment created by the introduction of computers into the classroom seems almost automatically to increase the amount of student cooperation in classroom learning tasks. However, he warned that teacher support and modeling are essential if these new attitudes toward learning are to be encouraged successfully.

Guidelines for Computer-Assisted Learning in Reading

Although research has demonstrated that computer instruction is effective in enhancing a variety of reading skills and concept areas (Reinking, 1988), educators have been concerned with the appropriateness of the possible roles computers can play in language arts instruction. Many educators feel that the emphasis should be on the use of computers for meaningful reading and writing instruction (Simic, 1993; Buckley, 1995; Guthrie and Richardson, 1995). The following guidelines focus on how teachers can integrate computers into reading/writing instruction.

1. ***Computer instruction should focus on meaning and should stress reading for understanding.*** Children should have opportunities to work with whole texts; therefore, teachers should select software programs that offer students the opportunity to process large amounts of text, rather than bits of unrelated language. In this way, students can use, extend, and apply what they know about reading comprehension.

Children should also have the opportunity to use word recognition programs that stress the use of word meanings along with phonics and structural analysis. The study of individual words and phrases must be offered within a contextual framework that help them make sense.

Moreover, children should have the opportunity to apply the skills being addressed in a meaningful way. Software that denies children opportunities to use what is "taught" do little to further learning.

Computer materials should be within the range of the students' conceptual development. The tasks should be challenging but not frustrating. Student interests, prior experiences, and the purpose for the activity all play a role in determining whether the computer activity is worthwhile and meaningful.

2. ***Computer instruction in reading should stimulate higher level thinking and should foster active involvement on the part of the learner.*** The children should be aware of what the task constitutes and why doing it is important. They should be able to make decisions that influence the computer activity. Software that builds in opportunites for children to make choices and verify their predictions help them to learn to think rather than merely react to someone else's ideas. Children should also have opportunities to monitor their own learning; therefore, activities that allow students to self-check and correct errors aid in the development of independent learners.

3. ***Computer instruction should support and extend knowledge of text structures.*** Children should encounter a variety of text structures and materials—narrative, expository, commercially prepared, teacher-authored, and student-authored. They should have the opportunity to experiment with text in many creative ways for many purposes.

4. ***Computer instruction should make use of content from many subject areas.*** The computer should enable children to apply reading strategies to all curricular areas. Software that is related to social studies, science, and mathematics requires the use of reading strategies. In order to progress as competent readers, students need to use what they know about reading comprehension in all of their school subjects. Computers need to be utilized in conjunction with other instructional modes—they should not be used as separate and isolated means of learning. Their use needs to be integrated with books and other learning materials. The computer needs to be seen as one additional way to share and retrieve information—as one additional way to practice skills and

apply learning in an interesting and meaningful way.

5. ***Computer instruction should link reading and writing.*** Children should have an opportunity to create text for the sharing and use by others. When students compose they must keep the reader in mind. This involves using what they know to make text comprehensible to others. Revision and proofreading involve the combined application of both reading and writing skills.

(adapted from Simic, 1993).

Joan Cavagnaro Talks About Computers in Her Whole Language Classroom

The single most effective use of computers in a whole language classroom is that of word processing. "Free writing is a flowing of ideas from head to paper without the anxiety connected with editing, spelling, and punctuation" (Doyle, 1988, 236). Once the student has completed this flowing of ideas, the computer becomes an irreplaceable tool that allows the student to enter the text and continue with ease through the writing process.

The following poetry writing project completed with first graders outlines a suggested process to follow. During a thematic unit on trees, we talk about and read many poems that center on trees. Once we decide to write our own poems, we brainstorm many different thoughts, ideas, and feelings that could be expressed in such a poem. The first step in the actual writing of the poems is for the students to record their ideas on paper; this becomes their first draft. An illustration may accompany the draft, but it is not required. Then I confer with each student, looking for complete thoughts and ideas. In most cases the students are now ready to enter this first draft in the computer.

Using the program *Children's Writing and Publishing Center,* the students are able to enter their own text. Since keyboarding is a new concept at this grade level, peer assistance helps students of all abilities. Using their own user ID, students save their work on the network and print out a hard copy of their poem. A second conference with students focuses on clarity and completion of their thoughts and ideas. Since revision can be made easily using the computer, students are willing to make changes. It is beneficial for the teacher to access a student's text and model this final editing process. Students view firsthand the ease of making revisions as the teacher talks them through the process. During the publishing process, each student creates an illustration that is mounted with a neat, important-looking copy of the poem. As the *Tree Poems* book is completed, a copyright page and table of contents are added. A quick look through the book displays equity for all the students that participated in the project. Once students are aware of this equity in the final published product, they develop a willingness to take chances and experiment with their writing.

Using the same word processor, I developed a writing activity that solicited parent cooperation. In lieu of the standard famous Americans who are routinely discussed during the months of January and February, we decide to do a minitheme on "Famous Americans." After brainstorming what it means to be famous and who is considered famous, each student chooses a person to research and then gathers biographical information, which is shared with the class. With the assistance of our librarian, the students are able to have at least one book that centers on the person they have chosen. I create a study sheet that is sent home with the students to help them and their parents focus on why the person was famous and to get an idea of when the person lived (see Figure 11.1). The study sheets are returned and discussed with the students, and, with the help of parent volunteers, each summary is entered in the computer and a printout made (see Figure 11.2). The art teacher assists by helping the students illustrate important events in the lives of these people, and a book results. When I repeat this project, I hope to use a time-line program to illustrate the time span that can be illustrated by such a project.

The shared book experience can be enhanced by using the computer. Using Big Books promotes the all-important concept of shared reading when the teacher rereads a story from a Big Book, until the students are able to read aloud as the teacher points to the print. Eventually each child can read the story without the support of the group. Although there are many

FROM THE CLASSROOM OF . . .

Kathy Pike and Jean Mumper New Paltz, New York

LET'S WRITE THE NEWS

Children need many opportunities to write for real reasons and for different audiences. A blank book, either standard size or enlarged, can be placed in the Writing Center, which may be titled *Let's Write the News.* Children are encouraged to bring in pictures from the newspaper, paste them into the book, and write the accompanying text. Of course, the text can go through the various stages of the writing process before being published in the class book. The computer could be used for publishing the children's writing of the news.

There could be variations to this activity. Entire articles could be pasted in and the children could write sequels, reactions, interviews with people featured in the articles, and so forth. Or articles could be pasted in the book and the children "hired" to illustrate what was described in the article.

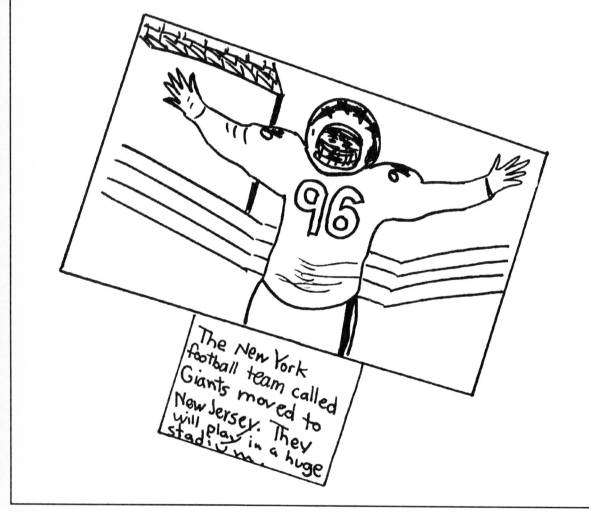

96
The New York football team called Giants moved to New Jersey. They will play in a huge stadium.

Figure 11.1 Sample Study Sheet

Name: ______________________

Famous American:

____

Why is this person famous?

What other interesting facts have you discovered (Please use the back of this sheet)?

Figure 11.2 Sample Summaries from Study Sheet

George Washington
by Karen Vining

George Washington was the first president. His father died when he was eleven. He was the leader of the army. He loved to ride horses, watch the boats, and dance. He could dance all night and still go to work in the morning. One day people dressed up like Indians and emptied tea into the water because there were too many taxes. George Washington's soldiers didn't have enough uniforms, guns, or food. They won the war against England. George Washington married Martha. He died when he was 67. He had gotten wet and sick. He rolled in his bed for many days and just before he died he said, "I die hard, but I am not afraid to go." When he died, nobody knew what to say but one man stepped up and spoke. He said George Washington was first in war, first in peace, and first in the hearts of his countrymen.

Michael Jordan
by Michael Gillis

You become famous when you can do something better than anyone else. The famous person that I'm writing about is Michael Jordan. He is a great basketball player. He can shoot from almost anywhere on the court. The number on his shirt is 23. He plays for the Chicago Bulls. In 1984 he was co-captain of the Olympic Team and they won a gold medal. He scores at least 37 points a game. He is a very low-key person. He was born on February 17th. he has two sisters and two brothers including him makes three boys. He is an awesome basketball player and I'm practicing to be one too.

John Paul Jones
by Mike Frantum

John Paul Jones won many battles at sea. He captured the British. John Paul Jones was not a very nice man and did bad things to other people. When he died his body was buried at the Navy Academy Chapel.

good Big Books available on the market today, the opportunity to write class stories and print them in Big Book size further involves students in reading text meaningful to them and using their language. The program *Superprint II: The Next Generation* allows teachers to print text in eight different sizes, from miniature to mega, thereby allowing them to create their own Big Books and individual student books.

When the school year begins, students are encouraged to experience their words in print. One of the first activities might be a sharing of the students' favorite season and what they like to do during that time of year. As the students illustrate their ideas, I confer with them and take dictation describing what they have drawn. Since this is the beginning of the school year, students are encouraged to write their thoughts, but the emphasis is not on their writing as much as it is on their ability to communicate verbally. Once the students see their thoughts in print, they realize the value of what they can create and share with their classmates. As I accumu-

FROM THE
CLASSROOM OF . . .
Kathy Pike and Jean Mumper New Paltz, New York

CLASS NEWS BOOKS

Particularly with young children or children needing practice in their oral language development, teachers record daily news activities. This is likened to the Language Experience Approach in which children's thoughts, words, and experiences are used as reading materials. Once the teacher has finished with the initial writing (generally on chart paper), the class news can be entered into the computer to make individual books. This is frequently done on a weekly basis so that children have something to take home regularly. These books can be illustrated with graphics on the computer or may be illustrated by the children in the classroom. One copy of the book could be saved for the class library or hung on a special hook in the Reading Center for all to enjoy.

Calico Corner News

Jose's cat had six Kittens on Monday. One is all black. He can lick your hand.	Weather: Mon Tu. W Th F	Katie's grandma came to visit. They made red jello. It was great!

(Classroom Chart)

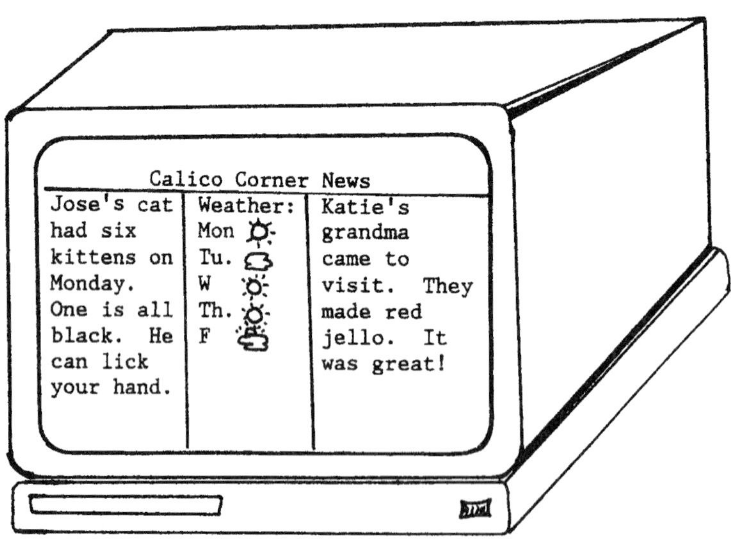

late students' ideas, I enter them into *Superprint II*. I use the students' drawings as a guide to select graphics from the program's extensive graphics library to help illustrate each student's page. A cover page, copyright page, and table of contents are also developed for the book. All the pages are printed in two sizes. The first size is super. As the students' pages are printed, they color them and I laminate each and add them to the book. All these pages result in one Big Book with large print that the entire class can read. At the beginning of the school year students are exposed to many sight words as well as to the names of all the students in the class as we read this book over and over. It quickly becomes a class favorite. The second size is miniature. As I print out each student's page, these are placed, two per sheet, horizontally on a sheet of 8 1/2 × 11-inch paper. A copy of each sheet is made for every student. As you fold each sheet in half add the cover, copyright page, and table of contents; and staple the raw edge. A miniature book is created for every class member. These become treasured books for independent reading. Other examples of activities using the computer can be seen in Figure 11.3. Children generated their own math stories, which were compiled, entered into the computer, and shared with the entire class. In Figure 11.4 the stories were written by the children after reading *The Important Book* by Margaret Wise Brown. This book varies the size and type of the print. By using various fonts on the computer, the children were able to create their own *important* versions. In Figure

LET'S PRETEND SLEEPOVER

Julie's kindergarten classes enjoy a pretend sleepover during the course of the school year. The children bring home invitations announcing the big event and listing the things the children should bring to school on the sleepover day. The children, Julie, the principal, and all the special area teachers who work with the kindergartners wear their pajamas and bring their sleeping pals, such as teddy bears or favorite blankets. Sleepytime music is played, cocoa and waffles are served, and the principal reads *Ira Sleeps Over.* Individual stories may be written for a class Sleepover Big Book or pictures can be taken and a photo essay of the experience can be created.

A variation of the pretend sleepover is to have a favorite stuffed animal sleep in the classroom for the night. The next day the children find their beloved friend somewhere special in the room. One little girl couldn't wait to go home to tell her parents that Teddy played with the computer all night. The stuffed animals could leave little notes for the kindergartners, and a class story could be written detailing the animal's experiences.

Figure 11.3

Name: ______________________

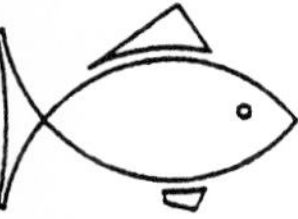

1. David K. had 14 fish. He sold 5 of them. How many of them does he have left?

2. Michael G. has one milk snake and Nicholas has two. How many snakes are there?

3. Karen has two brown cats and six dogs. How many animals does she have?

5. Amanda had 7 frogs. She gave 4 away. How many did she have? Then she gave one more away. How many did she keep?

5. David M. had four surfboards. A shark ate three of them. How many surf boards does David M. have?

Figure 11.4

The important thing about people is that everybody can do something their own way. You can play a game very good. You can swim very fast, so good that you can save a life. You can teach very good. You can share something. You can read a book. You can ride a bike. But the important thing about people is that everybody can do something their own way.

The important thing about paper is that you can draw on it. You can put it together and make a book . . . But the important thing about paper is that you can draw on it.

The important thing about school is that you can learn. You can learn the computer and you can paint. You can read books and you can write. You can send notes to eachother and you can count money. But the important thing about school is that you can learn.

The important thing about worms is that they make soil by eating plants. They tunnel in the ground. They help people go fishing. You can give them to birds and feed them to frogs. You can read about them and study them. But the important thing about worms is that they make soil by eating plants.

11.5 the class book, complete with graphics, was created after a study of the seasons.

Although the previous activities all result in a published class project, that is not always necessary. As children become writers, it is important for them to see their work valued, but as these same students develop their writing skills, the focus needs to be on the individual. This can be accomplished through the writing process each teacher establishes in the classroom. Computers have added a new dimension to a child's desire to write, but keep in mind that word processing is not a panacea. Just because a piece is written on the computer does not guarantee its quality. "Unless the writing process is clearly established in the classroom and students understand the teacher's expectations for revision and editing, a story composed on a word processor can be dull or poorly written" (Routman, 1991, 266). As with all communication and language processes in the classroom, using technology depends a great deal on the beliefs and philosophies of the teacher using them. The computer

Figure 11.5

In spring I like to ride my bike.

by Zachary

In summer I like to pick pretty flowers.

by Julia

In fall I like to jump in the leaves.

by Anthony

In winter I like to go sleigh riding.

by Michael

FROM THE CLASSROOM OF . . .

FLAT STANLEY: A FOLD-UP TRAVEL MATE

Pen pals, school exchanges, and expansion of geographic knowledge are all possible through the use of children's literature. One excellent idea came from the classroom of a special education teacher whose class read the book *Flat Stanley* by Jeff Brown. Stanley is a young boy who gets flattened by a falling bulletin board. Instead of being dismayed by his condition, Stanley finds he is able to go on unique adventures such as sliding through sewer grates, flying on a balloon, and fitting in an envelope and being mailed to far off places. Stanley makes a perfect pen pal since he fits inside an envelope and can be mailed to schools far from his home. Thus the Flat Stanley information exchange was born. A cardboard depiction of Stanley is folded to fit inside an envelope and sent to various schools. The following letter explains the program.

____
(Date)

Dear__________________________,

In my class, we read a book called *Flat Stanley*. It is about a first grade boy whose bulletin board flattens him one night in his bedroom. At first he is sad, but then he finds all sorts of things that he is able to do when he is flat. One thing he can do is fold himself up in an envelope and mail himself to visit friends in faraway places.

We made our own Stanleys in school and we are going to mail them to family and friends. We hope to learn about different places and landmarks and people.

I decided to mail my Stanley to you and hope you will show him a good time. Maybe you could take his picture next to a local landmark or send him back with a souvenir of your area. After your visit with Stanley, please mail him back to me and tell me about your visit. That way I can share the story with my classmates.

Thank you for helping to make this a fun learning experience for all of the children in my class.

Yours truly,

____

Dear Bill,
This is my
friend,
Flat Stanley is cut out of paper and decorated by the students.

is a tool and as such can be used to set high expectations for students as well as teachers. By setting high expectations for your students as well as yourself, you are likely to achieve them.

SUMMARY

From the studies available at this time, it appears there is a place for computers in a whole language classroom. It also appears that computer technology will find its place in many classrooms in the very near future. Computers provide alternative means of immersing a student in an environment filled with print and meaning. The role of computer use in a whole language classroom has unending possibilities. Computers can be used as tools to assist children in their efforts to explore the possibilities of language (Smith, 1986). At the same time a social connection is developing between children that supports learning in a whole environment rather than an isolated environment. Since computer technology has become part of our whole environment, applying it in the learning environment seems only natural, but the computer should be applied with caution. The teacher, having a sound understanding of how children learn, must select software that supports the goals that facilitate learning, rather than slick software that is essentially basals and workbooks adapted for computer use. Used thoughtfully and purposefully, computers can change traditional classrooms and further enhance children's thinking and learning (Genishi, 1988).

BIBLIOGRAPHY AND SUGGESTED REFERENCES

Balajthy, E. (1988). *Can computers be used for whole language approaches to reading and language arts?* Hershey, Pa.: Keystone Reading Association. (ERIC Document Reproduction Service No. ED 300 766.)

Beazely, M. R. (1989). Reading for a real reason: Computer pals across the world. *Journal of Reading, 32,* 598–605.

Becker, H., & Hativa, N. (1994). History, theory, and research concerning integrated learning systems. *Integrated Journal of Educational Research, 21,* 5–12.

Bradsher, M., & Hagan, L. (1995). The kids network: Student-scientists pool resources. *Educational Leadeship, 53,* 38–43.

Bruce, B.; Michaels, S.; & Watson-Gegeo, K. (1985). How computers can change the writing process. *Language Arts, 62,* 43–149.

Buckley, R. (1995). What happens when funding is not an issue? *Educational Leadership, 53,* 64–66.

Clements, D. H. (1987). Computers and young children: A review of the research. *Young Children, 43,* 34–44.

Collins, A. (1991). The role of computer technology in restructuring schools. *Phi Delta Kappan, 9,* 28–36.

Copen, P. (1995). Connecting classrooms through telecommunications. *Educational Leadership, 53,* 44–47.

DeGroff, L. (1989). *Computers in the whole language classroom.* Orlando, Fla.: Instructional Computing Conference. (ERIC Document Reproduction Service No. ED 318 452.)

Doyle, C. (1988). Creative applications of computer assisted reading and writing instruction. *Journal of Reading, 32,* 236–239.

Eberle, R. F. (1984). *Scamper on.* Buffalo, N.Y.: D. O. K. Publishers.

Genishi, C. (1988). Kindergartners and computers: A case study of six children. *The Elementary School Journal, 89*(2), 185–201.

Goodman, K. S. (1986). *What's whole in whole language?* Portsmouth, N.H.: Heinemann.

Guthrie, L., & Richardson, S. (1995). Turned on to language arts: Computer literacy in the primary grades. *Educational Leadership, 53,* 14–17.

Jansen, M. (1991). TLC: Its approach can transform K–6 classrooms. *T.H.E. Journal, 9,* 80–82.

Katzer, S., & Crnkovich, C. (1991). *From scribblers to scribes: Young writers use the computer.* Englewood, Colo.: Teacher Ideas Press.

Kurth, R. (1987). Using word processing to enhance revision strategies during student writing activities. *Educational Technology, 27,* 13–19.

McCarty, P. (1995). Four days that changed the world (and other amazing Internet stories). *Educational Leadership, 53,* 48–50.

Moore, M. (1989). Computers can enhance transactions between readers and writers. *The Reading Teacher, 42,* 608–611.

Moore, M. (1991). Electronic dialoguing: An avenue to literacy. *The Reading Teacher, 45,* 280–286.

Phenix, J., & Hannan, E. (1984). Word processing in the grade one classroom. *Language Arts, 61,* 804–812.

Raphael, J., & Greenberg, R. (1995). Image processing: A state-of-the-art way to learn science. *Educational Leadership, 53,* 34–37.

Reinking, D. (1988). Computer-mediated text and comprehension differences: The role of reading time, reader preference, and estimation of learning. *Reading Research Quarterly, 23,* 484–498.

Roblyer, M. D. (1990). The impact of microcomputer-based instruction on teaching and learning: A review of the research. *Educational Technology, 30,* 54–55.

Routman, R. (1991). *Invitations.* Portsmouth, N.H.: Heinemann.

Shaver, J. C., & Wise, B. S. (1990). *Literacy: The impact of technology on early reading.* Sarasota, Fla.: American Reading Forum. (ERIC Document Reproduction Service No. ED 327 832.)

Simic, M. (1993). *Guidelines for computer-assisted reading instruction.* ERIC Clearinghouse on Reading and Communication Skills, Bloomington, Ind. (ED352630).

Smith, F. (1986). *Reading without nonsense.* New York: Teachers College Press.

Van Dusen, L., & Worthen, B. (1995). Can integrated instructional technology transform the classroom? *Educational Leadership, 53,* 28–33.

Watson, D. J. (1989). Defining and describing whole language. *The Elementary School Journal, 90*(2), 128–141.

Wepner, S. (1990). Holistic computer applications in literature-based classrooms. *The Reading Teacher, 44,* 12–19.

Wepner, S. (1991). Technology-based literature plans for elementary students. *The Reading Teacher, 45,* 236–238.

SOFTWARE CITED

International Business Machines. (1991). *Stories and more.* White Plains, N.Y.: Author.

The Learning Company. (1989). *The children's writing and publishing center.* Fremont, Calif.: Author.

Lloyd, D., & Lee, B. (1990). *The new print shop.* San Rafael, Calif.: Broderland.

Pelican Software. (1989). *Superprint II: The next generation.* New York: Scholastic.

Snyder, T., & Kaemmer, D. (1986). *Timeliner.* Cambridge, Mass.: Tom Snyder Productions.

CHILDREN'S LITERATURE CITED

Brown, M. (1949). *The Important Book.* New York: Harper Trophy.

12 MEETING THE NEEDS OF ALL CHILDREN

Somewhere today a live ant is carrying a dead ant to be buried.

Ants live in communities and take care of each other. They help each other carry food. They also share food. If an ant finds another ant that is dead it will drag or carry the dead ant back to the nest and put it in a special place for dead ants.

Douglas

From the classroom of
Jean Mumper
Grade 3
Wallkill, N.Y.

Inspired by: *Somewhere Today* by Bert Kitchen

OVERVIEW

Educators, parents, politicians, and the business community have been exploring ways to provide quality education for all children. There are large numbers of children who are at risk of failure in school and in later life because their needs are not being met. In this at-risk population are children of poverty, minority groups, children from non-English-speaking homes, children with mental and physical disabilities, and children who are learning disabled.

Many students are at risk sometime during their school years and are able to overcome this and meet with success. But others remain at risk and experience repeated failure. There are common factors that lead to students being at risk. Many factors are beyond the control of the students and the schools. Some identified factors are living below the poverty level; being a member of a racial or ethnic minority; speaking a language other than English; experiencing school retention, poor attendance, low scores on standardized tests, illness; changing schools frequently; having excessive absences and low self-esteem; acting out with hostility or withdrawing; suffering from drug abuse; and being homeless. In many schools, where the student and teacher interactions are incompatible, the chances of failure increase (Reed and Sauter, 1990).

Some general practices have proven successful with children with special needs. This chapter addresses the issues involved with special needs students and explores programs designed to help such students achieve in school. The many practices described throughout this book, suitable for all students, are especially valuable for students with special educational needs.

Questions to Ponder

1. How can the needs of children at risk be met?
2. What techniques and methods can be used to increase literacy for at-risk students?
3. How can children who are non–native speakers of English be helped to achieve?
4. How can school programs build self-esteem for at-risk learners?
5. In what ways can schools provide greater challenges for the gifted and talented student?

STUDENTS AT RISK

Many students are at risk sometime during their school years but are able to reverse this process and participate successfully in regular class activities. But with overall dropout rates at 25 to 30 percent and for some inner-city high schools as much as 75 percent (Davis and McCaul, 1990), schools must focus on the inability of some students to escape the at-risk group. The National School Board Association Task Force (NSBA) has defined children and youth at risk as "those who are subject to environmental, family or societal forces, over which they have no control and which adversely affect their ability to learn in school and survive in society" (NSBA, 1989, 2). Many of these students share a common characteristic: they are vulnerable to failure. "There are three factors that contribute to children being at risk, the first being societal factors, which include children living at or below the poverty level, children of historically under-represented groups, and those living in unstable family and support systems. School environment is the second factor. Inappropriate curriculum, ineffective student-teacher relations, low teacher expectation, inadequate services, unrealistic standards, negative school climate and lack of sensitivity to diversity are the main factors" (Davis and McCaul, 1990). Internal student factors include low self-esteem, lack of interest and motivation, and low personal goals (Davis and McCaul, 1990). Lack of success in school related to these feelings can cause children to take part in negative behaviors—to give in to peer pressure, abuse drugs, engage in unacceptable social and sexual practices, and eventually drop out of school.

Because of economic disadvantages, poor children may not have the same background knowledge and experiences that more advantaged children have. The most recent research confirms that the single most effective factor in successful dropout prevention programs is good preschool education. Members of the 1992 National Governors' Association conference agreed unanimously that improving children's readiness for school is the most important issue to reach nationwide educational goals. They called for a bipartisan plan to improve children's readiness for school. The recommendations of the plan emphasized "more and better pre-school programs for all poor and disabled children; improved health and nutrition programs, and improved social services to help parents better prepare their children for school" (Celis, 1992, 22).

There have been successful attempts to help at-risk children learn to read and write and achieve in school. Following are some programs and some practices that have particularly benefited at-risk children.

Successful Programs

Reading Recovery

For some children, instruction in the regular classroom is not enough. Despite having supportive teachers and being in the best learning environments, some children fall behind. These children need additional help in order to make the breakthrough to becoming readers and writers. At-risk children can make sufficient progress to catch up with their peers, but this is not achieved by pressuring the children or having them struggle. Enabling children to catch up is best achieved by providing experiences that allow the children to move at their own individual paces. A program designed in New Zealand by Marie Clay—Reading Recovery—is just such a program (Clay, 1993b).

Reading Recovery is an early intervention program that is targeted to help young learners who are having difficulty in their first year of school. It is designed to give intensive extra support to help children learn to use the kinds of strategies that good readers and writers naturally use.

Reading Recovery is different from many traditional remedial programs in that it provides intensive one-to-one instruction, begins early in a child's schooling, and focuses on a child's strengths rather than his or her deficits. Children are immersed in reading and writing rather than receiving practice on isolated skills. Children are expected to make excellent progress during the duration of the program.

Based on a view of children as active, constructive learners, Reading Recovery is not designed as a classroom program but is used in conjunction with good classroom instruction. "The goal of Reading Recovery is to enable children to become good readers who have effective strategies and can use them in flexible ways to go beyond what they already know" (Pinnell, 1989, 169).

Reading Recovery provides individual tutoring to children experiencing difficulty in first grade, generally the lowest 20 percent of the first graders. These 6-year-olds who are experiencing difficulty are then administered a battery of diagnostic instruments to identify what they know about reading and writing. This series of tests, known as the Diagnostic Survey, consists of such subtests as letter identification, word tests, concepts about print, writing samples (including vocabulary, dictation, spelling, and writing a story), and some reading of text (Clay, 1993a). This information is coupled with information obtained from the classroom teacher. If children are identified as needing special attention, they are then enrolled in Reading Recovery.

Children who are admitted to Reading Recovery receive a 30-minute lesson daily from a specially trained teacher for a period of 10–20 weeks depending on the child's progress. During a Reading Recovery session, the teacher and the child sit side by side, reading and writing collaboratively. The teacher provides careful support that enables the young learner to work in the zone of proximal development, that is, to work at the outer limits of the child's knowledge. There are many opportunities to use oral interactions to support the child's literacy development. Teachers are trained to observe the children so that they may take advantage of the teachable moment and the discoveries about print that the children make. By selecting appropriate texts and adjusting the instruction, teachers facilitate children's growth in reading and writing.

When children first enter the program, they are engaged in reading and writing activities that permit the teacher to explore what they know. This Roaming the Known period lasts for approximately ten days and is a time for the teacher and child to develop a rapport and for the child to feel successful. Once this is established, formal instruction begins. Although teachers do follow a framework, the lessons and the program are individualized. Following is a framework for a Reading Recovery lesson:

Components of a Reading Recovery Lesson

1. **Taking words to fluency.** During the first few minutes of a Reading Recovery lesson, the child may be engaged in learning some high-frequency words. These words are identified from previous lessons as those the child was unsure of and needed to learn. The child might practice these words using a white board, using magnetic letters, writing the words in salt, or a combination of these techniques.

2. **Reading familiar stories.** As stories are introduced to a child, the books are placed in the child's book box for future use. Each day the child reads several familiar books. Some books are selected by the teacher because of the teaching and learning opportunities they present. Rereading allows the child to read quickly and fluently.

3. **Running Record on a familiar story.** In order to observe reading strategies and behaviors, the teacher takes a Running Record. For the Running Record, the child reads a book that was read for the first time during the previous lesson. The teacher records the reading using procedures described in Chapter 4. The teacher observes and watches for such behaviors as self-monitoring, omissions, substitutions, and so on. After the lesson, the teacher analyzes the reading, noting the child's reading behaviors and use of cues. This helps the teacher in instructional planning. (See Figure 12.1 for Sample Reading Recovery materials.)

4. **Working with letters.** If a child needs help with letter recognition or other identifying features of print, the teacher may plan some instructional activities, such as having the child use magnetic letters. This may also be done at any point during the lesson.

5. **Writing a story.** Each day the child is expected to write a story or message. Generally the message consists of one or two sentences and is written in a special book that is held so that one page appears on top of another page. The child's story is written on the bottom page, and the top page is used for the child to practice and work out the words. The message is written word by word, with the child writing the known words and trying the unknown words with the help of the teacher. Once the message is complete, the teacher writes it on a sentence strip, cuts it apart, and the child reassembles it. The writing of the message is a collaborative activity, with the child being supported through interactions with the teacher. When appropriate, the teacher may ask the child to write a word several times on the practice page. This provides an opportunity for the child to examine the details of the word, work on sound-symbol associations, and apply what was learned during previous sessions. The teacher then places the strip in an envelope for the child to take home. (See Figure 12.2 for a sample from a student's practice book.)

6. **Reading a new book.** The child is then introduced to a new book. First, the teacher and the child look at the book and talk about the illustrations and the story. Through these oral interactions, the child has an opportunity to become familiar with the story and the language that is used.

Through these daily sessions, students in the Reading Recovery program learn how to perform the same reading and writing tasks that they needed help with previously. The goal is to have the children achieve the average or above-average performance level of their classmates and to have developed a self-extending system and a repertoire of strategies to be used flexibly, for example, self-monitoring, searching for cues, cross-checking, and self-correcting.

Reading Recovery is not magical, although the results so far have been quite promising (Lyons and Beaver, 1995). Good teaching in the regular classroom setting is the first priority for educators (Clay, 1975). All children need effective and stimulating literacy experiences provided by caring, observant teachers who can further children's language abilities, and this is especially true for at-risk learners. Reading Recovery, coupled with good classroom instruction, is helping young children grow as readers and writers.

Figure 12.1A Sample Analysis of a Reading Recovery Session

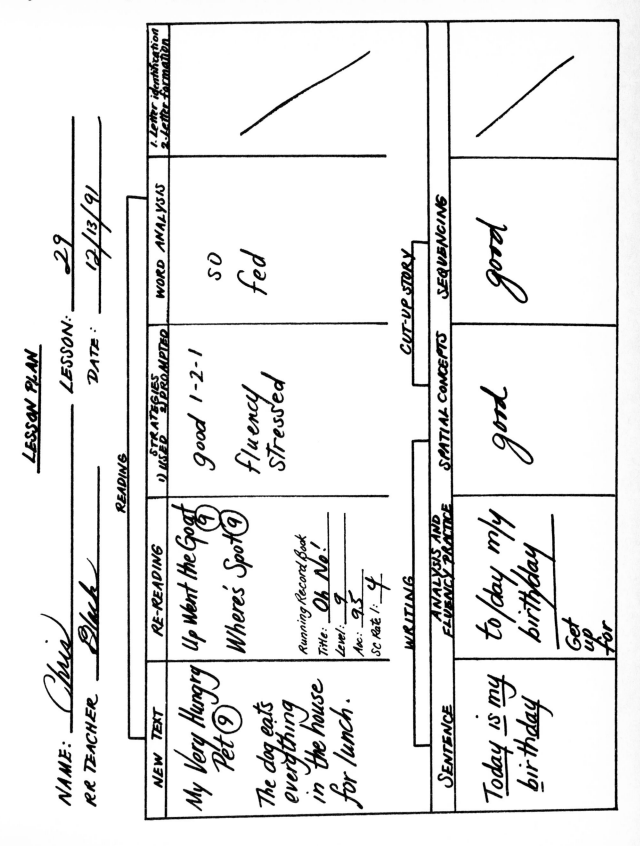

LESSON PLAN

NAME: Chris LESSON: 29

RR TEACHER Black DATE: 12/13/91

READING

NEW TEXT	RE-READING	STRATEGIES 1) USED 2) PROMPTED	WORD ANALYSIS	1. Letter identification 2. Letter formation
My Very Hungry Pet (9) The dog eats everything in the house for lunch.	Up Went the Goat (9) Where's Spot (9) Running Record Book Title: Oh No! Level: 9 Acc: 95 SC Rate 1: 4	good 1-2-1 fluency stressed	so fed	

WRITING | **CUT-UP STORY**

SENTENCE	ANALYSIS AND FLUENCY PRACTICE	SPATIAL CONCEPTS	SEQUENCING	
Today is my birthday	to/day m/y birth/day Get up for	good	good	

Figure 12.1B Sample Analysis of a Reading Recovery Session (cont.)

RUNNING RECORD

LESSON NO. 29

NAME Chris

TEXT LEVEL 9

RR TEACHER: Black

DATE: 12/13

Scores: RUNNING WORDS / ERROR 122 / 6 ERROR RATE 1:20 ACC. 95% S.C. RATE 1:4

Observation/Analysis of Cues and Strategies ✓ Easy 95-100% ___ Inst. 90-94% ___ Hard 50-89%

Good reading w/ with visual, meaning, & structure cues—

PAGE	TITLE AND LEVEL: Oh No 1	E (TOTALS 6)	SC (TOTALS 2)	CUES USED E	CUES USED SC
	✓ ✓ ✓ ✓ ✓ ✓				
	✓ ✓ ✓ ✓ ✓ ✓				
	✓ ✓ ✓ ✓ ✓ ✓ ✓				
	When ✓ ✓ ✓ ✓ ✓				
	Where (SC) ✓ ✓		1	(V)	(MSV)
	Oh				
	There's (SC) ✓ ✓ ✓ ✓ ✓		1	(MS)	(MSV)
	✓ ✓ ✓ ✓ ✓ ✓ ✓				
	✓ the/this —/blueberries ✓	2		(MSV)	
	✓ ✓ ✓ ✓ ✓ ✓ ✓ ✓ ✓ ✓ ✓ ✓ ✓ ✓ ✓ ✓ ✓ ✓ ✓ ✓				

everybody (T) ✓ ✓ 1

Figure 12.2 Sample from Student's Practice Book

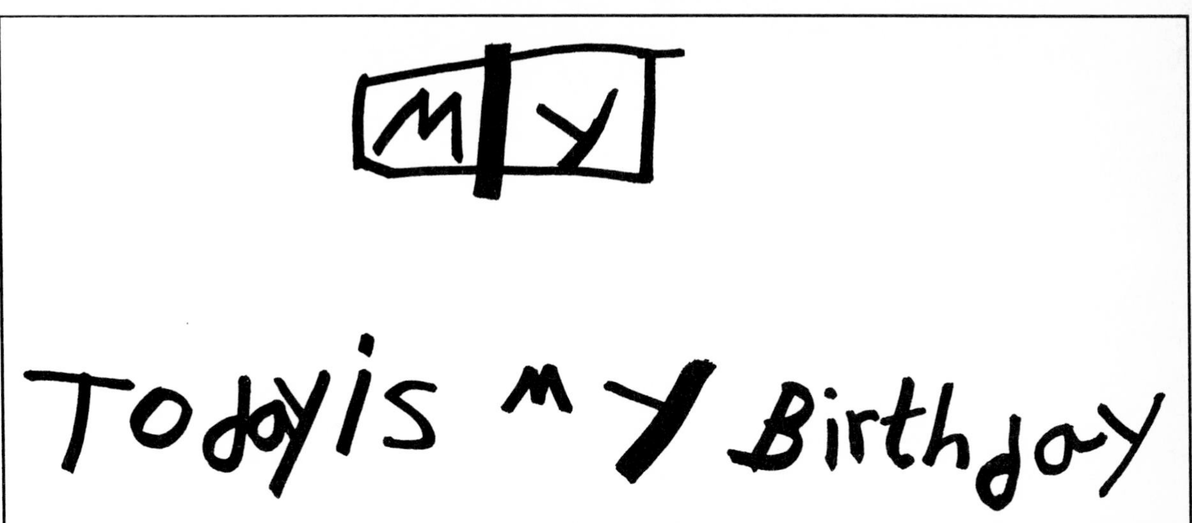

Early Intervention in Reading (EIR)

The Early Intervention in Reading Program (EIR) is another successful program for children at-risk in reading in grade 1, only the special reading instruction is provided by the students' classroom teachers. Unlike Reading Recovery, EIR provides supplemental support using small-group instruction. Like Reading Recovery, the program is similar in intent. The main objective is to provide quality supplemental instruction early in children's schooling so that they can get off to a better start and to prevent them from experiencing unnecessary failure (Taylor, Frye, Short, and Shearer, 1992; Taylor, Short, Shearer, and Frye, 1995).

EIR is almost exclusively a first-grade program, lasting the entire year. In addition to providing regular classroom instruction, classroom teachers work with five to seven of their lowest-achieving students for an additional 20 minutes of reading instruction. The students receive strategic instruction in word recognition and decoding skills, as well as extra help in the retelling of stories.

The small-group instruction provided to these lowest achieving students focuses on the repeated readings of picture books or summaries of these books, developing phonemic segmentation and blending abilities, and other word recognition skills (Taylor et al., 1992; 1995). Besides the supplemental instruction with the teacher, each student also works with a parent volunteer or a paraprofessional on rereading the materials from their small-group instruction.

Materials for the EIR program consist of picture books and summaries of these picture books on a chart and in booklet form. The materials range from 40 to 200 words in length and are divided into four levels.

Typically an EIR lesson with a book and accompanying activities lasts three days. On the first day, the teacher reads the story to the entire class, modeling fluent reading and appropriate book-reading behaviors. Then a summary of the story is read from a chart. Through skillful questioning and practice, the students learn to use all three cueing systems (semantic, syntactic, and graphophonic) to identify words. To enhance the development of phonemic awareness, the students write up to five words from the story using a series of boxes to record the individual phonemes.

On days two and three, the children write, with the teacher's guidance, a sentence related to the story in the back of their story summary book. The teacher supplies only those sounds the students cannot spell independently. This writing activity allows students to apply their knowledge of phonemic segmentation, blending, and phonics in the context of real reading and writing. After the third day, the children take a copy of their story summary home to read to their families. As the children progress through the program, the teacher introduces additional picture books that the children read in pairs or independently. This is to help the children make a transition to books they have never read before.

Early intervention programs such as Reading Recovery and EIR have been utilized as ways schools can prevent early reading failure. Although success in the early grades does not come with a guarantee of success throughout schooling, failure in the early grades virtually guarantees failure in the later grades and ultimately in life (Slavin, Madden, Dolan, and Wasik, 1994). Whatever the design, whatever the program, schools must regard early intervention and prevention as crucial for at-risk learners. However, early intervention with no follow-up in improved instruction in the regular classroom instructional program is not likely to produce lasting gains. Therefore it is imperative to link intervention and continued instructional improvement in order to prevent early school failure.

Effective Practices

Since whole language is a philosophy about teaching and learning, whole language teachers facilitate learning in the most effective ways for all children. Whole language teachers focus on what children can do; they focus on children's abilities, not their disabilities. Moreover, all children are considered to be capable learners, and whole language teachers are perceived as facilitators who provide the support needed by all learners. All children need learning experiences that are successful, and research suggests that disabled readers also benefit from whole language practices. In whole language classrooms, all students are immersed in productive learning environments in which the learning is relevant, purposeful, and enjoyable. By involving children in authentic reading and writing activities, whole language teachers create opportunities that allow children to capitalize on their abilities and develop new abilities. Involving children in meaningful reading and writing experiences is effective in developing lifelong learners. Some of these practices are described in the following sections.

Going Beyond the Language Experience Approach with At-Risk Students

The Language Experience Approach (LEA) has proven to be a highly effective practice with young children and with remedial readers. Using the children's natural oral language provides reading materials that relate to the children's interests and correspond to their syntactic abilities and background knowledge. Whereas using the children's own language based on their experiences and knowledge is valuable, frequently the stories that are produced do not use a variety of sentence structures or a wide range of vocabulary. The stories may read more like a list of sentences than a well-structured narrative or piece of expository writing.

Therein lies the problem. Children who are experiencing reading difficulty need models of good writing and need to be exposed to well-structured, well-written texts. Typically, remedial readers do not have sufficient prior knowledge with either narrative or expository text to draw on when composing their own writing pieces. In addition, remedial readers generally do not think about their writing in order to rework the text to make it more cohesive and meaningful. The traditional LEA does nothing to further the development of writing and understanding texts, nor does it help or encourage children to reflect on the meaning of the text. The traditional LEA does not help children understand or have experience with the writing process since LEA stories are generally first drafts that do not undergo any revision.

This does not have to be the case, however. The standard LEA can be modified to produce better models for furthering reading comprehension and for exposing children to the writing process model in order to provide a structure of stories and expository texts that can be internalized by the children. Knowing how texts are organized facilitates the understanding of the author's message.

The procedure begins with a concrete experience, similar to the regular LEA. The experience is discussed, drawing on the children's

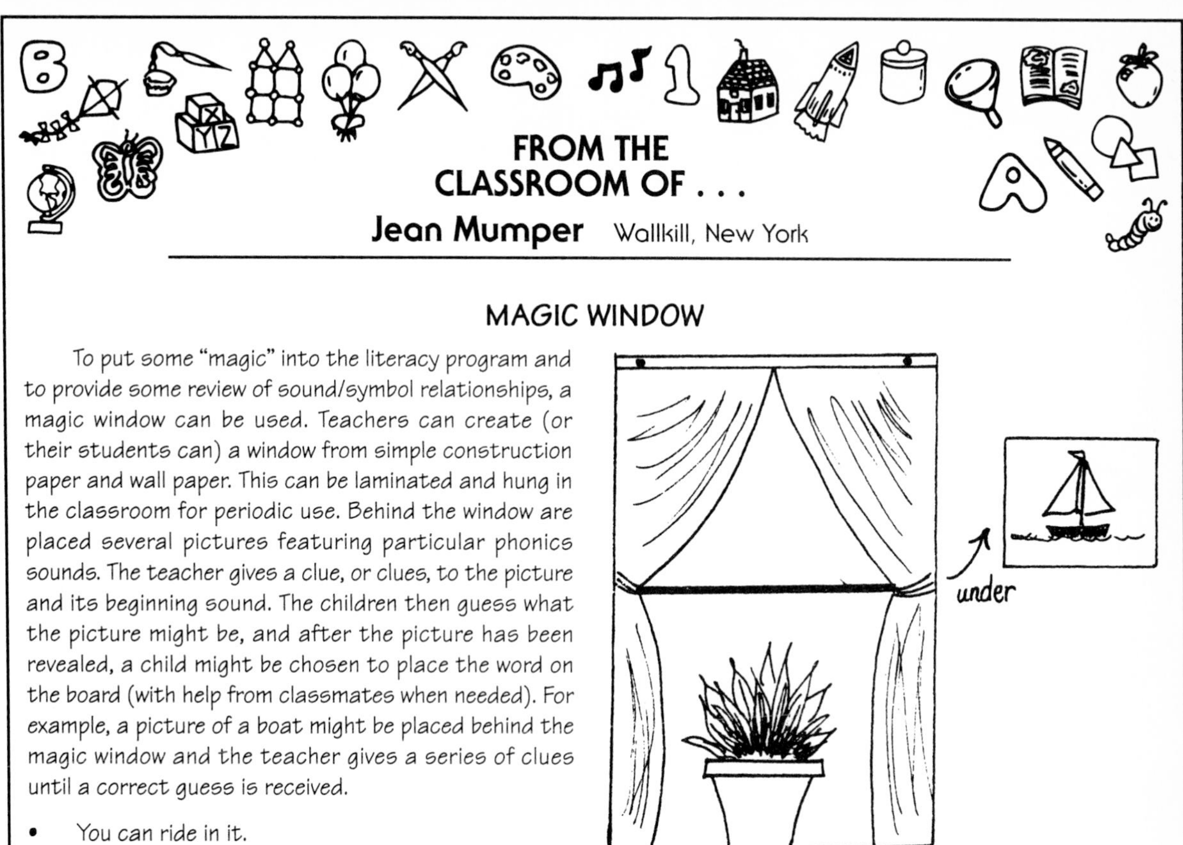

FROM THE CLASSROOM OF . . .

Jean Mumper Wallkill, New York

MAGIC WINDOW

To put some "magic" into the literacy program and to provide some review of sound/symbol relationships, a magic window can be used. Teachers can create (or their students can) a window from simple construction paper and wall paper. This can be laminated and hung in the classroom for periodic use. Behind the window are placed several pictures featuring particular phonics sounds. The teacher gives a clue, or clues, to the picture and its beginning sound. The children then guess what the picture might be, and after the picture has been revealed, a child might be chosen to place the word on the board (with help from classmates when needed). For example, a picture of a boat might be placed behind the magic window and the teacher gives a series of clues until a correct guess is received.

- You can ride in it.
- It begins with the letter "b" (or the sound /b/).
- It does not have wheels.
- It goes on water.

prior knowledge of the topic. The children then decide on a purpose for the writing (e.g., a narrative, a piece that will explain something, a persuasive argument) and discuss the intended audience. For example, the children may decide to write on the topic of hurricanes. The focus of the writing could be to explain proper evacuation procedures during a hurricane, and the audience could be people in their hometown. At this time, models of other language experience stories that contain easily identified purposes and audiences could be shared. The teacher could also think aloud, describing the strategies needed to compose this form of text. In the preceding example, the teacher could say that there might be a more effective way of presenting evacuation procedures than using a typical paragraph style. The teacher could give examples, such as manuals or handbooks.

Before beginning the dictation, the students should think about the piece they are about to write and make some notes. These notes could be placed on a semantic map, which will help the students organize their information as well as serve as a means of recording prior knowledge. While dictating, the students can stop and reflect periodically to determine whether what they have been composing makes sense and fits their purpose and audience. As the story is written, it should be read, reread, and rewritten. This gives the children insights into the recursive nature of the writing process.

Since the teacher is doing the scribing, spelling errors are of no concern, although teachers may ask for input while spelling the students' words. Because remedial readers frequently use nonstandard grammar, their dictated story may require editing after revision.

Teachers may use questioning to get the children to notice the grammatical errors or may give a minilesson on the necessary grammatical functions.

After the final version has been written, the story may now serve as reading material for the students. Follow-up writing or reading activities may be suggested to reinforce and extend the concepts presented in the original story. In the hurricane scenario, the students might want to write a narrative about a family surviving a hurricane or might want to research natural disasters. Using this modified LEA approach, students are not only given effective instruction in text structure and reading comprehension, but they are also given opportunities to learn about the writing process (Heller, 1988).

Scaffolding

Vygotsky (1978) has used the concept of the "zone of proximal development" to explain the social nature of learning. Experts (generally adults) can help children move from their actual developmental stages to their potential. This theory presupposes that what children are capable of doing in cooperation today, they will be able to do for themselves tomorrow. In essence, the message is that if children are provided support and encouragement, they will ultimately achieve independence. This type of support is called scaffolding.

Scaffolding is a temporary framework that provides students with a platform to the next step in their learning. It enables children to move a step forward; that is, it pushes children to the edge of their knowledge. Children and their mentors work in a partnership to construct meaning jointly (Graves and Graves, 1994). Through this partnership, the adult/expert works to support the learner/novice. Uncertainty is reduced, and children are able to experience successful learning experiences in reading and writing. Scaffolding is tailored to meet the students' individual needs and can be provided at any point during any learning act. As the children gain mastery, the scaffolding is removed. As children become more capable and competent learners, scaffolding no longer becomes necessary.

Scaffolding can take many forms in the elementary school classroom, from shared reading to peer tutoring to modeling by the teacher or other expert. During these activities, students are shown strategies to make them successful learners, are given support during the early practice stages, and gradually are released to perform the reading or writing activities independently.

To show how scaffolding can work, let's work at shared reading. For children to perform effectively as readers, they have to be aware of and use strategies that good readers use. During shared reading, the responsibility for the initial reading or readings falls on the teacher. As the story becomes familiar, children are encouraged to join in the reading through echo reading (joining in just after the teacher has read the text) or choral reading in which the words are read by the teacher and the students simultaneously. Either the teacher or the group provides the support—the scaffold—for a successful reading experience. In addition, the teacher can discuss the author's intended message and salient features of the print that might pose problems for the readers.

Scaffolding is an important activity to provide to at-risk readers. Children who are experiencing reading difficulties need this support to enable them to function as efficient readers would. The goal of any literacy program is to develop independent learners. Scaffolding is a way teachers can help their students develop competence. Through scaffolding, teachers coach, advise, offer support, challenge, and give vision to their students.

Other Effective Practices and Tips for Coping with Readers with Disabilities

To help provide a literacy program to meet the needs of all children, teachers have used many strategies that have proven to be helpful for readers with disabilities. These include:

- Activating students' prior knowledge through brainstorming
- Implementing whole class activities that have built-in individualization; for example, Sustained Silent Reading and journal writing
- Using open-ended projects that allow students to contribute at different levels with differing abilities

- Planning writing activities that encourage children to respond at their own levels; for example, patterned stories that enable students to write adaptations while borrowing the author's structure and pattern or participating in interactive writing experiences
- Using cross-age tutoring. Reading and writing for younger children gives readers with disabilities an opportunity to practice reading and writing at their own literacy level. On the other hand, young children experiencing difficulty can profit from the individual attention and modeling of older children. Not only does achievement improve, but self-concepts are enhanced as well. Activities that may be undertaken include reading aloud, taking dictation for LEA stories, helping with the writing process, reinforcing minilessons in reading and writing, and building background knowledge pertaining to a particular curricular area.

Figure 12.3 describes some other practices that work well with at-risk learners.

The practices previously discussed are only a few of the effective practices identified as benefiting readers with disabilities. Most, if not all, of the practices discussed elsewhere in this book serve remedial readers as well as more capable learners. If teachers provide the best classroom instruction in a language-rich environment, then all children can profit.

CULTURALLY DIVERSE STUDENTS

The United States is a culturally pluralistic society, whose ethnic, racial, and socioeconomic diversity is increasingly reflected in school populations today. The changing demographic statistics have already had a significant impact on schools, as more students than ever before come from linguistically and culturally diverse backgrounds. In the past, America was viewed as a melting pot, where languages and cultural differences were assimilated to form a new American culture. Unfortunately, it was the European American culture that was favored (Banks, 1994). Today, the concept of cultural pluralism has replaced assimilation. People now have a right to retain their cultural identity, and it is recognized that each culture makes contributions to and enriches all of society.

Children from diverse cultures arrive in schools with a range of language and literacy experiences, even though they are not the same as the mainstream students. Teachers who teach culturally and linguistically diverse children need to implement a literacy program that is both sensitive to and reflective of all the children's backgrounds and needs.

African Americans and Hispanics are the largest underrepresented populations in the United States, and a large number of them are also poor. In addition to the problems related to living at the poverty level that were discussed earlier, many children of minority groups participate in educational experiences that are totally irrelevant to their culture and everyday life. Teachers must educate themselves about the culture of the children they are teaching if it is different from their own. Teachers should be aware of the literacy activities that take place in the home, the parents' values, and the types of response activities that take place between children and adults. Literature and oral literacy activities that reflect the child's culture should be used in daily class activities. Writing and oral activities that give children a chance to talk about their families and their lifestyle should be encouraged. Teachers can explore their students' cultural response patterns so that they can then incorporate into the classroom curriculum similar ways of conversing and responding.

LINGUISTICALLY DIFFERENT CHILDREN

Students with English as a Second Language (ESL)

There are close to two million children in U.S. schools whose native language is not English. That number is projected to double by the year 2000 (Samuels and Farstrup, 1992). Some children speak only their native language; others speak some English or can understand English but not speak it. New immigrants entering schools quickly learn playground English as a means of coping with their everyday life. But school English has more abstract vocabulary and concepts that children have to learn. Teach-

Figure 12.3 Effective Practices for At-Risk Learners

PRACTICES	DESCRIPTION
Echo Reading	After the teacher reads a portion of a text, the student immediately repeats it, while looking at or pointing to the words. Echo reading allows teachers to model fluent reading and the students to practice it.
Choral Reading	The teacher and the students read in unison. Reading together, with the teacher's voice as a model, reduces the anxiety of reading alone.
Predictable Books	Predictable books, with their rhyming, repetitive or cumulative language, are easier to read. Because of the predictability and the support of the language, retelling stories either orally or in writing is more readily accomplished. Reading predictable books is useful to independent reading and as springboards for writing.
Shared Reading	Since the reader is supported by an "expert," success is ensured. Emergent learners develop print awareness and concepts about print, speech-to-print matching, phonics, phonemic awareness, and they acquire a sight vocabulary. All learners profit from the learning of the use of strategies while the reading is undertaken.
Repeated Reading	Repeated reading is the systematic practice of oral reading. The purpose is to help students acquire sight vocabulary and practice reading fluently and confidently.
Story Mapping	Story maps are graphic representations of the parts of a story. They show how the story parts are related and help readers organize story content.
Interactive Reading	A technique in which both the teacher and the students share the scribing. The teacher supports the writing of unknown words. An excellent technique to enhance phonics and phonemic awareness.
Listening Centers	In listening centers, students listen to literature read to them. By being able to hear and see the stories simultaneously over and over again, word recognition and concept development are enhanced.
Reciprocal Teaching	Reciprocal Teaching is a method for developing comprehension where a teacher models a sequence of meaning-making processes: summarizing; questioning; clarifying; and predicting.
Word Sorts	An activity where students sort words according to categories, either of their own choosing or their teachers'. Words can be sorted for phonic elements, rhyming words, words with similar meanings, common spelling patterns and the like. Word sorts help children see the features of words and the likenesses and differences between them.
Word Walls	Key vocabulary are highlighted on word walls, a space where words are showcased in the classroom. Words can be arranged alphabetically, phonetically, or thematically.

ers who work with second-language students are aware of the importance of helping them develop their ability to speak, read, and write English. It also appears logical that the most effective way to develop English is to totally immerse students in English. Although this idea of "more English leads to more English" seems to make sense, it runs contrary to research, which shows that the best way for bilingual students to develop their English proficiency and academic concepts is through their first language. It is recommended that children retain and use the language they know and build on that knowledge base before moving into English (Freeman and Freeman, 1992, 1993). Teaching isolated skills in English, even if the child could master the skills, has relatively little meaning to the linguistically different child. The general approach to bilingual programs is to teach children to read and write in their native language and at the same time teach English as a second language. Recent research in second language acquisition strongly supports bilingual education. There are several reasons for recommending the use of a person's first language:

- It validates them as individuals and builds on their strengths.
- It allows them to gain background knowledge and concepts, which will enhance future academic achievement.
- When students have developed proficiency in their first language, they can learn a second language quicker.
- Bilingual students come to value their first language and culture and maintain ties with their communities and families.
- The potential for clashes between the school's and the home's values is decreased.

(Freeman and Freeman, 1992).

There may be times when bilingual education is not possible. There may only be a few non-English-speaking children in the school, or there could be many languages and cultures represented in the non-English-speaking population. In addition, there could be a lack of funds and an inability to find teachers who speak the minority language. In these cases, many school districts offer English as a Second Language (ESL) programs instead. ESL programs usually remove the second language learner from the classroom for a prescribed time period to receive instruction in English.

As stated previously, the number of ESL students in U.S. classrooms is increasing, and many of these students do not read well in either their native language or in English. Teachers cannot be certain if the ESL students' difficulties are due to comprehension difficulties or to their limited facility with the English language. Therefore teachers face the daunting task of simultaneously building literacy and enhancing the learning of English. Fortunately, there are effective practices that can enhance the literacy abilities of ESL learners while they learn English. ESL students can be extended invitations to read, write, and talk using purposeful tasks within collaborative contexts. Language learning experiences can be organized to create authentic opportunities for oral and written expression and for helping students make connections with what they know and what the school can provide. These learning experiences can include using a thematic focus, constructing and sharing a classroom culture, reading aloud, developing vocabulary, publishing books, experimenting with language, and providing scaffolded instruction and cognitive strategy training (Ernst and Richards, 1994–1995; Gersten and Jimenez, 1994). "Students learning English as a second language gain substantially in classrooms where oral and written activities are regarded as integral to the process of negotiating knowledge, exchanging personal experiences and thoughts, and using language for authentic, meaning-making purposes" (Ernst and Richard, 1994–1995, 326).

Like all children, ESL children must have access to the best possible instruction and to real academic opportunity. ESL children learn English in the same way they learned their first language, primarily through immersion. (Chapter 2 discusses the language development of young children.) As you may have noticed, many of the techniques described in this chapter work well with native speakers and contribute to the development of all learners.

Non-standard-English Speakers

Think about talking to a person from Boston, from the South, or from the midwest. Can you tell where a person comes from just by listening to him or her speak? There is no one real way of speaking English, as dialects vary across geographic regions, ethnic backgrounds, and socioeconomic levels. All people speak in some form of dialect. However there are some dialects that are considered more acceptable and this is known as Standard English (SE). SE is the language of schools and the workplace. Other dialects are called nonstandard English (NSE), and students who use nonstandard English in more than 20 percent of their speech are considered nonstandard English speakers (Tompkins and Hoskisson, 1995).

Teachers have several roles to consider when working with NSE speakers. First, they must be sensitive to the needs of NSE children. They must also learn about the features of the NSE so they will be able to understand what the students will be facing as they learn to read, write, and spell in SE. In addition, teachers must accept and respect the child's language. Rejecting the child's language is tantamount to rejecting the child. "Dialect has no negative effect on reading achievement with the possible exception of teacher attitude" (Goodman and Goodman, 1987, 9). According to the Goodmans, constantly correcting children's syntax, incorrect verb forms, misplaced modifiers, and pronunciation eventually leads to children's withdrawal from participation. It is often the teacher's or the school's bias that doesn't accept the child's cultural language.

Although children's linguistic differences must be respected and accepted, teachers must also expose NSE speakers to SE. Teachers and other adults using SE need to provide a model from which NSE speakers can learn. Children need this modeling and immersion in SE for future academic and vocational success.

Using children's literature that involves SE patterns has been found to be successful in expanding the language competency of NSE-speaking children. Books with predictable patterns can be read, with the students repeating the language elements. Additional practice can be accomplished through drama, role-playing, and dictating or writing the story or a version of the story.

EFFECTIVE PRACTICES FOR THE LINGUISTICALLY AND CULTURALLY DIVERSE STUDENT

To help linguistically and culturally diverse children, teachers need to develop an understanding and appreciation of the culture and the language of their students. In addition there are practices and strategies that have proven to be effective in promoting literacy with these children. Second language learners, just as native speakers of English, learn how to read and write naturally when they are engaged in using language authentically for purposeful tasks (Lim and Watson, 1993; Ernst and Richard, 1994–1995). When a content-rich curriculum is implemented using a whole language philosophy of teaching and learning, the classroom develops into an optimal environment for learning a second language. "Students who are involved in natural, authentic, and content-rich settings will develop the language and concepts of the content while developing literacy and oracy skills" (Lim and Watson, 1993, 385).

Providing an Effective Classroom Environment

One exceedingly important practice is the establishment of a classroom environment that respects and supports all learners, encourages risk taking, and facilitates the development of language competence. In a classroom where there are children who do not speak English, children need to:

- feel respected and valued
- have their language and culture accepted
- develop a positive self-image
- be encouraged to interact with other class members
- have programs and materials in the class that reflect and celebrate cultural diversity
- be exposed to different ways of learning
- learn by themselves, with peers, and within the whole class

(Freeman and Freeman, 1992, 1993; Ernst and Richards, 1994–1995; Gersten and Jimenez, 1994)

Maintaining the Child's First Language

Recent research supports the theory that children who are encouraged to maintain their first language do better in school than do those whose first language is eliminated from school programs (Cummins, 1986; Freeman and Freeman, 1992, 1993). Teachers of second language learners should:

- encourage parents to assist in the classroom and school programs
- have translators available, if possible, for school meetings and conferences
- value the child's attempts to communicate in English
- speak slowly and embed the language in context-rich activities
- encourage risk taking
- focus on the meaning of what is said, not on how it is said
- give children time to answer questions
- use visuals and emphasize the development of concepts
- use materials and design curricular activities that provide all students with exposure to the contributions of all cultures
- ensure that environmental print reflects the children's first languages
- provide materials and resources in languages other than English
- encourage second language learners to publish stories and share their writing in languages other than English
- provide home-school activities

(Olsen and Mullen, 1990; Gibbons, 1991; Freeman and Freeman, 1992, 1993)

Cooperative Learning and Peer Teaching

Children new to English learn most from their English-speaking classmates, and second language learners may be more comfortable communicating on a one-to-one basis. This may be particularly true for "Newcomers," those children who have recently arrived in the United States and are unfamiliar with American life. To help with the adjustment to American schooling, these children can be paired with a buddy for the first few weeks while they become oriented to the school and class routines and while they learn survival vocabulary. From their first arrival, teachers should involve the new students in activities, frequently with their buddies or small groups of students. Since the children will need time to develop confidence in speaking English, they should not be called on to talk until they feel more comfortable in the class. As members of a cooperative group, they will learn through observation and exposure to the activities. As the students improve their ability to speak English, they can participate more fully in group activities. Flexible groups can be formed that change with interest and needs. The students should be given opportunities to interact in these groups as often as possible. To help non-English-speaking students interact with their peers, teachers should:

- plan ways of including second language learners in peer groups from the first day of school
- help children join with peers inside and outside school
- establish a mentor/buddy system for class activities
- provide opportunities for students to listen to, speak, read, and write English in nonthreatening situations with their classmates
- design activities and projects that include art, speaking, writing, and drama that can be undertaken cooperatively
- provide time for interaction at classroom centers

Reporting Back

It takes many years for limited English speaking (LEP) children to gain enough command of the English language to allow them to be successful in school. These nonnative speakers of English need to be given many opportunities to develop their competence in oral speaking. One activity that teachers may use to enhance language development is Reporting Back. Setting up Reporting Back situations in the classroom is a means of giving children practice at a more abstract level than language used in everyday situations. In Reporting Back activities, children first take part in hands-on experiences or experiments or listen to information read to them. They then report back to their classmates about what they have discovered.

Although hands-on experiences do provide children with opportunities to use language and to reflect on their learning, the language that is used is different in complexity from that used in reading and writing. However, even with more concrete experiences, Reporting Back activities provide a bridge between everyday talk and the more formal language associated with schooling. Teachers can initially engage the students in the hands-on activities and move to more complex ones, such as reading information from books or articles.

Becoming proficient in spoken language is necessary if children are to achieve in school. Reporting Back is one practice that allows children to be involved in purposeful oral language while structuring and organizing their newly acquired knowledge. Through interactions with other learners in such activities as Reporting Back, children are able to develop their own language skills (Gibbons, 1991).

Other effective practices—such as the cloze procedure, choral reading, scaffolded instruction, and using wordless books—are but a few practices identified as helping ESL students become successful language users. Most of the practices in this book, although not specifically designated for ESL students, will serve to create a classroom environment whereby all children can learn.

Content Area Instruction

It is necessary to modify how to plan and teach curriculum subjects for second language learners. In many schools, children are pulled out of the classroom for a daily period of instruction in English. It is important that the classroom teacher and ESL teacher cooperatively plan instruction and activities. New curriculum should not be introduced while the student is out of the room because additional stress is placed on the second language learner who misses the content being taught. Content area learning is more difficult for ESL students to understand because concepts are more abstract and the vocabulary is new and difficult. There are, however, certain practices teachers can implement to facilitate content area instruction.

- Allowing children to do more listening in the beginning
- Clarifying key ideas you must get across to students
- Simplifying vocabulary and speaking slowly
- Repeating key issues and ideas and summarizing frequently
- Using objects, pictures, and other concrete material to make the meaning clear
- Using graphic organizers and other visual aids to help students relate and organize information
- Using gestures and body language for emphasis to convey meaning
- Asking questions that don't require a yes or no answer
- Observing children closely to note whether children understand—for example, looking blank, looking puzzled, or sighing
- Providing support by thinking aloud to make the secrets of learning "public"

With more and more children for whom English is a second language entering school, teachers must be increasingly sensitive to the issues involved and learn more about the techniques and practices that ensure these students a smooth transition into the total school program. These children need time and encouragement to reach levels of competency to succeed in school. By combining meaningful and natural language experiences and opportunities with content-laden instructional practices, optimal language and subject matter learning is enhanced. As the instructional focus moves away from addressing language as an object and away from content as solely facts to providing content-rich, purposeful language experiences, second language learners will gain competency and fluency in English, as well as gain confidence in themselves as learners (Lim and Watson, 1993).

SPECIAL EDUCATION: THE INCLUSION MOVEMENT

It is impossible to cover the subject of special education within the confines of this chapter. However, since special education students are often second language learners as well as

FROM THE CLASSROOM OF . . .

Kathy Pike and Jean Mumper New Paltz, New York

BOOKWORDS

Key Words is an effective practice for building vocabulary. Here children choose a word that is highly meaningful for them and place this word on a card. Frequently, these words deal with the children's family, friends, favorite television shows or characters, and the like. To help children develop an interest in words from literature, *BOOKWORDS* may be undertaken instead. In this activity, children choose a word they would like to learn from a piece of literature. On the back of the card, the children can copy the sentence and page number from the book or write an original sentence if desired. For example, in the book *When Goldilocks Went to the House of the Three Bears*, published by Bookshelf, children may choose the word *tiny*, the word *slept*, or the word *growled*. These words may be used for developing oral language, for word sorting activities, or for writing resources.

being considered at risk, they do have special needs.

Frequently, children with learning disabilities (for whatever reason) are placed in self-contained classrooms with from six to twelve children. There is usually one teacher trained in special education and at least one aide, depending on the severity of the children's needs. In high-need classes, social workers, speech teachers, school psychologists, and other adults are part of the educational team on a regular basis. Special education classes tailor the curriculum to the individual child's needs and attempt to cover subject matter appropriate to the age group.

There is a growing movement to place students in the least restrictive environment, and this may not be in a self-contained special setting (Allington, 1993). Instead, children may receive their instruction in general education classrooms where they are placed in age-appropriate settings. This movement is a current trend that fosters the inclusion of special students in regular classes for a full school day. The special education teacher, sometimes referred to as a consultant teacher, and the aide form a team with the classroom teacher. Up until this time, mainstreaming was the accepted method of moving special education students into regular classrooms. A child who was good in math, science, or any other subject would leave the classroom for a specified period of time and join a regular class at the appropriate level for instruction in that particular subject. After the designated time in the regular class, the special education student would return to the home room. There are obvious drawbacks to separating students with special needs since they have to join society after leaving school. Since the goal of education is to educate students for later life, the inclusion movement aims to eliminate the separation of students and provide a more realistic situation (Baker, Wang, and Walberg, 1994–1995).

The hope is that students without special needs will be sensitized to the needs of children with special needs. The special needs child will no longer feel like an outsider in the school community. But, as with all new movements in education, there is resistance to change, and many problems have to be worked out before inclusion can be put into practice successfully.

THE GIFTED AND TALENTED

> The general objects—are to provide an education adapted to the years, the capacity, and the condition of everyone, and directed to their freedom and happiness—We hope to avail the state of those talents which nature has sown so liberally among the poor as the rich, but which perish without use, if not sought for and cultivated.
>
> (Thomas Jefferson)

One of the United States's most precious resources is being squandered—the gifts and talents of many of its students—as these students are not being challenged to perform at their best (United States Government, 1993). The problem is even more problematic among economically disadvantaged and culturally diverse groups, who have limited access to advanced educational opportunities. Schools must challenge their top performing students to attain greater heights if the nation is to attain a world class educational system and is to be competitive with other industrialized countries. Some effective programs for gifted and talented students do exist but many of these are limited in substance and in scope.

To provide educational opportunities for students with high potential, there are certain goals to be considered:

- More challenging curriculum standards must be set.
- More challenging, accelerated learning opportunities must be provided.
- Inquiry, problem solving, investigation, report writing, and product development must be stressed in school activities.
- There must be more learning opportunities for disadvantaged and culturally diverse students with outstanding talents.
- There must be opportunities for able students to work together and with students of different abilities.
- Talented youths must be provided with opportunities to work with tutors and mentors.
- The definition of gifted must be broadened.

(United States Government, 1993; Feldhusen, 1995)

There has been a need to rethink the definitions and assessment of gifted and talented youngsters in order to serve a broader range of talented students. New research has challenged the view that intelligence is fixed and can only be measured by standardized tests. Today, it is known that intelligence takes many forms and therefore requires that many criteria be used to measure it.

Howard Gardner has had a major impact on the thinking about human abilities. His concept of multiple intelligences, which will be described in this chapter, now constitutes an approach to gifted and talented education that recognizes the diversity of potential talents.

Too often, despite the recognized need for educating children with unique talents, gifted education has been a thorny issue and even has been considered elitist. However, it must be remembered that most children who are very able do not perform at high enough levels, as they are restrained by the lack of depth and challenge in regular classroom instruction and by the limitations of the specialized programs designed for them. Frequently, classroom teachers make few accommodations for them, even though there is evidence that they have already mastered major portions of the curriculum. In addition, the ways that bright children are identified using mainly test information and grades limits the access to the special opportunities that could benefit them. Other issues in gifted education include equity versus excellence, tracking versus grouping, assessment and evaluation, and curriculum compacting and modification. Funding for gifted education, the implementation of programs, and meeting the needs of the students, the teachers, and the community are added concerns in gifted education today.

Definition and Identification of Students with Outstanding Talent

Today's knowledge and thinking have reconceptualized the field of gifted education so that a broader, more encompassing definition of giftedness is now utilized. The following definition, based on the definition in the federal Javits Gifted and Talented Education Act, reflects today's knowledge and thinking:

> Children and youth with outstanding talent perform or show the potential for performing at remarkably high levels of accomplishment when compared with others of their age, experience, or environment. These children and youth exhibit high performance capability in intellectual, creative, and/or artistic areas, possess an unusual leadership capacity, or excel in specific academic fields. They require services or activities not ordinarily provided by the schools. Outstanding talents are present in children and youth from all cultural groups, across all economic strata, and in all areas of human endeavor.

In addition to the above definition, there are some markers that help in the identification of high-potential students including:

- curiosity
- advanced vocabulary and outstanding reading ability
- intenseness, with a tendency to get absorbed in activities
- exhibition of higher-level thinking and comfortableness with abstract reasoning
- sensitivity
- many interests and hobbies
- ability to make connections between ideas and activities
- preference to work alone or with older children or adults
- original ideas and thinking
- outstanding sense of humor
- talent in the fine arts
- great imagination
- ability to perform well on standardized tests

(Winebrenner, 1992)

Identifying gifted and talented students will depend on what the school community wants them to achieve and what resources they are willing to provide to cultivate and develop the talents. Outcomes must be clearly defined to develop programs that provide learning opportunities for the gifted. Figure 12.4 is a sample of one identification form. It synthesizes information from a variety of sources and assessment tools. Another means of identifying and meeting the needs of gifted students is to utilize the multiple intelligences model which is described in the following section.

Multiple Intelligences

Standardized tests no longer are considered the major criterion for identifying gifted and talented students. With the work of Howard Gardner and his research study on Multiple Levels of Intelligence, a new perspective appears for identifying gifted and talented children. He defines intelligence as the "capacity to solve problems or fashion products which are valued in one or more cultural settings" (Gardner, 1983, 34). He further proposes that at least seven intellectual capacities are used—each capacity having its own distinctive mode of thinking (Blyth and Gardner, 1990). The seven intelligences are musical, bodily kinesthetic, spatial, logical-mathematical, linguistic, intrapersonal, and interpersonal.

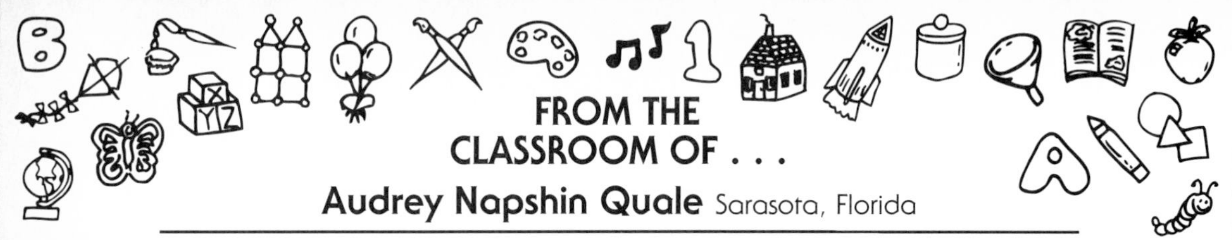

FROM THE CLASSROOM OF . . .

Audrey Napshin Quale Sarasota, Florida

CHALLENGE BOARD

One of the most rewarding things about teaching is getting students excited about learning. The use of a *Challenge Board* does that easily. The Challenge Board activity is one in which students raise questions for their classmates, or themselves, to explore and answer. The questions can be related to current subject matter or any topic that might be difficult, insightful, or intriguing. Challenge Board questions are color coded: a red star for "Look it Up" type questions; a yellow star for "Think about It" questions, and a green star for "Everyone Try It" questions.

A portion of a bulletin board or blackboard is dedicated to the Challenge Board activity. When students generate their questions, the questions are placed on the board. A box is provided for classmates to deposit their written answers.

At the end of the day, the class is gathered together for the "Brain Stretching" time. During this time, Audrey reads aloud the answers to questions posed on previous occasions. To conclude the session, she then shares any questions that have come up on that particular day. The students are encouraged to brainstorm answers. Any unsolved questions are added to the Challenge Board. If there are any questions that remain unanswered at the end of the school year, they are compiled and become part of a Summer Challenge Sheet which the students take home.

The Challenge Board process is designed to: promote student curiosity; give students an opportunity to conduct meaningful research; promote critical thinking; and create a lifelong love of learning. Students can be turned on to the wonderment of learning through their own challenging questions and insightful answers.

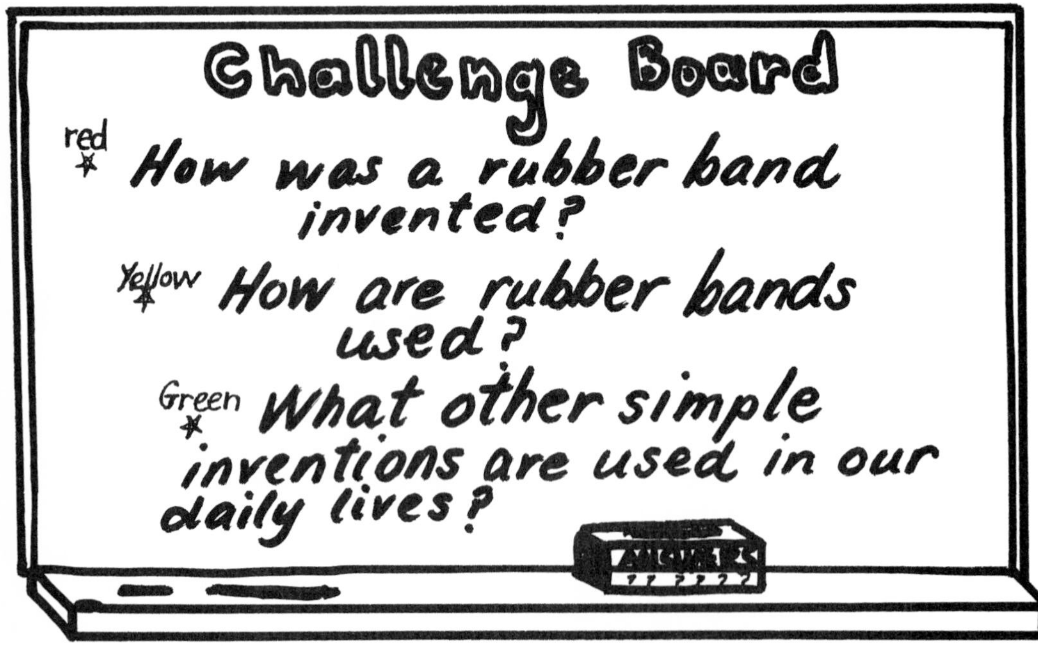

Challenge Board
red
How was a rubber band invented?
Yellow
How are rubber bands used?
Green
What other simple inventions are used in our daily lives?
ANSWERS

Figure 12.4

NAME__________________________GRADE______ DATE____________ EVALUATOR ____________

OFTEN | SOMETIMES | RARELY

ASSESSMENT FORM

Part I: HOW STUDENT LEARNS

- Has an advanced vocabulary for age/grade.
- Demonstrates a wealth of information for age/grade.
- Exhibits quick mastery and recall of facts.
- Asks challenging questions/uses higher level thinking.
- Transfers acquired knowledge and manipulates ideas.
- Perceives similarities and differences; comprehends abstract ideas/makes connections.
- Uses logical/analytical reasoning.
- Performs above grade level academically.
- Chooses complex and challenging activities.
- Is a reader; may choose reading in place of play or doing class work.

Part II: MOTIVATIONAL CHARACTERISTICS

- Exhibits high level of intensity.
- Is persistent in completing tasks.
- Prefers working independently, exploring and challenging own abilities.
- Requires little direction in completing tasks and solving problems.
- Is a perfectionist/is self-critical.
- Is a risk-taker.
- Appears very able, but may seem to be bored; is under-achieving.
- Is an alert observer.
- Can appear distracted or to be daydreaming.
- Follows through and completes tasks promptly.

Part III: CREATIVE RESPONSES

- Asks provocative questions.
- Is extremely inquisitive.
- Generates many ideas or solutions.
- Possesses original ideas.
- Demonstrates imagination/is innovative.
- Is a risk-taker.
- Changes, elaborates, and manipulates ideas.
- Has a keen sense of humor.
- Is often a non-conformist.
- Enjoys intellectual or thought-provoking challenges and activities.

Part IV: INTER/INTRA PERSONAL CHARACTERISTICS

- Is reliable.
- Is socially mature.
- Is well-liked by peers.
- Often challenges ideas.
- Is a leader.
- Is influential and can convince others.
- Is sensitive to others.
- Fulfills responsibilities.
- Is well-organized.
- Is competent in self-expression.

1. **Musical intelligence.** These children are sensitive to sounds in the environment. They are aware of tone, pitch, and rhythm. Children with this intelligence love to sing, hum, chant rhythmically, and clap or move using patterns in rhythm. Time should be made available for these students to participate or lead musical activities and attend concerts or other musical events. To enhance those who possess musical intelligence, a center in the classroom could contain tape recorders, tapes, metronomes, earphones, and objects that will allow the students to produce various sounds, for example, blocks, bottles, rattles.

2. **Bodily kinesthetic intelligence.** These children have an uncanny ability to use their bodies in a fine-tuned way. They can do things with their bodies effortlessly that most have to learn painstakingly. Children with this intelligence love athletic activities, acting, miming, and handling all kinds of objects and materials. They may take objects apart and put them together easily. They are usually moving in their seats and around the room, touching and fiddling with things. They are the future athletic stars and inventors. To meet the needs of those who possess bodily kinesthetic intelligence, students should be given opportunities to create and participate in performances, to role-play, to use movement to demonstrate a scientific or mathematical principle, to dance or move to interpret poetry or a historical event. Learning centers that appeal to these learners should include materials to allow for activities and opportunities for tactile experiences, for example, clay, sandpaper, and various textural materials.

3. **Spatial intelligence.** These children are able to see the physical aspects of the world and interpret their impressions accurately into different and new forms. These children usually remember where everything is. They draw and construct real-world representations. They love all kinds of doodads and inventions. These children actively seek out arts and craft activities. They are good at puzzles, mazes, and other manipulative challenges. They love photographs, videotapes, color, and design. These students need time to work on art projects, build with construction materials, draft and design, visit art galleries and museums, and view art slides and videos. A learning center for those who possess spatial intelligence should contain varied art supplies, puzzles, computer graphics, art and picture books, holograms, and games of an imaginative nature.

4. **Linguistic intelligence.** Children with this intelligence have a love affair with words, their meanings and usage. They love to read and write. They are great spellers and have strong vocabulary development. They are very good students in school and are also the riddle, joke, and trivia experts. These students gravitate toward activities involved with language. They need time to read a variety of print materials, participate in discussions and debates, and write for different purposes and for different audiences. In addition to the library center, a language center appeals to their specific talent. Within this center are taped stories and books, puzzles, and language games besides a variety of writing tools and materials.

5. **Logical-mathematical intelligence.** These children see order and pattern in the world. Reasoning ability is strong in working through problems. They love to figure things out conceptually and are whizzes at computing and problem solving. They love puzzles, mental challenges, numbers, number games, and all aspects of computers and related technologies. These students should have opportunities to investigate how things work; play computer games; play chess, checkers, and other strategy games; create math and science problems; and conduct experiments. A center for meeting the needs of those with logical-mathematical intelligence should include computer games, logic puzzles, materials to conduct investigations, calculators, challenging problems to solve, and journals for the recording of observations and experiments.

6. **Intrapersonal intelligence.** These children march to their own tune. They are perceived as impractical, loners, independent, daydreamers, and imaginative. They are very much in tune with the inner self and their feelings. Personal journal entries of these children may be voluminous. These children should be permitted to work alone if they choose to do so, and their individuality should be respected. While working in centers or other class activi-

ties, these students with intrapersonal intelligence could be given materials that they can critique or interpret based on their own personal assessments and could be provided with stories that allow them to put themselves in the main character's thoughts.

7. **Interpersonal intelligence.** This child is seen as a future president or—at the other extreme—as a gang leader. These children have the gift of gab and are masters of the art of persuasion. They are very outgoing and popular and make friends quickly and easily. They love to work in cooperative group activities. These students need to have opportunities to capitalize on their finely honed social skills. They are ideal candidates for peer teaching and will be empathetic to the learner. They may take over group activities, but given leadership roles they will share the time with other group members. They do well as members and officers of clubs and organizations. They particularly enjoy group discussions, brainstorming, class government, and areas for socializing and playing games.

Most students possess each of the seven intelligences to some degree, but the combinations and degrees of the intelligences differ. Educators must determine which students show promise and which students are at-risk in each intelligence and then plan accordingly. Gardner believes that under the right conditions children have the capacity to develop their multiple intelligences to a greater extent than is currently being done. Schools must nurture their students' interests and abilities and give them plenty of enrichment and learning opportunities to develop their intelligences and then must help them set vocational and avocational goals appropriate to their particular set of intelligences.

Javits 7+ Gifted and Talented Program

In Community School District 18 in Brooklyn, New York, a demonstration project is in place to explore ways of identifying and providing differentiated appropriate curriculum for gifted students in an underserved population. The traditional assessments usually used to identify gifted and talented children—such as paper-and-pencil tests—are not used in this program. The theoretical foundation for the project is based on Howard Gardner's research (1983). The gifted and talented classes will serve economically disadvantaged students, limited English proficiency students, and physically challenged students.

The program is federally funded. Director Joyce Rubin designed the implementation of the program cooperatively with classroom teachers, administrators, and other staff members. Student selection was based on multiple criteria, including interviews, as well as Gardner's seven intelligences theory. The curriculum is called Teaching for Discovery and provides a series of units designed to expand and individualize the curriculum, allowing children to discover their special interests and abilities. These units were created to enable the teacher to make a match between his or her students and an appropriately differentiated curriculum. Figure 12.5 presents a 7+ curriculum matrix.

Making Provisions for the Gifted in the Regular Classroom

In many schools where whole language programs are fully implemented, students have opportunities for choices that capitalize on their gifts and talents. They also become active in peer teaching programs and can be given leadership roles in various projects. Certain aspects of recognizing and educating gifted and talented students have become evident in schools today. These practices value and respect the need to educate all children.

Some schools have recognized that high potential students require a differentiated instructional program and that their needs can be met within the regular classroom. Appropriate, differentiated instructional programs are necessary for the academic growth of gifted children and for the continuation and preservation of their desire to learn. There are ways that this may be accomplished: compacting the curriculum and modifying the curriculum.

Compacting the Curriculum

Many high-potential students are able to achieve many of the regular curricular goals and objectives without direct instruction and without teachers spending a great deal of time on them. Curriculum compacting is a technique

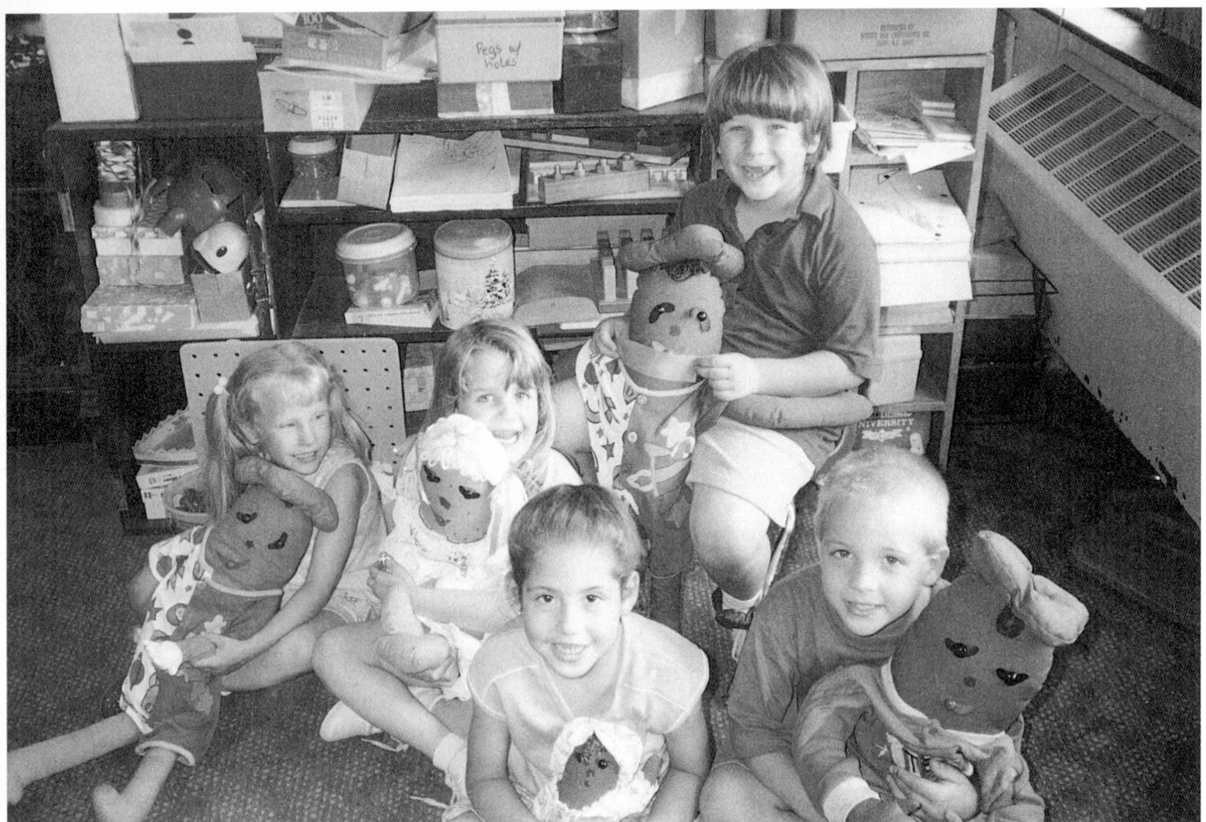

Students in the inclusion class of Merry Johansen in Wallkill, N.Y. enjoying the Pickle Puss Family of dolls.

that is designed specifically to make appropriate adjustments in any curricular area for all students at all grade levels (Renzulli, 1977; Reis and Renzulli, 1992). Curriculum compacting is a procedure that is used to streamline the regular curriculum for those students who are capable of learning it at a faster pace and to substitute more challenging content. The compacting process consists of three phases: (1) determining the goals and objectives of the regular curriculum, (2) assessing students for mastery of these objectives, and (3) substituting more challenging and more appropriate options.

When curriculum compacting is undertaken, the able students have time available for participating in a differentiated curriculum. However, this should not be more of the regular instructional program, but rather it should focus on modifications, both content and process, that reflect the students' instructional needs.

Modifying the Curriculum

There are several kinds of modifications that can be provided to gifted learners. Content modifications allow students to read more complex and in-depth reading materials, provide opportunities for students to select materials that reflect personal interests, and encourage students to explore topics that are not part of the regular curriculum.

Process modifications are those that emphasize the application of critical and creative thinking to challenging content. Whereas it is recognized that critical and creative activities should be available for all learners, the unique learning qualities of highly able students make these explorations all the more appropriate.

FROM THE CLASSROOM OF . . .

Karen Zgrodek and Stephanie Leechow Wallkill, N.Y.

PICKLE PUSS

Karen Zgrodek, a teaching aide in the primary inclusion class in Wallkill, N.Y., and her friend Stephanie Leechow, created a doll known as Pickle Pusss to help children, especially children with special needs, identify and share their emotions. Pickle Puss's eyes and mouth are attached with buttons, which allows them to turn creating various expressions. The doll has been helpful in enabling children to express their emotions and recognize that feelings are an important part of all of us.

In the classroom where Karen works, Pickle Puss has his own desk, or he occasionally shares a desk with the daily leader. Pickle Puss has his own backpack, which he tends to fill with treasures for the youngsters, e.g., a special book or toy. For example, when one child's kitten died, Pickle Puss brought a book about losing a pet. If a child is ill, Pickle Puss may accompany him or her to the nurse's office. He can even visit on weekends and children can help him keep a travel journal. He wears infant-sized clothing so the children can dress him for any occasion. He has assumed a definite personality and has been a valuable asset to the inclusion program in Wallkill. For information on how to acquire Pickle Puss, write to:

Pickle Puss Dolls
Best of Friends
5 Crest Haven Drive
New Windsor, N.Y. 12553

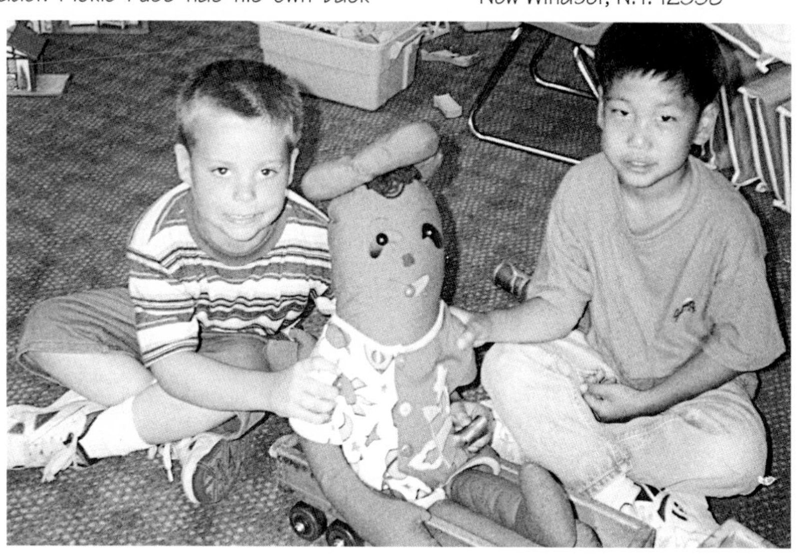

Figure 12.5 7+ Curriculum Matrix

Javits 7+ Gifted Program
Joyce Rubin, Director

Community School District

7+ CURRICULUM MATRIX

Conceptual Theme CULTURE Unit/Topic FRIENDS AROUND THE WORLD

Understanding/Generalization, Families are major transmitters of cultural heritage.

Intelligence → / Curriculum Area						
Social Studies	Learn and play multicultural games, dances	Students create movements that represent their names	Conduct surveys to get information about multicultural heritage	Explore the reasons behind the celebration of particular calendar dates	Listen to and compare music from different cultures	Locate geographical regions on a map
Communication Arts	Expand vocabulary by creating original verses to game of Bafta Hindi	Create name Acrostics	Interpret meaning of lyrics for "We Are The World"	Read Mojo Means One - A Swahili Counting Book Counting in sequence, read and write the numerals 1-10	Create original music to accompany the retelling of a story	Create a self-portrait for the "What's in A Name" big book
Mathematics	Play Lynx and Cat, a South African game	Engage in planning sessions to design the mural "Friends Around The World"	Construct an international counting big book	Use recipes for estimating, measuring, and modifying	Adapt the tune of "Ten Little Indians." Children count in various languages	Create a mural solving problems of size, shape, and balance
Science	Use sound clues to play the game Bird In The Cage	Share your ideas about how the mural should be organized	Examine relationship between climate and clothing; climate and home.	Examine different ways of charting data from surveys	Examine natural sources of musical instruments	Interpret pictures that represent geographical locations

Figure 12.6 Effective Practices for Differentiating the Curriculum

PRACTICE	DESCRIPTION
Compacting	Compacting is a flexible, instructional technique that enables high-ability students to skip work they already know and substitute more appropriate and challenging content.
Independent Projects	This process is built on student interest where teachers and students identify problems, topics, or issues to be investigated. Projects encourage planning and research skills at advanced levels, and allow capable students to work with complex and abstract ideas.
Mentorships	Students are matched with mentors within the students' talents and interest areas to develop and carry out projects or tasks. Mentorships help students develop skills of production in a particular field and to develop an awareness of careers.
Higher Level Questioning	By providing students with open-ended questions that require higher level thinking and metacognitive awareness, teachers will challenge students' thinking.
Learning Centers	Learning centers for highly able students should provide opportunities for advanced thinking, the development of complex projects, the use of research and technology, and student independence. Explorations should satisfy curiosity, allow student choice, be meaningful, and be of sufficient depth and breadth to challenge thinking.
Tiered Assignments	Various levels of activities can be provided students to encourage broader literacy activities and problem solving and to ensure that students are given opportunities to explore ideas at a level that promotes continued growth.
Contracts	Contracts—agreements between teachers and students—allots students freedoms and options about how to complete tasks. Contracts can make skills more relevant to high ability students by integrating them in more meaningful, interesting tasks.

Critical thinking requires the analysis and evaluation of textual materials before, during, and after reading, while creative thinking requires the learner to go beyond the text by creating and applying novel ideas and insights. Another process modification is the introduction of advanced research skills.

Curriculum modification has several advantages for both gifted students and their teachers. First, curriculum compacting can be utilized to provide appropriate instruction for any student who demonstrates proficiency in any curricular area. Modified curriculum is not exclusive to the gifted learner. Also, when modifications are provided, a variety of individualized activities can be made available, again to all learners. Finally, allowing gifted learners to select materials and projects that are of interest to them promotes enthusiasm for learning (Dooley, 1993).

It must be remembered that instruction for bright students differs from regular curricular offerings in several ways. First, in an appropriate differentiated curriculum, the knowledge is highly specialized and is related to real-world problems. Able students conduct authentic research, not just mere writing of reports, and hone such process skills as interviewing, gathering information through questionnaires and surveys and analyzing data statistically. Second, these students produce knowledge, not just simply consume it. Teachers assume different roles as well. They must be managers helping students locate specialized resources; guides who help students discover knowledge; and brokers who help students locate the specialized audiences to share their expertise. Finally, creativity is genuine, as students are encouraged to generate as many ideas as possible about the topic they are investigating. These principles of differentiated curriculum necessitate a high degree of self-evaluation and accountability on the part of both teachers and the students. This perspective of gifted education promotes open-ended instruction and genuine inquiry (Cooper, 1995).

Schools must assume responsibility for the academic progress for all children, including those who exhibit outstanding performance. The needs of the gifted cannot be overlooked. Through such practices as providing students with activities to develop their multiple intelligences, compacting the curriculum, and differentiating the curriculum by making modifications to both the content and the processes, an appropriate instructional program can be offered that will challenge gifted and talented learners. Figure 12.7 outlines some effective strategies for differentiating the curriculum.

> One can never consent to creep when one feels the impulse to soar.
>
> (Helen Keller)

SUMMARY

We are aware that all children have needs. The children referred to in this chapter have very special needs. Their needs must be met to ensure that their full potential is realized. This goes for children who are gifted and talented as well as for children with learning difficulties. Gifted and talented children need opportunities to interact with each other and be involved in programs that support and expand their talents. Learning disabilities, speaking English as a second language, family backgrounds, and economic and societal issues all contribute to placing these children at risk. Some principles can be applied to all of these students. One that is of utmost importance is building self-esteem—making children feel good about themselves. Seeing these children as individuals and creating learning environments to suit their individual needs are other vital issues. Following the tenets of the whole language philosophy of actively engaging children in the learning process can guarantee some measure of success in school.

BIBLIOGRAPHY AND SUGGESTED REFERENCES

Allington, R. (1993). Michael doesn't go down the hall anymore. *The Reading Teacher, 46,* 602–604.

Armstrong, T. (1994a). *Multiple intelligences in the classroom.* Alexandria, Va.: Association for Supervision and Curriculum Development.

Armstrong, T. (1994b). Multiple intelligences: Seven ways to approach curriculum. *Educational Leadership, 52,* 26–28.

Au, K. (1993). *Literacy instruction in multicultural settings.* New York: Holt, Rinehart and Winston.

Baker, E.; Wang; M.; & Walberg, H. (1994–1995). Synthesis of research: The effects of inclusion on learning. *Educational Leadership, 52,* 33–35.

Banks, J. (1994). *An introduction to multicultural education.* Boston: Allyn & Bacon.

Berthoff, A. (1990). Paulo Friere's liberation pedagogy. *Language Arts, 67,* 363–369.

Blyth, T., & Gardner, H. (1990). A school for all intelligences. *Educational Leadership, 45,* 33–36.

Cells, W. (1992). Governors announce plan to help preschool children. *The New York Times,* August 8, 22.

Chall, J. S.; Jacobs, H. D.; & Baldwin. J. (1990). *The reading crisis: Why poor children fall behind.* Cambridge, Mass.: Harvard University Press. 149, 155.

Clay, M. (1975). *What did I write?* Portsmouth, N.H.: Heinemann.

Clay, M. (1993a). *An observation of early literacy.* Portsmouth, N.H.: Heinemann.

Clay, M. (1993b). *Reading Recovery: A guidebook for teachers in training.* Portsmouth, N.H.: Heinemann.

Cooper, C. (1995). Integrating gifted education into the total school curriculum. *The School Administrator, 52,* 8, 12–15.

Davis, W., & McCaul, E. (1990). *At-risk children and youth: A crisis in our school and society.* University of Maine, Farmington: Institute for the Study of At-Risk Students.

DeFord, D.; Lyons, C.; & Pinnell, G. (Eds.). (1991). *Bridges to literacy: Learning from Reading Recovery.* Portsmouth, N.H.: Heinemann.

Dooley, C. (1993). The challenge: Meeting the needs of gifted readers. *The Reading Teacher, 46,* 546–551.

Ernst, G., & Richard, K. (1994–1995). Reading and writing pathways to conversation in the ESL classroom. *The Reading Teacher, 48,* 320–326.

Field, M., & Aebersold, G. (1990). Cultural attitudes towards reading: Implications for teachers of ESL/bilingual readers. *Journal of Reading, 33,* 406–410.

Feldhusen, J. (1995). A call for overhaul: Gifted education overlooks talent. *The School Administrator, 52,* 10, 11, 13.

Flores, B.; Tefft-Cousin, P.; & Diaz, E. (1991). Transforming deficit myths about learning, language, and culture. *Language Arts, 68,* 369–379.

Freeman, Y., & Freeman, D. (1992). *Whole language for second language learners.* Portsmouth, N.H.: Heinemann.

Freeman, D., & Freeman, Y. (1993). Strategies for promoting the primary languages of all students. *The Reading Teacher, 46,* 552–558.

Gage, N. (1990). Dealing with the dropout problem. *Phi Delta Kappan, 72,* 280–285.

Gardner, H. (1983). *Frames of mind: Theory of multiple intelligences.* New York: Basic Books.

Gardner, H. (1989). *To open minds.* New York: Basic Books.

Gersten, R., & Jimenez, R. (1994). A delicate balance: Enhancing literature instruction for students of English as a second language. *The Reading Teacher, 47,* 438–449.

Gibbons, P. (1991). *Learning to learn in a second language.* Newtown, N.S.W., Australia: Primary English Teacher Association.

Goffin, S. (1989). How well do we respect the children in our care? *Childhood Education, 66,* 68–74.

Goodman, K., & Goodman, Y. (1987). *Language and thinking in school.* 3rd ed. Katonah, N.Y.: Richard C. Owen Publishers.

Graves, M., & Graves, B. (1994). *Scaffolding reading experiences.* Norwood, Mass.: Christopher-Gordon.

Gunning, T. (1992). *Creating reading instruction for all children.* Boston, Mass.: Allyn and Bacon.

Heller, M. (1988). Comprehending and composing through language experience. *The Reading Teacher, 42,* 130–135.

Hiebert, E., & Taylor, B. (Eds.). *Getting reading right from the start: Effective early literacy interventions.* Needham, Heights, Mass.: Allyn & Bacon.

Hough, R.; Nurss, J.; & Enright, D. (1986). Story reading with limited English speaking children in the regular classroom. *The Reading Teacher, 39,* 510–515.

Kucer, S. (1995). Guiding bilingual students "through" the literacy process. *Language Arts, 72,* 20–29.

Lazear, D. (1991). *Seven ways of knowing: Teaching for Multiple Intelligences.* Palatine, Ill.: Skylight Publishing.

Levin, A. (1988). *Accelerated schools for at-risk students.* (CPRE Research Report Series RR-010). New Brunswick, N.J.: Center for Policy Research Education.

Lim, H., & Watson, D. (1993). Whole language content classes for second-language learners. *The Reading Teacher, 46,* 384–393.

Lopez, M. (1978). Bilingual education and the Latino student. *Bilingual Education for Latinos.* Washington, D.C.: Association for Supervision and Curriculum Development.

Lyons, C., & Beaver, J. (1995). Reducing retention and learning disability placement through Reading Recovery: An educationally sound, cost-effective choice. In R. Allington & S. Walmsley (Eds.), *No quick fix: Rethinking literacy programs in America's elementary schools,* 116–136.

McCauley, J., & McCauley, D. (1992). Using choral reading to promote language learning for ESL students. *The Reading Teacher, 45,* 526–533.

Mobley, L. (1990). Reading strategies for non-English speaking students. *The Reading Teacher, 40,* 182–184.

Moll, L. (1988). Some key issues in teaching Latino students. *Language Arts, 65,* 465–472.

National Commission on Excellence in Education. (1983). *A nation at risk: The imperative for educational reform.* Washington, D.C.: U.S. Department of Education.

National School Board Association. (1989). *An equal chance: Educating at-risk children to succeed.* Alexandria, Va.: Author.

New Zealand Department of Education. (1988). *New voices: Second language learning and teaching.* Wellington, New Zealand: Author.

Olsen, L., & Mullen, N. (1990). *Embracing diversity: Teacher's voices from California classrooms.* San Francisco: California Tomorrow.

Pinnell, G.; Fried, M.; & Estice, R. (1990). Reading recovery: Learning how to make a difference. *The Reading Teacher, 43,* 282–295.

Reed, S., & Sauter, R. (1990). Children of poverty. *Phi Delta Kappan, 72,* K1–K12.

Renzulli, J. (1977). *The enrichment triad model: A guide for developing defensible programs for the gifted and talented.* Mansfield Center, CT.: Creative Learning Press.

Renzulli, J., & Reis, S. (1992). Using curriculum compacting to challenge the above-average. *Educational Leadership, 50,* 51–57.

Ritty, M. (1991). Single-parent families: Tips for educators. *The Reading Teacher, 44,* 604–606.

Salvage, G., & Stevenson, H. (1991). Risk taking, bit by bit, *Language Arts, 68,* 356–366.

Samuels, J., & Farstrup, A. (1992). *What research has to say about reading instruction.* Newark, Del.: International Reading Association.

Slavin, R.; Karweit, N.; & Wasik, B. (Eds.). (1994). *Preventing early school failure: Research, policy, and practice.* Needham Heights, Mass.: Allyn & Bacon.

Slavin, R.; Madden, N.; Dolan, L; & Wasik, B. (1994). Roots and wings: Inspiring academic excellence. *Educational Leadership, 52,* 10–13.

Stavin, R.; Stegler, J.; & Stevenson, H. (1991). How Asian teachers polish each lesson to perfection. *American Educator, 15,* 12–20.

Sutton, C. (1989). Helping the non-native English speaker with reading. *The Reading Teacher, 42,* 684–688.

Taylor, B., Frye, B., Short, R., & Shearer, B. (1992). Classroom teachers prevent reading failure among low-achieving first-grade students. *The Reading Teacher, 45,* 592–597.

Taylor, B.; Short, R.; Shearer, B.; & Frye, B. (1995). First grade teachers provide early reading intervention in the classroom. In R. Allington & S. Walmsley (Eds.), *No quick fix: Rethinking literacy programs in America's elementary schools,* 159–176. Newark, Del.: International Reading Association.

Tompkins, G., & Hoskisson, K. (1995). *Language arts: Content and teaching strategies.* Englewood Cliffs, N.J.: Prentice-Hall.

Trachtenburg, P., & Ferruggia, A. (1989). Big books from little voices: Reaching high risk beginning readers. *The Reading Teacher, 42,* 684–689.

United States Government. (1993). *National excellence: A case for developing America's talent.* Washington, D.C.: United States Printing Office.

Vacca, R., & Padak, N. (1990). Who's at-risk in reading? *Journal of Reading, 33,* 486–488.

Vygotsky, L. (1978). *Mind in society.* Cambridge, Mass.: Harvard University Press.

Wallace, C., & Goodman, Y. (1989). Language and literacy development of multilingual learners. *Language Arts, 66,* 542–551.

Whitmore, K., & Crowell, C. (1994). *Inventing a classroom: Life in a bilingual, whole language learning community.* York, Maine: Stenhouse Publishers.

Winebrenner, S. (1992). *Teaching gifted kids in the regular classroom.* Victoria, Australia: Hawker Brownlow Education.

Zarrillo, J. (1994). *Multicultural literature, multicultural teaching.* Orlando, Fla.: Harcourt Brace.

CHILDREN'S LITERATURE CITED

Kitchen, B. (1992). *Somewhere today.* Cambridge, Mass.: Candlewick Press.

13 HOME TO SCHOOL: SCHOOL TO HOME

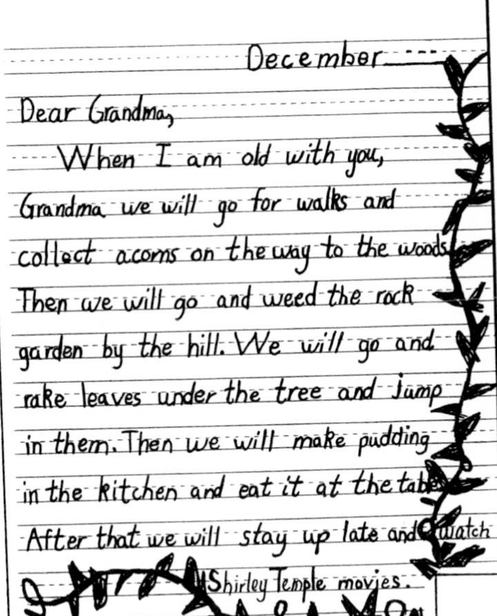

December

Dear Grandma,

When I am old with you, Grandma we will go for walks and collect acorns on the way to the woods. Then we will go and weed the rock garden by the hill. We will go and rake leaves under the tree and jump in them. Then we will make pudding in the kitchen and eat it at the table. After that we will stay up late and watch Shirley Temple movies.

Love, Robert

When I Am Old with You

We read a book in our classroom titled When I Am Old with You by Angela Johnson. It relates the sentiments of a child who looks forward to growing older with a grandparent.

Each student chose a special adult to whom to write. The enclosed letter relates their own words to you. They have enclosed a drawing and decorated the letter as well.

Please mail your response to the address on the envelope. All students have a mailbox in our classroom and they will be eager to hear from you.

I hope you enjoy the letter.

Jean Mumper ~ 3rd grade teacher

December 7/1995

Dear Robert,

Thank you for your beautiful letter.

Reading it reminded me of all the things we do together and how much fun we have doing them. I thought about the Christmas houses we're going to make and the good time we'll have working on them. But most of all Robert, I thought about what a lucky grandma I am to live close enough to be able to share so many good times. Some grandmas live so far from their grandchildren they are only able to visit a few times a year.

I am so happy that I'll have you to be old with me to share more good times, because I love you very much.

Love,
Grandma

After reading the story When I Am Old With You by Angela Johnson, each student wrote a personal letter to an older adult they loved. A cover letter explained the book and our writing activity. Every student did eventually receive a reply.

From the classroom of
Jean Mumper
Grade 3
Wallkill, N.Y.

Inspired by: *When I Am Old with You* by Angela Johnson

OVERVIEW

It has long been recognized that parents play key roles in their children's education both at home and at school. Parents are increasingly viewed as vital components in their children's successful literacy development. In order for schools to be effective, parents must assume an active role in all aspects of school life—from being their children's first teachers, to supporting school activities, to serving in an advisory capacity in the schools. With the growth and interest in the whole language movement, it is of particular importance to have a strong home-school connection. This chapter looks at the range of parental involvement possibilities and how these might be developed in the whole language classroom and in the whole language school. It provides specific suggestions and activities to illustrate how to encourage and strengthen the partnership between the home and the school to enhance the goal of creating lifelong learners. Areas that are stressed include communication between parents and the school, involving parents in the school, and involving parents in the home.

Questions to Ponder

1. What are the roles of parents in a whole language program?
2. Is parental involvement different in whole language classrooms from that in traditional classrooms?
3. How can schools help parents become more knowledgeable about whole language?
4. What are some of the concerns of parents regarding whole language and how might they be addressed?
5. How can parents become informed and involved in the assessment and evaluation of their children?

PARENT INVOLVEMENT: AN INTRODUCTION

There is an old African saying: "It takes an entire village to educate a child." That saying really reflects what educators have long believed about parent involvement in the schools; that is, literacy is promoted when schools and parents work together as partners. Through collaborative interactions, teachers and parents share the responsibility of educating children. Teachers and parents work together to promote children's academic, social, physical, and emotional growth. Research supports the notion that parent involvement is successful—that when parents are actively involved in helping their children, there are resultant long-term benefits (Ervin, 1982; Taylor, 1983; Boehnlein and Hager, 1985; Epstein, 1984, 1986; Henderson, 1987; Rich, 1988; Rasinski and Fredericks, 1989a; Strickland and Morrow, 1989; Morrow, 1993). Such positive outcomes as the following have been associated with the contributions of parents: higher academic achievement, improved school attendance, improved perceptions of the classroom and climate of the school by both students and parents, positive student attitudes, increased amount of time that parents and children spend together, and parent satisfaction with their children's teachers (Greenwood and Hickman, 1991). When schools include parents and value their contributions, parents increase their interactions with their children in the home and have more positive feelings about their own abilities to help their children (Epstein and Dauber, 1991). Moreover, an appropriate attitude toward learning can be nurtured, encouraged, and reinforced at home. There is a dual focus and emphasis in this partnership. Parents have to be integrated into the design of the educational system, and added support has to be provided in the home and to the home.

Parent involvement is of particular importance given the current interest in whole language. Because of the emphasis on meaningful and purposeful literacy experiences and the goal of creating lifelong readers and writers in a whole language program, it is increasingly important to have a strong home connection. Parental involvement should be an integral ingredient in any whole language program. Parents can broaden the dimensions of whole language and ensure that active learning, investigation, and discovery continue in the home as well (Fredericks and Rasinski, 1990a). This chapter is devoted to providing ways to stimulate parents' involvement and engagement in whole language activities both at home and at school. Prior to the discussion on ways to strengthen the bond between parents and the schools in a whole language program, the possible types of parent involvement are presented.

TYPES OF PARENT INVOLVEMENT

The quantity of literature regarding parent involvement is astonishing—from articles in magazines in supermarkets to those in professional journals. In light of all the information available to teachers and the current emphasis on and mandate for involving parents in education, teachers and schools need a framework for organizing parent programs. Epstein (1987, 1988) has suggested that successful efforts to involve parents in their children's education consist of five major types of parent involvement: providing for children's basic needs, communication from the school to the home, bringing parents into the school, assistance with learning activities at home, and decision making.

Basic Obligations of Parents

The most basic obligation of parents is the provision of food, clothing, shelter, safety, health, discipline, guidance, and the overall well-being of their children. Most parents meet these basic needs without help of interference from the schools, but when these obligations are not met, then the school must assist the family or alert social service agencies to investigate. Since parents vary in their abilities to fulfill these obligations, the school must adopt an active role in helping parents build positive home conditions to promote school learning. Ways to implement this responsibility include publications, workshops, and special programs on such topics as parenting, homework, attendance, television viewing, use of community resources, and other topics pertaining to home practices and conditions that have a bearing on success in school.

Parent Communication

Another type of parent involvement is communication from the school to the home. The school does have an obligation to help keep parents informed about their children's progress and school programs, and, in turn, parents are expected to act on the received information. These home-school communications can take many forms, including report cards, school calendars, special event notices, newsletters, and taped phone messages so that parents can gain an understanding of school policies and programs. Communications from the school ideally should be designed so that the school's messages and ideas go from the school to the home and from the home to the school.

Parent Involvement at School

A third type of parent involvement brings parents to the school building—usually as audiences for special events, participants in workshops and training sessions, and volunteers. Parents fulfill their roles in supporting school activities when they become spectators for assemblies, dramatic productions, or athletic events. When participating in workshops, parents assume the role of learners, since the focus of these training sessions is to educate parents on some aspect of parenting, the curriculum, or processes (such as the reading and writing processes) used in the classroom. To involve parents in more active roles in the school, teachers and administrators encourage them to serve as volunteers either in the classroom or elsewhere in the school on various projects (e.g., the school publishing center, literary anthology, or newsletter). The contributions of volunteers to the school community may be as follows:

- giving noninstructional assistance to teachers (e.g., on field trips, at class parties, and in the classroom)
- typing, keyboarding, or filing
- providing or acting as guest speakers
- listening to children read
- reading to children
- demonstrating hobbies
- participating in career awareness sessions
- providing remediation/enrichment after-school
- helping in the cafeteria, library, computer lab, or other areas requiring supervision
- serving as consultants on special issues or problems

- working with parent organizations in fund-raising, community relations, and political awareness

(Powell, 1986; Epstein, 1987)

The advantages of using volunteers are many. Volunteers lighten the work loads of teachers, resulting in improved teacher morale. By providing individualized instruction, volunteers have positive effects on students. By providing additional adult supervision, volunteers help alleviate discipline problems. Most important, volunteers not only strengthen the school's academic program, but they also become goodwill ambassadors for the school.

Parent Involvement in Learning Activities at Home

Another form of parent involvement is assistance with learning activities at home. These include requests for parents to provide guidance at home on learning activities that are coordinated with the classroom curriculum and ongoing projects. Such activities may involve listening to and discussing literature, responding to books through writing or the expressive arts, or sharing activities with their children. These sharing activities are outgrowths of curricular areas or themes currently being implemented in the classroom.

Parents as Decision Makers

A fifth type of parent involvement includes parents in the decision-making process which encourages them to assume active roles in governance and advocacy groups. The effectiveness of schools increases when schools are responsive to local needs, and there should be no barriers to reasonable parental participation in helping make policy decisions. Parents who are involved at this level are generally knowledgeable about the school's needs and the state of education. Among the activities that can be accomplished at this highest level of participation are:

- helping set school goals
- evaluating the effectiveness of school goals
- developing school policies on parent-related or child-related matters, such as homework and discipline
- developing and revising budget priorities and curriculum standards, and evaluating and selecting textbooks
- participating in such parent-school organizations as the PTA or PTO and serving on school committees, advisory councils, or other groups at the school, district, or state levels
- acting as child advocates
- participating in planning for school improvement
- participating on staff selection committees
- participating in other school-related activities that are mandated by state or federally funded programs
- providing workshops
- working to increase funding and influence legislation
- serving as watchdogs against discrimination in such areas as special education and bilingual programs

(Epstein, 1987; Comer and Haynes, 1991; Epstein and Dauber, 1991)

Schools that provide for the five types of parent involvement discussed help parents establish conditions at home that facilitate learning, understand the communications from the school, become effective volunteers, and share the responsibility for educating children. In addition, the parents' voices are included in decisions that affect the quality of the education provided to their children (Epstein and Dauber, 1991).

Each type of parent involvement discussed benefits both the school and the community. The school gains from the community contributions, and community members obtain satisfaction from their own participation and involvement. However, it must be noted that not all parents can assume the same degree of active participation in their children's education. There are barriers that schools must recognize and address when planning parent involvement programs. Parents may not wish to be involved or are unable to be involved because of their own level of literacy and schooling, their lack of fluency in English, their daily commitments and responsibilities, their level of comfort with the schools, and their desire to become involved in their children's education (D'Angelo and Adler, 1991; Greenwood and Hickman, 1991). Therefore, parent involvement programs must provide a wide range of activities that take into consideration parent interest, attitudes, abilities, energy, ideas, needs, culture, language, and lifestyles. An effective parent involvement program includes both strategies for keeping the less visible parents connected to the school and strategies for tapping and stimulating the potential of those parents who are active and highly visible.

A major goal of parent participation is to produce a climate of shared responsibility for academic learning. When parents are directly involved, there is a basic concern with instruction and an extended contact between the school and the parents (Sandfort, 1987). Parents who are involved in such programs generally voice only positive comments regarding the school (Long, 1985).

Now that both a rationale for parent involvement and a description of the possible types of parent involvement have been offered, it is time to discuss activities that have specific relevance to whole language. The rest of this chapter explores how schools and the home can develop effective partnerships in order to provide the most beneficial education possible for all children in order to help children become readers and writers. Specifically, the parent involvement programs and practices that are stressed are home-school communication, involving parents in the school, and involving parents in the home.

HOME-SCHOOL COMMUNICATION

There are several ways in which schools can establish and maintain effective home-school communication: face to face, through technology, and through the written word (D'Angelo and Adler, 1991). Each of these categories is addressed separately, with practical suggestions for implementation provided.

Face-to-Face Communication

Perhaps one of the most effective ways to communicate with parents is through face-to-face communication. This may take the form of home visits, parent-teacher conferences, back-to-school nights, or workshops and training sessions. The purpose of these activities is to give parents information about the organization and management of the classroom, the curriculum, assessment and evaluation procedures, and student progress.

Information nights, back-to-school nights, and open houses offer opportunities for parents and teachers to get to know one another and for parents to hear about the goals and objectives for the year, see some of the materials that will be used, receive relevant information on classroom procedures, and become familiar with the environment where their children will spend the duration of the school year. Since many parents will have experienced only traditional educational practices and may be unfamiliar with whole language, this is the time for teachers to allay parents' fears and give them a brief background in the common beliefs and practices associated with whole language. A slide or videotape presentation of children involved in meaningful reading and writing activities in whole language classrooms enables parents to see for themselves the learning that takes place. This should be accompanied by displays of children's writing, book and thematic projects, and other examples of whole language practices and activities. Teachers may also give parents packets containing the class schedule, information on management issues (e.g., book club procedures, lunch money, attendance, and the like), parenting tips, and information on the various curricular programs. At this time teachers may introduce learning activities that can be done in the home and may enlist parents as volunteers.

A variety of approaches can be used when conducting open houses to make the school visit appealing. When children are involved or their talents are featured, the attendance at open houses increases. Frequently schools will schedule special visits for future kindergartners and their parents. Sometimes these are held in the spring prior to the children's school entrance. On these occasions, Big Books may be read, puppets may greet the young ones, songs may be sung, and creative activities might occur. While the youngsters accompany kindergarten teachers to preview the classrooms, parents can remain in the meeting room to talk with current kindergarten parents. These seasoned parents become excellent publicity agents. Generally these welcoming sessions result in less anxiety and fewer tears on the first formal day of school.

During the school year, open houses and back-to-school nights can also feature student art displays in the halls and classrooms, student writings and projects, or the students themselves can participate in the event as guides and sources of information for parents regarding the various aspects of the class program. Sometimes the evening is combined with a family dinner that precedes the information portion of the event. For instance, in Jean Mumper's school in Wallkill, New York, all kindergarten children and their parents dine together (generally pasta or pizza is featured) during an annual fall get-together. The first-grade parents prepare the meal for the kindergartners and their families. The cafeteria is decorated with tablecloths and flowers, which provides a welcoming environment. After dinner, the children are invited to the auditorium to watch a movie while parents and teachers go to individual classrooms to discuss plans, curriculum matters, and daily routines.

There are many ways, in addition to those mentioned, to provide a welcoming environment for open houses or back-to-school nights. "Who Am I?" activities give parents something to look for when they arrive and also showcase their children. The format for the "Who Am I?" activity can involve having children draw themselves and write biographical data under their portraits, prepare silhouettes of themselves with biographical information written on the silhouette, or making paper bag figures of themselves that slip over the backs of their chairs. The parents' job is to locate their child through the illustrations and the written information. Figure 13.1 depicts several "Who Am I?" activities.

There are other ways to involve parents actively in these special sessions. Parents and their children can initiate a dialogue through writing, as in a dialogue journal. Parents can comment on their children's displays, the classroom environment, their children's writing, or a special project, or even offer words of encouragement. If parents prefer, they could leave a message for their child in the child's classroom mailbox, again focusing on the positive feelings they gained from the open house and from learning about their child's classroom.

Parents can also sign up for workshop or training sessions while attending open houses. Workshops can deal with any aspect of parenting or schooling, depending on the interests and needs of the parents. The teacher, the reading specialist, the school library media specialist, the school nurse, or any other school community member may be involved in setting up and implementing such workshops. Commercial programs, such as *Readers, Writers, and Parents: Learning Together* (Dundas and Strong, 1991), that outline a series of workshops to be conducted over time throughout the year and also provide the activities and needed resources are available. However, school districts need not purchase commercial programs but instead may design their own. Some effective family literacy programs include: Parents as Partners in Reading Program (Edwards, 1995); Parents That Read, Succeed! Program (Come and Fredericks, 1995); and Project FLAME-Family Literacy: *Aprendiendo, Jejorando, Educando* (Learning, Bettering, Educating) (Shanahan, Mulhern, and Rodreiguez-Brown, 1995). Many of these programs are designed to involve parents in literacy activities and events that support school-based goals, and some are designed to improve the literacy development of both adults and their children (Morrow and Paratore, 1993). An example of an effective program designed by the New York City Schools is described in Figure 13.2. This program demonstrates to parents the value of and procedures for reading aloud to their children. In addition, free books and learning activities are provided to parents.

Another promising workshop that demonstrates the value of functional reading and writing activities uses the newspaper. Many local newspapers support Newspaper in Education (NIE) programs and frequently provide free workshops and materials for parent groups. An example of one such program for *Newsday,* a newspaper based in New York City, is provided in Figure 13.3, along with some activities involving the newspaper that teachers themselves can demonstrate to parents.

In addition to the workshop topics described, other suggested topics include:

- The Reading Process
- The Writing Process

Figure 13.1 "Who Am I" Activities

Figure 13.2 Parent Read-Aloud Program (New York City Public Schools)

PROGRAM DESCRIPTION
This is a parent support system designed to involve parents in reading aloud at home. Parents meet monthly for workshops on the rationale of reading aloud, techniques for reading aloud, modeling of effective oral reading, and practice reading the actual books they will use with their children.

MATERIALS
Parent kits consist of articles on reading aloud, tips for reading aloud, workshop information, and a parent reading handbook. In addition, parents receive monthly kits with materials to use with their children. Parents with children in grades 1–3 receive kits containing four books with accompanying activities (which are optional), and parents with children in grades 4–5 receive kits with three books and accompanying activities. The books and activities are placed in attractive bags that have reading-related messages or decorations (available through Upstart Publishers).

PROCEDURES
Parents are invited to participate in the Read-Aloud program. During the first year of implementation over 800 parents participated, and the number has increased to over 5000 parents involved.

First Parent Read-Aloud Workshop
(The procedure varies somewhat for the primary and intermediate grades.)

- Rationale for reading aloud
- Procedures for read-aloud program
- Distribution and discussion of handout on hints or reading aloud
- Introduction of kit
- Modeling of oral reading from book in kit:
  Strategies for stopping points in the story are presented. Amount of time for reading aloud is discussed.
- Distribution of kits
- Introduction of books and activity sheets
- Establishing procedures for future workshops

For parents with children in the upper grades, the workshop presenters review the context and concepts of the books, especially for the nonfiction books. Background material is presented particularly in relation to special vocabulary. Strategies for handling longer pieces of text are provided, e.g., dividing the book into manageable segments in order to maintain interest and excitement. Parents are allowed to keep the materials given to them, and the books then become part of a family library.

(Courtesy of Sharon Gross and Marilyn Funes, New York City Schools.)

- Spelling Today
- Creating Home Literacy Centers
- What Is Whole Language?
- A Look at Authentic Assessment and Evaluation
- Strategies to Help Children at Home with Schoolwork
- Study Skills
- Reading Aloud
- Choosing Books for Children
- Making Books with Children
- Writing at Home
- How to Use Television Effectively
- Organizing the Home for Effective Learning
- How to Get the Most out of Parent-Teacher Conferences

When deciding to offer parents' workshops, it is helpful to poll parents as to the most desirable time for holding these sessions. School dis-

Figure 13.3A Newspaper in Education

The newspaper affords many opportunities for family enjoyment and education. When being introduced to the newspaper as an educational tool, parents need to be provided with a rationale for using the newspaper, need to become acquainted with the parts of the newspaper, and need to be given some activities that they may do with their children. The following are some activities that can be demonstrated at parent workshops, that parents themselves can do at the workshops, and that parents can take home to do with their children.

It's in the Bag: Newspaper Categories

MATERIALS
newspaper, large grocery bag, scissors, glue

PROCEDURE
A category is chosen and relevant items, articles, and pictures are found in the newspaper to support the category and its subdivisions. For example, if the category "People" is chosen, subcategories could include athletes, politicians, entertainment stars, and ordinary folks. Words could be constructed from individual letters found on the newspaper pages or used as they are written. At the end of the activity a story could be placed inside the bag for others to read.

Possible categories and their subcategories include:

Categories	*Subcategories*
clothing	man, woman, child, seasonal, evening, inner, outer
transportation	land, sea, air, space, recreational, wheels, work
rooms in a house	furniture, activities
foods	junk, nutritional, breakfast, lunch, dinner
sports	equipment, seasonal, athletes, indoor, outdoor
feelings	happy, sad, angry, disappointed, bored, curious
senses	seeing, hearing, tasting, smelling, feeling

Using the News

- Take a trip with a famous person in the news. Plot that person's journey on a map. Collect articles and pictures and place in that person's travel journal.
- Find the countries, continents, cities, etc. in the news on a map.
- Look for stories that are good or bad news.

Ads and the Newspaper

- Match prices in advertisements. Be a comparison shopper.
- Find foods you consider "fun" food.
- Write your own Crazy Ads.
- Role-play a job interview for a job advertised in the paper.

A Sporting Look

- Interview a favorite athlete. Collect pictures and articles about this person and make a scrapbook.
- Look at sports statistics and develop some for your class or school teams.
- Collect quotes from athletes.

(continued)

Figure 13.3B Newspaper in Education (cont.)

Weather or Not?

- Locate the cities in the world with the highest and lowest temperatures.
- Fronts—Where are they coming from and where are they headed?
- Keep a weather log for a period of time using information from the newspaper.

Entertainment

- Read a problem in an advice column. Write a response.
- Write your own horoscope and compare it with one in the paper.
- Survey favorite television shows and graph your results.

The Whole Thing (using the entire newspaper)

- Create a scavenger hunt. List items to be found.
- Make an alphabet book.
- Create an alphabet monster by ripping a piece from a page in the newspaper. Locate each letter, one by one, and connect the letters to create an alphabet monster. Write a story about your creation.
- Letters and numbers come in various sizes. Make a display of them.
- Start a collection of quotes.

(Courtesy of Particia Houk, Manager Educational Services of *New York Newsday,* and Nancy Becher, Professor at Hofstra University.)

tricts may have to experiment with several time schedules to find the one that works best for their parents and teachers. Some parents find it more convenient to stay at school when dropping their children off the first thing in the morning, while others prefer evening sessions. Schools may also have to make arrangements for child care during these sessions, particularly if they are held during the day and there are preschoolers in the home. Occasionally teachers may want to have both parents and their offspring together for a workshop, and right after school might work best in this case. If parents are unable to come to the school for workshops or are reluctant to do so, other means of informing parents will be necessary. These are addressed in the sections of this chapter about the use of technology and the written word to reach parents.

In addition to workshops, well-planned parent-teacher conferences and home visits have been successful in building healthy home-school relationships. However, it must be remembered that if the focus is to cover student progress, many parents, particularly those who were not good students themselves, feel threatened when coming to school to discuss their child's report card or academic success (or lack of it). Therefore, teachers must make parents comfortable and point out areas where their children have been successful as well as their needs.

To empower parents and help them assume more active roles in their children's schooling, teachers need to establish a collaborative relationship with the parents. Teachers and parents need to recognize each other's roles and contributions, respect these, and join together (Fredericks and Rasinski, 1990b). Instead of the teachers doing all of the talking and all of the suggesting, parents could be respected as coeducators who have insights and suggestions to offer in working toward the common goal of providing the best education for their children. Rather than teachers saying, "I suggest . . ." or "I think that you should . . . ," parents could be asked, "What do you think . . . ?" or "How do you feel about . . . ?" (Rasinski, 1989). Teachers could ask parents how they believe the classroom instruction could be modified to better meet their child's needs, what they have found to be effective at home, or what the parents could do at home to help their child. Teachers could propose possibilities as opposed to supplying all the answers. Parent-teacher conferences should be designed so that parents and teachers work together to establish goals, determine priorities, and find workable solutions.

In addition to gaining and providing information about their children's progress, parents can likewise be involved in assessing and evaluating their children. Many educators today are proclaiming that parents can and should play a significant role in the assessment process (Fredericks and Rasinski, 1990c). Involving parents in education can help eliminate some of the misinterpretations that can occur at reporting or conferencing time. It also helps parents provide direction for their children. However, although parents' contributions are welcome, their involvement should not be confusing or too elaborate.

Fredericks and Rasinski (1990c) propose several ways that parents can contribute to the assessment and evaluation process. At the beginning of the school year, parents can state their expectations for their children. They can also provide input on the value of home assignments, noting their appropriateness, difficulty, how their child understood the assignment or the procedures for doing the assignment, and even offer suggestions for improvement. Parents can be given a summary sheet on which they can periodically record their own observations and interpretations of their child's development as a reader and as a writer. This should be shared with the teacher as an ongoing means of communication.

Parents can also be invited to the school to observe their children involved in literacy activities. After such observations, parents can note their child's progress, identify strengths and needs, and discuss their findings with the teacher at an appropriate time. Parents can be provided with an observational guide that can be filled out periodically. An example of such a guide, modified from Fredericks and Rasinski (1990c), is presented in Figure 13.4.

Another way to include parents in the assessment and evaluation process is through student-led parent conferences (Little and Allen, 1988; Johnson, 1991; Austin, 1994). Since students are involved in choosing pieces to place in their portfolios, it is a natural outgrowth to have them share the contents with their parents. Of course, since this is a new undertaking for both the students and their parents, there has to be some initial training. The students can write a "Dear Reader of My Portfolio" letter explaining the contents of the portfolio. This can help them organize what they will tell their parents on the actual conference day, and it also provides the parents with some written documentation. Prior to the conference day, students should have an opportunity to have a dress rehearsal, which will entail a practice session with a classmate.

On conference day, several conferences can be scheduled simultaneously in different parts of the room. Tables with chairs for the students and their parents are placed around the room, with another table set up with refreshments. Conferences can last from 15 minutes to half an hour, depending on the age and experience of the student. The teacher is available in the room to oversee the process but is not available for meeting with the parents regarding their child's school progress. This way, the teacher's input does not overshadow that of the child's. Of course, parents can schedule individual conferences with the teacher at another time.

In addition to the letter describing the contents of the portfolio, students can fill out "Celebrations and Dreams" forms. On this sheet are listed several examples of work the student has considered outstanding (the celebration) and several dreams (goals) for the next term. Parents likewise write to their children, expressing their feelings (focusing on the positive) about the child's growth and development. They can also fill out a "Celebrations and Dreams" sheet, stating what they particularly liked (their celebrations) and things they'd like to see their child accomplish (their dreams). This type of conference has received positive feedback from all those involved—the students, the teachers, and the parents. A sample "Celebration and Dream" sheet is presented in Figure 13.5.

Using Technology to Communicate with Parents

If face-to-face communication is not possible as frequently as is desired, using technology can be an aid in communicating with parents. Of course, the telephone has been used for some time now to inform parents about things happening at school and to inform teachers about

Figure 13.4 A Look at Your Child: A Guide for Parents

Please think about your child's growth in reading and writing and indicate the appropriate response below using the following code.

1—Not at all
2—Sometimes
3—Frequently
4—Almost always

MY CHILD:

• understands what she/he reads	1	2	3	4
• enjoys listening to stories	1	2	3	4
• finds time to read alone at home	1	2	3	4
• can retell stories	1	2	3	4
• enjoys reading to others	1	2	3	4
• prefers to sound out unknown words	1	2	3	4
• guesses at unknown words and they usually are meaningful	1	2	3	4
• likes to write at home	1	2	3	4
• plans his/her writing using a web	1	2	3	4
• talks to others about what she/he read	1	2	3	4
• talks to others about his/her writing	1	2	3	4
• uses study skills regularly	1	2	3	4
• has improved in reading ability over the year	1	2	3	4
• has improved in writing ability over the year	1	2	3	4

My child is a good reader because ____________________
____
____

My child is a good writer because ____________________
____
____

I feel my child could improve ____________________
____
____

(Adapted from Fredericks and Rasinski, 1990.)

things happening at home. Unfortunately, many times these communications focus on the negative, as opposed to sharing positive happenings. Teachers need to take time to contact parents when their children have made worthwhile contributions in the classroom, and parents need to take time to contact teachers when they and their children have especially enjoyed something that occurred at school. Using the telephone to transmit good news helps build the home-school bond that contributes to effective schooling. Schools have also implemented "Dial a Teacher" programs in which recorded telephone messages are used to provide useful suggestions and information about any aspect of schooling. These brief messages could explain in a succinct manner some study skills, suggest books for read-alouds, promote the Parents as Reading Partners Program, or provide suggestions for helping children with word recognition. To implement such a program, a telephone number is reserved for this purpose, and messages are changed two or three times per week. Occasionally children could tape messages for parents or share some of their writing.

Hot lines (or telephone trees) can be established to give parents opportunities to contact each other to relay information or discuss mu-

Figure 13.5A Celebrations and Dreams Sheet

Celebrations and Dreams

Response to ______________________

Date ____________________

Student name ____________________

What I did well ____________________

____

____

____

____

____

What I want to improve ____________________

____

____

____

____

____

(continued)

Figure 13.5B Celebrations and Dreams Sheet (cont.)

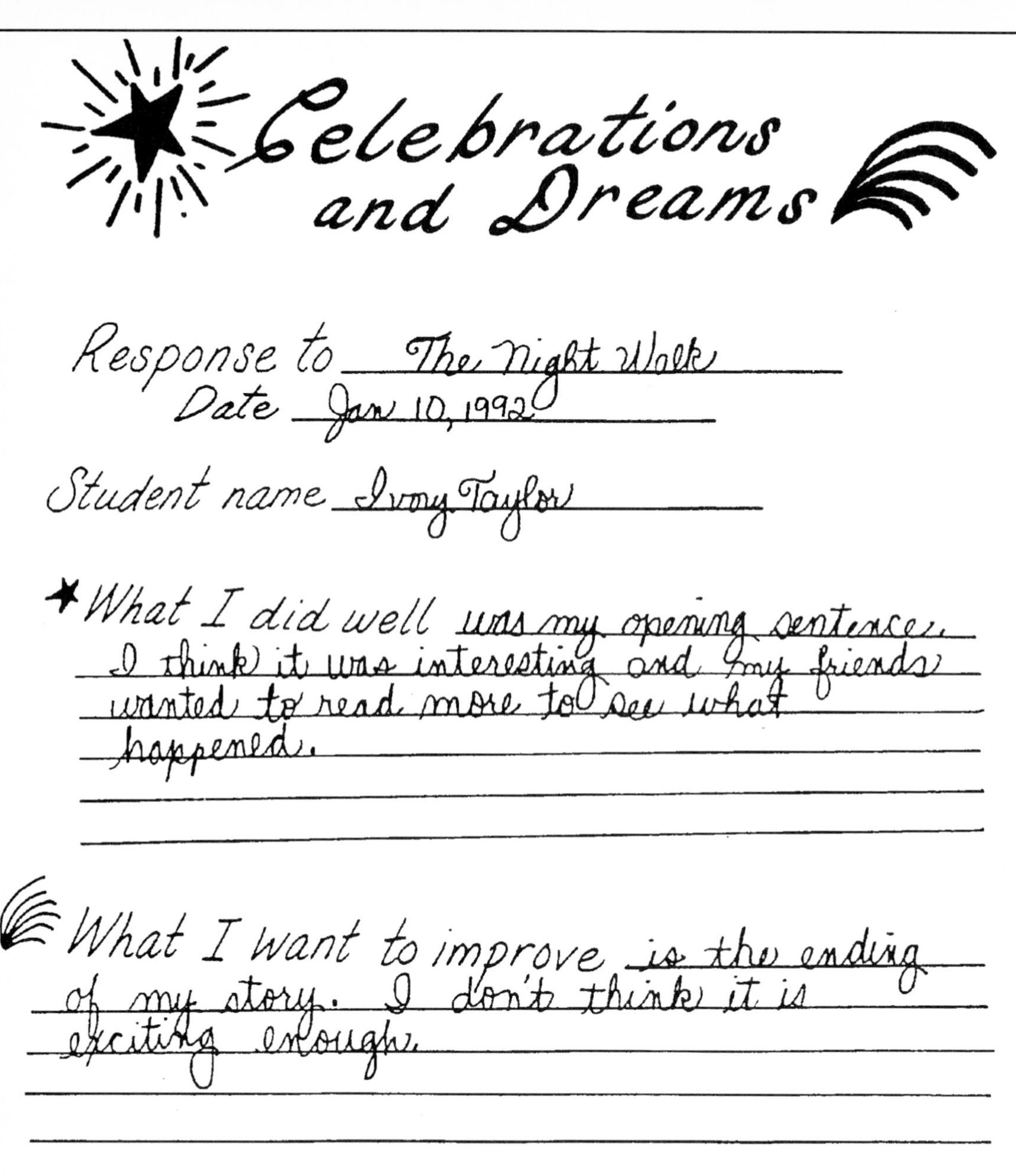

Celebrations and Dreams

Response to The Night Walk

Date Jan 10, 1992

Student name Ivory Taylor

★ What I did well was my opening sentence. I think it was interesting and my friends wanted to read more to see what happened.

What I want to improve is the ending of my story. I don't think it is exciting enough.

tual concerns. This means of communication enables parents to keep up to date on issues and events in their child's classroom.

The radio is another medium for delivering educational messages. Local radio stations may be contacted to sponsor such a program. These messages can deal with various topics, such as encouraging parents to become involved in their children's education, creating a learning atmosphere at home, or communicating with your child. Again, having the students themselves write and deliver some of the broadcasts is highly effective.

Not to be overlooked is the use of videotapes. The workshops or training sessions could be videotaped and the tape placed in a lending library for parents who were not able to attend. Most homes today have VCRs; thus using video technology is advantageous. For homes without such equipment, a viewing room at the school could be arranged, or a fellow Parent Teacher Association (PTA) member could sponsor a viewing session, with or without a faculty member present. Wonderful videos are also available for rent or purchase. For example, the International Reading Association has an excellent video on reading aloud, and Jim Trelease's popular presentation on reading aloud is available both on video and in a movie version.

Using the Written Word to Communicate with Parents

Historically, the written word has been the main medium for communicating with parents. The format of written communications varies depending on the needs of the parents and the desires of the school: standard report cards, narrative report cards, letters, notes, newsletters, pamphlets, announcements, newspapers, anthologies of student writing.

With the emphasis on the writing process and involving children in meaningful writing activities, many teachers and schools use students as the authors of many parent communications. Instead of the teacher describing the reading or writing program, students can provide descriptions that can be collected and distributed to parents in the form of informational pamphlets or incorporated into class newsletters. Students can issue invitations to parents to attend special events at the school, from plays and musical performances to workshops. Students can invite parents to come into school to read aloud in a classroom, to share an expertise, or to volunteer for a field trip.

Figure 13.6 illustrates several classroom newspapers that feature student writing and artwork to inform parents about what the class has accomplished that week. Another example of communicating with parents on a regular basis is shown in Figure 13.7. Joan Cavagnaro's first-grade class writes a weekly Class News, which is compiled from the daily sharings during the community meeting time. By using this technique, parents become informed about their child's interests and lives both at school and at home. Communications can come from the administration as well. Frequently these deal with announcements, special events, and school policies, but many principals use these to educate parents about the reading and writing program, testing tips, invented spelling, and the like. See Figure 13.8 for a sample of a communication from an administrator that deals with the topic of games as a way of facilitating school learning.

Speer Johnson (1989) describes a personal newsletter program she initiated with her fourth-grade class. Each week her class wrote a personal newsletter to their parents describing current class activities and future events. The parents read each newsletter, signed them, and returned them to the classroom, where they were stored for the duration of the school year. At the end of the year, the newsletters were bound and given to each student as a diary of his or her year in that class.

This personal newsletter not only served as an effective parent communication tool but also allowed the students to practice the language arts concurrently. In introducing the activity, the teacher and class brainstormed the possible events that could be included. These were placed on a semantic map, each idea written in a different color. The students then selected the parts of the web they wanted to share. The semantic map and color coding of the ideas on the map made the activity less overwhelming for the students, especially at the beginning of the year. Throughout the year, the students wrote 36 issues. The newsletters were not graded, but by observing what the students were doing, Speer

Figure 13.6A Class Newsletter—Jean Mumper Class

Kindergarten News

Mrs. Mumper's Rainbow Room

Vol. 1 No. 2 Ostrander Elementary School October 1991

The Firemen Visited

We climbed on the fire engine. They taught us to STOP, DROP and ROLL.

They sprayed water from a big hose. We talked about an evacuation plan.

* Please talk about this at home.

Ashley and Tim had a birthday this month. We had two parties in our classroom.

The Olive Taste Test

Our class tasted green olives. Most of our class liked them. See our graph.

Yes, I like olives	No thank you

A Visitor from:

THE COLLEGE AT NEW PALTZ

Mrs. Quick spent two weeks with our class. She helped us create an ocean in a box. She read us stories and played games with us. We will miss her.

The Favorite Book for October: Brown Bear, Brown Bear by Bill Martin Jr. We made our own version—Come see it!

– Bugs –

Sarah brought in some crickets. Katie brought a big grasshopper. Ryan found a dead butterfly.

Amy's new kitten visited our class for Show and Tell.

Mikhail, Laura, Angie, and Kenzie collected leaves for our science center.

Farmer John visited our classroom and showed us many different types of pumpkins.

Katie "My home is here," said the catepillar. The grass.	LAUREN "My home is here," said the spider. A web	MeLISSA "My home is here," said the dolphin. The ocean
"My home is here," said the octopus. SUSAN The ocean	"My home is here," said the turtle. RYAN A pond	"My home is here," said the bee. Heather A tree

In September we made applesauce. It was delicious! We learned this song to help us remember how to do it (Sing to the tune of "Sing a Song of Sixpence")

Wash an apple
Cut it up
Put it in a pot
When you cook it
You will see
It's applesauce you've got.

(continued)

Figure 13.6B Class Newsletter and Daily News Bulletin (cont.)

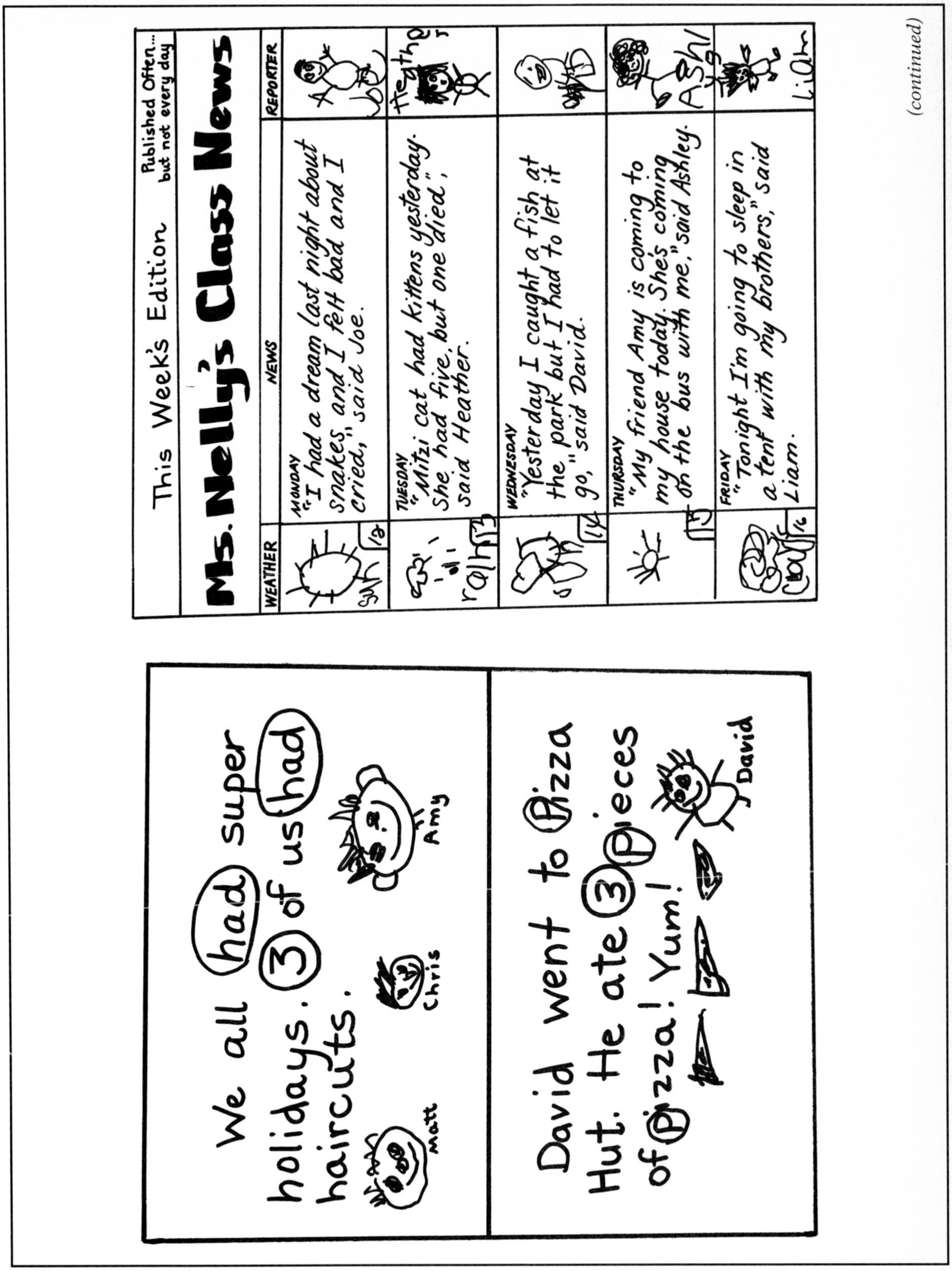

We all had super holidays. 3 of us had haircuts.

Matt Chris Amy

David went to Pizza Hut. He ate 3 pieces of pizza! Yum!

David

This Week's Edition — Published Often... but not every day

Ms. Nelly's Class News

WEATHER	NEWS	REPORTER
13	MONDAY "I had a dream last night about snakes, and I felt bad and I cried," said Joe.	Joe
14	TUESDAY "Mitzi cat had kittens yesterday. She had five, but one died," said Heather.	Heather
14	WEDNESDAY "Yesterday I caught a fish at the park but I had to let it go," said David.	David
15	THURSDAY "My friend Amy is coming to my house today. She's coming on the bus with me," said Ashley.	Ashley
16	FRIDAY "Tonight I'm going to sleep in a tent with my brothers," said Liam.	Liam

(continued)

Figure 13.C

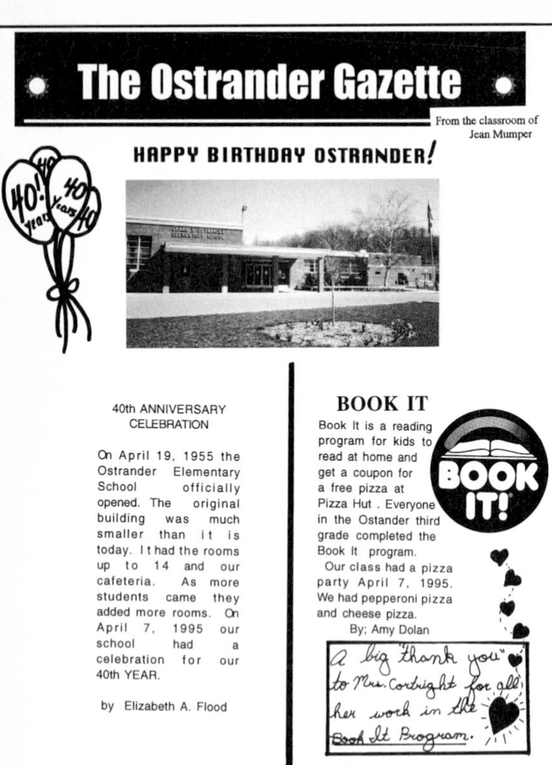

The Ostrander Gazette

From the classroom of Jean Mumper

HAPPY BIRTHDAY OSTRANDER!

40th ANNIVERSARY CELEBRATION

On April 19, 1955 the Ostrander Elementary School officially opened. The original building was much smaller than it is today. It had the rooms up to 14 and our cafeteria. As more students came they added more rooms. On April 7, 1995 our school had a celebration for our 40th YEAR.

by Elizabeth A. Flood

BOOK IT

Book It is a reading program for kids to read at home and get a coupon for a free pizza at Pizza Hut . Everyone in the Ostander third grade completed the Book It program.

Our class had a pizza party April 7, 1995. We had pepperoni pizza and cheese pizza.

By; Amy Dolan

A big "thank you" to Mrs. Cortright for all her work in the Book It Program.

Page 2 The Ostrander Gazette

AN INTERVIEW WITH...

MRS. McGOWAN is our school gym teacher.She loves her job.She did not always want to be a gym teacher, she wanted to be a Spanish or English teacher first. One of her favorite things is that she likes to help others.

She enjoys seeing students achieve their goals.

by Jonathon Horn

Our class put on a puppet festival.Over fifty people came! All students did a great job. After it was over we served our parents punch.We showed our parents our season pictures.We all had a good time.

by KARA FASCE and JONATHON HORN

OSTRANDER SCHOOL CELEBRATES 40 YEARS!

Come Sunday, March 19 to the St. Patrick's Day parade. Everyone can march. There will be a big school float ! The parade is at 2:OO. So please come to the fun and help celebrate 40 years of teaching and learning for our school. by Joshua Henke

Page 6 The Ostrander Gazette

SCIENCE AND MEDICAL NEWS

SLEEP

A-a-achoo WHY WE SNEEZE

Sometimes we get tiny pieces of dirt or dust in our nose. It tickles and makes an itching feeling .Since we can't scratch it, our body reacts by causing our muscles to move quickly. We blow air quickly out of our nose. This is what we call a sneeze.

by Andrea Craig

EVERYONE NEEDS SLEEP , EVEN IF THEY DON'T LIKE IT. AFTER EVERY DAY YOUR BRAIN AND BODY IS TIRED FROM THE ACTIVITY OF THE DAY. SLEEPING HELPS IT RECHARGE. IF PEOPLE DON'T GET SLEEP THEY GET CRANKY, AND SOMETIMES THEY CAN'T THINK RIGHT. IF THEY CATCH UP ON THEIR SLEEP THEY ARE OK. SCIENTISTS SAY THAT A GOOD NIGHTS SLEEP HELP PEOPLE TO REMEMBER MORE OF WHAT THEY LEARN.

by Elizabeth Flood

The Great Office Manager

Mrs. Koonz is our Office Manager. She has worked at Ostrander for 19 years and she worked at the Middle School for 7 years. She likes dealing with the public, the teachers, and all the students. Mrs. Koonz does not like to scold a student who is disobedient. "I love to dance" says Mrs. Koonz. She also likes to play golf and walks on the beach. She was born in Brooklyn N.Y. Her favorite place to be is in Florida. She likes to read The Cat in The Hat by Dr. Seuss and to sing the song "Memories." She likes to eat seafood and Italian food.

If Mrs. Koonz won a million dollars she would share it with her sons and families and build a house in the mountains. We hope her dreams come true.

by Zaccary Mills

Mrs. Koonz

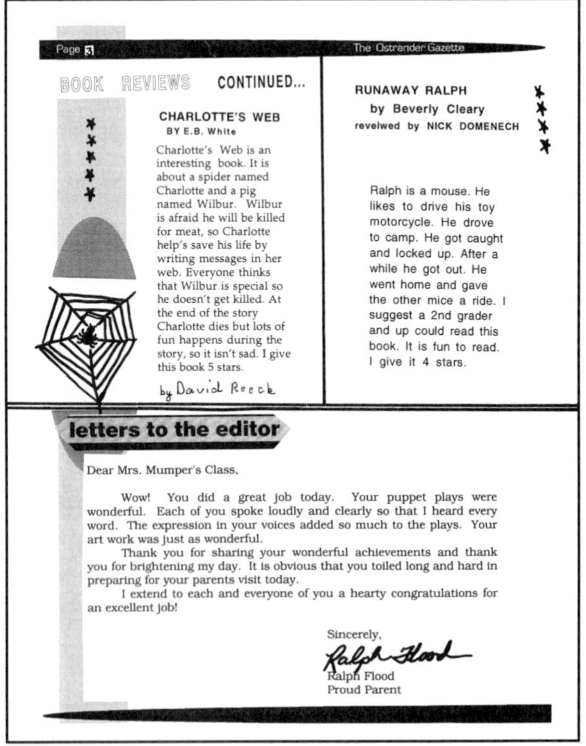

Page 3 The Ostrander Gazette

BOOK REVIEWS CONTINUED...

CHARLOTTE'S WEB

BY E.B. White

Charlotte's Web is an interesting book. It is about a spider named Charlotte and a pig named Wilbur. Wilbur is afraid he will be killed for meat, so Charlotte help's save his life by writing messages in her web. Everyone thinks that Wilbur is special so he doesn't get killed. At the end of the story Charlotte dies but lots of fun happens during the story, so it isn't sad. I give this book 5 stars.

by David Reeck

RUNAWAY RALPH

by Beverly Cleary

reveiwed by NICK DOMENECH

Ralph is a mouse. He likes to drive his toy motorcycle. He drove to camp. He got caught and locked up. After a while he got out. He went home and gave the other mice a ride. I suggest a 2nd grader and up could read this book. It is fun to read. I give it 4 stars.

letters to the editor

Dear Mrs. Mumper's Class,

Wow! You did a great job today. Your puppet plays were wonderful. Each of you spoke loudly and clearly so that I heard every word. The expression in your voices added so much to the plays. Your art work was just as wonderful.

Thank you for sharing your wonderful achievements and thank you for brightening my day. It is obvious that you toiled long and hard in preparing for your parents visit today.

I extend to each and everyone of you a hearty congratulations for an excellent job!

Sincerely,

Ralph Flood
Proud Parent

Figure 13.7 Class News—Joan Cavagnaro's Class

News Groups First Grade Mrs. C.

Week of February 25, 1991

On Monday Chucky told us about his trip to Disney World. He went on the "Run Away Train" and in the submarine. Chucky told us that he said "Hell-o" to Mickey Mouse for Mrs. C. His Mom and Dad drove to Disney World and it took them two days. Richard showed us a clay bear he made. He put it in the oven so it would get hard. He made it at his baby sitter's house. Craig showed us a Canadian coin that his Mom got out of her bank. He had to trade a US quarter for it. Amber told us that she got a new cat. The cat's claws had to be taken off. Now it can't go outside.

On Tuesday Brittany showed us a clown in a box that her Dad gave her. It is musical and can come out of the box. Chris F. showed us a Nintendo Power Magazine. He showed us how to get some clues. If you have a Nintendo you could use the magazine. Sarah brought in pictures of her dog. She brought in picture of Philip and herself when they were outside playing in the snow. Tamara showed us crystals she got from her friend's house. She found them in the woods. Mrs. C. told Tamara to always be sure she can see her house when she is in the woods because she could get lost.

On Wednesday Cherie showed us two dolls that came with a high chair and a stroller. It also came with food. The big doll could walk but the rechargeable battery was weak. Jacob told us he got a puppy. It is black and white. Craig thought it sounded like a border collie. Jacob's father named it Ottis. Lindsay showed us her Cabbage Patch Doll. Her grandma made a blanket for the doll. Lindsay said she has a bag of clothes for her doll. Andrew told us his brother, Daniel, got a hair cut. Lauren brought in Show White and the 3 Dwarfs. They move and they have little platforms that you can put them on. You can add on to this set. Her mother gave it to her on Valentine's Day.

On Thursday Alex showed beautiful rocks. She brought in a piece of special coal. Ten children examined them during the morning. Nichole showed us a newspaper article about her Uncle's house that had a fire that started in the basement. Nichole read part of the article to us. Leif showed us another comic book his Uncle Ron wrote. Steven showed us a magic mirror book. It makes a reflection of pictures. We talked about things being symmetrical. Ken showed us a car. It was broken. It had a man inside, it was yellow, the number on it was one. There were stickers all over it. His Dad tried to fix it, it worked, and broke again. Dad will try again.

On Friday Elise showed us a colored pencil. You can take one color out and put in another color. It had about 9 or 10 colors. She got it from Renai Richardson's birthday. Robert told us he is in Level 5. He is a Gold Star. He likes reading "Together We Go". Michael showed us twenty or thirty rocks, a horse and a parrot. It was called a rock garden. He showed us a rock necklace. Bree brought in little beads to make a necklace and a bracelet. You would need a lot to make a bracelet. Chris B. showed us 45 baseball cards. There were stickers with the baseball cards. He got them from his Grandma when she was visiting her two sisters in Florida.

LEARNING - THE FUN WAY

Learning occurs whenever students discover, compare, analyze, create, explore, classify, experiment, or interpret. "DOING" activities deeply involve students to a greater extent than merely listening or watching. Experience-based learning activities allow students to discover for themselves. Games and puzzles may be used to reinforce many other types of learning experiences. They are fun and enriching and provide wonderful opportunities for families to interact together. This issue of Connections is devoted to game-like activities for families to enjoy together in the home, on vacation, or any time an opportunity presents itself. In addition to the activities included in the pamphlet, we are providing you with a booklet filled with more learning games that will help your children improve their word recognition abilities. We hope you and your children enjoy learning and playing together.

PENCIL POKERS

Posterboard, felt pen, scissors and paper punch are needed for this game. Use simple line drawings of animals, objects, or people, such as those from a coloring book. Trace the design onto the posterboard with a felt-tipped pen, and cut it out. Punch holes randomly throughout the drawing. Write drill material on the front of the figure, one question next to each punched hole. On the back, write the answer next to the corresponding hole. The sudent reads the question, determines the answer and pokes a pencil through the hole, and then turns the figure over to get the correct answer. This game can be used to help syudents learn multiplication tables or for any other number of other basic skills.

Johnson was able to incorporate some of the students' needs into minilessons during Writers' Workshop (e.g., limiting and choosing activities, modeling various styles, varying print form, using interesting leads).

Family literacy programs and interactions can reduce parents' feelings of isolation from the schools while helping them support their children's learning (Shanahan, Mulhern, and Rodriguez-Brown, 1995). Shockley (1994) wanted to strengthen the home-school connection by including her families in a set of parallel literacy activities that matched school experiences with home opportunities. The activities she undertook included:

- *Tell Me About Your Child*

  At the beginning of the year, Shockley sent out a two-sentence request that read, "Welcome to first grade. Please tell me about your child." Families responded with heartfelt descriptions of their children.

- *Home Response Journals*

  Due to the success of the request for descriptions of their children, she then initiated home-school dialogue journals that allowed her "to stay in touch and be touched by the people who mattered the most to these young literacy learners" (Shockley, 1994, 501). The focus of this activity was to connect families with books, with each other, and with literacy experiences.

- *Family Stories*

  One of the regular features of her school day was storytelling, and during storytelling sessions connections were made with daily living, the interpretation of books, and their own writing. As an extension of this favored class activity, Shockley asked her families to write one of their family stories to contribute to a class book. All the families contributed and a class book was published. There was even a book signing celebration where family authors came and were honored by their offspring.

- *Parallel Reflections*

  At the end of the year, Shockley asked her students a literacy-related question each day and sent home a parallel question to be addressed by the families. For example, she asked her children, "How do you think you learned to read?" and then asked the families, "How do you think your child learned to read?"

Shockley and her families became real partners in both opportunity and purpose. By involving her parents in a set of meaningful activities, she was able to help parents connect with the school, which had a dramatic impact on both achievement and motivation.

There are additional ways to communicate to parents through the printed word. Schools frequently provide parents with handbooks or personalized school calendars that have pertinent meeting and special events dates along with information about the school district and its policies. These serve primarily as informational pieces about the schools, the district, and special curricular programs. To personalize these and to make them more appealing to parents, many teachers and schools include student samples (e.g., writing, drawing, pictures of students) along with the printed text. Involving the children increases the readability of the materials as far as the parents are concerned. One kindergarten teacher, Jane Eakins, sends home a monthly calendar, noting curricular endeavors, special events, and snacks coordinated with the theme. This calendar is stapled onto a sheet of construction paper along with a drawing from each child. Therefore the parents have a monthly calendar, illustrated by their own children, which may be prominently displayed in the home.

Activity calendars can be compiled by a classroom teacher, a committee of teachers, the school library media specialist, reading specialists, and interested parents. Suggestions for activities that may be done in the home either by the child alone or as a family collaborative undertaking are offered for each day of the week for an entire month. Activities capitalize on holidays and thematic studies, use the newspaper or materials easily available in the home, and involve all areas of the curriculum. Several professional sources, such as *Learning* and *Schooldays,* include monthly calendars and activities, and these may be helpful for ideas. An example of such a calendar appears in Figure 13.9. This activity combines two types of parent involvement: written communication and parent involvement in the home.

Figure 13.9 Activity Calendar

A Calendar of Activities

Select any 20 for this Month.

Set the table for dinner. Fold the napkins into △ triangles, make place cards with names.	Share one chapter of a novel with someone.	Write a note to someone and mail it.	Continue with another chapter of the novel. Read together with someone.	Cut out an interesting magazine picture. Make up a story about it.	Continue with another chapter of the novel. Ask someone to read it outloud while you listen.	Bake some cookies. Read or write the recipe.
Share the comics page in the newspaper with someone.	Visit the Public Library. Ask the librarian to show you the new children's books.	Help clean one drawer in your home.	Collect four different plant leaves. Notice how they are the same or different.	Copy a favorite poem and memorize it. Post it on the refrigerator.	Watch the weather report on T.V. or read it in the newspaper. Notice if it was correct.	Help write the grocery list for shopping.
Take a short walk. Write down five sounds you heard.	Pick a flower to give to a special person. Write a note to tell them why they are special.	Share a favorite book with someone. Retell the story using your own words.	Make a small book to write friends phone numbers in. Start by writing 5 phone numbers in the book.	Help vacuum or sweep one room in your home today.	Write the words for your favorite song.	Serve someone breakfast in bed today. Put a love note on the tray.
Make a get well card for someone who is ill.	Clean out or clean up the toy box or shelf in your room today	Cut up a magazine picture to make a puzzle. See if you can put it back together.	Play a board game or card game with someone.	Help address the bills or other mail.	Spend one whole day without any T.V. Write what you did instead.	Make a list of your ten favorite foods.
Look at the sky several times today. Notice where the sun appears. Are there clouds? Write or draw your observations	Read one article from the newspaper with someone.	Write all the words you can think of that mean HAPPY or SAD.	Take a walk around your home. Help clean up any litter. Read any signs, house numbers or mailboxes.	Make a list of items to take with you on a sleepover. Keep the list handy in your dresser drawer.	Help someone clean the car today.	Give someone you love a HUG. Tell the person why you love them.

Not to be overlooked are the innumerable books, magazine articles, commercial publications, and products (including video- and audiotapes) that can be purchased or collected and placed in a parent lending library. Such organizations as the International Reading Association and Reading Is Fundamental (RIF) provide excellent pamphlets for little or no cost. Frequently, local reading councils will put together parent resources, which can become part of the lending library. A bulletin board can be used to let parents know about conferences of interest, speakers in the area, new books, trips to take with their children, learning activities, and parenting tips. Of course, children's books could be on loan as well. Some suggested resources to include in the lending library are listed at the end of this chapter.

Teachers need to be aware of the range of communication opportunities and vary their approaches to meet the needs, interests, time constraints, and energy levels of all parents. Schools should aim to make every family a literacy family.

INVOLVING PARENTS IN THE SCHOOL

Encouraging parent participation in the classroom and in the school itself is another means of parent involvement. In this case parents are solicited to help fulfill the school's mission. Again participation can range from relatively passive involvement, such as helping in tutorial programs. Parents can fulfill many roles in the school, as mentioned earlier in this chapter. Whole language encourages parent participation in instructional matters and offers parents a myriad of opportunities to become involved in the classroom.

Prior to becoming involved in the daily classroom program, parents may prefer to visit for a morning or an afternoon to gain an understanding of the whole language program. At the annual back-to-school nights, some teachers invite parents to visit the classroom on a scheduled basis. Several days (or parts of days) can be designated for class visits. To make the visits manageable for teachers, a parent can be asked to develop and oversee the schedule. A parent interest inventory can be administered to find out parents' talents and interests that might be shared during the visit. The teacher might also suggest projects that parents can be involved in and make sure that the necessary materials are available when a particular parent arrives.

Teachers need not burden themselves with extra planning. Supervising a learning center, listening to children read, and assisting with an ongoing class project are excellent ways to involve parents without extensive teacher preparation. Parents may also be asked to share a children's book—one of their own choosing or from the class library—with the class before they leave. Comments from participating parents are offered in Figure 13.10.

In a whole language program, children become prolific readers and writers, and having extra help in the classroom allows teachers to personalize and individualize their instruction to a greater degree than was previously possible. Parents ease the work of publishing student writing since they assume some of the labor-intensive jobs. They can type final copies into the computer, transcribe invented spelling into standard spelling, take dictation for emergent readers or readers experiencing difficulty, help in bookmaking, and prepare writing journals. If schools publish newspapers, newsletters, or literary anthologies, parents can help with the composing, editing, and publishing.

Parents need not be involved only on the periphery of the classroom but can play an integral part in the instructional process as well. Because whole language is child centered and not teacher dominated, the children will not be reading the same book or the same page at the same time. Therefore parents can help provide individualized instruction and help children with guided reading and book-sharing projects. Parents can read aloud to children or listen as children read aloud. Parents should be encouraged not to teach or intrude in the children's learning, but rather to support and guide children.

Since many whole language classrooms integrate the curriculum using themes, other possibilities for involvement become open to parents. Parents can help collect resources or become resources themselves. This means they will demonstrate their talents or share their expertise, show slides of a country visited or a

Figure 13.10 Comments from Parents About Visitation Day

"The parent visitations were a most enjoyable way to see how the classroom operates."

"As for visits, we wished to be even more involved. Since we couldn't be due to busy schedules, we tried to let Marlo know we were always interested and concerned. I'm so glad you encourage and get participation."

"We both enjoyed participating in the Parent Visitation Days. The journals and books the children made were fantastic. The *pride* they took in this work was amazing. Like you said, they just couldn't wait to show everyone. When I went to vote on the budget, Erin *proudly* showed me everyone's work in the books. She was as thrilled with everyone else's pictures and words as she was with her own. Teamwork!"

"Eric's favorite activities for the year were the journal writings and the Parent Visitation Days. Eric will never forget his kindergarten class."

"Parent Visitation Day is always enjoyable. The parents look forward to them as much as the children."

"Travis loved Parent Visitation Day. He was so excited when it was my turn. I enjoyed that as much as he did. Letting me help with class projects and reading the story to the class made me feel good. I enjoy the children and you made me feel part of the class and I thank you for that."

hobby, give book talks pertaining to the thematic study, and so forth.

Many parents have talents that will enhance life in the classroom. In addition to serving as guest speakers, some parents may prefer to help design learning activities or set up learning centers. Since many classrooms use learning centers or stations, parents can use their creative talents to create learning packets, make educational games, or construct manipulatives. They may wish to become involved in helping design and set up the library corner, using carpentry and decorating talents to create an inviting, cozy corner for reading.

An interesting way to bring parents into the school and to increase their literacy abilities is to host parent reading-writing classes. Akroyd (1995) instituted such a program, entitled *Treasured Tomes,* for her families who came from 35 countries and spoke 21 different languages. Held in the evenings for a period of 10 weeks, the program had as its main objective to have parents write to their children using such writing forms as photo journals, memory books, diaries, and the like. Their childen accompanied them and read books while the parents wrote. The sessions consisted of 20 minutes for writing, reading and responding in groups of 2 to 3, and finally sharing as a community of writers. At the end of the 10 weeks, the families' stories were published and bound together as a book, and distributed to the participants. As Akroyd states, "Our parent reading-writing group filled 10 weeks with parents writing and sharing in different voices and different languages. We communicated through pages of facts and feeling and came to understand each other so much better. The pages that were produced were caressed by their owners and savored by the listeners" (584).

Whatever ways parents are used in the school or classroom, it is important to avoid merely assigning volunteers without consultation or discussion as to their interests and talents. Teachers and parents can approach parent participation as if they were colleagues and talk about the challenges and the problems presented in the literacy program. They can work together to decide what parents can do and with whom they will do it. It is desirable to adopt approaches and ideas that will capture and maintain parent participation and commitment to the school's literacy program. The focus should be on improved communication and mutual understanding between the home and the school.

INVOLVING PARENTS IN THE HOME

Parents are their children's first teachers, and much of parenting comes naturally when it comes to meeting the basic needs of their children. When children reach school age, parents frequently turn their education over to the schools. However, as demonstrated repeatedly, parents continue to contribute to their children's growth, development, and success. Parents are sometimes at a loss as to what to do in the home to encourage their children's literacy development. This then becomes an exceedingly important component of fostering parent involvement—helping parents help their children in the home. There are many possibilities for fostering learning in the home. Following is a sampling of them.

Creating an Environment for Learning at Home

During workshops or home visits, teachers can impress on parents the importance of setting up a home environment that is conducive for learning. Parents need to be shown how to create a home environment that promotes literacy development. Some of the ways parents can do this include establishing a home library center, creating places where their children can quietly study or read, finding a regular time for reading, making available an abundance of reading and writing materials, talking about what was read, and serving as models for their children as they engage in real reading and writing, both for functional purposes and for pleasure.

During these sessions, teachers can point out the many resources already available in the home that can encourage investigation and experimentation and stretch children's imaginations. Just think of all the catalogs and junk mail that arrive at each home on a regular basis. Our young learner Sarah, whose literacy development we have followed throughout this book, "teethed" on junk mail. Her parents saved the junk mail and placed it in a special box for Sarah, right beside the family desk (and bill-paying area). When her mother or father was busy paying bills, corresponding, or engaged in professional endeavors, Sarah was busily reading and responding to her daily mail! She would draw or write in her invented spelling, put marks in boxes, replace sheets of paper in envelopes, seal them, and give them to her parents to mail. Just think of all the literacy that Sarah learned watching her parents at their desk and then imitating their behaviors.

Taking advantage of items readily available in the home, such as junk mail, provides parents and their children with many hours of worthwhile learning experiences. Figure 13.11 lists resources found in the home and examples of print opportunities that are present in the home environment. This can be given to parents along with demonstrations of how to use them effectively.

As a testimony to seeing parents read and write in the home, Sarah's older brother David, then a senior in high school, recently shared a journal entry discussing someone who had influenced his life. It is interesting to note that he chose as that significant person his father engaged in reading. See Figure 13.12 for David's journal entry.

Parents can help their children become lifelong readers and writers by sharing a learning environment at home in which children are surrounded by an abundance of print. This gives ample opportunities to explore reading and writing in meaningful ways. As Rasinski and Fredericks (1991a) proclaim, "A literate home environment doesn't teach children how to read; rather it provides children with opportunities to enjoy reading and discover the many ways it can be used to enrich the experiences in their lives" (439).

Reading Around the Home

Having an abundance of reading materials available around the home was mentioned as one of the ways parents could create a suitable learning environment for their children. Parents should make sure that there are a large number of books and magazines around the home. Home libraries can be developed by purchasing inexpensive books through book clubs, at garage sales, and by trading books with other families. Schools can help put more books in children's home libraries by organizing Book Swaps or book exchanges. Children bring in books from home which are exchanged for Book Bucks. On a given day, children can use their Book Bucks to

FROM THE CLASSROOM

A "HOLE" LOT OF FUN

Have you ever noticed how many items have holes in them? Look around you and you'll be amazed at the number of holes that occur naturally in your everyday environment, for example, key holes, holes in sneakers for laces, a hole in the top of a soda can or bottle, a hole in the middle of a ring or a bracelet, etc. Teachers can capitalize on the "holeness" in the children's world and brainstorm where holes occur. The children's contributions can be kept on chart paper or a class book can be created. The book can be entitled *A Hole Can Be* accompanied with a hole somewhere on the page. The child is to choose an item having a hole, illustrate it, and provide a caption. In the example depicted below, a hole book was being created by kindergarten children and their fifth grade mentors. One little girl was having difficulty thinking of what she would like to draw. Her mentor then decided to provide hints and had her repeatedly look at his eyes. Sure enough, there was a hole—the opening in his eye known as the iris.

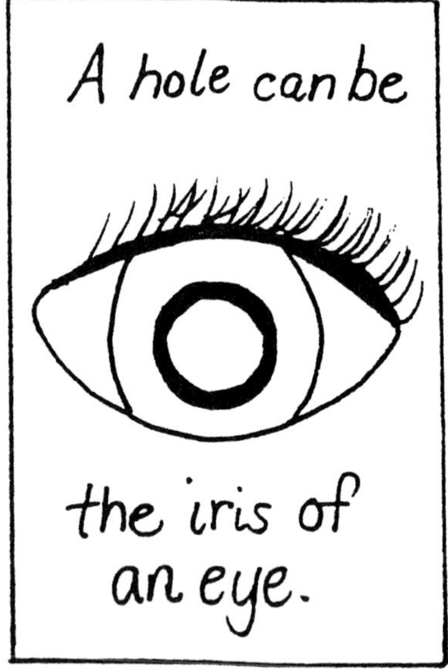

Figure 13.11 Resources in the Home

EDUCATIONAL MATERIALS	READING MATERIALS
pots, pans, and fitted lids	books of all kinds
sets of measuring spoons and cups	advertisements (in newspapers, through the mail)
cans of various sizes	board games
aluminum pie tins	directions for games and building models
plastic bottles and caps	recipes
empty milk cartons	television listings
buttons, nails, and screws of different sizes	cereal boxes (and other packaging)
magazine pictures	labels
silverware	bills of sale
plastic items, such as dishes, glasses, and coasters	sales receipts
clothing	coupons
puzzles	telephone directory
items that can be classified (according to color, shape, texture, sounds, hot or cold)	new purchase guarantees
spools	reference books
pasta, cereal, beans, other foods	manuals
scraps of material, yarn	magazines
clothespins	slogans on clothing
paper bags	greeting cards
Note: Some items are more appropriate for one age group than another. Safety must be considered at all times (e.g., avoid using small items that babies might swallow).	business cards
	checkbooks
	calendars

purchase books that other children have brought in (Sawyer, 1993). Parents can give children subscriptions to magazines for birthdays and special occasions. A listing of magazines appropriate for children is provided in Appendix I. In addition to purchasing books, parents should avail themselves of the public library and take advantage of the excellent selections in their children's school library.

There's more to reading at home than just literature. The mail carrier brings reading aplenty virtually every day, and this can be shared with the family. Reading occurs at mealtime—on cereal boxes, on labels, in recipes. These reading materials can be discussed and analyzed (e.g., the list of ingredients in certain products or the ways the manufacturer packages the products to entice future consumers), or they can become springboards for family activities.

Many possible extension activities can be created from materials in the home. For example, parents and children can make environmental print books. The fronts of cereal box packages can be collected and placed in a three-ring binder to become a book, possibly titled "Breakfast Reading." Some parents place inside these books only boxes of cereals they will permit their children to eat. Children can take these books to the grocery store and match a box on the shelf with one of the acceptable choices in the cereal book. A book can be made from collections of business cards. Children find small books especially appealing, and clever business cards are a source of novel reading material. Parents and children can make a bulletin board of "Things I Can Read" that includes logos from fast-food restaurants, toothpaste boxes, and labels from canned soups or pasta. The possibilities are endless.

Figure 13.12 David's Journal Entry

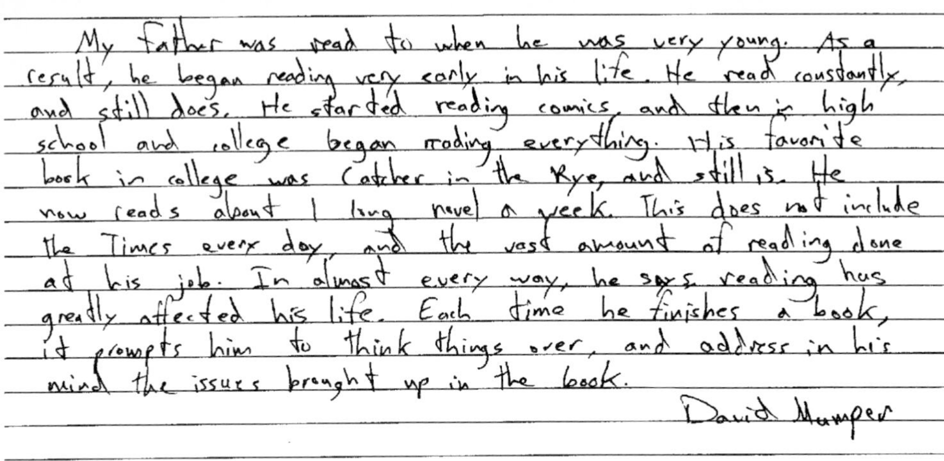

My father was read to when he was very young. As a result, he began reading very early in his life. He read constantly, and still does. He started reading comics, and then in high school and college began reading everything. His favorite book in college was Catcher in the Rye, and still is. He now reads about 1 long novel a week. This does not include the Times every day, and the vast amount of reading done at his job. In almost every way, he says reading has greatly affected his life. Each time he finishes a book, it prompts him to think things over, and address in his mind the issues brought up in the book.

David Mumper

David writing in his journal

Of course there are the daily newspapers and television guides that foster critical thinking and opportunities for family discussions. Sharing an interesting piece of news, an inspiring quote from a magazine or news story, a review of a movie or television series, or a humorous cartoon can contribute to family conversations at the dinner table. Many pleasurable family times can center around some form of reading material.

While reading and sharing literature together, parents and children can write comments to one another regarding the book or article, jot down interesting words or vocabulary, or note confusing passages. These can then become the focus of family dialogues about books.

To capitalize on the popularity of catchy slogans seen on such items as T-shirts, bumper stickers, bookmarks, and posters, parents and children can create their own or can comment on clever ones seen that day. Children can construct bookmarks to keep their places while reading, decorating them with wallpaper, book slogans, inspirational messages, or personalized illustrations. They can paint messages on T-shirts using fabric paint. Have you ever kept track of all the places that can be visited (or the colleges that can be attended) via the T-shirts you read in the grocery store, on the street, and in the classroom? Families can keep a listing of all the places visited through T-shirts, and these places can be located on a map. This activity is particularly enjoyable on a family vacation. Parents should be aware that the home presents many motivational opportunities for encouraging and sharing reading and writing—opportunities that translate into educational benefits for their children.

Paired Reading

An effective reading technique involving parents and children that was developed and popularized in England is the use of paired reading. In paired reading, parents and their children read together in a book of the child's own choosing, irrespective of reading difficulty. Through this technique, children get practice with reading and have the modeling of a fluent reader as well. Research has demonstrated that children participating in this program for 5–15 minutes a day make significant gains in their reading ability (Topping, 1987, 1989).

Paired reading is relatively simple. With a few training sessions and modeling by teachers, parents can use the procedure effectively. First, children choose the books or any other reading material that they would like to read and that is within the competence of their parent. With challenging texts, the child is supported by reading together with the parent, both reading the words aloud. Parents adjust their reading speed so that parent and child are reading together comfortably. The intent is to have the child say every word correctly. When the child makes and error; the parent merely repeats the word until the child repeats it correctly before proceeding.

When children are reading easier texts, they can indicate to their parents through some nonverbal signal (e.g., a nudge, a squeeze, or a tapping of the foot) that they would like to continue reading independently. Then the children proceed on their own until they encounter difficulty. At this point, the pair revert to reading together. Topping suggests that children be given no more than five seconds when encountering a difficulty without being helped. This keeps the momentum going and does not permit the child to become frustrated.

There is much emphasis on praise for correct reading, on self-correction, and the children's indicating that they would like to read alone. Paired reading helps children become fluent and confident readers, and despite the emphasis on exact word recognition, the participants gain in understanding as well. Because of the support of more expert readers (the parents) and the questioning and discussion that accompany paired reading, the children read with better comprehension.

Paired reading is flexible and can accommodate a variety of reading levels and interests. If parents are not able readers themselves, other siblings, or family members can be trained to use the technique. Teachers could also audiotape books with which children can read along. It is recommended that when introducing the procedure, there be a minimum of five sessions per week for at least five minutes each day. Parents and children need to commit to a trial period of six to eight weeks. At the end of that time, teachers and parents can meet, discuss successes and concerns, and make the necessary adjustments.

Paired reading is easy to do, works with children of all ages, and uses all kinds of reading materials from books to newspapers. Parents have been overwhelmingly supportive of this approach in their follow-up evaluations (Topping, 1987; Rasinski and Fredericks, 1991b). Paired reading has helped improve reading performance, increased children's desire to read, and strengthened the bond between the parents and their offspring.

Perhaps the overemphasis on correctness may discourage some whole language advocates from using this technique. The procedures were established to standardize the paired reading process and make the technique easier for parents to use. Teachers could modify the procedure somewhat and have parents correct only miscues that do not interfere with the meaning. However, this has not been tried or reported in the literature as yet. Are you up to the challenge?

In any case, paired reading brings children, parents, and books together in a supportive, productive relationship. Paired reading makes possible a form of parent involvement that is both effective and enjoyable.

Writing in the Home

In addition to providing meaningful reading activities, the home should offer opportunities for writing. An abundance of writing materials should be available, including an assortment of paper and writing implements, and children should be encouraged to write as frequently as possible for a variety of purposes. Meaningful writing opportunities that can originate from the home or that can be accomplished throughout daily life include:

- messages to family members
- greetings on birthdays and special days
- shopping lists
- menus
- letter writing—friendly and business
- writing directions on how to do something or how to go someplace
- writing captions for family photograph albums
- family journals or diaries
- noting meetings and appointments on a calendar

Families can correspond with one another via a dialogue journal in which family members can record their feelings, thoughts, and impressions or the day's events. This is an excellent way for parents to learn more about their children while fostering literacy at the same time.

When family outings are planned, children can read maps, write for information, write down directions, and help plan the trip. During the trip, children can keep a journal, jotting down the sites visited and their impressions of the trip. They can collect postcards and other mementos, take photographs, and include these in their travel journal. Samples from journals written during a family trip around the country are presented in Figure 13.13. These diaries remain pleasant reading for years to come and allow families to relive happy times together.

Children and their parents can likewise become authors themselves by writing original stories, poems, and articles. Family histories are fascinating. An excellent family project is to put together an "All About Our Family" biographical album. Children can concentrate on their immediate family or—if other generations are accessible and other information is available—can trace their family roots. Favorite family recipes can be compiled, which family members will treasure for years. Along with a recipe can be comments from those who were able to delight in the tasty treats.

These family histories or stories can be placed in fictional settings, as was recently done by the son of one of the authors. This family writer, the youngest of three boys, wrote a traditional folktale in which several brothers vie for the hand of a beautiful princess. The eldest has the brains; the middle son, the brawn; and the youngest, the kindness and goodness. Of course kindness and goodness eventually win out, and being a number-three son has its own rewards. This story is now placed in the family's treasure box to be savored over the years.

Wordless books and cartoons with words deleted (these can be covered with correction

Figure 13.13A Travel Journal Entries—Sarah and David

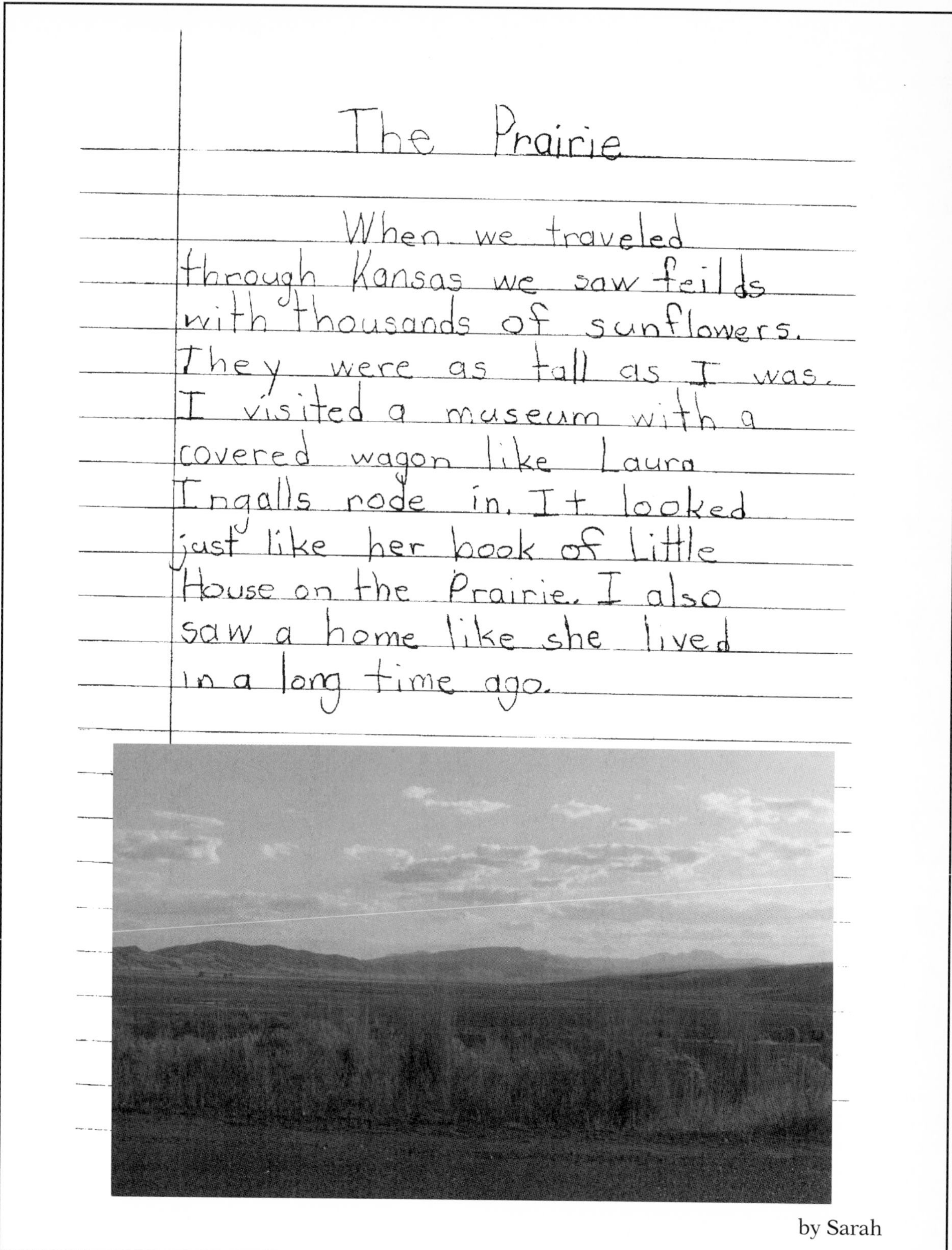

The Prairie

When we traveled through Kansas we saw feilds with thousands of sunflowers. They were as tall as I was. I visited a museum with a covered wagon like Laura Ingalls rode in. It looked just like her book of Little House on the Prairie. I also saw a home like she lived in a long time ago.

by Sarah

Figure 13.13B Travel Journal Entries—Sarah and David (cont.)

Sequoias

The giant sequoias grow in the Sierra Nevada mountains in California. Some of them have lived for over three thousand years. Some of them were twenty four feet across and three hundred feet high. Their bark can get to be two feet thick. The bark protects it from forest fires. In the sequoias groves no branches can grow on the bottom because there is no sunlight there. We walked a mile to a hut made out of a hollow sequoia. A man lived there thirty summers. You could stand up in the log house.

A U.S. forest Ranger led us on a hike around a marshy bog in the sequoia forest. He told many interesting stories about these huge trees. He told about how many of the trees had lived through many forests fires.

tape or markers) can inspire young authors while providing some structure. Because the events and illustrations are already given, children have to create only the text. Different family members can write their own versions, which can be shared during family moments together. A listing of wordless books is provided in Appendix C.

Just as with reading, writing opportunities abound in the home. Families just have to take advantage of them, value them, and make writing an integral part of family life.

Sharing/Learning Activities

Many teachers enjoy preparing learning or sharing activities that parents and children can do together in the home. These should not be likened to the worksheets and dittos associated with busywork, and they should not be unfinished classroom work with the parent's being responsible for overseeing that it be done. Rather, these should be opportunities for parents and children to explore, create, investigate, and learn together. In the past, children were assigned classroom projects to do at home. The finished projects were worthy of winning competitions when talented parents assumed the responsibility for the project and actually did most of the work. Instead, these sharing activities are outgrowths of classroom learning experiences or thematic studies. They are meaningful activities that relate to what is being explored in the classroom. They provide opportunities for parents to truly share in the educational process. Parents and children are encouraged to work together, with the child's efforts and emerging talents being celebrated. Examples of sharing sheets used in a kindergarten classroom are presented in Figure 13.14.

Another means of involving parents in sharing activities is through books sent home from the school. Frequently, children check out books from school libraries or borrow them from the classroom library, and no real attempt is made to connect parents and the reading of these books, aside, of course, from the suggestion that parents read aloud to their children on a regular basis. However, some teachers use book borrowing as real attempts to provide shared literacy experiences at home. One such procedure comes from the classroom of Jean Mumper. At the beginning of each day, children return borrowed books by placing them, title facing the class, along the chalk tray. The teacher adds new titles. Then the children who have returned books select one and place it in their backpacks. The books are kept in plastic bags that close (zip) at the top. Along with the books is a sharing sheet that has the title of the book at the top, the name of each child in the class along the side, and places for the parent (or child) to note the date shared, with whom, and comments.

Parents have been most receptive to these learning activities. In reviewing the various activities that they and their children participated in throughout the year, parents constantly acknowledge that they enjoyed the parent sharing activities "because they gave us something to work with and they were fun." Other comments from parents on the shared literacy experiences include:

"As for a parent's view, my favorite part was the sharing activities and the books borrowed from the class library. The excitement on my son's face was worth more than words can really say."

"I'd like to thank you for starting Kerry's school years with such enthusiasm and curiosity. She has gained a great interest in learning and is very excited about reading. I thought the sharing books were an excellent means of creating that excitement. The parent sharing activities were also very helpful in keeping us parents in touch with school life. We definitely enjoyed doing these activities together."

Poetry is another way of having children and their parents engage in sharing activities. Children could make poetry books that go home on a regular basis, perhaps weekly. Each week the children are given a poem to paste in their books, or to write in their poetry books. The parents and the children then share the poem and perhaps comment how the poem was used or celebrated that week. This way, the poetry book becomes a dialogue journal as well. At the front of the poetry books, there could be a letter to the parents explaining the program. One such letter from an early childhood educator in New Zealand follows:

FROM THE CLASSROOM

CLASSROOM MEMORIES

To capitalize on the portfolio movement, teachers and children can create a collection of children's work and projects over the entire year to be given to parents at the end of the school year. There can be photographs of the child at the beginning of the year, photographs during special events and activities, samples of writing, art work, etc. Parents will treasure these books for years and by taking them out periodically can watch their children grow throughout their elementary school years.

A variation of this activity, and one that is done in the Middletown, New York, School District, is to save four pieces of student writing each year. These are labeled, placed in folders, and saved until the end of the sixth grade. At that time, the students and their parents are gifted with a chronological history of the student's growth as an author.

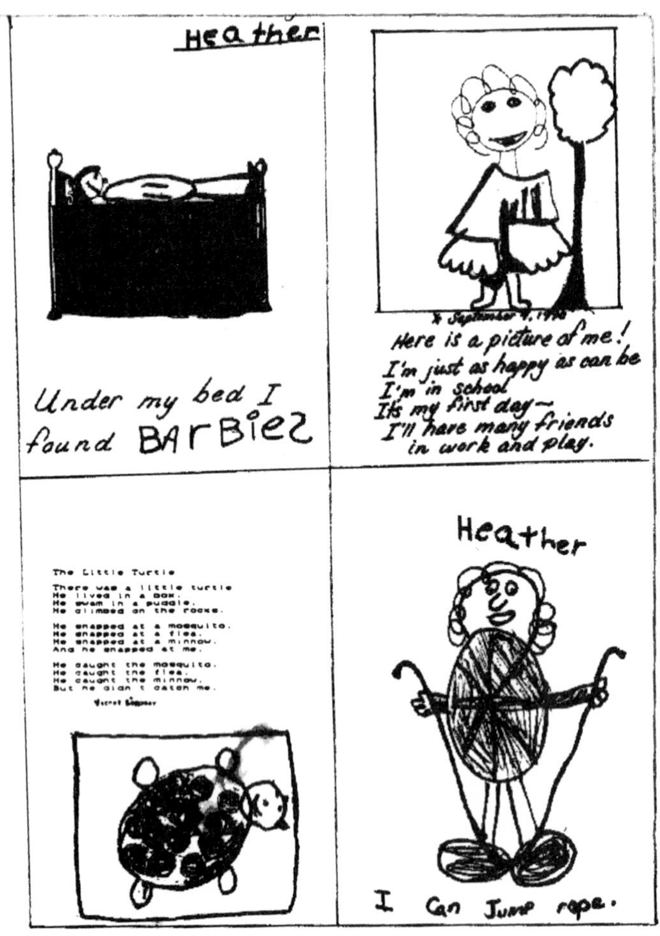

Figure 13.14 Initial Letter plus Samples of Sharing Sheets

Dear Parents,

Each week you will get a "Sharing Activity" to complete with your child during the following week. The activities will be related to a topic, theme, letter sound, or concept we will be highlighting during the week.

Your child will bring a sheet home each Friday and it is due back by the next Friday. You may, however, send them in any day. It actually helps to get a few each day! ☺

Hopefully, you will find these activities enjoyable. They will also give you a starting point to answer the question "What did you do in school today?".

We are partners in the educational process. Please feel free to call or plan a visit.

Sincerely,
Jean Mumper

Name:

Dear Parents,

For home sharing time this week I'd like you to read a favorite book, or your child's library book, together. When you are finished, ask him or her to tell the story back to you. Then compose 3 or 4 sentences with your child to tell me what the book was about. Write your child's words on the lines at the bottom (use the back if you need more space). Put a marker in the book to show the page your child liked best so he/she can share it in class.

Title (Your child should write this...) ______

Parents may write the sentences, but use your child's words.

______

Favorite page number is ______

They will share this page with the class.

Sharing Time for the week of Nov-2-8

Name COURtneY

Patterns

See if your child can see the pattern in each line below. "Say" each pattern out loud and point from left to right. Use real items to make the pattern when possible.

pencil "penny" ... what comes next?

"fork" "spoon"

On the back draw a pattern you made.

The person who helped was Mom

---

todd

Sharing Activity

← Opposites ⇒

Big ↔ Little
Large ↔ Small
Huge ↔ Tiny
Adult ↔ Child

Read these words aloud and ask your child to tell you another word that is opposite. There is no one correct answer. Talk about their responses, accept all reasonable choices and explore all possibilities.

Wet - dry
Hot - cold
Night - day
Hungry - full
Light - dark
Happy - sad
Fast - slow
Loud - soft
Hard - soft

Perhaps you can think of some more opposites. Give it a try and share them with me. Write them on the back. →

Name todd and Dad

Dear Parents/Guardian,

I now have a Poem Book.

I will paste in my favorite poems, songs, rhymes, and jingles.
Please help me to return the book each Monday.
I won't be able to read all the words at first, but please praise me for:

- looking at the pictures
- thinking about what is happening
- pointing at each word
- trying words that —make sense
  —sound right
  —look right

As I progress, I will rely less on memory and use more skills and letter clues.

Thanks heaps,

Love from,

____

Family Projects

To help break the parental barrier and to involve her parents in the education of their children, Burkhart (1995) developed a family projects curriculum collaboratively with the families of her students. Each month, families worked together on theme-related projects. Some of the project ideas included family trees, the weather, family biographies, family reading month, poetry month, measurement, and simple machines among others. Working together, Burkhart and her families learned the importance of a mutual relationship and its positive effects on the students. She was able to demonstrate that when parents participate in specific activities and projects that they have helped plan, they will continue to contribute to the success of their children.

Backpacks and Traveling Suitcases

Look around a classroom today and you'll see an assortment of backpacks, which practically every child uses to carry personal belongings to and from school. Capitalizing on the popularity and availability of backpacks, teachers have creatively adapted them into a form of parent involvement. One way to use backpacks along with thematic story is to house themes in backpacks. Small backpacks are purchased and can be decorated with some aspect of the theme's contents, such as a dinosaur for a dinosaur theme, foods for food-related themes, and babies for a "You Must Have Been a Beautiful Baby" theme. Backpacks can be decorated with fabric paint, sewn-on patches, or laundry markers.

The backpack contains four or five books centered around a theme, suggestions for activities parents and children can do together, and a journal in which parents and children can record how the books were used, activities carried out, and their personal reactions. These journals travel with the backpack theme and are available for other families to learn from and enjoy. Sometimes parents volunteer to put together a backpack theme themselves because of a special interest or talent. One family with roots in New Hampshire put together a backpack featuring books about the Granite State. In the journal, a grandmother who still resided in New Hampshire placed a recipe for delicious blueberry muffins. Figure 13.15 gives examples of several backpack themes with suggested books and activities.

Another means of encouraging a reading environment in the home is to make magazine packets that circulate among the children and their families (Farris, 1987). Bookbags, small suitcases, and backpacks make excellent containers for the magazine collections. The collections should contain something for every family member, for example, *Ladies Home Journal, Good Housekeeping, Readers Digest, Sports Illustrated, Time,* and *Newsweek* as well as magazines that appeal to children (e.g., *Sesame Street, Ranger Rick, National Geographic World, Cobblestone*). Magazines can be collected from personal subscriptions, donations from parents, garage sales, or whatever means are available. Suggested activities may accompany the magazine pack. This may mean that several of the magazines are available for cutting up (these could be housed in plastic food storage bags and clearly marked). Outdated and torn magazines are perfect for such activities.

Reutzel and Fawson (1990) describe another creative use of backpacks—the Traveling Tales backpack. The intents were to involve par-

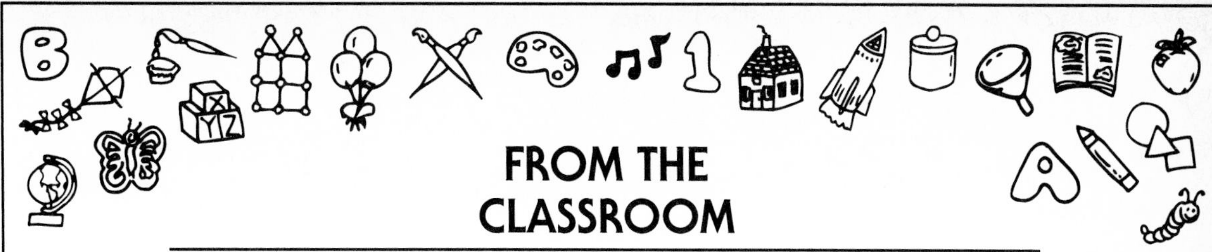

FROM THE CLASSROOM

SHARING SHEET

Book Title: *Huggles*

MRS. MUMPER/JOHANSEN
KINDERGARTEN A.M.
1992 - 1993
ROOM 3

After you have shared this book with your child please mark, date, and return.

Please Keep only 1 or 2 days!	*Date Shared*	*With whom*	*Comments:*
ANTONELLI, CODY			
BELL, AMANDA	2/18	Mom	☺
GIBSON, JUSTIN	2/8	Dad	Justin read it to Dad Dad enjoyed it the most
GOTTESMAN, AIMEE	1/26	Mom	Aimee enjoyed the ending!
GRAHAM, BRIAN	11/13	Mom + Dad	Brian enjoyed the ending + re-read it several times
GREEN, MATTHEW			
HAECKER, ERICK	11/14	Mom + Grandma	We All Laughed!
HECHT, ABBY	12/16	MOM	We Love Hugs!
HERMANCE, COURTNEY	1/25	Grandma	- We hugged!
HOWARD, BETTINA	1-2-93	mom	it's funny
KENYON, TERESA	2/22	Mom	Silly Story!
LEGHORN, STEVEN			
MACUR, DOUGLAS	3/3	Mom + Eve	"I loved it!"
MALLOY, KAITLYN	3/29	Mom	Kaitlyn enjoyed it
MARTIN, BROOKE	4/2	Mom	Cute!
MC CARL, DANIELLE	4/6/93	DAD	NEAT Book!
MIRO, LAUREN	2/6	Lauren	funny ending
ORPHAN, CHARLES (DANNY)			
REECK, MICHAEL	1/18	Dad	Very Enjoyable
SARVIS, JENNIFER	2/1	Sister	Loved it
SCHWARTZ, MICHAEL	1/8	Mom	Mike + mom Hugged
SMITH, RACHEL			
WALDEN, JASON	4/12	brother	liked it!
WIEGMANN, JEFFREY	1 Mar	Sister	He's Cool
WILLIAMS, CHARLES			

Figure 13.15A Backpack Themes

Note: The contents of backpack themes can vary. Typically, four or five books are included, accompanied by suggested activities and a journal. Other items that may be included are materials for projects, read-along tapes, and puppets.

Colors

BOOKS

Ehlert, L. (1989). *Color zoo.* New York: The Trumpet Club.
Lionni, L. (1959). *Little blue and little yellow.* New York: Astor-Honor.
Martin, Jr., B. (1983). *Brown bear, brown bear, what do you see?* New York: Holt, Rinehart & Winston.
Walsh, E. (1989). *Mouse paint.* San Diego: Harcourt Brace Jovanovich.
Testa, F. (1982). *If you take a paintbrush.* New York: Dial Books for Young Readers.

SUGGESTED ACTIVITIES

- Paste one paint chip sample onto a page. Find or draw things of that color. After you have done several colors, put the pages together to make a book.
- Draw your face on a folded sheet of paper. Cut out or have someone cut out a space for your eyes so that you can "see." Draw something that you saw inside the folded sheet. Make sure your picture can be seen by your cut-out eyes.
- Take a paper plate and plan a colorful meal. On the plate draw or cut out pictures of things that are a certain color; e.g., for a red meal find pictures of apples, cherries, and red gelatine dessert.

Frogs

BOOKS

Galdone, P. (1974). *The frog prince.* New York: McGraw-Hill.
Kalan, R. (1981). *Jump, frog, jump!* New York: Morrow.
Kellogg, S. (1977). *The mysterious tadpole.* New York: Dial.
Mayer, M. (1974). *Frog goes to dinner.* New York: Dial.
Scieszka, J. (1991). *The frog prince continued.* New York: Viking.

SUGGESTED ACTIVITIES

- Write the words to go with Mercer Mayer's wordless book.
- Use the frog puppet to act out your story.
- Talk about how the two Frog Prince books are different.
- Tell the story of *The Mysterious Tadpole* to another family member.

All About Me

BOOKS

Browne, A. (1988). *I like books.* New York: Knopf
Carlson, N. (1988). *I like me.* New York: The Trumpet Club.
Cohen, M. (1971). *Best friends.* New York: Macmillan.
Cowley, J. (1986). *My home.* San Diego: The Wright Group.
Parrish, P. (1988). *Amelia Bedelia's family album.* New York: Avon Books.

(*continued*)

Figure 13.15B Backpack Themes (cont.)

SUGGESTED ACTIVITIES

- Have someone trace around your body. Attach your head to a hanger so that you can hand up your body outline. Draw your face, hair, and some clothes. On your body write things you like to do, your favorite foods, and anything elese you'd like to write about yourself.
- Recreate a room in your home from a shoe box. Cut out or make furniture for your room.
- Make your own family album. Get a photograph of each family member (remember pets) or draw each member. Write some interesting information about each one.

Incredible Edibles

BOOKS

Barrett, J. (1978). *Cloudy with a chance of meatballs.* New York: Aladdin Books.
Cowley, J. (1986). *Yuk soup.* San Diego: The Wright Group.
DePaola, T. (1978). *Pancakes for breakfast.* San Diego: Harcourt Brace Jovanovich.
Gelman, R. (1977). *More spaghetti I say.* New York: Scholastic.
McGovern, A. (1968). *Stone soup.* New York: Scholastic.

SUGGESTED ACTIVITIES

- Make pancakes for breakfast, writing down the steps to make the pancakes.
- Write words for the book *Pancakes for Breakfast.*
- Draw a picture of some funny way you would like spaghetti. Soak some spaghetti in warm water and put it on your picture (no glue needed). The spaghetti will stick to your drawing and will be quite realistic.
- Go for a walk around your yard or neighborhood. Collect some junk to make yuk soup. Write a recipe for your soup.

ents with their children's writing and carry the process writing approach from the classroom into the home. A backpack was purchased and the words "Traveling Tales" were stenciled across the upper part of the backpack. The backpack contained traditional writing supplies—a variety of paper, writing implements, scissors, stapler, yarn, hole punch, wallpaper samples, glue, letter stencils, tape, and ruler. The items were organized in plastic zippered pouches with the contents of each pouch labeled so that the supplies could be returned properly.

Guidelines for the parents included procedural steps for them to follow. Parents were given information and suggestions on how to help their children choose topics, select the writing form (poetry, informational nonfiction, narrative), and choose the material that might be used. Parents were instructed to guide their children through the writing process from prewriting to publishing. Once the children were finished, they were encouraged to share their writing first with family members and then with their classmates. Parents were invited to the authors' sessions in the classroom so that they could also experience the sharing time. The Traveling Tales backpack proved to be an excellent means of involving parents in the writing process.

Backpacks are not the only containers that can be used in home writing activities. Rodriguez (1991) found other means to spark her first graders' enthusiasm for writing. She found an old briefcase that she converted into a Writing Briefcase by decorating the outside with stickers and filling it with writing tools and resources. The supplies were similar to those used by Reutzel and Fawson but also included a picture dictionary, magazine pictures, shaped books, word cards, and easy-to-read books. Parent correspondence was included as well—a letter explaining why writing is important to young children and how to use the briefcase and an information sheet briefly explaining the stages of writing development. One additional item was a notebook titled "All About the Author." Here the young authors provide information about themselves. Other children and parents both enjoy reading the autobiographies.

In addition to the Writing Briefcase, Rodriguez has a home writing activity called the Traveling Suitcase. This suitcase is a small overnight bag labeled with stickers from around the state, country, and world. Inside are the same writing materials as in the briefcase, along with items representing the places to which the suitcase has traveled. For instance, if the suitcase visited New York City, it could contain postcards, a small replica of the State of Liberty or the Empire State Building, ticket stubs for a tour around Manhattan, bumper stickers, toy taxis, and brochures. The children take the suitcase home and create a story about their travels.

The home learning activities described can be modified to suit the needs and interests of individual teachers and students. Involving parents in home learning activities fosters enthusiasm for reading and writing and helps connect the home and school in promoting future growth in literacy.

Textbooks in the Home

With the advent of a new school year, students receive new textbooks, particularly in the content areas. Although we are not advocating the sole use of textbooks for content area instruction, many classroom teachers still use them as part of their instructional program. In addition, content area instruction in the middle school, junior high school, and high school may still rely on textbooks; therefore students in the elementary school might profit from some experience in using texts. Traditionally, students take these books home to be covered. Sandel (1988) suggests that while covering the books, parents "uncover" them as well. It is suggested that prior to sharing the text at home with their children, parents attend a meeting to learn how the textbooks are to be used, how they are organized, and how parents may help their children discover this organization.

The objective of this shared textbook activity is to have parents and children look through the books together. By becoming knowledgeable about textbooks and how to use them efficiently and effectively, students can readily transfer their knowledge to future encounters with other textbooks. By having both parents and teachers provide demonstrations of the effective use of textbooks, students will approach other texts by asking themselves what they know about the book, what they know about the topics that will be covered, and what they expect to learn.

A memo is given to the parents to help them with the sharing procedure. Parents are encouraged to look at the books with their children and talk about them together. The parts of the book (table of contents, glossary, and so on) could be reviewed or demonstrated from. The parents could ask questions or give clues to have the children locate certain information (this could be likened to a treasure hunt). The text could then be skimmed to see whether the children can make connections with previous knowledge or with their own lives. For example, a chapter on immigration might remind the young reader of his or her grandparents' arrival in the United States, or a chapter on pollution might trigger memories of past recycling projects.

Textbook sharing allows parents and their children to experience yet another educational approach together. Children are helped to get to know their textbooks, and parents become acquainted with the curriculum and the topics that will be explored that year. Perhaps the joint exploration will inspire reading (and writing) on topics discovered on this journey through the textbook.

Connecting Reading and Writing with Real-Life Experiences

Parents can encourage literacy at home by connecting reading and writing with family experiences. The experiences can precede the literacy activity and act as motivators or background builders, or they can follow the literacy activities (Rasinski and Fredericks, 1991a). For example, if the family is planning a trip to the Boston area to take in the historic sites, they may wish to read such books as *Johnny Tremain, My Brother Sam Is Dead,* and *Make Way for*

Ducklings (which takes place on Boston Common) or any books pertaining to Boston or its history. The trip to Boston may inspire further reading about the Boston Tea Party, the historic ride of Paul Revere, or famous Revolutionary War battles.

Researching family histories or cultures may inspire families to read and enjoy the folklore of that culture. Each country has a rich heritage and history. Exploring this together as a family is both informational and pleasurable.

Of course, not all happenings in the home are enjoyable. Every family at some time endures personal hardships and sadness. Schools can help at this time by suggesting books that might help with the healing process. Suggested books for dealing with divorce, disabilities, and death are provided at the end of this chapter.

Parent involvement is essential to the well-being of the schools and to the well-being of the children who attend these schools. By working together as coeducators, parents and teachers are moving toward providing an educational system that develops readers, writers, and life-long learners both in the school and in the real world.

QUESTIONS PARENTS ASK ABOUT WHOLE LANGUAGE

Parents have a myriad of questions and concerns about this approach to learning called whole language. The following are questions asked by parents in our schools and questions we anticipate would be asked by any interested and concerned parent.

1. **What can I do at home to reinforce the whole language program?** The most important activity you can do is read aloud to your child every day. Other ways to reinforce whole language learning include encouraging your child in everyday literacy activities—writing items on grocery lists, taking telephone messages, addressing envelopes, marking important dates on the calendar, and keeping a daily diary or personal journal.

2. **How will I know what books are appropriate to read to my child?** Any book your child is interested in and able to enjoy is appropriate. For younger children we usually focus on picture books with minimal text and gradually, as children get older, increase the level to chapter books that are read over many sittings. Excellent resources for appropriate read-aloud books are Jim Trelease's *Read-Aloud Handbook* and The New York Times *Guide for Parents.*

3. **Should I have my child practice writing the alphabet letters?** Yes, but not in the traditional skill sheet way with isolated letters repeated over and over. Instead, encourage children at every opportunity to write letters in meaningful ways. Give them an inexpensive address book and let them write their friends' names and phone numbers. They are not only practicing letters and numbers; they are learning such important skills as alphabetization and organization. In a notebook, they can write words that are important to them—favorite cereals, games, books, toys, TV shows, or pets.

4. **If children aren't answering comprehension questions, how do I know they are comprehending what they read?** There are many ways to assess comprehension other than asking questions. Literature discussions afford children the opportunity to talk about what they've read. This can take the form of retelling, sharing a favorite part of the text, or just discussing the issues and feelings that evolve from the text itself. In addition, many children respond in literature response logs or learning logs following their reading of the text and these entries are used to assess student understanding.

5. **Who decides what is taught in a whole language classroom?** The material to be learned by students in a particular grade is usually mandated by the state and local school districts. In a whole language classroom, teachers address the required curriculum using the philosophy of whole language. Teachers often team plan and obtain student input. Subject matter is integrated whenever possible, and students learn in cooperative groups, pairs, and as a whole class. The methodology varies so that all students have opportunities to learn in an environment that guarantees success.

6. **What about test scores?** Simply stated, if children can read and write successfully, they will do well on tests no matter what method is used to teach reading.

7. **If my child is in a whole language classroom one year and then goes into a traditional classroom—or vice versa—won't that be confusing?** Not really. When children enter a new grade, they have no prior knowledge of what that grade is like. The child assumes that whatever is being taught is right for that grade. The child may find the skill work boring or ability grouping uncomfortable, but he or she will learn anyway. In contrast, if a child was in a traditional classroom and goes into a whole language classroom, adjustment is minimized since the class is now child-centered, and the teacher will focus on the child's unique abilities, interests, and needs.

8. **Since you sing the praises of whole language, can you guarantee that my child will learn to read and write?** All children can learn to read and write—some regardless of the method used. We acknowledge that there are many factors that put some children at risk. What we can guarantee is that in a whole language classroom, your child will love reading and writing and will probably become a lifelong learner.

COMMENTS FROM THE HOME ABOUT WHOLE LANGUAGE

Parents whose children have experienced the joys of whole language classrooms are quite favorable in their comments regarding this approach to literacy. What exactly are these parents saying? What are the benefits they see for their children and themselves as parents? In sharing their experiences, parents noted that they saw daily growth in their children's ability to communicate, both verbally and through writing. Their children grew in their knowledge of language and in the ability to respect themselves and others. Self-esteem was enhanced as the children gained in self-confidence. Because whole language provides children with opportunities for unlimited growth, the children were able to became self-directed learners, free to pursue their own interests and develop their own learning styles.

Parents appreciated the fact that their children were reading real books and using writing as a vehicle to both express themselves and communicate. Using literature, the children were able to provide thoughtful and perceptive analyses of books and grew to enjoy reading greatly. Parents were able to hear their children's voices in their writing and could see that their children had developed a sense of audience. The whole language classroom had afforded their children many opportunities to read and write.

Unlike their own histories as young learners in elementary schools, parents noticed that their children approached reading and writing naturally. They were unafraid to take risks, to experiment, or to make mistakes. In the whole language classrooms, mistakes were treated as opportunities. Parents wished that whole language had been available to them so that they could have read from the wealth of literature as their children are now doing—so that they today as adults could approach literacy (particularly writing) as readily as their children do.

As far as their personal involvement in the classroom, parents appreciated the increased opportunities to be involved in their children's education. They felt valued and knowledgeable. One parent acknowledged that she couldn't stay away from her child's classroom. She was wanted and appreciated by the teacher and the children and realized her contributions were valuable and respected.

Some parents even noticed that they now changed their practices in the home as a result of being involved in a whole language classroom. A parent reported that she now read, wrote, and talked more with her preschooler. Before she didn't recognize that early attempts at literacy were important and did not take the emergent literacy experiences seriously. Now she recognized that these experiences are serious business and provide a foundation for future learning.

Parents voiced their concerns too. Initially they were fearful that the perceived lack of structure would be harmful for their children's achievement in school. Later, as their children became more and more immersed in real literacy activities, they became concerned about their child's having to return and readjust to more traditional approaches to literacy. One teacher responded to this by saying that it was better to have had the opportunity to travel to Europe once than never to have gone at all. The voyage would leave lasting impressions and contribute to the children's growing world of knowledge.

Parents recognized that whole language allows children to build self-confidence at the same time that they are gaining the literacy skills that will follow them into adulthood. But children weren't the only ones to gain—parents profited as well. One parent proclaimed that through her exposure to and involvement in whole language as a parent, she too gained an insatiable thirst for learning about literacy. These comments came from parents whose children had the wonderful opportunity to grow as readers and writers with teachers who cared, who had an understanding of children's learning and language development, who were knowledgeable about the reading and writing processes, who recognized the important roles parents play in their children's education (Windsor, 1991). Perhaps the following words from a parent best summarize this section:

> When my son was in first grade, he had a teacher who taught using the whole language approach. He brought books home every night and couldn't wait until we sat down to read them. He also started writing his own stories—page after page of writing, using his own spelling. And this was a kid who could barely write his name in kindergarten! I was so pleased with his enthusiasm. In second grade, his classroom was very traditional, and the reading program used only the basal reader. I noticed his writing changed immediately. His stories were spelled perfectly, but included only two or three sentences, with very little creativity. He only brought home a library book once a week and the enthusiasm was missing. In third-grade, he had a whole language teacher and again I saw the sparkle in his eyes. During third grade, he kept a notebook of all his readings and made comments about them. He made books about baseball and soccer and wrote regularly to another third grade pen pal. I'm convinced the whole language program made the difference.

SUMMARY

An important aspect of today's schooling is the involvement of parents throughout the entire educational process. Parents are their children's first and foremost teachers, and it is hoped that they will continue to be involved in their children's education when the children enter schools. This chapter provided a rationale for involving parents and presented a variety of options and opportunities for parents to become involved depending on their interests, concerns, personal feelings about schools, time constraints, and the like. In addition to the traditional ways of involving parents, whole language programs offer a variety of involvement possibilities from volunteering in the classroom to being editors for the school publishing center. Questions commonly asked by parents were addressed as well as some comments shared by parents concerning their and their children's involvement in whole language programs. This chapter stressed the collaborative working relationship of parents and schools as they approached fulfilling the school's mission as coequals and coeducators. As Mark Twain exclaimed, "A person who chooses not to read is no better than a person who can't." This goes likewise for writing. Parents and teachers working together can create lifelong readers and writers who not only can read and write but choose to do so!

BIBLIOGRAPHY AND SUGGESTED REFERENCES

Akroyd, S. (1995). Forming a parent reading-writing class: Connecting cultures, one pen at a time. *The Reading Teacher, 48,* 580–584.

Austin, T. (1994). *Changing the view: Student-led parent conferences.* Portsmouth, N.H.: Heinemann.

Becker, H., & Epstein, J. (1982). Parent involvement: A study of teacher practices. *The Elementary School Journal, 83,* 85–102.

Boehnlein, M., & Hager, B. (1985). *Children, parents, and reading.* Newark, Del.: International Reading Association.

Burkhart, A. (1995). Breaking the parental barrier. *The Reading Teacher, 48,* 634, 635.

Cervone, B., & O'Leary, K. (1982). A conceptual framework for parent involvement, *Educational Leadership, 40,* 48, 49.

Come, B., & Fredericks, A. (1995). Family literacy in urban schools: Meeting the needs of at-risk children. *The Reading Teacher, 48,* 566–570.

Comer, J., & Haynes, N. (1991). Parent involvement in schools: An ecological approach. *The Elementary School Journal, 91,* 271–277.

D'Angelo, D., & Adler, R. (1991). Chapter 1: A catalyst for improving parent involvement. *Phi Delta Kappan, 72,* 350–354.

Dundas, V., & Strong, G. (1991). *Readers, writers, and parents: Learning together,* Katonah, N.Y.: Richard C. Owen Publishers.

Edwards, P. (1995). Empowering low-income mothers and fathers to share books with young children. *The Reading Teacher, 48,* 558–564.

Epstein, J. (1984). *Effects on parents of teacher practices in parent involvement.* Baltimore: Johns Hopkins University, Center for Social Organization of Schools.

Epstein, J. (1986). Parent reactions to parent involvement. *The Elementary School Journal, 86,* 277–294.

Epstein, J. (1987). What principals should know about parent involvement. *Principal, 66,* 6–9.

Epstein, J. (1988). How do we improve programs for parent involvement? *Educational Horizons, 66,* 58, 59.

Epstein, J. (1991). Paths to partnership: What we can learn from federal, state, district, and school initiatives. *Phi Delta Kappan, 72,* 344–349.

Epstein, J., & Dauber, S. (1991). School programs and teacher practices of parent involvement in inner-city elementary and middle schools. *The Elementary School Journal, 91,* 289–305.

Ervin, J. (1982). *How to have a successful parents and reading program: A practical guide.* Boston: Allyn and Bacon.

Farris, P. (1987). Promoting family reading through magazine packs. *The Reading Teacher, 40,* 825, 826.

Flood, J., & Lapp, D. (1989). Reporting reading progress: A comparison portfolio for parents. *The Reading Teacher, 42,* 508–515.

Fredericks, A., & Rasinski, T. (1990a). Whole language and parents: Natural partners. *The Reading Teacher, 43,* 692–694.

Fredericks, A., & Rasinski, T. (1990b). Conferencing with parents: Successful approaches. *The Reading Teacher, 44,* 174–177.

Fredericks, A., & Rasinski, T. (1990c). Involving parents in the assessment process. *The Reading Teacher, 44,* 346–349.

Gray, S. (1984). How to create a successful school/community partnership. *Phi Delta Kappan, 65,* 405–409.

Greenwood, G., & Hickman, C. (1991). Research and practice in parent involvement: Implications for teacher education. *The Elementary School Journal, 91,* 279–288.

Heald-Taylor, G. (1989). *The administrator's guide to whole language.* Katonah, N.Y.: Richard C. Owens Publishers.

Henderson, A. (1987). *The evidence continues to grow: Parent involvement improves student achievement.* Columbia, Md.: National Committee for Citizens in Education.

Henderson, A. (1988). Parents are a school's best friends. *Phi Delta Kappan, 70,* 148–153.

Johnson, T. (1991). Evaluation in the classroom: Describing and judging the repertoire. Workshop presented in Albany, N.Y., March, 1991.

Kaser, L.; Jeroski, S.; Gregory, K.; Cameron, C.; & Preece, A. (1991). Learner focused evaluation: Issues, strategies, and audiences. Preconference Institute, Annual Convention of the International Reading Association, Las Vegas.

Leitch, M., & Tangri, S. (1988). Barriers to home-school collaboration. *Educational Horizons, 66,* 70–74.

Little, N., & Allan, J. (1988). *Student-led Teacher Parent Conferences.* Toronto: Lugus Productions Limited.

Long, C. (1985). How to get community support. *Principal, 64,* 28–30.

Maring, G., & Magelky, J. (1990). Effective communication: Key to parent/community involvement. *The Reading Teacher, 43,* 606, 607.

Moles, O. (1982). Synthesis of recent research on parent participation in children's education. *Educational Leadership, 40,* 44–47.

Morrow, L. (1993). *Literacy development in the early years: Helping children read and write.* Boston: Allyn & Bacon.

Morrow, L. (1995). (Ed.). *Family literacy connections in schools and communities.* Newark, Del.: International Reading Association.

Morrow, L., & Paratore, J. (1993). Family literacy: Perspectives and practices. *The Reading Teacher, 47,* 194–200.

Morrow, L.; Tracey, D.; & Maxwell, C. (Eds.). (1995). *A survey of family literacy.* Newark, Del.: International Reading Association.

Nicoll, V., & Wilkie, L. (Eds.) (1991). *Literacy at home and school.* Rozelle, N.S.W., Australia: Primary English Teaching Association.

Potter, G. (1989). Parent participation in the language arts program. *Language Arts, 66,* 21–28.

Powell, B. (1986). Volunteers in the schools: A positive approach to schooling. *NAASP Bulletin, 70,* 32–33.

Rasinski, T. (1989). Reading and the empowerment of parents. *The Reading Teacher, 42,* 226–231.

Rasinski, T., & Fredericks, A. (1989a). Can parents make a difference? *The Reading Teacher, 43,* 84, 85.

Rasinski, T., & Fredericks, A. (1989b). Dimensions of parent involvement. *The Reading Teacher, 43,* 180–182.

Rasinski, T., & Fredericks, A. (1990). The best reading advice for parents. *The Reading Teacher, 43,* 344, 345.

Rasinski, T., & Fredericks, A. (1991a). The second best reading advice for parents. *The Reading Teacher, 44,* 438, 439.

Rasinski, T., & Fredericks, A. (1991b). The Akron paired reading project. *The Reading Teacher, 44,* 514, 515.

Reutzel, D. R., & Fawson, P. (1990). Traveling tales: Connecting parents and children through writing. *The Reading Teacher, 44,* 222–227.

Rich, D. (1988). Bridging the parent gap in education reform. *Educational Horizons, 66,* 90–92.

Ritty, J. (1991). Single-parent families: Tips for educators. *The Reading Teacher, 44,* 604–607.

Rodriguez, K. (1991). Home writing activities: The writing briefcase and the traveling suitcase. *The Reading Teacher, 45,* 160.

Sandel, L. (1988). Sharing textbooks at home. *The Reading Teacher, 42,* 177, 178.

Sandfort, J. (1987). Putting parents in their place in public schools. *NAASP Bulletin, 71,* 99–103.

Shanahan, T.; Mulhern, M.; & Rodriguez-Brown, F. (1995). Project FLAME: Lessons learned from a family literacy program for linguistic minority families. *The Reading Teacher, 48,* 586–593.

Snyder, G. (1991). Parents, teachers, children, and whole language. In V. Frose (Ed.), *Whole language: Practice and theory,* pp. 255–282. Needham Heights, Mass.: Allyn and Bacon.

Speer Johnson, J. (1989). Personal newsletters for parents. *The Reading Teacher, 42,* 737–738.

Strickland, D., & Morrow, L. (1989). *Emerging literacy: Young children learn to read and write.* Newark, Del.: International Reading Association.

Taylor, D. (1983). *Family literacy: Young children learning to read and write.* Portsmouth, N.H.: Heinemann.

Topping, K. (1987). Paired reading: A powerful technique for parent use. *The Reading Teacher, 40,* 604–614.

Topping, K. (1989). Peer tutoring and paired reading: Combining two powerful techniques. *The Reading Teacher, 42,* 488–495.

Wahl, A. (1988). Ready . . . set . . . role: Parents' role in early reading. *The Reading Teacher, 42,* 228–231.

Walberg, H. (1984). Families as partners in educational productivity. *Phi Delta Kappan, 65,* 397–400.

Windsor, S. (1991). Parents supporting whole language. In Y. Goodman; W. Hood; and K. Goodman (Eds.), *Organizing for Whole Language,* pp. 284–299. Portsmouth, N.H.: Heinemann.

CHILDREN'S LITERATURE CITED

Collier, J., & Collier, C. (1974). *My brother Sam is dead.* New York: Four Winds Press.

Forbes, E. (1943). *Johnny Tremain.* Boston: Houghton Mifflin.

Johnson, A. (1990). *When I am old with you.* New York: Orchard Books.

McCloskey, R. (1941). *Make way for ducklings.* New York: Viking.

RESOURCES FOR PARENT LENDING LIBRARIES

Barron, M. (1990). *I laen to read and writ the we I laen to tak: A very first book about whole language.* Katonah, N.Y.: Richard C. Owen Publishers.

Binkley, M. (1988). *Becoming a nation of readers: What parents can do.* Indianapolis, Ind.: D. C. Heath and Company.

Butler, D., & Clay, M. (1987). *Reading begins at home: Preparing children for reading before they go to school.* Portsmouth, N.H.: Heinemann.

Chan, J. *Why read aloud to children?* Micromonograph. Newark, Del.: International Reading Association.

Clay, M. (1987). *Writing begins at home.* Portsmouth, N.H.: Heinemann.

Davidson, M.; Isherwood, R.; & Tucker, E. (1989). *Moving on with big books.* New York: Scholastic.

Fields, M. (1989). *Literacy begins at birth.* Tucson, Ariz.: Fisher Books.

Gentry, R. (1987). *Spel . . . is a four-letter word.* Portsmouth, N.H.: Heinemann.

Glazer, S. (1990). *Creating readers and writers.* Micromonograph. Newark, Del.: International Reading Association.

Goldfinch, M.; Jones, A.; & McNeil, J. (1986). *Learning begins at home: Teaching children from birth to five.* Portsmouth, N.H.: Heinemann.

Goodman, K. (1986). *What's whole in whole language.* Portsmouth, N.H.: Heinemann.

Gunderson, L. (1989). *A whole language primer.* New York: Scholastic.

Hill, M. (1989). *Home: Where reading and writing begin.* Portsmouth, N.H.: Heinemann.

Kobrin, B. (1988). *Eyeopeners!* New York: Penguin Books.

Lipson, E. (1991). The New York Times *parent's guide to the best books for children.* New York: Times Books.

Meek, M. (1982). *Learning to read.* Portsmouth, N.H.: Heinemann.

Mooney, M. (1988). *Developing life-long readers.* Katonah, N.Y.: Richard C. Owen Publishers.

Mooney, M. (1990). *Reading to, with, and by children.* Katonah, N.Y.: Richard C. Owen Publishers

Ransbury, M. *How can I encourage my primary grade age child to read?* Micromonograph. Newark, Del.: International Reading Association.

Reed, A. (1988). *Comics to classics: A parent's guide to books for teens and preteens.* Newark, Del.: International Reading Association.

Routman, R. (1988). *Transitions.* Portsmouth, N.H.: Heinemann.

Sawyer, J. (1993). Motivating children's at-home reading with book swaps. *The Reading Teacher, 47,* 269–270.

Schickendenz, J. (1986). *More than the ABCs: The early stages of reading and writing.* Washington, D.C.: National Association for the Education of Young Children.

Silvern, S., & Silvern, L. *Beginning literacy and your child.* Micromonograph. Newark, Del.: International Reading Association.

Trelease, J. (1995). *The new read-aloud handbook.* New York: Penguin Books.

Wilson, G., & Moss, J. (1988). *Books for children to read alone: A guide for parents and librarians.* New York: Bowker.

In addition to the above resources, both the International Reading Association and Reading Is Fundamental have a series of worthwhile booklets and brochures available for parents.

International Reading Association
800 Barksdale Road
P.O. Box 8139
Newark, DE 19714-8139

Reading Is Fundamental
Publications Dept.
P.O. Box 23444
Washington, DC 20026

BOOKS TO HELP HEAL

Books Dealing with the Physically and Mentally Challenged

Abbott, D. (1994). *One TV blasting and a pig outdoors.* New York: Whitman.

Baldwin, A. (1978). *A little time.* New York: Viking (mentally challenged)

Cairo, S. (1985). *Our brother has Down's syndrome.* New York: Flyfly Books. (mentally challenged)

Carrick, C. (1985). *Stay away from Simon.* New York: Clarion Books. (mentally challenged)

Cohen, M. (1983). *See you tomorrow, Charles.* New York: Dell. (physically challenged—blindness)

Hanson, F. (1979). *What if you couldn't? A book about special needs.* New York: Scribner's.

Irvine, G. (1987). *The true story of Corky, the blind seal.* New York: Scholastic. (physically challenged—blindness)

Kline, S. (1994). *Marony, mummy girl.* New York: Putnam.

Lasker, J. (1974). *He's my brother.* Chicago: Whitman. (mentally challenged)

MacLachlan, P. (1980). *Through Grandpa's eyes.* New York: Harper & Row. (physically challenged—blindness)

Martin, B., & Archambault, J. (1987). *Knots on a counting rope.* New York: The Trumpet Club. (physically challenged—blindness)

Newman, L. (1994). *Fat chance.* New York: Putnam.

Paterson, K. (1994). *Flip-flop girl.* New York: Lodestar.

Peterson, J. (1977). *I have a sister—my sister is deaf.* New York: Harper & Row. (physically challenged—deafness)

Rabe, B. (1981). *The balancing girl.* New York: E. P. Dutton. (physically challenged)

Rounds, G. (1980). *Blind outlaw.* New York: Scholastic. (physically challenged—blindness)

Sobol, H. (1977). *My brother Steven is retarded.* New York: Macmillan. (mentally challenged)

Wallace, B. (1994). *True friends.* New York: Holiday.

Williams, K. (1994). *A real Christmas this year.* New York: Clarion.

Yeatman, L. (1985). *Buttons.* New York: Barron's. (physically challenged—deafness)

Yeatman, L. (1986). *Pickles.* New York: Barron's (physically challenged)

Yeatman, L. (1987). *Perkins.* New York: Barron's (physically challenged—blindness)

BOOKS DEALING WITH DIVORCE

Blume, J. (1972). *It's not the end of the world.* New York: Bradbury Press.

Brown, M., & Krasny, L. (1986). *Dinosaurs divorce: A guide for changing families.* New York: Joy Street/Little, Brown.

Cleary, B. (1983). *Dear Mr. Henshaw.* New York: Morrow.

Danzinger, P. (1982). *The divorce express.* New York: Delacorte.

Dragonwagon, C. (1984). *Always, always.* New York: Macmillan.

Duffy, B. (1994). *Coaster.* New York: Viking.

Gaeddert, L. (1983). *Just like sisters.* New York: E. P. Dutton.
George, J. (1994). *Julie.* New York: HarperCollins.
Greene, C. (1969). *A girl called Al.* New York: Dell.
Helmering, D. (1981). *I have two families.* Nashville: Abingdon.
Hurwitz, J. (1984). *DeDe takes charge.* New York: Morrow.
Irwin, H. (1980). *Bring to boil and separate.* New York: Atheneum.
Jukes, M. (1983). *No one is going to Nashville.* New York: Knopf.
Jules, M. (1984). *Like Jake and me.* New York: Knopf.
Park, B. (1981). *Don't make me smile.* New York: Avon.
Rofes, E. (Ed.) (1982). *The kid's book of divorce.* New York: Vintage.
Schuchman, J. (1979). *Two places to sleep.* Minneapolis: Carolrhoda.
Williams, B. (1983). *Mitzi's honeymoon with Nana Potts.* New York: Dutton.
Wolitzer, H. (1976). *Out of love.* New York: Farrar, Straus & Giroux.

BOOKS DEALING WITH DEATH

Avi. (1994). *The barn.* New York: Orchard.
Brown, M. Wise (1958). *The dead bird.* Reading, Mass.: Addison-Wesley.
Bunting, E. (1980). *The empty window.* New York: Warner.
Bunting, E. (1994). *The in-between days.* New York: HarperCollins.
Calvert, P. (1994). *Writing to Richie.* New York: Scribner's.
Clifton, L. (1983). *Everett Anderson's goodbye.* New York: Holt, Rinehart & Winston.
Coerr, E. (1977). *Sadako and the thousand paper cranes.* New York: G. P. Putnam's Sons.
Cohen, M. (1984). *Jim's dog Muffins.* New York: Greenwillow.
Graeber, C. (1982). *Mustard.* New York: Macmillan.
McDaniel, L. (1994). *Don't die my love.* New York: Bantam.
Miles, M. (1971). *Annie and the old one.* Boston: Little, Brown.
Nori, K. (1993). *Shizuko's daughter.* New York: Holt.
Orgel, D. (1986). *Whiskers once and always.* New York: Viking/Penguin.
Paterson, K. (1988). *Bridge to Terabithia.* New York: Scholastic.
Paterson, K. (1994). *Flip-flop girl.* New York: Lodestar.
Smith, D. (1973). *A taste of blackberries.* New York: Crowell.
Smith, S.M. (1994). *The Booford summer.* New York: Clarion.
Thesman, J. (1994). *Nothing grows here.* New York: HarperCollins.
Tolan, S. (1994). *Who's there?* New York: Morrow.
Trevor, W. (1993). *Juliet's story.* New York: Simon & Schuster.
Varley, S. (1984). *Badger's parting gifts.* New York: Lothrop, Lee & Shepard.
Viorst, J. (1971). *The tenth good thing about Barney.* New York: Atheneum.
Yarborough, C. (1994). *Tanika and the wisdom rings.* New York: Random.
Zolotow, C. (1974). *My grandson Lew.* New York: Harper & Row.

EPILOGUE

COMMENTS FROM A READER AND WRITER

Hi! I'm Sarah. I'm in college now, but I'm still in the process of becoming a reader and writer. Throughout *New Connections,* you watched me grow in my reading and my writing. In looking back at my elementary school years, I don't remember much about reading and books I read in school. I have to say that I remember only the ones that were my own books—the ones I heard over and over. But I loved hearing them *because* I knew the words. I would say I was reading because I could remember every single word. I loved the little book sets that came in boxed sleeves, like *The Nutshell Library* of Maurice Sendak and Beatrix Potter tales. When I could read by myself, I liked all the *Little House on the Prairie* books by Laura Ingalls Wilder. I used to dress up and act them out.

I kept many of the books I loved as a child, and I still have them in my room. I never wanted my mother to give my books away. I was mad when she gave some of my books to the church fair. Even today I love to read and write, and I do my share both in and out of school. My father remembers reading *The Best Nest* over and over again, and I guess I still have favorites. I love to read everything from Shakespeare to Edgar Allen Poe to Stephen King. Some of my favorite books now are *Catcher in the Rye* and *Lord of the Flies.* Just as I loved to write beside my mom and dad when I was very young and to make my own little books, I still love to write. Sometimes I lie on my bed and the words come to me. I love writing poetry and illustrating my poems. I thought you'd like to see my writing today, so I'm sharing some of my poems.

As I went through high school and go through college and meet new reading and writing demands and have more opportunities to read and write for fun at home, I find I am still growing as a reader and writer. Every day I can read something new and I can write. I know I will read and write—and enjoy reading and writing—throughout my life. But that's another chapter!

COMMENTS FROM A TRANSITIONAL TEACHER

Having taught in an elementary school for more than twelve years, I thought I knew everything about teaching children to read. About four years ago, I took a series of workshops on whole language teaching. Gradually I began to incorporate these new ideas into my classroom procedures. I also signed up for whole language conferences and presentations with guest speakers. My enthusiasm for teaching was rekindled.

As I used more good children's literature and encouraged my students to be risk-takers and writers, I was amazed at the results. My classroom is quite different from what it was four years ago, but the changes have been gradual and carefully implemented. The biggest changes I've seen in my students are in their independence and their love of reading. Students used to read only when it was necessary for an assignment—now they read at every opportunity and in each free minute!

COMMENTS FROM A WHOLE LANGUAGE TEACHER

I was trained to be a teacher during the seventies. Each area of the curriculum was taught separately. Reading instruction was aimed at specific ability groups through the use of basal series texts. Time periods were allocated each day for reading groups. I prided myself on being able to teach all my students to read. But I realize now that my pride was only partly justified. Yes, I taught children to read—but I didn't teach them to *love* reading. My students read for one major purpose: to write the correct answers on a worksheet or in the blanks of numerous workbooks.

I have always enjoyed handiwork and crafts, so my classes often included creative activities, but I did not necessarily try to relate the activities to my curriculum. During the eighties, after having taught for several years, I became more aware of the benefits of integrated teaching. I attended several workshops on whole language instruction. My interest led me to purchase several books about this philosophy. After incorporating some of the elements of whole language into my classroom, I was enthusiastic about adding more. I began with shared book experiences and provided a specific time for the children to read for pleasure. I read as well. This quickly became our favorite part of the day.

Next we incorporated activities to extend our favorite works of literature. When the book was finished, our fun began. We made our own books, created puppets to act out the stories, wrote to the authors, and read more and more. The children not only read more, but they also wrote more and with purpose. We no longer practice writing friendly letters; we write to real people. We don't practice punctuation separately; it is part of everything we write—our journals, our response logs, notes to friends, and our own stories and published books.

Parents used to come to school only on Open House Night and for scheduled report card conferences. Now they visit weekly on a scheduled basis and assist with classroom activities. They take an active part in the learning process.

The greatest change in my classroom in the past several years is in the enthusiasm of the children. They exchange books to read *daily.* They read during free time because they love it. Teaching is exciting for me even after fifteen years because I see joy in my classroom every day!

APPENDIXES

APPENDIX A

Predictable Books

Ahlberg, J. (1979). *Each peach pear plum.* New York: Viking.

Barrett, J. (1980). *Animals should definitely not act like people.* New York: Atheneum.

Barrett, J. (1970). *Animals should definitely not wear clothing.* New York: Atheneum.

Bayer, J. (1970). *A my name is Alice.* New York: Dial.

Becker, J. (1985). *Seven little rabbits.* New York: Scholastic

Birdseye, T. (1994). *She'll be comin' round the mountain.* New York: Holiday.

Bishop, C. (1938). *Five Chinese brothers.* New York: G. P. Putnam's Sons.

Brand, O. (1974). *When I first came to this land.* New York: G. P. Putnam's Sons.

Brandenberg, F. (1970). *I once knew a man.* New York: Macmillan.

Briggs, R. (1989). *Jim and the beanstalk.* New York: G. P. Putnam's Sons.

Brown, M. (1947). *Goodnight moon.* New York: Harper & Row.

Brown, M. (1972). *Runaway bunny.* New York: Harper & Row.

Brown, M. (1957). *The three billy goats gruff.* New York: Harcourt Brace Jovanovich.

Brown, M. (1952). *Where have you been?* New York: Scholastic.

Buller, J. (1988). *I love you, goodnight.* New York: Simon & Schuster.

Carle, E. (1977). *The grouchy ladybug.* New York: Crowell.

Carle, E. (1987). *Have you seen my cat?* New York: Picture Book Studio.

Carle, E. (1975). *The mixed up chameleon.* New York: Crowell.

Carle, E. (1989). *The very busy spider.* New York: G. P. Putman's Sons.

Carle, E. (1969). *The very hungry caterpillar.* Cleveland: Collins World.

Cauley, L. (1981). *Goldilocks and the three bears.* New York: G. P. Putman's Sons.

Charlip, R. (1964). *Fortunately.* New York: Parents Magazine Press.

Child, L. (1975). *Over the river and through the woods.* New York: Scholastic.

Christelow, Eileen. (1989). *Five little monkeys jumping on the bed.* New York: Clarion.

Cole, J. (1989). *Anna banana: 100 jump-rope rhymes.* New York: Morrow.

DePaola, T. (1978). *Pancakes for breakfast.* New York: Harcourt Brace Jovanovich.

De Regniers, B. S. (1990). *Jack and the beanstalk.* New York: Aladdin/Macmillan.

De Regniers, B. S. (1972). *May I bring a friend?* New York: Atheneum.

De Regniers, B. S. (1968). *Willy O'Dwyer jumped in the fire.* New York: Atheneum.

Duff, M. (1978). *Rum pum pum.* New York: Macmillan.

Elting, M. (1980). *Q is for duck.* New York: Clarion.

Emberly, E. (1974). *Klippity klop.* Boston: Little, Brown.

Ets, M. (1955). *Play with me.* New York: Viking.

Flack, M. (1932). *Ask Mr. Bear.* New York: Macmillan.

Fox, M. (1994). *Tough Boris.* San Diego: Harcourt Brace.

Galdone, P. (1979). *Gingerbread boy.* New York: Clarion.

Galdone, P. (1968). *Henny Penny.* New York: Scholastic.

Galdone, P. (1973). *The little red hen.* New York: Scholastic.

Galdone, P. (1984). *The teeny tiny woman.* New York: Clarion.

Galdone, P. (1972). *The three bears.* New York: Scholastic.
Galdone, P. (1973). *The three billy goats gruff.* New York: Seabury Press.
Galdone, P. (1970). *The three little pigs.* New York: Seabury Press.
Ginsburg, M. (1972). *The chick and the duckling.* New York: Macmillan.
Hayes, S. (1988). *Clap your hands: Finger rhymes.* New York: Lothrop, Lee & Shepard.
Hogrogian, N. (1971). *One fine day.* New York: Macmillan.
Hutchins, P. (1986). *The doorbell rang.* New York: Greenwillow.
Hutchins, P. (1972). *Good-night owl.* New York: Macmillan.
Hutchins, P. (1968). *Rosie's walk.* New York: Macmillan.
Hutchins, P. (1971). *Titch.* New York: Collier Books.
Joslin, S. (1958). *What do you do dear?* New York: Harper & Row.
Joslin, S. (1958). *What do you say dear?* New York: Harper & Row.
Keats, E. J. (1971). *Over in the meadow.* New York: Scholastic.
Kellogg, S. (1985). *Chicken Little.* New York: Morrow.
Kraus, R. (1989). *Leo the late bloomer.* New York: Harper & Row.
Kraus, R. (1970). *Whose mouse are you?* New York: Collier Books.
Krauss, R. (1945). *The carrot seed.* New York: Harper & Row.
Langstaff, J. (1955). *Frog went a-courtin'.* New York: Harcourt Brace Jovanovich.
Langstaff, J. (1974). *Oh, a-hunting we will go.* New York: Atheneum.
Langstaff, J. (1957). *Over in the meadow.* New York: Harcourt Brace Jovanovich.
Lobel, A. (1981). *On Market Street.* New York: Greenwillow.
Martin, B., Jr. (1986). *Barn dance.* New York: Holt.
Martin, B., Jr. (1983). *Brown bear, brown bear, what do you see?* New York: Holt.
Martin, B., Jr. (1989). *Chicka chicka boom boom.* New York: Simon & Schuster.
Martin, B., Jr. (1988). *Ghost-eye tree.* New York: Holt.
Martin, B., Jr. (1987). *Here are my hands.* New York: Holt.
Martin, B., Jr. (1991). *Polar bear, polar bear, what do you hear?* New York: Holt.
Mayer, M. (1987). *What do you do with a kangaroo?* New York: Scholastic.
McGovern, A. (1967). *Too much noise.* New York: Scholastic.
Mosel, A. (1968). *Tikki-tikki-tembo.* New York: Holt.
Munsch, R. (1986). *Fifty below zero.* Scarborough, Ontario, Canada: Firefly Books Ltd.
Numeroff, L. (1985). *If you give a mouse a cookie.* New York: Harper & Row.
Numeroff, L. (1990). *If you give a moose a muffin.* New York: Harper & Row.
O'Neill, M. (1973). *Hailstones and halibut bones.* New York: Doubleday.
Peppe, R. (1970). *The house that Jack built.* New York: Delacorte.
Piper, W. (1980). *The little engine that could.* New York: G. P. Putnam's Sons.
Polushkin, M. (1978). *Mother, mother, I want another.* New York: Crown.
Preston, E. (1978). *Where did my mother go?* New York: Four Winds Press.
Quackenbush, R. (1973). *She'll be comin' round the mountain.* Philadelphia: J. B. Lippincott.
Quackenbush, R. (1975). *Skip to my Lou.* Philadelphia: J. B. Lippincott.
Raffi. (1987). *Down by the bay.* New York: Crown.
Raffi. (1987). *Shake my sillies out.* New York: Crown.
Raffi. (1988). *The wheels on the bus.* New York: Random House.
Scheer, J., & Bileck, M. (1964). *Rain makes applesauce.* New York: Holiday House.
Schwartz, A. (1986). *In a dark, dark room.* New York: Harper & Row.
Scieszka, J. (1994). *The book that Jack wrote.* New York: Viking.
Sendak, M. (1962). *Chicken soup with rice.* New York: Harper & Row.
Sendak, M. (1963). *Where the wild things are.* New York: Scholastic.
Seuss, Dr. (1960). *Green eggs and ham.* New York: Random House.
Shaw, C. (1947). *It looked like spilt milk.* New York: Scholastic.
Shulevitz, U. (1967). *One Monday morning.* New York: Scribner's.
Slobodkina, E. (1947). *Caps for sale.* New York: Harper & Row.
Spier, P. (1961). *The fox went out on a chilly night.* New York: Doubleday.
Stevenson, J. (1994). *Fun/No fun.* New York: Greenwillow.
Turner, G. (1994). *Over on the farm.* New York: Viking.
Wells, R. (1973). *Noisy Nora.* New York: Dial.
Westcott, N. (1980). *I know an old woman who swallowed a fly.* Boston: Little, Brown.
Westcott, N. (1964). *The lady with the alligator purse.* Boston: Little, Brown.
Westcott, N. (1987). *A play rhyme.* New York: Dutton.
Wildsmith, B. (1987). *All fall down.* Toronto: Oxford University Press.

Wildsmith, B. (1972). *The twelve days of Christmas.* New York: Franklin Watts.
Williams, L. (1986). *The little old lady who was not afraid of anything.* New York: Harper & Row.
Wing, N. (1994). *Hippity hop, frog on top.* New York: Simon & Schuster.
Wondriska, W. (1970). *All the animals were angry.* New York: Holt, Rinehart & Winston.
Wood, A. (1984). *Napping house.* New York: Harcourt Brace Jovanovich.
Wood, A. (1990). *Quick as a cricket. Child's play.* Singapore: Play Spaces.
Wormell, M. (1994). *Hilda Hen's search.* San Diego: Harcourt Brace.
Zaid, B. *Chicken Little.* New York: Random House.
Zemach, H. (1969). *The judge.* New York: E. P. Dutton.
Zemach, H. (1975). *Mommy, buy me a China doll.* New York: Farrar, Straus & Giroux.
Zemach, M. (1965). *The teeny tiny woman.* New York: Scholastic.
Zolotow, C. (1958). *Do you know what I'll do?* New York: Harper & Row.
Zolotow, C. (1962). *Mr. Rabbit and the lovely present.* New York: Harper & Row.
Zolotow, C. (1965). *Someday.* New York: Harper & Row.

APPENDIX B

Books with Minimal Text and Wordless Books

Arnosky, J. (1982). *Mouse numbers and letters.* San Diego, Calif.: Harcourt Brace Jovanovich.
Bang, M. (1980). *Grey lady and the strawberry snatcher.* New York: Four Winds Press.
Briggs, R. (1978). *The snowman.* New York: Random House.
Brown, C. (1989). *Patchwork farmer.* New York: Greenwillow.
Carle, E. (1971). *Do you want to be my friend?* New York: Crowell.
Carle, E. (1973). *I see a song.* New York: Crowell.
Collington, P. (1987). *Angel and the soldier boy.* New York: Knopf.
Crews, D. (1980). *Truck.* New York: Puffin.
DePaola, T. (1981). *The hunter and the animals.* New York: Holiday House.
DePaola, T. (1978). *Pancakes for breakfast.* San Diego, Calif.: Harcourt Brace Jovanovich.
DePaola, T. (1983). *Sing, Pierrot, sing.* San Diego, Calif.: Harcourt Brace Jovanovich.
Goodall, J. (1975). *Creepy castle.* New York: Atheneum.
Goodall, J. (1988). *Little Red Riding Hood.* New York: McElderry.
Goodall, J. (1975). *Naughty Nancy.* New York: Atheneum.
Goodall, J. (1976). *Paddy Pork's holiday.* New York: Atheneum.
Goodall, J. (1973). *Paddy's evening out.* New York: Atheneum.
Heller, L. (1979). *Lily at the table.* New York: Macmillan.
Hogrogian, N. (1972). *Apples.* New York: Macmillan.
Hutchins, P. (1968). *Rosie's walk.* New York: Macmillan.
Kent, J. (1975). *The egg book.* New York, Macmillan.
Kightley, R. (1989). *Postman.* New York: Macmillan.
Koontz, R. (1988). *Dinosaur dream.* New York: G. P. Putnam's Sons.
Krahn, F. (1974). *April fools.* New York: Dutton.
Krahn, F. (1977). *A funny friend from heaven.* New York: J. B. Lippincott.
Krahn, F. (1977). *The mystery of the giant footprints.* New York: Dutton.
Krahn, F. (1976). *Sebastian and the mushroom.* New York: Delacorte.
Krahn, F. (1974). *The self-made snowman.* New York: J. B. Lippincott.
Krahn, F. (1975). *Who's seen the scissors?* New York: Dutton.
Lisker, S. (1975). *Lost.* San Diego, Calif.: Harcourt Brace Jovanovich.
Mayer, M. (1969). *Frog goes to dinner.* New York: Dial.
Mayer, M. (1969). *Frog where are you?* New York: Dial.
McCully, E. (1988). *The Christmas gift.* New York: Harper & Row.
McCully, E. (1985). *First snow.* New York: Harper & Row.
McCully, E. (1988). *New baby.* New York: Harper & Row.
McCully, E. (1984). *Picnic.* New York: Harper & Row.
McCully, E. (1987). *School.* New York: Harper & Row.
Ormerod, J. (1982). *Moonlight.* New York: Lothrop, Lee & Shepard.
Ormerod, J. (1981). *Sunshine.* New York: Viking.
Ponte, C. (1988). *Adele's album.* New York: Dutton.
Prater, J. (1986). *Gift.* New York: Viking.
Ramage, C. (1975). *The Joneses.* New York: J. B. Lippincott.
Schweninger, A. (1979). *A dance for three.* New York: Dial.
Smith, L. (1988). *Flying Jake.* New York: Macmillan.
Spier, P. (1988). *Rain.* New York: Doubleday.
Sugita, Y. (1973). *My friend Little John and me.* New York: McGraw-Hill.

Turke, H. (1987). *Bon appetit.* Natick, Mass.: Picture Book Studio.
Turke, H. (1987). *Butterfly Max.* Natick, Mass.: Picture Book Studio.
Turke, H. (1987). *Chocolate Max.* Natick, Mass.: Picture Book Studio.
Turkle, B. (1976). *Deep in the forest.* New York: Dutton.
Vincent, G. (1982). *Ernest and Celestine's patchwork quilt.* New York: Greenwillow.
Ward, L. (1973). *Silver pony.* Boston: Houghton Mifflin.
Wiesner, D. (1988). *Freefall.* New York: Lothrop, Lee & Shepard.
Winter, P. (1976). *The bear and the fly.* New York: Crown.

APPENDIX C

Alphabet Books

Ackerman, K. (1986). *Flannery Row: An alphabet rhyme.* Boston: Atlantic Monthly.
Anno, M. (1975). *Anno's alphabet: An adventure in imagination.* New York: Crowell.
Balian, L. (1984). *Humbug potion: An ABC cipher.* Reading, Mass.: Abingdon.
Base, G. (1986). *Animalia.* New York: Viking Kestrel.
Baskin, L. (1975). *Hosie's alphabet.* New York: Viking.
Bayer, J. (1984). *A my name is Alice.* New York: Dial.
Brown, M. (1974). *All butterflies.* New York: Scribner's.
Burningham, J. (1967). *John Burnigham's ABC.* Indianapolis: Bobbs-Merill.
Cameron, E. (1984). *A wildflower alphabet.* New York: Morrow.
Carle, E. (1974). *All about Arthur (an absoletely absurd ape).* New York: Franklin Watts.
Chess, V. (1969). *Alfred's alphabet walk.* New York: Greenwillow.
Chwast, S., & Moskoff, M. S. (1969). *Still another alphabet book.* New York: McGraw-Hill.
Crane, W. (undated). *Baby's own alphabet.* New York: Dodd, Mead.
Crowther, R. (1977). *The most amazing hide and seek alphabet book.* New York: Viking.
Deasy, M. (1974). *City ABC's.* New York: Walker.
Duke, K. (1983). *The guinea pig ABC.* New York: Dutton.
Duvoisin, R. (1952). *A for the ark.* New York: Lothrop, Lee & Shepard.
Eichenberg, F. (1952). *Ape in a cape: An alphabet of odd animals.* San Diego, Calif.: Harcourt, Brace & World.
Elting, M., & Folsom, M. (1980). *Q is for duck.* New York: Clarion.
Emberley, E. (1978). *Ed Emberley's ABC's.* Boston: Little, Brown.
Farber, N. (1975). *As I was crossing Boston Common.* New York: Dutton.
Feelings, M. & T. (1974). *Jambo means hello: A Swahili alphabet book.* New York: Dial.
Ferguson, C. (1964). *Abecedarian book.* Boston: Little, Brown.
Fujikawa, G. (1974). *A to Z picture book.* New York: Grosset & Dunlap.
Gardner, B. (1986). *Have you ever seen?* New York: Dodd, Mead.
Gardner, J. (1977). *A child's bestiary.* New York: Knopf.
Garten, J. (1994). *The alphabet tale.* New York: Random House.
Grossbart, F. (1966). *A big city.* New York: Harper & Row.
Harrison, T. (1982). *A northern alphabet.* Plattburg, N. Y.: Tundra.
Hoban, T. (1982). *A, B, see!* New York: Greenwillow.
Hoguet, S. R. (1983). *I unpacked my grandmother's trunk.* New York: Dutton.
Howland, N. (1994). *ABCDrive.* New York: Clarion.
Johnson, C. (1963). *Harold's ABC.* New York: Harper & Row.
Kitamura, S. (1985). *What's inside? The alphabet book.* New York: Farrar, Straus & Giroux.
Larcher, J. (1976). *Fantastic alphabets: 24 original alphabets.* New York: Dover.
Lillie, P. (1986). *One very, very quiet afternoon.* New York: Greenwillow.
Lobel, A. (1981). *On Market Street.* New York: Greenwillow.
MacDonald, S. (1986). *Alphabatics.* New York: Bradbury.
Matthiesen, T. (1966). *ABC: An alphabet book.* Bronx, N.Y.: Platt & Munk.
McGinley, P. (1948). *All around the town.* New York: J. B. Lippincott.
Neumeier, M., & Glaser, B. (1984). *Action alphabet.* New York: Greenwillow.
Niland, D. (1976). *ABC of monsters.* New York: McGraw-Hill.
Obligado, L. (1983). *Faint frogs feeling feverish: And other terrifically tantalizing tongue twisters.* New York: Viking.
Oxenbury, H. (1972). *Helen Oxenbury's ABC of things.* New York: Franklin Watts.
Pearson, T. C. (1986). *A apple pie.* New York: Dial.
Petersham, M., & Petersham, M. (1941). *An American ABC.* New York: Macmillan.
Piatti, C. (1966). *Celestino Piatti's animal ABC.* New York: Atheneum.
Rojankovsky, F. (1962). *Animals in the zoo.* New York: Knopf.

Rosenblum, R. (1986). *The airplane ABC.* New York: Atheneum.
Schmiderer, D. (1971). *The alphabeast book: An abecedarium.* New York: Holt, Rinehart & Winston.
Sendak, M. (1962). *Alligators all around.* New York: Harper & Row.
Sloane, E. (1963). *The ABC book of early Americana.* New York: Doubleday.
Stockham, P. (1974). *The mother's picture alphabet.* New York: Dover.
Van Allsburg, C. (1987). *The Z was zapped.* New York: Houghton Mifflin.
Viorst, J. (1994). *The alphabet from Z to A.* New York: Atheneum.
Weil, L. (1980). *Owl and other scrambles.* New York: Dutton.
Wildsmith, B. (1962). *Brian Wildsmith's ABC.* New York: Franklin Watts.
Willard, N. (1994). *An alphabet of angels.* New York: Scholastic.
Williams, G. (1954). *Big golden animal ABC.* Racine, Wis.: Golden Press.

APPENDIX D

Books for Younger Readers (Emergent and Developing Readers)

Aardema, V. (1981). *Bringing the rain to Kapiti Plain.* New York: Dial.
Ackerman, K. (1988). *Song and dance man.* New York: Knopf.
Ahlberg, J. (1978). *Each peach pear plum.* New York: Viking.
Ahlberg, J. & A. (1986). *The jolly postman.* Boston: Little, Brown.
Alda, A. (1994). *Pig, horse, or cow, don't wake me now.* New York: Doubleday.
Aldridge, J. (1994). *The pocket book.* New York: Simon & Schuster.
Alexander, M. (1969). *Blackboard bear.* New York: Dial.
Aliki. (1982). *We are best friends.* New York: Greenwillow.
Allard, H. (1985). *Miss Nelson is missing.* Boston: Houghton Mifflin.
Andersen, H. (1979). *The emperor's new clothes.* Boston: Houghton Mifflin.
Anglund, J. (1960). *A friend is someone who likes you.* New York: Harcourt Brace Jovanovich.
Auch, M. (1994). *Monster brother.* New York: Holiday House.
Asch, F. (1978). *Mooncake.* New York: Scribner's.
Aylesworth, J. (1992). *Old black fly.* New York: Holt.
Bang, M. (1985). *Paper crane.* New York: Morrow.
Bemelman, L. (1939). *Madeline.* New York: Viking.
Benchley, N. (1969). *Sam the minuteman.* New York: Harper & Row.
Berenstain, S. & J. (1978). *The Berenstain bears go to school.* New York: Random House. (Series.)
Bond, M. (1958). *A bear called Paddington.* Boston: Houghton Mifflin. (Series.)
Bonsall, C. (1980). *Who's afraid of the dark?* New York: Harper & Row.
Brandenberg, F. (1980). *No school today.* New York: Greenwillow.
Brett, J. (1989). *The mitten: A Ukrainian folktale.* New York: G. P. Putnam's Sons.
Bridwell, N. (1985). *Clifford's family.* New York: Scholastic.
Bright, R. (1975). *Georgie's Halloween.* New York: Doubleday.
Brown, M. (1976). *Arthur's nose.* Boston: Little, Brown. (Series.)
Brown, M. (1976). *Once a mouse.* New York: Scribner's.
Brown, M. (1947). *Goodnight moon.* New York: Harper & Row.
Browne, A. (1983). *Willy the wimp.* New York: Knopf.
Bruchac, J. (1994). *The great ball game.* New York: Dial.
Bunting, E. (1994). *Flower garden.* San Diego: Harcourt Brace.
Burningham, J. (1970). *Mr. Gumpy's outing.* Boston: Houghton Mifflin.
Burton, V. L. (1942). *The little house.* Boston: Houghton Mifflin.
Cannon, J. (1993). *Stellaluna.* New York: Scholastic.
Cannon, J. (1995). *Trupp.* San Diego: Harcourt Brace.
Carle, E. (1984). *The very busy spider.* New York: G. P. Putnam's Sons.
Carlson, N. (1982). *Harriet's Halloween candy.* New York: Carolrhoda.
Carrick, C. & D. (1985). *Patrick's dinosaur.* Boston: Houghton Mifflin.
Cherry, L. (1990). *The great kapok tree.* New York: Harcourt Brace Jovanovich.
Christelow, E. (1991). *Five little monkeys sitting in a tree.* New York: Clarion.
Clifton, L. (1980). *My friend Jacob.* New York: Dutton.
Clifton, L. (1983). *Everett Anderson's goodbye.* New York: Holt, Rinehart & Winston.
Cohen, M. (1980). *First grade takes a test.* New York: Dell.
Cohen, M. (1985). *Liar, liar, pants on fire!* New York: Greenwillow.

Cohen, M. (1982). *No good in art.* New York: Greenwillow.
Cohen, M. (1977). *When will I read?* New York: Greenwillow.
Cole, J. (1986). *The magic school bus at the water works.* New York: Scholastic.
Cole, J. (1989). *The magic school bus: Inside the human body.* New York: Scholastic.
Cooney, B. (1985). *Miss Rumphius.* New York: Atheneum.
Crews, D. (1978). *Freight train.* New York: Greenwillow.
Cuneo, M. (1994). *What can a giant do?* New York: HarperCollins.
D'Aulaire, I. & E. (1972). *Trolls.* New York: Doubleday.
Day, A. (1994). *Frank and Ernest on the road.* New York: Scholastic.
De Brunhoff, J. (1989). *The story of Babar the elephant.* New York: Random House. (Series.)
DePaola, T. (1981). *The comic adventures of old Mother Hubbard and her dog.* New York: Harcourt Brace Jovanovich.
DePaola, T. (1987). *Nana upstairs and Nana downstairs.* New York: G. P. Putnam's Sons.
DePaola, T. (1980). *Now one foot, now the other.* New York: G. P. Putnam's Sons.
DePaola, T. (1975). *Strega Nona.* Englewood Cliffs, N.J.: Prentice Hall.
De Regniers, B. S. (1964). *May I bring a friend?* New York: Atheneum.
Duvoisin, R. (1958). *Petunia beware.* New York: Knopf.
Ehlert, L. (1989). *Color zoo.* New York: Harper & Row.
Ehlert, L. (1992). *Moon rope.* San Diego: Harcourt Brace Jovanovich.
Ets, M. (1955). *Play with me.* New York: Viking.
Fatio, L. (1986). *The happy lion.* New York: Scholastic.
Flack, M. (1932). *Ask Mr. Bear.* New York: Scholastic.
Flack, M. (1933). *The story about Ping.* New York: Viking.
Flack, M. (1935). *Wait for William.* Boston: Houghton Mifflin.
Fox, M. (1989). *Koala Lou.* New York: Harcourt Brace Jovanovich.
Fox, M. (1994). *Sophie.* San Diego: Harcourt Brace.
Freeman, D. (1982). *Beady Bear.* New York: Viking.
Freeman, D. (1961). *Corduroy.* New York: Viking.
Gackenback, D. (1987). *Dog for a day.* New York: Clarion.
Gackenback, D. (1994). *Where are Momma, Poppa, and Sister June?* New York: Clarion.
Gag, W. (1928). *Millions of cats.* New York: Coward, McCann & Geoghegan.
Galdone, P. (1984). *Henny Penny.* New York: Clarion.
Gibbons, G. (1984). *Fire! Fire!* New York: Crowell.
Gibbons, G. (1989). *Monarch butterfly.* New York: Holiday House.
Gibbons, G. (1994). *Emergency.* New York: Holiday.
Ginsburg, M. (1982). *Across the stream.* New York: Greenwillow.
Ginsburg, M. (1972). *The chick and the duckling.* New York: Macmillan.
Goble, P. (1991). *Dream wolf.* New York: Bradbury.
Grahame, K. (1985). *The wind in the willows.* New York: Adama.
Greenfield, E. (1979). *Grandma's joy.* New York: Collins.
Grifalconi, A. (1991). *Osa's pride.* Boston: Little, Brown.
Grifalconi, A. (1986). *The village of round and square houses.* Boston: Little, Brown.
Haas, D. (1986). *The secret life of Dilly McBean.* New York: Bradbury.
Hall, D. (1979). *Ox-cart man.* New York: Viking.
Hamilton, V. (1994). *Jaguarundi.* New York: Scholastic.
Hawthorne, N. (1959). *The golden touch.* New York: McGraw-Hill.
Hazen, B. (1995). *Goodbye-hello.* New York: Atheneum.
Heller, R. (1981). *Chickens aren't the only ones.* New York: Scholastic.
Henkes, K. (1991). *Chrysanthemum.* New York: Greenwillow.
Henkes, K. (1993). *Owen.* New York: Greenwillow.
Hill, E. (1980). *Where's Spot?* New York: G. P. Putnam's Sons.
Hoban, L. (1981). *Arthur's funny money.* New York: Harper & Row. (Series.)
Hoban, R. (1960). *Bedtime for Frances.* New York: Harper & Row. (Series).
Hoban, T. (1994). *Little elephant.* New York: Greenwillow.
Hoff, S. (1958). *Danny and the dinosaur.* New York: Harper & Row.
Hurd, T. (1984). *Mama don't allow.* New York: Harper & Row.
Hutchins, P. (1986). *Rosie's walk.* New York: Macmillan.
Johnson, C. (1955). *Harold and the purple crayon.* New York: Harper & Row.
Jukes, M. (1984). *Like Jake and me.* New York: Knopf.
Keats, E. J. (1962). *The snowy day.* New York: Viking.
Kellogg, S. (1982). *Tallyho Pinkerton.* New York: Dial.

Komaiko, L. (1987). *Annie Bananie.* New York: Harper & Row.

Kraus, R. (1970). *Whose mouse are you?* New York: Macmillan.

Krauss, R. (1945). *The carrot seed.* New York: Harper & Row.

Kroll, V. (1993). *Naomi knows it's springtime.* Honesdale, Pa.: Boyds Mills Press.

Leaf, M. (1988). *The story of Ferdinand.* New York: Penguin.

Lee, D. (1974). *Alligator pie.* New York: Macmillan.

Lester, H. (1986). *A porcupine named Fluffy.* New York: Trumpet.

Lester, J. (1994). *John Henry.* New York: Dial.

Lindgren, A. (1950). *Pippi Longstocking.* New York: Viking.

Lionni, L. (1963). *Swimmy.* New York: Pantheon.

Lobel, A. (1979). *Days with Frog and Toad.* New York: Harper & Row.

Lobel, A. (1985). *Frog and Toad.* New York: Harper & Row.

London, J. 1994). *Let's go froggy.* New York: Viking.

MacDonald, B. (1947). *Mrs. Piggle-Wiggle.* Philadelphia: J. B. Lippincott.

Maestro, G. (1994). *Macho Nacho.* New York: Dutton.

Marshall, E. (1982). *Fox and his friends.* New York: Dial.

Marshall, J. (1972). *George and Martha.* Boston: Houghton Mifflin.

Martin, B. Jr. (1983). *Brown bear, brown bear.* Toronto: Holt, Rinehart & Winston.

Mayer, M. (1976). *There's a nightmare in my closet.* New York: Dial.

Mayer, M. (1982). *The unicorn and the lake.* New York: Dial.

McKissack, P. (1989). *Mirandy & Brother Wind.* New York: Random House.

McPhail, D. (1980). *Pig, pig grows up.* New York: Dutton.

Miles, M. (1971). *Annie and the old one.* Boston: Little, Brown.

Minarik, E. (1956). *Little Bear.* New York: Harper & Row.

Myers, L. (1994). *Turnip soup.* New York: Hyperion.

Ness, E. (1966). *Sam, Bangs and Moonshine.* New York: Holt.

Park, B. (1994). *Junie B. Jones and some sneaky peeky spying.* New York: Random House.

Parrish, P. (1963). *Amelia Bedelia.* New York: Harper & Row.

Peck, R. (1992). *Little Soup's turkey.* New York: Dell.

Peet, B. (1979). *Cowardly Clyde.* Boston: Houghton Mifflin.

Pilkey, D. (1994). *Dog breath: The horrible trouble with Hally Tosis.* New York: Scholastic.

Pinkwater, D. (1976). *I was a second grade werewolf.* New York: Dodd, Mead.

Polacco, P. (1990). *Thundercake.* New York: Philomel.

Polacco, P. (1994). *My rotten red-headed brother.* New York: Simon & Schuster.

Potter, B. (1901). *The Tale of Peter Rabbit.* New York: Frederick Warner. (Series.)

Prelutsky, J. (1986). *Read aloud poems for the very young.* New York: Knopf.

Quackenbush, R. (1987). *Quit pulling my leg, Davy Crockett.* New York: Simon & Schuster.

Raffi. (1987). *Down by the bay.* New York: Crown.

Raskin, E. (1968). *Spectacles.* New York: Macmillan.

Rey, H. A. (1973). *Curious George.* Boston: Houghton Mifflin.

Rounds, G. (1992). *The three little pigs and the big bad wolf.* New York: Trumpet.

Rylant, C. (1985). *The relatives came.* New York: Bradbury.

Rylant, C. (1994). *Henry and Mudge and the careful cousin.* New York: Bradbury.

Sachar, L. (1992). *Marvin Redpost: Kidnapped at birth?* New York: Random House.

Schwartz, A. (1984). *In a dark, dark room.* New York: Harper & Row.

Schwartz, D. (1985). *How much is a million?* New York: Lothrop, Lee & Shepard.

Seeger, P. (1986). *Abiyoyo.* New York: Macmillan.

Sendak, M. (1963). *Where the wild things are.* New York: Harper & Row.

Seuss, Dr. (1989). *And to think that I saw it on Mulberry Street.* New York: Random House.

Seuss, Dr. (1940). *Horton hatches the egg.* New York: Random House.

Shannon, G. (1981). *Lizard's song.* New York: Greenwillow.

Sharmat, M. (1989). *Go to sleep Nicholas Joe.* New York: HarperCollins.

Sharmat, M. (1972). *Nate the great.* New York: Coward, McCann & Geoghegan. (Series.)

Shaw, N. (1986). *Sheep in a jeep.* Boston: Houghton Mifflin.

Shulevitz, U. (1967). *One Monday morning.* New York: Scribner's.

Singer, I. B. (1984). *Zlateh the goat.* New York: Harper & Row.

Spier, P. (1979). *Star spangled banner.* New York: Doubleday.

Surat, M. (1983). *Angel child, dragon child.* New York: Raintree.

Sutherland, H. *Dad's car wash.* New York: Brace, Atheneum.

Titus, E. (1957). *Anatole and the cat.* New York: Mc-growttell.
Tresselt, A. (1947). *White snow, bright snow.* New York: Marrow.
Turkle, B. (1969). *Obadiah, the bold.* New York: Viking.
Turkle, B. (1969). *Thy friend, Obadiah.* New York: Viking.
Uchida, Y. (1975). *Birthday visitor.* New York: Atheneum.
Van Allsburg, C. (1986). *The polar express.* Boston: Houghton Mifflin.
Van Laan, N. (1989). *Rainbow Crow.* New York: Knopf.
Vinke, H. (1984). *The short life of Sophie Scholl.* New York: Harper & Row.
Viorst, J. (1972). *Alexander and the terrible, horrible, no good, very bad day.* New York: Macmillan.
Viorst, J. (1989). *The good-bye book.* New York: Atheneum.
Waber, B. (1972). *Ira sleeps over.* Boston: Houghton Mifflin.
Weiss, N. (1989). *Where does the brown bear go?* New York: Greenwillow.
Wells, R. (1985). *Hazel's amazing mother.* New York: Dutton.
Wells, R. (1994). *Lucy comes to stay.* New York: Dial.
Westcott, B. (1994). *Never take a pig to lunch.* New York: Orchard.
Westcott, N. (1989). *Skip to my Lou.* Boston: Little, Brown.
Wilder, L. I. (1953). *Little house in the big woods.* New York: Harper & Row. (Series.)
Wildsmith, B. (1976). *Wild animals.* New York: Oxford University Press.
Williams, J. (1979). *Everyone knows what a dragon looks like.* New York: Macmillan.
Williams, M. (1983). *The velveteen rabbit.* New York: Holt.
Williams, V. (1982). *A chair for my mother.* New York: Greenwillow.
Winthrop, E. (1994). *I'm the boss.* New York: Holiday House.
Wiseman, B. (1974). *Morris and Boris.* New York: Dodd, Mead.
Wood, A. (1985). *King Bidgood's bathtub.* New York: Harcourt Brace Jovanovich.
Wood, A. (1989). *Elbert's bad word.* New York: Harcourt Brace Jovanovich.
Yashima, T. (1976). *Crow Boy.* New York: Penguin.
Yolen, J. (1987). *Owl moon.* New York: Philomel.
Yorinks, A. (1986). *Hey, Al.* New York: Farrar, Straus & Giroux.
Zemach, H. (1990). *It could always be worse.* New York: Farrar, Straus & Giroux.
Zemach, H. (1969). *The judge: An untrue tale.* New York: Farrar, Straus & Giroux.
Ziefert, H. (1986). *A new coat for Anna.* New York: Random House.
Zion, G. (1956). *Harry the dirty dog.* New York: Harper & Row.

APPENDIX E

Books for Beyond Emergent Readers (Independent Readers)

Abells, C. (1986). *The children we remember.* New York: Greenwillow.
Armstrong, W. H. (1969). *Sounder.* New York: Harper & Row.
Banks, L. (1981). *The Indian in the cupboard.* New York: Doubleday.
Baylor, B. (1976). *Hawk, I'm your brother.* New York: Scribner's.
Baylor, B. (1986). *I'm in charge of celebrations.* New York: Scribner's.
Baylor, B. (1978). *The way to start a day.* New York: Scribner's.
Blume, J. (1971). *Freckle juice.* New York: Dell.
Blume, J. (1972). *Tales of a fourth grade nothing.* New York: Dutton.
Bulla, C. R. (1954). *Squanto, the friend of the Pilgrims.* New York: Scholastic.
Bunting, E. (1988). *How many days to America?* New York: Clarion.
Bunting, E. (1991). *The wall.* New York: Clarion.
Burch, R. (1982). *Ida Early comes over the mountain.* New York: Viking.
Byars, B. (1977). *The pinballs.* New York: Apple.
Byars, B. (1994). *The Golly sisters ride again.* New York: HarperCollins.
Christopher, J. (1981). *Fireball.* New York: Dutton.
Cleary, B. (1973). *Socks.* New York: Morrow.
Cleary, B. (1981). *Ramona Quimby, age 8.* New York: Morrow.
Coerr, E. (1993). *Mieko and the fifth treasure.* New York: Dell.
Cohen, B. (1983). *Molly's Pilgrim.* New York: Lothrop, Lee & Shepard.
Cole, J., & Deegan, B. (1986). *Magic school bus at the waterworks.* New York: Scholastic.
Collier, J. (1974). *My brother Sam is dead.* New York: Four Winds Press.
Coville, B. (1989). *My teacher is an alien.* New York: Minstrel Books.
Dahl, R. (1970). *Fantastic Mr. Fox.* New York: Knopf.
Danzinger, P. (1995). *You can't eat your chicken pox, Amber Brown.* New York: Grosset.

DeClements, B. (1985). *Sixth grade can really kill you.* New York: Scholastic.
DeJong, M. (1956). *House of sixty fathers.* New York: Harper & Row.
Estes, E. (1973). *The hundred dresses.* New York: Scholastic.
Farley, W. (1941). *The black stallion.* New York: Random House.
Filipovic, Z. (1994). *Zlata's diary.* New York: Viking.
Fleischman, S. (1986). *The whipping boy.* New York: Greenwillow.
Fox, P. (1973). *The slave dancer.* New York: Bradbury.
George, J. C. (1959). *My side of the mountain.* New York: Dutton.
Giff, P. (1979). *Fourth grade celebrity.* New York: Delacorte.
Giff, P. (1994). *Count your money.* New York: Dell.
Goble, P. (1988). *Iktomi and the boulder.* New York: Bradbury.
Hamilton, V. (1978). *House of Dies Drear.* New York: Macmillan.
Hautzig, E. (1968). *Endless steppe: A girl in exile.* New York: Crowell.
Henry, M. (1947). *Misty of Chincoteague.* New York: Macmillan.
Hinton, S. E. (1967). *The outsiders.* New York: Delacorte.
Howe, D. & J. (1971). *Bunnicula.* New York: Atheneum.
Howe, J. (1983). *The celery stalks at midnight.* New York: Atheneum.
Hurwitz, J. (1994). *School spirit.* New York: Morrow.
Kline, S. (1987). *Herbie Jones and the gift.* New York: G. P. Putman's Sons.
Lawson, R. (1939). *Ben and me.* Boston: Little, Brown.
Lester, J. (1968). *To be a slave.* New York: Dial.
Levitin, S. (1982). *Fisherman and the bird.* Boston: Houghton Mifflin.
Lindgren, A. (1950). *Pippi Longstocking.* New York: Viking.
Lord, B. (1984). *In the year of the boar and Jackie Robinson.* New York: Harper & Row.
Lowry, L. (1987). *Anastasia Krupnik.* Boston: Houghton Mifflin.
Lowry, L. (1989). *Number the stars.* Boston: Houghton Mifflin.
Mahy, M. (1982). *Haunting.* New York: Atheneum.
Maruki, T. (1982). *Hiroshima no pika.* New York: Lothrop, Lee & Shepard.
Mathis, S. B. (1975). *The hundred penny box.* New York: Viking.
McCloskey, R. (1976). *Homer Price.* New York: Viking.
Mohr, N. (1979). *Felita.* New York: Dial.
Montgomery, L. M. (1908). *Anne of Green Gables.* New York: Grosset & Dunlop.
Montgomery, R. (1981). *Haunted house.* New York: Bantam.
Morey, W. (1965). *Gentle Ben.* New York: Dutton.
Mowat, F. (1961). *Owls in the family.* Boston: Little, Brown.
Myers, W. (1988). *Scorpions.* New York: Harper & Row.
Norton, M. (1953). *The borrowers.* New York: Harcourt Brace Jovanovich.
O'Dell, S. (1978). *Island of the blue dolphins.* Boston: Houghton Mifflin.
Parrish, P. (1963). *Amelia Bedelia.* New York: Harper.
Pinkwater, D. (1983). *I was a second grade werewolf.* New York: Dutton.
Reiss, J. (1972). *Upstairs room.* New York: Harper & Row.
Taylor, M. (1976). *Roll of thunder, hear my cry.* New York: Dial.
Taylor, S. (1951). *All of a kind family.* New York: Follett.
Taylor, T. (1969). *The cay.* New York: Doubleday.
White, E. B. (1952). *Charlotte's web.* New York: Harper.
Yep, L. (1975). *Dragonwings.* New York: Harper & Row.
Yolen, J. (1988). *The devil's arithmetic.* New York: Viking.

APPENDIX F

Realistic Fiction

Abercrombie, B. (1990). *Charlie Anderson.* New York: McElderry Books.
Adler, D. (1994). *Hilde and Eli: Children of the Holocaust.* New York: Holiday.
Banks, L. (1995). *Broken bridge.* New York: Morrow.
Blume, J. (1980). *Superfudge.* New York: Dutton.
Bunting, E. (1978). *Fly away home.* Boston: Clarion/Houghton Mifflin.
Bunting, E. (1990). *Our sixth-grade sugar babies.* New York: HarperTrophy.
Burch, R. (1982). *Ida Early comes over the mountain.* New York: Viking.
Byars, B. (1989). *Bingo Brown.* New York: Viking.
Cameron, E. (1980). *Beyond silence.* New York: Dutton.
Cleary, B. (1983). *Dear Mr. Henshaw.* New York: Morrow.
Cleary, B. (1968). *Ramona the pest.* New York: Morrow.
Cleary, B. (1981). *Ramona Quimby, age 8.* New York: Morrow.

Cleaver, V. & B. (1969). *Where the lilies bloom.* Philadelphia: J. B. Lippincott.

Conford, E. (1983). *If this is love, I'll take spaghetti.* New York: Four Winds Press.

Corcoran, B. (1986). *I am the universe.* New York: Atheneum.

Danziger, P. (1980). *There's a bat in bunk five.* New York: Doubleday.

Feelings, T. (1994). *Soul looks back in wonder.* New York: Dial.

Fitzgerald, J. (1973). *The Great Brain reforms.* New York: Crown.

Fox, M. (1986). *Winfred Gordon McDonald Partridge.* New York: Viking.

George, J. (1959). *My side of the mountain.* New York: Dutton.

George, J. (1994). *Julie.* New York: HarperCollins.

Greene, C. (1983). *Ask anybody.* New York: Viking.

Hunt, I. (1966). *Up a road slowly.* New York: Follett.

Klein, N. (1974). *Taking sides.* New York: Pantheon.

Konigsburg, E. (1973). *From the mixed-up files of Mrs. Basil E. Frankweiler.* New York: Dell.

Little, J. (1991). *From Anna.* New York: Harper & Row.

Lowry, L. (1978). *Anastasia Krupnik.* Boston: Houghton Mifflin.

MacLachlan, P. (1982). *Mama one and Mama two.* New York: Harper & Row.

MacLachlan, P. (1985). *Sarah plain and tall.* New York: Harper & Row.

MacLachlan, P. (1994). *Skylark.* New York: HarperCollins.

Miles, B. (1976). *I would if I could.* New York: Knopf.

Naylor, P. (1989). *All because I'm older.* New York: Atheneum.

Paterson, K. (1988). *Bridge to Terabithia.* New York: Scholastic.

Paulsen, G. (1988). *Hatchet.* New York: Macmillan.

Paulsen, G. (1995). *The tent.* New York: Harcourt Brace.

Peck, R. (1975). *The ghost belonged to me.* New York: Viking.

Peck, R. N. (1976). *Soup and me.* New York: Knopf.

Perl, L. (1979). *Me and fat Glenda.* New York: Clarion Books.

Pfeffer, S. B. (1984). *Truth or Dare.* New York: Macmillan.

Robinson, B. (1972). *The best Christmas pageant ever.* New York: Harper & Row.

Robinson, B. (1994). *The best/worst school year ever.* New York: HarperCollins.

Rockwell, T. (1973). *How to eat fried worms.* New York: Dell.

Rosenberg, M. (1994). *Hiding to survive.* New York: Clarion.

Sachar, L. (1978). *Sideway stories from a wayside school.* New York: Avon.

Sachar, L. (1987). *There's a boy in the girl's bathroom.* New York: Random House.

Saint James, S. (1995). *The gifts of Kwanza.* New York: Whitman.

Scieszka, J. (1995). *2095.* New York: Viking.

Shreve, L. (1984). *Flunking of Joshua Bates.* New York: Random House.

Slepian, J. (1995). *Pinocchio's sister.* New York: Philomel.

Smith, D. (1973). *Taste of blackberries.* New York: Crowell.

Smith, R.K. (1984). *The war with Grandpa.* New York: Dell.

Stolz, M. (1960). *Dog on Barkham Street.* New York: Harper & Row.

Taylor, M. (1995). *The wheel.* New York: Dial.

Tripp, V. (1986). *Meet Samantha.* New York: Pleasant.

Voight, C. (1983). *Dicey's song.* New York: Atheneum.

Warner, G. (1942). *Boxcar children.* New York: Whitman.

Webster, J. (1988). *Daddy-Long-Legs.* New York: New American Library.

Wersba, B. (1989). *Wonderful me.* New York: Harper & Row.

Whitehouse, J. (1984). *I have a sister—my sister is deaf.* New York: Harper & Row.

Yolen, J. (1995). *And twelve Chinese acrobats.* New York: Philomel.

APPENDIX G

Fantasy Books

Alexander, L. (1968). *High king.* New York: Holt, Rinehart & Winston.

Babbitt, N. (1975). *Tuck everlasting.* New York: Farrar, Straus & Giroux.

Brittain, B. (1983). *Wishgiver.* New York: Harper & Row.

Cooper, S. (1973). *The dark is rising.* New York: Atheneum.

Dahl, R. (1964). *Charlie and the chocolate factory.* New York: Knopf.

Dahl, R. (1988). *Matilda.* New York: Viking.

Grahame, K. (1985). *The wind in the willows.* New York: Adama.

L'Engle, M. (1968). *A wrinkle in time.* New York: Farrar, Straus & Giroux.

Lewis, C. S. (1961). *The lion, the witch, and the wardrobe.* New York: Macmillan.

Lowry, L. (1994). *The giver.* New York: Bantam Books.

O'Brien, R. (1986). *Mrs. Frisby and the rats of NIMH.* New York: Atheneum.

Tolkein, J. R. R. (1938). *The Hobbit.* Boston: Houghton Mifflin.

APPENDIX H

Poetry

Adams, A. (1972). *Poetry of earth.* New York: Scribner's.

Adoff, A. (1982). *All the colors of the race.* New York: Lothrop, Lee & Shepard.

Adoff, A. (1985). *The cabbages are chasing the rabbits.* San Diego, Calif.: Harcourt Brace Jovanovich.

Baylor, B. (1983). *The best town in the world.* New York: Scribner's.

Bodecker, N. M. (1976). *Hurry, hurry, Mary dear! and other nonsense poems.* New York: Atheneum.

Brewton, J., & Blackburn, L. (1978). *They've discovered a head in the box for the bread and other laughable limericks.* New York: Crowell.

Brewton, S. (1973). *My tang's tungled and other ridiculous situations.* New York: Crowell.

Brooks, G. (1956). *Bronzeville boys and girls.* New York: Harper & Row.

Brown, M. W. (1961). *Four fur feet.* Glenview, Ill.: Scott, Foresman.

Carroll, L. (1985). *Jabberwocky.* Niles, Ill: Albert Whitman.

Ciardi, J. (1961). *You read to me, I'll read to you.* New York: J. B. Lippincott.

Clifton, L. (1977). *Everett Anderson's 1-2-3.* New York: Holt, Rinehart & Winston.

Cole, J. (1984). *A new treasury of children's poetry: Old favorites and new discoveries.* New York: Doubleday.

Cole, W. (1978). *Oh such foolishness!* New York: J. B. Lippincott.

Cole, W. (1981). *Poem stew.* New York: J. B. Lippincott.

Conover, C. (1987). *The adventures of Simple Simon.* New York: Farrar, Straus & Giroux.

De Regniers, B. S. (1988). *The way I feel . . . sometimes.* New York: Clarion.

De Regniers, B. S. (1986). *A week in the life of best friends.* New York: Atheneum.

De Regniers, B. S.; Moore, E.; White, M. M.; & Carr, J. (1988). *Sing a song of popcorn.* New York: Scholastic.

Esbensen, B. J. (1984). *Cold stars and fireflies.* New York: Crowell.

Farber, N., & Livingston, M. C. (1987). *These small stones.* New York: Harper & Row.

Fields, J. (1988). *The green lion of Zion Street.* New York: Macmillan.

Fisher, A. (1960). *Going barefoot.* New York: Crowell.

Fisher, A. (1979). *I stood upon a mountain.* New York: Crowell.

Fisher, A. (1964). *Listen, rabbit.* New York: Crowell.

Fisher, A. (1975). *Once we went on a picnic.* New York: Crowell.

Fisher, A. (1968). *We went looking.* New York: Crowell.

Fleischman, P. (1985). *I am phoenix.* New York: Harper & Row.

Fleischman, P. (1988). *Joyful noise.* New York: Harper & Row.

Frank, J. (1961). *Poems to read to the very young.* New York: Random House.

Frost, R. (1988). *Birches.* New York: Holt, Rinehart & Winston.

Frost, R. (1978). *Stopping by woods on a snowy evening.* New York: Dutton.

Frost, R. (1959). *You come too.* New York: Holt, Rinehart & Winston.

Giovanni, N. (1971). *Spin a soft black song.* New York: Hill & Wang.

Greenfield, E. (1981). *Daydreamers.* New York: Dial.

Greenfield, E. (1978). *Honey, I love and other love poems.* New York: Crowell.

Grimes, N. (1978). *Something on my mind.* New York: Dial.

Holman, F. (1970). *At the top of my voice and other poems.* New York: Scribner's.

Holman, F. (1985). *The song in my head.* New York: Scribner's.

Hopkins, L. (1983). *A song in stone: City poems.* New York: Crowell.

Hopkins, L. (1980). *Moments: Poems about the seasons.* New York: Harcourt Brace Jovanovich.

Hopkins, L. B. (1982). *Circus! Circus!* New York: Knopf.

Keats, E. (1965). *In a spring garden.* New York: Dial.

Kuskin, K. (1980). *Dogs & dragons, trees & dreams.* New York: Harper & Row.

Larrick, N. (1988). *Cats are cats.* New York: Philomel.

Larrick, N. (1968). *On city streets.* New York: M. Evans.

Larrick, N. (1983). *When the dark comes dancing: A bedtime poetry book.* New York: Philomel.

Lear, E. (1986). *The Jumblies.* Morristown, N.J.: Silver Burdett.

Lear, E. (1983). *The owl and the pussycat.* New York: Holiday House.

Lee, D. (1983). *Jelly belly.* New York: Bedrick.

Lewis, R. (1988). *In the night, still dark.* New York: Atheneum.

Livingston, M. C. (1985). *Celebrations.* New York: Holiday House.

Livingston, M. C. (1982). *A circle of seasons.* New York: Holiday House.
Livingston, M. C. (1986). *Earth songs.* New York: Holiday House.
Livingston, M. C. (1976). *4-way stop.* New York: Atheneum.
Livingston, M. C. (1984). *Sky songs.* New York: Holiday House.
Livingston, M. C. (1984). *A song I sang to you: A selection of poems.* New York: Harcourt Brace Jovanovich.
Livingston, M. C. (1985). *Thanksgiving poems.* New York: Holiday House.
Livingston, M. C. (1988). *There was a place and other poems.* New York: McElderry.
Livingston, M. C. (1989). *Up in the air.* New York: Holiday House.
Livingston, M. C. (1989). *Remembering and other poems.* New York: McElderry.
Livingston, M. C. (1990). *My head is red.* New York: Holiday House.
Lobel, A. (1983). *The book of pigericks.* New York: Harper & Row.
Lobel, A. (1984). *The rose in my garden.* New York: Greenwillow.
Longfellow, H. W. (1988). *Hiawatha.* New York: G. P. Putnam's Sons.
Longfellow, H. W. (1963). *Paul Revere's ride.* New York: Crowell.
Mahy, M. (1987). *17 kings and 42 elephants.* New York: Dial.
Martin, B., Jr., & Archambault, J. (1988). *Listen to the rain.* New York: Holt, Rinehart & Winston.
Martin, B., Jr., & Archambault, J. (1988). *Barn dance.* New York: Holt, Rinehart & Winston.
Marzollo, J. (1978). *Close your eyes.* New York: Dial.
McCord, D. (1969). *Every time I climb a tree.* Boston: Little, Brown.
McCord, D. (1977). *One at a time.* Boston: Little, Brown.
McCord, D. (1975). *The star in the pail.* Boston: Little, Brown.
Merriam, E. (1973). *Out loud.* New York: Atheneum.
Merriam, E. (1984). *Jamboree: Rhymes for all times.* New York: Dell.
Merriam, E. (1986). *Fresh paint.* New York: Macmillan.
Merriam, E. (1988). *You be good and I'll be night.* New York: Morrow.
Moore, C. (1980). *The night before Christmas.* New York: Holiday House.
Moore, L. (1982). *Something new begins.* New York: Atheneum.
O'Neill, M. (1961). *Hailstones and halibut bones.* New York: Doubleday.
Prelutsky, J. (1980). *The headless horseman rides tonight.* New York: Greenwillow.
Prelutsky, J. (1983). *The Random House book of poetry for children.* New York: Random House.
Prelutsky, J. (1984). *The new kid on the block.* New York: Greenwillow.
Prelutsky, J. (1986). *Ride a purple pelican.* New York: Greenwillow.
Riley, J. W. (1975). *The gobble-uns'll git you ef you don't watch out.* New York: J. B. Lippincott.
Ryder, J. (1988). *Step into the night.* New York: Four Winds Press.
Ryder, J. (1989). *Mockingbird morning.* New York: Four Winds Press.
Ryder, J. (1991). *Hello, tree!* New York: Dutton.
Rylant, C. (1984). *Waiting to waltz.* New York: Bradbury.
Sandburg, C. (1930). *Early moon.* New York: Harcourt Brace Jovanovich.
Sandburg, C. (1982). *Rainbows are made.* New York: Harcourt Brace Jovanovich.
Siebert, D. (1989). *Heartland.* New York: Crowell.
Silverstein, S. (1981) *A light in the attic.* New York: Harper & Row.
Silverstein, S. (1974). *Where the sidewalk ends.* New York: Harper & Row.
Snyder, Z. K. (1969). *Today is Saturday.* New York: Atheneum.
Thayer, E. L. (1988b). *Casey at the bat.* New York: G. P. Putnam's Sons.
Wilner, I. (1977). *The poetry troupe: Poems to read aloud.* New York: Scribner's.
Worth, V. (1972). *Small poems.* New York: Farrar, Straus & Giroux.
Worth, V. (1975). *Small poems again.* New York: Farrar, Straus & Giroux.
Yolen, J. (1986). *The lullaby song book.* New York: Harcourt Brace Jovanovich.

APPENDIX I

Children's Magazines

American Girl
P.O. Box 620190
Middleton, WI 53562

Boodle: By Kids for Kids
P.O. Box 1049
Portland, IN 47371

Boy's Life
Boy Scouts of America
P.O. Box 152079
1325 Walnut Hill Lane
Irving, TX 75015-2079

Calliope: World History for Young People
7 School Street
Peterborough, NH 03458

Chickadee
P.O. Box 11314
Des Moines, IA 50340

Child Life
P.O. Box 10003
Des Moines, IA 50340

Children's Digest
P.O. Box 10003
Des Moines, IA 50340

Classical Calliope
Cobblestone Publishing Co.
30 Grove St.
Peterborough, NH 03458

Cobblestone
Cobblestone Publishing Co.
30 Grove St.
Peterborough, NH 03458

Crayola Kids
Box 400425
Des Moines, IA 50340

Cricket
P.O. Box 51144
Boulder, CO 80321-1144

Current Events
Weekly Reader Corporation
245 Long Hill Road
Middletown, CT 06457

Current Health
Weekly Reader Corporation
245 Long Hill Road
Middletown, CT 06457

Dolphin Log
The Cousteau Society
930 West 21st St.
Norfolk, VA 23517

Faces
Cobblestone Publishing Co.
30 Grove St.
Peterborough, NH 03458

Good Apple Newspaper
Good Apple
P.O. Box 299
Carthage, IL 62321

Highlights for Children
2300 West Fifth Ave.
P.O. Box 269
Columbus, OH 43272

Hot Rod
Pederson Publishing Co.
P.O. Box 56831
Boulder, CO 80322-6831

Humpty Dumpty's Magazine
P.O. Box 10003
Des Moines, IA 50340

International Wildlife
National Wildlife Federation
8925 Leesburg Pike
Vienna, VA 22184

Jack and Jill
P.O. Box 10003
Des Moines, IA 50340

Kid City
P.O. Box 2924
Boulder, CO 80322

Kids Discover
P.O. Box 54205
Boulder, CO 80322

Kids Life and Times
Kids Life
P.O. Box D
Bellport, NY 11713

Ladybug
Box 592
Mt. Morris, IL 61054

Motor Trend
Pedersen Publishing Co.
8490 Sunset Boulevard
Los Angeles, CA 90069

National Geographic World
Department 00289
P.O. Box 2330
Washington, DC 20077-9955

Odyssey
1027 North 7th St.
Milwaukee, WI 53233

Oh!Zone
420 E. Hewitt Ave.
Marquette, MI 49855

Outdoor Life
Times Mirror Magazines
2 Park Ave.
New York, NY 10016

Owl
P.O. Box 11314
Des Moines, IA 50340

Pack O'Fun
Pac-O-Fun Inc.
701 Lu St., Suite 1000
Des Plaines, IL 60016-4570

Plays
120 Boylston St.
Boston, MA 02116

Ranger Rick
National Wildlife Federation
8925 Leesburg Pike
Vienna, VA 22180-0001

Scienceland
501 Fifth Ave.
Suite 2108
New York, NY 10017-5165

Spider
Box 639
Mt. Morris, IL 61054

Sports Illustrated for Kids
P.O. Box 830609
Birmingham, AL 35283-0609

Stone Soup
The Magazine by Children
P.O. Box 83
Santa Cruz, CA 95063

3-2-1 Contact
P.O. Box 53051
Boulder, CO 80322-3051

Storyworks
Scholastic
P.O. Box 3710
Jefferson City, MO 65102

U.S. Kids
Field Publications
4343 Equity Dr.
P.O. Box 16630
Columbus, OH 43216

Your Big Backyard
National Wildlife Federation
8925 Leesburg Pike
Vienna, VA 22180

Zillions: Consumer Reports for Kids
Box 54861
Boulder, CO 80322

Zoo Books
3590 Kettner Blvd.
San Diego, CA 92101

APPENDIX J

Language Arts Outcomes and Descriptors, K–6

Kindergarten

Reading Outcomes and Descriptors (K)

Attitudes

The students will:

1. be enthusiastic about learning to read.
2. choose literature for enjoyment.
3. show evidence of enjoying literature.
4. demonstrate proper care of books.
5. respond to literature with appropriate emotions.

Learning Indicators

The students will:

1. choose books for leisure time and independent reading.
2. focus on print.
3. understand and use one-to-one matching and conventions of print.
4. demonstrate directionality
    - left to right; top to bottom
    - identify cover and back of book
5. identify:
    - picture and text
    - words and letters (distinguish the difference between)
    - upper- and lowercase letters
    - some basic sight words
6. expand their listening and speaking vocabulary.
7. relate presented concepts to personal experience.
8. increase awareness of environmental literacy.
9. participate in shared group reading experiences.
10. contribute to class discussions.
11. predict what will happen next with some accuracy.
12. use strategies in reading
    - picture clues
    - beginning consonant sounds
    - retell story from picture clues
    - recognize language patterns (rhyme, repetition)
    - relate prior knowledge to new material

Speaking/Listening Outcomes and Descriptors (K)

Learning Indicators

The students will:

1. make relevant contributions to discussions.
2. speak and listen in a group.
3. use age-appropriate vocabulary.
4. follow simple oral directions.
5. listen to and recite simple finger plays, poems, and songs.
6. ask and answer questions.
7. express feelings and needs appropriately.

8. engage in dramatic play.
9. express ideas in complete thoughts.
10. speak audibly and clearly.
11. remember and retell story events in sequence and with details.

Writing Outcomes and Descriptors (K)

Attitudes

The students will:

1. show enthusiasm and enjoyment for writing.
2. take risks in writing.
3. willingly share writing with others.

Learning Indicators

The students will:

1. experiment with the writing process
   - prewriting
   - writing act
   - sharing
2. dictate complete thoughts for:
   - a caption for a picture
   - personal experience
   - a narrative (with support)
   - a patterned story (with support)
3. match illustrations with print.
4. use a mixture and drawings and "writing" to convey and support ideas.
5. demonstrate print awareness.
   - write left to right
   - write top to bottom
   - recognize that numerals and words have a form
   - recognize spaces between words
   - recognize a title
6. be familiar with the basic writing conventions.
   - use developmental spelling
   - identify punctuation marks
   - experiment with punctuation marks
   - discriminate between numerals (0–9) and upper- and lowercase letters
   - reproduce numerals (0–9) and upper- and lowercase letters
   - reproduce first name
   - use writing tools effectively

First Grade

Reading Outcomes and Descriptors (1)

Attitudes

The students will:

1. show an appreciation for literature.
   - choose literature for enjoyment at school and at home
   - enjoy listening to literature

Learning Indicators

The students will:

1. accumulate new vocabulary.
   - sight
   - meaning
2. use a variety of strategies to acquire meaning from print.
   - one-to-one correspondence (one spoken word is one written word)
   - language patterns (rhyme, repetition)
   - rereading
   - phonics (consonants, consonant blends, digraphs, long and short vowels)
   - context clues
   - picture clues
   - syntax (sentence structure)
   - prior knowledge
3. identify titles and authors.
4. recognize the difference between letters, words, simple sentences, and questions.
5. recognize the difference between real and make-believe stories.
6. demonstrate comprehension in a variety of ways:
   - make predictions
   - identify the components of story structure
   - identify the main idea
   - recognize cause-and-effect relationships
   - respond affectively to literature
   - draw conclusions
   - sequence a story
7. read orally with fluency and expression.
8. respond to literature through discussion, writing, art, and so on.
9. move to silent reading for comprehension.

Speaking and Listening Outcomes and Descriptors (1)

Learning Indicators

The students will:

1. make relevant contributions to discussions.
2. use and respond to developmentally appropriate language.
3. be willing to participate and listen in a group.
4. listen to and recite finger plays, poems, and songs.
5. ask and answer questions.
6. express feelings and needs appropriately.
7. engage in dramatic play.

8. make and listen to simple presentations.
9. begin to monitor and self-correct volume, rate of speech, intonation, and expression.
10. follow simple oral directions, retell what is heard, and respond appropriately.

Writing Outcomes and Descriptors (1)

Attitudes

The students will:

1. enjoy writing.
2. show an enthusiasm for writing.
3. take risk in writing.
4. understand that writing can help us tell others what we think.

Learning Indicators

The students will:

1. develop a piece of writing using the writing process
   - prewriting
   - drafting
   - simple revising
   - editing
   - publishing/sharing
2. recognize narrative story structure.
3. recognize expository structure.
4. write complete thoughts for:
   - a caption for a picture
   - personal experience
   - a narrative
   - a patterned story
   - factual information
5. develop print awareness.
   - use spaces between words
   - recognize a title
   - recognize a sentence
   - recognize a paragraph
6. use basic writing conventions.
   - use developmental and conventional spelling
   - continue to experiment with punctuation marks
   - reproduce numerals and upper- and lowercase letters
   - use upper- and lowercase letters appropriately
   - use writing tools effectively
7. move from dictation to independent writing of two or three simple sentences.

Second Grade

Reading Outcomes and Descriptors (2)

Attitudes

The students will:

1. show an appreciation for literature
   - choose literature for enjoyment at home and at school
   - enjoy listening to literature
2. be enthusiastic about reading.
3. expect reading to make sense.

Learning Indicators

The students will:

1. know the parts of a book.
   - author
   - title
   - illustrator
   - table of contents
   - index
   - glossary
   - copyright
   - dedication page
2. differentiate between different types of literature.
   - genres
   - author style
   - illustrator style
3. accumulate new vocabulary.
   - sight
   - meaning (multiple-meaning, homonyms, synonyms, antonyms, specialized vocabulary in math, science, social studies)
4. view reading as an active process, using experiences and strategies to create meaning.
5. recognize story structure.
6. interpret the reading selection in their own words, orally, dramatically, in writing, through art.
7. self-correct errors when reading.
8. read for specific purposes.
9. be able to predict with reasonable accuracy.
10. know how to locate and recall details, information, and the main idea.
11. use strategies to figure out unknown words.
    - context clues
    - phonics
    - structural analysis
    - picture clues
    - rereading
    - prior knowledge
12. demonstrate comprehension in a variety of ways.
    - identify the components of narrative structure
      - setting
      - characters

  - problem
  - plot
  - resolution
  - moral
- preview the material
- use prior knowledge
- identify the main idea and supporting details
- make predictions
- sequence a story
- recognize cause and effect
- respond affectively to literature
- draw conclusions
- make inferences

13. use strategies to facilitate comprehension.
    - predicting
    - monitoring
    - searching
    - cross-checking
    - self-monitoring
14. know reading is used in many forms, for example, magazines, ads, posters, books, newspapers, poetry, directories, and so forth.
15. read with fluency and expression at an independent level.
16. respond to literature through art, discussions, writing, drama, and so on.

Speaking and Listening Outcomes and Descriptors (2)

Attitudes

The students will:

1. enjoy sharing work, ideas, and experiences with others.
2. feel comfortable speaking in front of others.
3. value and respect what others have to say.

Learning Indicators

The students will:

1. know that language is used to explain thinking.
2. know language is used to share ideas and feelings.
3. be able to follow multistep directions.
4. make and listen to simple presentations.
5. seek and respond to clarification.
6. speak in complete thoughts.
7. use and respond in developmentally appropriate language.
8. interact and make relevant contributions in groups.
9. engage in role-playing.
10. be able to give others directions.
11. be able to listen to others and share ideas.
12. give positive feedback to a speaker.
13. assume a leadership role in a group.
14. express feelings and needs appropriately.
15. be able to use expression when speaking to an audience.
16. practice the elements of good listening and speaking in conversations and discussions.
17. listen to and recite songs, poems, and plays with expression.

Writing Outcomes and Descriptors (2)

Attitudes

The students will:

1. enjoy writing.
2. take risks in writing.
3. willingly share writing with others.

Learning Indicators

The students will:

1. develop a piece of writing using the writing process.
   - prewriting
   - drafting
   - revising
   - peer/teacher conferencing
   - editing
   - publishing/sharing
2. develop several sentences that relate to a topic.
3. begin to write a narrative using story structure.
4. begin to write expository pieces (informational).
5. use name, describing, and action words as a way of extending sentences and improving writing.
6. use letter-sound relationships when writing drafts, or in journal writing, to attempt conventional writing, and to use conventional spelling for completed work.
7. use a variety of writing resources, for example, dictionaries, reference books, charts, literature, and so on.
8. use basic writing conventions.
   - use both developmental and conventional spelling progressing toward conventional spelling
   - uses periods, question marks, and exclamation marks correctly and consistently
   - experiments with dialogue
   - uses upper- and lowercase letters appropriately

9. use a variety of writing tools effectively.
   - pencils
   - markers
   - pens
   - computers

Third Grade

Reading Outcomes and Descriptors (3)

Attitudes

The students will:

1. show an appreciation for literature
2. be enthusiastic about reading.
3. expect reading to make sense.

Learning Indicators

The students will:

1. choose and read appropriate books independently.
2. read a variety of genres: fiction, nonfiction, biographies, poetry, and so on.
3. accumulate new vocabulary.
   - sight
   - meaning (multiple-meaning, homonyms, synonyms, antonyms, specialized vocabulary in math, science, social studies)
4. view reading as an active process, using experiences and strategies to create meaning.
5. recognize the essential elements of story grammar (e.g., characters, setting, problem, events, conclusion, moral, mood).
6. interpret the reading selection in their own words, orally, dramatically, in writing, through art.
7. self-correct errors to maintain meaning when reading.
8. read for specific purposes (recreational, information).
9. draw on prior knowledge to construct meaning.
10. know how to locate and recall details, information, and the main idea.
11. use strategies to figure out unknown words.
    - context clues
    - phonics
    - structural analysis
    - picture clues
    - rereading
    - prior knowledge
12. demonstrate comprehension in a variety of ways.
    - identify the components of narrative structure
      - setting
      - characters
      - problem
      - plot
      - resolution
      - moral
    - preview the material
    - use prior knowledge
    - identify the main idea and supporting details
    - make predictions
    - sequence a story
    - recognize cause and effect
    - respond affectively to literature
    - draw conclusions
    - make inferences
13. use strategies to facilitate comprehension.
    - previewing
    - predicting
    - monitoring
    - searching
    - cross-checking
    - self-monitoring
14. know reading is used in many forms, for example, magazines, ads, posters, books, newspapers, poetry, directories, and so forth.
15. read with fluency and expression at an independent level.
16. respond to literature through art, discussions, writing, drama, and so on.
17. use a variety of reference materials to research a topic.

Speaking and Listening Outcomes and Descriptors (3)

Attitudes

The students will:

1. enjoy sharing work, ideas, and experiences with others.
2. feel comfortable speaking in front of others.
3. value and respect what others have to say.

Learning Indicators

The students will:

1. take appropriate turns in conversation and discussion.
2. develop and maintain topic.
3. be able to follow multistep directions.
4. speak for a variety of purposes, for example, literature response, reports, plays, Readers' Theater, debates, and so on.
5. seek and respond to clarification.
6. use increasingly descriptive vocabulary.
7. present orally with appropriate preparation.

8. interact and make relevant contributions in groups.
9. engage in role-playing.
10. be able to give others directions.
11. be able to listen to others and share ideas.
12. give positive feedback to a speaker.
13. assume a leadership role in a group.
14. express feelings and needs appropriately.
15. be able to use expression when speaking to an audience.
16. practice the elements of good listening and speaking in conversations and discussions.
17. listen to and recite songs, poems, and plays with expression.

Writing Outcomes and Descriptors (3)

Attitudes

The students will:

1. show an enthusiasm for and enjoy writing.
2. take risks in writing.
3. willingly share writing with others.
4. understand that writing conveys thoughts and meanings and is a tool for clarifying thinking and learning.
5. understand that people write for a variety of purposes and audiences.

Learning Indicators

The students will:

1. develop a piece of writing using the writing process.
   - prewriting (brainstorming, selecting a topic, rehearsing, organizing ideas, considering audience, purpose, and form)
   - drafting
   - revising
   - peer/teacher conferencing
   - editing
   - publishing/sharing
2. write a fictional piece using story structure (beginning, middle, and end).
3. write responses to literature, either generating own topics or responding to a provided prompt.
4. use increasingly descriptive vocabulary.
5. write expository text:
   - directions
   - simple reports
   - time lines
   - summaries
   - newspaper articles
   - letters
   - biographies/autobiographies
6. use name, describing, and action words as a way of extending sentences and improving writing.
7. maintain a working writing folder.
8. use a variety of writing resources, for example, dictionaries, reference books, charts, literature, and so forth.
9. take risks in writing
   - initiate own writing
   - try new topics, writing forms
10. consider the appearance and form of their writing.
    - write neatly using correctly formed letters
    - write legibly in cursive
    - use paragraphs
    - use complete sentences
11. be aware of and use the following conventions/mechanics.
    - Punctuation/Capitalization
      - use upper- and lowercase letters appropriately
      - identify punctuation marks
      - use ending punctuation marks
      - use commas in a series, addresses, dates
      - use contractions

    Spelling

      - recognize spelling errors
      - use resources to locate and correct spelling
      - occasionally use invented spelling for unfamiliar words

Fourth Grade

Reading Outcomes and Descriptors (4)

Attitudes

The students will:

1. show an appreciation for literature
2. be enthusiastic about reading.
3. expect reading to make sense.

Learning Indicators

The students will:

1. choose and read appropriate books independently.
2. read a variety of genres: fiction, nonfiction, biographies, poetry, and so on
3. accumulate new vocabulary.
   - sight
   - meaning (multiple-meaning, homonyms, synonyms, antonyms, specialized vocabulary in math, science, social studies)

4. view reading as an active process, using experiences and strategies to create meaning.
5. recognize the essential elements of story grammar (e.g., characters, setting, problem, events, conclusion, moral, mood).
6. interpret the reading selection in their own words, orally, dramatically, in writing, through art.
7. monitor own reading to maintain meaning.
8. read for specific purposes (recreational, information).
9. draw on prior knowledge to construct meaning.
10. know how to locate and recall details, information, and the main idea.
11. use strategies to acquire meaning from print.
    - context clues
    - phonics
    - structural analysis
    - graphic aids
    - rereading
    - prior knowledge
    - skimming and scanning
12. demonstrate comprehension in a variety of ways.
    - identify the components of narrative structure
      - setting
      - characters
      - problem
      - plot
      - resolution
      - moral
      - dialogue
    - preview the material
    - use prior knowledge
    - identify the main idea and supporting details
    - sequence a story
    - recognize cause and effect
    - respond affectively to literature
    - draw conclusions
    - make inferences
    - summarize
    - recognize point of view
    - make and support predictions
    - make and support evaluations
13. use strategies to facilitate comprehension.
    - previewing
    - predicting
    - monitoring
    - searching
    - cross-checking
    - self-monitoring
14. know reading is used in many forms, for example, magazines, ads, posters, books, newspapers, poetry, directories,
15. read with fluency and expression at an independent level.
16. reflect and respond to literature through art, discussions, writing, drama, and so forth.
17. use a variety of reference materials to gain information.
18. demonstrate an awareness of expository text (informational)
    - cause and effect
    - comparison and contrast
    - sequence
    - simple listing
    - problem and solution
19. recognize and use signal words while reading, for example, the use of such words as *because, therefore, consequently, first, next,* and the like. (These are essential for the understanding of expository text.)
20. read critically, applying such higher-order thinking skills as:
    - analysis (character traits and ongoing plots of stories)
    - synthesis (recognize relationships between various kinds of reading materials)
    - evaluation (make judgments about text)
    - application (connect values, themes and morals to own experiences, other pieces of literature, and other events.)

Speaking and Listening Outcomes and Descriptors Grades Four and Five

Attitudes

The students will:

1. enjoy sharing work, ideas, and experiences with others.
2. feel confident speaking in front of others.
3. value and respect what others have to say.

Learning Indicators

The students will:

1. interact and make relevant contributions in conversations and discussions.
2. plan and organize an oral presentation.
3. follow complex directions.
4. speak for a variety of purposes, for example, literature response, reports, plays, Readers' Theater, debates, and so on.
5. ask questions for clarification.
6. use increasingly descriptive and precise vocabulary.

7. present orally with appropriate preparation.
8. use proper grammar
9. engage in dramatic presentations.
10. be able to give others directions.
11. be able to listen to others and share ideas.
12. give positive feedback to a speaker.
13. assume a leadership role in a group.
14. express feelings and needs appropriately.
15. be able to use expression when speaking to an audience.
16. practice the elements of good listening and speaking in conversations and discussions.
17. listen to and recite songs, poems, and plays with expression.

Writing Outcomes and Descriptors (4)

Attitudes

The students will:

1. enjoy writing.
2. take risks in writing.
3. willingly share writing with others.

Learning Indicators

The students will:

1. develop a piece of writing using the writing process.
   - prewriting (brainstorming, selecting a topic, rehearsing, organizing ideas, considering audience, purpose, and form)
   - drafting
   - revising
   - peer/teacher conferencing
   - editing
   - publishing/sharing
2. write a fictional piece demonstrating use of:
   - introduction (use of effective leads)
   - characterization
   - conflict
   - events
   - resolution
3. use vocabulary that appeals to the senses to convey images or impressions.
4. write nonfictional pieces including:
   - reports
   - time lines
   - summaries
   - newspaper articles
   - letters
   - biographies/autobiographies
   - interviews
5. express in writing personal feelings, reactions, values, interests, and attitudes.
6. maintain a working writing folder.
7. use a variety of writing resources, for example, dictionaries, reference books, charts, literature, and so forth.
8. evaluate material based on definite criteria.
9. take risks in writing
   - initiate own writing
   - try new topics, writing forms
10. consider the appearance and form of their writing.
    - write neatly using correctly formed letters
    - write legibly in cursive
    - use paragraphs
    - use complete sentences
    - maintain verb tense and subject/verb agreement
11. is aware of and uses the following conventions/mechanics:
    Punctuation/Capitalization
    - use upper- and lowercase letters appropriately
    - use ending punctuation marks appropriately
    - use commas in series, addresses, dates, correspondence forms
    - use quotation marks
    - use contractions
    - use apostrophes to indicate possession

    Spelling
    - recognize spelling errors
    - use resources to locate correct spelling
    - use spelling strategies to spell unfamiliar words
12. use research skills in the content areas.
    - introduction to note taking
    - graphic organizers/outlining

Fifth Grade

Reading Outcomes and Descriptors (5)

Attitudes

The students will:

1. show an appreciation for literature
2. be enthusiastic about reading.
3. expect reading to make sense.

Learning Indicators

The students will:

1. choose and read appropriate books independently.

2. read a variety of genres: fiction, nonfiction, biographies, poetry, and so on.
3. accumulate new vocabulary.
   - sight
   - meaning (multiple-meaning, homonyms, synonyms, antonyms, specialized vocabulary in math, science, social studies)
4. view reading as an active process, using experiences and strategies to create meaning.
5. recognize the essential elements of story grammar (e.g., characters, setting, problem, events, conclusion, moral, mood).
6. interpret the reading selection in their own words, orally, dramatically, in writing, through art.
7. monitor own reading to maintain meaning.
8. read for specific purposes (recreational, information).
9. draw on prior knowledge to construct meaning.
10. know how to locate and recall details, information, and the main idea.
11. use strategies to acquire meaning from print.
    - context clues
    - phonics
    - structural analysis
    - graphic aids
    - rereading
    - prior knowledge
    - skimming and scanning
12. demonstrate comprehension in a variety of ways.
    - identify the components of narrative structure
      - setting
      - characters
      - problem
      - plot
      - resolution
      - moral
      - dialogue
    - preview the material
    - use prior knowledge
    - identify the main idea and supporting details
    - sequence a story
    - recognize cause and effect
    - respond affectively to literature
    - draw conclusions
    - make inferences
    - summarize
    - recognize point of view
    - make and support predictions
    - make and support evaluations
13. use strategies to facilitate comprehension.
    - previewing
    - predicting
    - monitoring
    - searching
    - cross-checking
    - self-monitoring
14. know reading is used in many forms, for example, magazines, ads, posters, books, newspapers, poetry, directories, and so forth.
15. read with fluency and expression at an independent level.
16. reflect and respond to literature through art, discussions, writing, drama, and so on.
17. use a variety of reference materials to gain information.
18. demonstrate an awareness of expository text (informational)
    - cause and effect
    - comparison and contrast
    - sequence
    - simple listing
    - problem and solution
19. recognize and use signal words while reading, for example, the use of such words as *because, therefore, consequently, first, next,* and the like. (These are essential for the understanding of expository text.
20. read critically, applying such higher-order thinking skills as:
    - analysis (character traits and ongoing plots of stories)
    - synthesis (recognize relationships between various kinds of reading materials)
    - evaluation (make judgments about text)
    - application (connect values, themes, and morals to own experiences, other pieces of literature, and other events.)

Writing Outcomes and Descriptors (5)

Attitudes

The students will:

1. enjoy writing.
2. take risks in writing.
3. willingly share writing with others.

Learning Indicators

The students will:

1. develop a piece of writing using the writing process.
   - prewriting (brainstorming, selecting a topic, rehearsing, organizing ideas, considering audience, purpose, and form)
   - drafting
   - revising
   - peer/teacher conferencing